D1154965

BENEDICT XVI

His Life and Thought

ELIO GUERRIERO

BENEDICT XVI

His Life and Thought

With a Foreword by Pope Francis
And an Interview with Pope Benedict XVI

TRANSLATED BY WILLIAM J. MELCHER

IGNATIUS PRESS   SAN FRANCISCO

Original Italian edition:
Servitore di Dio e dell'umanità: La biografia di Benedetto XVI
© 2016 by Mondadori Libri S.p.A., Milan, Italy

Cover photograph by Stefano Spaziani
Cover design by Roxanne Mei Lum

© 2018 by Ignatius Press, San Francisco
All rights reserved
ISBN 978-1-62164-183-4
Library of Congress Control Number 2017941963
Printed in the United States of America ∞

To von Balthasar, de Lubac, and Ratzinger,
my teachers

CONTENTS

FOREWORD

by Pope Francis

This extensive biography of my predecessor Benedict XVI is welcome: it offers a comprehensive, reliable, and balanced account of his life and of the development of his thought.

All of us in the Church owe a great debt of gratitude to Joseph Ratzinger/Benedict XVI for the depth and balance of his theological thought, which he has always lived out in service to the Church up to the highest positions of responsibility, as prefect of the Congregation for the Doctrine of the Faith during the very long pontificate of John Paul II and finally as universal pastor. The contribution of his faith and learning to a Magisterium of the Church that is capable of responding to the expectations of our time, especially in the course of the last three decades, has been of fundamental importance. And the courage and determination with which he has confronted difficult situations has shown the way to respond to them with humility and truth, in a spirit of renewal and purification.

But I wish to insist on the fact that in these first years of my pontificate, my spiritual bond with him remains especially deep. His discreet presence and his prayers for the Church are a continual support and encouragement for my ministry.

I have often remembered his last audience and his farewell address to the cardinals, on February 28, 2013, before leaving the Vatican, when he spoke these moving words: "Among you . . . there is also the future pope to whom today I promise my unconditional reverence and obedience." I could not know then that they would refer to me. But in all my meetings with him, I have been able to experience not only reverence and obedience but also cordial spiritual closeness, joy in praying together, sincere brotherhood, understanding, and friendship, and also availability to counsel. Who can understand better than he the joys but also the difficulties of service to the universal Church and to today's world and be spiritually close to the one called by the Lord to carry the weight of it? Therefore, his prayers and his welcome friendship are particularly precious to me.

For the Church, the presence of a pope emeritus besides the one in office is a novelty. And since they like each other, it is a good novelty. In a certain sense, it expresses in a particularly evident way the continuity of the Petrine ministry, without interruption, like the links of one and the same chain welded by love.

The holy pilgrim people of God have understood this very well. Every time the pope emeritus, accepting my invitation, has appeared in public and I have been able to embrace him in front of everyone, the joy and applause of those present have been sincere and intense.

I am very grateful to Benedict XVI for his willingness to participate in the opening of the Jubilee Year of Mercy by passing through the Holy Door right after me. In a recent interview of his (*L'Osservatore Romano*, March 17, 2016), in which he points out as "signs of the times" the fact that "the idea of God's mercy is becoming increasingly central and dominant" and that "man today is awaiting mercy", demonstrates once again in the clearest way how God's merciful love is the deepest unifying theme of recent pontificates, the most urgent message that the outgoing Church brings to the peripheries of a world marked by conflicts, injustices, and contempt for human persons.

Although situations and persons naturally vary, the mission of the Church and the ministry of Peter are always a proclamation of God's merciful love for the world. Joseph Ratzinger's whole life, his thought and his works, have been aimed at this goal, and with God's help I am striving to continue in the same direction.

INTRODUCTION

A biography of Joseph Ratzinger—Benedict XVI—must necessarily start off with historical-geographical background information. He was born in Germany in 1927 at the time of the inauspicious rise of Nazism, which was to leave so much horror behind. Like many German Catholics, he grew to reject every sort of violence, while also seeking to survive the tidal wave of barbarity that was extending dangerously from Germany to all of Europe.

The upheavals of war led him, during his years of formation, to approach two thinkers, Augustine and Bonaventure, who had put time at the center of their reflections. The African Father placed God's love at the origin of history and regarded his grace, proclaimed by Jesus, as a gift conceded to man's weakness. The ancient Parisian *magister* (schoolmaster), once he had become Minister General of the Franciscans and together with the historic change brought about by the *poverello* of Assisi, stressed the continuity in God's revelation that culminated in Jesus Christ and remains alive and at work in time despite institutional weakness and corruption. However, notwithstanding the millenarian illusions of Joachim of Fiore and his imitators in every era, one cannot entirely dispense with institutions. The reign of God proclaimed by Jesus is certainly near, through the presence of grace and the sacraments, but, once again, it is not within man's capabilities to achieve it or even merely to hasten its coming.

Supported by the thought of these two Doctors of the Church, but also of contemporary theologians such as Henri de Lubac and Hans Urs von Balthasar, at Vatican II Ratzinger was a staunch adversary of the naturalistic vision of Scholasticism that was still dominant in the congregations and in the pontifical universities of Rome. Some years later, however, with equal determination, he distanced himself from Rahner, Küng, the liberation theologians, and others who, in his opinion, by insisting excessively on novelty, ran the risk of breaking the flow of tradition. For Ratzinger, the latter is an uninterrupted course that, when traced back, leads to the apostolic origins and to Jesus himself.

In Munich, the cardinal was acquainted with the Integrierte Gemeinde, a small movement of Christians who had been persuaded by the Nazi horror to think again about the eternal Israel and about Christians' debt of gratitude to the people of the promise. This prompted him to develop the idea of the many religions and the one covenant established by God with mankind through the sons of Abraham. This perspective shaped his thought about the revelation that started in the covenant at Sinai and was brought to fulfillment by Jesus with the new law proclaimed on the Mount of the Beatitudes.

As prefect of the former Holy Office, Ratzinger sought to support the work of John Paul II, finally putting an end to the ill-fated consequences of Nazism and the war and calling Europe not only back to its Christian origins but also to the love and the beauty that are able to design and provide more welcoming structures for countries and cities, environments and landscapes.

As pope, just as he had already done in Munich, Benedict considered that his job did not consist solely in reforming old institutions; rather, looking farther, he invited the Church to faith and to metanoia, the change of heart required by the sexual and financial scandals.

He reminded all that doubt pertains not only to believers, who owe it to others to explain the reasons for their faith, but also to anyone who looks at creation sympathetically and to anyone who governs the world responsibly. Plato's landing place in the world of the spirit is still a serious possibility for someone who questions himself conscientiously and honestly, with the rationality that distinguishes him from animals. His legacy is found in the vigorous defense of the truth—a precious good for all mankind—in his encyclical on love, which views all men as searching for some meaning, for a possible coexistence in brotherhood.

Another momentous legacy of his pontificate is his resignation from the Petrine ministry. After having, together with his revered predecessor, called Europe back to its origins and its centrality, he started the process of opening the Church to new geographical and spiritual frontiers, and he finally led it into the third millennium about which John Paul II talked so much.

I did not write this volume to contribute to the cause of beatification of Joseph Ratzinger. Instead, I am convinced that the Church would do well to give up canonizing popes because, as Father von Balthasar asserted, this practice exposes her to the risk of canonizing herself and her history. The lives of pontiffs, however, are led, not beneath a bushel basket, but in full view of people throughout the world. It is appropriate to leave judgment on their conduct to the free research of scholars. This, too, could be a sign of the openness that is so dear to the heart of his successor.

I wanted to tell, instead, about an honest man, in love with Bavaria and books, who reluctantly left his professorial chair for an episcopal see. With this same attitude, he set out for Rome and experienced the restrained joy of the sower who sows the word in the hope that many will gather it in. His acceptance of his election as successor of John Paul II was once again an act of obedience to the decision of his confreres in the episcopate. In a famous essay, he had spoken about the martyrological structure of the Petrine primacy. In the somewhat contorted language of theologians, he meant to say that serving as pope requires a martyr's patience and ability to endure suffering. He did not imagine that he would have to experience it personally.

On the throne of Peter, too, however, he proved to be a consistent man and a staunch Christian. Although he was reproached for a deficit in government, this was accompanied by an invitation to reform and to imitate Christ that deserved a more wholehearted reception. The tenacity with which he confronted scandals that had been hushed up for too long did not win the support of those who too easily distanced themselves from them. In the political arena, finally, his program for a new humanism for the third millennium was received at least with skepticism by the Europe that was nevertheless the object of the German pope's concern and affection.

A judgment on Ratzinger's papacy cannot overlook the act of his resignation, long pondered and suddenly announced after the beginning of the Year of Faith. This was neither a movement of rebellion nor a pain-free step; rather, it was a prophetic gesture, carried out in the presence of God and with his support. This is the only way to explain his peacefulness afterward, the serenity of someone who knows that he has made a painful choice but the right one. Even more significant is Ratzinger's behavior as pope emeritus. His obedience and closeness to Pope Francis, especially at the most delicate moments, cuts the ground from under the feet of suspicious commentators and conveys the image of a man who, after being in command for a long time, had not forgotten the virtue of obedience.

In recent years, Pope Benedict has drawn close to Saint Benedict, the father of monastic humanism who was able to combine contemplative prayer and silent, harmonious work. In his book on *Truth and Tolerance: Christian Belief and World Religions,* he recalled the death of Saint Benedict, which according to Saint Gregory occurred in an upper room. Then he commented: "He can see the whole because he is looking at it from on high, and he is able to gain this vantage point because he has grown inwardly great. . . . And then the light of God can touch him; he can recognize it and can gain from it the true overview."[1]

Mater Ecclesiae monastery, too, where Pope Benedict is spending the last period of his life, is located on a height. There, like Saint Augustine, his lifetime traveling companion, he has found peace in God, and from there he remains in communion with his successor and the whole Church. At mankind, too, he looks with more serene eyes, with the love of Jesus, the good Samaritan who heals all sorts of wounds, with the mercy about which his successor speaks. To all he leaves the seed that was so patiently sown: to the Church, the invitation to a new, more committed imitation of Christ; to the world religions and to the States, the exhortation to collaborate with one another on the basis of sound legislation.

Having arrived at the conclusion of this study, I cannot fail to thank those who were close to me during these years of work with their suggestions and proposals. The list would obviously be too long if I tried somehow to approach completeness. I limit myself, therefore, to thanking above all the two pontiffs: Pope Francis, for his generous foreword for which I did not dare to hope; and Pope Benedict, who agreed to read my manuscript while responding to

---

[1] Joseph Ratzinger, *Truth and Tolerance: Christian Belief and World Religions,* trans. Henry Taylor (San Francisco: Ignatius Press, 2004), 161.

numerous requests for clarifications and giving valuable suggestions. After them, particular thanks go to Archbishop Georg Gänswein, who always replied to my questions clearly and precisely. No less important, however, is my gratitude to many who are not mentioned here. I conclude with a well-deserved word of thanks to my wife, my children, and my family members, who never failed to give me their support and understanding.

Monza, May 5, 2016

I

IN GERMANY DURING
THE THIRD REICH

The Ratzinger family

In Rickering, near Schwanenkirchen, in Lower Bavaria, a photo is preserved that depicts the entire Ratzinger family, which had gathered in 1931 to celebrate the eightieth birthday of the paternal grandmother, Katharina Schmid. At that time, the pope's grandfather, who also was named Joseph Ratzinger, had already died, while his two parents, Joseph and Maria, are at the right of the rather numerous group.

Joseph Ratzinger (his father) was born in Rickering in 1877, the second of eleven children of a farming family. He attended elementary school, where he became acquainted with two persons who had a particular influence on him: the chaplain, Father Rosenberger, communicated to him his profound religious experiences, and Maestro Weber, who directed the church choir, welcomed into the group of singers even little Ratzinger, who, from then on, had a serious and lasting passion for music and singing. When he finished elementary school, Joseph continued his education, as much as possible, by attending on Sundays a sort of secondary school that offered more in-depth courses in religion but also classes of a more general character. The first child was a girl, Anna. Therefore, it fell to the first male child, Joseph, to help his father with the heavy chores on the farm.

On October 20, 1897, the twenty-year-old was called up for military service in Passau. He was a good soldier, distinguishing himself as a sharpshooter. After his two years of conscription, he was appointed a non-commissioned officer and with that assignment stayed on for another three years in the army. When he returned home in

1903, he discovered that his parents had decided that the farm would be inherited by a younger brother and not by him. Therefore, he had to think again about his life and, after making suitable inquiries, decided to enter the police force. His service record described him as follows: "25 years old, Catholic, single, 5 feet 5 inches tall."[1] His first place of employment was Niederambach; numerous transfers followed, because at that time policemen were frequently moved around to keep them from putting down roots by remaining too long in one police station, which would have made possible further transfers too difficult.

At the beginning of the new century, Bavaria, in particular Munich, was not a bad place to live. It was no accident that Wassily Kandinsky had arrived from Moscow, Paul Klee from Zurich, Rainer Maria Rilke from Prague. Joseph, however, did not have the time to think about starting a family of his own: there were the needs of his parents' family, while his superiors advised him to wait to contract marriage.

During the First World War, he was in Ingolstadt, where the police forces were hiring more men because there were many industries in the area and they feared labor unrest. The war, in which Germany allied with Austria against France, Great Britain, and Italy, contributed to the downfall of the Habsburg Empire. Their defeat, which was at the origin of momentous repercussions throughout Europe, had incendiary consequences especially in German-speaking lands. Because of the social tensions in the German Empire, the inability of the classes in power to reform, and the ineptitude exhibited by the military commands, Germany and Austria were wracked, after their defeat, by dangerous internal upheavals. Revolution broke out beginning in Bavaria, of all places, where even before the official end of the war, in November 1918, the disorders were so serious as to lead to the Spartacist uprising and the so-called Bavarian Soviet Republic.

After the miserable end of the revolution, there were new elections the following year; the voters' preferences favored the Catholic party, which became the leading political association in Bavaria and the only regional party represented in the national German Parlia-

---

[1] For these facts, see Georg Ratzinger and Michael Hesemann, *My Brother the Pope*, trans. Michael J. Miller (San Francisco: Ignatius Press, 2011), 19ff.

ment, the Reichstag. At that point, the policeman Joseph Ratzinger decided that the time had come for him to start his own family. At the age of forty-three, he did not have any particular familiarity with worldly ways or women. He resorted, therefore, to a somewhat unusual method of getting engaged: an advertisement in the *Liebfrauenbote*, the Catholic newspaper in Altötting: "State employee, single, Catholic, forty-three years old . . . seeks matrimony, as soon as possible, a capable Catholic girl."[2] The first attempt led nowhere, but at the second, a woman named Maria Rieger responded.

Born in 1884, the mother of the future pontiff was originally from Rimsting, on Lake Chiem, the "sea of Bavaria", where Ludwig II had built his own Versailles. Maria's father, Isidor Rieger, was Swabian-Bavarian; her mother's name was Maria Peintner, who was originally from Tyrol. They ran a little bakery, which, however, was not enough to support the rapidly growing family. Maria, the first of seven siblings, quickly had to take on responsibilities. At first, she cared for her little sisters and brothers at home; then, having scarcely embarked on adolescence, she took a course to become a cook and soon went to work for an orchestral director in Salzburg so as to contribute to the family income. For her, too, proximity to a musical maestro fostered an unforgettable interest in singing.

The job, however, did not last long because the musician was not able to pay. The hard-working Maria tenaciously looked for new employment until she landed at the Hotel Neuwittelsbach in Munich, where they were looking for a pastry cook. In 1912, meanwhile, her father, Isidor Rieger, died, leaving her with an even greater duty to provide for the little band of her brothers and sisters, the youngest of whom, Clothilde, was only twelve years old. In 1920, when she read Officer Ratzinger's advertisement, Maria was thirty-six years old. She probably sought advice from her pastor, who gave her a favorable letter of reference, and the two young people began to visit each other.

Joseph was a severe, authoritative, just man; Maria—a beautiful, generous, good-hearted woman. Soon the two fiancés, who were no longer that young, learned to know and to love each other. On October 20, 1920, Joseph presented his official request for marriage.

---

[2] Emanuela Zanotti, *Il sorriso di Benedetto: Pellegrinaggio nella terra d'infanzia di papa Benedetto XVI* (Siena: Cantagalli, 2007), 29f.

After receiving the expected consent of his fiancée, Joseph, despite his age, had to ask for permission from the police force. Their wedding was celebrated on November 9, 1920, in Pleiskirchen, where their first two children were born, too: Maria in 1921 and Georg in 1924.

Beloved Bavaria

At the time when Joseph Ratzinger was elected pope in 2005, the world media insisted on the novelty of the German pope who succeeded the Polish one. The information was correct, but not precise. Before being German, Joseph Aloysius Ratzinger is Bavarian by birth and culture. In September 2006, he declared, while preparing to visit Bavaria: "I love the beauty of our land, and I like to take long walks. I am a Bavarian patriot; I particularly like Bavaria, our history, and of course our art."[3]

It is appropriate, then, following the reconstruction of a famous historian,[4] to take a look at the culture and geography of this *Land*, which, precisely because of its past, claims cultural and economic autonomy within the German Federal Republic. The first historical documents about Bavaria go back to the sixth century, when the duchy came to be governed by a family of French descent. Subsequently incorporated into the empire of Charlemagne and his successors, it regained its independence in the tenth century, when the Carolingians had to retreat from the eastern region of their empire. After several centuries of uncertainty, in 1180 the duchy was conferred by Frederick Barbarossa on Otto of Wittelsbach, whose family governed the country uninterruptedly for about 750 years, until the night of November 7–8, 1918.

As was already mentioned, even before the war was officially over, the toll of human lives taken by the first worldwide conflict and the privations subsequent to the defeat caused such great discontent among the population that unexpected, violent revolutions followed. One exceptional observer, Eugenio Pacelli, at that time nuncio in Bavaria, wrote: "The revolution in Bavaria broke out as

---

[3] Interview granted on the occasion of his apostolic journey to Bavaria in 2006.

[4] Andreas Kraus, *Geschichte Bayerns: Von den Anfängen bis zur Gegenwart*, 3rd ed. (Munich: Beck, 2004).

swift as lightning."[5] Not letting himself be deceived by reports in the conservative press, the nuncio blamed the events not so much on a foreign plot as on the psychological reactions of a famished, exhausted populace after the humiliation of defeat and many human losses.

Led by a secessionist group of the Socialist Party, the Spartacists, the revolution declared King Ludwig III deposed and, under the presidency of Kurt Eisner, gave rise to a Soviet-style republic, the *Räterepublik*, or Soviet Republic, which nevertheless fell miserably after only one month. Meanwhile, the nuncio, Pacelli, on the advice of the new archbishop of Munich, Michael von Faulhaber,[6] who had arrived in the city almost simultaneously with the diplomatic envoy from Rome, left the capital so as not to have to meet Eisner and give even the impression of recognizing in some way the head of the revolutionaries.

The disorders in the Bavarian capital, however, were not yet over. On January 12, 1919, there were regional elections that gave a solid majority to the ordinary parties, the Bavarian People's Party and the Social-Democratic Party. After several days, Pacelli considered it advisable to return to his post, but the following month, the assassination of Eisner by a young army officer, a nobleman and, moreover, a Catholic, started a new wave of violence and disorders that led to the second revolution in Munich. And so a second Soviet Republic was formed, as ephemeral as the first. In August 1919, the disorders came to an end with the accession of Bavaria to the German Empire and the Weimar Republic. Thus the *Land* of Bavaria took another step toward full adherence to the German

---

[5] Pacelli to Gasparri, November 15, 1918, in *AAES*, Bavaria, 42.

[6] Michael von Faulhaber (1869–1952) was archbishop of Munich and a cardinal. Consecrated bishop of Speyer in 1910, in 1916 he received the Iron Cross for his presence among the soldiers on the Western Front during World War I. In 1917, he was appointed archbishop of Munich and cardinal, an office that he held for thirty-five years until his death in 1952. A staunch opponent of Nazism, he was one of the supporters of the Friends of Israel Association. A friend of Nuncio, then Cardinal Pacelli, he was among the promoters of the Concordat with the Reich. At the same time, he wrote an initial document that served as the outline for the composition of the anti-Nazi encyclical *Mit brennender Sorge*. He was also a staunch opponent of the regime's euthanasia program, but at the end of the war, he protested against the Allies for their indiscriminate bombardment of Germany. Much loved in his homeland, in 1951 he ordained as priest the future Benedict XVI, who always had respect and veneration for him.

Confederation, even though it still claimed political and cultural autonomy, in particular with the Catholic People's Party.

Although the special character of the region is so tenaciously claimed and defended, it is impossible to overlook the fact that modern Bavaria is made up of three bands of territory with different historical origins: Swabia in the southwest, Franconia in the north, where originally Protestantism prevailed, while in the center and the southeast there is ancient Bavaria, the *Altbayern* about which the pope speaks in his memoirs in often lyrical tones dictated by a never-forgotten love. From Passau and Salzburg, this Bavaria looked toward Austria, Bohemia, and Czechoslovakia, toward Poland and the Slavic world, not with the intention of attacking and conquering à la Hitler and his lawless followers, but to keep alive a dialogue of culture and faith that had been uninterrupted for centuries.

The Church as a living space

To early twentieth-century Germany, which was involved in the *Kulturkampf,* the divisions caused in the universal Church by modernism and by the relentless reaction of Pius X and his overzealous counselors remained rather irrelevant. On the other hand, the theologians and the bishops with pastoral responsibilities realized before anyone else the danger posed by the subjectivism and individualism of modern times. They began, moreover, a significant new development in theology, which in the late nineteenth century and even at the beginning of the twentieth was deeply indebted to the neo-Scholastic view of faith as something bound up with the intellectual assimilation and verbal articulation of the truths of faith.

Among the first to react to the rationalism of this intellectual approach was the Benedictine monk Odo Casel (1886–1948), who by developing a theology of the sacraments and mysteries glimpsed the dawn of a new day that went beyond rationalism and materialism to ecstasy and mysticism. The banner waved by Casel was taken up by the liturgical movement, in particular by Romano Guardini (1885–1968),[7] who gave new momentum to the movement that

---

[7] On this Italian-German theologian and thinker, see Hanna-Barbara Gerl-Falkovitz, *Romano Guardini: Leben und Werk* (Ostfildern: Matthias-Grünewald-Verlag, 1985), especially chapter 5. Citations are from the Italian edition, *Romano Guardini: La vita e l'opera* (Brescia: Morcelliana, 1988).

had originated in France and soon landed in Germany, where it ran the risk, however, of being confined to the monasteries, to Beuron or Maria Laach.

The monks themselves, nevertheless, in particular Abbot Ildefons Herwegen, were the ones who took the initiative to extend the movement beyond the circle of the monasteries. For this purpose, Abbot Herwegen inaugurated a series of books, Ecclesia orans, "the Church at prayer", and an annual anthology of liturgical essays, the *Jahrbuch für Liturgiewissenschaft*, with which he sought to inculcate a sense of the beauty and aesthetic qualities of liturgical celebrations. Therefore, it was no accident that Guardini began to come from Mainz and Bonn to visit the Abbey of Maria Laach, where he met and became friends with Father Kunibert Mohlberg. To this Benedictine monk, Guardini showed copies of several letters in which he explained to a friend the origin of certain religious truths, in particular, the foundation of the liturgy itself, without going into specific arguments but offering a more in-depth sense of the whole.

Unbeknownst to Guardini, Father Mohlberg showed his letters to Abbot Herwegen, who was enthusiastic about them. With small modifications, the letters became the first chapters of *The Spirit of the Liturgy*.[8] The work was an immediate success; in less than five years, it ran to twelve editions. The reason for the unexpected reception must be sought above all in the utterly non-clerical language used by the author. Aiming to address everyone, he strived to explain every single liturgical text and action with reference to ecclesial reality as a whole, to the catholicity of the faith and of the Church. Max Scheler wrote to Guardini after reading the book: "I find your little work nothing short of classically perfect for your purpose, and I am especially glad also that it is being so widely read."[9]

The chapter on liturgy as being playful especially piqued the readers' interest. Guardini explained: The truth, like a work of art, does not pursue a purpose, but this does not mean that it does not have meaning. Its gratuitousness is at the origin of its beauty. Another very important point is the chapter on the priority of the *logos* over *ethos*, with which Guardini aimed to go beyond Kant. He wrote:

---

[8] *Vom Sinn der Liturgie* was published in Germany in the series Ecclesia orans in 1918 and in an English translation as *The Spirit of the Liturgy* by Sheed & Ward in 1935. The latter was recently reprinted by Biretta Books (2015).

[9] Gerl-Falkovitz, *Romano Guardini*, 125.

"Truth is truth because it is truth. The attitude of the will to it, and its action towards it, is of itself a matter of indifference to truth."[10] Scheler commented in his above-mentioned letter: "The chapter on *logos* and *ethos* has become necessary, in a very special way, precisely in an era like ours in which the passage by Saint John must be restored."[11] Ultimately and above all, Guardini inserted his reflections on the liturgy into the life of the Church. She possesses something more, which is derived from time, in shaping and binding. This tie to the life of catholicity and dogma is what guides us toward interior freedom. "Truth . . . can make prayer efficacious, and impregnate it with that austere, protective strength without which it degenerates into weakness."[12]

This obviously did not prevent Guardini from giving fair consideration to popular piety. The reference to the tie between liturgy and Church life signaled a gradual distancing from Maria Laach and an approach to the youth movement Quickborn (which means "gushing spring"). Guardini recalled in 1949:

> In 1919, some of us had taken a walk, and after their return they told us about an old fortress on the Main, called Rothenfels, where many unusual things were happening. Indeed, no one was in charge, they said, and yet there was perfect order. They worked and celebrated liturgy there, but everything came from the persons themselves who took part in it; the young men and the young women were together, in serious and in joyful times, but everything happened decently and properly. And so at Easter in 1920, I myself went up to visit.[13]

Founded in 1909, Quickborn had quickly gathered a good number of young people. Its growth was slowed by the war but resumed vigorously in 1919 after the acquisition of Rothenfels Castle, on the Main, to the west of Würzburg. The fortress became the most important meeting place for the young people of Quickborn. After approaching them almost out of curiosity, Guardini soon became their undisputed guide, the organizer capable of keeping the young

---

[10] Romano Guardini, *The Spirit of the Liturgy*, trans. Ada Lane (New York: Sheed & Ward, 1935), 59.

[11] Gerl-Falkovitz, *Romano Guardini*, 125. The passage from John referenced by Scheler is chapter 1, verse 1, of his Gospel: "In the beginning was the Word."

[12] Guardini, *Spirit of the Liturgy*, 9.

[13] Gerl-Falkovitz, *Romano Guardini*, 175.

people fascinated with his reflections on the liturgy, the Trinity, and the life of the Church. A philosopher who in turn became famous, Josef Pieper, recalled: "In August of 1920, I saw Romano Guardini for the first time, from a distance in the interior courtyard of Rothenfels fortress. . . . We were fascinated by something that we had never noticed before and by how much this man was able to tell us, in an almost incredibly simple way of speaking."[14]

Besides speaking, Guardini also knew how to listen, to understand the new ideas that were taking shape in souls. From 1920 to 1922, he was the spiritual director of the convent of the Sisters of the Sacred Heart in Pützchen, near Bonn. There he had the time to prepare his thesis for his adjunct professorship, but soon, after his first meetings at Rothenfels, these visits and meetings multiplied. He then gave a series of conferences that were the basis for another famous book: *Vom Sinn der Kirche*, published in English under the title *The Church and the Catholic*. The first of the five conferences on which the volume was based started with a sentence that soon became famous: "A religious process of incalculable importance has begun—the Church is coming to life in the souls of men."[15] The liturgical movement was thus embedded in the experience of the reality of the Church and acquired its foundation and depth. Previously, the faithful struggled to feel that they were a community in the liturgical celebration. The Church was viewed mainly as a religious institution of an official, juridical kind. The new sense, in contrast, made them experience the Church as a community that transcends and unites the individuals. She is the living communion of the faithful, the Mystical Body of Christ.

Joseph's first years

In Germany and Bavaria, the 1920s were not peaceful times. Inflation increased as far as the eye could see, the country was becoming impoverished, and disorders abounded. Georg Ratzinger recalled: "At that time my father was paid daily, but no sooner did he have his money in his hands than it was no longer worth anything, because

---

[14] Ibid., 195.

[15] Romano Guardini, *The Church and the Catholic*, in: *The Church and the Catholic* and *The Spirit of the Liturgy* (New York: Sheed & Ward, 1940), 11–116 at 11.

the prices had gone up again."[16] Joseph and Maria, nevertheless, did not let themselves be overcome with discouragement. Even though they could not afford luxuries on a policeman's salary, the chief of police was one of the leading figures of the countryside, while Maria made a great contribution to the family budget by cultivating a garden from which she harvested all sorts of vegetables. Furthermore, she knitted constantly, making caps, sweaters, socks, scarves, and gloves. Finally, with her skills as a cook, she was able to organize a tasty meal even starting with very simple ingredients. These qualities, combined with good humor, allowed the family to lead a tranquil life even in difficult times.

Another strong support was the staunch adherence of the two spouses to Catholicism. Brother Georg recalled: "Every day we prayed together, and in fact before and after each meal (we ate our breakfast, dinner, and supper together). The main prayer time was after the midday dinner, when the particular concerns of the family were expressed."[17] The parents were firmly convinced of God's help in the joyful and sorrowful events of life, and they lived their faith, not in isolation, but rather as part of the life of the Church as a whole and of the community in their village. On their wedding day, the pastor had given them a *Schott*. This was the term used at that time in Germany to refer to the missal for laypeople originally edited by the monk Anselm Schott of Beuron, the great Benedictine monastery in Baden-Württemberg. The standard-bearer of the liturgical movement, Schott had already published in the late nineteenth century a missal for the laity with the Latin text of the Mass side-by-side with the German translation, so that the faithful could participate in the liturgical life of the Church. Later attempts to design a missal for the laity were referred to by the name of the first editor. From the beginning, therefore, the Ratzinger family lived within that liturgical and ecclesial movement that found in Romano Guardini its most effective supporter and spokesman.

In 1925, the police officer Joseph Ratzinger was transferred to Marktl am Inn, a village of about two thousand inhabitants, almost all Catholics. On the marketplace, at number 11, there is still today a large house built in 1700 in the typical style of Southern Bavaria.

---

[16] G. Ratzinger and Hesemann, *My Brother the Pope*, 31.
[17] Ibid., 45.

The Ratzinger family came to occupy the first floor of it, and that is where, in the early hours of April 16, 1927, their third child was born, who was named Joseph Aloysius. The first name, as was the custom in the family, was his father's, the second, the equivalent of Louis, was given to him in honor of an uncle who had become a priest and had taken the name of the young Italian Jesuit Saint Aloysius Gonzaga.

Brother Georg recalled:

> That night, or else in the early morning hours, I was suddenly lying alone in bed. No one had awakened me, as they usually did, and instead I heard the noise of hectic activity. Doors slammed, rapid footsteps resounded in the hall, people were talking loudly. When I heard my father's voice, I said, "Father, I want to get up!" But Father said, "No, you must wait a while; today we have a little baby boy!"[18]

It was Holy Saturday, but there was snow, and it was very cold. But it was a unique opportunity: in those days, the Paschal liturgy with the blessing of the water and the baptismal ceremony was celebrated on the morning of Holy Saturday. Leaving in bed the children and their mama, who was still suffering from childbirth, the father quickly went to the church with the newborn. Little Joseph was thus baptized in the new holy water, and his baptism and his life were immersed in the Paschal atmosphere, in those hours in which the mysterious passage of Jesus from death to life occurs for the faithful. Cardinal Ratzinger later commented in his memoirs: "I have always been filled with thanksgiving for having had my life immersed in this way in the Easter mystery, since this could only be a sign of blessing."[19]

Having a rather weak constitution, little Joseph lived surrounded by the attentions of his mother and of the neighbors. The cardinal admitted in his memoirs that he remembered nothing about that village which he would have to leave soon, but emphasized its proximity to Altötting, the Marian shrine of that region, to which the family and he himself were accustomed to travel on pilgrimage. This circumstance, nevertheless, lends itself to another observation

---

[18] Ibid., 38.

[19] Joseph Ratzinger, *Milestones: Memoirs 1927–1977*, trans. Erasmo Leiva-Merikakis (San Francisco: Ignatius Press, 1996), 8.

made by a journalist of the *Süddeutsche Zeitung* on the occasion of
the election of Benedict XVI. Marktl is located exactly halfway between Altötting and Braunau, between paradise and inferno, between the shrine of the Blessed Virgin and the birthplace of Adolf
Hitler, whose ill-omened shadow was already starting to extend over
Germany. Little Joseph was not yet two years old at the time of the
first of many moves during his childhood.

The next stage of his life was spent in Tittmoning, a town about
twelve miles farther south, on the bank of the Salzach River; the
bridge over it also marks the border with neighboring Austria. This
is the place that the future pope remembered as his "childhood's
land of dreams".[20] Imprinted on his memory were the large square
with its elegant fountain, the magnificent town hall, and the imposing houses, among them the one destined for the family of the chief
of police, which was situated in the historical center and directly
fronted the square. Though no doubt splendidly located, the house
was not ideally suited to family life. Originally, it had been owned
by the canons of the collegiate church, and now it urgently needed
repairs. The floor was cracked, and the steep wooden stairs creaked.
These features, however, affected the mother, who was forced to
move around in a small kitchen and narrow corridors, but not the
children, who found it all mysterious, particularly the bedroom, the
former chapter room, which in contrast was particularly spacious.

Another thing that made Tittmoning so fascinating was the beautiful old church, which had been staffed in the preceding centuries
by the secular canons. Their founder, the mystic and visionary
Bartholomew Holzhauser, was the author of apocalyptic works. The
memory of this presence was preserved in the title by which the
pastor, the dean, and the chaplains were called: canons. Another attraction was the twelfth-century fortress that loomed over the city,
which for a time in the seventeenth century had been the summer
residence of the bishops of Salzburg. In the immediate vicinity are
the Marian shrine of Ponlach, or Maria Brunn, where the mother
often brought her three children for devotions to the Blessed Virgin, but also for a relaxing, healthful walk in the steep woods along
the height that leads to the shrine. The city was a little more elevated; below was the bridge over the Salzach. It was necessary to
pay a small toll, but the mother was close friends with the female

---

[20] Ibid., 10.

employee at the border, who often winked at it. Thus they came to a foreign country, where nevertheless the people spoke the same language and the same dialect.

In that beautiful border city, Joseph also had his first experience outside the home. While his sister and brother went to school, he was enrolled in the kindergarten run by English Sisters; the directress was a small but energetic nun. It was not a joyful experience: the smallest of the Ratzinger siblings would have preferred to stay at home with Mama. With hindsight, however, the pope maintained that the effort to get used to common life did him good. In Tittmoning, finally, the love of the two brothers for music began, promptly seconded by their parents. In the border city, Georg knew a gentleman who owned a harmonium, and he often went to his house so as to be able to play that mysterious instrument which attracted him. At last, when the family was about to leave for a new destination, by means of an ad placed in the newspaper, Herr Ratzinger purchased a used harmonium for his two sons. Thus were born in Georg a love that led him to become a musician and in Joseph an interest that never diminished and was constantly cultivated over the years.

The ascent of Nazism

In the late 1920s, Germany was a defeated, impoverished, and divided country. The Treaty of Versailles, which according to the victors would guarantee international order, in Germany was considered in reality "an international absurdity", as Pacelli wrote to Gasparri in 1920.[21] In 1923, the French government informed the German government of its intention to send into the Ruhr district a team of auditors to verify the strict application of the reparation programs established at Versailles. After the Spartacist rebellion in 1919, Bavaria had become a place of refuge for the counterrevolutionaries. There, too, a certain Adolf Hitler had begun to take his first steps; he wanted to make the southern *Land* "a center of renewal within the corrupt Marxist Reich".[22] The attempt to start an uprising from a beer hall in Munich in late 1923 ended with Hitler's arrest,

---

[21] Cf. Philippe Chenaux, *Pio XII: Diplomatico e pastore* (Cinisello Balsamo: San Paolo, 2004), 111.

[22] Marlis Steinert, *Hitler* (Paris: Arthème Fayard, 1991), 148.

but the National Socialist seed had already been scattered on the ground.

The following year, 1924, had led to the signing of the concordat between Bavaria and the Holy See, which guaranteed for Catholics the teaching of religion in State schools, the recognition of religious congregations as corporations under public law, and a whole series of favorable provisions. For Catholics, it seemed like the beginning of a more positive era. The economic crisis of 1929 soon put an end to the illusion. Galloping inflation and repeated strikes exasperated and discouraged the people. In 1930, the National Socialist Party of German Workers (NSDAP) won six million votes in the elections for the German Parliament. It was not yet the most popular party in the country, but it would soon become the leading party as a result of the failure of the last governments of the Weimar Republic, led by a representative of the Catholic Party, the so-called Center, which was headed by a cleric, Monsignor Ludwig Kaas, a friend and co-worker of the nuncio, Pacelli.

Seeing the advance of the Nazis, a growing number of the lay faithful wondered whether it was permissible for Catholics to belong to that party, which was overtly anti-clerical and anti-Catholic. The question was answered in the negative by the Vicar General of Mainz, whose position was adopted by L'Osservatore Romano, which wrote: "Membership in the National Socialist Party is incompatible with a Catholic conscience."[23] Still more important in our context was a statement by the Bavarian Bishops' Conference, with Michael Cardinal von Faulhaber presiding, that spoke about the Nazi Party and the Christian faith as fundamentally irreconcilable.[24] This explains the fact that in the Catholic districts of Bavaria, the National Socialist Party received a lower percentage of the votes in the fatal elections of 1933 compared with other German regions. After that, however, the Vatican authorities and the bishops necessarily had to deal with the Nazis, and the barriers gradually gave way.

The first signals that came from the chancellery, initiated by von Papen, Hitler's Catholic vice-chancellor, were immediately understood by the Vatican. There was the model used in Italy, where several years previously a concordat had been signed to defend the

---

[23] "Il partito di Hitler condannato dall'autorità ecclesiastica" ("Hitler's Party condemned by Church authority"), L'Osservatore Romano, October 11, 1930.

[24] See Chenaux, Pio XII, 168.

interests of Catholics against an authoritarian partisan State; there was the precedent of the concordat with Bavaria, which had been crafted by the nuncio, Pacelli, who had recently become secretary of state. On March 23, 1933, Hitler declared that he was intent "on continuing and developing the amicable relations with the Holy See".[25] Several days later, Cesare Orsenigo, the nuncio in Berlin, announced to Pacelli the arrival of von Papen in Rome. Meanwhile, the leaders of the Center, after voting to give Hitler full powers on March 23, 1933, decided to dissolve their own political organization on July 5 of the same year. But the Bavarian People's Party had preceded it by just one day.

Was this acting too hastily? Some politicians thought so, for example the University of Cologne professor Benedikt Schmittmann, who came from Germany to Rome for the express purpose of warning the secretary of state, with whom he had been acquainted in Germany. Most importantly, several German bishops were convinced of it, among them Cardinal von Faulhaber, who wrote and sent to Pacelli a memorandum in which he distinguished "what is praiseworthy" from "what is not" in the Nazis' program. The positive part (reference to Christianity, anti-Bolshevism) was far outdone by the negative: the propagation of hatred and the idea of race. Therefore, repeating expressions from the pastoral letter of the German bishops, von Faulhaber made it clear that the Christianity of which Hitler spoke no longer had anything to do with Christ, but was a different religion, a world view (*Weltanschauung*) that was Christian in name only.

In Rome, nevertheless, where other statements different in tone were arriving, the urgency of safeguarding Catholics seemed to be the overriding concern. For example, Archbishop Conrad Gröber of Freiburg wrote: "Hundreds of people, who are liable to be arrested for reasons of public security and now find themselves in serious danger along with their families, would be very grateful to the Holy See if they could be spared this fate."[26] This consideration was precisely what led Secretary Pacelli to accelerate the pace, while Pius XI, who at first had been the chief supporter of the initiative, started to have misgivings about the excessive haste.[27]

---

[25] Orsenigo to Pacelli, March 24, 1933, *AAES*, Germany, 162.
[26] Gröber to Pacelli, *AAES*, Germany, July 1, 1933.
[27] Cf. Chenaux, *Pio XII*, 174.

In any case, the signing of the concordat was greeted favorably in Rome; and this was also because the dangers connected with the agreement seemed to be averted by subsequent events, which occurred so rapidly as to justify even the haste with which the signing had been arranged. The disbanding of the Center Party, which came about by an independent decision, seemed to nullify the provision that prevented the clergy from becoming involved in politics, while, conversely, the concordat could become a bulwark against Nazi attempts to infiltrate the clergy. Moreover, the concordat ensured Catholic associations and organizations and, above all, protected the rights and freedoms of the Church in the educational field. As had already happened in Italy, however, disputes began immediately after the signing. In Germany, the concordat was presented as an implicit recognition of the German government; in Rome, *L'Osservatore Romano* published an article that ruled out the idea that the concordat signified "the recognition of a definite current of political doctrines or views".[28]

The attempt to arrive at a *modus vivendi* lasted only until the summer of 1933. The violent attacks of the Nazis on Catholic organizations, on youth groups, and on the clergy amply demonstrated how much their word and their signature on a concordat were worth to the Nazis. Consequently, above all in Bavaria, the episcopate returned to the previous position of clearly condemning the regime. Of them all, Cardinal von Faulhaber once again distinguished himself; particularly in his Advent sermons, he spoke up forcefully against the Nazis' repeated anti-Christian and anti-Semitic attacks. As had already happened in Italy, the main battlefield was control over the Catholic schools, which the regime attacked during the years 1935–1938.

The policeman's strategy

Among the protagonists of the *Kulturkampf*, the struggle between Church and State in Germany and Bavaria in the late nineteenth century, was an uncle of the father of the future pope, Doctor Georg Ratzinger (1844–1899). As a priest and politician, from 1875 to 1877 he was a member of the house of delegates of the Regional

---

[28] *L'Osservatore Romano*, July 26, 27, 28, and 29, 1933.

Council, and from 1877 to 1878 he belonged to the German Parliament. Elected once again to the Regional Council in 1893, he remained in that office until his death. As a conservative student of the famous Church historian Ignaz von Döllinger, one of the Old Catholics opposed to the acknowledgment of papal infallibility proclaimed in Vatican Council I, in 1870 he appeared suspicious to both the political and the ecclesiastical authorities. Unable, therefore, to count on an academic career, he became involved in Catholic journalism on social issues and dedicated himself to political activity. His most famous work is a *History of the Church's Care for the Poor.*

Among his works, though, it seems there were also some anti-Semitic writings that he published under a pseudonym. Nevertheless, neither his nephew nor his grand-nephews knew about them.[29] He criticized Prussia's ambition to become a great power and sensed that militarism would have inauspicious consequences. In keeping with his uncle's teachings, the policeman Joseph was against the policy of including Bavaria in a federation led by Prussia, preferring an agreement with Austria and, above all, with France. As an agent of law and order in Tittmoning and an observer of Bavarian and national politics, he was in a position to understand what was happening in the thirties in Germany and all around him and his family. Indeed, he used to read the daily newspaper from Munich, the *Münchner Tagblatt,* which was sympathetic to the Catholic People's Party and hostile toward the Nazis.

He was, moreover, a reader of the periodical *Der gerade Weg* (The straight way), the mouthpiece of Catholics involved in politics. In particular, the editor-in-chief, the journalist Fritz Michael Gerlich, distinguished himself in denouncing Hitler's followers; as early as 1932, he wrote: "National Socialism is a plague. . . . [It] means: hostility toward neighboring countries, tyranny at home, civil war, international war. It means lying, hatred, fratricide, and boundless misery."[30] It is perhaps superfluous to add that, after the Nazis seized power, he was beaten, tortured, and finally interned in Dachau, where he died.

---

[29] G. Ratzinger and Hesemann, *My Brother the Pope,* 24–26, esp. 26.

[30] Ibid., 64.

The head of the Ratzinger family knew, moreover, that in Munich the regime had started to gather strength with a view to seizing power. More than once, after all, he had had to intervene to defend unarmed persons against the attacks of gangs that extolled Hitler and Greater Germany. His repeated interventions made him well known in Tittmoning as a relentless anti-Nazi, and there were those who waited for an opportune moment to settle the score. His superiors therefore recommended a change of climate, and he willingly accepted the suggestion. Another transfer followed, therefore, which took place in mid-December 1932. From Tittmoning to Aschau, from a little town on the border with Austria to a village on the Inn River.

In his memoirs, Cardinal Ratzinger did not conceal a certain disappointment with an essentially peasant village where the only meeting places were a beer hall and two hotels, while the charming little church in that locality certainly could not compete with the basilica in Tittmoning. On the plus side, the lodgings of the police chief and his family, in a little modern villa owned by a rich farmer who had rented it to the police force, were plainly superior to their former ones. On the ground floor were the offices, on the second story, the finally comfortable home of the Ratzingers, who could also make use of a garden that immediately attracted the attention of Mama Maria. In keeping with a longstanding custom, the family immediately introduced themselves to the pastor, Alois Igl, who was assisted by Georg Rinser, the uncle of the author Luise. Igl was a very kind, welcoming person, like his housekeeper, who always had little gifts for the visitors. The Ratzinger brothers, too, went to visit her often. After a few days, the harmonium bought in Tittmoning arrived; Georg and Joseph happily spent hours learning to play it. Georg, in particular, quickly demonstrated an outstanding musical talent, and he began to play in church at the age of only ten.

A short time after their arrival in Aschau, Hitler came to power. The head of the Ratzinger family reacted to the news in a personal way that was curious but logical. He told his relatives: "War is going to break out soon; we need a house." And, in fact, that same year he purchased with his life's savings a house in Hufschlag, near Traunstein. There he took the appropriate steps to fix up the place and to go into retirement as soon as possible. At around that same time, the younger son, Joseph, started his schooling. A photo from those days best depicts the situation. The children on benches, turned around

toward the camera with their backs toward the schoolmistress. Behind her, on the blackboard, is written a simple addition problem
and a reading exercise. In the center of the wall—the crucifix, and
beside it two photos: one of Hindenburg, the head of State, the
other of Hitler, head of the government.

For the children, according to the memoirs, life continued almost
unchanged, centered on the school year that was still pervaded by
Catholic spirit and teaching. Of course, among the teachers there
were some, in particular the young ones, who sided with the Nazis
and little by little proposed initiatives aimed at changing the traditions of the village. One young Nazi instructor, for example, organized a May festival that was supposed to be the start of the renewal of the Germanic religion. Therefore, he set up a Maypole
with sausages hanging at the top of it. Then he read a prayer that he
had composed and started the contest, but the farmers laughed at
these initiatives, and the boys seemed more interested in the edible
prize than anything else.

The liturgical year revealed quite a different depth: it set a rhythm
for time and gave it the sense of being a course that is rich in meaning and laden with promises. Christmas and Easter were the hinges
on which the seasons of life and growth turned. The boys' chief
occupation was school, in which study was accompanied by a progressive immersion in liturgical life. Joseph, in particular, early on
received from his parents an illustrated *Schott*, in which the draw-
ings helped the reader to understand the individual gestures, the
principal liturgical actions. This first book was then replaced, as he
prepared for his First Holy Communion in 1936, by a new *Schott*
in which the individual parts of the liturgy were synthesized and
explained. Next came the *Schott* for Sundays, and finally the complete daily missal. "It was a riveting adventure to move by degrees
into the mysterious world of the liturgy, which was being enacted
before us and for us there on the altar. . . . This mysterious fabric
of texts and actions had grown from the faith of the Church over
the centuries."[31]

This fascination with the liturgy then turned into an attraction
to priestly life, which was manifested also in several miniature devotional objects used in games: little chalices, candles, candlesticks.
With the passage of years, there was no lack of special signs that

---

[31] J. Ratzinger, *Milestones*, 19–20.

left impressions on the child's memory and imagination. The first is connected with a place: the Marian shrine in Altötting, the Catholic heart of Bavaria. Located on the main square is the Gnadenkapelle, the Chapel of Grace, in which the miraculous statue of the Black Madonna is venerated. Bernard Lecomte, a former Vatican reporter for *Le Monde*, drew a parallel between Kalwaria Zebrzydowska and Altötting, two Marian shrines where a Black Madonna is venerated. Little Karol Wojtyła used to go to the first with his father, and Joseph with his family to the second: the two future popes from Central Europe who were called to pacify their countries and their continent in the delicate transition from the second to the third millennium.[32]

Joseph, in particular, went to Altötting in 1934, on the occasion of the canonization of Brother Konrad, a humble lay brother born in Parzham, in the neighborhood of Passau, on December 22, 1818. He soon lost both his parents, but the orphan did not become embittered; he kept his meek character and love of nature. Whenever he could, he used to recollect himself in prayer, and at the age of eighteen he sought admission to the secondary school run by the Benedictines in Metten so as to become a priest. Since he failed in his studies, he had to return to farming. In 1841, he entered the Capuchin monastery in Altötting as a lay brother; there he took his vows and spent the rest of his life, performing the humble service of porter. Smiling and always with a rosary in his hand, he dispensed spiritual and material aid to pilgrims, to the poor, and to children. He died in 1894, three years before the death of the principal champion of "spiritual childhood", Saint Thérèse of the Child Jesus, so dear to France, which would be attacked by the Nazis. Pius XI, at the recommendation of Cardinal Pacelli, first beatified and then canonized Brother Konrad, convinced that the faith of simple people is the best antidote to the cult of violence supported and practiced by Nazism.

Around the mid-1930s, indeed, the signs that even little Joseph could observe in everyday life were not speaking of peace. Even in such a remote village as Aschau there were steadfast Nazis, and the Hitler Youth (Hitlerjugend) was introduced, the youth organization that was supposed to teach the schoolboys the spirit of

---

[32] Bernard Lecomte, *Benoît XVI* (Paris: Perrin, 2006), 19.

the new rulers. Joseph's siblings, too—Maria, who in 1935 was fourteen years old, and Georg, who was eleven—had to put on the brown shirt and march through the streets of the village for the glory of the new Germany. Their father was fully aware of the danger to their young consciences posed by these demonstrations of violence and hatred, and he protested, accusing Hitler of being a vagrant, a scoundrel who was leading Germany to ruin. Another disturbing sign was the construction of a lighthouse on Winterberg, a hill overlooking the village. "At night, when it combed the sky with its glaring light, it appeared to us like a flash of lightning announcing a danger that still had no name."[33]

At the seminary

Joseph Ratzinger, Sr., was increasingly convinced that war was now imminent. He needed, therefore, to resign as soon as possible, since police work is such a risky job. In reality, he would have liked to submit his resignation on the very day when Hitler seized power, but the settlement of several thousand marks, which was paid out only when the officer reached retirement age, was indispensable in order to complete the purchase of the house. He held out, therefore, until he turned sixty and then immediately submitted his resignation, and the family moved to Hufschlag. The house, located in a strategic position, about nine miles from Lake Chiem along the road to Tittmoning, had been bought several years before and was now ready. Most importantly, it was near Traunstein, the location of the archdiocesan Seminary of Saint Michael, which Georg, the first of the two Ratzinger brothers, had already entered.

The family arrived at their destination one early April morning in 1937, when nature in flower was truly enchanting. Here it is appropriate to reprint a quotation from the memoirs of the future pope that still conveys the boy's enthusiasm: "The structural condition of this house caused Father all kinds of trouble, but for us children it was a paradise beyond our wildest dreams. . . . After all our wanderings this is where we finally found our true home, and it is here that my memory always returns with gratitude."[34]

---

[33] J. Ratzinger, *Milestones*, 16.
[34] Ibid., 22.

The structure of the old farmhouse, built in the Salzburg style in 1726, was very simple. In the front were the living quarters, and at the back there was a stall and a shed for wood and hay, where little Joseph liked to take refuge together with a cat that kept him company. The roof was covered with wooden shingles weighed down with stones to keep the wind from carrying them away. The house was located in the middle of a site measuring about three-quarters of an acre with two gardens, one in the front and the other at the back. A well in front of the house supplied the family with water and added a touch of poetry and enchantment to the place. Here Mama Maria started a garden from which she harvested spices and vegetables for the whole family. In the back, there were fruit trees that produced apples, plums, and cherries.

Their arrival in Hufschlag also meant a serious change in the life of Joseph, who at the age of ten had finished elementary school and was getting ready to start secondary school. At that time, the school year in Germany was divided into three parts: it began in spring, was interrupted in the summer months, then resumed in September until Christmas and, after the holidays, continued until March.[35] Soon after their arrival, therefore, Joseph had to start attending the school. With his father's approval, and following the example of his brother, who had entered the seminary in Traunstein and was attending the humanistic *gymnasium*, he too enrolled in the humanistic *gymnasium* in Traunstein. It was the last year of the old system that made a division between the science curriculum and the humanities in the secondary schools. The following year, the Nazis introduced a scholastic reform in which the two *gymnasiums* were combined. In addition, instruction in Greek and religion was abolished, while more classroom time was allotted to science courses and modern languages.

From his childhood, Ratzinger was glad to be able to follow the old system. Moreover, for the first two years, he continued to live at home; he walked a good half hour to school each day, which allowed him to admire nature and at the same time to repeat what he had studied in the evening or just that morning. A few weeks after the arrival in Hufschlag, when he was ten years and a few months old, Joseph received the Sacrament of Confirmation from

---

[35] G. Ratzinger and Hesemann, *My Brother the Pope*, 98.

the hands of Cardinal von Faulhaber on June 9, 1937. It was an encounter that made a tremendous impression on the boy, who would always remember the great cardinal with gratitude.

Notwithstanding his father's growing concerns about the ever more menacing political situation, the two years during which Joseph attended his first classes at secondary school as a day student were a time of serenity and growth. At school, he was able to broaden his horizons with Latin and Greek, two languages that revealed to him a rich, enthralling world of culture and civilization, which kept him far away from the false illusions of the regime.[36] At home, on the other hand, he was able to enjoy his parents fully: his mother, who was always obliging and generous, and his father, who little by little confided in his son and who gladly accompanied him on long hikes in the woods, telling him stories about his own life but also fantastic tales that nevertheless contained great human and Christian wisdom. The only difficulty of any importance was caused by the physical education classes; Joseph, who was the smallest in his class and one of the smallest boys in the whole school, did not like them at all. He much preferred walks in the woods or pilgrimages with his parents to the many Marian shrines in the vicinity.

In 1939, nevertheless, an important change occurred. The pastor, Stefan Blum in Haslach, who also had jurisdiction over Hufschlag, having ascertained that the youngest of the Ratzingers intended to follow in turn the path of formation for priestly life, recommended that Joseph, too, who was then twelve, should enter the seminary as soon as possible. The basic reason for the pastor's recommendation was the increasing conflict between the Church and Nazism. Young Joseph was not against entering the seminary, since his brother had already lived there for four years and spoke favorably about it to him. Moreover, while visiting Georg, he had had the opportunity to get acquainted with other seminarians and had become friends with some of them. For the family, on the other hand, this was a considerable economic sacrifice, since the father's meager pension was not enough to pay for tuition, room, and board for his two sons. That same year, though, their older sister, Maria, had finished school and had started to work for a large business in Traunstein.

---

[36] J. Ratzinger, *Milestones*, 23.

Their mother, moreover, during the summer went back to working as a cook at a hotel in Reit im Winkl. The generosity of the two women in the family, therefore, allowed the younger Ratzinger brother to enter the seminary, also.

Meanwhile, Joseph Jr. was successfully attending second-year classes at the secondary school; his application for admission was forwarded by Ratzinger Sr. on March 4, 1939. It was accompanied by a letter of recommendation by the spiritual director of the *gymnasium*, Hubert Pöhlein, saying that Joseph was a good boy, a diligent and reliable student who participated in the lessons with constant interest. The note from his physician, Doctor Paul Kellner, stated that the boy was in good health, although he was a little underweight. Submitted together with the application for admission was a request for a reduction of the boarding costs, since Joseph's brother was already attending the seminary and considering the family's not exactly prosperous circumstances. The response granting admission arrived before the end of March together with the agreement to reduce the costs—which in general was granted relatively often. In 1938–1939, only eleven students paid the full costs, while the other 123 had discounts depending on their need.[37] In Cardinal von Faulhaber's view, no one should give up the priesthood for economic reasons, and this reinforced the feelings of gratitude among the students and their parents.[38] The official day for new students to enter the seminary was April 16, 1939, right after Easter.

Founded in 1929 at Cardinal von Faulhaber's behest in order to increase the number of vocations to the priesthood, the seminary in Traunstein was an imposing building that housed around 150 boys in the late 1930s. Designed as a place to welcome new aspirants to the priestly life who came from the families of farmers or merchants, it offered the boys the opportunity for a good human and educational formation. For this reason, it was not called a minor seminary but, rather, a house of studies, and from the beginning it was endowed with several sports facilities. From its opening until 1956, the rector of the seminary in Traunstein was the priest Jo-

---

[37] Peter Pfister, ed., *Joseph Ratzinger und das Erzbistum München und Freising: Dokumente und Bilder aus kirchlichen Archiven, Beiträge und Erinnerungen* (Regensburg: Schnell und Steiner, 2006), 28.

[38] Ibid., 56.

hann Evangelist Mair, a severe but fatherly man.[39] He was assisted by several prefects who were responsible for discipline and studies.

According to the strict customs of the time, the daily routine began at 5:20 with the wake-up call and twenty minutes of personal hygiene. At 5:40, everyone had to be in church to attend Mass. Morning review followed until 7:10, when a light meal was eaten. After packing their satchels, all the boys went to school. Lessons began at 8:00 at the humanistic *gymnasium* with which Joseph was already familiar from having attended it for the two preceding years. Latin was taught by a classical philologist who had a son who was a priest and who was therefore well disposed toward the seminarians, as were the majority of the teachers besides. After noon, they returned to the seminary for lunch, and then, in good weather, they went to the sports field.[40] In fact, based on the new regulations in the area of physical education, it was necessary to spend at least two hours a day on sports; for Joseph, this was a veritable torture and difficult to forget.[41]

At 3:00 P.M., study hall began, which lasted until 7:00 P.M., interrupted by a break for a snack. Dinner was at 7:00 P.M., followed by a half hour of free time that was spent playing parlor games or devoted to conversation or to reading. One unusual characteristic of the seminary in Traunstein was the attention to music education, to which, as we know, the two Ratzinger brothers were very much inclined. At the seminary, therefore, they were able to pursue their common hobby. At 8:05 P.M., a quarter hour of spiritual reading began, while at 8:20, evening prayer was recited. At around 9:00 P.M., in silence, the students filed into the dormitories, which were large rooms, each containing forty-two beds. In the corridor, each student had his own closet, where he kept his personal belongings. Similarly, in the study hall, everyone had a desk with the books, notebooks, and other materials necessary for scholastic activities. It was an austere environment that prepared them for study and for life.

Joseph's stay at the seminary, however, was not destined to last long. The seminary had initially had the support of the population

---

[39] Ibid., 25f.
[40] Ibid., 28.
[41] Cf. J. Ratzinger, *Milestones*, 25–26.

and of the local authorities. With the coming of Nazism, however, the atmosphere changed rapidly. Any kind of support by the State was lacking, and Traunstein therefore found itself in a very difficult economic situation. In 1936 in Bavaria, Adolf Wagner became Minister of Education and Culture; he was a relentless Nazi who knew Hitler personally and was therefore powerful and feared within the Party. Wagner issued increasingly restrictive legislation about seminaries, encouraging denunciations, on the basis of which the staunchest Catholic teachers were accused and had to resign from their positions or else were transferred from office. In anticipation of the outbreak of war, moreover, a policy started of confiscating seminaries and other ecclesiastical properties. Traunstein, too, fell under the ax.

The modern building with its large rooms, a spacious kitchen, and a health clinic was too tempting an opportunity. It was therefore requisitioned as a treatment center at the beginning of the war, in September 1939. Therefore, with the new school year, Ratzinger started again to attend the school as a day student. From then on, a tight battle began between the State authorities and those of the Church, which led repeatedly to confiscations and restitutions of the building. Joseph's presence, too, at seminary was marked by these continual changes. After having started the year at home, on November 18, 1939, the seminarians, Ratzinger among them, were housed in the health spa in Traunstein, which they had to abandon, however, on April 1, 1940, to go back to attending school from home. The following school year, they were able to reenter the seminary, but as of December 12, they were sent to Sparz to the institute of the English Sisters. In autumn 1941, every place suitable for housing them was confiscated, and the Ratzinger brothers had to go back to attending school from home.

The seminary's fight for survival, which went through several phases, was accompanied by the fight over membership in the Hitler Youth. Introduced immediately after the seizure of power by the Nazis, membership in the Nazi organization for youth gradually became an obligation for young Germans. Until 1939, the seminarians were exempted from this obligation. With the outbreak of the war, however, the obligation to enroll was introduced. In order to avoid possible reasons for retaliation, from that year on, the seminary rector used to enroll the seminarians as a group in the Hitler Youth, not as volunteers, but rather as conscripts.

At that time, however, young Ratzinger was not yet fourteen years old, and therefore the obligation did not affect him directly. The problem arose on the completion of his fourteenth year. In 1941, he was therefore enrolled in the *Hitlerjugend* by his seminary superiors. In the archives, there is no document to this effect. The context and the testimony of the pope himself,[42] however, lead us to think that he was in fact enrolled in the organization by his superiors.[43] All told, the period of time spent by Ratzinger in the seminary was rather brief: around two years, from 1939 to 1941, spent first in the house of studies in Traunstein, then in the health spa in Traunstein, and then in the institute of the English Sisters in Sparz.

Despite the initial difficulties and the continual displacements, Ratzinger gave a positive evaluation of his experience in seminary, where he learned to adapt to common life and to form a community together with the others. "For this experience I am very grateful because it was important for my subsequent life."[44]

Toward world war

Nazism clearly had doctrinal roots with strong anti-Catholic elements, particularly in the areas of morality, the theory of the State, and exaggerated nationalism. Hitler's willingness to enter a concordat, the common enemy of Communism and the influence that it had on the people, to some extent even on the Catholics, who were represented in the government by von Papen, had suggested to the Holy See and the German episcopate an initially cautious attitude. As the years went by, however, given the flagrant violations of the concordat, Pius XI and his collaborators became increasingly convinced that it was fundamentally irreconcilable with the faith. Hence the idea for an encyclical took shape: *Mit brennender Sorge*, which severely condemned National Socialism; both its contents and the way in which it was brought into Germany, printed, and read simultaneously from the pulpit in churches throughout the country were a real challenge to the regime. The blow was felt by the Nazis, but it did not actually change their principles or conduct.

---

[42] Cf. Joseph Ratzinger, *Salt of the Earth*, trans. Adrian Walker (San Francisco: Ignatius Press, 1997), 52. The original German edition was published in 1996.

[43] Pfister, *Joseph Ratzinger*, 50.

[44] J. Ratzinger, *Milestones*, 27.

On the contrary, Hitler responded domestically with restrictive measures affecting the Catholic schools, while in foreign policy he drew closer to Mussolini, an approach that in the Vatican was considered hostile and dangerous.

In March 1939, meanwhile, Pius XI was succeeded by Pius XII, the secretary of state and former nuncio in Germany, who was elected to try to salvage peace and to avert war. He devoted the entire first part of his pontificate to this task. The expression contained in his appeal to rulers and to the peoples on August 24, 1939, "Nothing is lost with peace. Everything can be lost with war", defines the purpose of his activities. It illustrates, nevertheless, the disproportion between the desired end and the actual possibilities for influence on the part of the Holy See. The führer, in fact, thought that the moment had come to implement the policy of expansion in Europe that from the beginning had been one of his plans, and he was certainly not willing to give it up just because of an appeal from the pope. As early as 1933, when the Nazis came to power, the question of the Sudetenland in Czechoslovakia, a territory with the presence of a strong German minority, had become one of Hitler's chief claims.

Over the course of 1938, German pressures became ever stronger. In late September, a conference was held in Munich, promoted by Mussolini, in which the leaders of the United Kingdom and France, in order to avoid war, appeared conciliatory and advised Edvard Beneš, president of Czechoslovakia, to accept Hitler's demands. He spoke about protection for the German minority but in reality aimed to invade the bordering country. The Munich agreement notwithstanding, German troops occupied Czechoslovakia on March 15, 1939, and the very next day Hitler traveled to Prague to proclaim the protectorate of Bohemia and Moravia.

The Nazi dictator, however, had no intention of stopping. In late August, after an unfortunate pact with the Soviet Union, he began the invasion of Poland. The war that Joseph Sr. and the entire Ratzinger family feared so much was now a reality. There was nothing left but to face it while trying to save their lives, dignity, and faith. One harmless consequence of the war, for the two brothers, was the possibility of pursuing their musical hobby more intensively. As a result of the *Anschluss* (annexation), it had actually become easier to get to nearby Salzburg, where the Mozart concerts continued, while the prices were greatly reduced because fewer foreigners attended.

The year 1941 was the 150th anniversary of the great musician's death. Traveling the distance from Traunstein to Salzburg by bicycle, the two young Ratzingers were able to hear some extraordinary concerts. Georg commented: "For the first time in our lives, we had the privilege of attending a concert with top-quality interpretations of musical masterpieces. . . . So Mozart, I think, is my brother's favorite composer even today."[45] The year 1940 marked the triumph of the Nazis, with the occupation of Denmark and Norway and the invasion of Belgium, Holland, Luxemburg, and France, while Italy, too, decided to participate in the conflict by extending the front in the war to Greece and the Balkans.

In Germany, where the opposition was compelled to remain silent, there was an almost unreal calm. Joseph became an increasingly relentless reader. Among his favorite authors were two nineteenth-century German writers: he read *The Rider on the White Horse* and other novellas by Theodor Storm, and he was thrilled with *Mozart on the Way to Prague* by Eduard Mörike. Then, almost naturally, he became fascinated by Goethe and his writings, which were filled with a love for classicism and the joy of life. The solitude of war fostered in him also an enthusiasm for writing and poetry, in which he expressed his love for nature but also his enthusiasm for the liturgy. He began to translate some liturgical texts from Latin and Greek, and he also tried his hand at Latin verse.

In 1941, the conflict spread farther with the attack on the U.S.S.R. and the subsequent intervention of the United States in the war. Now Germany, too, was being tested by the war, with the introduction of ration cards and the return of more and more wounded men from the various fronts. The gloomy predictions of Joseph Sr. were coming true. Neither the victories abroad nor the fiery speeches of the dictator, however, could totally conceal the horror of what was happening inside the country, too. Various persons told stories about friends and relatives who had disappeared, and the Ratzinger family itself was overtaken by inexpressible sorrow. One of Joseph's cousins, the son of his mother's sister, who was only a few months younger than he, was born with Down syndrome.

---

[45] G. Ratzinger and Hesemann, *My Brother the Pope*, 110.

One day the Nazis came to take him away from home; some time later a notice arrived saying that the young man had died.[46] Similarly, an acquaintance of the family, Frau Westenthanner, whom they had met in Aschau, drifted gradually into dementia after her husband's death. She was therefore taken into custody by several government officials who brought her to Linz, where, according to the official report, she died, but everyone knew that she had been killed.

Georg Ratzinger recalled: "It was general knowledge that in the vicinity of Linz the Nazis gathered people who were mentally ill (or thought to be such) and, to their way of thinking, no longer useful to society, and then killed them."[47] A series of crimes that were being added to those caused by a war that was quite far from over.

Joseph goes to war

In the summer of 1942, the nightmare of war drew closer to the Ratzinger family. Georg, who by then had turned eighteen and was preparing for his matriculation exam, was called to perform the so-called "obligatory work service". With his squad, he had to travel to Wartenberg am Roll, in the Sudetenland, to build a sports camp. More than anything else, the experience was a gloomy preparation for the call to arms, which arrived at the end of the year. He later had to take part in the war in Holland, in Italy—in La Spezia and then in Montecassino after the famous abbey had been bombarded by the Allies—in Prague, and again in Italy, near Bologna, where he was wounded.

Joseph's turn came in 1943, when the military victories of the first two years of war were now a distant memory. Since they needed soldiers on ever more extensive fronts, the Nazis thought that college students who already lived together, far from home, could continue their studies in academic settings relocated to the vicinity of anti-aircraft artillery, the *Flak*. The seminarians from Traunstein born in 1926 and 1927 entered the service to take part in the defense of Munich. They lived in barracks like regular soldiers, wore uniforms, and performed approximately the same tasks. In addi-

---

[46] Ibid., 134.
[47] Ibid.

tion, they could take a certain number of courses taught by professors from the Maximilian Gymnasium in Munich; alumni from that school made up the majority of the enlisted students.

Then-Cardinal Ratzinger recalled in his first book-length interview with Peter Seewald: "I was sixteen years old, and for a whole year, from August '43 to September '44, we did our service. In Munich we were attached to the Max *Gymnasium*, so we also got lessons on the side. The subjects were reduced, but we still got a useful amount of instruction. On the one hand, this was naturally not pleasant, but, on the other hand, the camaraderie of the time also had its excitement."[48]

The first destination of the group was Ludwigsfeld, north of Munich. There the students had to provide aerial defense of a branch of the Bavarian Motor Works (BMW), which produced motors for aircraft. Cardinal Ratzinger also recalled in his interview with Seewald:

> A battery was divided into two main elements, the artillery and the range-finding section. I was in the range-finding section. We already had the first electronic and optical instruments to locate the approaching aircraft and to give the readings to the artillery. Besides the regular drills we had to be at the instrument at every alarm. What then became increasingly unpleasant was that there were more and more night alarms, and many nights were pretty much ruined.[49]

Subsequently, the young seminarians were transferred to Unterföhring, then to Innsbruck, and finally to Gilching. It was a difficult time for Joseph, who was so young and unsuited to military life and yet compelled to go to war. He tried to adapt as well as he could to the situation. He got an assignment to the reconnaissance services and then to telephone communications, used every free moment to read and study, and was not afraid to declare that as an adult he would like to become a priest. Eventually he won general esteem and respect. After a year of deployments in Germany and Austria, the students were discharged from the *Flak* in September 1944.

When he arrived home, however, Joseph found waiting for him a call to obligatory work service for the Reich. After an interminable trip riding in the bed of a truck, he reached the Austrian region

---

[48] J. Ratzinger, *Salt of the Earth*, 56.
[49] Ibid., 56–57.

of Burgenland, southeast of Vienna. Among the very large number of youths who had been called up for forced labor to build a southeastern rampart that was supposed to stop the advance of the Soviet troops, there were several classmates from the *gymnasium* in Traunstein. Joseph could therefore fraternize with friends and acquaintances. But despite the enchantment of nature, the two months spent in the Burgenland were among the hardest of his involvement in the war. Indeed, most of the officials who directed the work came from the so-called "Austrian Legion". That is to say, they were Nazis from the very beginning, ideologically driven SS-men, who harassed the youths with all sorts of abuses. One evening they woke the lads, who were exhausted by fatigue and mistreatment, and subjected them to a sort of interrogation. They asked for seemingly generic information, while in reality trying to identify recruits to enlist in the SS, whose numbers, like those of the soldiers, were starting to dwindle. When it was his turn to state the courses he had completed and the profession to which he aspired in life, Joseph openly declared that he wanted to become a priest. He was covered with insults and ridicule but fortunately was not pressured further to enter the SS.

Then there was the training with the shovel, the so-called *Spatenappell*, which had something almost religious and sacred about it. The shovel not only had to be perfectly clean, but it had to be grasped, lifted, and carried the right way, in tempo. In short, the lads were soldiers with a spade, and, before and after work, they always had to conduct a sort of para-liturgy. There was less of all that when the front came closer and nearby Hungary fell miserably, with the lads right on the border with it. Now the shovel suddenly lost its sacredness and from one day to the next became a normal working tool. This was a sign that demonstrated once again the empty falsehood of Nazism, a theatrical production backed by nothing but a big lie. The work had been suspended, the SS-men were no longer to be seen anywhere around, and the lads were left alone in the camp.

Finally, on November 20, their suitcases with their personal belongings were returned to them, and they were discharged. The train that brought the *gymnasium* student back home made slow progress because of the continuous air-raid alarms. Debris and ruins on every side testified to the defeat of Nazism, which was now manifest in all its devastating crudeness. Vienna, which only two months before had not yet been touched by the war, now showed obvious signs of the bombardments. Even worse was the situation in his beloved Salzburg, where the train station and the cathedral had been hit. Joseph arrived home on a splendid autumn day, and the joy of his arrival made him light-footed for once. The train did not stop at Traunstein. Without thinking twice, the lad jumped down from the train. As cardinal, he later wrote in his memoirs: "It was an idyllically beautiful fall day. There was a bit of hoarfrost on the trees, and the mountains glowed in the afternoon sun. Seldom have I ever experienced the beauty of my homeland as on this return."[50] Forced labor was usually followed directly by enlistment in the army. Joseph, however, did not find the dreaded postcard summons and therefore was able to stay with his loved ones for three weeks, during which he recovered physically and spiritually.

The conflict, however, had not yet ended, and before Christmas the dreaded postcard arrived summoning him to appear in Munich to enlist. In the Bavarian capital, he had the good fortune to deal with a kind-hearted official, an anti-Nazi who no longer believed in the "final victory". Turning to the young recruit, he asked him, "What shall we do with you? Where is your home?" Joseph replied eagerly: "In Traunstein. We have a barracks there." "So go to Traunstein, and don't start right away, but enjoy a few nice days first."[51] Obeying was pleasant this time. He knocked at the door of the barracks in the village in mid-December. The atmosphere was different, more humane. The uncertainty, though, made everything precarious, and a gloomy atmosphere brooded over Christmas in the barrack-room. Indeed, the troop was made up of very young lads and men in their forties who were married with children; they experienced intense homesickness, since they rarely received news from their families. Their suffering touched the heart of the future pontiff.

In January, Joseph was transferred to various barracks of neighboring villages, and in February he was sent back home on account of illness. In the following months, training sessions began. Strangely, the young men were not sent to the front, which was drawing ever

---

[50] J. Ratzinger, *Milestones*, 34.
[51] G. Ratzinger and Hesemann, *My Brother the Pope*, 123.

closer. They received instead new uniforms in which they had to march through the town, perhaps to convince the populace that Hitler still had young armed forces available and ready to fight.

Meanwhile, the months passed. On April 16, Joseph had turned eighteen, and the prospect of being called to the front became increasingly real. At a certain point, toward the end of that month or in the first days of May, he decided: "I will leave the barrack", and he headed for home. It was a very dangerous act, since the soldiers had orders to shoot deserters on sight or to hang them. And in fact, as he emerged from a tunnel, he found himself confronting two soldiers on guard. But they, too, were tired of the war. One of them called him over, saw that he had one arm in a sling from a wound, and said to him, "You are wounded, move on." Even at home, though, the danger was not dispelled. After a few days, two Nazis took up residence in the policeman's house; seeing Joseph, they began to ask embarrassing questions. The father could not restrain his anger and expressed all his bitterness over the destruction into which the country had been dragged by Nazism. A night passed during which Joseph's fate seemed to be sealed, but the following day the two men left without further explanation.

Finally, the Americans entered Traunstein and chose the Ratzingers' own house for their headquarters. So the fact emerged that Joseph was a former soldier. They therefore made him put on his uniform, declared him a prisoner of war, and forced him to take up quarters together with around a hundred other prisoners in the garden in front of the house. It was a sight that caused great suffering, especially for his mother, who was forced to see her defenseless son being supervised by American soldiers who were fully armed. Then the order was given for them to march, and every so often the column swelled with the arrival of new groups of prisoners.

After three days of uninterrupted marching on the empty highway, the column, whose end was no longer in sight, camped in Bad Aibling, where the prisoners spent a few days outdoors on the military airfield. From there, they were then moved toward Ulm, where, on an extensive agricultural field, around 50,000 survivors of the German army from all over Bavaria were gathered. It was not easy to manage such a great number of men. Provisions were scarce, as was the news that arrived from outside. Soon, though, there were many acts of charity and initiatives to help pass the time.

Joseph had a notebook with him, in which he wrote thoughts and poems, and he attended Mass celebrated by several priests and participated in debates on religious topics.

In this connection, we cannot fail to mention young Joseph's true passion for knowledge. Despite the repeated relocation of the seminary, the difficulties in obtaining books, and finally the calls to assist in anti-aircraft defense, in 1944 he received a *Semestervermerk*, a certificate stating that he had completed his years of study at the *gymnasium*. The following year, at Easter 1945, he received his diploma. In his case, though, it was not what is described as a war diploma. As already mentioned, he had read avidly not only the Latin and Greek classics and those of German tradition but also contemporary authors in the field of both literature and philosophy. An indirect confirmation of this is provided by the testimony of the theologian Alfred Läpple.

Speaking about his first meeting with Joseph Ratzinger in late 1945, Läpple recalled that he had immediately noted his great interest in philosophy and faith and that he had wondered how he could satisfy such a desire for knowledge.[52] Now, though, young Ratzinger was still a prisoner, and his future was more uncertain than ever. Visible on the horizon, nevertheless, was the slender form of the bell tower of the cathedral in Ulm, which, despite the bombardments, had remained standing and was a beacon of hope. In the anxieties of the present, it reached for the sky like a sign of continuity and of a not-too-distant return to life.

In June, they started to release the first prisoners, the peasants who had to cultivate the fields so as to provide food for the famished country. On the 19th of that month, Joseph received his precious discharge papers that put an end to his experience of war and military life. Two American trucks transported the group of liberated prisoners to just north of Munich. From there, they had to fend for themselves. Together with a companion, who was also originally from Traunstein, Joseph was preparing to make the journey home on foot, calculating the number of days necessary to cover the distance, when after a few miles a milk truck stopped. The disastrous war had taught the driver empathy, and he asked the two lads what their destination was; it turned out that he, too, was headed for

---

[52] Interview reprinted in Pfister, *Joseph Ratzinger*, 117.

Traunstein. Joseph thus arrived home even before sunset that same Friday, while his mother and sister were in church for the Feast of the Sacred Heart. His father, when he saw his son in front of him, was beside himself with joy. The following days were spent in serenity and rest and in telling one another what they had been through. There was still anxiety about Georg, about whom there was no longer any news.

In the book *The Salt of the Earth*, Peter Seewald asked then Cardinal Ratzinger what "providence" meant to him. The future pope replied: "I am quite firmly convinced that God really sees us and that he leaves us freedom—and nevertheless leads us. . . . For me this means in a very practical way that my life is not made up of chance occurrences but that someone foresees and also, so to speak, precedes me, whose thinking precedes mine and who prepares my life."[53] This is also the interpretation that he gives to his childhood and his participation in the war.

---

[53] J. Ratzinger, *Salt of the Earth*, 42.

II

PATH TO THE PRIESTHOOD

Back to everyday life

The joy over Joseph's homecoming on June 19, 1945, was repeated on July 1 with the unexpected arrival of his brother, Georg, who had returned from Italy. As soon as he arrived, Georg sat down at the piano and intoned "Holy God, We Praise Thy Name",[1] a hymn from the rich German tradition that praises God for the immense goodness with which he guides human history toward salvation. After their initial surprise, the whole family joined in with him. Having emerged unharmed from the conflict, beyond all reasonable hope, the Ratzingers could wholeheartedly express their thanks to God.

Soon, though, they had to think about the duties of everyday life. Economically, the family found themselves, like everyone in Traunstein, but also in Munich and throughout Germany, in a state of extreme poverty. In order to keep the population alive, ration cards had been introduced, as during wartime. Moreover, in order to be able to work, everyone had to obtain a new identity card and, for the young men who had been prisoners of war, discharge papers.[2] Only after having completed these bureaucratic procedures could one think about an occupation by which to earn a living so as not to burden the meager family budget.

Before the war, both brothers had been at the seminary in Traunstein and were acquainted with the rector, Johann Evangelist Mair. They called on him to greet him dutifully, but also to confirm that they wished to continue along the path on which they had set

---

[1] The original German hymn begins "Grosser Gott, wir preisen Dich."

[2] Georg Ratzinger and Michael Hesemann, *My Brother the Pope*, trans. Michael J. Miller (San Francisco: Ignatius Press, 2011), 139.

out. The priest welcomed them warmly and invited them to earn their living by working with him. Toward the end of the war, the seminary buildings had been converted into a hospice to take in refugees from East Germany and Rumania. Therefore, they needed thorough cleaning and repairs. The Ratzinger brothers' arms could be useful in clearing things out and bringing in tables, desks, and other furniture. In exchange, they received their daily food and a little more. Joseph, in particular, was happy. It was an opportunity to be immersed in the beloved atmosphere of study, to borrow books, and to meet classmates from years past. The two brothers left home in the morning by bicycle, and they returned in the early evening. This alternation of manual work and familial serenity was the best treatment to cure the physical and spiritual wounds of the war. Their intense work made it possible to reopen the seminary in Traunstein as early as November 20, the feast of Saint Corbinian, patron of the diocese.

Nevertheless, Traunstein was not the place where Georg and Joseph were to resume the path that would lead them to the priesthood. Their application for admission to higher studies was accepted, and they went to the major seminary in the city of Freising. From there, they sent to the rector in Traunstein a letter that summarized their thoughts about their time in minor seminary and about what had happened to them during the war. The two brothers said: "The years that we spent in the slavery of military service enabled us to appreciate the beauty and sublimity of our vocation more deeply than would have been possible in normal circumstances and perhaps, at least to a small extent, made up for the objective loss in the field of knowledge."[3] The idea is clear: military service had been a state of oppression that had nevertheless, as was the case for many men, strengthened rather than weakened their vocation.

The two brothers, however, were intensely aware of what they had missed in their education. We might also add that Joseph was the one who felt this deficiency more keenly, though he hoped to compensate for it through total dedication. In order to continue their formation, they had to attend classes in philosophy and theo-

---

[3] Peter Pfister, ed., *Joseph Ratzinger und das Erzbistum München und Freising: Dokumente und Bilder aus kirchlichen Archiven, Beiträge und Erinnerungen* (Regensburg: Schnell und Steiner, 2006), 52.

logy at the *Hochschule* for those subjects together with students from all over the Diocese of Munich and Freising.

Freising, the city on the hill

The older of the two dioceses that were joined in the nineteenth century was undoubtedly Freising. It was founded by Saint Corbinian in the early eighth century, upon his return from a pilgrimage to Rome, where he had been consecrated a bishop. Having settled on the hill of the city, he dedicated a church to Saint Stephen, which became the initial nucleus of the diocese instituted after his death by Saint Boniface. According to the *Life* written by Bishop Arbeo, who brought his body back to the city and laid it to rest in the cathedral, where it is still venerated today, Corbinian ordered a bear that had mauled his horse to carry his baggage for him across the Alps.[4] To this day, the bear carrying the saint's baggage is the symbol of the city. In 1818, at the time of the Restoration, the present Archdiocese of Munich and Freising was instituted, which joins the most populous industrial city with the city rich in civil and religious history.

At the end of the conflict, the major seminary had been requisitioned and converted into a military hospital for prisoners of war. Only with the gradual release of the internees was it possible to welcome the seminarians. Joseph's and Georg's turn came after the 1945 Christmas vacation. When the two brothers arrived at the beginning of 1946, notwithstanding the war and the carpet bombing of the Allies that had reduced all Germany to a pile of debris, the cathedral in Freising, built on the famous height, still stood in its majesty and was a sign of hope for those who had survived the war and destruction. Alongside it, the seminary and the college appeared to Joseph to be a peaceful oasis, a spiritual place for contemplation.

Welcoming the young men was the new rector, Michael Höck, an anti-Nazi from the beginning, a priest-journalist who had not hidden his aversion to the dictatorship of the führer. Born in 1903, Höck had studied at the German College in Rome under the aegis of Cardinal von Faulhaber. After being ordained a priest in 1930,

---

[4] Joseph Ratzinger, *Milestones: Memoirs 1927–1977*, trans. Erasmo Leiva-Merikakis (San Francisco: Ignatius Press, 1996), 154.

he returned to his country the following year and was appointed prefect of the seminary.

After Hitler's rise to power, in 1934 Höck was appointed editor-in-chief of the diocesan newspaper in Munich. Repeated warnings did not prevent him from manifesting his dissent more and more openly, until in 1940 the regime prohibited the publication of the newspaper and Höck was put on trial. Although acquitted, he was also arrested by the police and, after passing through various prisons, was interned in the camp in Dachau. He managed to survive and was liberated by the Americans in April 1945.[5] Cardinal von Faulhaber, who had great esteem and affection for him, appointed him rector of the seminary in Freising. The appointment of a man who had returned from a concentration camp could be risky, but for his seminarians he "was the right rector at the right time for the right seminarians".[6]

To be his right-hand man, he chose as prefect of studies Alfred Läpple, who at the outbreak of the war in 1939 was a few months short of finishing his studies to be ordained a priest. He had already begun studying for his doctorate when the Nazi authorities ordered the faculty of theology at the University of Munich to be closed. This was in retaliation against Cardinal von Faulhaber, who had refused to give permission to teach to Hans Bairon, a priest who had joined the Nazi Party.

At the outbreak of the war, Läpple was forced to leave everything and to enlist in the Luftwaffe. He was taken prisoner by the Americans in the German region of Westphalia and was transferred to France, near Le Havre, to a large camp where almost 50,000 prisoners were amassed. Among them were a large number of priests and Protestant pastors. Because of his knowledge of languages, Läpple was chosen as an interpreter and took advantage of this position to convince the authorities of the camp to assemble the priests, seminarians, and pastors in a single block. There they could celebrate Mass, hold ecumenical meetings, and also give mini-courses in theology. He was finally liberated in November 1945. He then telephoned the school to reestablish contact; the new rector Höck answered and told him: "Alfred, you are precisely the one I was

---

[5] Cf. G. Ratzinger and Hesemann, *My Brother the Pope*, 146.
[6] Cf. Alfred Läpple, *Benedetto XVI e le sue radici* (Venice: Marcianum Press, 2009), 15.

waiting for! You will have a fine, important job, for which you are just the right man."[7]

At his arrival, the rector, whom all the other priests affectionately called Michi, accompanied him to the banquet hall, which was more commonly called "the red room". In the past it had been the place for solemn institutional meetings; now it had been invaded by the desks of about fifty young students, to whom the rector introduced the new prefect, a sort of tutor for their studies. They could turn to him for suggestions about the curriculum, but also for practical counsels about their vocation. There was also a spiritual director at the seminary, the Jesuit Franz von Tattenbach. Of noble descent, this priest had been a sort of mediator between the Jesuit Order and the authorities of the Reich during the Nazi period, without compromising with the regime in the least. Following the lead of Rector Höck, he gave structure to the spiritual life of the house. "I maintain that those two men, Höck and Tattenbach, were the ones who most influenced the postwar generation of theologians."[8] Every evening he would give a meditation subdivided into points according to the Jesuit model.

The space available at the old seminary was greatly reduced because of the presence of many prisoners of war who were still there waiting to be liberated. The seminarians, therefore, slept in large dormitories in groups of forty. The already severe life of the aspirants to the priesthood was really Spartan because of the austerity imposed by the circumstances. The wake-up call was at 5:30, followed by morning prayers and Mass, which had particular relevance in the devotional life of the seminarians. It was celebrated by the priest in silence, and the young men followed it with pocket missals that gave the Latin text or a translation in German. This was followed then by meditation, breakfast, and classes at the school. When the students returned to the seminary, there was a short period of adoration in the church. After the break for the midday meal, finally, the schedule provided for a rather short time for recreation and then a more extended one for study. On feast days, all participated in the Solemn Mass in the cathedral; after supper, the seminarians could attend a conference or a musical concert, and then immediately they

---

[7] Ibid.

[8] Alfred Läpple, interview on April 30, 2006, reported in Pfister, *Joseph Ratzinger*, 124.

went to bed to rest, but also to protect themselves from the intense cold due to the lack of any form of heat whatsoever.

The curriculum was still modeled on the one that had been established at the time of the French Revolution. The courses on subjects more closely pertaining to pastoral ministry were held in the seminary. For the disciplines that were considered to be of a predominantly scientific character, the seminarians went to the nearby college for philosophy and theology. There were around 120 aspirants to the priesthood that year, equally subdivided: half had behind them a long, dramatic involvement in the war and were more advanced in age; the other half was made up of young men who had been affected only marginally by the hostilities. The former considered them inexperienced boys. The latter found it easier to learn the new currents in theology. All, however, were united by their great love of the Church, which they considered the true bulwark against the Nazi barbarity, and by their desire to leave behind them the tragedy of the conflict so as to start a new life.

Some have criticized the future pontiff for devoting little space in his memoirs, or in his writings, to the horror of the war and of the Nazi crimes.[9] Läpple gave the following explanation for this decision, with which he agreed: "There was nothing to discuss, no response of ours could have explained how it could have happened that some Christians had set up the concentration camps. . . . It was like starting over again from zero. It was as though the end of the war had given us life for a second time as a gift. We were happy about this; this was the predominant feeling."[10]

However, in those days, the Nuremberg trials were being held, the newspapers were filled with pictures of the camps and with the confessions of the Nazi criminals, and among the Catholics themselves there were many who wondered about the responsibilities of those who had remained silent or had been too accommodating.

Among these was the writer Ida Friederike Görres, author of a *Letter on the Church*, which, according to Läpple, "precipitated

---

[9] See in particular the excessively critical book by Matthew Fox, *The Pope's War: Why Ratzinger's Secret Crusade Has Imperiled the Church and How It Can Be Saved* (New York: Sterling, 2011), 31–36, which accuses the pope of selective memory because, in speaking about his youth, he does not recall the Nazi crimes in Traunstein and more generally in Bavaria.

[10] Cf. Gianni Valente, *Ratzinger professore* (Cinisello Balsamo: San Paolo, 2008), 20.

vehement debates at the seminary in Freising".[11] Even more critical was an article by Franz Josef Schöningh, editor of the journal *Hochland*, which in no uncertain terms accused the leaders of the ecclesiastical hierarchy of having "fallen into the snare of a slimy 'diplomat' because he was wrapped up in rosaries."[12] This article, in turn, aroused a heated debate at the seminary in Freising. The predominant feeling among those who had faced the horror of the battlefields and of the concentration camps was, nevertheless, the need to give thanks for having escaped the slaughter, the need to look elsewhere, to try to make a fresh start.

The polemic was reprised in 2006 by an American weekly newspaper that accused Ratzinger of having been too prone to forgive the German nation and too soft on the Nazis.[13] Rupert Berger, a seminary classmate of Ratzinger from the same district who was ordained a priest with him, responded to this critique as follows: "In this respect I cannot say much. One thing is certain: he hated the Nazis as I did, and in 1945 we had the sense of finally being free. I think, nevertheless, that he feels, as I do, Bavarian first and then German. For us, Bavaria comes first; here Germany has to give way. In theology, in contrast, he was more oriented toward France."

As for the relatively few condemnations of Nazism, immediately after its downfall, this was also the official policy of the Church, supported by Cardinal von Faulhaber, who was loved and respected by all the faithful, who saw in him the tenacious opponent who had been able to stand up to the dictator as few others could. On April 5, 1946, at the conclusion of the winter semester, the first one after the war, the prelate decided to celebrate a Pontifical Requiem Mass in Freising for the repose of the souls of the twenty-three priests, seventy-two students from the major seminary, and thirteen students from the minor seminary who had fallen in the war.

Among the crowd that packed the cathedral were the relatives of the fallen; the entrance procession was long and solemn. Behind the cross, the cortege started with the seminarians from Freising, wearing cassock and surplice; next came numerous representatives of the

---

[11] Läpple, *Benedetto XVI*, 69. It should be added that, because of this article, Görres was prevented from speaking in public to groups of Catholics. Later, Ratzinger corresponded with her for many years and gave the homily at her funeral in 1971.

[12] Ibid., 70.

[13] Timothy Ryback, "Forgiveness", *The New Yorker*, February 6, 2006.

clergy, in the middle of whom was the Auxiliary Bishop Johannes Neuhäusler, who, with Höck, had been in the concentration camps in Sachsenhausen and Dachau. Last of all, the cardinal advanced, blessing the people. In his homily, he spoke about the war, about the sacrifice made by so many brothers that must not be forgotten, and above all he exhorted his listeners to pastoral activity understood primarily as an educational task. "As future priests, those who came back will have to collaborate in the grand enterprise of reeducating our people. *Metanoeite,* learn to change your way of thinking, to change yourself personally. Our people were injected with ideas and principles coming from a lunatic or from hell."[14] The notions that the seminarians had to uproot from themselves and from the German people were: the racist principles that are at the origin of war between nations, the idea that war can lead to the enrichment of a nation, the idea of suppressing non-Aryans and then Christians.

Läpple related that, immediately after the Mass, he met the seminarians, who were profoundly impressed and agreed completely with the cardinal's talk. "They all sat silently at their desks, thinking: seeing that I was able to return, 'I can only be grateful and give thanks over and over again.' In the seminary in Freising, that basic spiritual state continued to be a gradually growing interior impulse."[15]

Philosophical formation

Although they were avoided in public, uncomfortable questions were not censored at all in the seminary. Again according to Läpple's testimony, Joseph, only a few days after his arrival, went to see the prefect and asked him how he had been able to keep the faith during wartime. "I answered him that it had been my mother's prayers. And that I knew that Christ loved me, and if he had saved me, then Christ himself would be the one to complete my life."[16] This traditional faith of the people was like a firm anchor of salvation, a sure basis to which the believer can have recourse in difficult times. Then, however, the prefect placed into the young man's hands a

---

[14] Läpple, *Benedetto XVI,* 21.
[15] Ibid., 24.
[16] Valente, *Ratzinger professore,* 28.

text he had composed during the long years of war and imprisonment. It had taken its definitive form in August 1945, in the camp
in Foucarville, near Le Havre.[17]

The title of the document, "Theology as Crisis and the Adventure
of the Theologian", opened new vistas for Joseph.[18] The traditional
apologetics with its rational formulas had proved to be inadequate
now. Modern man is not the only one to be shaken in his faith;
the theologian, too, cannot avoid confronting the doubt that his
contemporaries seek to stifle by immersing themselves in the noise
of life and the anxiety of work. The theologian, in contrast, leaving
neo-Scholastic thought behind because merely rational assurances
are no longer enough, must look at existence, at *his* existence, because theology is not just a course of studies to complete as soon as
possible, but rather an encounter, a dialogue through which he must
tune in to God's wavelength. And if God is love and generosity, it
is necessary to respond to him with the same attitude.

It was necessary, therefore, to develop an existential theology, of
which Kierkegaard had already spoken, appealing to the individual
conscience to which the prefect, and Joseph following him, had
been directed by Läpple's previous studies. The latter, indeed, was
the student of Theodor Steinbüchel, professor emeritus of moral
theology at the University of Munich and future rector of the University of Tübingen from 1946 until his death.

Specifically, in Ratzinger's memoirs, we read that the works that
had the greatest influence on his philosophical formation were two
texts by Steinbüchel: *The Philosophical Foundations of Catholic Moral
Theology*, published in 1938 but reprinted immediately after the war,
and *The Revolution of Thought*.[19]

The first work, in two volumes, was a classic manual of Catholic
moral theology, in which the author sought above all to describe a
Christian vision of man starting from the Scholastic axiom *Gratia
non destruit sed perficit naturam*, "Grace does not destroy nature but
rather brings it to perfection." This principle, the author said, allows
us to salvage every human value fully and to affirm the proper value

---

[17] Here Läpple had organized a sort of seminary course in theology for the Catholic
and Protestant clergy assembled in a special block of the camp.

[18] The text is reprinted in its entirety in Läpple, *Benedetto XVI*, 29–40.

[19] See J. Ratzinger, *Milestones*, 43.

of a natural ethics from which theological morality then sets out. To the latter, then, belongs a leading role because it alone is capable of defining man, the object of both nature and grace. The task, therefore, is to understand, first of all, the image of man as transmitted by revelation, and subsequently human morality is built up by a strictly philosophical method. Steinbüchel's work anticipated in some respects the theological anthropology of Vatican II, according to which Jesus Christ "fully reveals man to himself and brings to light his most high calling".[20] At the same time, Steinbüchel's work presented, in Ratzinger's view, an excellent introduction to the thought of Heidegger, Jaspers, and Nietzsche.

Even more important, for the future pope, was his reading of *The Revolution of Thought*, which in his opinion was an attempt to abandon the mechanistic image of the world so as to make room again for metaphysics in philosophical reflection. The point of departure was dialogic philosophy as understood by the Austrian Catholic thinker Ferdinand Ebner and the prophet of Chassidism, the Jewish thinker Martin Buber.

According to Ebner, the way to overcome the solitude of man who is encapsulated in his ego is dialogue. Only the thou of another person liberates man from solipsism and brings him into a dialogue, which is a path toward truth, freedom, and love. Buber was even more explicit: "I and thou exist in this world because man exists, and in particular the I exists only due to its relation with the thou."[21] Continuing this argument, Ebner arrived at the statement that at the foundation of the human I-thou relationship there is a divine I-Thou relationship.[22] The original Thou is the Thou of God, from whom comes the speech that is addressed to man and demands a response. Thus, language is of divine origin, and all of man's spiritual life is, in the final analysis, a dialogue with God. Christian existence is subject to the word of God, who awaits a response that is to be given responsibly and freely. This is the fundamental revolution of thought that Steinbüchel adopted as his own, followed by both Läpple and Ratzinger. In keeping with this new

---

[20] Vatican Council II, Pastoral Constitution *Gaudium et spes*, no. 22.

[21] Martin Buber, *Das Problem des Menschen* (Heidelberg: Schneider, 1948), 168–69.

[22] See the extensive introduction by Silvano Zucal to the Italian edition of the *Frammenti pneumatologici* by Ferdinand Ebner (Cinisello Balsamo: San Paolo, 1988), esp. 81f.

philosophical orientation, the professor of moral theology entrusted to Läpple, even before the war, the topic for a doctoral dissertation in philosophy: *The Individual in the Church: Characteristics of a Theology of the Individual according to Cardinal John Henry Newman.*

Having quickly become friends—so much so that at his own priestly ordination in 1947, Läpple invited young Joseph to serve as master of ceremonies—the prefect and the seminarian discussed these topics often. And, naturally, Newman and the subject of the doctoral thesis became another tile in the mosaic of the philosophical and theological personalism that would be at the foundation of the future pontiff's thought. Then-Cardinal Ratzinger would write in 1990 on the occasion of the centenary of Newman's death:

> For us at that time, Newman's teaching on conscience became an important foundation for theological personalism, which was drawing us all in its sway. . . . We had experienced the claim of a totalitarian party, which understood itself as the fulfillment of history and which negated the conscience of the individual. Hermann Göring had said about his leader: "I have no conscience. My conscience is Adolf Hitler." The appalling devastation of mankind that followed was before our eyes.[23]

Therefore, although in Ratzinger's writings we find no facile denunciation of the crimes committed by the Nazis in Germany or in the occupied countries, he does have a lively interest in promoting the formation of a free personal conscience capable of relating each of the events of history and the vicissitudes of life to the truth, which is sought persistently and incessantly. This is the best antidote to any dictatorship.

As we saw from the authors that he read and studied, Ratzinger's philosophical formation was concentrated mainly on contemporary philosophical currents. For a complete formation, however, he could not completely do without the classic philosophers of Christianity: Thomas and Augustine. Ratzinger's encounter with the medieval saint, the father of Thomism, was continued in the form of a joint project with the prefect Läpple. Both had read a work by Saint Thomas, *Disputed Questions on Truth*, translated into German by Edith Stein, about whom they knew nothing at the time. They had

---

[23] Mentioned in Valente, *Ratzinger professore*, 22.

only valued the beautiful translation, which had among other things an excellent introduction by a scholar, Martin Grabmann (1875–1949), who was as humble as he was innovative. To his readers, he revealed a medieval era that was surprisingly varied, quite far from the widely accepted cliché of a monotonous, closed universe.

The two young men then decided to try the second disputation by Saint Thomas, the *Disputed Questions on Charity*, keeping in mind the working method of Stein and Grabmann. The young Ratzinger, who had an excellent knowledge of Latin and Greek, was to translate the text, research and check all the biblical citations, and check the other citations drawn for the most part from Aristotle and Saint Augustine. Although this work was performed during his free time, Ratzinger, in a letter to Läpple on the latter's eightieth birthday, said that he considered it a useful "introduction to the world of sources".[24]

The subject of charity would return often in the works of the future pope, who dedicated his first encyclical to the subject. Joseph's heart, nevertheless, was never truly touched by the argumentations of Aristotle and Saint Thomas. The lectures of his philosophy professor Arnold Wilmsen, which followed the neo-Scholastic method learned in the Roman universities, left him even colder. "It seemed that he himself no longer asked questions but limited himself to defending passionately . . . what he had found."[25] Joseph, in contrast, needed precisely to ask questions and to get answers. For this reason, he enthusiastically read Saint Augustine, whose *Confessions*, even more than dialogical thought, seemed to respond to his need to rediscover himself in turbulent times, to reflect on his own life in dialogue with God.

The years in Munich

With the summer semester of 1947, Joseph had completed the two-year course of philosophical studies required by the seminary curriculum then in force. After passing the examination for admission to the theological faculty, the candidates for priesthood in the Diocese of Munich and Freising found themselves facing an alternative.

---

[24] See Läpple, *Benedetto XVI*, 56.
[25] See J. Ratzinger, *Milestones*, 44.

Most of them, particularly those destined for pastoral work, continued the course they had begun at the seminary in Freising. A few others, however, headed for a predominantly academic formation at the University of Munich. With two other companions, his countryman Rupert Berger and Hans Finkenzeller,[26] the younger Ratzinger brother, who had a passion for books and research, chose the path of university formation and for this purpose wrote to the cardinal archbishop to get the necessary authorization. Having obtained permission, he enrolled in the faculty of theology at the University of Munich, which could boast of a long history as a stronghold of Catholic thought in Germany.

In the second half of the nineteenth century, the Munich school went from a predominant interest in metaphysics and mysticism to historical research under the influence of Ignaz von Döllinger, a priest and a renowned Church historian in Munich. After being excommunicated for his refusal to adhere to the dogma of papal infallibility proclaimed at Vatican Council I, von Döllinger joined the Old Catholic Church. An important follower of his was Otto Bardenhewer, the author of a history of ancient Christian literature that for a long time was a fundamental text for patristic studies. Another disciple of von Döllinger and Bardenhewer was the aforementioned Martin Grabmann, who applied the historical method to the study of medieval thought.

At the time when he requested permission to attend the University of Munich, young Joseph had certainly heard about the prestige of the faculty of theology and of the so-called Munich school. On the other hand, he was not aware of the tragic state of many of the university buildings, including that of the faculty of theology itself. The Georgianum, too, an old college that used to house the theologians who intended to study at the State university, was little more than a heap of rubble. With his companions, Joseph found very dubious accommodations indeed in the former hunting lodge of the King of Bavaria in Fürstenried, south of Munich.

According to Ratzinger's memoirs, written when he was a cardinal, the setting was picturesque but the quarters were cramped, and, because of the lack of space, the seminarians slept in bunk beds, located alongside shelving that was loaded with books and

---

[26] See G. Ratzinger and Hesemann, *My Brother the Pope*, 161.

documents. "When I opened my eyes on the first morning, half asleep as I still was, I thought for a moment that we were back in the war again and that I had been transported to our Flak battery."[27] In comparison with the seminary in Freising, the situation was certainly more precarious: food was scarcer, the atmosphere among the professors cooler, and the student body too diverse for the sense of common purpose that was felt in Freising. The rector of the house, however, Joseph Pascher, who was also a professor of pastoral theology, brought warmth to the life of the aspirants to the priesthood.

Unlike the formation in Freising, where the spiritual life of the seminary followed the traditional model centered on individual piety, Pascher introduced a new style centered on the communal celebration of Mass. Although liberal-minded about other questions, he was inflexible about daily participation in the Eucharistic liturgy, which no one could miss. According to his own statement, young Ratzinger initially harbored some misgivings about the overzealous promoters of liturgical renewal, seeing in them an excessive fondness for philology and research into original texts, behind which was an ill-concealed rationalism.[28] Of course, Ratzinger himself had learned to follow the liturgy with the *Schott* missal, to enter into the spirit of the liturgical renewal, but for him the liturgical gestures and signs were secondary to attention to the texts and reflection on the theological content expressed by them. Nevertheless, the recollection with which Pascher celebrated and lived the Eucharist won Joseph over, and he in turn became a promoter of the liturgical movement.

Mitigating such an austere life was the marvelous park of the castle with two gardens, one in the English style and the other in the French style, where the seminarians could stroll and reflect. As we turn our attention from the premises of the seminary to those of the faculty, it is necessary to continue the litany of hardships. Due to the lack of space, lectures were held in the greenhouse of the castle garden, with contrasting but in any case uncomfortable effects depending on the season. In the summer, the heat was suffocating; in the winter, because of the lack of heat, the

---

[27] See J. Ratzinger, *Milestones*, 47–48.
[28] Ibid., 56–57.

cold was just as severe and inclement. Because of the shuffling of personnel caused by the dictatorship and the war, the professors came from many regions of Germany, and this obligatory gathering, too, was a sign of a communion and a future guaranteed by the Church.

As mentioned earlier, the theology faculty had been closed by the Nazi regime in 1938. Consequently, it was necessary to start almost from scratch in recruiting professors. It was possible to provide them because of the closure of two other German-speaking faculties of theology after the war, the one in Breslau in Silesia and the one in Braunsberg in East Prussia, which was occupied by Soviet troops and had been ceded to the government of the new Communist Poland. In short, the conditions and circumstances were certainly burdensome, but young Joseph, attracted by the intellectual adventure, could not wait to hear those professors, to follow their research, and to engage with their discoveries.

The star of the faculty was Friedrich Wilhelm Maier, a professor of New Testament exegesis, one of the leaders of historical-critical research applied to the Gospels. He was able to galvanize the students, and his lectures were the only ones for which the greenhouse in the garden proved to be too small for the number of listeners. In the professor of the Old Testament, Friedrich Stummer, on the other hand, Ratzinger recognized the seriousness of historical-philological work. In general, he credits the two professors of exegesis with having taught the students to pursue theology while always starting from the Bible, from the word of God, which challenges the theologian every time. Notwithstanding this recognition, Ratzinger's greatest expectations concerned the dogmatic theologians, the professors of theology in the strict sense. At the faculty in Munich, there were essentially two professors of dogmatic theology: Michael Schmaus and Gottlieb Söhngen.

The former, originally from the Diocese of Munich, had taught also at the University of Münster in Westphalia and was renowned throughout Germany. He had detached himself from Scholastic thought and had written a volume, *Catholic Dogma*, that was inspired by the liturgical movement and the rediscovery of the Church Fathers that had taken shape in the 1930s and 1940s. After the war, he still excelled in the clarity of his presentation, but, despite his great erudition, he was no longer successful in applying the fruitfulness of traditional Christian doctrine to the contemporary way of thinking.

In contrast, the innovative method of Gottlieb Söhngen, the professor of fundamental theology, seemed all the more attractive; according to Ratzinger, he "questioned himself radically while at the same time he was a radical believer".[29] Originally from Cologne, he deeply loved his city and his region. Initially he had studied philosophy, taking a particular interest in the phenomenology of Husserl, who, after the dissolution of the metaphysical thought elaborated by Kant and his followers, once again created an opening to thought about transcendence. Then he had gone over to theology, adopting the new findings of the liturgical and ecclesiological movement and reflecting in greater depth on the sense of mystery pioneered by Odo Casel.

In his lectures, Söhngen did not follow a written text, but he had in front of him only notes with exclamation points and question marks. When he had a particular insight, he would come down from the lectern and teach extemporaneously. This then created a special atmosphere in which the students stopped taking notes so as to enter fully into communion with the professor. Rupert Berger, Ratzinger's countryman and classmate in Munich, recalled in particular a lecture from the winter semester in 1947 during which Söhngen stated: "Although revelation itself ended as a *factum historicum* with the apostles, it remains a living event, 'a living presence through the life-giving Spirit' and a *viva vox* [living voice] that always occurs anew in particular in the celebration of Mass."[30]

This brings us to one of the fundamental points of the theology to which Ratzinger would hold fast throughout his life, one of the key elements of his faith and thought. As the reader will have gathered, Joseph quickly became a disciple and friend of Gottlieb Söhngen, with whom he also shared an interest in music. In his study, the professor had a grand piano on which, with almost professional skill, he often played classical music, particularly Chopin. Sometimes he invited the young theology student to the Prinzregent Theater,

---

[29] Recorded by Valente, *Ratzinger professore*, 38.

[30] See Rupert Berger, "Erlebte Liturgie in Ratzingers Studienzeit", in *Der Logosgemässe Gottesdienst, Theologie der Liturgie bei Joseph Ratzinger*, ed. Rudolph Voderholzer (Regensburg: Pustet, 2008), 86.

where the state orchestra had found shelter after the destruction of the war. In short, between the late 1940s and the beginning of the new decade, the theological faculty in Munich appeared to be a lively, open laboratory where various theological approaches and mentalities were present and confronted each other.

Almost instinctively, Ratzinger aligned himself with the more open professors, those with a vision of mature, responsible people, of a society in which Christianity would be a stimulus for building a community of free men held together by mutual respect more than by the rigor of the law and by force.

In the summer of 1949, meanwhile, construction work at the Georgianum and at the theological faculty was proceeding at a good pace, and all signs indicated that they could return to the city for the next semester. The theology students, therefore, prepared to leave the old, uncomfortable castle of Fürstenried, which, nevertheless, evokes the memory of heroic, fruitful times when they were quartered there. Ratzinger, in particular, admits that he made several decisions there that were decisive for his life. First of all, with regard to celibacy. The lack of space forced the young aspirants to the priesthood to rub elbows sometimes with the young women who also took courses offered by the faculty. Years later, in an interview granted to the journalist Seewald, the cardinal would confirm that he had had to consider very seriously there the sacrifices required by celibacy, until he managed to say yes with conviction in the autumn of 1950 on the eve of his diaconal ordination.[31]

Another serious crisis for the young man was the awareness that he felt strongly attracted to theological research. Was this love of study, however, sufficient to justify a priestly vocation? Alfred Läpple recalled that he reflected at length, during spiritual exercises before priestly ordination, on a passage by Saint John Chrysostom that said, "The man is not the one who makes the sacrificial offerings become the Body and Blood of Christ, but Christ himself, who was crucified for us. The priest, who represents Christ, (only) pronounces the words, but their active force and the grace come from God."[32] After his First Mass and the reception afterward, he then discussed

---

[31] Joseph Ratzinger, *Salt of the Earth*, trans. Adrian Walker (San Francisco: Ignatius Press, 1997), 56.

[32] See Läpple, *Benedetto XVI*, 73.

the matter in depth with his younger friend, who, when they were able to take a long walk together, questioned him at length about what he had experienced at the moment of the Consecration, when he had acted in the name of Christ and in the name of the Church.

Joseph, therefore, could not agree to become a priest solely out of love for study and theology. At the center, there had to be his dedication to Christ and to the Church, his availability (*disponibilità*) for service, for the care of souls. He pronounced his assent interiorly,[33] and from then on, he not only had no doubts about his vocational choice, but over the course of his life he constantly held fast to this availability, which would bring him along paths he could not even have imagined then.

New horizons of the mind

In the interview with Peter Seewald, Ratzinger recalled what he read during those years: "People were reading Gertrud von le Fort, Ernst Wiechert and Dostoevski, Elisabeth Langgässer, everything that was around in the way of literature at the time."[34] The works of Dostoevski impressed him by their literary vigor, in which a philosophical and theological interest is not lacking; the poems of Gertrud von le Fort (1876–1971), in contrast, enjoyed a certain popularity in Catholic circles because of their mystical-ecclesiological content. The works of Wiechert and Langgässer, finally, had relevance to the tragedy of the Holocaust. Ernst Wiechert (1887–1950) was a writer with a strong religious consciousness and a deep attachment to nature. Interned in Buchenwald, he managed to survive, although weakened physically and mentally. In 1948, he moved to Switzerland, where he wrote about that part of his life and about his desire to retreat from the world.

The writings of Elisabeth Langgässer (1899–1950) were along these same lines. Being half-Jewish on her father's side, she experienced exclusion from higher education and met with serious difficulties in publishing her writings. She was also sentenced to forced labor, while her daughter Cordelia perished in the concentration camp. After the hostilities, therefore, she wrote realistically and

---

[33] Ibid.
[34] J. Ratzinger, *Salt of the Earth*, 60.

pessimistically about the horror of the war and was very critical of proponents of so-called "internal emigration", of those who proved to be too lukewarm in denouncing the Nazi horror. She described this attitude as "playing with flowers and blossoms over the horrible abyss of the mass graves that are covered precisely with flowers and blossoms".[35]

Another book he read, which is not mentioned by Ratzinger in this context, was *The Satin Slipper* by Paul Claudel. He discovered this French author through two Jesuits, de Lubac and von Balthasar, whom we will have reason to mention fairly often in this book. Before he fled in great haste to escape the Nazis, de Lubac resided at the theological house of studies of the Society of Jesus on Fourvière hill in Lyon. There he was visited by Paul Claudel, who traveled from his castle in Brangues; he then discussed the poet's *Satin Slipper* at length with von Balthasar, who was so impressed by the concept of Catholicism present in the work that he immediately made plans to translate into German this masterpiece of French drama.[36]

Ratzinger also was fascinated by his reading of Claudel's work, specifically in the version by von Balthasar. In it he found corroboration of his conviction about the primacy of love in the Christian vision. Modeled on the example of the mission of Jesus within the Divine Trinity, the single or married Christian's vocation to love, too, can rise to relevance for the history of peoples and of the cosmos. An extensive citation from and commentary on *The Satin Slipper* would appear in Ratzinger's most famous work, *Introduction to Christianity*,[37] which would simultaneously mark the summit of his fame as a progressive theologian but also his separation from that trend.

In the field of theology, strictly speaking, his friendship with Söhngen once more opened up for Ratzinger the new horizons for theological research that were being cultivated in those years

---

[35] The quotation is recorded by Ernst Klee, *Das Kulturlexikon zum dritten Reich* (Frankfurt am Main: Fisher, 2007), 353.

[36] His German translation was published as *Der seidene Schuh* (Salzburg: Otto Müller, 1939). See also what the Swiss theologian writes in *Our Task*, trans. John Saward (San Francisco: Ignatius Press, 1994), where he speaks about the "the writer's boldness in giving planetary dimensions to the love of a man and a woman, and his determination . . . to describe the painful transfiguration of Eros into pure Agape", 43–44.

[37] Joseph Ratzinger, *Introduction to Christianity*, trans. J. R. Foster, rev. ed. (1990; San Francisco: Ignatius Press, 2004), 43–44.

especially in France. He was particularly enthusiastic about one volume that he received as a gift from the prefect, Läpple. The book was *Catholicisme: Les aspects sociaux du dogme* [translated as *Catholicism: Christ and the Common Destiny of Man*] by Henri de Lubac. The volume best synthesized the new vision of the Church rooted in tradition that was becoming prevalent in French circles.

Responding to the challenge posed by the two forms of totalitarianism, Marxist and National Socialist, de Lubac showed that the Catholic vision is not at all individualistic; it is not limited to the private life of the individual but, rather, is intrinsically communitarian in solidarity, without resorting to the use of force or violence. De Lubac wrote in the introduction to the work, which was published in 1938: "Catholicism is essentially social. It is social in the deepest sense of the word: not merely in its applications in the field of natural institutions but first and foremost in itself, in the heart of its mystery, in the essence of its dogma. It is social in a sense which should have made the expression 'social Catholicism' pleonastic."[38]

He then proved his thesis in three parts. The first, dogmatic, part highlighted the vision of the Church as the communion founded by Jesus, her sacramental structure designed to include all aspects of life, her salvific offering addressed to all, her aim being universal salvation in eternity. The second part examined the relation between Christianity and history, between Scripture and tradition, or, rather, the way in which the word of revelation passes through history and affects it. The third part addressed the contemporary situation, with the fragmentation in which the world and the Church herself seemed to be wandering, and gave evidence for the ever more acutely felt need for a new Jerusalem capable of bringing a comprehensive humanism.

Written on the eve of the war, the work presented itself almost as a prophecy by a witness who, among other things, had fought against the Nazis, had participated in Le témoignage chrétien[39] (Christian

---

[38] Henri de Lubac, *Catholicism: Christ and the Common Destiny of Man*, trans. Lancelot C. Sheppard and Sister Elizabeth Englund, O.C.D. (San Francisco: Ignatius Press, 1988), 15.

[39] Le témoignage chrétien was the liaison agency for the Christians in the Lyons area who were involved in the Resistance. Father de Lubac was its founder (together with his confrere Jean Daniélou) and the coordinator until he was discovered and was forced to go into hiding.

witness) in France, and had been one of the few voices from the prewar period who had warned about the harmful effects of anti-Semitism for Christian society and for civilization itself. In the post-war years, then, he had immediately published a work, *Surnaturel*,[40] that he had composed in the hiding place where he had taken refuge so as to flee the Nazis. In it, he summarized his vision, which had matured in a confrontation with the modern French philosophical thought of Bergson and Blondel, which spoke about a nature that was no longer closed in a stable, well-defined order but open to dialogue with God, reawakened to itself precisely by the voice of God.

De Lubac then showed that this vision was not in conflict with the thought of the Fathers of the Church; on the contrary, it was in fact present in the Christian tradition, in the thought of Origen in the East and of Saint Augustine in the West. This simple, indisputable assertion, nevertheless, seemed to overturn the foundations of a way of thinking that had been settled for centuries. Theology was no longer the science that, starting from dogma that was already well defined, regulated the life of mankind and of the *societas christiana*, but was, rather, more humbly, reflection aimed at studying the conditions for accepting God's call, which reached man through the voice of revelation.

The caretakers of orthodox belief reacted indignantly. Father de Lubac was denounced to Rome as a dangerous subversive, and, in the 1950 encyclical *Humani generis*, Pius XII spoke about a *nouvelle théologie* (new theology) and theologians who "destroy the gratuity of the supernatural order" (no. 26).[41] Together with four confreres, de Lubac was suspended from teaching, and his most important books were removed from bookstores and even from the

---

[40] *Surnaturel* was published in France in 1946. Later de Lubac revised this work, which had been written in a single burst and made two volumes out of it, which he affectionately called his twins: *The Mystery of the Supernatural* and *Augustinianism and Modern Theology*, both published in English by Herder and Herder. In them, he responded to the main objections raised by his adversaries, particularly to the objection that if God calls man to the supernatural, the creature is obliged to respond to him and his freedom is diminished. The Jesuit's response exalted simultaneously the generosity of God's grace and the even greater freedom of the creature who can accept the gift of grace or not.

[41] The English translations of all papal, conciliar, and curial documents are taken from the Vatican website (http://w2.vatican.va) and can easily be accessed there.

libraries of the Society of Jesus. This blow that had been dealt to the
new orientations in theology was noticed in Munich, also. Alfred
Läpple recalled Söhngen's reaction when he heard the news:

> The professor did not want to provoke anyone and did not mention
> the incident in the lecture hall in front of the students. But after
> the lecture, Ratzinger and I went with him into his study, where
> there was a large grand piano. . . . This time, in front of us, without
> saying a word, he furiously threw down onto the desk the books
> that he was carrying with him from the lecture. Then he sat down
> at the piano and took out all his anger on the keyboard.[42]

Sincerely grieved, Söhngen was nevertheless a believer who was
able to suffer for his Church and with his Church. He submitted,
therefore, to the judgment of the authorities as he did also on another occasion that same year. Originally from Cologne, he came
from a family in which the parents belonged to different confessions. He was therefore particularly attentive to the first meetings
of the incipient ecumenical dialogue, which were headed by Lorenz
Jäger, the Catholic bishop of Paderborn, and Wilhelm Stählin, the
Lutheran bishop of Oldenburg. With a view to the proclamation
of the dogma of the Assumption of the Blessed Virgin Mary, the
theological faculties were invited to give their opinion.

In Munich, most of the professors and students declared themselves against it, specifically so as not to offend the sensibilities of
the Protestants, who considered Catholic devotion to the Blessed
Virgin to be already excessively distorted by sentimentalism. Among
the professors, Söhngen in particular repeatedly spoke out against
the proclamation, calling it inopportune. Consequently, in a public debate, Edmund Schlink, a Reformed professor of systematic
theology at the University of Heidelberg, asked him: "What will
you do if the dogma is nevertheless proclaimed?" Söhngen replied:
"If the dogma is proclaimed, I will remember that the Church is
wiser than I." Ratzinger, who related the episode in his memoirs,
commented: "I think that this small scene says everything about the
spirit in which theology was done here—both critically and with
faith."[43]

---

[42] Related by Valente, *Ratzinger professore*, 46.
[43] J. Ratzinger, *Milestones*, 59.

A course without respite

Their arrival at the Georgianum, on Ludwigstrasse in Munich, in the final months of 1949 allowed Ratzinger and his companions to become more involved in the cultural debate of the time, to observe close up the fervor of the reconstruction that over the next few years would give rise to the German economic miracle. At first he and his companions took lodgings in a wing that was more or less ready while work was still going on briskly around them. The situation was similar at the faculty of theology, where the new arrivals could follow courses in disciplines related to theological knowledge. Rupert Berger explained that he attended together with Ratzinger lectures given by Alois Dempf, an anti-Nazi, professor of philosophy and history, and by Philipp Lersch,[44] a professor of psychology. This was an opportunity that would be taken many times by the future pontiff in his vision of theology as a discipline that is open to dialogue and is invited to the symposium of the sciences to learn the many facets of the one truth, so as to pose the questions that refer to a horizon of transcendence. The students, moreover, could now listen to Romano Guardini, who on Sundays used to preach at the Church of Saint Louis at the university, while on Wednesday mornings he gave his lectures on the Catholic vision of the world in the great auditorium of the university to an overflow crowd.

The time was approaching, however, for the final examinations, which in those days covered all the subjects studied in the three-year curriculum. Although with regret, Ratzinger soon had to set aside his personal interests so as to concentrate on his studies. In the testing of these oral exams in the summer of 1950, as was widely anticipated, he distinguished himself by his ability to go to the heart of theological problems and to establish connections between the dogmatic nucleus and applications to the life of the faithful and by the exemplary clarity of his presentation. From then on, events followed one another rapidly. In confirmation of the results of his oral exams, Ratzinger received in July from Söhngen a proposal to which he may have already given some thought: during the next year he had to prepare a thesis on an assigned topic for an open competition. If his research paper won, he would receive a modest

---

[44] Pfister, *Joseph Ratzinger*, 87.

sum of money and, most importantly, he would have opened the door to a doctorate and could continue his studies with a view to a university career.

The year that was about to start was crowded with obligations. Diaconal ordination was scheduled for October, and therefore the year of preparation for the practical aspects of priestly ministry began. The idea of adding an academic research paper on short notice to a program that was already so full was an almost impossible challenge. Ratzinger, nevertheless, decided to accept the proposal also. The first months, from July to October, were the ones during which he could devote himself entirely to the scientific work: in-depth study of Augustine's thought, extending his research to his precursors in North Africa: Tertullian, Cyprian, Optatus of Milevis. Then he returned to Freising, where in October 1950 he received ordination to the subdiaconate and the diaconate from the hands of Auxiliary Bishop Johannes Neuhäusler (1888–1973).[45] In Freising, he met again his former prefect, Läpple, who was teaching the theory of sacramental practice. As mentioned already, the subjects in the curriculum for that year were of a predominantly practical nature. He had to prepare to preach and to administer the sacraments, to teach catechism and the Christian virtues, to become involved in the communal and administrative life of a parish. It was a serious commitment, which he did not want to shirk at all, and, besides, it proved to be invaluable already in the year following his priestly ordination.

He was therefore able to devote himself to research almost exclusively in his free time, but he had support from his parents and friends. His brother, Georg, who was going to be ordained a priest together with him, took care of the practical aspects concerning the celebration; his sister, Maria, who at that time was working as a secretary in a law firm, prepared the typewritten copy of the thesis; his friend Alfred Läpple was generous with his advice and suggestions, while everyone at the seminary proved to be understanding and helpful.[46] According to custom, the research paper had to be submitted in late April so as to allow the professors to evaluate it before the conclusion of the academic year. Having handed in the

---

[45] Ibid.
[46] J. Ratzinger, *Milestones*, 99.

manuscript, Ratzinger could now reserve the months of May and June exclusively for study and recollection with a view to ordination.

Priestly ordination

The great bell of Saint Corbinian Church rang mightily on June 29, 1951, the Feast of Saints Peter and Paul, when in the cathedral in Freising forty-four deacon candidates made their entrance for priestly ordination. Presiding at the ceremony was the much-revered Cardinal von Faulhaber; a great crowd of lay faithful attended, among whom, in reserved places, were the relatives of the priests-to-be. Among the candidates were the brothers Georg and Joseph Ratzinger; in the first pews, their parents and sister watched apprehensively those two boys who, having survived the war, were about to be commended to the Church definitively so as to dedicate their lives to mankind.

After the beginning of the Mass, the rite of priestly ordination itself followed. While the candidates lay prostrate on the ground, the Litany of the Saints was chanted, as though to invite the hosts of saints, the heavenly Jerusalem, to participate in the rejoicing over the fruitfulness of the Church on earth, for the harvests that the new laborers would gather and sow together. Then an assistant of the bishop called each of them to the altar, and each one individually replied *adsum*, "I am present, I am ready." Finally von Faulhaber, after invoking the Holy Spirit, imposed his hands on the head of each of the candidates, who thus became priests.

A moment after the cardinal had imposed his hands on him, the future pope saw "a little bird—perhaps a lark—[that] flew up from the high altar in the cathedral and trilled a little joyful song." Although he has repeatedly said that he is not a mystic, he had the clear sensation that it was a voice from on high telling him: "This is good, you are on the right way."[47] After the cardinal, all the priests present extended their hands over those young men who had just become their confreres, qualified to celebrate the Eucharist, to distribute the sacrament that recalls Christ's sacrifice and renews his presence. Next came the kiss of peace to ratify their entrance into

---

[47] Ibid.

the priesthood, in communion with the Church of Munich-Freising and in the apostolic succession, in communion with the universal Church.

At the end of the Mass, first Georg and then Joseph blessed and embraced their parents, sister, and friends, while all present congratulated Maria and Joseph on the rare event of having two sons ordained priests at the same time. That same evening, the entire Ratzinger family returned to Traunstein, where on July 1 the other new priest from the area, Rupert Berger, was to celebrate his First Mass.

The two brothers, in contrast, celebrated their First Solemn Mass on July 8. In those days, there was no provision for concelebration, and therefore Joseph performed the rite at seven o'clock, and Georg at nine. This schedule and celebration were not exactly ideal from the liturgical perspective, but Joseph had an indelible memory of it anyway. The parish church of Saint Oswald was festively illuminated, and "the joy that almost palpably filled the whole place drew everyone there into . . . the sacred event."[48] At that time, the cardinal commented [years later in his memoirs], the conciliar Constitution on the Sacred Liturgy had not yet been published, which speaks about "active participation". Nevertheless, that participation was indeed present in the Christian communities. There was a confirmation of this after the Mass, when, according to a practice that was widespread then, the two brothers went to the parish office to get a list of those who wanted a visit from the new priest. Georg and Joseph were pleasantly surprised to note that everyone in the area wanted to meet and to have the blessing of the new priests, which they regarded as a special grace.

Joseph, therefore, spent the few days of vacation that he had left visiting his neighbors from house to house, receiving everywhere a warm welcome that was directed, not primarily to him personally, but rather to his role as a representative of Christ, as a bearer of his word. Thus he experienced the truth of the Pauline verse that he had selected for the prayer card commemorating his First Mass: "Not that we lord it over your faith; we work with you for your joy" (2 Cor 1:24).[49]

---

[48] Ibid., 99–100.

[49] The commemorative card with the inscription and the photo of Ratzinger, who seems even younger than his twenty-four years, is reproduced at the beginning of vol-

The care of souls

After the exciting days following priestly ordination came the first pastoral assignment, which Ratzinger both looked forward to and feared, feeling that he did not have particularly practical aptitudes, the characteristics required of an assistant priest. No sooner was he appointed than he had an adventurous beginning. Although he had been assigned to the parish in the Bogenhausen district of Munich, starting in early August, because of an emergency he had to present himself first at Saint Martin parish, in the district of Moosach. The pastor had fallen ill, while the assistant priest, the pastor's sister who served as the housekeeper, and the sacristan were all on vacation and unreachable by the means of communication at the time. In short, it was a baptism by fire, all the more so because, as Ratzinger would observe humorously when he had become archbishop of the city, during that month "almost all the canonical problems came up that someone with the care of souls can encounter."[50]

When the vacation and the emergency stint were over, the young man appeared at the parish of the Most Precious Blood in Bogenhausen, one of the middle-class districts of the Bavarian capital, the location of the Villa Stuck Museum, dedicated to Franz von Stuck, the professor of Paul Klee and Giorgio de Chirico, the monument to Richard Wagner, the Prinzregent Theater, and the villa belonging to Thomas Mann. For his superiors, this was the right parish in which to assign a minimum of pastoral work to a young priest who was destined for other duties. Ratzinger, on the other hand, could not help being struck by the fact that this was the parish in which the assistant pastor Hermann Josef Wehrle had served along with the rector of the little Church of Saint George, the Jesuit Father Alfred Delp.

Wehrle, the descendant of an old Catholic family, was put to death by the Gestapo on September 14, 1944, because, in a conversation of a pastoral nature, he had told the Baron Major Ludwig von Leonrod that knowledge about a plan to kill a tyrant was not a sin and therefore he was not obliged to report it. Arrested after the failed

---

ume 12 of the *Complete Works* of Benedict XVI, a collection of his writings dedicated to the theology of the priesthood and priestly spirituality.

[50] See *Kardinal Ratzinger: Der Erzbischof von München und Freising in Wort und Bild*, ed. K. Wagner and A. H. Ruf (Munich: Pfeiffer Verlag, 1977), 65.

attempt on Hitler's life on July 20, 1944, the Baron, under torture, had related the incident, and this detail not only had not spared him, but also led to the arrest of the priest, who was sentenced to death as well.[51] The Jesuit Alfred Delp, on the other hand, was the son of a mixed marriage: his mother Catholic, his father Lutheran. After a period of wavering between the two Christian confessions, he opted for Catholicism and decided to enter the Jesuit Order. Ordained a priest in 1937, he was editor of the journal *Stimmen der Zeit* until it was shut down by the Gestapo. He then became rector of the Church of Saint George, which was dependent on the Precious Blood parish in Bogenhausen. Then he came into contact with the members of the Resistance in Kreisau. Arrested after the attempted assassination on July 20, 1944, he was sentenced to death for having belonged to that group.[52] The sentence was executed by hanging in Plötzensee Prison in Berlin on February 2, 1945.

The example of the two martyred priests was a powerful stimulus for their younger colleague who was starting his priestly ministry in their parish. One thing that people remembered about Wehrle was that in his suit a note had been found with the words: "I have just been sentenced to death. What a beautiful day: today the Exaltation of the Cross." About Delp, Läpple relates several sentences that remained engraved on his memory and on that of many priests of the postwar years.[53] Ratzinger was particularly impressed by the following: "Bread is important. Freedom is more important. But the most important thing is unbroken fidelity and adoration that is never betrayed."[54] The parish community bore the imprint of Max Blumschein (1884–1965), pastor of the Precious Blood parish from 1934 to 1956. The arrest of the two priest-martyrs had affected him deeply, and, according to Ratzinger's memoirs, he had

---

[51] See *Testimoni di Cristo: I martiri tedeschi sotto il nazismo*, ed. Helmut Moll (Cinisello Balsamo: San Paolo, 2007), 340–42.

[52] The circle in Kreisau, which had a Christian-Social character, took the name of the place in which a group of intellectuals and opponents of the Nazi regime met with a view to building a new Germany after the defeat that was now considered inevitable. After the attempt on Hitler's life on July 20, 1944, the organizer of the group, Count Helmuth James von Moltke, and several other members were arrested and sentenced to death.

[53] Läpple, *Benedetto XVI*, 100.

[54] Ibid.

an ardent interior love for Christ and dedicated himself unsparingly to his ministry.

The example of his generosity was a powerful force that led the young assistant priest to dedicate himself with just as much self-denial to the households entrusted to him. The chief duty of an assistant priest was to teach religion to the children from the second to the eighth grades. There were sixteen hours of instruction, and it was necessary to add to these the time required for preparation. Ratzinger, indeed, did not and never would improvise; his lessons were always carefully prepared. For this reason, too, he managed to establish a good rapport with the youngsters and experienced joy in abandoning intellectual abstraction so as to be immersed in the concrete and at the same time imaginative world of the children.

Teaching was the principal occupation of the newly ordained priest, but certainly not the only one. Every Sunday, he had to celebrate Mass at least twice and to give two homilies. His preaching ability was precisely the trait that struck a young parishioner who later chose priestly life and had Ratzinger as a professor. Monsignor Hermann Theissing has testified:

He expressed himself very simply, and yet he was able to preach in an excellent way. And soon he had his listeners, which was no mean feat, because we had the Jesuits from Kaulbachstrasse, and, above all, in the background there was still Alfred Delp, who was an excellent preacher. Although I had been acquainted with Delp only as a little boy, in the 1950s everyone was still compared with him. Ratzinger preached very simply but made a great impression.[55]

In this regard, Ratzinger himself related to Theissing that in one of their many strolls through the city (neither of them owned an automobile), the pastor, Father Blumschein, told him: "You can preach at every Mass, except the one at 7:30; there are Jesuits at that one, smart guys." Soon, though, the pastor was convinced that Ratzinger was not at all inferior to the Jesuits.

Early every morning, from 6:00 to 7:00, he was in the confessional, and then he dedicated his entire Saturday morning to the Sacrament of Penance. Moreover, there was his work with the youth groups. "We also had a musical group in which he participated,

[55] Hermann Theissing, interview on February 22, 2006, in Pfister, *Joseph Ratzinger*, 132.

singing with us. And again, like one of us he even went on bike trips."[56] Finally there was preparation for and the celebration of extraordinary occurrences such as Baptisms, First Holy Communions, weddings, and funerals. These events then gave rise to important friendships, so much so that the young aficionado of theological studies, who had had doubts about his vocation because he was more attracted to scholarly research than to pastoral work, began to wonder whether it was not better to stay in pastoral care: "The feeling of being needed and of accomplishing an important service had helped me to give all I could, and this gave me a joy in the priesthood."[57]

Traveling, then, by bicycle through the streets of Munich, the young priest, who had seen close up the ruins and devastations of the war, could now touch with his own hands the rapid progress in the rebuilding of the country. As an attentive observer, he also analyzed the causes of that unexpected rebirth, of that dream that took shape over the course of a few years.

They were years of great sacrifices, but also of a desire for peace and reconciliation. Europeans no longer wanted to punish or humiliate their enemies, as had happened after World War I, but they aimed to build a society on the basis of law and morality, the equality of men and solidarity among nations. There was a sense that human rights could be guaranteed on this foundation and that the very idea of Europe, which had been born of the encounter between the Christian heritage and the modern States, could acquire new vigor.

Young Father Ratzinger, nevertheless, was not an enthusiast devoid of a critical mind. On the contrary, precisely in those hours of religious instruction, he realized that the way in which many of the children lived and thought could certainly not be described as Christian. Following social conventions, they still participated in the rites and public demonstrations of the Church, but their thoughts and their hearts followed habits and life-styles that were certainly not informed by the Gospel. This observation in the field was later the subject of an article, "The New Pagans and the Church",[58] which

---

[56] Ibid., 131.

[57] J. Ratzinger, *Milestones*, 102.

[58] The article was published in 1958 in the journal *Hochland* 51 (1958–1959): 325–28. It was then included in an anthology entitled *Das neue Volk Gottes* (The new people of

caused an uproar. Ratzinger wrote that the Christian community "is in an entirely new way a Church of pagans. No longer, as once long ago, a Church of pagans who have become Christians, but a Church of pagans who still call themselves Christians but in reality have become pagans."[59]

This was the reality that had already been denounced during the war by two French priests with the publication of a little volume that was provocative even in its title: *France, a Mission Land?*[60] In the German-speaking world, this was the phenomenon against which Hans Urs von Balthasar had spoken up a few years earlier; a theologian in Switzerland, he invited the Church not only to take note of the gradual de-Christianization of the countries that merely formally continued to call themselves Christian, but also to demolish within the Church the bastions of triumphalism,[61] to get rid of high-sounding institutions, of practices and devotions that had dangerous side-effects. They not only no longer conveyed the message of the Gospel, but were obstacles in the way of seeing the source, the heart of Christ pierced by the soldier's lance and, above all, by the love of God that had induced him to come to the world to save, not Christendom, but all mankind.

In his turn, Ratzinger did not fear to speak in his article about the urgent need to rid the Church of worldliness, so that she might be able to recognize that she was a little flock, made up of a remnant of witnesses capable of living and transmitting the Gospel of Christ.[62] Having become acquainted with the assistant priest, in his great simplicity and modesty,[63] the youngsters of Bogenhausen had no

---

God) (Düsseldorf: Patmos-Verlag, 1969). Italian edition: *Il nuovo popolo di Dio* (Brescia: Queriniana, 1971), 351–64.

[59] J. Ratzinger, *Il nuovo populo*, 362.

[60] Henri Godin, Yvan Daniel, *France: Pays de mission?* (Paris: Cerf, 1943).

[61] Hans Urs von Balthasar, *Razing the Bastions*, trans. Brian McNeil (San Francisco: Ignatius Press, 1993).

[62] It is interesting to note that during those same years in Italy, Don Luigi Giussani, who like von Balthasar in later decades would have ties of friendship with Cardinal Ratzinger, made a similar observation, for the most part from the same position as instructor of religion, which prompted him to begin Gioventù Studentesca (Student youth), the first nucleus from which the movement Communion and Liberation started.

[63] "He lived in astonishing simplicity. In his room there was no large writing desk with many photographs, as was the case with the other assistant priests, but only a little table with a few notebooks on it, a shelf for books, and a bed. That was all": Hermann Theissing, in Pfister, *Joseph Ratzinger*, 130.

idea that they had among them a theologian who soon would make a name for himself. Therefore, at the end of summer 1952, when Ratzinger announced to them that he was about to leave them, they asked him where he was going. He replied that in September he had to travel to Freising to teach. "Then we looked at him and commiserated with him. 'You will have to take exams and do a research paper.' Then he answered, 'I did that already. Now I have to prepare a doctoral thesis.'" Then they were very much surprised.

Return to Freising

Ratzinger did not know it, but his departure from the Precious Blood parish had already been determined the previous year. Cardinal von Faulhaber had made the decision in July 1951 in a meeting with Alfred Läpple. After earning his doctorate on July 2 of that year, the former prefect in Freising had had a meeting with the cardinal to discuss his own future. The latter urged him to continue his studies with a view to teaching at the university, asking him, however, to remain for another year in Freising as teacher of the theory of sacramental practice for the candidates for priestly ordination in 1952. Then the cardinal asked Läpple the name of a possible substitute, and the latter did not hesitate to mention Ratzinger, who, therefore, had to remain in Bogenhausen just long enough to get the minimum of pastoral experience that the cardinal deemed necessary for every priest, even if he was destined for a university career.

Not being sure that the cardinal would take his suggestion, Läpple did not tell his friend about his conversation.[64] The young assistant priest heard the news during the summer of 1952 with mixed feelings. On the one hand, it was the desired solution with respect to returning to the studies he loved; on the other hand, especially in the first few months, he noticed the lack of that fullness of human relations which had been established in his pastoral work. He was helped by the fact that, basically, he had not been away from the seminary setting for long. Now, though, he was no longer the brilliant seminarian of two years before, but was, rather, the youngest teacher on the faculty.

---

[64] For this reconstruction of the sequence of events, see Läpple, *Benedetto XVI*, 97–100.

The first thing about the new professor that struck observers was precisely his youth. Then there were several still more important characteristics. In the first place, his language. Elmar Gruber, one of his students and admirers, who in turn became an excellent teacher and the author of volumes about religious instruction, stated: "I took down his lectures in shorthand and transcribed them. There was a lot to learn. In the first place, his language was fascinating. It was a fascinating, completely new language. . . . During the vacations I literally memorized the transcribed lectures, just to immerse myself in that language."[65] Then there was the train of thought, which Gruber described as "meditative-reflective", which was produced by his profound spirituality based on Sacred Scripture and the Church Fathers. Gruber also recalled Ratzinger's introductory lecture in Freising on truth. The truth is a person, Ratzinger maintained, and one arrives at it by love.

Gruber also commented that this is a proclamation of faith completely different from doctrinal teaching. By following Ratzinger's lectures, which were rich in symbols and images, one entered fully into the depths of the reality that was symbolized. Man can experience more than he can understand. As for his rapport with the other professors and with the students, his dominant trait was modesty, which stood out even more against the brilliance and profundity of his presentation. Theissing, too, recalled:

> The faculty in Freising, at that time called the *Philosophisch-Theologische Hochschule*, generally—and this must be admitted plainly—was not the best in terms of formation. Sometimes we played Battleship on pieces of paper, every professor distributed his own hand-outs, and therefore there was no real need to be present. And suddenly Ratzinger arrived and the lecture halls filled up. No one said, "You don't go to Ratzinger's classes."[66]

This surprised his colleagues and, at the same time, stirred up quite a few feelings of envy. The seminary was still headed by Rector Höck, who by his kindness tried to put everyone at ease. His right-hand man was still the Jesuit Franz von Tattenbach, who was admired for his spirituality, but also because he had managed to visit his confrere Alfred Delp in Tegel Prison in Berlin. In his

---

[65] Elmar Gruber, interview on February 23, 2006, reported in Pfister, *Joseph Ratzinger*, 141.

[66] Hermann Theissing, in Pfister, *Joseph Ratzinger*, 129.

presence, with the dispensation of his superiors, the priest-martyr had made his solemn vows in the Jesuit Order.[67] Now, in the community made up of the instructors and the students of the seminary in Freising, Tattenbach was a spiritual director who was always ready to listen in every need. Contributing also to the familial atmosphere was the rector's niece, Barbara Höck, who was there for her uncle, to whom she had devoted herself entirely ever since he had been interned in the concentration camp.[68]

The young professor therefore had help in adjusting to the new environment, even though, as during the previous year, the work load prevented him from thinking about the past for long. His first duty was teaching, for which he lacked experience but certainly not ability. Then there was regularly scheduled pastoral care: celebrating Masses in the cathedral and being available for confessions. Another sort of duty was working with a youth group based on a shared interest in popular music. The young people involved learned the lyrics of popular songs and played various instruments to perform them: zither, guitar, flute, clarinet, double bass.

Every year, then, at the beginning of Advent, there was a concert called *Dombergsingen*, which became an important gathering. "Most of the musical groups from Upper Bavaria, Swabia, and Salzburg that later became famous through radio and television debuted in the Red Room of the seminary in Freising."[69] One year later, in Advent of 1953, Ratzinger gave these groups a short talk that became famous for its humor more than anything else. Surprising the listeners, the young professor declared that Saint Augustine was acquainted with yodeling. Commenting on Psalm 33, which invites the just to exult over God's creation and his interventions in the history of Israel, the African Father of the Church spoke about the *jubilus*: "But there is no doubt that he means the same thing: the expression of a wordless joy that is so great that it transcends speech."[70] The young professor drew the conclusion that from the fifth and fourth centuries before Christ, via fourth- and fifth-century Africa during the Christian era, music was already circulating through Bavaria and the entire Alpine

---

[67] Roman Bleistein, *Alfred Delp: Storia di un testimone* (Cinisello Balsamo: San Paolo, 1994), 169–71.

[68] Läpple, *Benedetto XVI*, 101.

[69] Ibid., 108.

[70] Ibid., 110.

region! An encouragement for the yodelers of yesterday and today and for many European and American singers.

His weightiest duty, in any case, was preparing for his doctorate, an extremely burdensome ordeal. First, he had to submit his thesis and receive favorable evaluations from the readers. Then, within the next six months, he had to pass courses in four specialized subjects, taking in each instance a one-hour oral examination and a written test. After concluding these, the doctoral candidate had to give a lecture in the *aula magna* (great auditorium) and defend theses that he had previously prepared in Latin. Only if everything went well would he receive the title of Doctor. As previously mentioned, the topic for the doctorate had been proposed by Professor Söhngen, who had chosen the theme: "People and house of God in Saint Augustine's teaching on the Church".

The topic was part of a debate that was becoming widespread in Germany and Central Europe in those years. In 1943, Pius XII had published an encyclical, *Mystici corporis*, that summarized the best results of the liturgical movement and of the new vision of the Church and tried to incorporate them into the universal Magisterium of the Church. Published while the war was still in progress, the encyclical was universally well received and seemed to have calmed dissent that threatened to cause a deep division in the Catholic world. It showed that a synthesis is possible between the traditional view of the Church, which, based on a comparison with surrounding society, insisted on the visible elements of the ecclesial institution, and the new concept popularized by the liturgical movement, which highlighted, instead, the elements of communion and fraternity resulting from the divine origin of the community founded by Jesus Christ.

At the same time, however, several studies were published in Germany, in particular by the Dominican friar Mannes D. Koster, maintaining that "mystical body" is a definition suited to grace, but not to the Church. It describes the intimate communion among the faithful in the Church, not the visible, communal, and juridical institution of the people of God. Moreover, "mystical body" is a metaphor, whereas scientific theology, going beyond images, must arrive at scientific definitions. The last-mentioned observation then allowed Koster to extend his critique to the entire reinterpretation of the Fathers of the Church that had been done in those years. The liturgy, too, which is the faith of the Church at prayer, he continued, is scarcely acquainted with the expression "body of Christ" and, in order to describe the Church in all her aspects, he resorted to the expression "people of God". Hence the title of the research paper entrusted by Söhngen to Ratzinger. By comparing the two definitions—"body of Christ" and "people of God"—he was to assess the reinterpretation of the Fathers made in recent years, the specific content of the two definitions, and the relation between them.

Söhngen had then added the expression "house of God", which was supposed to function as a connection between the two more common expressions. This was obviously a compelling problem, which touched on a central point in the Catholic vision, which still caused excellent minds in the Church to be victimized and excluded. In past years, nevertheless, Ratzinger had been tirelessly analyzing the thought of Saint Augustine and, after *Catholicism*, had read another work by de Lubac, *Corpus mysticum*, which already in its title alluded to the expression in the title of the encyclical by Pius XII. Based on texts by the earliest Christian authors, the French Jesuit had demonstrated that the expression designated above all the Eucharistic celebration, which is at the same time the memorial of Christ's sacrifice and a festive gathering of the Christian community during which the risen Christ made himself present once more among his disciples. Thus, from the outset, the opposition between institutional reality and spiritual element was overcome.

This was the heuristic principle of the young doctoral candidate. The comparison with the doctrine of the Church in the writings of Saint Augustine allowed him not only to respond to the questions posed by Professor Söhngen, but also provided him with the very nucleus of his theological vision, which then developed over the course of the years.

"People and House of God in Saint Augustine"

Erich Przywara, a friend of Hans Urs von Balthasar and certainly no stranger to Ratzinger's cultural world, in a famous work[71] on the African Father of the Church wrote that, by making classical

---

[71] Erich Przywara, *Augustinus: Die Gestalt als Gefüge* (1932; 2nd ed., 1934). The work was translated into Italian as: *Agostino informa l'Occidente* (Milan: Jaca Book, 2007).

antiquity and the Gospel converge in his writing, he places himself at the origin of the European spirit. He then went on to assert that the result is a banquet of fruitful antitheses from which philosophers and theologians have drawn for centuries without ever exhausting their potential. Ratzinger, therefore, was taking his place in a long line of famous interpreters that runs from Duns Scotus to Nicholas of Cusa, from Luther to Jansen, from Descartes to Kierkegaard. Following their lead, he took for granted the division between the early Augustine, who still labored under the baggage of the philosophical concepts that he had acquired in the years before his conversion, and the mature Augustine, who, after entering the hierarchy, was prompted by his very office to reflect more responsibly on the nature of the Church.

To tell the truth, Ratzinger saw a turning point already in the passage from Manicheism to neo-Platonism. For the Manichees, all that exists is the reality of the world as it is perceived by men, and through it runs the clear distinction between good and evil, light and darkness. The neo-Platonists, in contrast, consider reality, as seen in our eyes, as only the obscure part of the true reality, the pale reflection of another world that is present, nevertheless, to our mind, which is itself the reflection of this unchangeable reality. This is a first step toward the approach to the Christian vision, so that Ratzinger exhorted the reader not to conclude too hastily that this position is irreconcilable with the Gospel. "Precisely in the gradual change that occurs in this point it is possible to point out Augustine's path, which leads from a theology configured in an almost purely metaphysical way to an increasingly historical understanding of Christianity."[72]

Now, though, the concrete, historical form of Christianity is the Church, which appears as a royal road and the universal salvation of the people. In agreeing, therefore, to belong to the Church, Augustine rejected the way of the neo-Platonists, which was reserved for only a few philosophers, so as to enter into the common way of the faithful, the way given by God to meet the needs of creaturely infirmity from which philosophy cannot protect us. "There is no other way to wisdom than that of deciding to follow the Word of God

---

[72] Cited and translated into English from the Italian edition: Joseph Ratzinger, *Popolo e casa di Dio in sant'Agostino* (Milan: Jaca Book, 2005), 27f.

who descended into the lowliness of our flesh. His masterly teaching of humility is the authentic salvific act of God for our sake."[73] This humility of God allowed Augustine to accept the authority of Mother Church, of whom he had a concrete image in his own mother, Monica, and it enabled him to accept also the weakness of a large number of the faithful, whose salvation is reckoned by the measure, not of their knowledge, but of their love.

On the other hand, if the multitude of the faithful casts shadows on the face of the Church, the same legions of Christians give it a light that cannot be overlooked. The multitude of believers, among whom there are also many martyrs, was for Augustine an obvious sign that God alone could post. We are, nevertheless, in a passing stage that allows us to speak about the multitude of believers but not yet about the people of God. The analysis of the second expression in the research paper also confirmed this first finding. The definition of the Church as house of God brings us back to the visible sphere, to the temple where the cultic action par excellence is carried out: the sacrifice. The temple of the spiritual God, however, is in turn spiritual. The sacrifice, like the prayer addressed to this God, occurs in the chambers of the heart.

The idea of spiritual worship is completed by the concept of indwelling. Nowhere is God so present to man as in the temple. This presence, however, cannot be merely spatial; otherwise, we would be witnessing a materialization, which for Augustine was intolerable. God, therefore, dwells in the inner man, as Christ dwells in the man of faith. So far, the Church and the sacraments were absent from the discussion. In this same interior sphere, Ratzinger found two concepts, love and unity, which in turn are present at a stage that is not yet definitive, but they would prove decisive for Saint Augustine's concept of the Church. Initially, the African Father spoke only about the love of God, the supreme good, to which he then added the remark that love of neighbor is the surest path to the love of God.

Another important concept for the early Augustine was unity, which he got from Plato, via Plotinus. To the now-Christian thinker, however, the One is important not only in the intelligible sphere but also in the real world. The more something is one,

---

[73] Ibid., 19.

the more real it is. Similarly, the more at one a man is, the more peaceful he is in himself and the more real he is. Similarly, friends and lovers aspire to unity. This is the path by which Augustine, once he became a bishop, would elaborate his mature vision of the Church.

Having arrived at this point, Ratzinger, intending to sketch the spiritual world encountered by Augustine upon his return to Africa, proposed a digression on the concept of the Church elaborated by three North African Fathers: Tertullian, Optatus of Milevis, and Cyprian of Carthage. The most original of the three, in Ratzinger's view, is the first, who developed his thought in the debate with Gnosticism. In opposition to the Gnostics' polemics against corporeal and sensible reality, Tertullian insisted on the visible, concrete elements of the ecclesial constitution. Christ clothes man in his entirety, body and soul, through the sacraments. Being salvific signs, they transmit Christ's grace and the power of the Holy Spirit and determine the ethical and canonical aspect of the life of the Church. The vision of the historical and ecclesial nature of Christian salvation in Tertullian, which came down to Augustine through Optatus of Milevis and Cyprian of Carthage, was for Ratzinger the corrective that the author of the *Confessions* needed in order to arrive at his mature view of the Church. The bishop of Hippo was almost constrained to elaborate further his vision of the Church from two different contexts, of a doctrinal and a historical nature, in which he happened to find himself: the first was the bitter clash with the Donatists; the second was the debate with pagan civilization, now in its decline, in his work on the city of God.

The defense of the Catholic Church against the Donatists had as its foundation the conviction that the true Church must be a Church of the multitudes, according to the early Augustine, and of all peoples, according to his mature works. Only in this way, indeed, is it the Church that will fulfill the biblical prophecies concerning the salvation of all nations. In this way, Ratzinger continued, "the multitude of peoples that inhabits the orb consisting of earth and water thus appears as the one people of Abraham gathered from the variety that separates into intimate unity by the work of the one descendent of Abraham: Jesus Christ."[74] Present in this people is

---

[74] Ibid., 145.

the *caritas* that comes from the Holy Spirit and nourishes the communion of saints.

Consequently, in contrast to what the Donatists maintained, holiness is not a moral virtue acquired by the asceticism of individuals but, rather, an objective quality given by the Holy Spirit to the Church and transmitted by her to the faithful by means of the sacraments. Augustine thus avoided the temptation of the Donatists, which later would be that of the Cathari, also, to expel sinners from the Church. By way of *caritas* and mercy, he fully restored the value of the visible Church. Ratzinger summarized: "The Catholic Church appears as the fulfillment of Christ, as his body, and thus as the spiritual Christ who has remained present."[75] And although the faithful cannot have direct access to this ecclesial body of Christ, they can approach its sacred sign, the sacrament of the Eucharist.

In the sacrament of the Body and Blood of Christ, we find the interior way in which the Church and the saints are the body of Christ, brought about by the charity given by the Holy Spirit. What is more internal and pneumatic, nevertheless, is also more external; what is more mystical is also more common. This is the position at which Augustine arrived in his last work, *The City of God*, in which he contrasted the earthly city and the city of God. The former has its own foundation in itself and is satisfied with its own precarious position; the latter is the heavenly Jerusalem, which, nevertheless, has a pilgrim colony on earth. In short, "the people of God is the community that represents the unity of those who offer the sacrifice with Christ; the house of God means this interior 'oneness' in the Spirit of Christ, which certainly is not realized without the 'oneness' in the body of Christ."[76]

Having attempted a summary of the thesis, we can understand the enthusiasm with which Professor Söhngen welcomed the work of the young doctoral candidate: Now my student knows more than I do; I prepared the way, but he will make his voice heard more loudly.[77] In reality, Ratzinger not only solved the initial problem by confirming that the expression "body of Christ" was an adequate definition of the Church, as was the correct interpretation of the

---

[75] Ibid., 157.

[76] Ibid., 184f.

[77] G. Ratzinger and Hesemann, *My Brother the Pope*, 159.

Church Fathers proposed by de Lubac and by other patrologists of that time. He had in addition identified a pneumatic center, an incandescent nucleus from which it was possible to develop a new vision not only of the Church but of all of theology, with repercussions on Christology, the liturgy, doctrine on the sacraments, particularly the Eucharist and its ministers, eschatology, and finally the Christian presence in the world.

This also explains the gratitude and loyalty of the future pope, who would grapple with the thought of the North African Father for decades and would have recourse to his fruitful ideas for the rest of his life. But we will talk about this later. Now it is appropriate to conclude with a minor episode. In July 1953, Ratzinger concluded his doctorate with the theological faculty in Munich with his public debate. The young doctor had to give a lecture in the great hall in the presence of the rector and the dean of the faculty, then answer questions about the thesis that he had presented in Latin. Participating in the event were his family and friends, too. His father and mother were especially happy for this son of theirs, who, after priestly ordination, gave them another great joy.[78] During the summer, Joseph was finally able to take time for a bit of rest together with his brother, Georg. The latter had met in his parish Franz Böckle, a priest originally from Chur, who organized a trip to Switzerland for the two brothers.

The chair of dogmatic and fundamental theology at the College of Philosophy and Theology in Freising had already been offered to him for the following year. Nevertheless, he turned it down. After the great effort of the previous year, he wanted to remain in Munich to confer again with Professor Söhngen, so as to start his research for his *Habilitation*, the degree that would qualify him as a university lecturer.

---

[78] Ibid., 176.

III

THE TEENAGER OF THEOLOGY

Toward an academic career

A priest in 1951, an instructor at the diocesan seminary in Freising as of 1952, a doctor in theology in 1953, and invited the same year to hold the chair of dogmatic and fundamental theology at the College (*Hochschule*) for Philosophy and Theology associated with the seminary, Ratzinger was running at breakneck speed. He himself was aware of it and therefore asked the academic authorities in Freising for a sabbatical year in which to do the exploratory reading necessary to identify a topic for study to present then as the academic thesis required in order to obtain the *Habilitation*, to qualify to teach as a university lecturer.

Ratzinger, in short, aimed to teach on the theological faculties of universities in Germany. Teaching at the college, which depended on the diocesan curia, was only a rite of passage before facing the riskier challenge of the open sea of the State universities. The academic authorities in Freising consented. They found a substitute for a year, and meanwhile Ratzinger shuttled between Munich, where he did research at the university, and Freising, where he continued to teach pastoral sacramental ministry to the seminarians in their final year and to carry out pastoral work in the cathedral parish.

As he continued his academic course, he still had as his guide Professor Söhngen, who was convinced more than ever that he had a talented disciple. For the purposes of his doctorate, he had conducted invaluable research on one of the major representatives of the patristic era, with a view to a complete and correct formation. Söhngen thought that it would be good that Ratzinger continue with a study on Saint Bonaventure, one of the great thinkers of the medieval period.

For Söhngen, nevertheless, history was not enough; he attentively watched the contemporary debate, also. After the crisis of the war, thinkers—philosophers and theologians—were less and less attracted by metaphysical thought and turned their attention to history. In theology, in particular, there was a debate over the concept of salvation history as it is connected with the concept of revelation. Whereas Scholastic theology conceived of revelation as the communication of a series of truths crystallized into dogmas, now the accent was placed on God's historical action in which the truth is revealed gradually.

In that general cultural context, it was then necessary to add a theme connected in particular with the development of the ecumenical dialogue between Catholics and Protestants in Germany. From the Reformation period on, the followers of Luther tended to consider speculation on a metaphysical basis as rather detached from the specific content of the Christian faith, which not only shows the way to eternity but also is centered on the encounter of man with God who works in history. And once again a question arose that would be the center of Ratzinger's reflection until his mature period: How can what happened in the past become present? How can something that is unique and unrepeatable have universal significance? The topic was fascinating, and Ratzinger went to work enthusiastically.[1]

His love of research, however, led the instructor and student to underestimate the sensibilities of Professor Michael Schmaus, the dean of the faculty of theology, who was considered the greatest expert in medieval theological thought, not only at the University of Munich but in all Germany. He therefore found it offensive that Ratzinger should turn to Söhngen as a director for such research without first consulting him. This is the origin of a tenacious hostility that very nearly nipped in the bud the career of the aspiring professor, who, unaware of faculty politics, was walking straight ahead on his own path.

During the summer of 1954, he finished gathering the materials, read the works of Saint Bonaventure and the monographs on his thought, and elaborated the basic lines of the research. What

---

[1] Joseph Ratzinger, *Milestones: Memoirs 1927–1977*, trans. Erasmo Leiva-Merikakis (San Francisco: Ignatius Press, 1998), 104.

remained was the painstaking work of drafting the text of his research, which was then to be published as a requirement for qual-
ifying as a university lecturer. As he had promised, however, he
decided that he could accept at least partially the offer from the
College in Freising. For the moment, he would teach the course in
dogmatic theology, while he obtained permission to postpone for
another year the course on fundamental theology.

During the summer semester of 1954, therefore, as an extraordinary professor of dogmatic theology, he taught a course on God.
"It was a joy to move through this great question and the richness of the tradition concerning it."[2] His enthusiasm was noted
also by the students, who in great numbers attended the lectures of
the young professor, which probably annoyed the older instructors.
The biggest challenge of the year, nevertheless, was writing the text
that then went into *The Theology of History in St. Bonaventure*.[3] He
had to cope not only with the shortage of time and the conceptual
difficulties but also with unexpected problems of a practical nature.
The handwritten text with a thick apparatus of footnotes had to be
typewritten so as to be presented in duplicate to the secretariat of
the university.

Keeping to a careful schedule, Ratzinger laboriously completed
his manuscript during the summer of 1955. The typist to whom he
gave it, however, was not only excessively slow but made the project
more difficult with numerous typographical errors and other mistakes and omissions. In short, Ratzinger, already under stress from
an enormous work load, was on the verge of a nervous breakdown.
After the additional work of correction, he submitted the two required copies to the secretariat of the university in the autumn of
1955.

At the same time as he submitted the thesis, there was a change
of a practical sort in his life. Several months before, an emeritus
professor had died, freeing up an apartment of the diocesan curia
nearby the cathedral in Freising that was traditionally reserved for
the instructors at the college. Söhngen had closely followed the

---

[2] Ibid., 105.

[3] The first edition of the volume was published in Munich, by Schnell und Steiner,
in 1959. An English translation was made by Franciscan Herald Press in 1971 (reprinted
in 1989).

thesis of the aspiring professor and had not concealed his great appreciation for the results he had obtained. The oral examination for the *Habilitation*, therefore, seemed to be little more than a formality.

Ratzinger, therefore, decided to anticipate slightly the final decision and moved into that spacious apartment, which was conveniently located near the place where he was teaching. Not only that. In a sort of restricted family council, the three siblings decided that the time had arrived to think about different accommodations for their parents. *Vater* Joseph and *Mutter* Maria were still very fond of the house in Traunstein, which they had acquired by so much sacrifice and had beautified and made a welcoming home over the course of the years. They were, however, elderly now, and the house was too isolated for them to be able to continue to live there alone. With one accord, the three siblings decided that it was time for them to go live with Joseph, who could now provide a sufficiently spacious apartment. They also divided up the tasks. Joseph had the necessary remodeling done to his apartment. Georg helped their parents to make the decision and to prepare for the move. Maria would then resign from her job so as to rejoin her brother and their parents and thus to recreate the family atmosphere to which they were all so attached.

The move took place on November 17, 1955, on a day marked by melancholy but also by the warmth of many students who came to lend a hand. "That year we experienced a very happy Advent, and, when my brother and sister also joined us at Christmas, the strange new house again became a real home."[4] This was, though, the calm that made even more threatening the storm that was about to hit the aspiring professor.

Bonaventure, Joachim of Fiore, and the theology of history

The mishaps connected with Ratzinger's *Habilitation* exam are similar to the difficulties connected with understanding the question addressed in the doctoral thesis and then in the book that Ratzinger derived from it. The subject, nevertheless, was crucial for the formation of Ratzinger's thought and for the contribution that he made to the development of Catholic thought at the time of Vatican II.

---

[4] J. Ratzinger, *Milestones*, 106.

We must therefore dwell again somewhat on this topic. The years of Bonaventure's life coincided with one of the most turbulent and at the same time fertile periods in Church history.

Giovanni di Fidanza, his baptismal name, was born in Città di Bagnoregio (Viterbo) around 1217. He completed his initial studies at the convent of the Friars Minor in his town and distinguished himself by his lively intellect. In 1236, we find him in Paris, where he is learning to read Scripture and the *Sentences* of Peter Lombard, at first under the guidance of Alexander of Hales and then of other masters, including Jean de la Rochelle, Odo Rigaud, John of Parma, and William of Meliton.[5] The most direct connection is the one with Alexander of Hales, the founder of the Franciscan school to which Bonaventure belonged, which had "its own, unmistakable, and in a certain sense inimitable structure that was apparent in its originality".[6]

Under the influence of Alexander and of his school, in 1243 he entered the Franciscans, then resumed his studies and became a bachelor of theology and of the Sentences; later, he was declared a master in 1254. A brief period of teaching followed, and then in 1257, unexpectedly, he was elected General of the Order. In fact, it was precisely the Franciscan Order that found itself at that same time at the origin and the epicenter of great tensions in the Church. To simplify matters, we can say that, in the institution founded by the Little Poor Man of Assisi, two camps clashed: the Conventuals, who sought somehow to adapt the strong innovative spirit brought about by Francis to the demands of everyday life and of ecclesial tradition, and the Spirituals, who did not want to quench the fire of renewal that the saint had brought.

The latter increasingly tied the Franciscan adventure to the teaching of Joachim of Fiore, who had prophesied the advent of a new age, the third and definitive eschatological age under the sign of the Holy Spirit. The Calabrese abbot had also made a calculation according to which the new age would be introduced by a preparatory phase, the duration of which happened to coincide approximately with the years of the life of Saint Francis.

---

[5] Cf. Jacques-Guy Bougerol, *Introduzione a san Bonaventura* (Vicenza: Libreria Edizioni Francescane, 1988).

[6] Cf. Inos Biffi, *Figure medievali della teologia* (Milan: Jaca Book, 1992), 77f.

On the basis of these premises, the Spirituals understood the Order in radically eschatological, purely spiritual terms, going so far as to deny the importance of any visible form whatsoever, not only of the Order itself, but also of the Church. Bonaventure's predecessor in the Generalate, John of Parma, had declared himself in favor of this approach and had been compelled to resign by the Church authorities, who feared the disorders to which such a position could lead. Bonaventure, who for his part favored a spiritual view of the Order and of the Church, had been elected specifically to make peace between the two camps, to save the Franciscans from excommunication, and to contribute to peace within the Church.

Before Ratzinger, scholars maintained that, after having taken severe measures against his predecessor,[7] the theologian originally from Bagnoregio had no longer been confronted with the vision of the Calabrese abbot and the group of the Spirituals. After reading his biography and his writings, however, Ratzinger attributed great importance to the new General's decision to spend a period of solitude in Verna in 1259, as though intending to make a second novitiate so as to draw closer to the spirit of the founder and to understand in depth the meaning of the Order he had been called to lead. Now, after the retreat in Verna, Ratzinger observed, Bonaventure's writings showed signs of this new spiritual attitude.[8]

The work in which he directly confronted Joachim is made up of a series of discourses on the early chapters of Genesis, which speak about the creation of the world. Given in Paris in 1273, these sermons came to be called the *Hexaemeron* because, in accordance with the biblical account, they explain God's creative work in the succession of the days of the week: for six days the Lord worked, and on the seventh, the Sabbath, he rested. It is, therefore, an exegetical work that remained unfinished, because, among other reasons, in that same year Bonaventure was appointed cardinal and no longer had time to review and correct the text that had been set down in writing by the students during the lectures. Hence the difficulty of

---

[7] Joseph Ratzinger, *The Theology of History in St. Bonaventure*, trans. Zachary Hayes, O.F.M. (Chicago: Franciscan Herald Press, 1979, 1989), 166n3.

[8] Among these, Ratzinger includes *The Mind's Road to God*, a journey from philosophy to the ecstatic excesses of Christian wisdom, the *Life of Saint Francis*, the *Collations on the Ten Commandments*, and those *On the Seven Gifts of the Holy Spirit*.

interpreting the work, but also the originality of a thought that had reached the fullness of its development.

The exegesis of the time distinguished four senses in Scripture: the literal sense was the basis from which were then developed the allegorical or typological sense, the tropological or moral sense, and finally the analogical or eschatological sense. The traditional teaching was then enriched by Bonaventure with the inclusion in his explanation of *sacramental figures*, persons, types, or images through which, in his opinion, the entire Bible speaks about Christ and the Antichrist. In a bold step, the Franciscan General then transposed to biblical interpretation the patristic, Stoic concept of *rationes seminales*. " 'As new seeds come from plants, so also new theories and new meanings come from Scripture.' . . . Scripture points to the future; but only he who has understood the past can grasp the interpretation of the future. . . . In this way the exegesis of Scripture becomes a theology of history; the clarification of the past leads to prophecy concerning the future."[9]

Now, finally, the Franciscan General could address the speculations of Joachim of Fiore. The Calabrese abbot maintained that corresponding to the days of creation there are two cycles of seven ages of salvation: those of the Old Covenant, which conclude with the first coming of Jesus, are the prototype of the seven ages of the New Covenant, which is destined to conclude with the seventh day of Christ's Second Coming. At this point, though, Joachim introduced a third age, that of the Holy Spirit, the preparation for which, as already mentioned, coincided approximately with Saint Francis' lifetime. Hence the conclusion of the Spirituals, who said that Saint Francis had actually started the age of the Spirit, the final hour, the seventh, which was the eschatological hour of the Church. Hence their rigorism, their desire to go back to the Gospel without any variation whatsoever, but also the revolutionary mission, through which laws and hierarchies were to fall away.

Saint Bonaventure, according to Ratzinger, did not reject Joachim's vision of the future outright; he strived, instead, to supply it with content that is more realistic and compatible with Christian history and wisdom. Along with the Spirituals, he maintained that Saint Francis is in fact the angel who announces the contemplative era,

---

[9] J. Ratzinger, *Theology of History in St. Bonaventure*, 7–9.

the seventh day that will precede the Lord's definitive manifestation. He was therefore realistic enough to see also the weaknesses of
his Order that, therefore, did not coincide with the eschatological
order announced by Francis. Together with the Dominican Order,
it found itself on the threshold of a new age that would be a time of
contemplation so that a revelation might be given to the people of
the new or last age. Now, Ratzinger asked, what can be the meaning
of this revelation? If Bonaventure was thinking of a completely new
revelation, independent of Jesus Christ and the Gospels, then he
would not have avoided the notion of a new Gospel, which had
already been condemned by the Church.

As he proceeded with his investigation, Ratzinger pointed out
above all that in Bonaventure there is no one concept to define
the essence of revelation. He spoke, instead, of multiple revelations
in which God, the revealer, speaks to an individual who becomes
the depositary of the revelation. This allows us also to identify a
dynamic, future-oriented character of revelation itself. Especially in
the *Hexaemeron*, Ratzinger continued, revelation means "the unveiling of the future",[10] but also the unveiling of the mystical, hidden
sense of Scripture and the unveiling of the divine reality that is accomplished without images in the mystical ascent.

The final revelation of which Bonaventure spoke is none other,
therefore, than the spiritual wisdom that is capable of grasping the
threefold spiritual sense of Scripture. What it is necessary to believe is not grasped through the reading of Scripture. "The letter
by itself is merely the water which is transformed into wine in the
spiritual understanding. . . . Here, therefore, 'revelation' is synony-
mous with the spiritual understanding of Scripture; it consists in
the God-given act of understanding, and not in the objective letter
alone."[11]

One of the major Italian experts in medieval theology further explained: the distinction between divine revelation and human investigation is at the origin of the field of scriptural theology. This begins with the *fides Christi* (faith in Christ), which is a gift from God
and the core of divine revelation.[12] Yet Scripture does not coincide

---

[10] Ibid., 58.
[11] Ibid., 63.
[12] Cf. Inos Biffi, *Figure medievali della teologia*, 104.

with theology in the strict sense. The sacred writer, indeed, could not wrap his spiritual vision in mere spirituality. He wrapped it, instead, in the "swaddling clothes of written language".[13] Theology, therefore, always starts from Scripture, but then comes to wisdom, to a spiritual understanding of Scripture. In a word, the revelation of which Bonaventure spoke is not the gift of a new Scripture, in addition to the Old and New Testament, but, rather, a new understanding of the old and ever-valid Scripture. The great cultural flourishing begun in Paris by the Franciscans and the Dominicans seemed to be a further confirmation of this beginning of a new revelation or spiritual understanding of the written word.

The danger of the novelty or subjectivism of the individual theologian was not taken into serious consideration by Bonaventure. Indeed, the deep sense of Sacred Scripture does not depend on the individual but is transmitted in a broad, cosmic-hierarchical context, in the teachings of the Fathers and in the theology of the Church. It is true, on the contrary, that for the theologian as for the simple believer, there are various degrees of revelation, which does not designate the simple knowledge of Scripture but, rather, "simple, inner familiarity with the mystery of the Word of God".[14] Mysticism, like revelation, is not an individual grace independent of the age. "Rather, it involves the entrance into that form of knowledge which the Apostles had; and thus it will be the true fulfillment of the New Testament revelation."[15] And just as apostolic revelation ended with John, the apostle of love, so too the final revelation will unfold in "love as the fulfillment of desire, that is, as the science of charity, which is overflowing with the fullness of God".[16]

In Bonaventure's view, therefore, God is at the origin and at the end of every person's story, but also of history and of the cosmos. It is not far from the truth to say that he adopted the neo-Platonic vision of reality as a descent that comes from God and leads back to him. The Franciscan General, however, added his own adjustments. For him, God is above all "the intelligible sphere whose center is everywhere while its circumference is nowhere".[17] This definition,

---

[13] Saint Bonaventure, *Breviloquium*, prologue.
[14] J. Ratzinger, *Theology of History in St. Bonaventure*, 71.
[15] Ibid., 93.
[16] Biffi, *Figure medievali della teologia*, 109.
[17] J. Ratzinger, *Theology of History in St. Bonaventure*, 144.

for Bonaventure, tells of God's infinity and eternity, which is expressed in the lack of a circumference. Beyond the lack of a circumference, however, internal coherence and unity are also part of eternity. Coherence is represented by the center of the circle, in which its radical unity is expressed. Bonaventure then transferred the description of the intelligible circle, first of all, to the individual person, whose spiritual journey, however, is made within the circular concept of the history of the world. "Through man and through the grace that sanctifies man . . . the world must be drawn back into the *circulus aeternitatis*."[18]

The center of the center, nevertheless, is Christ. He is the center of all things and the center of all sciences through his Cross.

> The lost middle of the circle is found again by means of two lines that intersect at right angles, that is, by a cross. This means that by His cross, Christ has definitively solved the geometry-problem of world history. With His cross He has uncovered the lost center of the circle of the world so as to give the true direction and meaning to the movement of the individual life and to the history of mankind as such.[19]

After this laborious but certainly fruitful journey, we can understand, first of all, the attitude of the two readers toward Ratzinger's study. The bold thesis of the prospective university lecturer revolutionized the understanding of Bonaventure's thought, imposed a significant revision on the prevailing interpretation of philosophical and theological thought in the Middle Ages, and offered a solid point of departure for going beyond the prevailing concept of revelation at that time. Indeed, it was too much for a scholar like Schmaus, who was considered and in turn thought himself to be one of the major experts in medieval thought, to accept in its entirety without reacting. On the other hand, Söhngen, who had already passed judgment on his student's doctoral thesis, regarded it as a confirmation of his decision. Ratzinger not only proved to be capable of designing an independent scientific research project—one of the academic requirements for a candidate to qualify as a university lecturer—but again and again displayed an extraordinary talent for highlighting original and innovative aspects present in the works of

---

[18] Ibid., 145.
[19] Ibid., 146.

the great theologians of the past. In short, he was able to read the great thinkers of the past empathetically and was then able to derive from them nourishment to enrich and elaborate the contemporary theological debate. As for Ratzinger himself, from his research on Saint Bonaventure, he gained an enormous wealth of insights that flowed into his method and also into the content of his theology.

First of all, the concept of revelation is not static, not metaphysical, but rather bound up with God's interventions in the history of Israel and of all mankind. The central and definitive revelatory event is that of Jesus Christ, who was sent by the Father into the world to save man created in his image and likeness and was raised by him from the dead in the power of the Spirit of love. This work of God had witnesses in the Old Covenant and witnesses in the New. Their testimony is entrusted to Scripture, which, in turn, is entrusted to the Church. The revelatory event, however, is prior to the texts of Sacred Scripture, which in any case must be read in light of Jesus' Resurrection and in communion with the Christian community to which Jesus himself entrusts his Eucharistic body and his written revelation as a living deposit to be preserved and handed down over the generations.

Present in the Church, therefore, there are seeds that allow us to discover revelation and to go ever deeper in our understanding of it. For this reason, we can certainly say that revelation is completed, but we must also add that revelation is in a state of becoming because the Spirit can always give a superior capacity for insight and immersion into the mystery of God. Hence, the expectation of a revelatory future that of course does not go beyond Scripture and the person of Jesus Christ, yet can allow us to enter in greater depth into the word, the sacrament, and the person of Jesus and of his Church.

The interpretation of Scripture, then, does not refer exclusively to the past, but also entails the hope of an eschatological interpretation in parallel with the hope founded on a future coming of Jesus. The relation between Scripture and tradition, therefore, is not static and cannot even be determined in a definitive way. Certainly, the Holy Spirit has permitted the Church over history to arrive at some benchmarks, dogmas, that are indispensable; the Spirit, nevertheless, can always give a greater wealth of insight through the Magisterium, theological work, and, above all, the lives and teaching of the saints and mystics. Taking again as an example the person of Saint Francis, who was so beloved and venerated by Saint Bonaventure: the dogma of the Incarnation was indeed present in the Christian tradition of the first millennium. It is certain, nevertheless, that with the desire to see depicted in the manger scene the manner in which the Son of God came into the world, Saint Francis promoted a deeper piety with respect to the Incarnation and infancy of Jesus.

The drama of the Habilitation

After the manuscript was submitted, not a word was heard from the second reader, Schmaus. In February, an understanding female secretary announced that the professor had finally taken up Ratzinger's thesis. At Easter, Schmaus convened in Königstein (Hesse) a meeting of German-speaking professors of dogmatic theology. Also invited was Ratzinger, who recalled meeting on that occasion Karl Rahner, the great Jesuit theologian, with whom he would collaborate during the council. Rahner himself asked to meet Ratzinger, who, despite his young age, had been invited to write several articles for the encyclopedic work *Die Religion in Geschichte und Gegenwart*, published by Lutheran theologians. Since Rahner was preparing to organize among Catholic scholars a similar work, an updated edition of the *Lexikon für Theologie und Kirche*, he was interested in knowing the editorial criteria followed by the Protestants. This was certainly the occasion for an interesting meeting.

After the conference, Schmaus finally summoned Ratzinger for a brief conversation, during which he announced to him in no uncertain terms that he intended to reject his *Habilitation* thesis because the concept of revelation contained in it was dangerously close to modernism,[20] while the work as a whole did not fulfill the required scientific criteria. It threw cold water on the young theologian, who was generally regarded as launching out on a more than promising future in the academic field. He was especially anxious about questions of a practical nature. Of course, he could abandon a teaching career and return to pastoral work, but only a few months earlier, his parents had sold their house so as to follow him to Freising.

---

[20] Alfred Läpple, *Benedetto XVI e le sue radici* (Venice: Marcianum Press, 2009), 95.

Another move certainly would not have been easy to explain or to manage.

Upon his return to Munich, there were emotional meetings with Professor Söhngen, seeking the true reason for the rejection and possible solutions. Some friends alerted them that from Freising, where there was no lack of envious colleagues, rumors had arrived in Munich accusing Ratzinger of modernism, of subjectivism in his manner of interpreting and evaluating dogmas. Then there were the sensitivities, anxieties, and fears of Schmaus. The author of a Catholic *Dogmatics* that had enjoyed great success and was read widely in German-speaking countries had indeed returned to his teaching career, but he felt that his impact on the younger generations was beginning to decline. They now preferred the younger Söhngen, who realized that, after the war, it was no longer the hour for grand syntheses. One needed, instead, to be content with fragments and above all to pose questions.

This was exactly Söhngen's method. Ratzinger himself would recall him in 1971, while giving the eulogy at the funeral of his beloved professor in the Church of Saint Agnes in Cologne: "His fundamental spiritual attitude was to pose questions radically and critically. Even today it is not possible to question more radically than he did. But at the same time, he was a radical believer. The thing about him that fascinated us students over and over again was precisely the unity of these two elements."[21] Schmaus was aggrieved, therefore, by the growing influence of Söhngen on the younger generation, just as he now found it difficult to tolerate the reputation of his rival's prize pupil as a "child prodigy" in theology.

Moreover, Ratzinger had not refrained from arguing that in Munich research on the medieval era, of which Schmaus himself was the leading representative, had stopped before the war and had disregarded the new trends coming especially from the works of the philosopher from Louvain, Fernand van Steenberghen. This observation wounded Schmaus' pride, and he reacted by pointing out the many typing errors in the text, which allowed him to come to the conclusion that the work lacked the necessary scientific rigor.

The session of the faculty council that examined Ratzinger's *Habilitation* thesis at the end of the summer semester was stormy. The

---

[21] Ibid., 80f. Ratzinger's entire homily was published in Italian by *30Giorni* 1/2 (2006).

reader and the second reader set forth their different perspectives; the faculty council tempered Schmaus' severe judgment by deciding that the text should be returned to the author, who could present it again after having corrected the errors that had been pointed out. Certainly not a glorious outcome, but after the preceding months, in which it seemed that the path to an academic career had been compromised, it opened up again a glimpse of a future. Then, taking in hand his own manuscript, marked up by Schmaus with extremely polemical annotations, Ratzinger noticed that the corrections were concentrated in the first two parts of the text, where he spoke about the method he followed and about the concept of salvation history in thirteenth-century theology. The last part, in contrast, which was more specifically dedicated to Bonaventure's theology of history, was almost devoid of critical remarks.

Ratzinger then had an insight that was at the same time a gamble. He would abandon the first two parts of the work and would present as his thesis only the final part, which was considered more original and innovative, after of course providing the necessary introductory materials and correcting the errors noted by Schmaus. The instructor was thus cornered. After having evaluated that part positively, he could no longer reject it, as he might have liked to do. Ratzinger submitted his plan to Söhngen, who gave his approval without further ado. The work necessary for the rewriting was done during the summer vacation of 1956. To the general surprise of the faculty at how little time was required for the revision, the two corrected copies were resubmitted in October of that same year. More months of impatient waiting followed, and, finally, on February 11, 1957, Ratzinger learned that his thesis had been approved. He breathed a sigh of relief, but the trial had not yet come to an end.

To obtain the coveted qualification to teach as a university lecturer, at that time the candidate had to give a public lecture with a subsequent response by the reader and the second reader. Ratzinger prepared for the lecture while noticing the growing tension. Indeed, failure was still possible, and this time in public. That had occurred twice since the end of the war, and in both instances it had then weighed heavily on the life of the failed professor.

On February 21, the day scheduled for the lecture, the large auditorium selected for the occasion was packed. "An extraordinary tension was almost palpable in the air."[22] After Ratzinger had finished his lecture, the two professors took the podium; they very soon forgot about the candidate completely and started what seemed to be a grand medieval disputation. The professors challenged each other to a duel of citations, then turned to the public and sought their consent and approval. Then the council withdrew to a session that, in turn, seemed endless.

After the nerve-wracking wait, finally the dean emerged from the council hall. He approached the little group of people remaining, made up of Joseph, his brother, and several friends, and informally announced that he had passed the examination and the coveted *Habilitation* had been granted. The stress had been so great that only slowly was Ratzinger able to return to his everyday work without fear of having dragged his parents into an inglorious adventure.

Professor at the College of Philosophy and Theology in Freising

After obtaining the *Habilitation* to teach at the university level, Ratzinger was appointed a lecturer (*Privatdozent*) at the University of Munich, and, according to a plan made long before, on January 1, 1958, he was appointed ordinary professor of dogmatic and fundamental theology at the College of Philosophy and Theology in Freising. In the house on the Domberg (cathedral hill), the atmosphere was finally relaxed. Joseph lived there with his parents, and, in keeping with their plans, they were joined by his sister, Maria, who had resigned from her job in order to support her parents and brother. Finally, after so much uncertainty, the new professor could dedicate himself full-time to teaching and research, while his sister kept house, and even their parents found a job to their liking. Among the tasks of the new professor was that of examining the students, and to ease the rigorous atmosphere that accompanied tests at that time, Joseph preferred to invite to his residence those who were to be examined. His parents had formed a little welcoming committee. "Our father then invited the theologians in and led them into the living room where they could wait. Our mother brewed a cup of tea for each one and offered a few cookies with it,

---

[22] J. Ratzinger, *Milestones*, 112.

so that everything went smoothly and humanely."[23] In short, there was finally a period of serenity and optimism, in keeping with the euphoria in a country that, after having gone through the tragedy of war, was up and running again, economically and civically.

In 1957, the Federal Republic of Germany reached its goal of full employment; in the elections that year, the Christian Democratic Party crossed the threshold of an absolute majority of the votes.[24] The Church, too, now seemed headed for a recovery that seemed both quantitative and qualitative. Appearances, nevertheless, do not deceive the eyes of the attentive observer. In 1958, Ratzinger returned to his article on "New Pagans"[25] and published it as a warning not to be fooled by appearances. He rejected the rigorist solution, which proposed restricting the sacraments to a small core group of staunch, observant believers, nor did he agree with the intransigent separation of the Church from the surrounding society. At that time, his solution looked to a Christocentrism through which both the few and the many might be saved. The young professor wrote: "Damnation belongs to all men universally; salvation belongs to Christ alone. . . . He alone takes all the evil upon himself and thus frees for us the place of salvation. All the salvation that can exist for man is based on this original exchange between Christ, the One, and us, the many, and the humility of faith is to recognize this."[26] The Church and the faithful are thus called to humility and seriousness. Grace alone conferred on the Church the task of representing the many; commitment alone can enable the faithful to carry out their mission of witnessing to Jesus' Gospel of salvation.

Evil in the world: Reinhold Schneider and Hermann Hesse

An indefatigable reader, Ratzinger did not limit his interests exclusively to the field of philosophy and theology, but also attentively followed contemporary writers whose works could stimulate his

---

[23] Georg Ratzinger and Michael Hesemann, *My Brother the Pope*, trans. Michael J. Miller (San Francisco: Ignatius Press, 2011), 185.

[24] Cf. Gianni Valente, *Ratzinger professore* (Cinisello Balsamo: San Paolo, 2008), 58.

[25] See chapter 2.

[26] Joseph Ratzinger, *Il nuovo popolo di Dio* (Brescia: Queriniana, 1971), 361.

thinking. The first who deserves to be mentioned in this connection is Reinhold Schneider (1903–1958). After his studies in economics, Schneider was hired as an administrative employee by an art dealer who had interests in the Iberian Peninsula. His many travels in Europe, particularly in the Iberian countries, prevented him from succumbing to the fascination of Nazism. On the contrary, his literary output can be summarized as a historical-geographical journey through Europe in conscious contrast to National Socialist fanaticism. After the war, even though he continued to write about saints and about Christian and Catholic themes, he felt increasingly attracted by Indian thought. In *Winter in Vienna*, his final work, which many considered an apostasy from Christianity, he wrote: "Firmly convinced that the Church was divinely founded and will last until the end of history, I nevertheless prefer to withdraw into the crypt. I hear the song from afar. I know that He is risen, but my life force has sunk so low that it is no longer capable of getting up from the tomb, of holding and desiring anything besides death."[27]

Among the many works by Schneider, two in particular interested Ratzinger: the novel *Las Casas before Charles V*,[28] on the Dominican friar who defended the indigenous peoples of the West Indies, and *The Great Renunciation*, the play devoted to Celestine V, the pope who abdicated from the papacy seven centuries before Benedict XVI. The two works represent Schneider's earliest and latest literary work. The first is from 1938, when the cultural climate was dominated by National Socialism; the second is from 1957, when the writer, in view of the tragedy that Europe had experienced, had given in to a vague pessimism that even doubted whether the witness of the saints was effective. The theme of the novel devoted to Bartolomé de Las Casas is the testimony of conscience, as Ratzinger himself explained in a conference entitled "Conscience in Its Time", held at the Reinhold Schneider Society in the early 1970s.[29]

---

[27] Reinhold Schneider, *Winter in Wien* (Frankfurt: Insel Verlag, 1983), 489f.

[28] The original edition, entitled *Las Casas vor Karl V* (Frankfurt: Insel Verlag) was published in 1938. Italian edition: *Bartolomeo de Las Casas* (Milan: Mondadori, 1942), which was reprinted by Jaca Book in 1978.

[29] The text was then published in Ratzinger's volume *Church, Ecumenism, and Politics*, trans. Michael J. Miller et al. (San Francisco: Ignatius Press, 2008), 160–72.

In the novel, testimony is given in the presence of Charles V by Las Casas, but also by Bernardino, like the former friar a former Spanish conquistador, who had been brought back to humanity and to repentance by a slave woman, Lucaya. The girl was slender and perhaps for that reason was not assigned the heavy labors to which the other Indians were subjected; her personality, nevertheless, radiated an attraction that conquered Bernardino. He watched her with growing attention and realized that his fascination was born of the suffering that she experienced due to her profound communion with her people:

> I must also relate that once, while a guard was beating a native, a spectacle that left me altogether indifferent, I heard Lucaya sobbing nearby. I found her behind a tree, disconsolate, with her face bathed in tears. . . . If a baby died at the exhausted breast of his mother, if a man was dejected and crushed by fatigue, I could guess those events from Lucaya's face even before the supervisor reported them to me.[30]

An Indian woman in the depths of her soul, Lucaya in reality was also a fervent Christian: she was in communion with the sufferings of her people and was in communion with the sufferings of Christ on the Cross. And Lucaya's helpless testimony had been precisely what touched Bernardino's conscience, just as then the testimony of Las Casas touched the heart of Charles V. And here is Ratzinger's comment in the conference: "The corrective could spring only from faith itself. . . . This is the only thing that justifies this faith as the truth: the fact that as a matter of principle it cannot be a multiplication of power but is, rather, a wake-up call for the conscience, which limits power and protects the helpless."[31]

As was already mentioned, the second work by Schneider that Ratzinger read attentively was *The Great Renunciation*. Two questions run through the play: What can the individual do when injustice triumphs? The other: Is Christianity a force for peace, or, as in the Book of Revelation, do the powers of hell assemble and fight with renewed vigor when the Just Man appears? Schneider tried to answer them by relating the incident of Pietro da Morrone, who had been elected pope with the name of Celestine V in June 1294. Soon, however, Pietro realized that he was unsuccessful at bringing

---

[30] Schneider, *Bartolomeo de Las Casas*, 77.
[31] Joseph Ratzinger, "Conscience in Its Time", in *Church, Ecumenism, and Politics*, 166.

peace, either in religious matters or among the States. Therefore, he resigned in December of the same year, 1294, after only a five-month pontificate.

The play was dominated by Schneider's final pessimism: Europe, like the world at the time of Celestine, was covered by a thick layer of black lava from which its inhabitants could not manage to free themselves. There was no lack of efforts by individuals: Latino Cardinal Malatesta, Prince Luigi di Napoli, Pietro Celestino, all men of good will, Christians who would like to remedy the irresistible contagion that was emitted by the hearts of men and spread like the plague. Their intentions, nevertheless, deteriorated and were corrupted. Celestine V, in particular, was a holy man who agreed to ascend the throne of Peter, hoping to restore peace in the Church, but his expectation proved to be illusory. How could he think of healing a corrupt institution that had been invaded by the worm of power? What could his holiness do against the much more effective work of the evil one? His pontificate only exacerbated an already compromised situation, and ultimately there was nothing left for him to do but resign.

Another German-language writer who was important for Ratzinger was Hermann Hesse; in particular, he read and liked *Steppenwolf*, a novel from 1927, and *The Glass Bead Game* [also published in English as *Magister Ludi*] from 1943. Like Schneider, Hesse looked sympathetically to India, to its flight from appearances in order to return to the whole, to "the dissolution of painful individuation".[32] Especially the more recent work was pervaded by a cultural pessimism that left little room for hope. For this reason, Ratzinger distanced himself from *The Glass Bead Game*, in which a fictitious world prevailed, a sort of mathematics of the mind. In contrast, he found in *Steppenwolf* a truly extraordinary ability to diagnose society's ills and to give a prognosis: "It anticipated, in a certain way, the problems that we subsequently lived through in the sixties and seventies. The novel, as you know, is actually about one person, but one who analyzes himself into so many different personalities that the analysis finally leads to self-disintegration."[33]

---

[32] Hermann Hesse, *Steppenwolf*, trans. Basil Creighton (London: Penguin Books, 1990), 73.

[33] Joseph Ratzinger, *Salt of the Earth*, trans. Adrian Walker (San Francisco: Ignatius Press, 1997), 70.

Ratzinger's encounter with writers who turned to the New World of America or to the Indian East in order to flee from Europe's wars and decline certainly merits attention. It testifies to an open mind that is alert to the pressures that come from the world of culture. At the same time, Ratzinger also gained from it corroboration for the construction of his theology, for Christian personalism, for the unity of the love of God in creation and in salvation history, which became the motive for a reliable hope, notwithstanding the ceaseless activity of the powers of evil. Ratzinger's attention to eschatology, too, resulted from the gravity of his encounter with the apocalyptic catastrophes that ravaged the earth in the twentieth century. The harshness of the trial, nevertheless, did not cause him to forget the promise of the Risen Christ: "Behold, I am with you always, to the close of the age" (Mt 28:20).

Christian brotherhood

In 1958, as proof of his growing fame, Ratzinger was invited to the theological convention of the Austrian Institute for Pastoral Work, which was held in Vienna. The topic assigned to the young theologian concerned Christian brotherhood. Following the method of fundamental theology, a practice that he would often adopt in those first years of teaching, he addressed the subject matter first from an extra-biblical perspective, both ancient and contemporary, and then examined the question in depth in the First Covenant and in the New Testament. In ancient Greece, *adelphós*, brother, meant someone who belongs to the same *polis*, nation. The rest, in contrast, are barbarians. This is the origin of a fundamental distinction in the *ethos*: one's ethical obligation toward those inside is different from one's obligation toward those outside. The problem appears in intensified form in the Old Testament. Indeed, corresponding to the Greek *polis* is the Old Testament theocracy in which political unity is understood as religious unity, also.

He then returned to the ethical dualism between the nation and the nations. "For the individual, a brother was one who belonged with him in the unity not of just any people, but of the unique Chosen People of God. That meant that brotherhood did not depend merely on common racial descent, but on common election by God."[34] This election, nevertheless, gradually transcends the national tie. First the conviction is affirmed that God, father of the nations through creation, is in a particular way father of Israel through election. Nevertheless, this distinction, too, is destined to be overcome. The God of Israel, indeed, the God of all peoples, is also the father of all. Besides Israel, he wants to save all mankind. And although this is not possible through the people of the twelve tribes, redemption becomes effective through Jesus Christ and the people constituted by the twelve apostles.

Christ, Ratzinger then wrote, makes visible the fact that God is grace, that from all eternity Christ is the only Just One, the only one worthy of election. Through grace, nevertheless, an unheard-of exchange occurs: "Christ becomes rejected, takes the fate of the rejection of all upon himself, and thus renders all in his place—in him and through him—elected, just as he had become rejected in us and through us."[35] In Christ, the pairs of brothers about which the Bible speaks are elected: Cain and Abel, Ishmael and Isaac, Esau and Jacob, Israel and the other nations. The unheard-of exchange, nevertheless, also concerns the followers of Christ in the past as in the future. After the coming of the Son of God and after his death on the Cross, the two robbers on the cross, Judas and Paul, the synagogue and the Church, the Church and the nations are elected with him. It is true that in the Old Covenant one gets the impression at first that the election of one entails the non-election of the other. If we look attentively, however, the elect are chosen also for the non-elect.[36] As is clear, moreover, from the example of Esau and Jacob, the two brothers stand not only for themselves but represent the respective peoples that originated from them. Similarly, the Church is, as such and in her totality, the bearer of this vicarious election that is extended to all the nations. The Church, therefore, cannot remain self-enclosed, inside her bastions, but necessarily has a missionary and sacramental dimension. She, indeed, has the gift, which becomes a task: "to show forth by signs the hidden mystery of God, to proclaim publicly in the visible world the share of God

---

[34] Joseph Ratzinger, *Die christliche Brüderlichkeit* (Munich: Kösel Verlag, 1960). The book was published for the first time in English in 1966 by Sheed & Ward. It was reprinted as: *The Meaning of Christian Brotherhood* (San Francisco: Ignatius Press, 1993), 7.

[35] J. Ratzinger, *Meaning of Christian Brotherhood*, 77.

[36] Ibid., 78.

in the drama of history".[37] As the channel and instrument of grace, the Church, nevertheless, is not simply interchangeable with God's grace. The latter acts freely with individuals, with Christian communities besides the Catholic one, with the world religions, with believers and nonbelievers. To the Catholic Church, however, is reserved the objective representation of the vicarious work in union with the Cross of Christ.

Catholics, for their part, who are called by grace to witness to the faith and to charity, must be ready and willing to be vicariously rejected so that others might be elect in their place. "One stands in the place of the other, and it is an expression of God's faith in us that he draws us into this system of vicarious election."[38] This apparently simple argument salvaged the specificity of the Catholic Church but also the just relation of brotherhood with other Christians. For a generation that had learned to appreciate the solemnity of Karl Barth's theological speculation, the eros of the witness that emanated from the pages of *Resistance and Surrender* by Dietrich Bonhoeffer, reading these pages was a joy and a liberation. The social dimension of the faith was reevaluated, also.

Once again, Ratzinger's reasoning had an elementary simplicity. He wrote: Christian brotherhood is based on the faith of our real filiation with respect to the Heavenly Father. Contemporary theologians, however, in explaining the Lord's Prayer, the Our Father, dwell almost exclusively on the second term and end up neglecting the plural possessive adjective that also has great importance. "The Christian prayer to the Father 'is not the call of a soul that knows nothing outside God and itself', but is bound to the community of brothers. Together with these brothers we make up the one Christ."[39] This, too, was a powerful antidote offered to anyone who had to confront the new ideas of Marxist origin, which rebuked Christians, even those seriously committed to social work, of being basically petty bourgeois. Ratzinger, instead, helped them to feel that they were brothers, not counting on their own strength, intellect, and arrogance, but on the communion with Christ that is open not only to the strong, to those who were politically involved

---

[37] Ibid., 89.
[38] Ibid., 79.
[39] Ibid., 51–52.

in a struggle that did not reject recourse to violence, but to all, especially to the weak, the poor, the humble, and the persecuted. These were not the defeated of history, but those through whom Jesus had primarily come into the world and with whom he had completed his course of suffering and death in solidarity.

Professor in Bonn

Once he was named a lecturer, Ratzinger could receive "calls" from all the theological faculties present in the State universities of the German Federal Republic. Usually several years passed between the *Habilitation* and the call, but the professor of dogmatic theology in Freising was accustomed to rapid advancement, and there were already rumors about prestigious calls. The first proposal was from the canon of the cathedral responsible for catechesis, who wanted him to be a professor at the Pedagogical Institute in Paising, near Munich, where his friend Alfred Läpple already had the chair. There the new professor would have to teach religion to elementary school teachers, who in turn were called to explain the religion to their little pupils. The archbishop, too, Joseph Wendel, who had succeeded the unforgettable Cardinal von Faulhaber, would have been happy with this solution. During the war there had been few ordinations in the archdiocese, and the archbishop preferred to have his priests remain in the diocese rather than accept positions at State universities.

The candidate in question, nevertheless, did not like this solution. Properly speaking, Paising was not a true university, and, furthermore, he did not consider himself suited for the job that was proposed. Earlier in 1956, right in the middle of the stormy events that had accompanied his *Habilitation*, the dean of the theological faculty in Mainz had informally asked Ratzinger whether he would be interested in accepting the chair of fundamental theology at his university.[40] At that time, Ratzinger had refused categorically. He did not feel like giving up his *Habilitation* thesis and abandoning his parents, who had moved in with him shortly before. In the summer of 1958, in contrast, he received a call from the University of Bonn offering him the chair of fundamental theology. Now the situation

---

[40] J. Ratzinger, *Milestones*, 113.

was different: he had finally obtained the coveted *Habilitation*, while his brother, Georg, for his part, had finished his studies in Munich. He was then appointed choir director of the parish of Saint Oswald, in Traunstein, and received as a benefit with his position a nice little house in the center of the town that was already familiar to the Ratzingers.

It was a coincidence that Joseph could not help but consider providential. The idea of moving their parents once more, which previously had seemed so difficult, now appeared like a return home that might be more than welcome. He spoke about it with Georg, who said that he was enthusiastic about the possibility of hosting their parents, who, for their part, while not underestimating the difficulties connected with the new change of location, insisted that their younger son accept an opportunity that a few months earlier seemed like only a distant hope. Joseph, therefore, could see his way clear to accepting the call from Bonn, all the more because it was the chair to which his beloved Professor Söhngen had aspired throughout his life. He did not know it, but the decision proved to be one of the most important in his life.

Shortly after that, he was summoned by Cardinal Wendel, who intended to confirm his appointment to Paising and to congratulate him. Ratzinger thanked him for selecting him but politely informed him that he intended to accept the invitation from Bonn. All that the cardinal could do was to say that he himself was pleased that one of his priests should be named to such a prestigious chair. For Ratzinger, though, it was the conclusion of a stage of his life that was impassioned and worrisome at the same time, while a new phase was opening that took him far from home and started him on a career that was both swift and full of twists and turns. It was also a separation from his parents, whose closeness had been a precious support in moments that certainly had not been easy, and it was a separation from his beloved Bavaria. Awaiting him now were the ways of academia and the circumstances by which God was leading him to destinations and changes that he could not even imagine.

From the sources of the Danube to the Rhine in its full course, from the birthplace of Mozart to that of Beethoven, from Bavaria to the Rhineland, from Munich, the historic capital of Bavaria, which was already starting to recover its former prosperity, to Bonn, the capital of the German Federal Republic, which was intended to be temporary until it was possible to unify the country—a cause that the Germans did not want to give up. The geographical distance between the two cities was certainly no less than the cultural difference. Whereas the Danube passes through and connects Catholic and Orthodox countries, the Rhine is the mighty waterway that runs through predominantly Protestant regions and through countries, Belgium and Holland in particular, that after the tragedy of war were in turn heading for a phase of renewed prosperity and wide cultural influence. Ratzinger, however, was young, and the challenge elated him. He wrote in his autobiography: "The great river with its international shipping traffic gave me the feeling of openness and breadth, of the meeting of cultures and nations that for centuries had occurred here and made one another fruitful."[41] In Bavaria he felt at home; in the Rhineland he felt that he was at the center of Europe, which, after the war, was seeking new horizons of an economic and political sort.

The move took place in April 1959. The young professor was accompanied by his sister, Maria, who, from then on, would be her brother's faithful assistant. She kept house and prepared the meals, but she was also a trusted advisor, an attentive observer. Her brother first presented his thoughts and his lectures to her, and she called him back to the essentials and to clarity. Temporarily Joseph went to live at the Albertinum, the house of studies where the majority of the students from the Catholic faculty of theology resided. This circumstance, too, had its beneficial sides. At the house of studies, Ratzinger had the opportunity to get to know his students closely, how they lived and thought, and this promoted reciprocal understanding and respect.[42] The lectures began on April 15, 1959, and soon the students noticed the breath of fresh air that they brought. First of all, there was his way of presenting himself: with his ever-present beret, he seemed, according to the description of one rather caustic student, "the second or third assistant priest from some huge city parish",[43] and yet he was already a full professor. Above all, his way of teaching, devoid of all rhetoric, inspired enthusiasm: he went directly to the point and expressed his thought with rare

---

[41] Ibid., 115–16.
[42] Ibid., 115.
[43] See Valente, *Ratzinger professore*, 58.

clarity and precision. One of his first students wrote: "The lectures were prepared down to the millimeter. He used to give them by paraphrasing the text that he had prepared with formulas that sometimes seemed to build up like a mosaic, with a wealth of images that reminded me of Romano Guardini. In some lectures, like in the pauses during a concert, you could have heard a pin drop."[44]

The God of faith and the God of the philosophers

The magisterial lecture, the one that officially inaugurates the academic career of the new professor, was scheduled for June 24, 1959, toward the end of the summer semester. According to the tradition of the German theological faculties, the instructors and students of the entire faculty attended. Ratzinger, consequently, chose a subject, "The God of faith and the God of the philosophers", that at that time was already central to his reflections, and he has not abandoned it over the course of the years. He wrote in 2004 in the preface to a new edition of the text: "When I reread this inaugural lecture . . . I fully realized, for the first time, the extent to which the questions posed then have remained to this day, so to speak, the guiding thread of my thought." Ratzinger's magisterial lecture was greeted by students and instructors with unanimous and even enthusiastic applause. In reality, the new professor had given his best: clarity and simplicity of exposition, the ability to go to the heart of problems. Instructors and students had the sense that they had in front of them, not just a skillful professor of theology, but rather an original thinker who was destined to leave a lasting impression in the field of education and on the life of the Church.

Ratzinger's fame quickly crossed the threshold of his new university to spread to the city of Bonn, to the Rhineland, and to the entire German Church. And soon he received an invitation to publish his lecture, which was available to readers as early as 1960.[45]

---

[44] The statement is by Horst Ferdinand, recorded in ibid., 65.

[45] *Der Gott des Glaubens und der Gott der Philosophen* was first published in Germany by Schnell und Steiner (Munich-Zurich) in 1960. In 2004, Professor Heino Sonnemans took the initiative to republish the text, and Cardinal Ratzinger wrote a new preface. However, the book with the new preface was published by Paulinus (Treviri) only after Ratzinger was elected pope in 2006; this new edition is based on the Italian translation, entitled *Il Dio della fede e il Dio dei filosofi*, published by Marcianum Press (Venice) in 2007.

It is appropriate to pay particular attention to this text, because its contents are at the basis of any philosophical-theological reflection whatsoever. Ratzinger, moreover, would constantly return to the subject at regular intervals to defend conjointly the mystical, personal, and supernatural aspect of the faith, guaranteed by God's revelation, and man's rationality, to which is delegated the task of translating the unique faith event into the universality of human reflection. Only this ceaseless work of mediation is a guarantee both of the gratuitousness of God's revelation and also of the reliability of the foundation on which the truth claim of every human assertion is based.

Precisely this claim, which he defended persistently over the decades,[46] cost the author the gradual loss of the growing majority of relativists—believers and nonbelievers. The latter wanted to restrict faith-based thought to the confines of religion, and the former were content to remain unperturbed in a sort of limbo where people repeated a teaching that made no demands on its followers, who became increasingly marginalized.

At least as ancient as the first testimonies of religion and of human thought, the topic "the God of faith and the God of the philosophers" became central to modern reflection, according to Ratzinger, in 1654, the year when Pascal had written on a slip of paper—found in his pocket immediately after his death and entitled *Memorial*— these words: "Fire. God of Abraham, God of Isaac, God of Jacob, not of the philosophers and the scientists." Pascal had experienced the living God, the God of the Bible, who was at the origin of wonderment toward reality that was very different from the contemporary "geometric spirit" of Descartes, which was well known to the same French scholar, who was a mathematician and a physicist.

---

[46] At the beginning of the preface to the third edition mentioned in the preceding note, Ratzinger himself recalled some of his later speeches on this topic. We might add to these a reference to the famous conversation with Jürgen Habermas at the Catholic Academy of Bavaria, in which the then-cardinal pointed out the implications—social as well—of the demand for truth and the cardinal's collaboration in the important encyclical by John Paul II, *Fides et ratio*. One of the cornerstones of the encyclical expresses the cardinal's firm conviction: "The Church remains profoundly convinced that faith and reason 'mutually support each other'; each influences the other, as they offer to each other a purifying critique and a stimulus to pursue the search for deeper understanding" (no. 100). The encyclical has been published in English by Pauline Books and Media (Boston, 1998).

Ratzinger added that, in Pascal's time, rationalistic philosophy was still too strong, and for this reason the earthshaking challenge presented by the *Memorial* was not yet taken up. Only the total dissolution of metaphysics started by Kant with the transposition of the religious element to the extra-rational, extra-metaphysical sphere finally brought Pascal's thought into the limelight, while exaggerating the contrast between the two poles: religion is experienced fact, philosophy is theory; the God of religion is alive and personal, the God of the philosophers is empty and inert.

Having arrived at this point, but before proposing a synthesis of his own, Ratzinger synthesized two proposals, one Catholic, the other Protestant, which somehow exemplify the way of dialogue and the disjunctive way in the relation between reason and faith. To represent the Catholic tradition, for once the young professor did not call on his beloved Augustine or a theologian from the patristic tradition, but rather Thomas Aquinas, who, at the height of the medieval era, achieved a careful, accurate synthesis between ancient thought and Christian tradition. According to Ratzinger, where modern thought introduces a perfect parallelism between religious thought and God, Aquinas introduces a distinction between religious thought and the God of faith that allows him to salvage Christian specificity. Both natural religion and the vision of the gods that was characteristic of philosophy have for Saint Thomas an identical content. From this perspective, "philosophy is the highest possibility of the human mind."[47]

Along this line of thought, nevertheless, the Christian religion is not, as contemporaries maintain, in opposition to the philosophical vision. The distinction, rather, is thought of in terms of the plan of grace that does not destroy but rather elevates and perfects nature. This allowed Saint Thomas to affirm that the God of Aristotle and the Christian God are the same. Aristotle recognized the true God, whom Christians can understand more deeply in faith, just as in eternal life they will be able to comprehend him in even greater depth in his nature as love. In short, we are looking at one cognitive act divided into three degrees of increasing intensity.

To represent the Protestant thought of the first half of the twentieth century, in contrast, Ratzinger chose the Swiss theologian Emil

---

[47] J. Ratzinger, *Il Dio della fede e il Dio dei filosofi*, 21.

Brunner (1889–1966). A promoter of dialectical theology, Brunner was firmly convinced of God's radical otherness, in contrast both to the liberal thought of the Reformed theologians and also to the so-called *analogia entis* (analogy of being) of the Catholics. Both these visions, in the opinion of the more famous Karl Barth and of Brunner as well, ended up obscuring the specificity of the Christian God, his absolute otherness, his freedom. For Brunner, the critique of the vision of God proper to all philosophical vision, and to all theology, which on this point also accepts only dialogue with philosophical thought, stands out particularly against what he described as the actual datum of the revelation of God's name in the Bible. Whereas a name underscores otherness and oneness, philosophical thought opts for the universal and the abstract, so that instead of an analogy, we need to talk instead about opposition and contrast. Nor, according to Brunner, was there in the Bible a gradual weakening of the revelation of the name in the passage from the Old to the New Covenant. On the contrary, the most theologically developed text of the New Covenant, the Gospel of John, considers the revelation of God's name the task of Jesus par excellence.[48]

Revelation, furthermore, is given in terms of the ability to call upon God: if God makes his name known, he does not thereby express his essence, properly speaking; rather, he manifests the possibility of calling upon him. Hence the major difference: in philosophy, man is the one who seeks God and delineates a concept of him; in faith, God is the one who reveals himself and offers to man, not a thought, a generic truth, but rather communion and love. Brunner deduced this also from what he described as the fatal error in the translation of God's name by the so-called "Septuagint" writers. In the passage where God defined himself: "I am who I am", underscoring the mysterious, unique element of his person, the Septuagint translated: "I am he who is." In this way, they eliminated the mystery of the one God, they likened him to the other gods. Ratzinger, certainly, did not share the radical position at which Brunner arrived. He nevertheless maintained that this radicalization somehow liberated the field so as to pose anew the question about the *analogia entis*, in order to seek to formulate in a new way the

---

[48] Ibid., 25.

relation between rational knowledge and the knowledge of faith, between natural being and the reality of grace.

The challenge of a personal God

After clarifying the terms of the question, the young professor went on to explain his synthesis. Courageously, he went beyond not only Brunner and Saint Thomas but the entire Christian tradition to try to define *ex novo* both the philosophical concept of God and that of pre-Christian religion.

An initial observation makes clear that it is not possible to define the philosophical concept of God while completely abstracting from the religious context. Even in the pre-Christian era, indeed, the concept of God in Greek philosophy was in a relation with religion. In Ratzinger's view, this is what results in particular from the threefold vision of God that is present in the Stoic distinction of mythical, political, and natural theology. According to Varro, whose explanation was followed by Ratzinger, the mythical vision of God coincides with that of the poets who speak about the gods and their passions. Political and civil theology, in contrast, is of the people and pertains to the *polis*, with respect to its laws and institutions. Among other things, these two types of visions of God are relatively close, all the more because both are expressed in man's cultic practice.

Natural theology, finally, is the theology of the philosophers and those who study the natural sciences. The object of natural religion is the cosmos in which, immersed in the physical reality, the reality of the divine, too, appears to man: this leads man to inquire about the nature of the gods and, therefore, about theological metaphysics. Once again, Ratzinger concluded, we find ourselves facing the distinction between the God of faith and the God of philosophers. Faith has to do with one or more living persons to be encountered, revered, prayed to; philosophy, in contrast, discovers the truth of reality and thus tends also to define the truth of the divine being.[49]

At this point, though, we observe an untenable distinction between the two visions of God in ancient theology. The philosophical vision is interested in the abstract truth about the cosmos and

---

[49] Ibid., 39f.

about God; religion goes its own way independently of the truth. This, according to Ratzinger, is the obligatory way of polytheism, not only the ancient variety, which in its multifarious forms is then forced to acknowledge the unity of the absolute. Nevertheless, since the absolute in itself is not a person and cannot be invoked, polytheism is forced to resort to the gods, to reflected images of the absolute. All that remains in play, then, is the challenge of monotheism, which addresses the Absolute itself as God, so that he is at the same time the Absolute in himself and man's God.

This "bold challenge" of monotheism, nevertheless, is possible because the believer knows that he was called upon first by a personal God, by the God of Abraham, Isaac, and Jacob. Otherwise, his identification of the God of revelation with the God of the philosophers would be untenable *hubris*. Only through the divine initiative did the mute, ineffable God of the philosophers become the God who in Jesus Christ speaks to man and listens to him. Within biblical theology itself, this passage becomes visible in the gradual purification of the concept of creation. A real affinity could be established between the God of natural religion, of the philosophers, and the God of creation from nothing. For this reason, the idea of creation, like no other, lent itself to explaining the particularity and at the same time the universality of the biblical faith in God in the world of the nations.

Therefore, when the Fathers of the Church made a synthesis between biblical faith and the Hellenistic mind, which at that time best represented the philosophical mind in general, they did nothing but attend to a demand that is not only legitimate but necessary and present both in the pre-religious, philosophical concept of God and also in the gravity of the revelation of God. The meeting place of the religious vision with the philosophical one is the question of truth. Precisely the search for truth, which is an intrinsic part both of the philosophical question and also of the faith journey, allowed Ratzinger to conclude with an invitation to the seriousness of the application both in the philosophical and the theological field. This made room for the critique of the synthesis worked out by the individual Fathers of the Church. Well founded as a demand, it could and must sometimes be carried out with a more in-depth analysis of certain specific aspects, particularly of a sometimes not exactly critical tendency toward apologetics.

For this reason, too, the medieval patristic synthesis exempts neither philosophers nor theologians from the work of continuing their
investigation of the truth. On the contrary, the reconciliation between the thought of faith and the thought of the philosophers must
always be renewed with a ceaseless effort by both parties: philosophy
tends constantly toward the understanding of reality, of the world
in which rational man is called to live; theology, according to the
psalm verse cited by Saint Augustine, is always seeking the face of
God. If each one pursues its own goal, they are destined to meet,
without either of the two ever being able to maintain that it has
reached its own goal definitively. The path of theology, in particular,
will never be concluded because "it consists principally in seeking
again and again the face of God 'until he comes', and he himself
is the answer to every question."[50] Only in eschatology, then, will
the abstract, absolute God of the philosophers also be revealed as
the extremely personal God who did not remain in heaven in his
ineffability, but revealed himself, came to meet man, and brought
him back to his house, to his supernatural destiny.

As already mentioned, the young professor's inaugural lecture met
with the admiration of instructors and students, forever silencing
the misgivings connected with the tormented *Habilitation*.

The departure of Vater Joseph

After the conclusion of the summer semester, the first one that
he had spent in Bonn, Joseph and his sister rejoined their brother,
Georg, in Traunstein for the summer vacation after the labors of
moving house and teaching. They were preparing for a magnificent
August full of intimacy and relaxation, good reading and much music. Once again, however, the idyll was rudely interrupted. Shortly
after mid-month, one night *Mutter* Maria called Georg, who lived
on the upper floor, asking him to come down because *Vater* was
ill. He came promptly, gave his father a few drops of lemon balm
[a calming herb], which seemed at least for the moment to comfort
him, and then they called a doctor. The latter discovered nothing
particularly serious, and life went on, at least for the moment.

---

[50] Ibid., 55.

Vater Joseph returned to his usual activities: on August 23, he went to the seminary to hear a sermon by his younger son, the professor. After lunch, he accompanied his wife on a long walk. Upon their return home, as they passed the parish church, they went in for a visit to the Most Blessed Sacrament, and he prayed with an unusual fervor that did not escape the notice of his wife. The three siblings, meanwhile, reassured, took the occasion to make an excursion to Tittmoning, the little town on the border with Austria. The trip took place in an atmosphere of joyous memories and enchantment with natural beauty.

In the evening, however, news awaited them that brought them back to reality abruptly. Upon returning home, *Vater* Joseph had felt unwell, fainted, and fell to the ground heavily. It was a major stroke from which he did not recover. He died two days later, on August 25, surrounded by the affection of his wife and children. Having always had close ties with his family, Joseph felt the blow: his family had lost one of its pivotal members. Nevertheless, there was consolation in the serene, edifying way in which his father died and in the awareness that a member of the family had entered into eternity with God.

Professor friends

Among the professors who favorably welcomed the young theologian from Bavaria, we should mention, first of all, the great historian of the Council of Trent, Hubert Jedin (1900–1980). Originally from Silesia, the tenth child of an elementary schoolteacher and of a mother who was born Jewish and converted to Catholicism, Jedin, according to some accounts, had been responsible for the call of Ratzinger to Bonn.[51] It was natural, therefore, that the two professors should establish a friendly relationship, rich in cultural and also human exchanges.[52]

---

[51] See Valente, *Ratzinger professore*, 63. The call was probably promoted once again by Söhngen, who had known Jedin in Rome at the seminary near the Teutonic Cemetery, and in 1951, as dean of the faculty of Catholic theology in Munich, he himself had invited Jedin to succeed Franz Xaver Seppelt on the chair of history. See Hubert Jedin, *Storia della mia vita* (Rome: Morcelliana, 1987), 102 and 263.

[52] From a conversation of the author with Benedict XVI.

Actually, the two had complementary characters and training. In the years of his priestly formation, the historian had been fascinated by dogmatic theology as well as his own field;[53] the theology professor, as we know, had shown more than an occasional interest in the development of thought about the theology of history. With time, a deeper understanding developed between the two professors based precisely on the concept of Church history and of the empathy necessary to approach and understand it. Jedin, who in those years coordinated the group of scholars who were working on a new manual of Church history to replace that of Joseph Hergenröther, was a staunch supporter of the necessity of understanding and expounding in greater depth the "internal history of the Church".[54] This conviction is, indeed, fundamental to the *Handbook of Church History*,[55] which opens with a methodological introduction by the editor-in-chief that declares almost provocatively: "Church history treats of the growth in time and space of the Church founded by Christ. Inasmuch as its subject is derived from and rooted in the Faith, it is a theological discipline; in this respect it differs from a history of Christianity."[56]

In Jedin's view, this statement must not limit or impede at all the empirical-historical verification of its vital manifestations on the basis of the historical sources. The theological aspect concerns the divine origin of the Church and the understanding of her as a place for the transmission of grace with the assistance of the Holy Spirit. Starting from the definition of the Church as body and seed, Jedin could then continue: "As the grain of wheat germinates and sprouts, produces stalk and ear, yet always remains wheat, so does the Church's nature manifest itself in changing forms during the course of history, but remains always true to itself."[57]

Jedin's point of departure is clearly theological and springs from a hermeneutic of tradition that is very close to the Ratzingerian

---

[53] See Jedin, *Storia della mia vita*, 65.

[54] Ibid., 281.

[55] The first volume of the manual, which by the end consisted of seven volumes, was published by Herder (Freiburg im Breisgau) in 1962. An English translation, *Handbook of Church History*, ed. John Patrick Dolan, was published in 1965 by Burns & Oates (London). An expanded ten-volume English edition entitled *History of the Church* was published by Crossroad (New York) in 1980.

[56] Jedin, *Handbook of Church History*, 1:1.

[57] Ibid., 1:1–2

vision that was disputed so much by Schmaus on the occasion of the *Habilitation*. The theme would soon reappear at Vatican II, particularly in the debate about the sources, Scripture and tradition, which underlies the Constitution on Divine Revelation, which for Ratzinger is the council's most important document.

His friendship with Jedin then proved to be invaluable for the extraordinary knowledge that the historian had of the councils, conciliar rulings, and the city of Rome—the monuments but also the restaurants where you could have a good meal and where meetings and discussions took place that were certainly not irrelevant for the proceedings of the council.[58] Indeed, Jedin had lived for a long time in the Italian capital, first as bursar at the Teutonic College, then as a refugee, and finally, for about ten years, as a scholar conducting archival research with a view to publishing his great work on the history of the Council of Trent.[59] Therefore, in 1959, when the convocation of Vatican II was announced, he had the opportunity of further intensifying his friendship with Jedin, but we will have to speak of this again in the next chapter.

Broadening the horizon, another professor with whom the young theologian from Bavaria struck up a friendship and a professional exchange was the exegete Heinrich Schlier (1900–1978). Born in Bavaria of a Protestant family, Schlier had been the student of the famous Lutheran biblical scholar Rudolf Bultmann, who, in turn, had been the student of Martin Heidegger and had applied his teacher's existentialist philosophy to biblical exegesis. A member of the Confessional Church in the Nazi years and during the war, Schlier had then been called to the chair of New Testament studies and ancient Church history with the Lutheran-Evangelical faculty at the University of Bonn.

His rethinking of the application of Bultmann's method to the study of the New Testament and to the consequences for the life of the faithful is precisely what led Schlier in 1953 to convert to Catholicism. Of course, he did not intend thereby to renounce all that he had learned from Bultmann. He had realized, however, that the program of demythologization advocated by his teacher and by

---

[58] From a conversation of the author with Benedict XVI.

[59] The work *Geschichte des Konzils von Trient* was published by Herder (Freiburg im Breisgau) in four volumes in the years 1949, 1957, 1970, and 1975; a two-volume edition in English was published by B. Herder Book Co. (St. Louis, 1957–1961) with the title *A History of the Council of Trent*.

his school ultimately emptied the Gospel message of all meaning. Reducing the Resurrection to a mere interior event occurring in the consciousness of the disciples based on their faith meant that every other event connected with Jesus was referred to a merely anthropological measure. Consequently, the figure of the Messiah himself could not be demythologized and reduced to the level of a wonderworker or a prophet.

Although he did not entirely renounce Bultmann's existentialism, which proved to be fruitful for the actualization of the saving work of Jesus and its application to individuals, Schlier was nevertheless of the opinion "that we cannot attempt to reconstruct the historical Jesus while abstracting from the Gospels. The evangelical accounts, as they are read in the Church, are what allow us to reconstruct even vital features in the historical experience of Jesus. Based on this shared insight, Ratzinger and Schlier became friends."[60]

Facilitated by their common Bavarian origin, his friendship with Schlier proved to be invaluable for the young theologian, who would soon have the opportunity to deepen this hermeneutical principle and to tell others about it at Vatican II. Subsequently, in the sixties and seventies, the two scholars would repeatedly collaborate at the Gustav Siewerth Akademie in Bierbronnen, in the Black Forest, organizing weeks of study for young theologians. Schlier, moreover, would often be a guest at the periodic philosophical-theological meetings of the group of Ratzinger's students. The latter would then refine the exegetical method worked out in those years during the long period in which he would serve as prefect of the Congregation for the Doctrine of the Faith and president of the Pontifical Biblical Commission. Finally, he would espouse it clearly in the methodological foreword to the first part of his *Jesus of Nazareth*,[61] before applying it convincingly in the reconstruction of the figure and message of the Teacher from Nazareth.

Outside of the two faculties of theology, Lutheran and Catholic, Ratzinger struck up a special friendship with the Indologist Paul Hacker (1913–1979). According to Ratzinger's own account in his

---

[60] Valente, *Ratzinger professore*, 69.

[61] Joseph Ratzinger, *Jesus of Nazareth: From the Baptism in the Jordan to the Transfiguration*, trans. Adrian J. Walker (New York, London, et al.: Doubleday, 2007), xi–xxv. It is also interesting to note that upon the publication of this first part of the three-volume work, in 2007, the debate among scholars focused precisely on this point.

memoirs, Hacker had an extraordinary preparation in the linguistic field. After studying Slavic languages initially, he had then specialized in Indian languages, literature, and religions, displaying an extraordinary talent for linguistic analysis. As an ordinary professor of fundamental theology, Ratzinger also had to discuss world religions in his courses. He insisted then particularly on Hinduism, since he could count on the support of his friend Hacker. Later on, a student friend would report the laments of a student from those years: "Many a student lamented the fact. . . . They used to say: 'Ratzinger is totally immersed in Hinduism, he talks to us about nothing but the *bhakti* and Krishna, and we can't take it any more!' "[62]

Although it started in Bonn, the friendship between Ratzinger and Hacker continued in Münster, where the two met in the mid-1960s. At that time, Hacker, who for some time had adhered to Hinduism, was a fervent Lutheran and was grappling tirelessly with Luther. Later on, he became a Catholic and, after a brief interval in which he was part of the progressive camp, became a harsh critic of Vatican II. All this, Ratzinger concluded, certainly did not promote the acceptance of his book on Luther, which, nevertheless, had remarkable value.[63]

Again according to his memoirs, among the professors on the Catholic faculty in Bonn with whom he likewise had good relations were Theodor Klauser, founder and editor of the *Reallexikon für Antike und Christentum*, and Johann Auer, with whom he later had the opportunity to collaborate in Regensburg.

His first students

As already mentioned, the success of the new professor of fundamental theology with the Catholic theology faculty at the University of Bonn was swift and brilliant. And soon a group of students gathered around him who kept in contact with him over the years. The first one who should be mentioned is Vinzenz Pfnür (1937–2012). Originally from Berchtesgaden, a town in the far south of Bavaria, about twelve miles from Salzburg, he began to study theology in 1956 at the College of Philosophy and Theology in

---

[62] Valente, *Ratzinger professore*, 70.
[63] J. Ratzinger, *Milestones*, 117–18.

Freising, where he knew Ratzinger and had him as a professor. Then he followed the new professor to Bonn, where he concluded his academic formation. He earned his doctorate in Münster in 1970 with a thesis supervised by Ratzinger and Erwin Iserloh. Then he became a professor of Church history with the Catholic faculty of the University of Münster. He was an organizer and a staunch supporter of Ratzinger's *Schülerkreis*, the group of students who met regularly with their former professor, even when he was later called to assume pastoral and magisterial duties in the Church.

Pfnür was the one to draw into Ratzinger's orbit a very young Lutheran student, Peter Kuhn. The display of academic erudition was not what impressed Kuhn, but rather the lucid simplicity of his language, his ability always to go to the heart of the questions being addressed.[64] Later on, Kuhn became Ratzinger's assistant during the turbulent period in Tübingen and would continue to be part of the group of students even when the professor was appointed archbishop, cardinal, and prefect of the former Holy Office. Kuhn then gradually shifted his interest to the study of Judaism, so much so that he became professor of Judaic studies at the Salesians' Institute of Philosophical-Theological Studies in Benediktbeuern. He was only the first of Ratzinger's students to come from the world of Protestantism. They were attracted by the young professor's breadth of perspective.

Another student of Ratzinger who would go far was Hansjürgen Verweyen, future professor of fundamental theology at the University of Freiburg. His principal work deals with the ontological presuppositions of the act of faith, a topic that was dear to Ratzinger, also. After earning his bachelor's degree and doctorate, he taught for a time at Notre Dame University in Indiana, a position that he landed with the help of his professor. Nevertheless, he developed his thought independently, which led him to positions that were sometimes very critical with regard to his former teacher. The latter, though, did not break off contact with him, just as he did not react too forcefully to the accusations of another one of his assistants, Werner Böckenförde, preferring somehow to disappoint his followers rather than to react to accusations with excessive vehemence.[65]

---

[64] Valente, *Ratzinger professore*, 64.

[65] Ibid., 74f.

At the conclusion of this chapter describing the transition from Freising to Bonn, it is appropriate to emphasize once again the swiftness and the substantial character of the change that had taken place in the young professor's life. Within the course of a year, Ratzinger went from a much-disputed *Habilitation* thesis to a solid reputation, despite the fact that he was still quite young. Moreover, Bonn was not only the capital of the German Federal Republic but was also a commercial hub and a center of cultural exchange. Ratzinger wrote in his memoirs: "Cologne was close, Aachen not far, Düsseldorf and the Ruhr region belonged to the area drained by this same Rhine. . . . Here fresh impulses came from everywhere, especially since Belgium and the Netherlands were near and the Rhineland has traditionally been the gate to France."[66]

From nearby Cologne would come a further change that would have a decisive impact not only on the professor's academic career but on his whole life.

---

[66] J. Ratzinger, *Milestones*, 116.

IV

IN ROME FOR THE COUNCIL

Meeting with Cardinal Frings

In 1958, the year of Ratzinger's transition from Freising to Bonn, a major historical event took place that was destined to influence Professor Ratzinger's life decisively. The diplomat-pope Pius XII died and was succeeded by the patriarch of Venice, the elderly Angelo Giuseppe Roncalli, who took the name of John XXIII. After the long pontificate, which in its early years had had to confront the monstrous upheavals of the war, while in the second decade it had gradually slipped into gloomy immobility, the cardinals in the consistory desired a quiet transition, while the faithful wanted a significant change. On January 25, 1959, only a few months after his election, he announced the convocation of an ecumenical council.

The surprise was so great that the cardinals gathered at Saint Paul's Outside the Walls in Rome received the words of John XXIII with embarrassed silence, which for a moment hurt the pontiff. Convinced, nevertheless, of the divine origin of his initiative, he did not think at all about abandoning or postponing the preparation for an event that, despite the initial coolness of the cardinals, was greeted with enthusiasm not only by the faithful but also in secular circles in Europe and throughout the world. In May 1959, an antepreparatory commission was established, and the following year the proximate preparation began with the formation of ten commissions to draft schemas to be presented at the council. The work of preparation and the interest in the council crossed the threshold of Rome, of Italy, and of the West.

In Germany, too, the interest was lively, and Ratzinger took part in it diligently and passionately. Repeating several considerations that had been aired during the pontificate of Pius XII, many canonists and theologians thought, however, that a council would now be little more than superfluous. The pope, who had been declared infallible by Vatican I, could now settle doctrinal problems by himself; the bishops and the faithful could, at the very most, assemble to render such a faith event more solemn, as had happened on the occasion of the proclamation of the dogma of the Assumption in 1950. Even in Germany, there were some who upheld this thesis (the Church historian Ernst Benz, for example) and the idea that the need for the council depended solely on considerations of whether it would be politically opportune.[1] The pope, they argued, wanted to give an impressive idea of the Church's unity and at the same time to guarantee the support of the bishops, who now were arriving from ever more distant lands. In short: a centripetal movement to counteract the centrifugal forces of an organism that, for the first time, was gaining a substantial presence outside of Europe. Benz was a Lutheran Church historian, and his thesis sprang from his opposition to the primacy and to the definition of papal infallibility, which would make any attempt at an ecclesiology of communion useless.

Ratzinger was not of the same opinion; he courageously took a stance at a conference held in that same year, 1959, at the Catholic Academy in Bensberg, not far from Bonn.[2] For the young professor, "the Church is by her essence the mediation of the living presence of the word of God in the world, the 'tent of the word'."[3] From this presence of the word, mediated through the hierarchical structure and the life of the community, follows the infallibility of the Church, despite the failings and weaknesses that accompany her advance through history. The hierarchical structure comes first because of the need to guarantee the authenticity of access to the sources, but nevertheless it is secondary to and dependent on participation in life with Christ, in communion with him. The teaching of the Church lives by the faith that is present in her. "Infallibility,

---

[1] Benz' article, "Die Konzilsankündigung des Papstes Johannes XXIII", was published in *Evangelische Welt* 13 (1959): 114ff.

[2] The conference given in Bensberg was then published in one of Ratzinger's most important books on ecclesiology, *Das neue Volk Gottes* (The new people of God) (Düsseldorf: Patmos-Verlag, 1969). The author cites the Italian translation, *Il nuovo popolo di Dio*, 4th ed. (Brescia: Queriniana, 1992), 161–85.

[3] J. Ratzinger, *Il nuovo populo*, 162.

therefore, belongs first of all to the entire Church. . . . The ecclesiastical authority exists in the context of the whole living Church, which in her entirety is the body of Christ."[4]

Then Ratzinger raised the question about the council and the exercise of the Magisterium in order to be able to transmit the word that is given to the Church. From this perspective, "the council is an assembly at the service of the government of the entire Church."[5] This means that it is a meeting of those who have responsibility for governing the Church, that is, of the bishops. But is this not the primary duty of the pope, the successor of Peter, who was defined as infallible by Vatican I? To this objection, Ratzinger responded: There is an ordinary and an extraordinary Magisterium. The officials of the particular ordinary Magisterium are the diocesan bishops, assisted by their priests. The officials of the universal ordinary Magisterium, on the other hand, are the bishops together with the pope. The exercise of the universal ordinary Magisterium, therefore, has two extraordinary forms: the council, which consists in the unanimous proclamation of the pope and the bishops, and the pope when he speaks *ex cathedra*. From this, Ratzinger drew the conclusion that the bishops are not mere ecclesiastical administrators in the part of the Church's territory that is entrusted to them but, rather, successors of the apostles and as such part of the apostolic structure of the Church instituted by Christ himself. On the other hand, the pope, too, as successor of Peter, is part of the apostolic college and can speak in its name. Hence, the conclusion that pope and bishops should not be considered voices that are potentially in opposition but, rather, as complementary agents of the one universal ordinary Magisterium of the Church.

Although this is the formal element, which over the centuries has given cause for contrasting abuses, such as late-medieval conciliarism, and papism between the late nineteenth and the early twentieth century, the positive element consists of the wealth of content of what Ratzinger called the universal ordinary Magisterium. It has its origin in the "genuine voice of the bride of Christ who relates the word to the Lord from whom she received it."[6] The universal

---

[4] Ibid., 164f.
[5] Ibid., 175.
[6] Ibid., 183.

ordinary Magisterium of the pope and the bishops, therefore, vitally depends on the whole Church and gives voice to her, just as every bishop in communion with the pope and with his brothers in the episcopate breaks the bread of the word in his diocese. Hence, the usefulness of the council, even after the proclamation of papal infallibility, as the ordinary expression of the universal Magisterium; hence, the importance of the individual bishops as members of the apostolic college and not just as local administrators.

Ratzinger's conference clarified several essential points and directed the listeners' attention to the positive things that could result from the conciliar sessions. In this sense, he was altogether in line with the intention that had prompted Pope John to undertake this bold initiative, which many considered even dangerous. Another element in keeping with the pontiff's ecumenical concern was overcoming the narrow perspective present in the definition of the council given by canon law and in the theological views that were predominant then in Rome. Such a broader perspective led to unprecedented overtures not only toward Lutheran and Reformed Christians, as one might expect from a German theologian, but also toward Orthodox thought that was manifested in citations both from the Fathers of the Church and from contemporary Orthodox authors.

The conference in Bensberg had a success that could be compared with that of the inaugural lecture held the preceding year in Bonn. Present at the event, moreover, was an extraordinary auditor: the archbishop of Cologne, Josef Frings, who since 1946 had been a cardinal and president of the German Bishops' Conference. His attention had been drawn to the conference in Bensberg and to the theological acumen of the new professor from Bavaria by his secretary, the priest Hubert Luthe, a former classmate of Ratzinger in Munich. The archbishop, who enjoyed great authority in Germany, was now more than seventy years old and in rather poor health. Nevertheless, he was one of the group of bishops who perceived the importance of the opportunity offered to the Church and was determined to play the role of a protagonist so that the conciliar sessions would not be devoid of the innovating impulse that the pope wanted and thus might bring about a true renewal. At his side, he had a historian like Jedin, who published a *Brief History of the Councils,*[7] which familiarized many readers with the conciliar institution.

After the above-mentioned conference, Frings had a long conversation with Ratzinger[8] and later consulted him repeatedly on topics pertaining to the theology of the council. At Frings' prompting, and perhaps that of his colleague and friend Jedin, Ratzinger in turn realized the ecclesial importance of the council that was about to be celebrated in Rome and did not fail to prepare conscientiously. The first test of the synergic collaboration between the archbishop and the theologian occurred in 1961, when Ratzinger was commissioned by Frings to prepare for him the text for a conference on the socio-cultural context in which Vatican I had taken place and also the one in which Vatican II was about to be celebrated. He had been asked to give this conference by the Columbianum Institute in Genoa, where the bishop, Giuseppe Cardinal Siri, was one of the acknowledged leaders of the Italian episcopate and, in general, of the conservatively oriented bishops. Frings was therefore aware of the delicate nature of the request that had been made of him, but he did not want to avoid the challenge, and he turned to the young professor to draft the text. The conference, submitted by Ratzinger during the summer of 1961, was then presented by Frings the first time in late August, to the German bishops during the meeting of the German Bishops' Conference that year, whereas it was read in Genoa on November 20, in an Italian translation, by Bruno Wüstenberg, an official of the Secretariat of State, because of an ocular disease that was causing the progressive deterioration of the cardinal's eyesight.

The argument by Ratzinger-Frings started from a decisive observation. The socio-cultural context of the second half of the nineteenth century was very different from the current one. That era witnessed the first symptoms of liberalism, which was about to burst onto the intellectual scene through historicism and would lead to

---

[7] The *Kleine Konziliengeschichte* (Freiburg im Breisgau: Herder, 1959), sold almost 100,000 copies in Germany and was translated into seven languages. The work was published in English as *Ecumenical Councils of the Catholic Church: An Historical Outline* (New York: Herder and Herder, 1960).

[8] See Joseph Ratzinger, *Milestones: Memoirs 1927–1977*, trans. Erasmo Leiva-Merikakis (San Francisco: Ignatius Press, 1998), 120.

the crisis of modernism. In the early 1960s, in contrast, the consequences of the two world wars generated a profound distrust of Western civilization, which had long been identified with Christianity. Moreover, the rapid growth of technology was further weakening the Greco-Christian thought characterized by the primacy of the *logos* and speculation. Along with the dangers in the new cultural context, Ratzinger-Frings also saw the opportunity to broaden the horizons anew, to cross once again the frontiers of the West so as to think about the universal, catholic horizon of the nations. This resulted in a growing relativization of Western culture, but, in Ratzinger's view, this diminution, too, could be a stimulus to enter into new cultures, to find a new *koiné* (common language) in which all cultures and all peoples could be addressed. Even Marxism could be a stimulus to "present in a new light the salvation that is offered to humanity in Christ, not only for eternal life, but also with respect to life here below."[9] After these general considerations, the conference then advanced several concrete proposals about the chief purposes of the council. The assembly of bishops should free itself from outmoded forms of magisterial practice, such as the Index of Forbidden Books, and stop proclaiming new dogmas and new condemnations. On the contrary, it should place itself at the service of the Church's vitality and aim to promote new forms of Christian piety in keeping with the demands of the biblical-liturgical renewal.

Frings' conference in Genoa was certainly not revolutionary, but for those times it was not lacking in boldness, especially since it was presented in Cardinal Siri's archdiocese. Therefore, it did not go unnoticed, and the text of the intervention reached the pope. As Cardinal Frings would recall later,[10] on February 23, 1962, while he was in Rome for a session of the preparatory commission, he received a summons to an audience with the pope. Not knowing what to think, he feared that he would be rebuked by the pontiff due to the influence of the conservative cardinals in the Curia. He then said to his secretary: "Put my red cape on me; who knows, it might be the last time." Therefore, he was very surprised when the pope confided to him that he had read the Genoa conference the previous

---

[9] Related by Gianne Valente in *Ratzinger al Vaticano II* (Cinisello Balsamo: San Paolo, 2013), 32.
[10] Ibid.

evening and had greatly appreciated it. Moreover, it corresponded completely with his intentions in convoking the council. Being an honest man, the cardinal admitted that he was not the author of the text, but the pope praised him also for his ability to choose capable, trusted collaborators.[11] Although Frings already intended to bring Ratzinger with him to the council, from that moment on there were no more doubts: the young Bavarian professor would be the theological consultant of the cardinal of Cologne at Vatican II.

The purpose of the council

The machinery of the council, which the pope wanted to set in motion at top speed, was meanwhile proceeding laboriously amid structural difficulties and deliberate delays. In 1959, the secretary, Tardini, had invited the bishops, the superiors general of the religious orders, the universities, and the Catholic faculties to submit proposals for possible subjects to discuss at the future council. A total of 2,812 responses arrived in Rome; they were evaluated by the antepreparatory commission and then forwarded to the authorities in the Curia, who in turn drafted proposals and exhortations. The following year, on June 5, 1960, with a *motu proprio* personally composed by the secretary of state, Cardinal Tardini,[12] John XXIII started the true and proper preparatory phase. First of all, he established the name of the council, which would be called Vatican II; then he created ten commissions to draft schemas of decrees to be presented to the council Fathers. As had happened already with Vatican I, the commissions relied on the work of the Roman congregations, whose members ended up having a predominant role. Among the commissions, there was then a central one made up of the presidents of the individual commissions (generally this was the prefect of the Roman congregation on which the work of the individual commission was based), the presidents of the national

---

[11] For the entire episode, see ibid., 32f.

[12] For this reconstruction of the preparatory phases of Vatican II, see *Storia della Chiesa*, ed. A. Fliche and V. Martin, vol. 25/1, *La Chiesa del Vaticano II*, ed. M. Guasco, E. Guerriero, F. Traniello (Cinisello Balsamo: San Paolo, 1995), chap. 3, pp. 129–57. The text was written by Roger Aubert, the author of most of the two volumes of this history of the Church that are dedicated to Vatican II. The citation reprinted here is found on pp. 139f.

and regional episcopal conferences, and experts from the Roman universities or from other study centers in Italy and abroad.

As president of the German Bishops' Conference, Cardinal Frings was therefore a member of the central commission and, as already mentioned, was determined to participate at the council as a protagonist. In April 1962, he officially appointed Ratzinger his theological collaborator for the council, and therefore he regularly forwarded to him the schemas drafted in Rome. The young theologian was supposed to study them and formulate proposals for improving them.[13] The first schemas arrived from Rome in the initial months of 1962. Among Ratzinger's colleagues, his friend and colleague Hubert Jedin was also involved in the preparation of the conciliar proceedings. He was well acquainted not only with the history of the council, but also with Italy and the Roman Curia and, as a member of the preparatory commission for education and schools, was also informed about the preparations and the orientation that the Roman authorities wanted to give to the conciliar event. The two often met to discuss, to exchange information, and to formulate an initial strategy.[14]

Jedin, moreover, an expert on ecumenical councils, pointed out to Ratzinger and Cardinal Frings the importance of the rules for the council, which were not only a sort of customary—a handbook of correct procedures—but always proceeded from the ecclesiological vision of the compilers.[15] Prepared in a curial environment, the rules that were about to be drawn up in Rome, and which in fact would be distributed to the Fathers at the start of the

---

[13] Ratzinger's proposals to Frings have been studied by Gianni Valente in *Ratzinger al Vaticano II*.

[14] Hubert Jedin, *Storia della mia vita* (Rome: Morcelliana, 1987). See in particular chapter 5, on his arrival in Italy, and chapter 14, on his participation in the council.

[15] As Ratzinger writes toward the beginning of his account of the second session (Joseph Ratzinger, *Theological Highlights of Vatican II* [New York and Mahwah, N.J.: Paulist Press, 1966, 2009], 61f.), and, as he confirmed in speaking personally with the author, he had had the occasion to ask the historian of the Council of Trent for advice on this subject. Jedin, then, had written about the subject in an article, "Die Geschäftsordnungen der beiden letzten ökumenischen Konzilien in ekklesiologischer Sicht" (The statutes of the last two ecumenical councils from an ecclesiological perspective), *Catholica* 14 (1960): 105–18, in which he explained that the statutes are applied ecclesiology, a previous practical decision on the basis of which the various forces can play their role at the council.

council, contained a predominantly juridical view of the Church, set solidly in her defense of papal primacy and of the infallibility of the pope's Magisterium. Hence Cardinal Frings' determination to be informed and, even before the proceedings started, to make the changes considered necessary on the basis of the new ecclesial sense. Ratzinger would return to this subject in his report on the second session, evaluating positively the changes made to the rules by Paul VI.[16] In the meantime, he started to send to the cardinal his observations on the preparatory documents. Probably on his advice, Frings criticized the first chapters of the schema *De ecclesia* and its definition of "Church militant", which it would be better to replace with "pilgrim Church" or "wayfaring Church".

In late May, however, the theologian returned to the cardinal several theological schemas marked up with marginal notes and accompanied by a letter that described very well the work and the type of language adopted by the Secretariat for Christian Unity. "If the Council could be guided sufficiently to adopt these texts, it would certainly be worth the trouble and some true progress would be achieved."[17] Even more relevant was a preconciliar text by Ratzinger that was at the origin of a new initiative by Frings. In one of the meetings of the central commission, the cardinal became the spokesman for the discontent that was spreading among the German and European bishops concerning the manner in which the council was being prepared. Proceeding in this way would merely end up canonizing the theology of the prevailing school in Rome, while thwarting the pontiff's desire for renewal and repressing the new forms of thought and of piety in the fields of liturgy and ecclesiology. He also criticized the plethora of documents they had received and suggested setting aside those that pertained less to the purposes of the council. Finally, he recommended drawing up a specific document that would summarize the purposes of the council before it started.

The cardinal received a response from the secretary general of the council, Archbishop Pericle Felici, who maintained that the prelate's observations could not be taken into serious consideration. As for the purposes, if it considered it opportune, the council itself would

---

[16] J. Ratzinger, *Theological Highlights of Vatican II*, 62ff.
[17] See Valente, *Ratzinger al Vaticano II*, 35.

be able to provide the clarifications requested. Unconvinced, the cardinal also asked his theological consultant to prepare the draft of an introductory constitution that would specify the objectives and purposes of the council, whose opening session was now imminent. Ratzinger set to work and wrote a brief, three-page document in Latin, which is preserved among the papers of Cardinal Döpfner of Munich.[18] As Gianni Valente writes, among the texts produced in the months immediately preceding the start of the council, Ratzinger's text holds a unique place. It does not propose an alternative way of proceeding, it does not offer more or less detailed critiques, but goes to the heart of the conciliar purpose, which is not separate from the very purpose of the Church. The council must raise the desire for God that is present in man and direct it toward Jesus Christ. The reform of the Church is dependent on the interior renewal that can be brought about only by Jesus Christ, her spouse and Lord. Ratzinger, in short, turned once again to his beloved Augustine to emphasize the yearning for God that is present in man, so as then to arrive at the centrality of the figure and message of Jesus, which had been emphasized in Germany by the liturgical reform, by the biblical renewal, and by the volume *The Lord* by Romano.

The start of the council had been scheduled for October 11, 1962; as the date drew near, the work intensified. In early July 1962, the pope ordered that a copy of the preparatory schemas be sent to all the council Fathers-to-be. In late July, Secretary of State Tardini asked the Fathers to send to Rome their proposed revisions. Only a few Fathers responded, among them Cardinal Frings, who was still making use of Ratzinger's work. The latter became bolder in his judgments, extended his critiques, and suggested avoiding theological discussions and concentrating instead on the essentials. The cardinal, who was more and more pleased with his collaborator, wrote to him on August 29, 1962, asking him officially to accompany him to Rome, and in the same letter he invited him to prepare in advance a report on the doctrinal schemas, particularly on the draft of the Constitution on Divine Revelation, to be given in Rome on October 10, the vigil of the inauguration of the council, to all the German-speaking Fathers present in the Italian capital. Ratzinger,

---

[18] The text was published by Jared Wicks, "Six Texts by Prof. Joseph Ratzinger as peritus before and during Vatican Council II", *Gregorianum* 89/2 (2008): 233–311.

therefore, could enjoy only a few days of summer vacation. In the month of September, he had to reread the documents, prepare the conference, and broaden its horizons toward the catholicity of the Church. From September 9 to 11, we then find him in Mainz, a guest of Bishop Hermann Volk, along with other German-speaking experts. Directed by Karl Rahner, the theologians exchanged their opinions on the documents they had received, concentrated on possible improvements, and prepared for their common work.

Arrival in Rome

Ratzinger's journey to Rome started in Cologne. On October 9, before departing for the Eternal City, the aged Cardinal Frings wanted to inaugurate the conciliar period in the cathedral of his city. After a prayer recited in front of the main altar, he descended to the crypt to let his assistants show him the niche in which he would later be buried. Ratzinger, who obviously was present at the event, would recall it years later as follows: "I can still see the pensive, recollected way in which he touched the place of his future burial, which because of his weak eyesight he could no longer see clearly. In that moment, he was projected into the future so as to be able to accomplish his immediate tasks, precisely on the basis of the responsibility of such contemplation."[19] Shortly afterward, the little group left for Rome, where it arrived on the evening of that same day.

As was decided beforehand, Ratzinger took up residence in the Pontifical German College of Santa Maria dell'Anima, near the Piazza Navona. German seminarians who were studying at the Roman universities customarily lived there; it was the home base for bishops and priests visiting the Eternal City. Rahner and Bishop Volk of Mainz lived there, too. From there, moreover, it was easy enough to reach Saint Peter's for the council sessions. The first appointment, as already mentioned, had been scheduled for the following day at the college itself. Without even being able to take a look around, Ratzinger had to expound his analysis of the doctrinal schemas, in particular the schema *De fontibus* on the sources of

---

[19] The episode was reported by Ratzinger in 1976, on the ninetieth birthday of Frings. The text is reprinted by Norbert Trippen, "Il cardinale e il professore", *L'Osservatore Romano* [Italian edition], October 1, 2008.

revelation. Although his initial judgments had been cautious, this time Ratzinger was severe. The document prepared by Roman professors and prelates lacked three fundamental points: the relation between Scripture and tradition, the inerrancy of Sacred Scripture, the relation between the Old and the New Testament.

The decisive critique was the one regarding the first point. If one starts by trying to define formally the relation between Scripture and tradition, there is no escaping the now-classic dilemma that penalizes one of the two terms in play. Instead, Ratzinger suggested starting from a historical concept of revelation, at the origin of which is God who, in his goodness, decides to reveal himself to men through his word that becomes incarnate. The word of God is then entrusted to the Christian community, which transmits it through Sacred Scripture and tradition. "Revelation is not something that comes after Scripture and tradition; on the contrary, it is God's speech and action that comes before all the historical formulations of his word."[20] In short, Ratzinger once again emphasized the importance of what he had had the opportunity to analyze in depth by studying in particular the concept of revelation in Saint Bonaventure. In the patristic and medieval tradition, there is no abstract concept of revelation; instead, attention is paid to the manifold revelations of God, who manifests himself to the community in its pilgrimage through history. The concept of divine inspiration and of the inerrancy of Scripture also fits into this interface between God and the community of believers. Although God makes use of prophets, apostles, and evangelists to reveal himself concretely, the believing community as such is then the one to which the word is addressed. Called to accept it and to put it into practice, the community must then protect it and hand it down through the generations.

One final point demonstrates the uniformity of God's revelatory action in history, to which the Bavarian theologian would pay more and more attention in his work. One cannot separate the Old from the New Testament or select from the Old Covenant only those passages that seem more directly connected with Christian history. Throughout the Old as well as the New Testament, it is the same God who reveals himself and becomes incarnate in order to save

---

[20] Ibid.

mankind. At the conclusion of his talk, the young theologian formulated a principle that once again corresponded to the pope's intention in convoking the conciliar assembly. Here it is a matter, not of making one theological school among many prevail, but rather of proclaiming God's saving action to the world. As always, Ratzinger aimed right at the target, but the attention of his listeners was already turned to the following day, to the day of the inauguration of what could be for the Church the most important event of the century.

In the report that he later wrote after the first council session, nevertheless, the theologian was not particularly enthusiastic about the inaugural day.[21] Like many, he was thrilled by the impressive number of council Fathers coming from all corners of the earth, each of whom seemed to bring with him the expectations of so many Christian communities spread throughout the world, but also of many people of goodwill who, as rarely before in history, looked to the capital of Catholicism with confidence and hope. The great Vatican basilica and the ancient liturgy seemed, on the one hand, capable of responding to the expectations; on the other hand, the interminable length of the liturgy, the repetitions of chants and gestures whose significance escaped many of those present, too, seemed to establish the distance of the Church from modern times and hence to illustrate the immensity of the task that the 2,500 council Fathers present were called to confront. Once again, the positive element came from the pope, from his enthusiastic opening discourse, and from the vast prospects that, once again, he proposed to the Fathers for the council. It was not a matter of entering into theological debate, of favoring one or another theological current; instead, it was necessary to aim at a fundamental change so as to promote a lively exchange with the contemporary world and its needs. At the end, though, Ratzinger praised an apparently unostentatious gesture that was appreciated especially by the Fathers of the Eastern Churches. In signing the profession of faith, the pope wrote after his name

---

[21] Unlike de Lubac, Congar, and other theologians, Ratzinger does not seem to have kept a diary of the conciliar sessions. After each session, nevertheless, he published a well-considered report of the most significant events. For the sake of convenience, these reports will be cited from *Theological Highlights of Vatican II*, an abridged English translation of the reports that were originally published in German after each session by Bachem (Cologne). See note 15.

only the title "Bishop of the Catholic Church". "No pretentious titles;" Ratzinger commented, "just the simple official designation which united him with his brethren."[22]

The first session

The council, which was solemnly inaugurated by Pope John XXIII on October 11, 1962, and was declared finished by Paul VI on December 8, 1965, took place in four sessions that were held each year in autumn. According to the rules, during the sessions, three types of meetings were foreseen: the public sessions, with the pope presiding; the general congregations, during which the Fathers discussed the documents proposed to them; and the sessions of the ten commissions responsible for rewriting the documents according to the directions of the Fathers. The first public session on October 11 was followed by the first general congregation, which was held on October 13. On the day's agenda was the election of members of the ten planned commissions, and soon the atmosphere became rather overheated and frantic. Ten ballots were distributed to the Fathers, each with blanks on which to write sixteen names, together with a list of those who had already participated in the preparatory commissions. The initiative was quickly viewed as a curial trick to nudge the vote toward individuals who favored the direction that Rome hoped to take. Several prelates spoke out against this way of proceeding, first of all Cardinal Liénart of Lille, France, and then Cardinal Frings; they demanded a postponement of the voting so as to allow the Fathers to get to know each other a little better and thus to be able to vote with greater knowledge of the matter. The thunderous applause that greeted the two speeches, notwithstanding the prohibition against applause, were for Ratzinger an eloquent sign: "The Council had shown its resolve to act independently and autonomously, rather than be degraded to the status of a mere executive organ of the preparatory commissions."[23]

After this first obstacle was overcome, a structural difficulty remained: how to get an assembly to function when around 2,900 bishops, superiors general, and experts had a right to participate and an average of between 2,000 and 2,200 persons attended the ordi-

[22] Ibid., 22.
[23] Ibid., 23.

nary sessions, many of whom, according to Ratzinger, had no parliamentary or synodal experience. It was a gigantic body, which in any case could not have produced fruitful work. Suggestions were made about bishops being able to elect delegates, while others proposed working in groups. These proposals were rejected and, according to Ratzinger, rightly so: from the beginning, councils represented the true catholicity of the Church. It could not be renounced because of practical difficulties. The solution that gradually emerged as they proceeded now to the debate on the liturgy was to establish informal groups that were in agreement about the points proposed for discussion and then were represented in the council hall by a Father who was delegated to speak in their name.

The true work of the council, properly speaking, started on October 20, when the schema on the liturgy was proposed for discussion. In Ratzinger's view, the decision to open the council proceedings with this schema was a wise one. This document had been drafted better than the others inasmuch as it could already make use of the fruits of the ecclesial liturgical movement that had found an initial synthesis in the Magisterium of Pius XII. There was, then, a further consideration that made this commencement even more significant. It was, basically, the acknowledgment that the liturgy is "the true source of the Church's life, and the proper point of departure for all renewal".[24] Here, according to Ratzinger, are the most important findings contained in the schema that was the basis for the Constitution on the Sacred Liturgy:

- The return to the origins, with the elimination of many feast days of saints so as to highlight the centrality of Sunday, oriented toward Easter. This led also to the elimination of many repetitions, which had been seen also in the celebration of the inaugural Mass.

- Greater attention given to the word, as distinguished more clearly from the sacrament. According to the language of the council, this should lead to the preparation of a table of the word alongside the Eucharistic table.

- The decentralization of liturgical legislation, granting to the episcopal conferences or to individual diocesan ordinaries the possibility of making decisions pertaining to individual countries or individual dioceses.

---

[24] Ibid., 31.

• Making room for vernacular languages in the liturgy. Ratzinger, in turn, declared that he was in favor of vernacular languages in the Church, not so much to facilitate the participation of the laity in the liturgy as to bridge the gap between Scholastic philosophy and theology, which were still expressed in Latin, and the thought that had developed in the Enlightenment era. Too close a connection with a dead language made thought sterile, also.

These are Ratzinger's essentially favorable reflections about the schema on the sacred liturgy, the first document to be discussed, which furthermore was approved by a very large majority. Later on, Ratzinger was much more cautious about the liturgical reform, particularly about some forms of its application, which, to his way of thinking, departed from the spirit of the conciliar constitution.

The voting for the schema on the liturgy took place on November 14, 1962, and immediately afterward the Fathers turned to a discussion of the schema on revelation, which quickly proved to be more difficult. In reality, the schema on the sources of revelation had been severely criticized by Ratzinger himself in his presentation to the German bishops on October 12. Besides the individual points highlighted by Ratzinger, the schema still reflected the anti-modernist mind-set; it was polemical with regard to the Lutherans; it leaned toward dialectics in the relation between Scripture and tradition. On the basis of these considerations, although it was forbidden by the rules, Cardinal Frings had directed Ratzinger himself to prepare a sort of prologue of an alternative document to be proposed to the council itself. Hubert Jedin was then directed to study the rules to see whether their wording allowed some way of presenting a new draft schema and at the same time abbreviating the over-long discussions.[25]

In the meantime, the meetings followed each other at a brisk pace. As early as October 15, a meeting had been held at the German College dell'Anima, with Karl Rahner, Bishop Volk, his theological advisor Semmelroth, and Ratzinger participating. The last-mentioned, at one point, pulled out of his briefcase a text designed as the first chapter of a new draft. Semmelroth was enthusiastic about it and maintained that they absolutely had to use it. Rahner,

---

[25] Jedin, *Storia della mia vita*, 304.

too, had prepared a document of his own and then the two works were combined to form one Rahner-Ratzinger schema, which, as the latter would write,[26] had no possibility of being approved. The theologian Yves Congar was of the same opinion; in his diary, he lamented the Germans' way of working: after making a decision among themselves, they rush ahead without bothering about others. Moreover, "in spite of the fact that the Rahner-Ratzinger text contains some EXCELLENT things, . . . it is nonetheless very personal, not very conciliar."[27] On the other hand, it had been presented at a previous meeting to two influential cardinals, too, Siri and Montini, who gave it a rather tepid reception. In his diary, Congar lucidly saw the value of this schema, even though it was destined to failure: the debate sparked by it would be useful. "Putting another text before the Fathers will help them to realise how inadequate the official schema is, and what really needs to be said."[28]

This is precisely what happened. The wide circulation of the Rahner-Ratzinger text is precisely what got members of the episcopate belonging to the episcopal conferences of Africa, Latin America, and part of Asia as well involved in the opposition to the official text. It should be noted, on the other hand, that the body of the text drafted by Rahner in his rather theoretical style ended up prevailing over Ratzinger's salvation-history prologue. For this reason, too, the definitive version needed a better blend. In any case, it led to the surprising vote on November 20, in which the Fathers in favor of rejecting the text (1,368) far outnumbered those against doing so (813). The conciliar rules per se required a two-thirds majority in order to reject a schema, so the voting favored what from then on became a minority at the council, whereas the majority of the Fathers were thwarted. This created, therefore, a regrettable situation that was resolved by an intervention by the pope the day after the voting. He declared that the schema *De fontibus* was rejected, entrusting the redrafting of it to a mixed commission presided over by Cardinals Ottaviani and Bea.

After the vote on November 20 and the pope's decision to entrust

---

[26] J. Ratzinger, *Milestones*, 128–29.

[27] Yves Congar, *My Journal of the Council*, trans. Mary John Ronayne, O.P., and Mary Cecily Boulding, O.P. (Collegeville, Minn.: Liturgical Press, 2012), 162.

[28] Ibid.

to the theological commission and to the Secretariat for Promoting Christian Unity the job of reworking the text of *De fontibus*, the conciliar assembly started to examine the shorter documents. Actually, they began to deal with the schema on the Church, too, but for some time now the majority of the assembly had been convinced that this schema, too, would have to be reworked and presented again in a second session. Speaking in the hall on December 5, Cardinal Frings was once again very severe: in the schema on the Church, only a small part of the Church's tradition was taken into account, the patristic era and the Eastern tradition were almost entirely disregarded. Moreover, how could the chapter on the Magisterium ever be entirely separated from the one on the episcopate? Or were the bishops not the Doctors and teachers in the Church? These observations of the cardinal of Cologne, according to de Lubac, were once again inspired by Ratzinger.[29] But now, as Ratzinger observed in his account of the first session, a growing weariness[30] was taking hold of the Fathers, and the suspension of the assembly on December 8 was gladly welcomed by all.

In his greeting to the council Fathers, the pope, perceiving a widespread sense of disappointment because of the lack of concrete results, encouraged them. The temporary outcome was explained by the complexity of an assembly that first had to learn to work together.[31] Adopting the pope's observation as his own, Ratzinger concluded his account of the first session with an observation that is only apparently paradoxical: the most important result of the council consisted precisely in the lack of approved documents, in the decision to rework several documents *de novo* before proposing them in the hall for debate. The council had spoken up, thus demonstrating its irreplaceable character. Certainly, the assembly had shown the human side of the Church, also, which is destined to last until the Lord's return. For this reason, too, it was not possible to think about an immediate reunion of Christians. Taking the recommendation of Pope John, nevertheless, the conciliar assembly had made it possible to draw attention to how much there was in common already

---

[29] Henri de Lubac, *Vatican Council Notebooks*, trans. Andrew Stefanelli and Anne Englund Nash (San Francisco: Ignatius Press, 2015), at 1:452.

[30] J. Ratzinger, *Theological Highlights of Vatican II*, 50.

[31] Hubert Jedin, "The Second Vatican Council", in *History of the Church*, ed. H. Jedin, K. Repgen, and J. Dolan (New York: Crossroad, 1981), 10:96–150 at 113.

between Christians in the West and in the East. For this, Ratzinger concluded, we can only thank the Lord and look confidently toward the future.[32]

Transfer to Münster and the second session

When the first session of the council was finished, Ratzinger returned to Bonn. He had to face a backlog of work at the university, the duties that resulted from his participation in the conciliar proceedings, to which was added the proposal of a new academic position, to which he could not give an answer at first. In the summer of 1962, shortly before the beginning of the conciliar proceedings, Hermann Volk, ordinary professor of dogmatic theology in Münster, Westphalia, had been appointed bishop of Mainz. For his successor, the academic authorities were thinking of the young professor from Bonn who was in Rome for the council and was collaborating closely with his predecessor. The latter, who held him in high esteem and considered him a friend, pressured him to accept the position, but Ratzinger was uncertain. On the one hand, he already had numerous duties, but, on the other hand, he was attracted by the possibility of going to a university that in the field of theology was more prestigious and had a greater tradition than Bonn. Above all, he would have the opportunity to teach what had always been his favorite subject: dogmatic theology.[33]

What tipped the scales in favor of transferring to Münster, however, was the sense that the idyllic time in the federal capital was over. Although the students still admired him, among the faculty members there was a growing distrust of the young professor who, although just arrived, had already skipped over all the academic hierarchy and had been invited to the council and was in great demand as a speaker and writer. Therefore, a certain theological envy spread, which solidified and took the form of a true opposition to the theologian who had come from the South. There were skirmishes in the early months of 1962, when two Orthodox students, Damaskinos Papandreou and Stylianos Harkianakis, made a request to conclude their studies by writing their doctoral theses under the

---

[32] J. Ratzinger, *Theological Highlights of Vatican II*, 53–54.
[33] J. Ratzinger, *Milestones*, 129–30.

direction of the Bavarian theologian. According to the norms then in force, there was no provision for non-Catholic students to become doctors of theology in a Catholic faculty. The faculty council, therefore, acted correctly in asking Ratzinger himself to ask for permission from the cardinal of Cologne, to whom the Catholic faculty of theology in Bonn reported.

The discussion, nevertheless, brought to light an unexpected animosity toward the young professor. In the following months, moreover, Ratzinger presented to that same council the topic selected for the *Habilitation* thesis of Johannes Dörmann, another student of his, who intended to study in depth the new findings of Johann Jakob Bachofen in the field of anthropology. The request was rejected, and the decision was communicated to Ratzinger in a letter that he received while he was in Rome for the first session of the council. The objection was that the subject matter proposed did not strictly concern theology. Ratzinger, nevertheless, understood that some of his colleagues also wanted to send a message to him personally; he thought of his own *Habilitation* and finally decided to accept the invitation of his colleagues in Münster. There he would be able to look after his students without doing them harm.

Meanwhile, he gave his final course in Bonn, which dealt with divine revelation, filling his lectures with stimulating ideas and approaches that had emerged from the conciliar debate. It was also an opportunity to treat in greater depth the topic that was to be addressed again at the council. From time to time, there were also meetings with Fathers and experts of the council in order to rewrite texts, propose new ones, and prepare for the second session.

THE CHRISTOCENTRIC APPROACH OF PAUL VI

Pope John's death had caused anxiety about the resumption of the conciliar proceedings, but on June 21, 1963, a new pope was elected: the archbishop of Milan, Giovanni Battista Cardinal Montini, who took the name of Paul VI. The pontiff, originally from Brescia, announced on the day after his election his commitment to continue Vatican II and to bring it to its conclusion. Like many others, Ratzinger, who meanwhile had been appointed a *peritus*, that is, an official expert of the council, drew a sigh of relief and intensified his work of preparing for the next session. It was inaugurated by the new pope on September 29, 1963, with a "very simple ceremony to emphasize that the resumption of the proceedings was not a new beginning but rather the continuation of the work begun the preceding year."[34] In the months that had passed between his election and the new beginning of the work, the pope had also made some improvements to the council rules. Four moderators had been introduced to direct the general congregations, the coordinating committee became a permanent organization, and a press office had been instituted to convey accurate information to journalists.

In his account of the second session, Ratzinger started precisely with the observation that, since the press now had detailed information about the debate in the hall, this debate could now concentrate on theological questions. Actually, the first innovation had been anticipated by the new pope even before the resumption of the council. In a speech made to the Roman Curia on September 21, Paul VI had spoken about the reform of the Curia. This topic was of interest to the council, according to Ratzinger, inasmuch as the opposition between the universal episcopate and the Curia was not something new but had already appeared at the preceding councils from the Middle Ages down to Vatican I. Previously, however, the popes, although agreeing about the need to reform the Curia, had always reserved this prerogative to themselves. Now, in contrast, by announcing the opportunity before the council reconvened, the pope was in a way giving full freedom to the conciliar debate, allowing the bishops to advance proposals, while reserving for himself the final decision. Thus he established a relation between "a daring step into the future [and] the preservation of the past".[35]

The other innovation, to which Ratzinger attributed even greater importance, resulted from the decisively "Christ-centered" character[36] of the inaugural speech of Paul VI, given with a *pathos* that revealed in him the union of theological intelligence and spiritual witness. Ratzinger, in short, was sincerely moved when the pope mentioned the mosaic of *Christ the Pantocrator* in the apse of the Basilica of Saint Paul, before whose majesty the small statue of

---

[34] See Rogert Aubert, "La svolgimento del Concilio", chap. 6 of *Chiesa del Vaticano II*, 255.

[35] J. Ratzinger, *Theological Highlights of Vatican II*, 60.

[36] Ibid., 67.

Pope Honorius III almost disappeared, like his successor Paul VI and the Fathers themselves gathered in the basilica. The true head of the council, as of the Church, Paul VI concluded, is therefore Christ. His presence could not diminish human dignity. With this speech, Ratzinger continued, Paul VI put the assembly of bishops in continuity with the spirit of John XXIII, who had always maintained that the idea for the council came, not from his own initiative, but from an inspiration of the Holy Spirit.

THE CONSTITUTION ON THE CHURCH

After the opening ceremony, the council immediately faced the new draft constitution on the Church composed by a group of Belgian theologians headed by Monsignor Gérard Philips with the decisive support of the cardinal of Brussels-Malines, Léon-Joseph Suenens, supported by Paul VI, because, like the pope, the cardinal, too, was moved by the desire to give an "organic plan to Vatican II".[37] According to Ratzinger, the Belgians had succeeded in combining the traditional elements of Scholasticism supported by the Italian and Spanish theologians and the modern findings of ecclesiology of the German and French school. The result was a very good point of departure, even though weak elements were not lacking. These, moreover, had already been pointed out by Cardinal Frings, who spoke in the hall once again on September 30, 1963. After expressing his appreciation for the pastoral and ecumenical sensitivity and the thrilling plasticity of the biblical images, the cardinal of Cologne still considered the theological part concerning the bishops and the eschatological perspective inadequate. These were precisely the points that Ratzinger would work out in greater depth as a member of the fifth theological subcommission.

The overall judgment, however, was still largely positive, as was the favorable judgment of the Fathers who spoke during the initial sessions. Returning now to Ratzinger's evaluation after the conclusion of the second session, the theologian identified a first guideline of the constitution on the Church in the approach that it took to salvation history. The Church is not a self-enclosed institution, defined once and for all, but rather is on a journey and represents the

---

[37] See *La Chiesa del Vaticano II*, 495.

history of God with mankind. Now, if the Church is understood in this way, Ratzinger continued, the result is an eschatological vision of her that frees her from anxiety and the temptation to perfection, and thereby at the same time she appears more human, more earthly, sinful, liable to criticism, in need of renewal and above all of God's unceasing mercy.

Another characteristic feature of the schema was the presentation of the Church as a sacramental sign. This means that she refers to God and is the sign of God among men. The more she refers beyond herself and is transparent to God and Jesus Christ, the more effective she is. This vision, however, requires those who are called to an ecclesial ministry to understand themselves as servants of the sacred sign of God in the world. This is the transition to the treatment of the hierarchical structure of the Church, which is subdivided into bishops, priests, and deacons. Ratzinger immediately addressed the argument concerning the bishops, explaining that the difficulty lay not so much in the term "collegiality" as in the reality of the collegiality of bishops, which is derived from the college of apostles. On this subject, there were two approaches among the council Fathers.

The first emphasized the membership of the bishops in the apostolic college, while the second insisted on union with the head of the apostles, Peter. With his work in the fifth subcommission, Ratzinger staunchly advocated the first approach. Thus, he summarized the nucleus of his most important contribution to the document that would become *Lumen gentium*, the Dogmatic Constitution on the Church. The point of departure of all reflection resulted from the fact that Jesus chose twelve apostles, a number that had a very precise significance: it referred to the twelve sons of Jacob-Israel, who gave rise to the twelve tribes of Israel. In reality, the twelve tribes lasted for only a few generations. They continued to exist, nevertheless, in the popular imagination, supported by prophetic preaching, as an expectation and hope of the full reconstitution of the twelve tribes and, therefore, of the entire Israel of God. Another significant detail should be noted: until Easter, the Twelve are always designated as a group by this name. Afterward, they receive the name of apostles, envoys, "those who are sent". Once we have clarified the symbolic value of the number and of the post-Paschal title of the apostles, Ratzinger said, the meaning of the apostolic college and of membership in it becomes clear.

The initial function of the apostles was to be, by the very symbolism of their number, a sign that the hope of Israel was finally
fulfilled, that the new Israel was definitively restored. The symbolic
value of the number, as Saint Luke highlights well in his account
of the election of Matthias, also says that no one of the apostles
could carry out his mission and be significant in the birth of the
new Israel, of the Christian community, without the other eleven.
Now applying this consideration to the bishops, the successors of
the apostles, the Constitution on the Church says that the bishops are bishops not only as individuals but also as members of the
apostolic college. In a graphic formulation: "The bishops are essentially a college; the episcopal office is a collegial office; essential
here is that the office of the individual bishop be correlated with
the office of his fellow bishops."[38] And what about the function of
Peter, from whom the Fathers of Vatican I derived the primacy and
the infallibility of the pope? On the one hand, he is independent
of collegiality because of the special mission—that of keeping his
brethren united—that was conferred on him directly by the Lord;
on the other hand, he continues to be part of the Twelve; he is not
foreign to their community but, rather, a member of it.

This solution, according to Ratzinger, is not merely theoretical.
Without detriment to the special function of the pope, it situates
the successor of Peter organically in the community of the bishops,
whose communion with one another testifies to the communion
among all the local Churches. Another consequence is that the ministry of the individual bishop is not limited to the local community
entrusted to his specific pastoral care, but, rather, his responsibility
extends to the whole Church. In summary, Ratzinger concluded,
by freeing the apostolic college from the excessive juridical burden
accumulated over the course of the centuries, the council succeeded
in restoring the original spiritual structure of the Church.

Another important point in the document, the theologian said, is
the institution of the permanent diaconate, which the Fathers from
Latin America in particular had advocated. In this, Ratzinger saw
two positive features: on the one hand, a greater balance between
the sacramental table and the table of the word and, on the other
hand, the dynamism of the Church in Latin America and in the mission countries. In the second session, the driving force had come

---

[38] J. Ratzinger, *Theological Highlights of Vatican II*, 81.

from these countries, whereas in the preceding year, the initiative had been from the countries of Central and Northern Europe.

On the other hand, the German *peritus* was not satisfied with the chapter dedicated to the laity. He maintained that it had started from a negative definition: "The layman is neither a priest nor a religious", without then managing to develop a specific concept of the lay believer, who, nevertheless, has his own dignity and reason for existing in the Church. The positive element is represented by the emphasis on the universal vocation of Christians to holiness, which over the years surely would have repercussions on the understanding of the dignity of the individual believer, but for the moment the theology of the laity still seemed in need of development.

Ratzinger saw another positive element in the inclusion of the document on the Blessed Virgin in the document on the Church. On this matter, opinions were divided: some wanted a separate Marian document, while others preferred including it in the document on the Church. Ratzinger was in favor of the second recommendation, which then prevailed, because in that way ecclesiology opened up to the heavenly Church, thus emphasizing both her spiritual and her eschatological dimension. Of course, this inclusion says something also about the mystery of the Blessed Virgin. She is the humble Virgin who owes everything to God's grace. She embodies the Church of the poor, the Church on her pilgrim way through history and the hope born from the root of Israel. Ratzinger also saw this inclusion of Mariology in the Constitution on the Church as an open door to dialogue with the Christian denominations so that it might more easily be possible to reach an agreement with them on this original, living core of Marian devotion.

Another positive element, in Ratzinger's view, was the formula used by Paul VI to ratify the documents of the council. The question was not merely formal. In short, whenever the popes had approved conciliar documents in the past, they had employed some formula suited to the mentality of the times. It was not possible, therefore, for Paul VI to repeat the formula from Vatican I if he wanted to take into account the ecclesiology that had been discussed during the preceding months.[39] Instead, he returned to an older formula that considered the pope as a member and the head of the college

---

[39] In this regard, see the reconstruction of the debate on the subject in Jedin, *Storia della mia vita*, 315f.

of bishops. In this way, Ratzinger concluded, through recourse to ancient formulas, the renewal of ecclesiology had been confirmed. At the same time, subsequent developments were not denied, either. Ratzinger is very fond of this criterion and throughout his life has sought to adhere to it.

At the conclusion of the second session, Ratzinger noted, among the Fathers, the growth of a kind of pessimism. There were some who feared that everything would remain as it had been before, while others feared what would happen next. The truth, the Bavarian expert concluded, is that "No Council . . . could by itself bring about the renewal of Christianity. It could only furnish an impulse pointing beyond itself to the routine of daily Christian service. The only appropriate conclusion lay in the individual's daily practice of faith, hope and charity."[40]

In order to continue the theological work, after the conclusion of the council, the Dutch editor Paul Brand was thinking about starting a theological journal that would function as a forum connecting the various exponents and the different theological schools that were playing such an important role for the conciliar assembly. The initial meetings were held in Rome even during the first session of the council. The project then took shape during the second session. The theologians most directly involved were Karl Rahner and Edward Schillebeeckx, but the invitation was extended also to Kasper, Metz, Küng, de Lubac, Le Guillou, and, naturally, Ratzinger. The last-mentioned was not one of the most active contributors, but in 1963 he participated in a meeting of the "dogma" section to which he had been assigned, and in the first issue of the journal, which was named *Concilium* and was published in various languages and countries in Europe, there was an essay by the Bavarian theologian entitled "The Pastoral Implications of the Doctrine of the Collegiality of Bishops".[41] Repeating the views that he had already supported during the second session of the council, Ratzinger stated that the fraternity or communion among the bishops results from the mystery of the communion of love of the Triune God and is ordered to the fraternal communion of the whole Church. "Ultimately there

---

[40] J. Ratzinger, *Theological Highlights of Vatican II*, 123.

[41] The article was then republished in the anthology by Joseph Ratzinger, *Il nuovo popolo di Dio*, 221–45.

is collegiality among the bishops because there is fraternity in the Church, and the collegiality of bishops fulfills its purpose only if it serves this fraternity and is itself exercised in a fraternal way."[42]

In the midst of such hectic activity, in late 1963, there was another painful loss in the life of Ratzinger the theologian. As he related in his memoirs, at the beginning of that year, his brother, Georg, with whom their mother, Maria, lived, told him about the increasing difficulties that she had in eating and keeping down food. She often vomited and was plainly losing weight.[43] Finally, in August of that year, the doctor confirmed their worst fears. It was incurable stomach cancer. They could only wait and return to the mother a little of the affection that she had always generously given to her children. For her part, *Mutter* Maria did not get upset. Until October, she continued to keep house. Then she had to be admitted to the hospital. In early December, Georg wrote to his brother that their mother was getting worse and all signs indicated that the end was not far off. Joseph arrived promptly and spent the last two weeks at his mother's bedside. He recalled in his memoirs: "Her goodness became even purer and more radiant and continued to shine unchanged even through the weeks of increasing pain."[44] She died on December 16, 1963, comforted by the love of her children. It is worth quoting, though, a later statement by Ratzinger: "The radiance of her goodness has remained, and for me it has become more and more a confirmation of the faith by which she had allowed herself to be formed."[45] Later on, when the German theologian would repeatedly invite his listeners or readers to consider the faith of simple people, he would always have in mind the example of his parents.

On the other hand, Congar, too, would have a similar experience, and he explained it with equal clarity in his diary. He wrote on November 26, 1963, less than a month before the death of Ratzinger's mother:

Yesterday evening, I telephoned Sedan at 8.20 P.M. My mother was still alive, but would certainly not last the night. At 10.40 P.M., I

---

[42] Ibid., 235.

[43] J. Ratzinger, *Milestones*, 130.

[44] Ibid., 131.

[45] Ibid.

had a telephone call from Sedan: "She is with the good Lord". If it were a question of the mystical history of the Council, my mother would have an important place in it. During years of suffering, she has never ceased to pray for the Council, for my own work. The Council has been borne along by many prayers and suffering offered for it. But who knows, who could write this history?[46]

Although he stated in *My Journal of the Council* that he did not intend to speak about his personal feelings, Congar returned to the subject on December 1 to emphasize once again the strength of the ties that are not only valuable for a generation but are passed down from one generation to the next.[47] This is one of the arguments that Ratzinger would often use to stress the importance of the faith of simple people and the need to defend and protect it from excessive, gratuitous innovations.

The third session

The account of the third session, like the preceding one, originated in conferences. It should be noted, however, that one of the two conferences that make up the text was given almost at the beginning of that period of the council, while the other was read several months after the conclusion of the session. This explains the sometimes different accents in his general evaluation, whereas repetitions can be noticed here and there. Prevalent in the first part of the account is a largely positive judgment on the work conducted thus far; in the second, one can observe an attitude that is more worried about the persistence of an influential minority that had access to the pope and was at the origin, in particular, of the so-called *Nota praevia explicativa* that was appended to the Constitution on the Church through the intervention of Paul VI.

THE COLLEGIAL PRINCIPLE AND THE SACRAMENTAL NATURE OF EPISCOPAL ORDINATION

Ratzinger's account began with a general observation: the subjects tackled in the third session were richer and more systematic. It

---

[46] Congar, *My Journal of the Council*, 455.
[47] Ibid., 457–58.

started with the schema on the pastoral ministry of bishops, then continued with the declaration on religious liberty. Surprisingly, Ratzinger did not dwell on the debate about the new document on revelation. After having worked with great zeal on the schema about the two sources, his attention was focused now on the problems connected with the conciliar statements on the episcopal ministry. The Constitution on the Church, according to Ratzinger, emphasized the hierarchy's ministry of service, a ministry that is explained in the proclamation of the word and in the service of the Eucharistic table. "The Church, made up of communities whose function is divine worship, is accordingly built up from a community of bishops, one of whom as successor of Peter is responsible for the unifying function."[48]

Ratzinger was more concise in listing the other topics discussed in the council hall. He said he was in favor of religious liberty, exhorting the Church to free herself from excessively close embraces with the State, as was still the case in Italy and Spain. He urged ecumenism to remain soberly on the ground of biblical testimony and also emphasized attention to history in the development of doctrine. As for the relation between the Church and the world, he limited himself to describing the two camps that had clashed at the council: the first, rather optimistic one was based on a theology of incarnation; the other, in contrast, was inclined to take a more critical attitude in terms of the theology of the Cross. For the moment, Ratzinger seemed not to take a position, though later on he would side more and more resolutely with the latter approach.

In the second part of his commentary on the third session, which corresponds to the second conference, Ratzinger dwelt above all on the relation between the pope and the episcopal college; in this section, he discussed the famous "Black Thursday" that occurred on November 19, 1964. After pressures exerted by the conciliar minority, which feared that chapter 3 of the Constitution on the Church excessively limited the papal prerogatives defined at Vatican I, the secretary of the council, Archbishop Felici, introduced to the Fathers a *Nota praevia explicativa*, a preliminary explanatory note, ordered by the pope, which seemed to attenuate the prerogatives of the episcopal college that were acknowledged by the

---

[48] J. Ratzinger, *Theological Highlights of Vatican II*, 138.

conciliar document. The Fathers and experts present in the Hall were greatly dismayed. Among the experts, it was precisely Ratzinger and Congar who proposed voting against it.[49] In his account of the session, however, Ratzinger's commentary was calmer. First of all, he pointed out a curious anomaly present in the conciliar rules that seemed to deny that the pope is part of the episcopal college and as such can intervene in the council. Now, the pontiff's intervention with the explanatory note introduced changes that could have been proposed by a bishop supported by a rather restricted group of Fathers. Moreover, with his intervention, the bishop of Rome sought to reconcile opposing tendencies in such a way as to be faithful to his task of keeping his brethren united. That said, Ratzinger concluded, no one looked forward to a repetition of the procedural maneuvers on display that day and that week.[50]

Another important result of the chapter dedicated to the bishops in the Constitution on the Church was the definition of the sacramental nature of episcopal consecration or ordination. Ratzinger wrote that this was not about flattering the bishops after they were mistreated by Vatican I. From a deeper perspective, it was necessary to draw this consequence from the definition of the sacramental nature of the Church. If she is a salvific sign, then the successors of the Twelve also participate in her sacramental nature, which is conferred on them with episcopal consecration or ordination. As a result, membership in the episcopal college is not primarily the consequence of a juridical act coming from the pope but results from the sacramental act of consecration. For this reason, the bishop, like the apostles, is not ordained exclusively for the local Church, but his consecration entails membership in the college of bishops.

Ratzinger, nevertheless, did not want to end up exalting the episcopate unduly just because in the previous century the primacy of the pope had been exalted excessively. As though to caution against this danger, he reported not only the observations of the Fathers of the curial minority but also the warnings of observers from the Christian ecclesial communities. Kristen Skydsgaard, for example, an observer at the council from the Lutheran Church of Denmark, called for a less poetic and enthusiastic view that was more attentive

---

[49] See Aubert, "Lo svolgimento del concilio", 307. See also Valente, *Ratzinger al Vaticano II*, 136f.

[50] J. Ratzinger, *Theological Highlights of Vatican II*, 159–60.

to the reality of sin. In this regard, he cited an anecdote that caused general hilarity. Seeking information on episcopal collegiality, Cardinal Ottaviani asked a famous exegete about the subject. The latter replied that he knew nothing about it. The cardinal then asked an old priest, who, after careful reflection, responded, in contrast, yes: the apostles had acted collegially in the Garden of Gethsemane when all together they had abandoned the Lord. Skydsgaard continued: "We smile, because this was only a story; but suddenly we no longer smile but freeze up. Suddenly all this is very close to us: the denial, the falling away, the cross, but also the resurrection, the gift of grace, the boundless love and power of God. Without this dimension we do not comprehend the mystery of the Church."[51]

Similarly, Nikos A. Nissiotis too, an observer from the Orthodox Church, called attention to the fact that this doctrine not only did not exist in the Orthodox tradition but ran the risk of fostering an increasing clericalization of the Church.

According to the British theologian Aidan Nichols,[52] the report on the third session of Vatican II is the "high point" of Ratzinger's so-called "progressivism". Later on, second thoughts would lead him to change his position and to distance himself from some of his traveling companions, such as Karl Rahner and Hans Küng. For the moment, I limit myself to noting the fact; it will be necessary to return to it at greater length at the conclusion of this chapter.

The concluding session

Like other experts, during the interval between the third and fourth session of the council, Ratzinger was remarkably busy. In particular, he was appointed as an expert to the subcommission charged with rewriting the text on the missions. The commission, which was headed by Servite Bishop Johannes Schütte and had Father Congar as another excellent member, met twice during the early months of 1965. At the first meeting, Ratzinger was not present but sent a document of high theological caliber[53] that posited the Holy Trinity itself as the foundation of missionary work. Starting from the

---

[51] Ibid., 174.

[52] See Aidan Nichols, *The Thought of Pope Benedict XVI: An Introduction to the Theology of Joseph Ratzinger* (London: Burns & Oates, 2007), 67–68.

[53] For the following discussion, see Valente, *Ratzinger al Vaticano II*, 142.

Gospel of John, in which the Son is sent by the Father, he was able to affirm that the Church does not go on mission by her own power. Christ himself, who receives the fullness of charity from the Father, is the one who works through the Church and draws the hearts of men to himself and to the Father. This work is then completed by the Holy Spirit, who fosters the missionary proclamation, the acceptance of the Gospel seed that is sown, and the *plantatio Ecclesiae*, the growth of the Church, which, in turn, has as its purpose, not the institutional Church, but once again the proclamation of the word of God.

Ratzinger's document made a great impression on the members of the subcommission, who decided to adopt as a basis the text prepared by Father Congar but made use of Ratzinger's text for the first theological chapter. The understanding between Congar and Ratzinger was, moreover, excellent. Reporting on the second meeting of the subcommission that was held in Nemi between March 29 and April 3, 1965, the Dominican friar is particularly caustic. Against the background of the harsh judgment reserved to the other participants, the praise lavished on the German professor stands out even more: "Fr. A. Seumois really is an ass. . . . Mgr Yago says nothing and appears to be very bored; Mgr Perrin scarcely follows what is going on and is no help; Mgr Cavallera agrees; Mgr D'Souza says nothing. . . . Fortunately, Ratzinger is there. He is reasonable, modest, disinterested, a great help."[54]

For his part, the theologian from Münster was worried about the criticisms of the schema on the sources of revelation and feared that the majority of the council Fathers might distort it. Upon his return to Rome, he spoke about it with Father de Lubac, another expert with whom he was in ever closer agreement.[55] Between one trip and the next for the conferences that gave rise to the conciliar reports, there were his courses at the university, which also examined in greater depth the principal topics discussed at the council. In short, Ratzinger took very seriously his participation in Vatican II, so that, when he arrived in Rome on September 14 for the inauguration of the fourth and last session, he got to work immediately.

---

[54] Congar, *My Journal of the Council*, 748.

[55] See Henri de Lubac, *Vatican Council Notebooks*, vol. 2, trans. Anne Englund Nash (San Francisco: Ignatius Press, 2016), 338.

At the end of the third session, the atmosphere had been rather gloomy. Everyone noticed the consequences of the "black week" with the explanatory note and the impression that the pope intended to give too much consideration to the arguments of the curial minority. According to Ratzinger, Paul VI immediately afterward had given ample proof that he did not intend to disregard the conciliar decisions. Moreover, at the opening of the fourth session, after an excellent introductory speech in which he spoke about, among other things, "the art of loving [that] is often converted into the art of suffering",[56] the pope pleasantly surprised those present with the announcement of two extraordinary events: the institution of the synod of bishops and the acceptance of the invitation to visit the United Nations Organization on the occasion of the twentieth anniversary of its founding. For Ratzinger, these were two important signs. With the institution of the synod, the pope confirmed his intention to approve the spirit of the council; with the visit to the U.N., he emphasized the Church's intention, which was at the basis of schema 13, to be open to the world. Ratzinger, therefore, distanced himself from the experts who maintained that the synod, meant to be an organ of collegiality, had become an instrument of the Roman Primate. The synod, Ratzinger observed, would accomplish its task if it succeeded in making the living voice of the universal Church heard within it. On the other hand, the very term "synod" referred to the essential structure of the early Church, so that the new episcopal organization was not arising from incidental demands but, rather, appeared as an expression of a structural element of the Church's constitution. It would accomplish its task completely when it became an integral part of the Church's life.

RELIGIOUS LIBERTY

The work on the numerous documents that still needed to be approved definitively began on September 15 with the discussion, for the third time, of the document on religious liberty. Here again, it was necessary to overcome the objections raised by the conciliar minority: the first objection disputed the alleged equivalence of truth and error; the second maintained that religious liberty tended

---

[56] J. Ratzinger, *Theological Highlights of Vatican II*, 202.

to obscure the love of truth; the third, which emerged over the course of the third session, lamented the lack of biblical foundation. Ratzinger responded to the objections precisely by starting from this final observation. To the supposed lack of explicit Scripture passages, he contrasted the New Testament message itself, at the center of which is the Cross that does not side with the powers of this world but, instead, testifies to God's powerlessness. In the account of the temptations in the Gospel of Matthew, the idea of a politically powerful Messiah is rejected as a diabolical temptation. Therefore this objection was untenable.

In the debate in the hall, moreover, one idea emerged that Ratzinger considered particularly fruitful. The Christian faith forcefully claims the freedom to conduct missions throughout the world. It follows, logically, that if one claims the right to Christian witness in the world, one cannot then deny freedom of belief as a fundamental form of religious practice even in countries having an ancient Christian tradition. In this way, the idea of mission ends up being at the origin of the idea of religious liberty.[57] Another significant contribution came from the staunch support of the schema by the council Fathers from Eastern Europe, who had faced long years of imprisonment precisely because of the denial of the freedom to practice religion. The idea of religious liberty, therefore, slowly made headway among the Fathers, and this explains the outcome of the final vote, which led to the approval of the conciliar Declaration by a large majority. The result, moreover, demonstrates that, although the opposition of the minority was tenacious, it was quantitatively small.

THE CHURCH IN THE MODERN WORLD

Central to the debate at the fourth session was the so-called "schema 13", which gave rise to the fourth conciliar constitution, *Gaudium et spes* on the Church in the Modern World. The document had resulted from the combination of a series of documents on contemporary man prepared by the Roman commissions. According to Ratzinger, the Roman texts were juridically irreproachable, but the answers were so obvious that they had little to do with reality. It was therefore necessary to put together various documents that

---

[57] Ibid., 209.

dealt with modern man and to rewrite them according to the new spirit of the council as Pope John wished. The task of preparing a new text was entrusted to the Belgian Cardinal Suenens and was supported by many Fathers of the majority group, among them Suenens himself and Frings. By the autumn of 1964, the schema started to take shape; it consisted of seven chapters. The first part (three chapters) outlined a sort of Christian anthropology; the second part addressed contemporary topics that were considered particularly burning issues: marriage and the family, war and peace, social problems, the relation of Christians to the culture and technological mentality of our time.

At the first presentation in the hall, in 1964, the German bishops, influenced in particular by Rahner and Ratzinger,[58] had expressed serious doubts. Now, according to Ratzinger, even after a working meeting held at the beginning of 1965 in Ariccia to take into account the proposed revisions suggested by the council Fathers, the schema still reflected the original cast given to it by the group of French compilers, and it had obvious limitations. On the one hand, it aimed to distance itself from Scholastic language so as to find a biblical foundation; on the other hand, it tried to draw closer to the modern situation and to its language. As a result, the document was neither biblically based nor truly relevant to the contemporary mind-set. The same difficulty appeared in the autumn of 1965, and Ratzinger once more pointed out the unresolved problems: the juxtaposition of two realities, the world of experience and the world of Christian faith, put together without any particular internal connection. Even its Christology, which is the central nucleus of Christianity, gave the impression of being derived from a secondary world that was set alongside the first without any particular ties to it.[59] Then there was the excessive optimism with regard to technology, hardly tempered at all by any attention to the limits of all human progress. Ratzinger asked: What is the relation between technological progress, viewed from the perspective of a popularized Teilhardism, and Christian hope?

This simple-minded outline needed to be corrected. Therefore, during the autumn months, while other documents were being discussed in the public sessions, a commission was established that

---

[58] See Aubert, "Lo svolgimento del concilio", 327.
[59] J. Ratzinger, *Theological Highlights of Vatican II*, 221–22.

was to work at top speed. For this reason, the commission was sub-divided into as many as ten subcommissions, each of which had to review different chapters and points. At de Lubac's urging,[60] Ratzinger was appointed to the fourth subcommission, which was working on chapter 3 of part 1. The most significant contribution of the Bavarian theologian, however, was in the preamble itself of the constitution, in what eventually would be numbers 9 and 10 of *Gaudium et spes*. Above all, this latter paragraph repeated almost ver-batim a text presented by Ratzinger on October 17.[61] At the very beginning, the reader can see the intent to correct the schema's failings with an Augustinian approach: "The dichotomy affecting the modern world is, in fact, a symptom of the deeper dichotomy that is in man himself." Hence the classic questions of fundamental theology are enumerated in the middle of the paragraph: "What is man? What is the meaning of suffering, evil, death, which have not been eliminated by all this progress?" Then, at the beginning of the final paragraph, the decisive Christian response follows: "The Church believes that Christ, who died and was raised for the sake of all, can show man the way and strengthen him through the Spirit in order to be worthy of his destiny: nor is there any other name under heaven given among men by which they can be saved."[62]

Thus rewritten, the document did not totally eliminate the crit-icisms. Nevertheless, in his final assessment, Ratzinger was able to point out also the positive sides of the fourth constitution. Against the recurring magical view of the universe, which in antiquity often led to idolatry and magic, the sober perspective of science can be a good ally of faith, which considers the universe to be created by God's Spirit-filled Word. Therefore the cosmos, which contains the traces of the *Logos*, is rationally structured and can be understood by reason and should be respected as the garden entrusted to man's

---

[60] In his council diary, de Lubac writes on October 6, 1965: "Talked next with Bishop Volk (Mainz); we were looking for a practical means by which the essential remarks made about the schema might be seriously taken into consideration. . . . We agreed on the following point: he should have at least Dr. Joseph Ratzinger, a theologian who is as peaceful and kind as he is competent, invited to collaborate with the group drafting the schema." *Vatican Council Notebooks*, 2:387.

[61] Cf. Valente, *Ratzinger al Vaticano II*, 158ff.

[62] Translation taken from *Vatican Council II*, vol. 1, *The Conciliar and Postconciliar Docu-ments*, new rev. ed., ed. Austin Flannery, O.P. (Northpoint, N.Y.: Costello, 1996), 910–11.

care. Hence the autonomy of technology, which helps to identify the laws that govern the world and can help to improve man's life in the world. Ratzinger then listed two other more specific points in which the constitution, by distancing itself from tradition, introduced significant innovations. As far as marital and familial ethics are concerned, *Gaudium et spes* sought to construct a personalist vision without ignoring the social dimension of matrimony. The norm built on the natural law is complemented by a reference to the word of the personal God, who gave as a model for spousal love the perfection of his love revealed by Jesus in his love for the Church.

The other significant point concerned the teaching on war and peace. Since the days of the bishop of Hippo, indeed, the conditions in which war could be declared just have changed profoundly. Faced with such a scenario, the council then renounced a somewhat static definition so as to suggest actions that are more in keeping with the teaching of Jesus. Therefore, once the purpose is established, achieving peace, it is necessary to respect international law, to establish conventions in order to humanize war, to renounce the power of arms, to work for disarmament and for the institution of international authorities. A result, Ratzinger concluded, that may seem meager. Nevertheless, it corresponds to the current situation, which is fraught with uncertainties, fear, and threats. A man who faces reality with an attentive, penetrating eye is not far from the mystery of God's mercy that is revealed in Jesus Christ.

The solemn conclusion of the council

On December 7, 1965, the last four conciliar documents were approved definitively: the Pastoral Constitution on the Church in the Modern World, the decrees on the Ministry and Life of Priests and on the Church's Missionary Activity, and the Declaration on Religious Liberty. Immediately afterward, Ratzinger concluded, a spirit of joy and of profound thanksgiving spread among the council Fathers, who, meeting for the last time in Saint Peter's Basilica, exchanged the kiss of peace, conscious that they had attended a historical event, a gift of grace. These feelings became even more intense as the morning session continued, when Cardinal Bea, in the attentive, participatory silence of all the Fathers who were present and of many guests, read the joint declaration that Pope Paul VI and the Orthodox Patriarch Athenagoras I had previously signed and that was being read at the same time by the secretary general of the [Orthodox] synod in Saint George Church in Istanbul. With this declaration, the pope of Rome and the patriarch of Constantinople abrogated the excommunication that in 1054 the Roman legates, headed by Humbert Cardinal of Silva Candida, had hurled against Patriarch Michael Cerularius and two other dignitaries of the Orthodox Church, to which the patriarch and the Orthodox synod had responded with a similar measure. The thunderous applause that accompanied the kiss of peace between Paul VI and Metropolitan Meliton of Heliopolis finally gave vent to the profound emotion of those present. "The millennium of hostility was spanned by the rainbow of reconciliation; the kiss of peace concluded the millennium which began with the curse of anathema."[63] The closing ceremony on the following day, December 8, 1965, in contrast, did not warm Ratzinger's heart. The grand Baroque ritual seemed to the theologian a bit pompous and superficial.

If we try now to summarize concisely the contribution made by the Bavarian *peritus* to the work of the council, we must first recall the clear negative judgment that he gave to the document *De fontibus* (On the sources). When communicated to Cardinal Frings and the German bishops, it led not only to the rejection of the original document but also the formation of the conciliar majority. After having drawn up an alternative schema with Karl Rahner, which in reality served as a transitional document, the elaboration of the Constitution on Divine Revelation was entrusted to a mixed commission composed of several cardinals, members of the theological commission, and the Secretariat for Promoting Christian Unity.[64] This commission achieved appreciable results already in the months immediately following the first council session, so much so that it was approved in March during the second meeting of the coordinating commission.[65] It was then reworked by two subcommissions in which Ratzinger did not participate. The contribution of the Bavarian theologian, nevertheless, was decisive in giving the document the salvation history character that is also its chief merit as the basis

---

[63] J. Ratzinger, *Theological Highlights of Vatican II*, 259.
[64] Cf. Aubert, in *La Chiesa del Vaticano II*, 238.
[65] Ibid., 247.

for the renewal of theology and preaching and for the dialogue with the separated brethren.[66]

Another significant contribution was Ratzinger's collaboration on the Doctrinal Constitution on the Church. Here he worked above all on chapter 3, in particular on the theological definition of the apostolic college, on the bishops' membership in it, and on the sacramental nature of episcopal ordination. Along the same lines was his contribution to the Decree on the Mission Activity of the Church and to the Constitution on the Church in the Modern World. In the first document, he pointed out the Trinitarian origin of the concept of mission, which is already present in the Gospel of John; in *Gaudium et spes*, given the optimistic, predominantly social approach of the original drafters, he sought to recover once again the salvation-history perspective, based on the Incarnation of the Son of God. This perspective is able to serve as a foundation for a more realistic Christian anthropology that is capable of taking into account the fragility of human nature and its inclination to sin, which only the grace brought by the Son and bestowed in the Holy Spirit can remedy.

In the fragmentary nature of the contributions of the Bavarian theologian, we can therefore recognize also the uniformity of an approach to which Ratzinger would remain faithful, both in the years of his academic career and also in the longer period of his episcopal ministry as bishop of Munich, prefect of the Congregation for the Doctrine of the Faith, and as successor of the apostle Peter in the See of Rome.

The solemn conclusion of the council now gave way to the accomplishment of a task that had been spelled out in Rome and now had to take shape and substance in all Christian communities. Now, nevertheless, the world witnessed a new, unexpected phenomenon. Many of the faithful who had initially greeted the conciliar event enthusiastically now gave in to unjustified discouragement, not because of any lack of concrete results, but because of the illusory expectations raised by biased Church leaders and journalists. Quoting the Protestant observer Oscar Cullmann, Ratzinger recalled that "on the whole our expectations, insofar as they were not based on illusions and apart from some exceptions, were fulfilled and in some

---

[66] Cf. Congar, *My Journal of the Council*, 518.

respects surpassed.''[67] Looking, then, at the first attempts to implement the conciliar reforms, the German theologian recalled the
abuses in the liturgical field that were present in many Catholic communities, which did enormous damage to their worship. Moreover,
he noted that many were worried more about modernity than about
truth. Finally, he considered even more dangerous the phenomenon
of the ecclesiastical "impressionist painters" who tended to depict
the preconciliar era in dark colors, reserving the brighter colors for
the conciliar era and modern times. For Ratzinger, this was a way of
distorting history that could lead to erroneous, unfair judgments.
In this regard, he cited the remark by the great scholar of world religions Friedrich Heiler, who concluded his essay on the Catholic
Church for the volume *The Religions of Humanity*,[68] which serves as
an introduction to the series with the same title, with the following
observation: Notwithstanding the weight of the past, notwithstanding the debatable character of dogmas, it is nevertheless necessary
to realize that "many millions of people considered the Church of
Rome their spiritual mother, in whose bosom they feel protected in
life as well as death." The observation struck Ratzinger deeply, and
he would recall it many times, particularly in debates with Church
leaders and theologians: they are not called, above all, to form a sort
of avant-garde to guide the faithful through changing times, but,
rather, are called to be ministers and dispensers of the word and
the sacraments, which are the real treasure from which the Church
draws over the centuries to nourish the faith of those who, with a
sincere and humble heart, entrust themselves to her care.

A final consideration is offered by the flattering judgment by Congar of Ratzinger's character: "He is reasonable, modest, disinterested, a great help."[69] These character traits enabled Ratzinger to
make "the Rhine" flow into the Tiber, that is, the findings of the
theology from Germany and more generally from Central Europe;
they also allowed him to bring back to his own country from the
council an increased attention to the faith of those who are simple of
heart. "To serve and to live this faith is the noblest vocation in the

---

[67] J. Ratzinger, *Theological Highlights of Vatican II*, 260.

[68] Friedrich Heiler, *Die Religionen der Menschheit* (Stuttgart: Reclam, 1959), 750. English translation: *The History of Religions as a Way to Unity of Religion* (Tokyo: Maruzen,
1960).

[69] Congar, *My Journal of the Council*, 748.

renewal of the Church."[70] In this regard, Ratzinger compared the immediate postconciliar period with the so-called "intertestamental" period. Between the legalism of the Pharisees and the liberalism of the Sadducees, Israel's faithfulness was preserved by the poor in spirit: Zachary, Elizabeth, Joseph, and Mary kept the torch of Israel's faith and hope alive and, like precious torchbearers, brought it from the Old to the New Covenant. The poor and the simple of heart are the Church's most valuable treasure. Service to their faith is the best thing that can be done to renew the Church. This was not yet Ratzinger's very vocal parting of ways with his fellow experts who had supported the conciliar majority, but it is certainly a consideration and a warning that went in that direction.

---

[70] J. Ratzinger, *Theological Highlights of Vatican II*, 263.

V

THE WORLD TURNS ITS BACK ON GOD

Professor in Münster

Münster, in Westphalia, on the northwestern border of Germany, is today a city populated mainly by young people, who find there an ideal place to study at the Wilhelms-Universität, one of the most renowned in Germany. Its history, in contrast, is marked by three dramatic events in which religion always played an important role. Founded in Carolingian times, the ancient Monasterium at the time of the Reformation was briefly conquered by the Anabaptists. In 1535, however, the city was regained by the troops of the bishop-prince Francis of Waldeck, who had the leaders of the revolt tortured and exposed their bodies in cages hanging on the tower of the church of Saint Lambert. That was the end of the kingdom of Münster, "a repugnant mixture of piety, greed for pleasure, and thirst for blood", as the historian Leopold von Ranke wrote. The next significant event in the history of the town took place in the following century: the Peace of Westphalia, the main treaties of which were signed in Münster. The agreement not only recognized the ancient right of princes to have their subjects profess their own religion, as established in Augsburg, but also allowed states to establish agreements, even in religious matters, without necessarily consulting the pope. The last event, of which Ratzinger had certainly heard in his youth, was the fierce resistance to Nazism put up by Bishop Clemens August Graf von Galen, in particular to the provisions condemning the physically and mentally disabled to death. For his courageous resistance to Nazism and his obstinate defense of life, Bishop von Galen was later created cardinal and then proclaimed Blessed by Benedict XVI in the first year of his pontificate.

Ratzinger arrived in Münster in 1963, and his first course of dogmatic theology closely followed the academic programs. The teaching of dogmatic theology started, according to a classic pattern, with an introduction to the dogma and the doctrine of the Eucharist. The seminar, in contrast, focused on the interest of the day: Scripture and tradition, for which, as we know, Ratzinger was particularly well prepared both by his study of Saint Bonaventure and by the contribution that he made to the drafting of the Constitution on Divine Revelation. Ratzinger's success among the students was immediate. Vinzenz Pfnür related: "There were around 350 students enrolled in the course, but an average of 600 attended the lectures. Students from other fields, too, such as philosophy and jurisprudence, came to listen to Ratzinger. We printed the handouts for the ecclesiology course on the centrality of the Eucharist, and we sold 850 copies of them."[1] Another of his first students, Peter Kuhn, continued: In Münster a small print shop was organized. Ratzinger's courses were mimeographed and then sold throughout Germany, a sign that the theologian's fame was expanding throughout the country.

Even in the University of Westphalia, however, there was no lack of critical voices. Among these, I would like to recall Hansjürgen Verweyen, an early disciple of Ratzinger who, while appreciating the young professor, immediately expressed misgivings. Verweyen's criticism was directed, in particular, against Ratzinger's seminar on the Constitution on Divine Revelation, held in the 1965–1966 winter semester. The text of the seminar later went into Ratzinger's commentary on *Dei Verbum* contained in the second supplementary volume of the *Lexikon für Theologie und Kirche*. The German scholar, having been a longtime professor in the United States, also reflected the thoughts of many American scholars when he said that at least from the time of the Reformation, the relationship between Sacred Scripture and tradition had been one of the major problems of the Church. The council sought to address this fundamental issue in the Constitution on Divine Revelation, *Dei Verbum*. Ratzinger himself, in his memoirs,[2] recalled his efforts and those of Cardinal Frings

---

[1] Related by Gianni Valente in *Ratzinger professore* (Cinisello Balsamo: San Paolo, 2008), 117.

[2] Joseph Ratzinger, *Milestones: Memoirs 1927–1977*, trans. Erasmo Leiva-Merikakis (San Francisco: Ignatius Press, 1998), 124–30, esp. 128.

to overcome this impasse, which threatened to distance Catholics from the development of Bible studies.

Verweyen did not question Ratzinger's word, nor did he underestimate his competence; he doubted the success of his efforts, however. As a proof of this statement, he reported some critiques by Ratzinger himself, contained in the commentary on the Constitution on Divine Revelation.[3] Then, he went on: "We have to wonder whether or not Ratzinger's position, often reaffirmed, that tradition at the council was understood completely in terms of Scripture can really stand."[4] Actually, Verweyen claimed, at least in no. 9, the minority of those who were not willing to give up the affirmation of a material coupling of Scripture and tradition prevailed. Then Verweyen went on to tell about a harsh confrontation with the professor, during the winter semester of 1965–1966. He conceded, finally, that both in the *Catechism of the Catholic Church* and in the *Compendium of the Catechism*, these uncertainties of the conciliar document are not present. His criticism, therefore, was an indirect acknowledgment of Ratzinger, under whose direction the two above-mentioned doctrinal documents had been elaborated.

Can the Christian scandal be eliminated?

At the end of 1965, at the conclusion of Vatican Council II, Ratzinger returned to Germany. In his heart, he still had the applause that accompanied the kiss of peace between Paul VI and Metropolitan Meliton of Heliopolis, representing Patriarch Athenagoras. The embrace appeared to many and to him in particular as a sign of hope, like the beginning of a task that, with the time of the great doctrinal elaboration over, was now supposed to take shape in every diocese, in every Christian community.[5] Yet, even before the end of the council, looking at the way in which it was interpreted in the ecclesial community of Germany, the theologian, who had now

---

[3] Joseph Ratzinger, "Introduction and commentary on the prologue and the first two chapters of *Dei Verbum*", in *Lexikon für Theologie und Kirche*, 2nd supplementary volume (Freiburg im Breisgau: Herder), 519f.

[4] Hansjürgen Verweyen, *Joseph Ratzinger-Benedikt XVI: Die Entwicklung seines Denkens* (Darmstadt: WBG, 2007), 37.

[5] See Joseph Ratzinger, *Theological Highlights of Vatican II* (New York and Mahwah, N.J.: Paulist Press, 1966, 2009), 259.

reached the height of fame and whose opinion was listened to very attentively, noticed something that did not convince him. According to the image chosen as the title of a famous book, the Rhine had poured its waters into the Tiber, but now it seemed tired and disappointed. The changes brought about in Rome appeared limited, restrained by the Curia. It was up to the theologians and the individual communities to carry on the debate and the innovations that in Rome had only been mentioned.[6] While acknowledging the role that theologians had had and still had in this evolution, Ratzinger initially seemed above all worried about what was happening in Christian communities, in dioceses, and in parishes. In two conferences addressed primarily to the ecclesial community, he made his concerned voice heard.

The first conference was in June 1965, when the last session of the council had yet to begin. Invited to a meeting of the Association of Catholic Students of Münster, the theologian, who was not yet forty years old, invited his audience to reflect on the meaning of ecclesial renewal. The pleasant sensation created by the watchword of the *aggiornamento* desired by John XXIII was now gone. It had been replaced in the Christian communities by a deep division that did not bode well at all.[7] On one side, Ratzinger continued, there were the innovators who push the Church to adapt to today's common mentality; on the other, there were the defenders of an antimodernist Catholicism, the Cassandras who already saw the weakening of the central power, the spread of a large number of heresies. In the center, there were those who had long since fought for the renewal of the Church, those like de Lubac and von Balthasar who sacrificed themselves for her renewal and now wondered whether this was the way to raze the bastions, as stated in the title of a famous essay by the Swiss theologian.[8]

For this purpose, the theologian from Basel followed up the small volume published in 1952 with a new pamphlet in 1963, *Love Alone*

---

[6] See J. Ratzinger, *Milestones*, 133–34.

[7] The conference "What Does the Renewal of the Church Mean?" was then published in Joseph Ratzinger, *Das neue Volk Gottes* (Düsseldorf: Patmos, 1972), 91–106.

[8] The original title of the famous work by Hans Urs von Balthasar was *Schleifung der Bastionen*, which was published in Germany in 1952 by Johannes Verlag (Einsiedeln). The most recent English edition is *Razing the Bastions: On the Church in This Age* (San Francisco: Communio Books, Ignatius Press, 1993).

Is Credible,[9] which was supposed to represent "the positive, constructive complement to my earlier book".[10] Von Balthasar wrote that the movements of history come from outside, the revolutions that imply the elimination of forms connected with the authority of other eras or even just with abandoned or outdated habits. Instead, from the inside, holiness itself is what tends toward simplicity and sobriety and tries to break the shells of the past so as to show itself, fresh and rejuvenated, to the modern and contemporary world.[11]

In his lecture, Ratzinger followed the pattern outlined by von Balthasar, relying, however, in his argument, on the model of the early Christians and the Fathers of the Church, already followed by de Lubac in *The Splendor of the Church*, a work from 1953. The principle of Christian renewal, Ratzinger wrote, is the definition of Christianity, not of renewal. Otherwise, we become like merchants, constantly investigating the tastes and desires of the public, the better to sell them their own merchandise. On the other hand, Christianity, from the very beginning, presented itself as the New Covenant, as the New Testament that completes the Old one and aims at the essential renewal of mankind. Here, Ratzinger quoted the beloved Saint Augustine: "The old canticle celebrates the selfishness of the flesh, the new one celebrates the love of God." And he commented: "True renewal is not in the letter; its success depends on the ability of new forms to become the instrument that brings about the decisive transition from the old man to the new, from egotism to love. The new liturgy, too, will become and will be an old song unless it is continually open so as to become the instrument of the unifying love of Jesus Christ."[12] On the other hand, individual Christian renewal is not enough; it must extend to the Church, which has an ideal model in the early Christian community. From the comparison with the early Church, it is possible to determine what is wrong in the present-day Church and to make the necessary corrections.

---

[9] Translated by D. C. Schindler (San Francisco: Ignatius Press, 2005).

[10] These two small but dense volumes by von Balthasar are now published in Italian in one volume entitled *La percezione dell'amore* (Milan: Jaca Book, 2010). The second volume has been translated by D. C. Schindler as *Love Alone Is Credible* (San Francisco: Ignatius Press, 2004), 13.

[11] Von Balthasar, *Percezione dell'amore*, xi.

[12] J. Ratzinger, *Das neue Volk Gottes*, 96–97.

Based on this criterion, Ratzinger identified two fundamental errors of the past epoch: the connection with the power of the Con-
stantinian and medieval eras; the attempts at integrism originating
from the opposition to the Reformation of the sixteenth century.
Coming now to the present day, the overzealous advocates of so-
called incarnation theology run the risk of falling back into the Con-
stantinian wedding of Church and State. Considering the Church
too detached from today's world, these theologians end up proposing again a Church dangerously close to the contemporary world,
to the spirit of the age and of history. On the other side, there are
those who preclude the possibility of the Church living out her
Christian vocation in the contemporary world because they consider her necessarily bound to forms of the past. How to escape
from these two equally misleading paths? The main way is shown
by Jesus himself, who, in his time, found that he, too, had to avoid
two similar models. On one side, there were the Pharisees and,
within them, the group of Essenes or of Qumran; on the other, the
Sadducees. The former seemed to have all the requirements of a real
spiritual renewal, but in their rigor they ended up "depending on
the letter and formalism of a system"[13] and thus isolated themselves
from the world and therefore from true life.

In our time, Ratzinger saw this danger in a Church separated from
the world, self-enclosed, forgetful of the fact that her Lord died at
the gates of the city. "Outside, in front of the guarded gates of the
city and the sanctuary: that is the place for a Church that wants
to follow the Crucified."[14] The other attitude, equally wrong, is
that of the Sadducees. In our days, Ratzinger saw it proposed again
by those who try to combine the faith too closely with the world,
eliminating from it anything that the world may not like. Faith is no
longer yeast and no longer salt; rather, it is confused with the world
and thus deprived of interest and effectiveness. The great theme of
hermeneutics, Ratzinger stated, tends to turn into a methodology
that, after too much interpretation, ends up emptying and eliminating the very contents of the Christian faith. Once again here,
Ratzinger called for the sobriety and simplicity of the early Church,
which ultimately is the echo of the simplicity of the one God. "To

---

[13] Ibid., 101.
[14] Ibid., 102.

become simple in this sense would be true renewal for us Christians, for each one of us and for the entire Church."[15]

In the course of this chapter, I have already had reason to speak about Hans Urs von Balthasar. In this regard, Victor Hahn, another of Ratzinger's disciples, related an episode that took place in that period of time and had as its protagonists Johann Baptist Metz, Hans Urs von Balthasar, and Ratzinger himself. Detaching himself from Rahner's transcendental theology, in those years Metz was beginning to start a current of thought commonly known as "political theology", which was dangerously close to what Ratzinger called "incarnation theology". Against that approach, von Balthasar had taken a firm stance when he was invited to hold a debate in the presence of the students in Münster. Ratzinger was chosen as the moderator of the debate. Hahn remembered: "Between one intervention and the next of the two contenders, Ratzinger summarized their thoughts with an expository richness that made even the most obscure passages of the two speakers clear and interesting. At the end, the audience respectfully applauded both Metz and von Balthasar. But the longest and most enthusiastic applause was reserved for the moderator."[16]

As Hahn reported, on that occasion Ratzinger acted as arbitrator between the two contenders. From what we have said, however, it is clear that he felt closer to the Swiss theologian, to whom he was bound by a friendship that would soon lead the two to an intense collaboration.

The council tested by the faithful.
Conference at the Katholikentag in Bamberg

The Katholikentage, or "days of the German Catholics", which officially started in 1848, have a great tradition in Germany. Historians identify three moments in which the meetings played an important role in the history of Catholicism in modern Germany: during the Kulturkampf in the late nineteenth century; in the years between the two wars in the early twentieth century; during the period of reconstruction when the Katholikentage resumed in Mainz in 1948

[15] Ibid., 106.
[16] Valente, Ratzinger professore, 118.

with the motto "Germany, mission land". "As in all areas, also in the religious the reconstruction proceeded from the bottom up. There struck the great hour of the parish principle."[17] Ratzinger had had the chance to witness this fervor of initiatives and works in the short period of his pastoral care in Munich, immediately after his priestly ordination. This same fervor he now saw in crisis, and for this reason he raised his voice. In 1966, the Catholic gathering was held in the town of Bamberg, in the Frankish part of Bavaria, and the theme, one year after the conclusion of the council sessions, was almost obligatory: "Catholicism after the Council". Even the choice of the speaker was almost obligatory: Ratzinger was one of the few experts who had taken part in all stages of the council, had been an esteemed interpreter of it, was Bavarian, and had already given various conferences on the subject in numerous German cities and universities.

In his talk,[18] the theologian first critically examined the very concept of Catholicism. In accepting an outdated terminology, one ran the risk of adhering to the medieval concept of the Church and empire, something that everybody wanted to overcome. That being said, Ratzinger did not want to play the sophist. The theme proposed by the organizers ultimately asked the question: What is the situation of Catholics after the council and as a result of the council? He answered the question with a clear statement that was surprising at that time: "Let us say it frankly: a certain uneasiness prevails, an atmosphere of coolness and also of disappointment."[19] The world that, for a moment, had viewed the Church with some interest, has long since gone its separate way again. Clerics, which should certainly be understood to mean bishops and priests, but also theologians and all those involved in ecclesiastical activities, particularly in the liturgical field, feel that they are protagonists more than ever.[20] They are advocates of conciliar hermeneutics, but by dint of interpreting, they run the risk of emptying the faith of its contents.

---

[17] Ludwig Volk, "The Church in German-speaking Countries", in *The Church in the Modern Age*, vol. 10 of *History of the Church*, ed. Hubert Jedin, Konrad Repgen, and John Dolan (New York: Crossroad, 1980), 10:531–56 at 547.

[18] The conference has now been published in the volume *Das neue Volk Gottes*, 129–51.

[19] Ibid., 130.

[20] Ibid., 137.

Wherever clerics and experts clash and debate, the faithful divide into two antagonistic parties. For some, the council did too little, its texts were the result of compromises, of tactics that ended up prevailing over the breath of the Holy Spirit; for others, it was a cause of scandal, ultimately a surrender of the Church to the spirit of the times. For Ratzinger, however, it was not about taking a stand between two parties but, rather, about analyzing in greater depth the reasons for the uneasiness in the circles where it was most evident: in the liturgical field, in the relationship between the Church and the world, and in the ecumenical field.

THE LITURGICAL FIELD

The field in which the council had arrived relatively soon at a convincing synthesis was that of the liturgy. Prepared by the liturgical-ecclesial movement, the liturgical constitution had been approved at the end of the second session, in 1963, and had been the first ripe fruit of Vatican II. "But precisely this liturgical renewal, so much desired and welcomed with so much joy, has become, in many ways, the sign of contradiction."[21] At the time, according to Ratzinger, there were three main objections to the liturgical renewal. The use of the vernacular language removes the veil of mystery from the sacred, just as it eliminates the sense of communion with one's contemporaries from other countries and continents, and with the faithful of past centuries. The prevalence of the communal aspect is an obstacle to silence, which is better suited than a lot of talk to the mystery in which God can make his voice heard more incisively. Lastly, the communal liturgical celebration was transformed many times into an iconoclast attack on the beauty that had been generated and transmitted over the centuries.

Ratzinger replied to the objections of the conservatives by fully defending the validity of the constitution and of the liturgical renewal. "The Christian liturgical celebration is by its essence the proclamation of the good news of God to the community that is present, the acceptance of it by the community in response, the common speech of the Church to God."[22] The liturgical reform

---

[21] Ibid., 132.
[22] Ibid., 133.

of the council thus appeared to Ratzinger not only legitimate, but even necessary. This does not mean, he added, that all its practical implementations are equally legitimate and acceptable. He imputed to the liturgists, for example, a certain taste for archaism that has resulted in the elimination of every form of orchestral music from the liturgy, while, on the other hand, the door of the house of God has been opened to any other impromptu, enthusiastic jazz group. The risk is that more attention will be paid to the liturgical form than to the worship of God. The consequence is a new form of ritualism and clericalism, an iconoclastic fury that eliminates the law of continuity that cannot be transgressed with impunity. The real liturgical reform, Ratzinger concluded, requires, instead, a high degree of tolerance and demands the long-suffering of love.

THE NEW RELATION BETWEEN THE CHURCH AND THE WORLD

To exemplify the Church's situation in the contemporary world, Ratzinger evoked the image of New York's neo-gothic cathedral surrounded and overlooked by steel giants, the skyscrapers. Where once the spires of the medieval cathedrals recalled the eternal, now the Church appears dominated, almost lost, in the modern world. Hence the desire, expressed first of all by the youth movement, to be freed from the past of the Christian institution. In turn, the council, with the Constitution on the Church in the Modern World, had wanted to sweep away the dust of the past so as to make room for fresh air. Soon, however, when they tried to define in new terms the Church's relationship with the modern world, they realized that there were other problems to be considered than the mere suppression of ancient forms. From a theological point of view, according to Ratzinger, two stages of development have to be discussed.

First, there is the incarnational phase, which reminds us that God is not alien to this world; on the contrary, he became a man and is not a God of the afterlife but a God of this world. Incarnate Christianity is not an escape from the world and expectation of the afterlife; rather, it is joyfully engaged in the present time, rejoices over all that is beautiful, great, and noble in this world. At this point, however, the second phase, which Ratzinger defined as eschatological, comes into play. This reminds us, first of all, that the incarnational phase does not have in the New Testament the central position that we are tempted to attribute to it now. The central position is occupied instead by the profession of faith in the Resurrection, which, in turn, is inseparable from the theme of the Cross. If we want to be more precise, the theology of the Incarnation itself results in the theology of the Cross and Resurrection. Consequently, an orientation of the Church to the world cannot mean a departure from the Cross, a detachment from the scandal of the Cross. On the contrary, the elimination of all secondary scandals, the razing of the bastions, as von Balthasar put it, ends up emphasizing the primary scandal of the Cross, the scandal of God, who, for love of mankind, faces the Cross and the Resurrection.

As I have already mentioned, Ratzinger was invited to collaborate on the Constitution on the Church in the Modern World precisely to curb the excessive anthropological optimism of the original document and to highlight the saving action of the Son of God, who died and rose for all mankind.[23]

ECUMENISM

The third area considered by Ratzinger in his report is ecumenism. The point of departure is an invitation to gratitude and patience. Who, Ratzinger asked, just ten years ago, could have even hoped that in such a short time the Catholic Church would have developed internally such a sense of her inadequacy, a feeling that is necessary in order to develop ecumenical sensitivity?

That being said, it is inevitable that when we move from doctrine to daily life, we encounter difficulties and resistance. Some Protestants have the feeling that Catholic openings are in reality dictated by tactics. On the Catholic side, there are those who complain that the goodwill that has led to so many openings is not really matched by a similar feeling from the Lutheran-Evangelical side. Still in Catholic circles, there are, on the other hand, the impatient individuals who no longer see any difference and ask their Church to dare the paradox of pluralism and to consider themselves, at this point, one Church among others. The latter, Ratzinger concluded, end up promoting integrism, just as the exaggerations of the liturgical

---

[23] See in the preceding chapter the paragraph on the constitution *The Church in the Modern World*. To Ratzinger, in particular, we owe no. 10 of the current constitution.

movement are harmful to the proper implementation of the liturgical reform. In all three areas being examined, the gratitude for the breath of the Spirit that set in motion the conciliar renewal is at the origin of patience, which is the concrete, everyday form of love. In this love, however, faith and hope are also present, the theological virtues that do not come from man but are a gift from God. Only in this way can a believer escape triumphalism, even the postconciliar variety, thus sharing the experience of Simon of Cyrene. Forced to help Jesus carry the Cross, he gradually realizes that he himself is supported and carried by Jesus on his journey. "And thus all reflections on the situation of the Church after the council always lead once again to the same point: to love, by which the Church lives, inasmuch as she receives it from the Lord and is continually called upon to give it herself."[24]

In his memoirs, Ratzinger described himself at the Bamberg conference as "more emphatic", while his bishop, Cardinal Döpfner, "expressed surprise at the 'conservative streak' he thought he detected".[25] Even more severe in his judgment was the above-cited Verweyen, who, having taught for a long time in the United States, became the spokesman for critiques coming from the American universities. Thus Verweyen said that during the Bamberg conference, Ratzinger talked about the people's disappointment, like after a big party. Actually there never was a party. The great turning point that many seemed to see with the pontificate of Pope John XXIII and with the contemporary election of John Kennedy, the Catholic president of the United States, was just a transient illusion. According to Verweyen, what had happened was an "hour of humanity", but the disciples of Jesus had once again missed their appointment because they were overcome by sleep.[26] As for Ratzinger, he was, together with Frings, part of a group that, during the council, firmly pledged to take significant steps forward, while also being concerned that these changes should be approved by the large majority of the council Fathers. With the arrival of Paul VI, though, the Frings-Ratzinger group found itself in great difficulties because the traditionalists organized and constantly gained importance in

---

[24] Joseph Ratzinger, *Das neue Volk Gottes*, 150.

[25] J. Ratzinger, *Milestones*, 134.

[26] Verweyen, *Joseph Ratzinger*, 39.

comparison with the varied progressive constellation.[27] The flaws in Verweyen's text are the very inexact reconstruction of historical events but, above all, the prejudice that views searching for as wide an agreement as possible among the council Fathers as a surrender to the traditionalists. Along this line, he interpreted as an obvious surrender the invitation to patience with which Ratzinger concluded his account of the famous Black Thursday and the exhortation not to give in to skepticism because the council is on the right path anyway.[28]

Tübingen

In Münster for only three years, at the height of a fame that now reached the general public, too, Ratzinger received a new call. The *vocatio* this time arrived from Tübingen, having originated from a surprising name, the Hans Küng who would become so controversial as a critic of the future developments of the Catholic Church. At the council, the two German-speaking theologians, almost of the same age, often shared goals and the strategies of their bishops; both took part in founding the journal *Concilium*, but they were also aware of their basic difference. Whereas Küng, in the wake of Rahner, tended to abstraction and deduction, Ratzinger, since his first publications dedicated to Saint Augustine and Saint Bonaventure, favored reflection of a historical kind. In this sense, the call of Ratzinger to Tübingen was in line with the tradition of the Catholic faculty of the city in Baden-Württemberg, which in the nineteenth century gave birth to the famous Catholic school of Tübingen, with a predominantly historical character. Johann Sebastian von Drey (1777–1853) is considered its founder, but the most prestigious name associated with it is certainly Johann Adam Möhler (1796–1838). Author of two famous works, *Unity of the Church* and *Symbolism or Exposition of Doctrinal Differences between Catholics and Protestants*, Möhler was a firm proponent of tradition as the organic development of dogma through history and of the Church understood as a mystical body.

---

[27] Ibid., 40f.
[28] J. Ratzinger, *Theological Highlights of Vatican II*, 159–61.

As we can already anticipate, Ratzinger was certainly not distant from the vision of his old precursor, whose openness to ecumenism he shared, but in doctrinal clarity, without hiding the difficulties generated by controversy and history. In his memoirs, he alluded to the charm of the Swabian city and its tradition;[29] it seems, however, that the impetus to make the move came mainly from his sister, Maria, who had not become acclimatized to the city in Westphalia and dreamed of at least coming closer to her hometown.[30] In short, Ratzinger decided to accept the call to Tübingen and began teaching there as early as the summer semester of 1966. He gave a course in Christology designed entirely as a dialogue with existentialist thought, whose representative in the faculty was Ernst Käsemann, a disciple of Rudolf Bultmann.

Initially, the attendance and enthusiasm of the students were in keeping with what had happened in Bonn and Münster. Besides being numerous, students were motivated by a lively interest, so much so that they came from other fields of study. Ratzinger, as usual, always went right to the essentials, made no concessions to rhetoric, was always attentive to his interlocutors, and accurately quoted the Church Fathers and other sources.[31] He also made a very clear distinction between freedom of theological research and the life of the Church. While he called for caution in making changes within the Christian community, especially in the liturgical field, the Bavarian professor did not hesitate to sign the declaration of Nijmegen, an appeal in which 1,360 theologians, from fifty-three different countries, demanded academic freedom and respect for the "plurality of theological schools and forms of mental openness" from the Vatican institutions, in particular from the Congregation for the Doctrine of the Faith. Even more surprising and interesting, in particular with reference to the future resignation of Pope Benedict XVI from the papacy, is Ratzinger's signature on a petition by the professors of theology in Tübingen who asked the bishops to renounce the lifelong episcopate and to set a time limit for residential bishops. For the writers of the article that explained

---

[29] J. Ratzinger, *Milestones*, 136. See also the speech at the presentation to the Pontifical Academy of Sciences, Rome, November 13, 2000.

[30] See Georg Ratzinger and Michael Hesemann, *My Brother the Pope*, trans. Michael J. Miller (San Francisco: Ignatius Press, 2011), 201.

[31] See Valente, *Ratzinger professore*, 127.

the meaning of the petition that was published by the prestigious *Theologische Quartalschrift*, the theological journal of Tübingen, the optimum duration of the appointment was eight years. Only for special reasons could the assignment be renewed or extended.

One of the promoters of the initiative and authors of the article, the professor of fundamental theology Max Seckler, testified that initially Ratzinger was the only professor of theology who did not want to sign. Then Seckler visited him to have coffee and managed to convince him to give his assent. According to Martin Trimpe, one of Ratzinger's students, the latter acted more than anything else to avoid conflicts and because he did not consider the matter particularly relevant. It cannot be ruled out, however, even in the light of the future decision to renounce the pontificate, a certain sensibility of Ratzinger, not for the abolition of the episcopate for life, but for a time limit to the exercise of the ministry. When some students marveled at finding his signature on that petition, Ratzinger suggested they write one or more articles against that proposal. And that was what Peter Kuhn and Martin Trimpe did: against the thesis signed by their professor, they published in *Hochland* a long article in two installments.[32]

Introduction to Christianity: *Best-seller around the world*

In the winter semester of 1900, the Lutheran, liberal-minded theologian Adolf von Harnack gave in sixteen lectures, at the University of Berlin, a course designed for students from all the faculties entitled "The Essence of Christianity",[33] which recalled the title of a work by Ludwig Feuerbach, published in 1841. The lectures were soon collected in a volume that became a classic of Lutheran theology, one of the cornerstones of liberal thought against which Karl Barth thundered. Where Feuerbach proved to be destructive, Harnack turned out to be reductive, subjecting God to the measure of man, who ended up taking the upper hand over God's own holiness. Later, in the late 1920s, in Tübingen, a Catholic dogmatic theologian, Karl Adam, also gave a lecture course on the nature of

---

[32] Ibid., 147.

[33] Adolf von Harnack, *What Is Christianity?*, trans. Thomas Bailey Saunders (New York: G. P. Putnam's Sons, 1901).

Catholicism.[34] In opposition to modernism, Adam argued that the Catholic Church is a community capable of acting and suffering, of praying and loving, of growing and preserving unity. Moreover, it has grown enormously since A.D. 33, the year of Jesus' death, but at the same time has preserved its identity through the centuries and in those peoples where it has spread. Adam's book, too, had a long-lasting success.

However, the author to whom Ratzinger felt closest and who inspired him was certainly Romano Guardini, who in turn published, in 1938, a book entitled the *Essence of Christianity*.[35] The Italian-German author, in the initial pages, wondered: "What is the particular quality peculiar to it alone, by virtue of which Christianity is founded and is distinguished from all the other religious possibilities?"[36] Guardini then rejected a wide range of false answers that ended up reducing Christianity to natural categories. The meaning of Christianity, therefore, must be derived from within, in particular from its essential core, Jesus of Nazareth. "Through the Incarnation of the Son of God, through the mystery of faith and grace, all creation is required to give up its—apparent—autonomy and to submit to the dominion of a concrete person, namely, Jesus Christ, and to make him its own fundamental norm."[37] Ratzinger's long confrontation with Christology would show how seriously Ratzinger had taken his reading of Guardini.

In any case, lectures directed to students from all the faculties were a gigantic undertaking in theology. On the wave of the growing popularity he had among students, in the summer semester of 1967, Ratzinger in his turn ventured to offer a similar course. In response as well to the request by the council Fathers, who asked for a simple, uniform exposition of the Catholic faith,[38] the subject was

---

[34] Karl Adam, *The Spirit of Catholicism*, trans. Justin McCann (Steubenville, Ohio: Franciscan University Press, 1996).

[35] Romano Guardini, *Das Wesen des Christentums* (Würzburg: Werkbund Verlag, 1938). Citations are from the Italian edition, *L'essenza del cristianesimo* (Brescia: Morcelliana, 2009).

[36] Ibid., 7.

[37] Ibid., 12.

[38] The same motivations were at the origin of the *Catechism of the Catholic Church* (Vatican City: Libreria Editrice Vaticana, 1992), and subsequently in the *Compendium* of that same catechism (Vatican City: Libreria Editrice Vaticana, 2005). Both editorial projects were directed by Ratzinger, amid the skepticism of many theologians. Its widespread circulation nevertheless proved that the project was initiated for the right reasons.

a general introduction to Christianity in the form of a commentary on the Apostles' Creed. It was presented in the sober form that was so dear to the author, with arguments drawn from tradition and the Fathers, but also from personalist philosophy and the Hassidic tradition. Just as he transferred to Tübingen, Ratzinger changed his assistant, and, instead of Werner Böckenförde as his right-hand man, now there was Peter Kuhn, an expert in Judaic language and literature. Students from all fields attended the two weekly lectures that took place on Wednesday and Thursday afternoon, from 5:00 to 6:00 P.M., but priests assigned to pastoral work, religious, and simple lay people also attended. Faithful to his own way of writing and arguing, Ratzinger introduced into his presentation, however, a series of anecdotes that impressed the audience and contributed to the success of the initiative.

CLEVER HANS

Among those who are not devoted to work, the example of Clever Hans became famous, the prototype of the theologian who is optimistic at all costs, who exchanges the truths of the faith for current opinions that are less and less convincing. In the end, like Hans, who started his trip with a load of gold that he trades for products of less and less value until he finds in his hands a whetstone that he then throws away, the theologian, too, ends up becoming a bearer of opinions that are completely useless. Another story that caused a sensation was the example of the theologian who, in order to make himself heard, changes his clothes and language, ending up in the situation of the clown that Kierkegaard had talked about in his day. Urged by a circus owner to ask for help from nearby villagers because a fire has broken out in the camp, he runs, without taking the time to change his costume. His haste, however, is not rewarded with success. When he arrives in the nearby village, his distressed pleas for help are welcomed by the loud laughter of the villagers. They think he is reciting his lines well, that his desperate attempts to urge them to action are just a trick to convince them to watch the show.

Hence Ratzinger's conclusion: it is not enough for a theologian or a preacher to change his clothes in order to be taken seriously. In a time when the reasons for non-belief are presented and diffused with a previously unknown vigor, the theologian must rigorously

dig into the grounds of his faith and present them frankly, even at
the risk of being ridiculed. Besides, the abyss of doubt yawns not
only in front of the believer. Even the nonbeliever must grapple
with the hypothesis that God may exist, that the believer is not
chasing fairy tales, but that he may have reasonable arguments at
the foundation of his faith. Ratzinger made use of a Jewish story,
related by Martin Buber, to suggest this idea humorously.[39] A well-
educated scholar went to visit a *tzadik* to cause a crisis in the latter's convictions, to wreak havoc with his apologetics. Upon being
admitted in the room of the just man, he was about to repeat his
arguments, which had already caused many other learned men to
question their certainties. The *tzadik*, however, did not seem to pay
him much attention. He continued to pace back and forth in his
room and only after a while glanced at him and exclaimed: "Who
knows, maybe it really is true."[40] The learned scholar sought, in
vain, the strength to reply. That observation: "Who knows, maybe
it really is true", was already making its way inside his mind.

These courageous and acute observations attracted a growing
number of auditors at Ratzinger's lectures. Peter Kuhn then had
the idea of going beyond a mere transcript for the handouts and
brought his huge tape recorder to the auditorium. The lectures,
thus recorded, were then transcribed, and, with a few corrections,
the text of the *Introduction to Christianity* was ready for the press.[41]
Published for the first time in 1968, the book was a dazzling success.
In Germany it was reprinted a dozen times in just one year; abroad
it was translated into about twenty languages. Very few books of
theology can boast such a wide readership.

THE CHRISTIAN, A CASTAWAY CLINGING TO THE CROSS

The examples admonishing the reader to consider the importance
of theology are accompanied by a powerful exhortation to rely on
faith, which, far from resulting in a protected circle or a Church
outside which there is no salvation, is support for universal brother-

---

[39] Ratzinger's comment on the little story by Buber is on pp. 46–47 of *Introduction to
Christianity*, trans. J. R. Foster (San Francisco, Ignatius Press, 2004).

[40] Martin Buber, *Werke* (Munich: Kösel; Heidelberg: Schneider, 1963), 3:348.

[41] In the original German, the book was published by Kösel (Munich, 1968) with the
title *Einführung in das Christentum*.

hood. The starting point of Ratzinger's argument is that every Christian is called to plunge into the abyss of faith, experiencing every man's condition of poverty and indigence. "The believer is always threatened with an uncertainty that in moments of temptation can suddenly and unexpectedly cast a piercing light on the fragility of the whole that usually seems so self-evident to him."[42] Even a saint like Thérèse of Lisieux, who grew up sheltered by a faith protected by membership in a remarkable family and by the high walls of the Carmel, cannot escape, at the height of her mystical experience and her earthly journey, the "worst temptations of atheism".[43] In the uncertainty that surrounds it and threatens the foundations of its faith, the soul of the believer experiences its own extreme poverty, but also the brotherhood that creates a bond with every other human being.

In this descent into the skin of sinners and nonbelievers, the believer finds himself in the situation described by Paul Claudel at the beginning of "*The Satin Slipper*",[44] the work made known in Germany by Hans Urs von Balthasar, who promoted its first performance in Zurich during the war, seeing in it a clear allusion to the world situation at the time.[45]

The beginning of the play tells the story of a Jesuit missionary whose ship has been sunk by pirates. He is adrift, clinging to a board from the sunken ship like Jesus to the Cross, but the board is not attached to anything, so that he ends up sinking in the middle of the ocean, halfway between the old and the new world. According to Ratzinger, this is the real situation in which the believer lives in our time. Only a miserable wooden board binds him to life, to God, but everything makes him think he will soon be swallowed up in the abyss, like all the other castaways from the ship. The believer, however, following the example of Saint John of the Cross or Saint Thérèse of Lisieux, does not let go of the board, knowing that it has the strength and power to bring to safety not only him but also his brother and all those who can somehow cling to it. The Jesuit Father, in fact, has a brother, Rodrigo, who is the prototype

---

[42] J. Ratzinger, *Introduction to Christianity*, 42.
[43] Ibid.
[44] Paul Claudel, *The Satin Slipper* (London: Sheed & Ward, 1945).
[45] Elio Guerriero, *Hans Urs von Balthasar* (Cinisello Balsamo: San Paolo, 1991), 86.

of the worldly man, an adventurer wandering between God and the world. Rather, Ratzinger continued (repeating an idea of his friend von Balthasar), the Jesuit, like every believer, clings to the Cross not only for himself but also for his brother who considers himself a nonbeliever, who has turned his back on God and, tired of waiting, employs all his energies to acquire the riches of this world. The brother can thus be saved, drawn by the power of those ropes and that unstable board. Even the nonbeliever, in reality, cannot stay compact and hermetically sealed in his non-faith, but he, too, is subject to the doubt that exposes him to the temptation to believe. "Anyone who makes up his mind to evade the uncertainty of belief will have to experience the uncertainty of unbelief, which can never finally eliminate for certain the possibility that belief may after all be the truth."[46]

Ratzinger's observation was a warning for the generation that was bound to face the tormented period of 1968. To the many who were about to leave the Church because they did not want to be members of a community that, both because of its historical past and because of some reductive theological views, seemed to exclude the poor, the weak, the damned, Ratzinger showed an inclusive brotherhood extending to all the sons of Adam.

GOD'S REVELATION

Introduction to Christianity rightly begins with a reflection on the act of faith. Faith is the recognition that reality is more than the sense objects that we can touch and shape, more than *factum*, something that we can transform with our hands; it is the realization that the invisible precedes the sensible and, indeed, is more real than the visible. Moreover, faith is the confident acceptance of the meaning of what is real; it is a confident stance on the ground of the *Logos*, the word of God that, for Christians, is a person whose name is Jesus Christ. And not only that. As John's Gospel says, the Word was with God and the Word was God. In the beginning, therefore, there is not an abstract thought but, rather, a relationship that, as the evangelist hastens to point out, is a relationship of love that unites the Father and the Son with one another. In love, the Father

---

[46] J. Ratzinger, *Introduction to Christianity*, 45.

generates the Son; in love, he creates the world in the image of the Son. That is why creation is full of signs that refer to God, which mankind has recognized over the centuries and transmitted through religions.

Not only that: when confronted with man's sin, as dramatically recorded in the Book of Genesis, Father and Son conceive their plan for redemption. The Son offers to come into the world; the Father accompanies the mission of the Son in the spirit of their common love. Thus, salvation history begins as a mystery of love with well-defined persons (Abraham, Moses) and with a people that likewise has a precise name: the sons of Jacob or Israel. God makes a covenant with this people, entrusts to it his law and his name. God then comes out of his secrecy and his fullness and reveals himself.

Ratzinger also stressed, however, the importance of negative theology, in which love prevails over knowledge: "We are now touching a realm . . . in which any false forthrightness in the attempt to gain too precise a knowledge is bound to end in disastrous foolishness; a realm in which only the humble admission of ignorance can be true knowledge. . . . Love is always *mysterium*—more than one can reckon or grasp by subsequent reckoning."[47]

THE LOVE THAT MOVES THE SUN AND THE OTHER STARS

The second part of the book, reflection on the Son of God, is introduced by the final verse of Dante's *Comedy*, "The love that moves the sun and the other stars", and by the entire conclusion of canto XXXIII of the *Paradiso*. The mystery of God is revealed to Dante through the human figure that shines with the very hue of the circle of God (XXXIII, vv. 130–31). Moreover, not only the Trinitarian doctrine, even Christology begins with a mystery, the scandal of the historicity of the Word that comes into the world and dies in it. The theology of the Incarnation and the theology of the Cross fuse, as is again evident in the most obvious way in John's Gospel. But this way, the meaning of everything comes to rely on a little branch that floats in the ocean of history.

To counter this objection, contemporary theologians and exegetes have ended up following the positive method of the natural sciences,

---

[47] Ibid., 162.

which are limited to cataloguing rather than interpreting or inquiring about meaning. Yet in the field of history and that of theology,
positivism creates an antithesis between meaning and history, between *Logos* and event, which leads to the denial of theology itself and of the reflection on God. The first step in this direction
was taken by Harnack in his *What Is Christianity?* Harnack focused
his attention on Jesus, stripping him of his supernatural revelatory
attributes, which are considered later additions by the evangelists.
The central statement of his work is: "Not the Son but only the
Father belongs in the Gospel."[48]

Ratzinger ironically commented: "How simple, how liberating
this seems! . . . Jesus versus Christ, and this means 'away from
dogma, onward to love'."[49] Not only that. A few decades after the
publication of Harnack's book, the anthropological optimism that
his work promoted ended up being trampled under the boots of the
marching armies. Therefore, it was necessary to change direction,
to escape the mirage of historicism so as to respond to the thirst for
the supernatural, to the question of meaning. That is what Rudolf
Bultmann did: during the years of World War II, he stated that, as
far as Jesus is concerned, the important thing was that he existed;
for the rest, faith was not based on such uncertain historical bases
but solely on his preaching, the *kerygma*, contained in the Gospels.

Ratzinger wondered: Once the question about Jesus and his person had been deemed irrelevant, was any progress made? Preaching
is important, but it loses legitimacy and meaning when it is detached
from his person. During the rest of the sixties, with the so-called
"theology of the death of God", there was once again an insistence
on Jesus as a person: we have lost God, but we have Jesus, who
is a sign of trust. "In the midst of a world emptied of God, his
humanity is to be a sort of proxy for the God who can no longer
be discovered."[50]

For Ratzinger, however, the oscillation between Jesus and Christ
that characterized the first half of the twentieth century was not in
vain. It stimulated closer consideration of the good reasons behind
the transformation of the title "Christ", Messiah, into a proper

---

[48] Ibid., 199.
[49] Ibid.
[50] Ibid., 200.

name as we understand it. Christ is, indeed, a title that indicates an office, a commission, but it is also a person, because in Jesus it is not possible to distinguish between person and office. Jesus did not accomplish a mission different from his person. Calling him Christ means affirming that he identified himself with his office, with his commission, with his word. He is the *Verbum*, the Word; he acts and gives himself; he is self-giving. Jesus said about his death on the Cross: "And I, when I am lifted up from the earth, will draw all men to myself" (Jn 12:32).

Ratzinger commented: "This sentence is intended to explain the meaning of Jesus' death on the Cross. . . . The event of the crucifixion appears there as a process of opening, in which the scattered man-monads are drawn into the embrace of Jesus Christ, into the wide span of his outstretched arms."[51] This brings us back to the Cross again. "As the crucified criminal, this Jesus is the Christ, the King. His crucifixion is his coronation. . . . His existence is thus his word. He *is* word because he is love."[52] Thus we return to the Cross about which Claudel spoke in his *Satin Slipper*. The Jesuit, like every Christian, clings to it in faith and love. Jesus Christ, indeed, is not a wreck accidentally lost in the ocean; rather, he is a person who comes from the Father for the love of mankind. Through the Cross to which Christians adhere by faith, love is revealed, which is the nature of God, the meaning of the world and of history, the path by which every man can reach God.

THE SPIRIT AND THE CHURCH

The third part of the book and of the Creed is introduced by the statement relative to the Holy Spirit. Ratzinger hastened to make a clarification. Holy Spirit here refers, not to the third Person of the Holy Trinity in his being within the divine life, but, rather, the Spirit understood as a divine gift left by Jesus to mankind. He is "the power through which the risen Lord remains present in the history of the world as the principle of a new history and a new world".[53] In this way, the article referring to the Holy Spirit

---

[51] Ibid., 239–40.
[52] Ibid., 206.
[53] Ibid., 332–33.

becomes interwoven with the one about the Church and her sacraments. It is what can be inferred from the following article on the
communio sanctorum, which must be interpreted above all as a communion of holy things, of the Eucharist.

The other article, the one on the remission of sins, primarily concerns the first sacrament of the Christian initiation, Baptism, but
soon the focus extends also to the remission of the sins of wayfarers,
of those who travel through history and always need forgiveness for
their faults and weaknesses. The connection between Holy Spirit
and Church already partially eliminates the difficulties that emerge
as soon as the Church is defined as one, holy, catholic, apostolic.
The characteristics of the Church do not depend on the observance
of the covenant with the Redeemer but, rather, are given by God in
the form of grace that continues despite the infidelity of mankind.

Lastly, the article about the resurrection of the body expresses the
New Testament hope of the resurrection of the person, the unique
human composition of body and soul. The fact, then, that "the
awakening is expected on the 'Last Day', at the end of history, and
in the company of all mankind indicates the communal character of
human immortality, which is related to the whole of mankind." [54]

Return to Bavaria

The international success of *Introduction to Christianity* [55] could not
stop the wave of protests that was spreading with astonishing speed
throughout Europe in 1968. Universities and cultural centers were
the first to be conquered. In a very short time, Tübingen became
one of the centers promoting the protest, which in Germany was
particularly rapid and violent. In his memoirs, Ratzinger examined
rather extensively the origins and causes of the protest, surely, as was
his custom, prompted by the desire to understand, but also because
that sudden detachment of the young people from the Church has
long been a wound that has healed only with the passage of time.

---

[54] Ibid., 351.

[55] In G. Ratzinger and Hesemann, *My Brother the Pope*, 204, interviewer Michael Hesemann writes: "Upon reading it, Karol Wojtyła, Archbishop of Kraków, believed he had
found a spiritual brother. Paul VI, too, was enthusiastic when the Italian edition was
published."

The causes of a cultural revolution that has few precedents in history have been examined and described at length. Here I would like to recall the reasons given by the future pontiff, with a particular focus on the situation in Germany. The change began in 1967, when Ratzinger was still giving the course from which *Introduction to Christianity* originated and it was still possible to celebrate solemnly the 150th anniversary of the faculty of Catholic theology at the University of Tübingen. On the international stage, the Americans' failure to liberate Vietnam gave way to a new ideology: the Vietcong, defenders of the poor and fighters for freedom.

In Germany, the 1966 elections made necessary the *grosse Koalition*, the grand coalition of Christian Democrats and Socialists, led by the Christian Democrat Kurt Georg Kiesinger (1904–1988). Born in Ebingen, not far from Tübingen, Kiesinger was an experienced, often controversial politician. He had been president of Baden-Württemberg for eight years, but above all he had been a member of the Nazi Party, and during the war he had worked for the Ministry of Foreign Affairs in the office for propaganda. For some time, the country's most influential weekly magazine, *Der Spiegel*, had declared a war on him, and novelists Heinrich Böll and Günter Grass had spoken out against him. The case was the beginning of a wave of revision that induced young people to blame their fathers for their past, the horror of the Shoah, that too easily had been set aside during the decades of the reconstruction. The atmosphere was explosive, and Tübingen became one of the centers for the neo-Marxist mobilization. Catholics were indiscriminately lumped in with the culprits, as guilty of collaboration with the torturers or, in any case, of having offered little or no resistance to Nazism.

The mastermind of the uprising was Ernst Bloch, who was teaching on the faculty of philosophy in Tübingen and already in the fifties had published a three-volume work, *The Principle of Hope*, in which he maintained that hope and utopia are at the origin of human action. A staunch atheist, he referred to secularized Jewish-Christian Messianism as the new driving force in history. In a short period of time, students adhered with enthusiasm to these very generic, vague theses and subjected to a critical review all of past history, especially Christian history. One might have expected a reaction from the theological faculties to such a radical protest. Instead, the

Lutheran-Evangelical faculty, in particular, became the loudspeaker for the most extreme theses. They began to circulate leaflets that contained the slogan "Cursed be Jesus", while the Cross was denounced as "a sado-masochistic glorification of pain".[56]

Ratzinger had had no protests against him personally, but remaining silent and pretending that nothing was happening seemed to him like a betrayal. Moreover, in 1968, when the protest reached its heights, he was the dean of the Catholic faculty of theology. In that same year, Küng, who had been ousted, took a leave. Ratzinger, on the other hand, made friends with two Lutheran-Evangelical professors, the patrologist Ulrich Wickert and the missiologist Wolfgang Beyerhaus, who, like him, thought that they should never surrender to the outrageous tactics of students who made violence the ultimate weapon in their arguments. "They would interrupt the lecture screaming or went onto the rostrum to force the professor to answer to their 'revolutionary' questions."[57] Then they stormed the academic senate yelling, and some professor tried to seek a dialogue making attractive promises. Ratzinger, on the contrary, collected his paperwork, said goodbye, and left. In those months, the dean of the Catholic faculty of theology received a new offer.

In 1967, finally implementing an old project, the Free State of Bavaria had opened in Regensburg the fourth university of the southern region of Germany. From the beginning, the management had thought about Ratzinger for the chair of theology, but, at the time, he had just arrived in Tübingen and so refused the offer. Two years later, as they made progress in the work of consolidating the new university, they thought about a second chair of dogmatic theology, and again Ratzinger's name was at the top of the list of the possible instructors. Between the end of 1968 and the beginning of 1969, he received the new proposal, again in an informal way, and this time his response was favorable.

Ratzinger had not found things bad in Tübingen, where, among other things, his requited passion for cats was born, but the atmosphere in the faculty of theology had become overheated. Regensburg, on the other hand, where his brother Georg was already living, offered the possibility to return home, to reunite the family,

---

[56] Ibid., 203.
[57] Testimony by Martin Trimpe, recorded by Valente, *Ratzinger professore*, 139.

and, after the busy years of the preparations for and the proceedings of the council, to develop his own theological thought in the quiet of a brand new university. The move took place in November 1969. As on other occasions, his students came to his aid. The first trip was particularly adventurous. Books and clothes were packed in a van, Ratzinger and his sister, Maria, were accompanied by a student priest, the Augustinian Father Lehmann-Dronke, driving a car that, needless to say, was full of books. Upon their arrival at the outskirts of Regensburg, the car was stopped by the police because of the obvious overload, but then the amused policeman let pass the two priests, who had claimed to come from Bierbronnen.[58]

Regensburg, city on the Danube

Regensburg, about sixty miles north of Munich, cannot boast a great tradition at the university level, but it was very attractive for the professor who was, by then, at his fifth university campus. First of all, there was the European river par excellence, the Danube. In Regensburg, the Danube is not yet such a heavily traveled river as the Rhine in Bonn, but it has greater solemnity and already gives an idea of all the cities and states through which it is about to pass. If the Rhine put the professor in communion with the countries of Northern Europe, here the Danube was the gateway to Austria, Hungary, and the countries of Central Eastern Europe. Then there was its history. Regensburg had fortunately been spared the bombing and could still show the *Porta praetoria* (Praetorian Gate), built in the second century by the emperor Marcus Aurelius as a defense and, at the same time, an entrance into the Roman Empire. There was Saint Peter's Cathedral, an important example of the French Gothic style in Germany, where the *Domspatzen*, "the cathedral sparrows", sang. The boys' choir had been conducted for quite a few years by his brother, Georg, and the professor, who loved music, made friends with the singers. Georg said that his brother used to keep Saturdays and Sundays free for visits with his family. "He also made an effort to keep in close contact with the Domspatzen."[59]

---

[58] In German, *Bierbronnen* means "beerspring". Obviously, the policeman concluded that books and beer had gone to the heads of the two priests.

[59] G. Ratzinger and Hesemann, *My Brother the Pope*, 207.

In the early days, Joseph lived in a rented house and commuted to the university by public transportation or with the not-so-new cars of his students. The faculty of theology took the place of the diocesan College of Philosophy and Theology, and, at first, it inherited its headquarters as well, in the cloister of the Dominicans where, at the origins of the order, Saint Albert the Great had taught. Pretty soon, however, even the faculty of theology had its own house in Pentling, where the remaining premises of the university were located. With the help of a capitular canon, Professor Ratzinger, too, found a lot right near the university, bought it, and, with the help of the architect Hans Scheininger, built a comfortable cottage.

In the middle of the yard surrounding the house, a bronze fountain was built, in the shape of boat, in which the three Ratzinger siblings sat invoking the Virgin. A gesture of Marian piety, but also a sign of his great fraternal love and his ties to his family, which one must always take into account in his life. In one corner, on the other hand, was placed a sketch of a cat,[60] a sign of an affection for felines that would accompany the future pontiff over the years. All these were signs that pointed to his intention to make this house the safe harbor of his academic journey and his life.[61] His brother, Georg, said: "Even when the house was completed, my brother always came first to my place on Sundays to have a midday meal together at the refectory of the Domspatzen. Only then did I ride with him out to Pentling, where we drank coffee together with our sister and spent a pleasant evening. There we could converse and relax."[62] Every morning without fail, the professor went to say Mass in the rectory, accompanied by Maria. The parishioners, when they saw them arrive, would say to one another, jokingly: "Look, Joseph and Mary are arriving!"[63]

In the faculty, the situation was very different from Tübingen.

---

[60] "In Tübingen . . . [there was] an itinerant cat that . . . came to visit him every day and was fed by him. It even accompanied him to his lectures and to Mass. It was a black cat, a very intelligent pussycat. Once a man on the street spoke to him and asked him . . . how he had trained the cat so well that it walked beside him." G. Ratzinger and Hesemann, *My Brother the Pope*, 205.

[61] In a meeting that I had with the cardinal in 2005, a few months before his election to the papacy, he told me, with obvious pleasure, that he was looking forward to returning to his house in Regensburg.

[62] G. Ratzinger and Hesemann, *My Brother the Pope*, 206–7.

[63] Valente, *Ratzinger professore*, 151.

There was no great tradition here, but neither was there the haughtiness of the Swabian city. Professors represented all trends, but all felt free in their choices; they had no cumbersome models to contend with.

The other dogmatic theologian was Johann Auer, with whom Ratzinger had been acquainted since the time he was a student in Munich. Auer already had made a career for himself, but he certainly did not have Ratzinger's fame; yet the two had a mutual esteem and, in time, would find ways to collaborate quite intensively. Representing the new trends was the professor of fundamental theology, Norbert Schiffers, who was close to liberation theology. And, as if to refute in advance those who over the decades accused him of being opposed to exegetical research, Ratzinger also had good relations with the exegetes Franz Mussner and Heinrich Gross.

Moreover, Ratzinger had learned from the conciliar experience the importance of dialogue and attention to others. Rigorous in his thought, he was polite and accommodating in practical matters, and, for this reason, colleagues chose him for increasingly difficult academic duties. He would have liked to avoid them so as to take up again the thread of his theological research, which was too often interrupted, but, in the end, he did not escape from the vote of his colleagues, who chose him at first as dean of the faculty and then as vice-rector of the university. As always, he gave the best of himself during his lectures, which he prepared with meticulous care. As an appendix to his book on Ratzinger's years as a professor, Gianni Valente compiled the complete list of the courses and seminars given by the professor. Just scanning the index, you can get a sense of the rigor of the system. In the lectures, the subjects from systematic theology predominate; in the seminars, more space is given to sources and current topics.

Clearly, the professor of dogmatic studies did not spare himself when he recommended to his students that they keep their critical mind alert. One of his students, Joseph Zöhrer, said that once, during a lecture, a student tried to present, too emphatically, a thesis based on a quotation from Rahner. Ratzinger replied ironically: "It is strange that, after legitimately declaring your own skepticism about the formula *Roma locuta; causa finita*, now you move, without batting an eye, to the formula *Rahner locuto; causa finita*."[64]

---

[64] Ibid., 154.

The professor and his students

One academic tradition that Ratzinger had fully developed over the years was that of the *Doktorvater*, the professor who accompanies those students who are preparing for a doctorate and to qualify for academic teaching. Remembering the ups and down of his own *Habilitation*,[65] he wanted to be really close to those young men who, after completing their university lectures and examinations, set out on the open sea of research. Moreover, because he always had so many students, he had many doctoral theses to follow. Consequently, he could not assist each student individually, but he organized the *Schülerkreis*, literally "the circle of students", the group of students working on their doctoral theses. The intent was not to start a theological school, much less a pressure group to favor academic or ecclesiastical careers, but to help young men to acquire their own research methodology.

Initially, Ratzinger's group of students was not much different from the others. In Bonn, he had still been too young to give his own imprint to it; in Münster, too involved with council-related duties. In its unique form, the group took shape in Tübingen, but it really acquired its own character and functionality in Regensburg. Students usually gathered every other week, generally on Saturday morning. The meeting began with the celebration of Mass. Then, after a brief introduction by the instructor, each student in turn explained the purpose and status of his research. This way, the professor could assess the progress of the work and the methodological ability acquired and then politely gave suitable recommendations. Usually he did not intervene very much, nor was he very critical. This task was carried out, sometimes with excessive zeal, by the doctoral candidates themselves.

One feature appreciated by everyone was the great freedom guaranteed by the *Doktorvater*, who rarely rejected a topic or imposed one of his own. A brief review of the subjects most frequently chosen by Ratzinger with and for his students confirms the range of the professor's interests but also his generous willingness to tackle

---

[65] J. Ratzinger, *Milestones*, 112–13.

new issues.[66] I will recall the most important. First of all, the theses of historical character, dedicated to the great theologians and thinkers of the past: Ignatius of Antioch, Irenaeus, Athanasius, Hilary, and Augustine; then, there were studies on the medieval masters: Bonaventure, Thomas Aquinas, Alexander of Hales, Rupert of Deutz, Honorius of Regensburg, and Gerhoh of Reichersberg; another core of historical theses concerned theologians and thinkers linked to the Protestant Reformation and the Council of Trent. Finally, there were the contemporary themes, in which two currents can be recognized: critical confrontation with philosophers and writers like Nietzsche, Camus, Jaspers, and Bloch; studies on theologians like de Lubac, von Balthasar, Congar, Rahner.

This variety might lead you to think that the approach was fragmented. However, according to Stephan Horn, who after Kuhn was Ratzinger's assistant in Regensburg, the professor, unlike Rahner or Pannenberg, was not interested in investigating reality starting from his own point of view. On the contrary, he drew abundantly from the Scriptures and tradition in order to enter into a critical and constructive dialogue with the problems of the day. His intent was to add to the breadth and richness of the living tradition, considered not only in its organic development, in its heights and depths, but also in the elements of fracture and polarity that give birth to other questions and other possible insights.

Firmly rooted in tradition, Ratzinger proved to be particularly attentive and open to ecumenical dialogue. He had already been introduced to it by Professor Söhngen at the time of his studies in Munich. Subsequently, however, he did not miss a chance to attend ecumenical working groups. In Bonn, he got in contact with the first core group of ecumenical dialogue founded by Pastor Wilhelm Stählin and by the bishop of Paderborn, Lorenz Jäger; in the federal capital, he also got in touch with the two young Orthodox theologians whom we have already mentioned, Damaskinos Papandreou and Stylianos Harkianakis, with whom he would maintain friendly relations throughout his life.

---

[66] Stefan Otto Horn, "Il cardinale Ratzinger e i suoi studenti", in Josef Clemens and Antonio Tarzia, *Alla scuola della verità: I settant'anni di Joseph Ratzinger* (Cinisello Balsamo: San Paolo, 1997), 11.

Stephan Horn reprinted the text of a letter sent by Cardinal Ratzinger to Metropolitan Papandreou to thank him for the wishes the latter had sent to him for his fiftieth birthday. The cardinal wrote:

Your presence at the lectures profoundly and incisively marked my life. Before then, I knew the Eastern Church from books, from icons, and even from participation in great liturgical events. However, only through personal meetings did it come closer to me with its vital force and become a tangible presence that has proved to be effective in my theological thought, in my faith, and in my life, while, before then, it remained for me concealed in something a bit exotic and archaic.[67]

The variety of the topics of the dissertations chosen by the professor for his students was matched by the diversity of the origins of Ratzinger's *Schülerkreis*. The early seventies were the golden age of theology, and Germany was considered to be its homeland. Among Ratzinger's students, therefore, there were priests and religious, lay men and lay women, Germans, Europeans, Americans, Africans, and Asians. For this reason, too, meetings were always fascinating, an opportunity to become acquainted with new worlds, new ways to approach theology and the problems of faith.

Then there were the meetings with the great theologians of the time, made possible by the esteem surrounding Ratzinger. Following Peter Kuhn's suggestion, this custom began in 1967, still during the Tübingen years, with a trip to Basel. There, a few hundred yards away, on the two banks of the Rhine, lived two of the greatest theologians of the time: Karl Barth and Hans Urs von Balthasar. The group of students had the opportunity to meet them both, and the experience made a lasting impression. Karl Barth, already advanced in years, was conducting at the time a seminar on *Dei Verbum*, the conciliar constitution on Divine Revelation, with an earnestness and a commitment that astonished the students. They had prepared many questions, but Barth was, instead, interested in posing questions to Ratzinger, who at the council had participated in the preparation of that document.

The following year, the group from Tübingen crossed the border into France and traveled to Alsace to meet Yves Congar. The

---

[67] Ibid., 12.

experience of the war and of long sufferings endured within the Church had made the theologian of the Ardennes frank, almost to the point of severity, in personal encounters; since the time of the council, he had been particularly respectful of Ratzinger's intelligence and wisdom in dealing with complex and controversial issues. For this reason, he welcomed his students courteously and spoke with them about ecclesiology and pneumatology, about dialogue with Churches and Christian communities.

Among subsequent meetings that are worth remembering were those with the Protestant theologian Pannenberg, with the future Cardinal Kasper, and with Rahner in 1977, a few months after Ratzinger's elevation as cardinal, to talk about his Christology. Stephan Horn wrote about this meeting: "An intense discussion developed. In no other case was I so sorry that the dialogue had to be interrupted after just two days."[68] Again, an indirect disproof of Ratzinger's alleged close-mindedness, of his seeking refuge in a theology sheltered from the troubles and investigations of modern theologians.

Another initiative, primarily intended for the students of the *Schülerkreis*, or at any rate for students of theology, was started by Ratzinger in the seventies, starting from the awareness of the limits of a theology developed only on writing desks. The abandonment of the clerical state by some priests or else by students almost at the end of their studies of theology was obvious proof of those limitations. Von Balthasar had already spoken, in the fifties, about this division between theological reflection and life, but, even before that, Ratzinger remembered the example of Guardini, who had not only done great work at the university, but had opened, in the Rothenfels Castle, a spiritual center that gave concreteness and expansiveness to his academic work. Thus he became the educator of a whole generation of young German Catholics, who only in this way were able to resist the lures of the Nazi ideology.

Ratzinger had something of this sort in mind, but in a more limited form because of the different historical situation, when one of his students, Johannes Lehmann-Dronke, told him about an old farm, owned by the Countess von Stockhausen, that had been turned into a center for studies, located in an enchanting place near Lake

---

[68] Ibid., 15.

Constance. Hence the idea to start, along with his friend Heinrich Schlier, the Protestant exegete who had converted to Catholicism, a summer course of theology "in which the serene and informal coexistence in everyday things made the dialogue and the common prayer more fruitful". Together, the former disciple of Bultmann and the conciliar theologian taught the concrete way to approach the figure of Jesus, not only in a correct perspective from the exegetical-theological point of view, but also in a prayerful attitude, which is the indispensable method by which to overcome the historical distance and to recognize Jesus as the Christ. He is the dead and risen Lord of whom Guardini spoke, the contemporary who gives himself to the faithful in the sacraments and to whom, according to Ratzinger, even today's believer can open his heart in trust and adoration.

The experiment was carried out assiduously by the two professors until 1978, the year of Schlier's death. Stephan Horn remembered: "It was fascinating for the students not only to be able to discuss with the professors, but also to be able to go out for brief walks with them and, above all, to enter into spiritual harmony. It was natural to celebrate Holy Mass every day and to sing Compline at night. There was also the opportunity to recite the Rosary together in the village church."[69] The *Schülerkreis* was so important to Ratzinger that he would continue the meetings with his students even long after having left the university and, obviously in a scaled-down form, even during the time when he was a cardinal and then pope. Then-Cardinal Ratzinger declared in 1995, during an interview with Peter Seewald: "For me a very important experience, also humanly speaking, was the fact that I didn't work with the doctoral candidates individually; rather, every week we worked together for about two hours, and each one took turns presenting the results of his research and submitting them to discussion. I think that everyone gained by that."[70]

---

[69] Ibid., 18.

[70] Joseph Ratzinger, *Salt of the Earth*, trans. Adrian Walker (San Francisco: Ignatius Press, 1997), 65.

VI

JOY OVER A RENEWED
ENCOUNTER WITH THEOLOGY

At home in a new place

The move to Regensburg assured Ratzinger of the peace and quiet that he desired, which also restored to him the joy of a renewed encounter with theology. After such a frantic sprint through various university posts and the council sessions, the theology professor, whose volume *Introduction to Christianity* was making its way around the world, had finally landed in a place that seemed definitive. In Regensburg, moreover, the Ratzinger family was back together: Joseph and Maria found Georg there, who, for his part, as director of the chorus of *Spatzen* (sparrows), was in a happy phase of his life. Several of his performances of Schütz, Bach, Vivaldi, and Monteverdi had received international recognition. In 1976, the millennium of the famous choir was celebrated with great solemnity.

Ratzinger, furthermore, after the difficult years in Tübingen, had the impression that he had finally acquired his own vision of dogmatic theology,[1] which seemed to open up for him the path to a period of fruitful production, an opportunity to write regularly and not just occasionally. He felt therefore newly at home, not only in the physical sense of a place where he could build a dwelling in which to spend the rest of his life together with his siblings, but also in the sense of a cultural and spiritual home, convinced that he had found and could develop his own theological method, harmoniously based on Scripture, the Fathers of the Church, and tradition. By living in Regensburg, therefore, he was not relegated to a far-off

---

[1] Joseph Ratzinger, *Milestones: Memoirs 1927–1977*, trans. Erasmo Leiva-Merikakis (San Francisco: Ignatius Press, 1998), 150.

corner of Germany, distant from the major centers of culture, as his detractors hoped. On the contrary, he was increasingly involved in responsibilities that prepared him for tasks that were at the moment unforeseeable.

The International Theological Commission

Among the many initiatives undertaken by Paul VI to implement the desires expressed by the council Fathers during Vatican II was the institution in 1969 of the International Theological Commission. Just as the synod of bishops, in collaboration with the Secretariat of State and the Roman Curia, was supposed to assure the participation of the bishops in the government of the universal Church, so too the Congregation for the Doctrine of the Faith was supposed to take into account the major role played by the theologians at the council and to assure them of a hearing, which was to provide input for the decisions made by the former "Holy Office". The commission was made up of thirty theologians from various schools and nations, chosen by the pope based on information provided by the prefect of the congregation. Among the first appointees, who are called to remain in office for five years, were above all the theologians who played a decisive role at Vatican II, including, of course, Ratzinger. Several times a year, therefore, the professor from Regensburg had to go to Rome to debate new perspectives of theology concerning issues that were particularly delicate for the life of the Church. This allowed him to remain in contact with the major theologians who had already distinguished themselves at Vatican II but also with up-and-coming scholars.

The proceedings of the Theological Commission, nevertheless, were not a calm debate among colleagues; rather, they reflected the atmosphere of great uncertainty that was tearing apart the life of the Church in the immediate postconciliar period. Its work therefore made slow progress and proceeded amid harsh criticism and disputes. Some Central European theologians, unlike those who were collaborating with the journal *Concilium*, were impatient with the tiresome work of applying the reforms headed by Paul VI. They wanted to proceed in haste with ever more daring changes. Some asked for the abolition of priestly celibacy; others fought for a Church that would adopt as her own the laws of parliamentary democracy. And when anyone objected that such provisions were not present in the documents that had been approved at the council, they answered by invoking a "spirit of the council", which, however, is difficult to define.

The pope, for his part, had to remain faithful to the task of preserving the unity of the Church, which was threatened by opponents of a conservative stripe, who, on the contrary, were hostile to any change, especially in the liturgical field. Within the Theological Commission, the viewpoint of the progressives was upheld with growing radicalism by Karl Rahner, the Jesuit theologian with whom Ratzinger had had the opportunity to collaborate during the first session of the council, and Johannes Feiner, a Swiss ecumenist, editor-in-chief of *Mysterium salutis*, an encyclopedia of dogmatic theology that had a wide readership in those years. After increasingly heated debates, the two theologians polemically left the commission, which, in their opinion, was good for nothing, since neither the congregation nor the pope was taking their work into account in any way. Various theologians of the commission, nevertheless, did not agree with the position of Rahner and Feiner. Being more thoughtful, Henri de Lubac, Hans Urs von Balthasar, Joseph Ratzinger, Marie-Joseph Le Guillou, and Jorge Medina felt increasingly uneasy about an aggressive theology that distanced itself more and more decisively from tradition and from the Fathers of the Church in search of an *aggiornamento* that, in their view, ends up being a surrender to the world.

On the one hand, they wanted to support the pope and those who were working at the laborious task of purifying and renewing the Church; on the other hand, they noticed the urgency of defending the faithful who were bewildered by the often ungenerous accusations that were being leveled against the Church. De Lubac, who had had to suffer so much for having looked forward to and promoted the return to the Fathers of the Church, certainly did not intend to give up their theology, which is centered on the sense of mystery. Moreover, he was literally wounded by the lack of love for the Church evident above all in his Order, the Society of Jesus, and then among the many churchmen who in the decades before the council had been overzealous activists and had now become inexorable critics of the Church and of Paul VI.[2]

---

[2] I refer here to many conversations that I had with Father de Lubac in view of the publication of the Italian edition of his works by Jaca Book of Milan.

Hans Urs von Balthasar, for his part, though completely misunderstood, maintained his program of "razing the bastions". The dismantling of the ancient wall was supposed to allow all nations to see the Heart of Jesus Christ burning with love, his descent into hell in order to bring the good news of salvation to all mankind, not to lead the faithful to take the broad path of mimicking the world in the world. That is how one ends up sprinkling every modern custom with the waters of baptism. The theologian from Basel was among the most decisive. He, who had not been invited to the council because of a snub that de Lubac had described as "disconcerting" and at the same time "humiliating",[3] maintained that at a time when most people have become inflexible with the Church, ready to denounce her every defect, the first task of the theologian and of the Christian believer is to live in communion with the Church and then to speak up in her defense. Notwithstanding all the human weaknesses, she is the bride of Christ, the mother whom Jesus on the Cross left in Mary to his disciples.

Communio: *A program for the theology and the life of the Church*

Ratzinger had a great affinity for von Balthasar and de Lubac. He wrote in his memoirs: "Never again have I found anyone with such a comprehensive theological and humanistic education as Balthasar and de Lubac, and I cannot even begin to say how much I owe to my encounter with them."[4] Like those two masters, who were originally from Switzerland and France, respectively, he did not read works of theology and philosophy exclusively, the disciplines at the heart of dogmatic theology, but was attracted also by music, literature, law, and, more concretely, the life of the Church, the liturgy, because of its importance in relation to God and the life of the simple faithful. In short, the three theological friends, on the occasion of a meeting of the Theological Commission, found themselves together one evening with Le Guillou and Medina in a Roman tavern. They spoke once again about their uneasiness, but also about the need to make their voice heard. Some of them, among

---

[3] Henri de Lubac, *The Church: Paradox and Mystery*, trans. James R. Dunne (Shannon, Ireland: Ecclesia Press, 1969), 103.

[4] J. Ratzinger, *Milestones*, 143.

them von Balthasar and Ratzinger themselves, had been among the collaborators on *Concilium*, but now they felt the need to distance themselves from it and were speculating about a new journal entitled *Communio*. Its supporters were not thinking primarily of polemics against *Concilium*. They did, nevertheless, want to speak frankly and to have the courage to take as their point of departure, in their articles, communion in the sacraments and in the faith that they shared with the bishops, but also with the people of God, with the simple faithful for whom, as Jesus said, the Father has a special love (Mt 11:25f.).

From this perspective, the new journal intended to make accessible and to develop the new ecclesiology proposed by the conciliar Constitution on the Church. Based on these fundamental convictions, several guidelines for the new publication were established. Precisely out of the respect due to the readers, the journal, which did not mean to address specialists exclusively, but also the simple faithful, would not have one central editorial board and not even just one edition but, rather, a group of editorial centers corresponding to the number of countries or linguistic areas in which it was present. Nevertheless, the role of coordinator among the various editions was immediately assigned to von Balthasar, and, as long as he lived, the Swiss theologian was universally considered to be the one who inspired *Communio*.

That being said, each editorial center was fully autonomous and, in fidelity to the common inspiration of them all, could draw on the patrimony of articles made available by all the editions. At the same time, however, it could and should also produce articles from its own language area, so as to be closer to the thinking of its own readers. The result was that the issues of *Communio* offer both articles in common and articles proper to each language edition. This makes for a dense, surprising forest in which it is not easy to untangle oneself, which nevertheless forms an abundant, luxuriant whole. Moreover, from the very start, both clerics and laymen were invited to join the various editorial boards. Ideally every editorial board was supposed to be composed of one-half clerics and one-half laymen, just as every issue was supposed to contain on average an equal number of international articles and national articles.

At first, the journal was to be published simultaneously in Germany and in France. Because of difficulties that arose in the latter country, for the first issue, scheduled for the beginning of 1972, there were two editorial boards, located, however, in Germany and in Italy. In the German-speaking area, besides von Balthasar and Ratzinger, who together with de Lubac are to be considered the founders of the journal, others joined the initiative: Karl Lehmann, Rahner's former assistant and at that time professor of dogmatic theology in Freiburg; Hans Maier, then minister of public schools in Bavaria; the psychologist Albert Görres and Otto B. Roegele, a professor of journalism in Munich. An invaluable role was played then by Franz Greiner, former editor-in-chief of the periodical *Hochland*. He was the coordinator of the group and took care of the printing, administration, and circulation of the journal.

Talk about a possible Italian edition of *Communio* started in late 1970. Then, in early 1971, there was the meeting of four young people[5] from the Communion and Liberation movement with von Balthasar,[6] who, at the end of their conversation, told them: "Ratzinger. You have to talk with Ratzinger. Today he is the decisive man for the theology of *Communio*. He has the pivotal role in the German edition . . . if he agrees."[7] After a few weeks, during Lent, Angelo Scola explained,[8] the little group made their second journey, this time to Regensburg. Ratzinger welcomed them courteously, listened to what they had to say, and marveled at their enthusiasm. At the end of the meeting, he gave his assent, not so much because of their theological convictions as because of their ecclesial enthusiasm, because of their membership in or else closeness to Communion and Liberation.[9]

After another working meeting conducted in Zurich in 1971, the Italian editorial board was now ready in turn to move on to the production phase. The first editorial group included, besides the

---

[5] They were Angelo Scola, future bishop and cardinal, Eugenio Corecco, professor of canon law then bishop of Lugano, Giuseppe Ruggieri, the first editor-in-chief of the journal, and Sante Bagnoli, an editor.

[6] See the amusing, impassioned account of that meeting made by the current archbishop of Milan, Angelo Scola, who was part of the small group, in Josef Clemens and Antonio Tarzia, *Alla scuola della verità: I settant'anni di Joseph Ratzinger* (Cinisello Balsamo: San Paolo, 1997), 169ff.

[7] Ibid., 170.

[8] Ibid., 171.

[9] J. Ratzinger, *Milestones*, 144.

three young people mentioned above,[10] Father Giuseppe Colombo, a well-known theologian from the theological faculty in Milan; the psychologist Giacomo Contri; Virgilio Melchiorre, an instructor of philosophy at the Catholic University of Milan, and Father Luigi Serenthà, a Milanese theologian. On the Italian editorial board, too, the presence of laymen was rather important; although the C&L members of the editorial board had taken the initiative at first, from the very beginning there was an almost equal number of editors who had had no experience in the movement. The first editor-in-chief, Father Giuseppe Ruggieri, was not a member. Simultaneously with the German edition, the first issue of the bi-monthly Italian journal appeared in January 1972. Made up, as mentioned before, of international and Italian articles, the first issue featured in particular two articles, by von Balthasar and de Lubac respectively, that outlined the purpose and the program of *Communio*.

The Swiss theologian began:[11] The observation post of the journal is the Christian community in its dynamic, irreducible tension between God and the world. In the first Christian centuries, the tension manifested itself in the consciousness of the little group that had been formed and nourished by the love of God, manifested and bestowed by Jesus Christ and called to move about in a dark, hostile world. At the same time, however, the Church has always felt that she is catholic, that is, the herald and bringer of salvation to people throughout the world. This simple faith, sustained by the Holy Spirit, was what enabled Christians to grow and to spread in the Hellenistic world until Christianity basically became coextensive with civil society. This congruence continued throughout the Middle Ages, endangering the tension between the faith and the world since, even though the Church had reached almost complete equality in society, at least in the West, the penetration of the world with the Christian leaven remained a very problematic task that was far from accomplished.

After many warnings from the saints, the Protestant Reformation started the breakdown of the simple congruence, highlighting the frailty of a society that could describe itself as Christian in name

---

[10] Strictly speaking, the editor was not part of the editorial board.

[11] Hans Urs von Balthasar, "Communio: un programma", *Communio* [Italian edition] I (1972): 3–12.

only. In our days, too, there is no need to do away with the tension between the Church and the world. Geographically, this is a statement that needs no proof. Spiritually, on the other hand, the program of *aggiornamento* cannot eliminate the tension between God and the world, between the Christian community and civil society, but at most can make it more evident, more fraught with the scandal that comes from the Cross of Christ, from the wounded side from which gush the blood and water of the sacraments of salvation. In the Christian community, too, the tendency toward the universal must remain alive, because if it is not universal, Christianity ends up on the dung-heap of religious rejects. Von Balthasar concluded: "We will try with *Communio*. Not on the lookout, much less starting from a capitalistic ownership of the truths of the faith. We have already said how this truth in which we believe leaves us exposed. Like sheep in the midst of wolves. This exposure is not about bravado but about Christian courage."[12]

De Lubac's article entitled "Credo sanctorum communionem" integrated the programmatic proposal of the Swiss theologian with the teaching of the Fathers of the Church. The communion of saints, the French theologian explained, should be understood primarily in the neuter plural, as a communion or sharing of holy things, the mysteries of Christian worship. Participation in these mysteries, above all in the Eucharist, is what generates interpersonal communion among Christian believers, who have been sanctified by Baptism. "The communion of saints among themselves is the fruit of the communication of the holy things to each one of them."[13] This truth, de Lubac concluded, had been proclaimed and extolled by Vatican II. The new journal, therefore, was situated in turn along the conciliar line, without racing ahead but rather in a spirit of service.

Ratzinger's first article in the Italian *Communio* appeared in issue 3 of 1972 and bore the title "Beyond Death".[14] As we will have reason to observe later in this same chapter, in fact, Ratzinger was working at that time on the set of problems related to eschatology,

---

[12] Ibid., 12.

[13] Henri de Lubac, "Credo sanctorum communionem", *Communio* [Italian edition] 1 (1972): 29.

[14] Joseph Ratzinger, "Al di là della morte", *Communio* [Italian edition] 3 (1972): 9–18.

the events concerning the end of the world and of mankind, and anticipated in the journal several very interesting approaches.

Nevertheless, what I urgently wish to note at the conclusion of this section on *Communio* is the echo of von Balthasar's call to Christian courage in Ratzinger's writing. In the preparatory meetings for the journal, the future editors had spoken about it several times. For Ratzinger, the heart-felt invitation by the theologian who wrote *The Glory of the Lord* had become a significant legacy, which would inspire several of his more important decisions. It was also a warning that he often repeated to bishops, priests, theologians, and all who have authority in the Church. I reprint here a quotation from a conference given to commemorate the twentieth anniversary of the journal, given at the Gregorian University in Rome in 1992. On that occasion, as editor-in-chief of the Italian edition of *Communio*, I was at his side and could observe how the cardinal, engrossed, almost trembled with emotion while pronouncing the words that are worth reprinting at length. After telling about the origin of the journal and about its spread to more than ten countries or language areas, he continued:

> There is still no reason to be self-satisfied. I cannot help but think about a sentence of Hans Urs von Balthasar: "It is not a matter of bravado, but of Christian courage, to expose oneself to risk." Have we been courageous enough? Or have we in fact preferred to hide behind theological learnedness and tried too often to show that we too are up-to-date? Have we really spoken the Word of faith intelligibly and reached the hearts of a hungering world? Or do we mostly try to remain within an inner circle throwing the ball back and forth with technical language?[15]

It remains to be said that *Communio* has had a broad circulation with numerous national or language editions. In Europe, it has appreciably helped our continent to breathe with both lungs, to use an expression of John Paul II, who sponsored the Polish edition of the journal; in the United States, the editorial board included members of the John Paul II Institute in Washington; in Latin America, it had a more difficult life, yet it has kept alive the bond of catholicity in countries like Argentina and Brazil. Various editors of the journal

---

[15] Joseph Ratzinger, "Communio: A Program", *Communio* [English edition] 19 (Fall, 1992): 436–49 at 448–49.

have later gone on to important careers in the life of the Church, just as many who have collaborated with the journal worked with Ratzinger either in the years when he was prefect of the Congregation for the Doctrine of the Faith or during his pontificate.

Jews and Christians, one covenant

The idea of the *Shoah*, the Holocaust, of how the extermination of Jews was possible in a country that called itself Christian, of how Christians were able to tolerate or at least not to do everything in their power to oppose it, worried not only the young Germans in 1968. Even before then, it had aroused the interest of a group of young German Christians who had founded an association called the Junger Bund, the Young Alliance. It came to be headed by a young woman, Traudl Weiss, who previously had been active in traditional Catholic associations, together with the priest Aloys Goergen. During the first years of the association, the main driving force had been the priest, but the events of 1968 made a change necessary. Traudl, who in the meantime had married the lawyer Herbert Wallbrecher, went with her husband in 1967 on a long trip to Israel. They struck up friendships with people from the Jewish world, and this gave rise to a spiritual affiliation that led to the rediscovery of truths that were so obvious as to be banal: Jesus and the Twelve were Jews, God's covenant with his people was never abolished, Israel remains the root on which the Church grew.

These are the basic ideas from which then developed the Katholische Integrierte Gemeinde, the Catholic Integrated Community, founded by the couple with the support of the auxiliary bishop of Paderborn, Johannes Joachim Degenhardt. The community, however, was focused, not solely on the past, but, rather, on rediscovering the ancient heritage, intended to live in the present and to have an effect on worldly reality. Although religions generally think about the interior, spiritual realm, Judaism is quite attentive also to the reality of the world, to the society surrounding it. Therefore, the members of the Integrated Community took initiatives at the social level, also, for which they alone were responsible. The communities then appeared as little oases of common life that ideally were inspired by the first Christian community in Jerusalem. The concrete model, on the other hand, was that of the Israeli *kibbutzim*, with which the representatives of the community maintained relations that became more intense with time. Most of the members of the community lived in extended families composed of twenty to twenty-five persons. They were a concrete, peaceful example of the utopian communities for which so many young people in 1968 longed.

They were viewed as such by Ludwig Weimer, a young man from Lower Franconia who was studying philosophy, theology, and German, first in Würzburg and then in Munich. He therefore entered the Integrated Community and became one of its staunchest members. After completing his studies in theology with a thesis entitled "Religion and Revelation in Ernst Bloch", he moved to Regensburg to obtain his *Habilitation* to teach at the university and came to join the group of students that had Professor Ratzinger as their advisor. The latter assigned to him a demanding thesis on the relation between grace and freedom, which kept the young man busy from 1974 to 1979. In turn, Weimer introduced his professor to the Integrated Community. This gave rise to a bond of friendship that never diminished, despite the difficulties encountered by the community both in Germany and in Rome.

Professor Ratzinger, who was so dedicated to teaching and study, was for his part seeking something concrete, a place in which Christian teaching became lived praxis, with regard to both prayer and everyday life. Then there is the other even more significant aspect. Like many of his compatriots, the professor of dogmatic theology perceived the enormity of the extermination, of the atrocities committed by his people at the expense of the Jews, and he wanted to help somehow to eradicate anti-Semitism, the fruit of prejudice and ignorance. Nothing could be better, therefore, than rediscovering the Hebrew roots of the Christian faith, not from the perspective of surpassing it, but from that of complementing it.

As a tree that was grafted onto an old trunk bears the fruits of the graft but also receives the sap that comes from the root, so it is with the Christian faith. It was grafted onto the root of Jesse, the father of David, and has at its foundation the ancient root that it can never renounce. Thus, in-depth study of the themes belonging to the Old Covenant can only benefit Christians, who, when they acknowledge their debt, must necessarily set aside their prejudices and cultivate feelings of solidarity with the people from whom the Messiah came: the Savior.

Especially in its beginnings, however, the path of the Integrated

Community was not a smooth one. The basic idea of Traudl, who with the passage of years became the real guide of the group, was that the faith must permeate the life of the community entirely, in its individual and social aspects, in private and in public. The children of the members always received a biblical name, in the political field they constantly sided with Israel, and the entrepreneurship of some members of the group, including the lawyer Wallbrecher, Traudl's husband, was promoted. These policies were based on the conviction that there should be a religious foundation for every department of life, but, as one can easily imagine, they met with suspicions and prejudices. Outsiders accused them of being a wealthy sect, while within the ranks of the Church herself some looked with suspicion at a community that was not only autonomous with respect to the many powerful German ecclesiastical structures, but many times critical also about the organizational model of the Church herself and about the diocesan administrative structures that often collaborate with and compete with the public ones.

Another ground for accusation was the originality of the liturgical reform adopted by the community, which incorporated ancient and recent models of the Hebrew liturgy. Then there were the rumors of those who, after being drawn to the experience of integration, then abandoned it, accusing those in charge of abusing authority and of imposing their own authority to the point of plagiarism and psychological subjection. In vain, Traudl and her husband requested a meeting with the archbishop of Munich to explain their position, the interior impulse that was guiding them on their path. Several times they wrote to the authoritative Julius Cardinal Döpfner, who was also president of the German Bishops' Conference, but they never received a response, and then, in 1976, they launched a sensational protest. Members of the community entered simultaneously into four German cathedrals and started a "demonstration of continuous prayer".

The news was reported prominently by the newspapers, and the symbolic gesture of the occupants was for the most part ridiculed and criticized. Among the few who dared to take up the defense of these very unusual demonstrators was Professor Ratzinger, who maintained that praying is a right of every believer. In the end, Cardinal Döpfner received the leaders of the community and offered them words of reconciliation. In the houses of the community, the enthusiasm for the cardinal's encouraging words was still undiminished when, a few days later, news arrived that once again called everything into question. At 8:00 in the morning of July 24, Cardinal Döpfner, who was only sixty-two years old, died of a heart attack.

It was a great loss for the city of Munich, for Bavaria, and for the German Church, but also for the universal Church, since quite a few thought of him as the successor of Paul VI. It was, moreover, a loss for the Integrated Community, for which the survival and approval of the archbishop of Munich was indispensable. A period of uncertainty followed that ended in the early months of 1977 with the surprising nomination of Ratzinger as archbishop of Munich. This initial good fortune was followed a year later by more substantial support. Despite the fact that only eighteen months had passed since their arrival in the diocese, and that not many in the Curia regarded the Integrated Community sympathetically, on December 7, 1978, having just returned from Rome where he participated in the conclave that elected the new pope from Poland, Ratzinger officially approved the statutes of the community in the Diocese of Munich provisionally for a five-year period.

According to the statutes, the community, to which both families and individuals belong, seeks to "make the Gospel present in the world separated from the Church in such a form that those who are distant can also find a new way to the Church's faith".[16] The members of the community undertake common initiatives in the economic, healthcare, and educational fields. The community, which has various centers in Germany, Austria, and Tanzania, was recognized as an apostolic community as described in the Vatican II decree *Apostolicam actuositatem*. With that same document, Cardinal Ratzinger confirmed the election of Traudl Wallbrecher as head of all the Integrated Communities, while he appointed the priest Peter Zitta, originally from the Diocese of Vienna, as ecclesiastical assistant of the Integrated Community in the Diocese of Munich.[17] In particular, he was responsible "for the doctrine, for the administration of the sacraments according to the ecclesiastical precepts, and for the unity of the community".

---

[16] Cf. Peter Pfister, ed., *Joseph Ratzinger und das Erzbistum München und Freising: Dokumente und Bilder aus kirchlichen Archiven, Beiträge und Erinnerungen* (Regensburg: Schnell und Steiner, 2006), 335.

[17] Ibid.

A final appointment followed, that of the priest Dieter Katte, as liaison between the community and the presbyterate of the diocese. The series of decrees by the archbishop was complemented by a letter sent to the general leader, Traudl, and to all the superiors of the individual houses; the letter explained two points that were to be considered "fundamental intrinsic presuppositions" for the recognition:

- With this step, the way of life of the Integrated Community is considered a possible way of living the faith concretely in the Catholic Church. For its part, the community takes its place in the Catholic Church without any pretense of exclusivity, therefore recognizing other old and new forms of accomplishing this purpose;

- the celebration of the Holy Eucharist is the central form in which unity with the universal Church is brought about. Therefore, it is important that it be celebrated with full respect for the ecclesiastical ordinances. And, therefore, it is necessary that the liturgy of the word not take precedence over the part that is more strictly sacramental and also that ultimate responsibility for the proclamation of the word in the Eucharist must be reserved to the priest.

Notwithstanding the conditions spelled out with the indispensable juridical precision, given the conditions at that time, the approval of the community by the young archbishop was a courageous gesture. It showed openness to the lay world that, notwithstanding the repeated statements of an ecclesiological character made in the Constitution on the Church, the clergy generally regarded with mistrust. Above all, the Integrated Community would prove to be for Ratzinger the opportunity to come into closer contact with the Jewish world. This closeness provided occasions to give concrete expression to grief over the crimes committed against the Jews for which the German people had made themselves responsible during the war.

Ratzinger, like the generation of those who had seen the horrors of war with their own eyes, had thrown himself into his studies immediately after the war, which was his way of participating in the rebuilding of his country. Now, in contrast, the hour had come for an opportune, mature reflection on the meaning of the Holocaust. During the long years in which he would then journey with the Integrated Community,[18] this grief would then be transformed positively into a progressive appreciation of the heritage of Israel's piety and thought. Not only that; the dialogue would prove to be fruitful for the future pontiff's own work: Mary, Daughter of Zion, the continuity between the synagogue and the Church, the many religions and the one covenant, the dialogue with the Orthodox Jew Neusner concerning Jesus in the first volume of *Jesus of Nazareth*— all these are topics that come from the encounter with the heritage of the faith and culture of Israel that was facilitated by his closeness to the Integrated Community. Above all, the topic of the many religions and the one covenant, to which we must return later, represents a turning point for Catholic theology, the import of which has not yet been fully evaluated either on the Jewish[19] or on the Catholic side.

Eternal life: The soul is indispensable

Eschatology is one of the major theological topics at the end of the second millennium and the beginning of the third about which Ratzinger spoke up not only independently but almost completely alone. Whereas Catholic theology and, even more so, Catholic preaching seem to have put this subject in a corner and mentioned it only in passing and with more or less embarrassment, Ratzinger dedicated attention that was neither sporadic nor transitory to the final realities. Moreover, it was easy for him to show that the themes related to death and eternal life, which are certainly present in the early days of Christianity, have by no means become less important in our time. As the French historian Jean Delumeau testified, the

---

[18] In 2006, on the occasion of the thirtieth anniversary of Ratzinger's first encounter with the community, Father Ludwig Weimer, together with Traudl Wallbrecher and Arnold Stötzel, published a book entitled *30 Jahre Wegbegleitung Joseph Ratzinger/Papst Benedikt 16. und die Katholische Integrierte Gemeinde* (30 years of accompaniment: Joseph Ratzinger/Pope Benedict XVI and the Catholic Integrated Community) (Bad Tolz: Ursfeld, 2006). Two other volumes by Father Weimer on Ratzinger's dialogue with the Jewish world are: *Maria non senza Israele: Una nuova visione del dogma sull'Immacolata Concezione* (Bari: Ecumenica, 2010); and *L'ebreo Gesù di Nazaret: Un contributo al dialogo tra Jacob Neusner e Benedetto XVI* (Milan: Marietti, 2011).

[19] This, at least, was Rabbi Neusner's opinion when I met him in 2007.

aspiration to eternity is a fundamental idea of every religion, not only Christianity, and it certainly cannot be set aside by new waves of theology.[20]

In the preface to the first edition[21] of his volume dedicated to eschatology, Ratzinger recalled that twenty years had passed since 1957, when at the age of thirty he had given the course on eschatology for the first time. Since then he had not only addressed over and over again the topics that emerge from it, but had made a true *retractatio*, an abrupt reversal with respect to the question of the soul. In his early years of teaching, indeed, he had adopted the program of so-called de-Platonized eschatology that entirely denied the idea of the soul, which was considered to be of Platonic origin and foreign to the world of the Bible. Later on, however, he had changed his mind, rediscovering "the inner logic of the Church's tradition".[22]

An article entitled "Beyond Death" published in *Communio*[23] set forth clearly the reasons for his retraction. Ratzinger remarked: the rejection of the soul causes problems that are surely no less serious than the difficulties that it eliminates. If we no longer speak about the soul, then what does the resurrection of the body mean? And if the latter takes place "at the end of the ages", what will happen in the meantime between the death of the individual and the final resurrection? Will there be total sleep or complete death? But, in that case, what does that mean for the identity between the dead person and the resurrected person? The difficulties begin to be resolved if we overcome the concept of linear time, of final realities that follow the end of time when eternity will begin. The *eschaton*, eternity, begins for each one of us at the end of our time. And, therefore, this is one reason to take seriously our life in this world and our encounter with Christ. Every death lands in eternity, in the encounter with the Risen Christ, who has won eternity for us.

In order to justify the reasoning just presented, however, it is necessary to recover the concept of the soul. It is true, Ratzinger wrote, that this concept comes from Greek philosophy and was in-

---

[20] Jean Delumeau, *Alla ricerca del Paradiso* (Cinisello Balsamo: San Paolo, 2012), 5f.

[21] Joseph Ratzinger, *Eschatologie: Tod und ewiges Leben* (Regensburg: Pustet, 1977, 2007); trans. Michael Waldstein and Aidan Nichols, O.P., as *Eschatology: Death and Eternal Life* (Washington, D.C.: Catholic University of America Press, 1988), xiii.

[22] Ibid.

[23] J. Ratzinger, "Al di là della morte", 148–61.

troduced late and rather hesitantly into Christian tradition.[24] Nevertheless, we need to add that even intertestamental Judaism was acquainted with images that clearly differentiated life from the state after death. There is continuity, therefore, between the faith of Israel and the apostolic preaching, with the decisive correction that, for Christians, "everything must be seen and experienced starting from Christ and with reference to Christ".[25] This work, too, of carrying over to Christ the materials derived from the Jewish tradition took time. In the long term, therefore, Christian eschatology essentially came to coincide with the Jewish form of it, while limiting itself to placing the new center in Christ, the Risen Lord, in whom his followers live after death.

An awareness developed, therefore, of an eternal life that is granted to everyone after the death of the individual and before the definitive coming of the future world. In this way, the person's identity is preserved beyond the existence of his body. The conceptual instrument through which this identity is affirmed is the soul. The term is not unknown to the New Testament, which uses it to signify precisely that aspect of one's identity which goes beyond death. The expression, nevertheless, came from the Greek milieu and was connected with their dualistic vision of the world. For this reason, a long process of purification was necessary, which was carried out after the completion of the first millennium, above all by Saint Thomas Aquinas.

As contemporary scholars demonstrate, the Dominican saint's vision of the soul is radically new with respect to the ancient teaching of Plato and Aristotle. This does not mean that elements of dualistic thought have not in fact been introduced in contemporary popular thinking. For this reason, Ratzinger continued, it is necessary to continue the work of purifying, and, for this purpose, he advised recourse today to dialogical-personalist thought. The soul, which, for the Scholastics, was what differentiates man, what constitutes him in his humanity, in his vocation to the truth, is for supporters of dialogical thought fundamentally the call that God addresses to man, inviting him to a dialogue of love. Whereas according to Saint Thomas the human soul was the vocation to the truth and, therefore, incorruptible and eternal, for the dialogicians it is essentially

---

[24] Ibid., 155.
[25] Ibid.

the dynamic of love. It is "the dynamic of an infinite opening that simultaneously signifies participation in the infinite and in eternity: one who is inserted into the dialogue of love with God does not die. The love of God confers eternity."[26]

Eschatology

MY MOST HIGHLY DEVELOPED AND ACCURATE WORK

When Ratzinger arrived in Regensburg in the late 1960s, Johann Baptist Auer, professor of dogmatic theology and history of dogma, whom he had already met at the University of Bonn, was editing a *Small Catholic Dogmatic Theology* in paperback format that was supposed to serve as a *vademecum* for students. Auer had already finished the fifth volume, *The Gospel of Grace*, yet both the professor of dogmatic theology and the publisher, Friedrich Pustet, insisted that Ratzinger not only contribute something as an author but also join the whole project as co-editor. Initially, the newcomer sought to evade the commitment, but then he ended up accepting it. Two topics would be assigned to him to treat: the introductory volume, an *Introduction to Theology* that Ratzinger was no longer able to write because of his election as bishop of Munich, and the volume on eschatology. The theologian had given his first course on eschatology exactly twenty years before, in 1957 in Freising. The treatise on eschatology, therefore, was the one that he had worked on longest and that required less reworking for publication.

This circumstance prompted him to begin his collaboration with the *Small Dogmatic Theology* precisely with the volume on eschatology. As a result of the long preparation for it and the serenity that he rediscovered, Ratzinger always considered that book his "most thorough work and the one I labored over most strenuously".[27] Together with the volumes on Christology, with which it also has remarkable points in common, it is also the work in which the author is convinced that he is saying something new and original in the panorama of contemporary theology. Hence, his concern about the continual updates of the book. For the sixth edition, in 1989, he

---

[26] Ibid., 158.
[27] J. Ratzinger, *Milestones*, 150.

added an illuminating account of the debate that had followed the publication of the book and also his commentary on a declaration of the Congregation for the Doctrine on the Faith that clarified that "the idea of the soul [is] indispensable for the discourse and thinking that belong with faith".[28]

Finally, as one last confirmation of Ratzinger's interest in this work and in eschatology in general, in 2006, already as pope, he wrote a new preface to the work that was neither predictable nor conventional but intervened again in the debate and gave a more clearly christological orientation to his eschatology, in keeping with the growing interest in Christology, to which, even as pontiff, he would dedicate his attention and his efforts as a scholar and a writer.

TRANSITION FROM AWAITING THE END TO CHRISTOLOGY

After leading a tranquil life at the margins of the proclamation of the faith over the course of several centuries, eschatology, Ratzinger remarked, based on a similar statement by Hans Urs von Balthasar,[29] became almost unexpectedly a central, burning topic in theology starting in the early twentieth century. The exegetes were the ones to call attention to the centrality of the proclamation of the imminent coming of the kingdom in the preaching of Jesus.

The numerical data undeniably support the biblical scholars' statement: the term "kingdom" or "reign" occurs 122 times in the New Testament, 99 times in the Synoptic Gospels, a good 90 of which are to be attributed to Jesus himself. Hence the conclusion that the word "kingdom" has a fundamental importance in the Gospels. One confirmation of this is the petition for the coming of the kingdom in the Our Father, which must be understood as a prayer in view of the imminent end of the world. However, in the transition from the pre-Paschal preaching to the post-Paschal apostolic preaching, the proclamation of the kingdom was gradually replaced with preaching about Jesus.

This transition, nevertheless, far from being a betrayal, as the exegetes suggest, is the expression of the tradition's fidelity to the

---

[28] In the English edition of 1988, the two articles mentioned here are found respectively on pp. 261–74 and 241–60. The sentence quoted here is on p. 261.

[29] Hans Urs von Balthasar, "Lineamenti dell'escatologia", in *Verbum caro: Saggi teologici*, vol. 1 (Brescia: Morcelliana, 1968), 259f.

word and work of Jesus. The gradual replacement of the expression "kingdom of God" with the preaching of Jesus does not scandalize the faithful at all because the kingdom of God was not meant to indicate a transcendent reality concerning the afterlife and the future but, rather, God's action in history, in the present. Now, according to the Old Testament tradition, God's intervention had to come about through the Messiah, through Jesus, whose novelty results not only from the content of his message but also from the authority with which he pronounces it. According to the exegetes, therefore, he had never claimed the title of Messiah for himself; only the inscription on the Cross would attribute it to him unequivocally and definitively.

This linkage to the Cross, therefore, would lead to two inescapable consequences. The title Messiah-Christ must be situated at the basis of the entire Christian creed; with the linkage to the Cross, the title acquires a radically new meaning, along the lines of the tradition of the major prophets. "Appropriately enough, given this foundation, Jesus' proclamation of the Kingdom of God is shot through with a sense of the urgency of the present moment. It does not take as its subject speculations about the where and when of space-time. At its heart stands the person of Jesus himself. Its fundamental categories are grace and repentance."[30] This allowed Ratzinger to conclude that Jesus did not announce an explicit Christology, yet the lines of his preaching lead to it. He is the eschatological kingdom of God; he is God's victory in the form of humility, poverty, and welcome.

Hence, it is advisable once again to ask ourselves about the imminent expectation of the kingdom. This is certainly present, but it is not unambiguous, and it cannot be made a criterion for determining the antiquity and authenticity of Jesus' statements. Two principles for exegesis can be derived from it: the word of Jesus exists only and always as a word that is heard, as a word that is transmitted by the Church. In conformity with this, the Gospel is not found apart from the Church as an independent, self-enclosed reality. In particular with reference to eschatology, we can observe a distance between the literary schema and the contents, which are different in the individual Gospels. This happens because the content is still

---

[30] J. Ratzinger, *Eschatology*, 30.

open. The future does not happen independently of the faithful, apart from the Church and all mankind.

The literary data offer the narrative and interpretative schema; later history becomes part of the tension of the text itself. This explains the reason why the Gospel of John, written a generation after the Synoptic Gospels, could examine in greater depth the word that had been received and explain it with greater clarity for the readers. This process of assimilation and accompaniment of the word is destined to last for all of Church history. The Lord has his time. Christians know that Jesus came, and for them this is a reason for joy. They know also, however, that the time in which they live can be both the time of the oppression of God in this world and also the time of sowing the seed that bears fruit for all mankind. This is their knowledge but also their hope.

In our time, Ratzinger concluded, there have been various interpretations concerning the impact of eschatology on Christian life: from the existential reading of Barth and Bultmann, to the salvation-history reading of Oscar Cullmann, to the interpretation of realized eschatology of C. H. Dodd. Then there are the more recent views, those of the theology of hope and of political theology, which take the history of the world into greater consideration and end up transforming eschatology into a political utopia, proposing again the ancient error of the Zealots.

There is nothing else to do, then, but to return again to the figure of Jesus Christ. He is the Son, and his kingdom is built on self-emptying and self-gift. The answer to the question about the kingdom is therefore the Son. By becoming sons, the faithful can, in turn, enter into the kingdom. Not as objects, but as subjects, as persons who have become children through love. In this direction, there is an opening made by hope, which "exists only where there is love". Hope really can spring eternal because "in the crucified Christ, love prevailed and death fled vanquished."[31]

HOPE BEYOND DEATH

The contemporary world, according to Ratzinger, has a schizophrenic attitude toward death. On the one hand, in everyday life people tend to hide the reality of death as much as possible. On the

---

[31] Ibid., 66.

other hand, television and the other media propose a spectacular view of death in which the event is presented in an entirely natural way, eliminating any metaphysical or transcendent question whatsoever. The difference between the traditional approach to death and the contemporary one becomes particularly evident in the contrast between a petition from the litany of the saints and everyday thinking. Whereas in former times the faithful prayed, "Deliver us, O Lord, from a sudden death", most people nowadays would prefer a sudden, unexpected death. This flight from death out of fear of pain, however, has unfortunate consequences for human life itself, which becomes impoverished, deprived of its distinctive character, which is connected to the hope of immortality, the continuation of life after death.

On this point, the modern mind-set receives the support of exegetes who say that in the Bible death is not transfigured idealistically but is experienced in its full, crude realism. There can be no doubt: death swallows up the entire human being; only the resurrection guarantees the hope of a new life. As Ratzinger recalled in the above-cited article in *Communio*, this agreement between the modern mind-set and the conclusion of the more radical exegetes raises many more problems than it solves. In a particular way, "resurrection becomes a mere cipher whose content mutates according to the philosophical convictions of the writers concerned."[32]

In order to get out of this seemingly no-exit situation, Ratzinger followed several guidelines by Helmuth von Glasenapp. According to this great scholar of religions in all civilizations, in the beginning we find the mythical, contented satisfaction in this world that is perpetuated through the generation of children. Nevertheless, death is never absolute, both Hades and *sheol* allow a shadowy existence while awaiting a definitive fate. In the transition from the sixth to the fifth century B.C., nevertheless, in Greece as in Israel, there was a crisis that led to an increasing spiritualization. As an antidote to the dissolution of the *polis*, to the injustice of tyranny and violence, Socrates offers an alternative vision of man: in order to live in justice and truth, man must be more than just *bios*, simple biological existence. He thus becomes a sort of martyr, a witness to the spiritual truth about man that goes beyond death.

---

[32] Ibid., 75.

In the Bible, in contrast, the mythical view that well-being follows right action is challenged critically and definitively with the Wisdom books of Qoheleth and Job. The bitter skepticism of Ecclesiastes shatters any remaining hope placed in the expectation that well-being will smile upon the upright man. On the contrary, experience amply shows that the arrogant and the violent are the ones who enjoy life in this world. Hence, the rebellion of Job, who, against the advice of his friends, is not willing to acknowledge any guilt that could justify his disgrace but, rather, calls on God in the hope of renewed, definitive life. Along with the sapiential writings, there is also the way opened up by the major prophets, particularly by the songs of the Servant of God in Second Isaiah. For the suffering servant, sickness and death no longer have an exclusively negative meaning, but must be confronted positively on behalf of others, in vicarious substitution. Thus they become the way in which the suffering servant clears for sinners the path that leads to God.

The path thus pointed out is examined in greater depth by the psalms. In this regard, Ratzinger cited two passages that will then be repeated extensively in the New Testament. Psalm 16 arrives at full confidence in God, distancing itself definitively from the worship of local gods. This psalm says: "My body also dwells secure. For you do not give me up to Sheol, or let your godly one see the Pit. You show me the path of life; in your presence there is fulness of joy, in your right hand are pleasures for evermore" (Ps 16:9–11). Even though the psalm does not speak explicitly about immortality, God's vital force appears stronger than corruption and death and can show the way that leads to a new life. The other passage to which Ratzinger referred is taken from Psalm 73, which opens with a statement about the goodness of God and about the foolishness of the psalmist who wavers by envying the mighty upon seeing the success of the wicked to whom nothing bad ever seems to happen. Then, however, while praying in the temple, the psalmist has an extraordinary experience; based on it, he understands how empty and illusory is the happiness of a man far from God who amasses wealth and power. Then he decides to entrust himself completely to God: "You guide me with your counsel, and afterward you will receive me to glory. . . . My flesh and my heart may fail, but God is the strength of my heart and my portion for ever" (Ps 73:24–26).

A further step that already clears the way leading to the New Testament is taken by the so-called martyrological literature that is situated in the context of the persecutions of the Jews in the Hellenic period. Belonging to this literary genre are the Book of Daniel, the Book of Wisdom, and Second Maccabees. These are the most recent texts of the Old Testament, which aggravate, so to speak, the situation already described in Psalm 73. Here the believer is called to choose, not between two types of life, but rather between continuing life at the price of renouncing faith in God, or else renouncing his own life in the conviction that God's justice will be able to give him a better life. The Maccabee brothers confront death in the conviction that "he who dies into the righteousness of God does not die into nothingness, but enters upon authentic reality, life itself."[33]

Here emerges the experience in which communion with God signifies life beyond death. In order to express this concept, the Book of Daniel and the Second Book of Maccabees resort to the predominantly Oriental model of resurrection, while the Book of Wisdom cites the Western, Greek model of the soul. Ratzinger could therefore conclude his excursus on death in the Old Covenant with a statement that not only opens the door to hope in eternal life but establishes a connection between soul and resurrection. At this point, the New Testament does not need to develop a specific vocabulary to express the martyrdom of Jesus, his passage from death to life. The martyrdom and Resurrection of Jesus, the just man, concretely actualizes the vision of Psalm 73 and the confident hope of the Maccabees. There is, nevertheless, an extension of the meaning in the descent of Jesus into *sheol*, into the impure place where God is not glorified, indeed, into the place of cruel distance from God. When facing biological life that is thwarted by pain and death, man can react by closing in on himself or else by accepting pain and death in the love that comes from Jesus. "Man's enemy, death, that would waylay him to steal his life, is conquered at the point where one meets the thievery of death with the attitude of trusting love"[34] that is offered to him by the Son of God.

---

[33] Ibid., 91.
[34] Ibid., 97.

This love, nevertheless, does not exempt us from the possibility of pain and death, which indeed become our way of participating in Christ's martyrdom, in the love that is the nature of the One, Triune God. Flight from pain and death is flight from life. Only definitive life, eternal life in God, definitively makes us safe from death.

THE IMMORTALITY OF THE SOUL AND THE RESURRECTION OF THE DEAD

The New Testament's provenance from the world of Judaism dispenses the Christian authors to a great extent from the task of developing their own vocabulary relating to the state of those who have died in Christ. The essential novelty is precisely the expression "in Christ", whereby life after death becomes christological and acquires a life that is fundamentally related to that of the Risen Christ. Moreover, the good thief receives the promise that on the very day of his death he will be with Christ in paradise, while Saint Stephen on the point of death calls out: "Jesus, receive my spirit." For Saint Paul, finally, death is gain because earthly dissolution means being with Christ. Although this was the common faith of the first-generation Christians, the terminology used to express it was almost exclusively drawn from the language inherited from Judaism.

Two points were certain, according to Ratzinger: death in Christ guaranteed that the believer would survive between death and the final resurrection; the vehicle through which the believer continued being with Christ was indifferently called soul or spirit, as in the Judaic tradition. Nevertheless, the anthropological implications of these last two terms had not been examined in depth. Thomas Aquinas, at the height of the Middle Ages, was the one to develop a concept of soul capable of answering the many anthropological questions to which a response had not yet been given. The Dominican Doctor adopted the Aristotelian definition of the soul as form of the body, but transformed it radically by connecting the soul also to the spiritual element, which for Aristotle was absolutely ruled out. The soul, for Thomas, was therefore the element that in a human being is united both with the body and with the spirit. "The soul is the 'form' of the body. . . . Conversely, the form of the body is spirit, and this is what makes the human being a person."[35]

This doctrine was widely accepted in the Middle Ages in the West, apart from a decisive objection by Luther, and in Catholic countries it was retained for a long time as a convincing vehicle to express the anthropological presuppositions of faith in the Resurrection of Christ. In the twentieth century, however, the exegetes ended up blaming the soul for importing the dualistic view of man belonging to the Greek world. In order to avoid this danger, which implied disdain for the bodily element, they rejected the concept of soul and limited themselves to repeating the ancient terminology, of Jewish provenance, for the Resurrection of Christ. Ratzinger did not rule out the possibility that the dualism lamented by the exegetes may still be present in popular thinking. Nevertheless, the concept of soul elaborated by Aquinas had correctly overcome the Greek dualism, just as it was able to answer several questions that otherwise remain unanswered.

Again, Ratzinger explained that the unity of the human being on which the exegetes insist is certainly a significant fact. But who can imagine a resurrection of the body immediately after individual death, given the current findings of science? And if, on the contrary, the resurrection of the dead occurs at the end of the world, who or what guarantees the identity of the person who has died in Christ with the person who rises at the end of time? The refusal to answer these questions would end up relegating Christians to a sort of supernaturalism that would distance them from human rationality. Hence, the necessity of recourse to a convincing anthropological vision in order to explain what happens in the intermediate time between the individual's death and the end of the world, the universal end of history.

RATZINGER'S SOLUTION

Ratzinger's proposal foresees the revival of the concept of soul elaborated by Saint Thomas, while insisting on two significant emphases or corrections. The first concerns the dialogical character of immor-

---

[35] Ibid., 148–49.

tality. Whereas Saint Thomas, with the definition of soul as "form of the body", seemed to overemphasize the essentialistic nature of the soul, the German theologian, in order to preserve God's initiative, proposes speaking about the dialogical character of immortality. In this regard, he cited at length a famous homily by Saint Gregory of Nyssa on the beatitude of the pure of heart who shall see God.[36] The consuming Greek desire for the vision of God is humanly doomed to fail because, as the Bible repeats many times from the Pentateuch to Saint John, no one can see God; anyone who sees God dies. Therefore, according to Saint Gregory, man's situation can be compared to that of Peter, who, venturing out onto the water of the Sea of Galilee, is not able to float and is about to sink. Only the hand extended to him by the Lord can save him. Consequently, only the faith and love with which the believer grasps the hand extended by the Lord can save him.

Man is therefore a being who is capable of knowing and loving God only in faith. He attains immortality, not by self-enclosure, but by opening himself to God's offer of love. This way salvages both the primacy of God's initiative and the dialogical nature resulting from the christological vision and the link with matter, the human body. This latter transition suggests Ratzinger's other emphasis, aimed at avoiding the notion that immortality is the privilege of the faithful alone, from which those who do not believe are excluded. The search for God, which is equivalent to the tendency toward truth and love, is not something superadded to human nature. Instead, this openness, this tendency, is the deepest thing there is in a human being and at the same time is given by God in such a way as to be part of human nature, of what a man has in common with all other human beings. At the same time, this tendency toward the supernatural[37] is the *proprium* of his person, which distinguishes him from all other created beings.

---

[36] Gregory of Nyssa, *Oratio 6 De beatitudinibus*, PG 44:1263–66.

[37] In this reflection, too, Ratzinger relies on Father de Lubac, whose *Surnaturel*, published immediately after World War II, was a true revolution in Catholic thought. When he then adds that de Lubac arrived at this revolution above all through his return to the Fathers of the Church, we find another element in common between the most influential *periti* of Vatican II, who, right after the council, were labeled as conservatives and replaced by new, improvised masters.

RESURRECTION OF THE SOUL

After examining the concept of immortality, Ratzinger now set out to examine in greater depth the concept of resurrection, to which contemporary exegetes resort in order to express the life of the believer after death. This deeper understanding, in his opinion, is reached by answering two questions. The first concerns the state of the believer after death: the Gospels say that he is now with Christ. Afterward, though, will there still be something, the end of human history, a last day of mankind and of the world? The second question concerns matter: Does the final resurrection involve the human body and the whole cosmos, too? Saint Paul and Saint John clearly state that the resurrection of the body will occur at the end of the ages, when all of God's creation will enter into salvation. The literature of the first Christian centuries, in turn, underscores God's fidelity toward his entire creation, not only toward the spirit. In this regard, it is necessary to reject both the danger of the excessive spiritualism of the Greeks and the temptation of a naïve naturalism that appears repeatedly in the Carolingian era.

Thomas Aquinas, by purifying the concept of soul borrowed from Aristotle, took the step by which it became possible to formulate a non-sensualistic realism on the basis of which the soul can never renounce its relation with matter. Upon the death of the individual believer, therefore, the identity of his body is no longer determined by the body, which is destined for corruption, but is, rather, determined by the soul.

THE FINAL RESURRECTION AND THE RETURN OF CHRIST

At this point, though, two questions arise almost automatically: After death in Christ, will there still be an end of human history, a truly last day? Does Christ's Resurrection concern also the resurrection of matter, of the human body, and of the universe as a whole? In this regard, exegetes for the most part answer that the New Testament contains no instructive statements. Ratzinger objects that, like the Jewish world of its day, the New Testament is acquainted with an intermediate stage of being with Christ. Moreover, Saint Paul certainly renounces a naturalistic, physicalistic interpretation of the resurrection because flesh and blood cannot inherit the kingdom of

God.[38] This, nevertheless, does not prevent him from continuing to speak about the resurrection of the body, not in the sense of a return to the ensouled body, but modeled after Christ's Resurrection as corporeality that comes from the Holy Spirit.

Spiritualization, nevertheless, involves not only the human body but all of creation. On this point, the Christian tradition of the first centuries is thinking not so much of the development of human capabilities but rather about God's fidelity to his entire creation. On the other hand, man, who with death exits from history, does not lose contact with it. For Christians, the link to time of those who are dead is fundamental and results from the Christian vision of God, who cares for every fragment of time granted to man and to all creatures. In this regard, Ratzinger quoted an extraordinary homily by Origen. Commenting on the words of Jesus during the Last Supper, "I tell you I shall not drink again of this fruit of the vine until that day when I drink it new with you in my Father's kingdom",[39] the Alexandrian theologian observed: "As long as we do not act in such a way that we can mount up to the Kingdom, he cannot drink alone that wine which he promised to drink with us. . . . Thus it is that he waits until we should be converted."[40] But Jesus is not the only one who waits; the patriarchs, prophets, and saints are waiting. "You will have joy when you depart from this life if you are a saint. But your joy will be complete only when no member of your body is lacking to you. For you too will wait, just as you are awaited."[41]

This observation allows Ratzinger to draw another conclusion: man's sin is not the only thing that delays Christ's return to earth; so does his love for mankind, for sinners, which is shared by the saints' love. Although sin shackles time, love is openness to time, a petition for the gift of time for sinners. This is not only the reflection of great thinkers—Ratzinger referred in particular to Heidegger—but also the insight of a humble, simple saint like Thérèse of Lisieux, guided exclusively by her love. Ratzinger therefore concluded that Christians cannot have doubts about the intermediate time after

---

[38] 1 Cor 15:50.
[39] Mt 26:29; Mk 14:25; Lk 22:18.
[40] Origen, *Seven Homilies on Leviticus*, cited by J. Ratzinger in *Eschatology*, 185.
[41] Ibid., 186.

the death of the individual human being and about the communion of saints, but neither should they have doubts about the return of Christ and about the final judgment. In this regard, the only things that can be taken as certain are the call to vigilance and the certainty that Jesus' final coming, as in the case of his earthly birth, surpasses our ability to imagine it. This is why in reference to this subject, the Bible itself resorts to images that are for the most part liturgical and cosmic. Their purpose is to reveal and at the same time to protect from curiosity the love of him who on the Cross brought time to completion and at the same moment, with his two hands outstretched, holds it open, waiting to be able to embrace all mankind.

For her part, the Church experiences and celebrates the liturgy, the "feast of hope-filled presence directed towards Christ, the universal ruler".[42] This hope is not opposed to the judgment that is awaited as the revelation of man's liberty, through his choice with regard to the Father and his Son, Jesus. In reality, Christ does not judge but rather loves. The sole objective of his coming is the salvation of all, the purpose of his life is to build up a body in which all will be able to meet again in fullness, and this will be eternal life. This consideration makes room for the hope that every human being and the whole cosmos will be saved.

HELL, PURGATORY, HEAVEN

The hope for the salvation of all mankind cannot eliminate from the New Testament the many passages that clearly foresee the possibility of eternal perdition, of *hell*. It is equally true, however, that together with the authors who insist on describing the suffering of the damned, even in the first Christian centuries there were thinkers like Origen who opposed this conclusion in the name of the doctrine of God's mercy. In the centuries closer to our day, the possibility of eternal damnation has been called into question increasingly by saints and theologians. For his part, Ratzinger maintained that the possibility of eternal damnation is based on God's great respect for man's freedom. Irrevocable ruin exists inasmuch as man, in his freedom, can make that choice. Jesus Christ, nevertheless, entered

---

[42] Ibid., 204.

into the freedom of sinners and pierced it with the superior freedom of his love that descended into hell. For some modern saints, among them Saint John of the Cross and Saint Thérèse of Lisieux, therefore, the possibility of hell is transformed into the exhortation to suffer, in the dark night of faith, communion with Christ who has descended into hell. In a similar vision, the statements regarding eternal punishment remain as a terrifying possibility. Against them, however, stands the confident hope that is born of Christ's descent into hell to announce salvation even to sinners and of the will of the saints who, forgetting their own salvation, desire to accompany Jesus Christ in his descent.

Between hell and heaven there is an intermediate state that was described in the Middle Ages as "purgatory". Underlying this intermediate state is the conviction that, if a life has been decided definitively at death with regard to its proper destiny, a human being need not enter into it immediately. On this topic, nevertheless, there was a difference of opinion between the Latin Church and the Greek Church. Both exhorted the faithful to intercede for the deceased by means of prayers, almsgiving, and good works. Only the Latins foresaw the possibility of any punishment and expiation in the next world.

Again with reference to purgatory, Ratzinger asked himself what we ought to think of this doctrine today. He saw an interesting line of interpretation in a proposal advanced by the exegete Joachim Gnilka, who said that the fire of purgatory is Jesus Christ himself. He is the majesty of God that is manifested as judging fire, which transforms man and brings him into conformity with his own glorified body. What significance, however, does intercession for the deceased have in this regard? Man is not a monad, Ratzinger replied. In love, he is united with those who are dear to him and intercede for him, as he is with all the members of the body of Christ in the communion of saints. And for Christians, this is another reason for hope.

Heaven, for Ratzinger, who avoided the term paradise, is "that definitive completion of human existence which comes about through the perfect love towards which faith tends".[43] This completion or perfection does not concern the future exclusively but occurs in the

---

[43] Ibid., 233.

encounter with Christ, which is why, overcoming the categories of space and time, we can say that heaven exists when and to the extent that the believer is with Christ. Heaven, therefore, is a personal, christological category that also becomes theological inasmuch as Christ offers himself continually to God the Father and in this act of adoration brings every believer with him. At the same time, he introduces the believer also into the communion of all the elect, of all mankind. This communion, nevertheless, has at the same time a cosmic dimension, because all of creation is destined to become the mirror and image of God's greatness. It follows that heaven has two historical phases: the first starts with the elevation of the Lord, who inaugurates reconciliation between God and man and, with that, heaven; the second begins with the completion of the Lord's body. Indeed, the salvation of the individual, too, will be complete when the salvation of the universe and of all the elect is likewise accomplished. Then the entire creation will arrive at the perfection for which it was created.

ESCHATOLOGY CENTRAL TO THE CHRISTIAN'S LIFE AND TO THE CHURCH

I have already mentioned the attention with which Ratzinger followed the debate on eschatology after the publication of his volume until the time of his pontificate. In the appendix to the sixth German edition of his work, in 1989, he recalled the wide-ranging debate occasioned by the publication of his book. Nevertheless, he lamented the fact that most of the commentators, both critical and favorable, ended up restricting the set of problems to the question about the corporeal character of the resurrection, connected to the death of the individual immediately after the conclusion of his life. The resurrection at the end of time, in contrast, ended up coinciding with the theologies of hope or liberation that had in view, not the destiny of man as such, but rather a worldly, collectivistic future modeled on what Ernst Bloch had predicted several decades before.

The misunderstanding limited both the vision of God's salvific action and also Christian anthropology. Deprived of its power, eschatology ended up at the margins of Christian life, losing the central role that, according to the exegetes themselves, it had in the preaching of Jesus. Instead, the kingdom of God, in Ratzinger's view, starts precisely at the encounter with Jesus. The gift of the sacraments of Christian initiation clears, so to speak, the way that then leads to everyday life within the ecclesial communion. It is not diminished in the death of the individual, since he, because of the immortality of the soul, will continue to be part of the ecclesial communion and will already enter into his destiny, which will reach its full completion and revelation at Christ's return, when his body, too, will participate in the final resurrection. Only in this manner will Christian eschatology reacquire its central role in Christian faith and life. The extension of the time of waiting, however, is due to the persistence of sin but also to the love of God and of Christians themselves who interceded so that all mankind and all of creation might enter again into the communion of the saints and of God.

In his various interventions, finally, Ratzinger himself summarized and emphasized what he considered the original and characteristic points of his proposal relative to eschatology.

Dialogical immortality. The originality of Ratzinger's proposal results from what he described as "dialogical immortality". This immortality is granted by God, who freely turns to man, inviting him to the dialogue of love and, ultimately, to enter into the movement of love within the Divine Trinity. Only a God of love who creates man and comes to earth for the purpose of weaving a dialogue of love can be at the origin of a dialogical immortality.

Immortality of the soul and resurrection in Christ. The following may be a definition of eschatology generally shared by contemporary theologians: the beginning and completion of man's resurrection is Christ. But if the term "resurrection" referred to Christ has meaning through his union with the Father, who in the spirit of love delivers him from death soon after his descent into hell, the reference to man necessarily passes through his composite nature, soul and body. Otherwise, the expression "resurrection in Christ" is doomed to ambiguity because it suggests the resurrection of the individual at the moment of death, dematerializes the resurrection itself, since no one can believe that the human body is spared corruption immediately after death, and renders individual an event, the resurrection, that signifies a communion extending to all mankind and all of creation. When referred to man, one can say, instead, that after death, "our 'I' is, as it were, confirmed in God through Christ's resurrection and thereby tends expectantly towards the future resurrection."[44]

The mystery of man. Pascal had already insisted that man is more than man. Therefore, if we do not want to restrict this vision that has a solid foundation in Christianity, it is necessary to preserve the doctrine of the immortality of the soul in its fullness. Only this doctrine, indeed, affirms that, through the Risen Christ, our "I" is confirmed in God and oriented toward the future, final resurrection and preserves the realism of the Bible, which speaks precisely of the final resurrection extended also to the flesh, to the body of each human being.

The methodological question. In the second half of the nineteenth century, John Henry Cardinal Newman, whom Ratzinger would later declare Blessed, had insisted on what he called the development of dogma. With this expression, he did not mean a sort of modernist accommodation of dogma to contemporary thinking; rather, he was referring to the growth of Christian thought aimed at an ever fuller and ecclesial understanding of the truth of faith. In this perspective, Ratzinger said, a lively, uninterrupted circulation should be established between the life of the Church, exegesis, and Christian thought. The major findings of exegetical research should thus lead to a deepening of the faith, not to a continual questioning that ends up damaging the faith of the simple people to whom Jesus primarily addressed his announcement of salvation. Modern exegesis, in contrast, has made itself increasingly independent of the ecclesial tie so as to adhere fully to the presuppositions of historical research aimed at identifying and fixing the words of revelation in their historical context and even seeking to explain them on the basis of preceding terminology and thought. In this way, whereas the evangelists and the New Testament writers strove to transmit and entrust the teaching of Jesus to future Christians, exegetes turn their sights constantly to the past and end up entirely renouncing the connection with the life of the faithful. The result is that we no longer have that sort of uninterrupted growth which was at the

---

[44] Ibid., 267.

origin of the tradition formed by the contribution of the thought of the Church Fathers, of Scholasticism, and of the modern era and which together with the communion of the saints has made the life of the Church fruitful in time. Because of the preoccupation with tracking down what is ancient and attributing value only to words that were in fact pronounced by Jesus, all that remains of the Gospel and of the entire New Testament after being sifted by an often ruthless criticism are disjointed bits that we can scarcely manage to connect with one another. Hence the need for the work of the exegete, in the full sense of the scientific method, should keep in view also the life of the faithful and Christian thought in a shared ecclesial sense. Obviously, Ratzinger considered this topic indispensable, and he would return to it insistently both as prefect of the Congregation for the Doctrine of the Faith and as pope. This seems to me, moreover, to be one of the reasons at the origin of the enormous effort that he devoted to the composition of his writings on Christology and more generally to the writing of his three volumes on Jesus.

VII

ARCHBISHOP OF MUNICH

Upsetting news for Germany

In July 1976, Ratzinger had just completed the summer semester during which he gave his course on the "General Doctrine of Creation". In keeping with the commitments that he had made with Professor Auer and the publisher Pustet, he was now working intensely on the final draft of his manuscript on eschatology when, on July 24, a bit of unexpected and almost unbelievable news made the rounds in Bavaria and all of Germany: the cardinal of Munich, Julius Döpfner, had died unexpectedly of a heart attack at the age of sixty-two.

In order to explain the emotions that upset even non-Catholics and nonbelievers in Germany, it is necessary to keep in mind that, like Ratzinger, Döpfner was a *Wunderkind*, who, almost immediately after the war, had embodied the spirit of reconstruction of a country that had been destroyed and humiliated by Nazism and military defeat.[1] A bishop and a cardinal at a young age, he had represented, even abroad, the positive image of his country, which wanted to turn its back on the memory of two decades of a nightmare. Then he had played a leading role at Vatican II, where he had been one of the four moderators in charge of directing the conciliar proceedings. In the first sessions, together with the older Frings, with whom Ratzinger collaborated, he did not hesitate to take cutting-edge positions on the major controversial topics being discussed. Later on,

---

[1] Born in Hausen of a humble farming family in 1913, he had attended secondary school in Würzburg and completed his philosophical and theological studies in Rome at the Germanic College. After a short period of pastoral work, at the age of thirty-five, he was appointed bishop of Würzburg and in 1957 was promoted to Berlin, where the following year he was created a cardinal. He arrived in Munich in 1961, the year before Vatican II started.

distancing himself from those who tended to prolong the conciliar session endlessly, he proved to be a practical man by proposing a plan to expedite the proceedings.[2] Then he was a member of the commission for the revision of canon law, a member of the Council of the Secretary General of the synod and president of the German Bishops' Conference. Therefore, his talent and his authority were in great demand to keep united an episcopal conference that was in grave danger of becoming scandalously divided, particularly in 1968, after the publication of the encyclical *Humanae vitae*.

For this reason also, in view of the papal succession that was considered to be not far off, given the condition of Pope Paul's health, some people thought of him as a possible candidate if it became necessary to resort to a non-Italian pontiff. Now, instead, it was necessary to think about his successor in Munich, by tradition and extent one of the most important dioceses in Germany and in Europe.

A surprising nomination

After the emotion of the first days and the funeral of the lamented archbishop, the names of possible successors began to circulate in the diocese. Ratzinger's name, too, was on the list. The professor had no special pastoral experience or administrative abilities, but in Rome he enjoyed great confidence. He had not studied in the capital of Catholicism, but he had become well known there both through his effective participation in Vatican II and also through his work on the International Theological Commission. Paul VI, in particular, had been pleased with his efforts, along with those of Father von Balthasar, to resist the spread of the anti-Roman sentiment that had never completely subsided in Germany since the times of Luther and the Reformation. In his native land, in contrast, Ratzinger was starting to enjoy less of a good reputation. His disagreement with Küng and his decision to distance himself from Rahner were portrayed by the press as a struggle between progressives and conservatives, and this was turning popular opinion against him. In Mu-

---

[2] See Jan Grootaers, "Protagonisti del concilio", in *Storia della Chiesa*, ed. A. Fliche and V. Martin, vol. 25/1, *La Chiesa del Vaticano II*, ed. Maurilio Guasco, Elio Guerriero, and Francesco Traniello (Cinisello Balsamo: San Paolo, 1994), 418–25. The note related to the plan to accelerate the council proceedings is on p. 421.

nich, finally, he certainly could not present himself as a follower of the late cardinal. Not particularly close at the time of the council,[3] relations between them had been kept within the bounds of a rather formal politeness. Among the clergy, nevertheless, and also among the political and academic authorities, the theologian could boast of supporters. Above all, there were his numerous former students, many of whom had become his staunch followers. Then there were priests and laymen who found their views reflected in the journal *Communio* and did not agree with the excessive changes and experiments of the postconciliar Church, especially in the area of liturgy. Finally, there were the custodians of the Bavarian heritage who saw in Ratzinger the standard-bearer of a love for the Church and for local culture that seemed to be imperiled by a development so rapid that it seemed on the verge of demolishing an entire patrimony that had been built up over the centuries. Nevertheless, he still lacked pastoral and administrative experience, and it appeared that this would keep the theologian safe, since he certainly did not want to change his life once again.[4]

Ratzinger's declaration that the visit from Guido Del Mestri, nuncio of the Holy See in Germany, was altogether unexpected[5] must nevertheless be interpreted. Although it was not desired, the appointment as archbishop of Munich was a real possibility, and Ratzinger must have known about it, if only through the calls that were becoming more and more insistent. In any case, the nuncio Del Mestri handed him a letter with the request to read it at home and to reflect on it. It nominated him archbishop of Munich and Freising, the successor of Döpfner, von Faulhaber, and Saint Corbinian. At first, the theologian seriously considered declining. The letter, nevertheless, allowed him to consult his confessor, and Ratzinger thought it advisable to make use of this permission, convinced that he would have another reason to say no with a clear conscience. Contrary to his expectations, nevertheless, the confessor replied with conviction that, given the situation in the Church,

---

[3] See Guido Treffler, "Der Konzilstheologe Joseph Ratzinger im Spiegel der Konzilsakten des Münchener Erzbischofs Julius Kardinal Döpfner", in Peter Pfister, ed., *Joseph Ratzinger und das Erzbistum München und Freising: Dokumente und Bilder aus kirchlichen Archiven, Beiträge und Erinnerungen* (Regensburg: Schnell und Steiner, 2006), 151–83.

[4] See Joseph Ratzinger, *Milestones: Memories 1927–1977*, trans. Erasmo Leiva-Merikakis (San Francisco: Ignatius Press, 1998), 152.

[5] Ibid.

he had to accept. He appeared, therefore, at his new appointment with the nuncio and gave his assent to the nomination.

The news was given to the diocese on March 25, 1977, the Feast of the Annunciation. His brother comments: "At twelve o'clock noon, the bells throughout the city tolled. It was very moving, I must say."[6] The consecration was scheduled for May 28. In the weeks between the two dates, he needed to take leave of Regensburg and the university, meet his future collaborators, and think about episcopal consecration and about plans for his own episcopate. Significant in this regard are the motto and the episcopal coat of arms chosen by the new archbishop. He himself gives a significant explanation of them in his memoirs.

The episcopal motto, "Co-workers of the Truth", was taken from the Third Letter of Saint John. For Ratzinger, this meant continuity between the theological work that he had done until then and the magisterial duties that he was about to assume: "Despite all the differences in modality, what is involved was and remains the same: to follow the truth, to be at its service."[7] The coat of arms was more complex, consisting of three symbolic motifs: the crowned Moor, taken from the distinctive heraldry of the bishops of Munich, was for the new bishop the symbol of the universality of the faith that knows no distinctions of race or class; the conch shell, in contrast, is the sign of pilgrims, of those who know that Christians have no permanent dwelling place in this world. Moreover, it referred to Saint Augustine, to theological work, to the Trinitarian mystery, which is greater than all possible human understanding. Finally, there was the bear that, according to the legend, was compelled by Saint Corbinian to carry the luggage originally intended for the mule that accompanied the saint on his journey to Rome. For Ratzinger, this beast of burden was the symbol of his own episcopal responsibility. He commented: "Yes, indeed, I have become a draft animal, a beast of burden, an ox—and yet this is just the way in which I am with you, serving you, just the way in which you keep me in your hand."[8]

---

[6] Georg Ratzinger and Michael Hesemann, *My Brother the Pope*, trans. Michael J. Miller (San Francisco: Ignatius Press, 2011), 211.

[7] J. Ratzinger, *Milestones*, 153.

[8] Ibid., 155. The last sentence is taken from Psalm 73:22–23.

Among the duties of the bishop-elect, it is worth mentioning a visit on March 31 to Freising, where a meeting of the German Bishops' Conference was being held. There he was welcomed by Auxiliary Bishop Ernst Tewes and by the pastor of the cathedral parish in Freising, Michael Höck, the former rector of Ratzinger the seminarian during the years immediately after the war. A photograph depicts the new bishop of Munich, visibly moved and accompanied by the two prelates, praying at the tomb of Saint Corbinian. By the date of his consecration, the bishop-elect was exhausted because of his many duties. The day of his episcopal consecration, however, like the day of his priestly ordination, was grace-filled. The bishop of Würzburg, Josef Stangl, acting president of the Bavarian Bishops' Conference, together with the bishop of Regensburg, Rudolf Graber, and Auxiliary Bishop Ernst Tewes, vicar capitular, imposed hands on him. Ratzinger recalled in his memoirs: "The day itself was extraordinarily beautiful. . . . I experienced what a sacrament is—that what occurs in a sacrament is reality."[9] In his first homily, he stressed that the bishop, on whose head the missal had just been placed, is a man who has been appropriated by the word of Christ, thus becoming "a trustee of Another, of Jesus Christ and of his Church". Therefore, he cannot change his opinion as he pleases, he cannot act like a private person, but is subject to the inspiration that comes from the Holy Spirit, which makes him wise, fearless, and just and teaches him to love. In conclusion, he recalled his love for Bavaria, whose natural beauty had been enhanced over the centuries by the Christian faith. Then he warned about the naïve attempt to preserve its beauty without preserving the spirit that had produced it. A Bavaria where no one believed anymore would have lost its soul. He concluded by asking everyone for concord and a spirit of unity.[10]

The real critical point with which the new archbishop had to deal is already addressed in his first pastoral letter dedicated to unity, defined as "the fundamental form of building up the Church". The letter, which was read in all the churches in Munich on Sunday,

---

[9] Ibid., 152.

[10] The homily is reprinted in vol. 12 of the *Collected Writings* of Joseph Ratzinger; Italian edition: *Annunciatori della parola e servitori della vostra gioia* (Rome: Libreria Editrice Vaticana, 2013), 288–92.

June 19, 1977, was an urgent plea for unity "after the many disputes in recent years that have confused many Christians and made them unsure".[11] Each individual cannot decide what is true and what is false. The Church is a living organism in which the rule of growth and maturation is in force. At the same time—and this would be a perennial concern of his—for the new archbishop, this call to unity and peace must not be mistaken for weakness; it does not exempt us from the effort to walk along the path of truth.

Cardinal at age fifty

Several days after he was consecrated archbishop of Munich, Ratzinger received a second summons from the nuncio Del Mestri, who told him that he would be created cardinal in a mini-consistory that would be held on June 27 in the Vatican. He was probably more surprised by this new announcement than he had been by the notice of his appointment as bishop. Certainly, the archbishops of Munich customarily became cardinals, but such a short interval since the episcopal consecration suggested that the pope had a particular reason for his decision. In Rome, one of the chief co-workers with Paul VI was Bishop Giovanni Benelli, substitute to the secretary of state. As had happened to Monsignor Montini himself in 1954, the closeness between the pope and the substitute caused concern in the Vatican, and the pontiff finally had to yield to pressures urging him to dismiss Benelli, whose presence had become too cumbersome.[12] Paul VI, nevertheless, who had suffered because of his dismissal in 1954 and his failure to be appointed a cardinal during the remaining years of the pontificate of Pius XII, told Benelli upon appointing him archbishop of Florence that he would also hold a special consistory to appoint him a cardinal, so that he would not have to leave the Vatican without receiving the scarlet hat. At the same time, the pope asked Benelli to name some bishops who could receive the scarlet hat with him. It was therefore Benelli himself who recom-

---

[11] Pfister, *Joseph Ratzinger*, 281.

[12] According to the Vaticanist Benny Lai (*I segreti del Vaticano da Pio XII a papa Wojtyła* [Rome-Bari: Laterza, 1984]), Benelli's staunchest opponents included the pope's secretary, Pasquale Macchi, Secretary of State Cardinal Villot, and several representatives of Opus Dei.

mended the name of Ratzinger, who thus became a cardinal at age fifty. He would receive the cardinalatial biretta together with Benelli himself, Bernardin Gantin, former bishop of Cotonou, Benin, and now pro-president of the Pontifical Council for Justice and Peace, the Dominican Luigi Ciappi, theologian of the papal household, and the archbishop of Prague, František Tomášek, who had been cardinal *in pectore* since the preceding year.

Ratzinger therefore left for Rome on June 26 accompanied by his family, by four of his doctoral students from Regensburg, and by several representatives of the archdiocesan chancery. They would be joined the following day by a large group of the faithful, along with government officials, politicians, and cultural figures. On June 27, the consistory took place, during which the new cardinal received the pallium, the sign of his dignity as metropolitan within his ecclesiastical province and of his bond with the successor of Peter. The pope then placed on his head the cardinalatial biretta and assigned to him his titular parish of Santa Maria Consolatrice in the Tiburtino district.[13] In his address to the new cardinals, Paul VI emphasized their great fidelity in this postconciliar period of creative ferment that had its divisive elements, too. And he thanked Cardinal Ratzinger because "in many valuable publications he has shown how theological research—on the royal road of *fides quaerens intellectum*—cannot and must not ever walk without a deep, free, creative adherence to the Magisterium. . . . With our great confidence it guides an elect flock along the paths of truth and peace."[14] Cardinal Ratzinger would later recall: "After the liturgy in which he had conferred on us the ring as well, the pope expressed the desire to meet me in a private audience. This was a conversation without any specific agenda; he just wanted to get to know me personally."[15]

On that same occasion, as Ratzinger answered questions during an interview with Vatican Radio, his thoughts turned particularly to his co-workers and the faithful in Munich. He said that he wanted

---

[13] The new cardinal would take this appointment very seriously. He visited the parish every time he came to Rome and sent to it the faithful from Munich who went on pilgrimage to the Italian capital.

[14] See the Holy Father's address on the occasion of the consistory for the nomination of four cardinals, June 27, 1977.

[15] "Il Signore sceglie la nostra povertà", interview with G. Cardinale, in *30Giorni* 8 (2003).

to dedicate all his efforts to the local Church that was entrusted to him and stressed that the bishop must be a theologian, also, just as someone who studies theology must remain a believer if he does not want the matter that he investigates to dissolve in his hands.[16]

Upon returning to his native land, after the solemn festivities, Ratzinger returned to the theme of unity in the Church. In his first homily as cardinal, given on July 10 in Saint Michael's Church in Munich, in the presence of a thousand people, he recommended unity with the pope. Then he distanced himself from the separatist trends that had been started above all by liturgical celebrations that had often become a laboratory for arbitrary experimentation. Nothing could be preserved or gained by disputes that endangered peace and harmony in the communities. One cannot seek Christ except in the visible Church where we find Peter.[17] The new cardinal returned again to the theme of Catholic unity when commemorating Cardinal Döpfner on the first anniversary of his death on July 23, 1977. During the last decade, the great achievement of his predecessor had been to keep united a Church that had run the risk of being dissolved when unexpected difficulties arose. Love of unity was all the more necessary, given the development of a culture that denied its origins and no longer venerated the Crucified or even despised the sacred sign of our redemption.[18]

Pastoral care

After the festivities for his appointment as cardinal and after the summer vacation, the new bishop plunged into his pastoral work.

THE LITURGICAL REFORM

Given the divisions that were causing confusion and uncertainty, both in the Diocese of Munich and in the rest of Germany, the cardinal wanted to restore serenity and a certain unity of spirit, although in a plurality of forms. His adherence to Vatican II was indisputable; nevertheless, the council cannot be invoked to introduce arbitrary

---

[16] Joseph Ratzinger, "Un vescovo deve essere anche teologo", in J. Ratzinger, *Annunciatori della parola*, 293.

[17] Pfister, *Joseph Ratzinger*, 287.

[18] Ibid., 288.

changes without any theological basis that are dictated solely by the desire to adapt to the current mentality.

First confession. One of his first interventions was to support a decision by the Congregation for Divine Worship that asked for a first confession to precede First Holy Communion. Given the many objections that had been raised in the diocese, the matter was discussed by the priests' council in the presence of the cardinal. Ratzinger defended the Roman guideline above all in order to promote uniform practice. In the debate, nevertheless, numerous practical difficulties emerged, due to the insufficient understanding of the sacrament at the age that is suitable for children to receive Communion. Ratzinger concluded that it was necessary to leave children with the option of going to Confession as children. The Sacrament of Penance, however, has the power to adapt to the age of the penitent and to accompany every stage of life.[19]

The Eucharist. The center of liturgical life is of course the Eucharistic celebration, the Mass. Intervening in the debates of that time, the cardinal emphasized in a solemn homily on February 26, 1978, that it is necessary, first of all, to free the Eucharist from the control of individual priests and also of individual communities. It is the gift of Jesus Christ to the universal Church. It preserves its greatness only if we free it from our arbitrary will. In the same homily, the cardinal opposed the theory that the Church had strayed from Jesus' intention by turning the Eucharist, a simple fraternal meal, into a sacred action. The Church allegedly had then built cathedrals and developed increasingly solemn liturgical forms, contradicting the nature of Jesus' mandate. Ratzinger admitted that this argument may appear attractive and plausible, but even a modicum of reflection shows it to be profoundly false. Sunday, the Lord's Day, became the intimate place for the Eucharistic celebration of the fledgling Church. It is therefore situated in the new context of the Resurrection, and this was the origin of the adoration, the cultic character, and the praise, "the joy over the glory of the Risen Lord". In an unbroken tradition, the Eucharist then became open to the richness of the buildings, to the richness of the peoples. This openness, the

---

[19] Ibid., 296.

cardinal said, must, however, be verified in various places and in time. Hence the reform of the liturgy, which is not occurring for the first time in our century.

The cardinal then took a stance in the debate between promoters of Communion on the tongue and those who preferred to receive it from the priest in the hand, calling for tolerance for the two positions, both of which had justification from the historical as well as the theological perspective. He also asked for understanding both for the use of the vernacular and for recourse to the traditional Latin. Although the first is preferable for the understanding of the participants, the second is a sign of communion with the universal Church. He also recalled that the Eucharist nevertheless remains a mystery that goes beyond human understanding, and so the breathless search for a translation within the reach of everyone can only foster banal language. At a certain point, the difficulty in understanding is overcome by love, not by the fleeting insight of the moment.

In a later intervention on March 9, 1978, Ratzinger nevertheless took up a position against the liturgical conservatives, in particular against the followers of Archbishop Lefebvre. He was of the opinion that no one had anticipated the decision to introduce the new Missal while at the same time prohibiting the old one. Nevertheless, one could not call into question the fundamental direction of the reform. It was, on the other hand, conducive to greater tolerance to reintroduce some forms of the old rite in the new liturgy so as to reestablish continuity with the past. However, a reform of the liturgical reform was unthinkable.[20]

Sunday Mass. In 1981, the cardinal dedicated his Lenten Pastoral Letter to the observance of Sunday. It is based on the Resurrection of Jesus Christ from the dead. Therefore, Sunday worship is a profession of faith in the Resurrection, "a profession that Jesus lives, that God lives and gives life to man beyond death. It is the profession of faith that we can hope, the profession that love lasts, and therefore the profession that there is a right way of living."[21] Furthermore, Sunday refers to Christ's return; we can therefore

---

[20] Ibid., 310.
[21] Ibid., 408.

hope in the reign of Christ, in the reign of God, and therefore we can confidently face the future, which will be richer than the past. The precept to observe Sunday is therefore not an invention of the Church; it is the Church's response to what the Lord has done and is doing. He was the one to make this day his and ours, to make it the day of coming together with him in the Church's celebration. Therefore, the Sunday celebration of the Eucharist cannot be replaced with other liturgical and devotional ceremonies. Similarly, the bishops are not authorized to recognize possible ecumenical celebrations as the Sunday celebration of the Eucharist. Since the apostolic tradition, Sunday, shaped by this encounter with the Lord, is the day of breaking bread, of the Eucharist, and the bishop does not have the authority to replace this celebration with another liturgical ceremony.

PREACHING

The crisis in preaching. After the period of pastoral experience following his priestly ordination, Ratzinger had not had pastoral duties again. Over the years, nevertheless, he had not failed to preach on special occasions,[22] and above all in 1973 he had published a volume, *Dogma and Preaching*,[23] in which he explicitly addressed the topic of the relation between preaching and dogma. He began the foreword to the volume: "The path from dogma to preaching has become very difficult. There are no longer any patterns of thought and assumptions that carry the content of dogma into everyday life."[24] Given this difficulty, the author continued, many leave dogma aside completely and end up speaking in their own name, abandoning any connection whatsoever with objectivity. It is a danger that can lead to the dissolution not only of dogmatic

---

[22] Besides the volume on preaching that I discuss in the following paragraphs, see also the volume *Teaching and Learning the Love of God: Being a Priest Today*, trans. Michael J. Miller (San Francisco: Ignatius Press, 2017), which reprints the homilies given by Ratzinger on the occasion of the anniversaries of priests also in the years before his episcopal consecration.

[23] Joseph Ratzinger, *Dogma und Verkündigung* (Munich: Verlag und Druckerei Manz, 1973); trans. Michael J. Miller and Matthew J. O'Connell as *Dogma and Preaching* (San Francisco: Ignatius Press, 2011).

[24] J. Ratzinger, *Dogma and Preaching*, 7.

theology but of theology in general. The theologian, therefore, cannot remain in the inaccessible cocoon of his scholarly activity, but must come to the aid of dogma and preaching with a reflection on the theory of preaching and with concrete models that can be replicated by the priest who has pastoral responsibilities.

Church and preaching. For Ratzinger, the Church and preaching cannot be separated from the stream that flows from the origin and makes fruitful the life of the faithful. It is necessary to begin again from the origins each time in order to renew not only synchronic communion but also diachronic communion that is capable of reaching across time and starting from Jesus Christ, from his Paschal Eucharist, which is at the foundation of Christian communion and proclamation. Contrasting, therefore, the preaching in the Old Testament with that of the New, together with the exegetes Ratzinger noticed two significant differences. The former is directed essentially to the people of Israel, which already exists as a community to which the preaching of the priests and prophets is addressed. The latter, on the other hand, is directed in principle to all peoples. Initially, therefore, the Church does not exist; the purpose of preaching is precisely to gather the peoples around itself and thus to make them Church.

Therefore, there is an indispensable connection between Church and preaching. Whether as a word addressed to those who already believe or as the proclamation addressed to nonbelievers, the Church is always the standard place of preaching. In the first case, in view of the fullness of the life and communion of those who are already gathered around the Eucharist of Jesus; in the second, as a landing place of those who receive the word and are called to Baptism and the Eucharist. While it is a place of preaching with respect to the listeners, the Church is the place to which the preachers belong, too. The latter cannot speak in their own name or as men in charge of a single community or of a group, but speak in the name of the Church, which is one and catholic in all ages. "Faith means emerging from the isolation of one's own existence and becoming 'one body' with Christ. . . . This 'Body' alone is the abode of his 'Spirit'. The Body is the acting subject of the Word."[25] The Bible,

---

[25] Ibid., 22.

too, understood as the fundamental form and norm of all preaching, is an ecclesial word and, therefore, can be understood as Bible only in the context of the Church.

Church and word of God. As place and subject to which the word of God is addressed, the Church is not, however, the word of God. The latter stands opposite the Church and leaves its mark on her life. At the same time, it is also a critical authority for the Church in reference to the concrete form of her existence. This means that the Church, in which the word dwells and lives, is obligated to be a space of life and not of death. The word entrusted to the Church comes alive in three ways: directed to the Church that already believes, whose faith must grow; as a proclamation so that the Church might grow; as the word handed down to future believers.

Criteria for preaching. Based on these premises, Ratzinger explained several distinctive criteria of Catholic preaching. The point of departure of all preaching is the Sacred Scripture of both the Old and the New Testament. Then, there are the professions of faith in which the Church has expressed for the faithful in a binding way the faith that she has received from the apostles. The creeds are then supplemented with the living Magisterium of the Church, the teaching of the pope and of the bishops united in the apostolic college. Finally, there is the faith of the people of God. We must not isolate the local communities from the context of the universal Church, as though the current thought of the community, its convictions, even if agreed on, could replace the word of Scripture and of the Magisterium. Nevertheless, "the simple faith of simple people deserves the respect, the reverence of the preacher."[26] This is a point to which Ratzinger continuously returns, both at the methodological level and in his preaching as bishop.

THEMES OF THE PREACHING IN MUNICH

As bishop of Munich, Ratzinger very much took to heart the task of preaching. Here we mention some sample topics connected with the city and the diocese of Munich.

---

[26] Ibid., 33.

Marriage and family. In 1980, the cardinal devoted his Lenten pastoral letter to the faithful of the archdiocese to the topic of marriage and the family. Our present and our future, the cardinal explained, depend on our attitude toward matrimony. Man and woman, according to the Bible, have the same nature and the same dignity. In the marriage covenant, there is a clear reference to God's covenant with mankind, to the pact of unity between Christ and his Church. The virtue of purity does not lead to the denial of one's own bodily nature but, rather, leads the capacity to love to its authentic greatness and anchors sexuality fully in human dignity. The height of freedom is man's ability to make up his mind, his ability to decide. Dedication to one person and fidelity to him is not the opposite of freedom but, rather, its true beginning. A child is not a threat, a diminution of freedom, a limitation of self-fulfillment. The future will surely founder if, out of fear of self-limitation, we deny ourselves the one force that can give us the future: children.[27]

An official chancery memorandum dated April 2, 1980, notes that the cardinal's letter had great success not only in the Archdiocese of Munich but also throughout Germany as well as in Austria and Switzerland. The cardinal's letter was presented to engaged couples and to young families and was being used also in seminaries and in religious instruction classes.

Prayer in the family. On November 18, 1978, though, Ratzinger recommended prayer in the family to the many faithful who had gathered in the cathedral in Freising for the feast of Saint Corbinian. On that occasion, the cardinal described the family as the living place of common life where one can speak, pray, sing, and be there for one another. The people and the Church cannot exist without the family, because "then we would lack the interior place of trust where one can learn to believe and where the words of faith acquire a human meaning."[28] The theme of prayer in the family therefore became a constant in the cardinal's preaching. He declared again in 1979: The family stays together only if it prays together. Reunification is possible only if the husband and the wife do not just discuss things between themselves but together present themselves to God.

---

[27] Pfister, *Joseph Ratzinger*, 371.
[28] Ibid., 331.

The cardinal then exhorted the faithful to return to the custom of praying and singing together as a family and to revive the practice of celebrating at home the feast days of the liturgical year and the beautiful Christian traditions.[29]

On another occasion, the cardinal spoke about prayer in families and in small groups. The Church, the cardinal wrote in a letter that was read in all the churches of the diocese, is not made up of priests and bishops alone but is realized precisely in the prayer of small groups. He also wrote: "If there is no more prayer in the family, the Church's liturgy, too, dies from within; little by little, the family dries up, and so does society itself, because then there is a lack of the strength of unification that can transform standing next to others into standing together."[30]

Defending life. A few months after his episcopal consecration, the cardinal was already exhorting all the Christian communities to help needy pregnant women. In a statement to the members of the association Pro-Life Action, the cardinal declared that every abortion is an enormous challenge for Christians. For this purpose, a house had been prepared where needy pregnant women could find shelter together with their babies and reside there for a time. Therefore, he invited Christians to be generous and to support the initiative with their donations. The house in Munich, the cardinal concluded, is a pro-life opportunity and a sign that we are doing what we believe in.[31]

Creation and ecology. In the above-mentioned Lenten pastoral letter for 1981, Ratzinger deduced love for the environment from the Christian view of creation. God's exhortation to subdue the earth does not mean to exploit or violate it. Rather it means to take care of the earth! Imprint on it the face of the Spirit that is in it! In this way, we will serve it and respond to its ultimate purpose. The word "culture" has the same root as "cult". It includes the connotations "cultivation" and also "veneration". This means cultivating the earth in such a way as to venerate in it the presence of God and thus to honor God himself. This same idea calls for moderation in

---

[29] Ibid., 243f.
[30] Ibid., 358.
[31] Ibid., 289–90.

cultivating the earth and a life-style that turns exploitation into care. It is important for Christians to develop this life-style decisively in our time.[32]

Europe. Another public topic dear to Ratzinger is Europe. The cardinal obviously sees Europe as being based on a Christian foundation. He addressed the subject in the first Pontifical Mass celebrated by him on the occasion of the feast day of the founder of the diocese, Saint Corbinian. Only the strength of Christian faith can open frontiers, overcome prejudices, combat hatred, and produce true unity. Greed for possessions, even with so many economic strategies, does not unite but rather arouses envy, which separates. Thinking then of the countries in the East that were divided from the West by the Iron Curtain, the cardinal concluded: "The international project of rebellion and hatred that is offered to us as a hope for unity can in reality create only dictatorship and anarchy."[33]

Bavaria. In the first chapters of this book, I have already had occasion to recall Ratzinger's love of Bavaria, understood as a countryside, but also as a State or at least as a territory with a strong local tradition. In this regard, as early as an interview on September 21, 1977, Ratzinger declared himself a staunch federalist with regard to both the form of the government and also the ecclesiastical structure.[34] His federalism then went hand in hand with the Christian liberalism that is present in the genuine unity between faith and life that could be experienced in Bavaria on major feast days. Christian faith implies love for creation and, therefore, also the serene, joyous acceptance of the beauty of creation. "I take very much to heart this joyous faith that is reflected in life without puritanism."[35]

Ratzinger then declared that he was against doctrinaire uniformity in the ecclesiastical field. For this reason, he had already spoken with the nuncio requesting that the Bavarian Bishops' Council be mentioned again in the *Annuario pontificio*, which was not just a book but rather the self-presentation of the Catholic Church.

---

[32] Ibid., 407f.

[33] Ibid., 298.

[34] Interview with the *Freisinger Tagblatt*, a local edition of the *Münchner Merkur;* cf. Pfister, *Joseph Ratzinger*, 291.

[35] Ibid.

Two months later, Ratzinger led to Rome the Bavarian Bishops' Conference for the first time on their *ad limina* visit to the pope as an autonomous group. Two years later, in 1979, there had already been two new successors to the See of Peter, and John Paul II left a lasting, distinctive imprint on the papacy. He had already been to the United Nations, where he had intervened in favor of human rights, which included also the right to the free practice of one's religion.

Citing this speech, Ratzinger invited the citizens of Munich and all Bavarians to remain faithful to the spiritual heritage of their land. The cardinal recalled that the crisis resulted from Marxism and from radical liberalism. These currents of thought aimed to situate persons in a place without history. The cardinal, in contrast, invited them to remain firmly attached to "our great tradition and to our culture, which, purified by faith, is a root that endures and supports".[36]

THE ADMINISTRATION OF THE SACRAMENTS

During the brief period in which he was archbishop of Munich, Ratzinger performed his episcopal ministry above all by participating intensely in the administration of the sacraments, particularly of those that are reserved to the bishop, such as the Solemn Pontifical Masses on the occasion of the major feast days, the administration of the Sacrament of Confirmation, the crown of Christian initiation, and the sacrament ordaining men as priests and deacons.

Solemn Pontifical Masses. As for the Solemn Pontifical Masses, which at that time many priests and lay people wanted to simplify, if not suppress, he underscored the continuity in tradition of a Church that had been capable of producing great art and great music. Both visual art and music had given expression to the praise of God over the centuries. We must not renounce this expression of the human spirit in the name of a misunderstood simplicity. The old-fashioned sensibility of the lover of classical music, who moreover had a brother who directed one of the most famous church choirs in Germany, played a major role here.

---

[36] Pfister, *Joseph Ratzinger*, 359.

Confirmation. In glancing at the list of pontifical Masses and other liturgical celebrations over which the cardinal presided during the four years of his episcopate in Munich, one is struck by the number of Confirmations he administered.[37] The cardinal evidently set great store by this sacrament, which in his view brings Christian formation to its completion and involves a definitive choice for life, a choice for Christ. He had developed a homily that, by his own admission, was like a template that he then would adapt to the different places and circumstances in which he conferred the sacrament.[38] Even in the somewhat stylized form in which it was published by *Communio*, it reveals a great ability to get the children's attention and to speak to their hearts. The ceremony, the cardinal began, is subdivided into three sections: the Confirmation promises, the prayer of the bishop in the name of the Church, and then the Confirmation properly speaking, when the confirmand's forehead is marked with the sign of the cross. It is a signpost that shows the way in our life. Confirmation is not a momentary ritual but, rather, a beginning that is meant to mature throughout life. It is also a promise that reaches into eternity. First, however, it is an invitation to courage and constancy, an invitation to build up our life with Christ.[39]

THE BISHOP AND HIS PRIESTS

Volume 12 of the *Collected Writings* of Joseph Ratzinger is devoted entirely to the theology and spirituality of the Sacrament of Holy Orders, in its three stages of bishop, priest, and deacon.[40] The original German edition runs to more than 900 pages and is further subdivided into theology and spirituality. This results from the attention that the author constantly gave to the subject, but also from the lively concern of someone who experienced and observed close

---

[37] Ibid., 204–35.

[38] The homily was published for the first time by the Italian edition of *Communio* in no. 64 (1982): 40–46. It was then republished in the anthology of all the articles by Ratzinger published by the same journal on the occasion of Ratzinger's election to the papacy: Joseph Ratzinger, *La vita di Dio per gli uomini* (Milan: Jaca Book, 2006). The homily, entitled "Omelia per una cresima", is found on pp. 68–73. The citations will reference this latter publication.

[39] J. Ratzinger, "Omelia per una cresima", 73.

[40] Selections from this volume 12 have been published in English as *Teaching and Learning the Love of God: Being a Priest Today*. See note 22 above.

up the profound crisis in which priests came to find themselves in the decades immediately after Vatican II. As a bishop, therefore, Ratzinger not only administered the Sacrament of Holy Orders to his priests and deacons, but he also paid particular attention to their formation and spirituality. Here I would like to mention just two homilies dedicated to priestly spirituality that he gave at the beginning and at the conclusion of his episcopal ministry in Munich and a homily on the occasion of a diaconal ordination.

The first homily was given in 1978, during a Chrism Mass, on the day that the Church dedicates to the consecration of the holy oils and at the same time observes the feast of priests. The oil that is distributed on that day is derived from the one sacrament of the death and Resurrection of Jesus. The priests who receive this one oil for the celebration of the sacraments in the diocese are servants of life. For this reason, Holy Thursday is also the feast of priests, whose duty it is to take the oil of life and to make it pour out over the whole body of the Church. They receive the oil from the bishop, who receives it from the one Spirit of Jesus, and they distribute it "so that once more the life-giving oil might overcome the dryness of everyday routine and bring alive in us the joy of Christ's victory".[41]

The concern for unity echoes also in his farewell to his priests. Here, the cardinal's greeting even assumed the emotional tone of an adieu, the tone of Saint Paul's greeting to his co-workers in Mileto:

> I would like to ask you for this above all else: Let us keep going, let us stay together! The priesthood is a ministry that can be performed only in the first person plural. Therefore I chose as my motto *Cooperatores Veritatis* [Co-workers of the truth], in which this We of our service is expressed: only by being brothers . . . of Jesus Christ, only by entering into the great fellowship of those who are called and by being the We of the presbyterate of a diocese can we as individuals carry out our ministry to the whole and for the whole.[42]

The cardinal then went on to invite the priests to support each other, to meet together, to speak among themselves, and to have confidence.

---

[41] Joseph Ratzinger, "Holy Oils: Signs of God's Healing Power and Diocesan Unity", in *Teaching and Learning the Love of God*, pp. 33–38 at 38.

[42] Joseph Cardinal Ratzinger, "By Surrendering Ourselves, We Also Find Ourselves", Farewell meeting with priests and deacons, 1982; ibid., 55–64 at 60–61.

We should also mention a homily for a diaconal ordination. Christ, the cardinal began, is God's Yes to mankind. He is not the rebellious man, the man who harbors the passion of rebellion against God, but rather the man who says Yes. The Cross is not an act of rebellion, but his final great Yes pronounced in the midst of the world's darkness. To be deacons means to trust in the Yes of Jesus Christ and to give people the courage to say Yes: the courage of fidelity, the courage of confidence, the courage of love.

Building a seminary. The plan to build a new seminary in Munich went back to Döpfner's years as archbishop. The first concrete step had been taken in 1967 with the formal publication of the announcement of the project and the identification of a suitable construction site. Then more than ten years passed before moving on to the execution phase. The decisive impetus had come in 1980 with the visit to Munich by John Paul II, who had urgently invited young men to follow the example of the holy bishop and founder of the diocese, Corbinian, and to become poor, chaste witnesses of the reality of God's presence among the brethren. Given the pope's invitation, Ratzinger had cut through the red tape, and within a year, on November 20, 1981, laid the first stone of the new seminary.

The building, designed to house around eighty seminarians, was not completed until 1983. When Ratzinger laid the first stone, however, it was a sign of trust and hope. Now he had to leave Bavaria. Only five days later, on November 25, his transfer to Rome was announced.

POPULAR DEVOTIONS

In interviews, as well as in his memoirs, Ratzinger always showed great respect for popular devotion. As archbishop of Munich, in his writings, as in practice, he sought to remain faithful to this conviction even in an era when the clergy proved to be rather reluctant to promote the forms of devotion inherited from the past. He made frequent visits to the Marian Pillar, the column in the center of Munich with the statue of the Blessed Virgin at the top. The visit was a custom of the bishops of that city, but Ratzinger lent a special solemnity to the event and composed a prayer that is a distillation of Marian devotion, but also of reflection on Bavarian history and on the current situation: "Our ancestors chose you as their protectress, as duchess of their country. Your motherly kindness stands above all human sovereignty as a sign of the new, liberating lordship of Jesus Christ. The paths of our land come from you and through you go to the One who is himself the Way. We pray you, be the protectress of our country, of our diocese in our time also."[43] Through formulas that seem conventional, we note the nostalgia for a world without so many debates, one that was poorer but more serene.

June 16, 1977, was the Solemnity of Corpus Christi. Ratzinger presided at the Solemn Pontifical Mass, after which the traditional procession took place, which is supposed to be the sign of the presence of Christ and of Christians in the city. It was a beautiful sunny day, and more than forty thousand persons walked in the procession. Represented in the cortege were all social classes of the city, from ecclesiastical dignitaries to state and municipal authorities, from representatives of youth groups to academic authorities, down to representatives of foreign workers and folklore groups accompanied by a musical band. In this case, too, Ratzinger's speech culminated in a lyricism that is not without apprehension that Christian civilization, as foreseen by Guardini, was destined to decline in a short time.

Two years later, in 1979, the preparations suggested that there would be a large crowd again for the Corpus Christi procession, but it could not take place because of bad weather conditions. The cardinal was compelled to celebrate the Pontifical Mass in the cathedral and to lead a procession on a reduced scale in the immediate vicinity of the cathedral. Nevertheless, the president of the Bavarian Parliament, Franz Heubl, and the powerful leader Franz Josef Strauss took part in the event. Also participating were ten Indian bishops led by the archbishop of Calcutta, Lawrence Cardinal Picachy. The Indian prelates were in Germany at the invitation of the German Bishops' Conference.

The speech that best clarifies Ratzinger's view of Christian, and not just popular, devotion goes back to 1981. When invited to give a conference on devotion to the Sacred Heart as part of the celebration of an international Eucharistic Congress that was being held in Lourdes from June 24 to 28, the cardinal stated that Christian devotion needs the senses. "Man needs to see, needs interior vision. . . . He must climb on the ladder of the body in order to find

---

[43] Pfister, *Joseph Ratzinger*, 279f.

the road to which faith invites him."[44] The great medieval mysticism and the extraordinary devotion to the Sacred Heart in the modern era cannot simply be replaced by rediscovering the Bible and the Fathers of the Church. Contemporary theology, he continued, is dominated by scientific rationality that pushes human emotions aside into irrationality. This results in disdain for the emotional aspect of devotion. Christian devotion, on the other hand, needs the senses that are centered in the heart. It corresponds to the image of the Christian God "who has a heart" and to a Paschal devotion, because the Paschal Mystery is by its very nature a mystery of the heart, in which the history of God's love for mankind is summed up. "The love that addresses us from the Gospels, from the Acts of the Apostles, and from the Book of Revelation appeals also to the sensory form of human love."[45] The word of God did not assume a fictitious, unimportant body.

Pastoral ministers are not judges of the faith. In a meeting with the deans of the archdiocese, there was a discussion about so-called "fallen-away" Christians and also non-believing Christians. Taking the podium, the cardinal recommended to the deacons and, through them, to the priests to take care of many persons' need for faith and not to turn into judges of faith. In many people there is still a "remnant of faith, or at least the need to believe". In an agitated situation, we need to be able to grasp both sides of the phenomenon, which means that we need to look sympathetically even at manifestations of faith that, strictly speaking, are not to be recommended. "We need to be able to accept positively even fragments of faith."[46] The cardinal then urged the priests to preserve unity and friendship among themselves. This could not be imposed by law but is attained by fraternal dialogue.

ECUMENISM

Although Cardinal Döpfner had not been one of the initiators of the ecumenical movement in Germany, after Vatican II he had started good relations with the separated brethren.

---

[44] Ibid., 122.
[45] Ibid., 123.
[46] Ibid., 412.

Dialogue with the Lutheran Church. Following this overture of trust
toward the Lutheran community of Munich, in 1969 Cardinal
Döpfner and the territorial Lutheran bishop at that time, Hermann
Dietzfelbinger, had started the practice of holding a joint ecumenical prayer service during the Octave of Prayer for Christian Unity.
When appointed archbishop of Munich, Ratzinger went to meet
for the first time the territorial bishop of the Lutheran-Evangelical
Church, Johannes Hanselmann, on July 15, 1977. According to the
joint communiqué released afterward, the meeting was cordial. One
result was the decision to hold a common ecumenical celebration in
the cathedral in Munich the following January, during the Octave
of Prayer for Christian Unity. The discussion then turned to ecumenical questions at the local level and efforts to have the Augsburg
Confession acknowledged by Catholics.

The meeting was in fact held on January 20, 1978. The common
prayer called for peace among Christians, who must not grow accustomed to division but, rather, must become a sign of peace and reconciliation among the nations. Then, the two Christian prelates
prayed together for their predecessors, and the celebration concluded with the recitation of the Creed and the Our Father. A
collection was taken up also to support a center in Ireland for reconciliation between Catholics and Protestants, which was to house
refugee families from Northern Ireland. Mothers and children from
the north and the south of the country who were in need of peace
and rest could spend vacation time there together. Moreover, working groups were organized for young Catholics and Protestants from
countries where both Christian confessions were present.

A speech defending the ecumenism of Paul VI goes back to early
July 1978. The cardinal asserted that Montini would go down in
history as the pope of ecumenism. Indeed, he had taken up the
initial ecumenical signals given by John XXIII and had developed
them extensively. Ratzinger then responded to the accusations from
some circles of the Lutheran Church in Bavaria to the effect that the
region was witnessing a gradual cooling of the ecumenical effort.
The ecumenical movement, he affirmed, is a matter of conscience
that must mature in the search for truth.[47] In a letter sent several
days later to the territorial bishop, Hanselmann, Ratzinger thanked

---

[47] Ibid., 319.

his predecessor, Hermann Dietzfelbinger, who had then turned seventy, for having worked for mutual understanding and union between the Catholic and Lutheran Churches.

In 1980, an important preaching exchange program was introduced as part of the annual ecumenical meeting: on that occasion, the sermon would be given by the bishop of the guest Church. In 1980, the meeting was held during the celebration of Evening Prayer in the Catholic cathedral in Munich, and the sermon was given by the Lutheran bishop, Hanselmann. The following year, on the other hand, the meeting took place in the Lutheran Church of Saint Matthew, and Cardinal Ratzinger gave the sermon. In his Lenten pastoral letter for 1981, nevertheless, Ratzinger recalled that participation in ecumenical worship cannot replace Sunday Mass. Given the differences in their understanding of priestly ministry, of the Paschal character of the Eucharist, and of the permanent presence of the Lord in the consecrated Hosts, the bishops were not authorized to allow intercommunion.

Dialogue with the Orthodox. The meetings with representatives of the Orthodox Church during Ratzinger's episcopate in Munich were not so regularly scheduled but seem to have warmed his heart more. After the election of John Paul II, the cardinal's meeting with Orthodox prelates intensified both numerically and qualitatively. In November 1979, the pope traveled to visit the Orthodox Patriarch Dimitrios I of Constantinople. On that occasion, the leaders of the two Churches decided to establish a commission of theologians to discuss the topics on which it was possible to reach an agreement. The first of the meetings planned was held on Patmos and Rhodes from late May to early June 1980. Cardinal Ratzinger, appointed a member of the Catholic part of the dialogue commission, spoke there on May 30.

On May 2, 1981, in turn, he welcomed to Munich a delegation from the Armenian Church headed by Patriarch Vasken I Baljian. On that occasion, Ratzinger stated that many of the differences that had arisen over the course of history can be attributed more to terminology than to substance. Concretely, he then promised the patriarch assistance for the integration of young Armenians residing in Germany and for Armenian liturgical celebrations in the Catholic churches. The following month, it was announced that the meeting of the Orthodox and Catholic commissions would be held in 1982 in Munich. The decision was made by mutual agreement by the Secretariat for Christian Unity and Cardinal Ratzinger.

In early September 1981, a delegation from the Russian Orthodox Church led by Archbishop Vladimir Sabodan arrived in Munich. In his welcome speech to the delegation at the airport, Ratzinger highlighted the role played by the Orthodox Church in the unification of the countries in the East and in the spread of Christianity even outside of Europe. For his part, Sabodan underscored the presence of Christ in both Churches and conveyed the greetings of Patriarch Pimen who, as a gesture of appreciation and friendship, had sent Ratzinger one of his pectoral crosses.

The year of the three popes

In 1978, Paul VI was eighty-one years old and had been pope for fifteen years. He had never been a man with an iron constitution, and especially in recent years he had sorely felt the weight that he had had to carry on his shoulders since the council. Since September 1977, he had suffered increasingly from osteoarthritis and often walked while supporting himself on his secretary's arm. He wrote in a note that dates back to the final months of his life: "In the evening of life the decisive experience. Strength diminishes, conflict increases. *Ut sim fidelis, ut sim fidelis.*[48] What should be pursued even more than the results of one's own activity is fidelity to the line of commitment and of love."[49] With this final sentence, which is the best summary of his entire pontificate, he left this world on the evening of August 6, 1978. Among the 111 cardinals convened in Rome in a timely fashion by the cardinal deacon, Carlo Confalonieri, Joseph Ratzinger of Munich and Karol Wojtyła of Kraków were among the youngest, selected by Paul VI both for their experience and also for their balance. They had participated in the council and had become reliable interpreters of it as well. For this reason, in 1976, not only had Wojtyła been called to preach the pope's retreat, but the whole Curia could see the pope diligently

---

[48] Latin: "May I be faithful, may I be faithful!"

[49] The quotation is recorded by Giselda Adornato, *Paolo VI: Il coraggio della modernità* (Cinisello Balsamo: San Paolo, 2008), 291.

taking notes during his conferences. The Polish cardinal was then repeatedly elected to the Secretariat of the Council of the Synod of Bishops until he became its senior member. As such, he presided over the Synod on Catechesis that was held in October 1977, in which another participant was the archbishop of Munich, who a few months later was nominated a cardinal with unusual rapidity.

That was the first occasion on which the two cardinals were able to get acquainted, after fleeting encounters at the council, and they immediately struck up a sincere friendship. A few months later, in 1978, they saw each other again for the election of the new pontiff. Among the German-speaking bishops in particular, the elderly Cardinal König of Vienna started to float the idea of a non-Italian pontiff. In particular, he might be Wojtyła of Kraków, who, in fact, received several votes in the initial ballots. For the moment, nevertheless, the proposal still seemed too daring. As was anticipated, the two most representative Italian candidates, Siri of Genoa and Benelli of Florence, received the greatest number of votes. Soon, however, there was a successful mediation that redirected to the patriarch of Venice, Albino Luciani, the votes needed to be elected. He was elected on the fourth ballot and took the name of John Paul I. Ratzinger was happy with the new pope, whose smile immediately showed that he was a man of God.[50] For his part, the pontiff immediately demonstrated his confidence in him by sending him as his legate to the national Marian Congress in Ecuador.

The cardinal of Munich traveled there on September 19 and remained there until the end of the month. He wanted to become acquainted firsthand with the Latin American subcontinent about which people spoke so much in Germany, but also to warn the bishops and the local Church leaders about the influence of rationalistic Western thought, in its Marxist version. He had received letters about this influence from Maximino Arias Reyero, a Latin American student of his who had become professor of dogmatic theology at the Catholic University of Santiago, Chile. For his part, Reyero later testified that in discerning what he described as the Marxist origin of liberation theology, which had such great success at that time throughout the Latin American subcontinent, Ratzinger's

[50] Pfister, *Joseph Ratzinger*, 322f.

book *The Meaning of Christian Brotherhood* had been of fundamental importance to him.[51] Upon arriving in Latin America, the cardinal of Munich adopted Reyero's concerns. Speaking at the conclusion of the Marian Congress in Guayaquil, he exhorted his Latin American listeners not to let themselves be robbed of their future, not to let themselves be deprived of their own culture of the heart. Then he invited the religious to remain faithful to their spiritual vocation and to the specific charism of their Order. The cardinal advised the priests as well to remain faithful to their spiritual vocation. There is not just a political and social liberation. Although he also has a social responsibility, the priest is more than a functionary and a social worker. For this reason, it is necessary that "the kingdom of God be proclaimed as the proclamation of Jesus, that the sacraments be administered as the Church received them from Christ".[52]

On September 28, the shocking news arrived from Europe of the death of Pope Luciani. After returning to his country immediately, the cardinal, like many of his colleagues, wondered about the meaning of this death. Only one month earlier, they had duly elected John Paul I, and now they found that they needed to elect

---

[51] Joseph Ratzinger, *Die christliche Brüderlichkeit* (Munich: Kösel, 1960); trans. as *The Meaning of Christian Brotherhood* (New York: Sheed and Ward, 1966; San Francisco: Ignatius Press, 1993). Reyero's testimony is contained in the *Festschrift* in honor of Ratzinger's seventieth birthday: Josef Clemens and Antonio Tarzia, *Alla scuola della verità: I settant'anni di Joseph Ratzinger* (Cinisello Balsamo: San Paolo, 1997), 27–35. Among other things, the Latin American theologian wrote: "It was not easy to distinguish in this movement [liberation theology] the Christian impulses and foundations from a practical implementation that was not that Christian. There was and still is confusion. There are many redeemable things in this way of doing theology and operating. The scandal of poverty and the pride of the powerful, the passivity of Christians, . . . the drive to make the Church closer to the people. . . . But there was also something that I could not accept. It was the division of people into good and bad, rich and poor, the exploiters and the exploited—the division that, in the Church, translated into the Church of the hierarchy and the Church of the people; it was the lack of reflection on the image of the one, unique Father for all. Then the Marxist interpretation of fraternity became clear to me: brotherhood without the Father; brotherhood that was based on one's own strength and practical reason; brotherhood that needs enemies in order to survive, a utopian, unreal fraternity." The length of this quotation from pp. 32f. seems justified because it explains nicely the very same idea that Ratzinger had of liberation theology, the basis of his position that earned him so much criticism in Latin America and then throughout the West.

[52] Pfister, *Joseph Ratzinger*, 325.

a new pontiff. What could be the meaning of this event? Maybe it was necessary to think about a more radical change.[53] Ratzinger was probably already thinking about his friend Wojtyła, but he did not need to campaign among the German cardinals. While he was in Ecuador, from September 19 to 25, the archbishop of Kraków together with several Polish bishops had been on an official visit in Germany, where he had spoken twice to the German Bishops' Conference assembled in Fulda and once in Cologne. Among other things, Wojtyła said during his homily in the cathedral in Fulda on September 22: This meeting will strengthen the two Churches in truth and in love and will help "to heal the wounds of the past, whether the more distant or the recent past".[54]

The German cardinals appreciated these words very much, which brought to an end the process of peacemaking between the two Churches that had begun on November 18, 1965, during the council, with a letter from the Polish bishops to their German confreres. This letter, in which the Polish bishops forgave and asked forgiveness of their German confreres, had elicited a lot of criticism in their fatherland, directed especially at Wojtyła.[55] He, however, had remained faithful to this message, convinced that it was necessary finally to get beyond World War II. This was the firm conviction of the cardinal of Munich, also.

In the October conclave, a tie reoccurred between Cardinals Siri and Benelli, who once again shared the majority of the votes in the initial ballots. This time, however, the solution of a non-Italian pope had become more familiar, and it was precisely the Germans who were among the staunchest proponents of the election of the Polish cardinal. First put forward on Monday morning, October 16, 1978, Wojtyła's candidacy rapidly gained support, and in the evening of that same day he was elected pope and took the name of John Paul II. Ratzinger was happy with the choice. During Wojtyła's whole pontificate, he made no secret of his feelings of admiration for the Polish pope, and later when he succeeded him, he continued to take the same attitude.[56] Here it is worthwhile recalling an

---

[53] Bernard Lecomte, *Benoît XVI: Le dernier pape européen* (Paris: Perrin, 2006), 76.

[54] Luigi Accattoli, *Quando il papa chiede perdono: Tutti i mea culpa di Giovanni Paolo II* (Milan: Mondadori, 1997), 47–52.

[55] Ibid., 48f.

[56] See, in this regard, the little volume I edited that reprints the most important statements regarding the figure and work of John Paul II made by Ratzinger either as cardi-

excerpt from the interview granted by Ratzinger to Peter Seewald concerning the first impression that Wojtyła made on him:

> The first thing that won my sympathy was his uncomplicated, human frankness and openness, as well as the cordiality that he radiated. . . . You sensed that here was a man of God. Here was a person who had nothing artificial about him, who was really a man of God. . . . You notice that about a person: he has suffered, he has also struggled on his way to this vocation. . . . This intellectual wealth, as well as his enjoyment of dialogue and exchange, these were all things that immediately made him likeable to me.[57]

In the last few years before his election, John Paul II had often been in Rome either as a member of the Secretariat of the Synod of Bishops or to participate in meetings of four Roman congregations. He had realized the difficulties in the functioning of the Curia and had often thought of the need to surround himself with trusted persons. Soon, therefore, he thought of bringing to Rome someone whom he now considered a friend and admired for his learning: the Ordinary of Munich. In one of their meetings, he told him that he wanted him in Rome to replace, at the head of the Congregation for Catholic Education, the French Gabriel-Marie Cardinal Garrone, who, having reached the age of seventy-seven, was retiring. For Ratzinger, this was another shock. He had been bishop of Munich for about a year, and it seemed to him a lack of respect for the faithful of his beloved Bavaria to abandon them after such a short time. Persuaded for the moment, the pope replied: "Let's consider all of this again."[58]

Difficulties with theologians

The second half of 1979 was a difficult period for Ratzinger in his relations with theologians, particularly with some of his colleagues and friends. Above all the Küng case was in the news again. For a decade now, the Swiss theologian had been on a path that gradually distanced him from theology and from the Catholic Church.

---

nal or as pope: Elio Guerriero, ed., *Giovanni Paolo II: Il mio amato predecessore* (Cinisello Balsamo: San Paolo, 2007).

[57] Joseph Ratzinger, *Salt of the Earth*, trans. Adrian Walker (San Francisco: Ignatius Press, 1997), 85.

[58] Ibid.

In 1970, he had published a book, *Infallible? An Inquiry*,[59] in which he clearly took a position against the papal infallibility defined at Vatican I. The following year, in his contribution to an anthology in which the more prominent theologians of the council distanced themselves from Küng, Ratzinger still remained pragmatic, a "possibilist". On the one hand, he recognized with Küng the need to break with the theology taught in the pontifical universities; on the other hand, he forcefully maintained that it was necessary to remain faithful to Catholic doctrine.[60] Ratzinger distanced himself much more clearly from Küng after the publication of *On Being a Christian*.[61] Having joined the group of theologians who had given birth to the journal *Communio*, Ratzinger collaborated on a collection of essays[62] whose main authors were precisely those contributors to the new journal. According to Ratzinger, Küng, in his desire to distance himself from Rome, was now expressing the partisan convictions of a school of thought, and not a truth of faith for which one can live or die.

The Swiss theologian, nevertheless, proceeded unperturbed along his path and in 1979 published an article in which he harshly criticized John Paul II. This was a frontal attack that received wide coverage not only in Germany but also in the United States, France, Latin America, and Italy. Consequently, the Congregation for the Doctrine of the Faith, at that time headed by the Croatian Franjo Cardinal Šeper, who for some time had already been examining the volume on papal infallibility, considered itself almost compelled to withdraw the Swiss professor's canonical mission, which in practice meant his authorization to teach theology on the Catholic faculties of the State universities in Germany. Thus, a decision was made that the bishop of Rottenburg-Stuttgart, in whose jurisdiction the University of Tübingen was located, then had to implement. This

---

[59] Hans Küng, *Unfehlbar? Eine Anfrage* (Zurich and Einsiedeln: Benziger Verlag, 1970); trans. Edward Quinn as *Infallible? An Inquiry* (Garden City, N.Y.: Doubleday, 1971).

[60] Joseph Ratzinger, "Contraddizioni nel libro 'Infallibile' di Hans Küng", in *Infallibile?: Rahner-Congar-Sartori-Ratzinger . . . contro Hans Küng* (Rome: Edizioni Paoline, 1971), 47–80.

[61] Hans Küng, *Christ sein* (Munich and Zurich: Piper, 1974); trans. Edward Quinn as *On Being a Christian* (New York: Doubleday, 1976).

[62] Hans Urs von Balthasar et al., *Diskussion über Hans Küngs "Christ sein"* (Mainz: Grünewald, 1976).

had caused a big commotion that had imperiled the teaching of theology at the State universities.[63]

Finally, a more or less agreeable solution had been found with the *Land* of Baden, whereby Küng could continue to teach in Tübingen: no longer on the Catholic faculty, however, but in the field of religious studies. Obviously, the incident was much talked about in Munich, too; it was portrayed by the newspapers, particularly by the *Frankfurter Allgemeine Zeitung*, as a sensational sign of the lack of freedom of expression in the Church. Invited several times to express his opinion, Ratzinger spoke on the occasion of a meeting with the young people of the diocese held in Freising on November 11, 1979. The facts are simple, the cardinal said. Küng was distancing himself on many points from the Catholic Church, and therefore he could no longer teach in the name of the Church. It was a question of clarity and honesty. On the other hand, Küng was denying the bishops' very right to grant a canonical mission, and therefore it was not clear why he insisted so much on it. He certainly had freedom of speech, but then he spoke in his own name, not in the name of the bishop of the Church. This was how one should understand also the recent speech by the Ordinary of Regensburg, who had withdrawn the invitation sent to Küng by the College of Catholic Studies in the neighboring city on the Danube. The college was a Catholic institution, and the invitation, although sent by the rector of the institute, had been made in the name of the bishop. The latter, therefore, had the right and the duty to intervene. Ratzinger then invited the young people not to take too seriously the air of martyrdom that surrounded Küng. Perhaps, with the exception of the pope, there was no bishop in the world who had as much access to the media as he did. Furthermore, a professor in Tübingen was not the most suitable spokesman for the Church of the poor.[64]

The repercussions of the sensational withdrawal of the *placet* from Küng had not yet died down when, in the following month, a new case burst onto the scene that collided head-on with the cardinal of Munich. Johann Baptist Metz, Ratzinger's former colleague in

---

[63] In a conversation that I had with him a few years after the event, this was the conclusion that Walter Kasper had reached; he gave a rather severe judgment on Küng's conduct on that occasion.

[64] Cf. Pfister, *Joseph Ratzinger*, 361.

Münster, who was famous for having started a so-called "political" approach to theology, had been suggested by the academic senate as first on a list of three names presented to the Bavarian Minister of Education, Hans Maier, as successor in the chair of fundamental theology at the University of Munich. Contrary to general expectations, nevertheless, the second on the list was appointed, Professor Heinrich Döring. A wave of protest against Maier followed, but also against Ratzinger, who was, not unjustly, thought to have influenced the choice made by his friend the Minister. The elderly Karl Rahner became the spokesman of the general indignation, even though he had sincerely admired his younger colleague at the time of the council.

In a letter that was made public by the press, the Jesuit theologian accused Ratzinger of not distinguishing adequately between his hierarchical responsibility and his theological views, and he challenged him to a public debate in defense of freedom of theological research. At first, the cardinal hoped that the outcry would die down, and for this reason he preferred to remain silent. Given the escalating polemics, however, he intervened with a long, articulate position paper. He responded to Rahner, saying that he had refused to debate publicly precisely out of respect for him. He did not deny his involvement in the appointment that bypassed Metz; indeed, he declared that he had followed the matter very attentively from the beginning. He then added that all three nominees suggested were qualified for the job and that he had not intended to do Metz any harm.

Yet the impression that one gets from reading the document is that for once the cardinal was short on arguments and that the risk keenly perceived by the former professor was destined to follow Ratzinger for a long time. In this specific case, Hansjürgen Verweyen maintained that Ratzinger had been misled by insufficiently distinguishing the concept of hope in Metz from the one in Moltmann's writings. In tracing the thought of the two authors back to an excessively broad and vague view of Marxism, he ended up lumping them together in a condemnation that appeared unfair to many people.[65] It must be recalled, nevertheless, that later on there

---

[65] Hansjürgen Verweyen, *Joseph Ratzinger-Benedikt XVI: Die Entwicklung seines Denkens* (Darmstadt: WBG, 2007), 71.

was a public reconciliation between Ratzinger and Metz on the occasion of a colloquium held in Ahaus near Münster in 1998.[66] Ratzinger, finally, in a report given in 2000 to the convention on the implementation of Vatican II, declared that he had been deeply impressed by the speech with which Metz had resigned from his chair of theology in Münster in 1993.[67]

These two incidents connected to the figures of Küng and Metz provoked a wave of discontent, especially among young people, which led to a disagreeable form of protest. On June 10, 1980, the cardinal had been invited to give a conference at the University of Munich. A group of students from the far left, probably backed by persons from outside the university, prevented him from speaking by shouting, booing, and whistling. For several hours, it seemed to the cardinal that he was reliving his experiences in Tübingen; nevertheless, there was no lack of votes of confidence.

The journey to Poland and the Synod on the Family

In the preceding pages, I have already mentioned the role played by the German bishops in the election of John Paul II and the intention of both Wojtyła and Ratzinger finally to overcome the rancor and the divisions due to the Second World War. These common purposes were confirmed in an important way in the second half of 1980. On August 6, Ratzinger announced to the citizens that in November the pope was going to visit Germany. On that occasion, he would also make a stop at the Marian Shrine in Altötting and in Munich, where he would celebrate Mass on the Theresienwiese, the same plaza where twenty years earlier the World Eucharistic Congress had been celebrated, which had given a strong impetus to the faith in the diocese. Upon his arrival, the pope would encounter a Church that was certainly alive; the cardinal, nevertheless, expected incentives and encouragement to overcome divisions and conflicts present in the Church and in society. From September

---

[66] Gianni Valente, *Ratzinger professore* (Cinisello Balsamo: San Paolo, 2008), 181.

[67] Ratzinger's report entitled "L'ecclesiologia della costituzione 'Lumen Gentium'" was published in the Italian edition of *L'Osservatore Romano* dated March 4, 2000, and in the volume containing the proceedings of the convention entitled *Il concilio Vaticano II: Recezione e attualità alla luce del Giubileo* (Cinisello Balsamo: San Paolo, 2000).

11 to 18, a delegation of German bishops went on pilgrimage to Poland to repay the visit from the Polish bishops in 1978. Ratzinger had not been able to participate in that event, since he had been in Ecuador as the legate of Pope Luciani. Now, however, not only did he travel to Poland, but on September 13, as the guest of Cardinal Macharski, Wojtyła's successor, he gave a solemn discourse in the cathedral in Kraków.

In his speech, he underscored the role of faith as a reconciling, unifying force. Europe became Europe only through the Christian faith. This faith contains within itself the Hebrew heritage, but also the best of the Greco-Roman intellectual tradition. The Germanic and Slavic peoples gave new forms to this faith, but they had received their history and identity from it. The encounter with Jesus Christ had laid the foundations of true humanism, of a new humanity that is at the basis of all true progress. In this context, the cardinal also recalled the barbarity of the Nazi practice of killing the mentally disabled. Christian culture had built not only cathedrals in honor of God but also hospitals for the sick and the aged. True European culture is not only a culture of reason; it is love of neighbor, of mercy, and of social justice.

Ratzinger concluded his speech with an impassioned invitation to preserve unity in multiplicity. The multiplicity of national cultures constitutes the richness of Europe. After the ravages caused by nationalism in the first half of the twentieth century, it is necessary to learn anew the true European spirit. He then asked the Blessed Virgin, the Mother of the Lord and Mother of Europe, to bless the path of reconciliation that Poles and Germans, together with all Europeans, now intended to follow. Upon returning to his country, on September 16, he celebrated a Solemn Pontifical Mass in thanksgiving for the eighth centennial of the House of Wittelsbach: again an appreciation of the Christian history of Europe. On September 26, finally, he left for Rome, where he was a *relator* at the Synod on the Family. The pope had entrusted this task to him because he wanted to re-launch the institution of the synod and to strengthen the Christian vision of the family, which in some quarters was being called into question, especially in the West and in Germany itself.

Ratzinger divided his speech into three points: the situation of the family in the modern world, God's plan for the family today, problems in pastoral ministry. Given the crisis of the traditional family, the cardinal of Munich called for a true Christian personalism. Only a correct anthropology can promote the equality of the sexes and the dignity of women. From the sacramental perspective, the love of one man and one woman corresponds to Christ's union of love with the one Church. This love is at the foundation of the fidelity and indissolubility of marriage. Finally, the cardinal spoke about educating young people to conjugal fidelity and about the difficulties faced by separated or divorced families. "With God's help, our synod must show the hope of the Gospel and proclaim the Good News to mankind."[68] In this context, the cardinal already spoke about mercy toward the separated, the divorced, and the civilly remarried. They are not outside the Church, which must show toward them her motherly heart.

With regard to the 1980 synod, Carlo Maria Cardinal Martini recalled an incident that had struck him. Throughout the month, Ratzinger showed that he was listening very attentively to the interventions of the synod Fathers who requested explanations relative to his report. He then responded very pertinently. In particular, the cardinal of Milan was struck by the fact "that in a particularly delicate moment of the synod proceedings, he admitted simply that, having worked until late the preceding night, he had not actually succeeded in putting together the text that was awaited, and thus he asked to postpone his speech. I did not know whether to admire his wisdom more or his sincerity."[69] I myself was witness to a similar incident that took place on the occasion of the presentation of a book to the institute of patrology, the Augustinianum in Rome. After I gave the floor to the cardinal, he admitted that he had not had the time to read the work. Nonetheless, he provided background information for the volume that made the following speeches almost superfluous.

Unity in multiplicity, the desire finally to overcome the consequences of the war, culture, peace, reconciliation, the European spirit, Christian anthropology, personalism, and the open, dynamic

---

[68] See Pfister, *Joseph Ratzinger*, 393.

[69] C. M. Martini, "Un servitore della fede e della tradizione", in Josef Clemens and Antonio Tarzia, *Alla scuola della verità: I settant'anni di Joseph Ratzinger* (Cinisello Balsamo: San Paolo, 1997), 186.

nuclear family were topics common to Ratzinger and to Wojtyła. On this set of shared values, which was stronger than any different views on individual subjects in theology or morality, they built an alliance that was destined to last over the years.

The visit of John Paul II to Munich

As previously announced, from November 15 to 19, 1980, John Paul II traveled to Germany. His itinerary included Cologne, Mainz, Fulda, Altötting, and Munich. The visit had a twofold purpose: to express gratitude and closeness to the Church that contributed to his election and to invite the Catholic community to unity, to set aside the recriminations against Rome that were due principally to *Humanae vitae* by Paul VI. For the German lay faithful and also for many priests and bishops, the encyclical was a difficult burden to bear, while for John Paul II it remained a pillar of his Christian vision of marriage. Ratzinger accompanied the pope on all the stages of the journey, which on November 18 brought him to the Marian Shrine in Altötting, the heart of Bavaria and at the same time the geographical, cultural, and spiritual center of Europe. There, Ratzinger, from his childhood, used to go on pilgrimage with his parents and siblings to venerate the Black Madonna of that locality, which certainly reminded John Paul II of another famous Black Madonna, the one in Częstochowa. There the pope held a meeting with German theologians, to whom he spoke with rare candor. Reading a text that many considered to have been inspired by Ratzinger, he said that theology is certainly a science, but it presupposes faith. For his part, the theologian teaches in the name and by the mandate of the Church, and if there are differences between the Church and the theologian, the latter is the one who must bow his head.

The next day, more than a half million persons participated in the Mass celebrated by the pontiff on the Theresienwiese, the esplanade famous for the Oktoberfest, the autumn beer festival. The view was extraordinary, and once again Catholic Bavaria lived up to its reputation. Not everything, though, went as it was supposed to. At the end of the ceremony, Barbara Engl, spokesman for the German League of Catholic Youth, took the microphone and said that it was difficult for young people to understand a Church that is timid, attached to the status quo, and against reforms.[70] The pope was surprised, looked at Ratzinger, exchanged a few words with him, and suddenly ended the ceremony without answering. It was in reality a provocation owing chiefly to the fact that the young people had not had the opportunity to converse with the pope as had been the case in Paris and Cologne. According to the planners, this neglect was due to the shortage of time. The gesture of protest, however, was also a sign that among German Catholic young people, even in Catholic Bavaria, there was a persistent uneasiness to which no one had successfully given a convincing response.[71] In any case, the pope was accustomed to quite different sorts of protest.

At the airport, before boarding the plane that was to take him back to Rome, he repeated with emotion the basic leitmotiv of his journey, which Ratzinger fully shared: it is necessary to overcome the tragic consequences of the Second World War; it is necessary to reestablish peace among nations, in particular between Germany and Poland. In a telegram sent several days later, he warmly thanked the cardinal and all the faithful of Munich for their welcome. For his part, Ratzinger wrote a letter to the faithful thanking them for the welcome that they had given to the pope and urging them not to let themselves be deprived of the joy that had been experienced during those days in the liturgical and devotional celebrations, in the streets and on the plazas. And as though to offset the protest of the youth spokesman Engl, he particularly thanked the young people who had prepared themselves with a night of prayer for their meeting with the pope.

"It was not easy for me to decide. The pope wants me in Rome."

On May 13, 1981, the Turkish terrorist Mehmet Ali Ağca fired at John Paul II. The assassination attempt failed, but the pope was seriously wounded, and in order to continue performing his ministry,

---

[70] See Lecomte, Benoît XVI, 79; Pfister, Joseph Ratzinger, 399.

[71] In reality, perhaps precisely in view of the pope's visit, there had been a meeting of the cardinals with the leaders of the League of Young Catholics on June 2. The latter had met Ratzinger a few days before the pope's arrival, showing him the demands they intended to make. The cardinal had invited them not to make general statements but to make true demands, specifying whether they were expressing a personal opinion or a general view. Obviously, no agreement was reached. Cf. Pfister, Joseph Ratzinger, 399.

he needed trusted co-workers more than ever. Precisely during those summer months when the pope was getting back to work at the Vatican, one of the most delicate jobs in the Roman Curia opened up. Franjo Cardinal Šeper left the Congregation for the Doctrine of the Faith both because he had reached the age limit and also because he had come down with a serious illness. And then John Paul II thought once again of Ratzinger and repeated to him the invitation from a few years before: "We want you in Rome." Ratzinger had turned down the first invitation in 1978, citing his recent appointment as archbishop of Munich. Now he did not feel he could answer again in the negative. Part of his decision to accept, certainly, was his concern about and affection for the wounded pope, but there was also the sense of exhaustion caused by pastoral work to which, perhaps, he was not exactly called. Moreover, the debates between conservatives and progressives certainly had not subsided in his diocese. Maybe it was better for him to return to theology.[72] He then asked the pope: As prefect of the congregation, could he continue to write theology and to publish books? For the pope, who was well acquainted with the love for writing and continued to write and publish even very personal books himself, that posed no problem.[73] At this point, the decision was made: Ratzinger would be the new prefect of the Congregation for the Doctrine of the Faith. Upon announcing his appointment to the faithful on November 26, 1981, the cardinal recalled once again his affection for Munich, which was also the diocese where he had been born, the capital of his beloved Bavaria. He emphasized the growth of mutual trust during the four years that he had spent in Munich as archbishop and his desire to bring to completion the many initiatives that had been started. He maintained, nevertheless, that he could not refuse the new responsibility, in the service of the universal Church. Through this ministry he would still remain united with his diocese and his faithful.[74]

---

[72] Cf. Lecomte, *Benoît XVI*, 81.

[73] J. Ratzinger, *Salt of the Earth*, 86.

[74] Pfister, *Joseph Ratzinger*, 435f.

VIII

FIRST YEARS IN ROME

In the service of the universal Church

Among the thousands of congratulatory notes delivered to the new prefect of the Congregation for the Doctrine of the Faith there was one sent by a former student of Ratzinger, the Orthodox Damaskinos Papandreou, future metropolitan bishop of Adrianople. After the greetings and good wishes, he posed to his former professor the acute question that Karl Rahner had already addressed to him: "What continuity will there be between the old professor and the new prefect?" Ratzinger did not avoid the question: "The prefect and the professor are the same person. The two titles, however, indicate two different functions, which have different duties."[1] Although clear to the cardinal, the distinction was fraught with tensions that would lead to disputes that caused a sensation within and outside the Church. Coming from Germany, one of the countries where the tensions within the Christian community were more passionate, Ratzinger was aware of the difficulty of the job that he was about to assume. He knew, also, that he could count on his good formation, his conscience, and the support of John Paul II, who had insisted so much on having him at his side. And then there was the insistent call to courage that he had addressed to the bishops and the priests. He said to Peter Seewald in 1996: "Even today I am glad that in Munich I didn't dodge conflict, because letting things drift is . . . the worst kind of administration I can imagine. From the very beginning it was clear to me that during my time in Rome I would have to carry out a lot of unpleasant tasks. But I think I

---

[1] See Bernard Lecomte, *Benoît XVI: Le dernier pape européen* (Paris: Perrin, 2006), 82.

may say that I have always sought dialogue and that it has also been very fruitful."[2]

There is a lot of Ratzinger in this admission. The clarity of thought, the awareness that he was going against the current and therefore would inevitably be exposed to criticism, but also the conviction that he was doing the job that he had been asked to do, his service to the truth for the universal Church. Ratzinger's arrival at the congregation, moreover, posed a methodological problem that should be mentioned right away.

As I have already recalled in the preceding chapter, he immediately made it clear to the pope that he wanted to keep writing and publishing. Moreover, he was a leader who was certainly not content merely to sign the documents published by his dicastery. At the same time, however, he fully respected the thinking of his collaborators. In this regard, Bernard Lecomte recalled a curious episode. For some time, the Lutheran World Federation and the Pontifical Council for Promoting Christian Unity had been working to draw up a joint document on the doctrine of justification, whereby man becomes just through God's gift and not through his good conduct fostered by the ecclesiastical institution. After numerous attempts, finally in early 1998, they came to approve a joint document that was publicly praised by Ratzinger, who belonged also to the Council for Promoting Christian Unity and had many Lutheran friends. Upon returning to the congregation, however, he realized that most of his consultors were against it. According to Lecomte, ultimately it took the pope's persistent efforts in order for the *Declaration on the Doctrine of Justification* to be presented solemnly at last in the Vatican Press Office on June 25, 1998.[3] It was accompanied by a document that piqued the curiosity of the experts: a response by the congregation expressing its reservations. On the other hand, especially at the beginning, the prefect accompanied the documents of his own dicastery with articles and also with explanatory interviews. I have tried to give preference to the latter in order to reconstruct Ratzinger's thought about the matters treated in the documents of the congregation, also.

---

[2] Joseph Ratzinger, *Salt of the Earth: The Church at the End of the Millennium*, trans. Adrian Walker (San Francisco: Ignatius Press, 1997), 83.

[3] Cf. Lecomte, *Benoît XVI*, 85f.

ARRIVAL IN ROME

After the official announcement of his appointment to the Congregation for the Doctrine of the Faith, Ratzinger remained in Munich for about four months. He had to take leave of his diocese and receive instructions in order to start his new and demanding job. He arrived in Rome in March 1982. He was accompanied by his sister, Maria, a walnut writing desk, an automobile that he had acquired in Freising and was very fond of, his beloved piano, and about two thousand books that made up his private library. He took lodgings on the fourth floor of a palazzo on the via della Città Leonina, in an approximately 3,000-square-foot apartment, across from the barracks of the Swiss Guard, a few steps away from Saint Peter's Square. A prestigious residence reserved for the cardinals who work in the Roman congregations, it was transformed into a genuine library, according to the unanimous testimony of those who had reason to visit it.[4] Soon his neighbor would be the Italian Pio Laghi, former nuncio in Washington, and later the Colombian Darío Castrillón Hoyos, a tenacious opponent of liberation theology.

Although the residence was prestigious, the cardinal did all he could to preserve his life-style, which was austere to the point of seeming ascetical. In the morning, he rose early, recited his private prayers, said Mass, then sat down for the breakfast prepared by Maria. His clothing, too, was as simple as ever. Over his black cassock in the winter months, he wore an overcoat of the same color; on his head, the indispensable beret; and under his arm, a rather worn-out briefcase containing dossiers that were sometimes extremely sensitive. To see him you might think of Father Brown, a simple, keen-eyed country priest, always ready to greet tourists or to answer their questions. I myself recall having met him once at the entrance to the Porta Sant'Anna at the Vatican. The Swiss Guard had stopped me, and I was showing him my identification when I saw the cardinal coming down from the other side. I tried to hurry up so as to go and greet him, but the Swiss Guard was not of the same mind. The cardinal then came over to greet us, embarrassing

---

[4] This is the testimony of several witnesses, among whom was the Vaticanist for the network RAI, Giuseppe De Carli, who repeated it several times on television. Cf. Paolo Mosca, *Il ciabattino del papa et altre storie* (Cinisello Balsamo: San Paolo, 2009), 44.

me and the guard, who sprang to attention. On Thursday morning, he used to go to say Mass at the Teutonic College of Santa Maria in Campo Santo, which had been established for German-speaking priests studying theology in Rome, and on Sunday mornings he sometimes went to the parish of Santa Maria Consolatrice, his titular church in the Eternal City. Returning to his weekday schedule: at around 8:30, like a faithful employee, he would leave his apartment to go to work. He did not have to go far, and therefore he regularly went on foot. Through the Piazza della Città Leonina, he reached the Bernini columns, which brought him onto Saint Peter's Square, and he found himself in front of his office, located in the Piazza del Sant'Uffizio, on the other side of the huge dome. After 1:00 P.M., he went back again, carrying under his arm the briefcase in which he had placed new dossiers to be studied at home.

Almost always he ate with Maria, who from time to time managed to prepare some Bavarian dishes for him. Again, it was his sister who went one day to the tailor Mancinelli in Borgo Pio to ask him to make a clerical suit for her brother to wear when he was traveling. "He never got tired of trying on clothing. He always had a kind word for my sons and my wife."[5] He did not like to frequent the Roman restaurants together with monsignors or other cardinals to forge alliances, to network, and to keep up with the gossip that often enlivens the little world of the Vatican. Sometimes, nevertheless, he would go to the Borgo Pio to the Cantina Tirolese, a restaurant where dishes typical of the Alpine region were served. "Ratzinger used to arrive there before eight o'clock, with his black attaché-case, in clericals, always in the company of friends. . . . There he found the atmosphere of the Bavarian Stuben [that is, Bierstuben = tap-rooms]."[6] Other times, on festive occasions, he went to the Passetto di Borgo with his sister, Maria. "Always with them were Bishop Mayer and his sister. They would eat and then chat for a long time in German."[7] More precisely, the four spoke in the Bavarian dialect. Paul Mayer and his sister, indeed, were originally from Altötting, the Bavarian shrine not far from the birthplaces of the two Ratzingers. Mayer had become a Benedictine monk, taking

---

[5] Ibid., 180.
[6] Ibid., 24f.
[7] Ibid.

the religious name of Augustine; he was a professor and rector of Saint Anselm's Abbey in Rome. Then he had been undersecretary of the preparatory commission of Vatican II. Conservative in his thinking, he then became a bishop, a cardinal, and prefect of the Congregation for Divine Worship.[8]

Ratzinger's favorite drink was orangeade; he avoided wine so as to stay lucid and be able to return to work immediately with the required attention. He often went walking in the old quarter across from the Vatican, and one could see him conversing with the local merchants.[9] In particular, he won the affection of a South American shoemaker who realized that he had Ratzinger among his clients when he saw him on television beside the pope. "He was a simple person; unless I spoke first, he would let me work without opening his mouth."[10] At home, his favorite pastime was the piano, which he played regularly, particularly pieces by his beloved Mozart. Then, as though to promote the friendship of the cardinal from Munich with the Romans, there was his love for cats. His brother has toned down somewhat the legend about Ratzinger the "cat-lover"; he did recall, nevertheless, that on Thursday mornings, when he would go to the Teutonic College of Santa Maria in Campo Santo to say Mass, there was always a cat who waited for the cardinal to be petted by him.[11]

THE HOLY OFFICE

Paul III Farnese, a pope who reigned between the Renaissance and the Reformation, was the founder of the Holy Office in 1542. Given the spread of reforming trends that were gaining more and more ground in Germany and in German-speaking countries, he instituted a commission of cardinals called the Sacred Congregation of the Roman and Universal Inquisition with the task of defending the Church from all forms of heresy. Always at the head of the papal congregations, it kept that title until the early twentieth century,

---

[8] In memory of his old friendship, Benedict XVI celebrated Mass and gave the homily on the day of the funeral of the almost century-old cardinal, in 2010.

[9] See Georg Ratzinger and Michael M. Hesemann, *My Brother the Pope*, trans. Michael J. Miller (San Francisco: Ignatius Press, 2011), 218.

[10] Mosca, *Il ciabattino del papa*, 40.

[11] G. Ratzinger and Hesemann, *My Brother the Pope*, 219.

when the progress of historical science, which threw a disturbing light on the systems adopted by the tribunals of the Inquisition, induced the pontiff at that time, Pius X, to change the name to the Sacred Congregation of the Holy Office.

The discontent that smoldered for decades in ecclesiastical circles made itself heard in particularly harsh, sorrowful tones at Vatican II. At the first session of the council, the German bishops and experts, with Ratzinger among them, had raised their voices to bring about a change in the practices and purposes of what was by then the oldest of the Vatican institutions. Taking these requests into consideration, on December 7, 1965, a few days before the conclusion of Vatican II, Paul VI redefined and expanded the tasks of that Vatican body. Instead of an exclusively corrective mandate, it received also and above all a proactive purpose. It was not enough to correct errors; it was necessary to promote the doctrine of the faith, to point out its positive aspects. Hence, the new name of Congregation for the Doctrine of the Faith. Ratzinger was fully in agreement with this new approach, indeed, he considered it an essential condition for being able to accept the job. While he was still in Munich, he had said that the particularly delicate questions would be worked out by symposia and colloquia. "It is a matter of connecting the particular impulses with the whole, making them fruitful and purifying them, finding solutions to the major topics of the day in a broad and truly Catholic exchange."[12] And in his interview with Seewald, he added: "First of all, I wanted to stress as vigorously as possible the collegial model rather than individual decision making and to underscore the role of the individual constituent elements. I also wanted to foster dialogue with theology and theologians, as well as with the bishops, for our immediate partners are actually the bishops."[13]

The process of renewing the congregation, however, had not yet been completed. In 1988, John Paul II specified further tasks for it, declaring that, in order to achieve its purposes, the congregation had to "promote studies aimed at increasing understanding of the faith, so that in the light of the faith solutions can be found for new

---

[12] Cf. Peter Pfister, ed., *Joseph Ratzinger und das Erzbistum München und Freising* (Regensburg: Schnell und Steiner, 2006), 436f.

[13] J. Ratzinger, *Salt of the Earth*, 86.

problems that have emerged from the progress of the sciences and of civilization", a formulation in which it is easy to recognize the stamp of the new prefect in charge of the congregation itself. With this intention, once he had arrived in Rome, Ratzinger renewed the personnel of the congregation, which, after a time, was composed of around forty employees assisted by around thirty consultors, most of them professors of the Pontifical Roman Universities. The cardinal's main collaborators were the internal employees, who divided the work among themselves according to their areas and fields of competence.

LISTENING TO THE BISHOPS AND CONFRONTING THE THEOLOGIANS

The cardinal's primary sources of information were the episcopal conferences and the bishops making their *ad limina* visits in Rome. They were chiefly the ones who informed the cardinal and his co-workers, and sometimes they asked them to intervene in support of previous decisions and concerns of a pastoral nature. Ratzinger confided to me that he spent most of his time listening to bishops from all parts of the world. Many were tired and confused, others felt alone and abandoned in remote dioceses, subjected along with their flock to violence or else attacked by the media without really knowing why or having the time to respond. He considered these meetings a true, genuine pastoral ministry in the attempt to inspire confidence and courage in those who were objectively working in difficult conditions. The gratitude of these bishops when they left Rome with renewed confidence and evangelical enthusiasm was the best form of recognition for the cardinal, whom the media stubbornly presented as a cold bureaucrat who executed sentences.

At the beginning of *The Ratzinger Report*,[14] Vittorio Messori found it amusing to quote the hasty, fanciful judgments of some of the Italian media. In reality, the misunderstanding of the journalists had its origin in an uneasiness that was present within the Church herself. Given the internal and external disputes, many preferred to avoid the contradictions by pretending not to see them. The shy, peaceful Bavarian cardinal, in contrast, thought that it was precisely

---

[14] Joseph Ratzinger with Vittorio Messori, *The Ratzinger Report*, trans. Salvator Attanasio and Graham Harrison (San Francisco: Ignatius Press, 1985), 9.

his job to intervene, to speak clearly, and to call the bishops to their ministry of proclaiming the Gospel.

Of course, Ratzinger wanted to engage in dialogue with the theologians, too, but this brought up the same objection that Karl Rahner had made in his day: Was the new prefect of the congregation, who was a highly renowned theologian, not seeking to impose his view of theology, to favor one school of thought, instead of promoting the innovative thrust of Vatican II? Was his intention to fall back on more consolidated lines after the humiliation of the challenges from secularization? The progressive theologians, too, saw the problems and contradictions in a society that was separating itself more and more from the Church and from the Christian world view, but they thought that this trend was unstoppable. From his perspective, Ratzinger honestly confronted the problem and sought to give more than a perfunctory answer. In an article entitled "Theology and the Government of the Church",[15] he first carefully defined the two terms of the question, then sought to relate them to each other. To theology is entrusted the study of the rational aspect of the faith, whereas the Church is the concrete living space of reason in search of meaning. The complexity lies in keeping both tasks in their reciprocal autonomy and fullness.

The first sort of mistake occurs when the Magisterium infringes on the autonomy of theological research; theology's mistake consists of deserting the Church or else no longer recognizing her Magisterium. "[Theology] no longer reflects the spiritual foundation of a living community; its subject in this case is merely the private reason of the individual researcher, . . . but in this way it ceases to be theology: by making itself totally autonomous, it achieves, not a higher status, but its own destruction as theology."[16] Nevertheless, the tension already pointed out could not be eliminated, especially in the initial years; on the contrary, there were new clashes that the cardinal sought to account for, in particular in the above-cited book edited by Vittorio Messori, *The Ratzinger Report.*

---

[15] The article was published in the Italian edition of the journal *Communio* 66 (1982): 36–47. Here it is cited from Joseph Ratzinger, *La vita di Dio per gli uomini* (Milan: Jaca Book, 2006), 205–15, an anthology in which all his articles that had been published in the Italian edition of the journal were collected after he was elected pope.

[16] See ibid., 214f.

COLLABORATOR WITH JOHN PAUL II

I have already mentioned that John Paul II and Ratzinger had great esteem and respect for each other. When Ratzinger arrived in Rome, these sentiments gave a concrete shape to their collaboration. In *Salt of the Earth*, the cardinal recalls two types of institutionalized meetings, so to speak, when the pope and his collaborator got together to address the most delicate questions. The specific problems of the congregation were discussed in their Friday meeting. In his interview with Seewald, the cardinal describes in considerable detail how these meetings were conducted: "First I wait; then the Pope comes in. We shake hands, sit down together at the table, and have a little personal chat."[17] The conversation was conducted in German. The pope already had with him the dossiers to be examined. The cardinal presented them to him once again, then the pope decided. Among the most delicate topics discussed together with the pontiff, Ratzinger recalled, were: liberation theology, the function of theologians in the Church, and bioethical questions.[18]

The second type of meeting was of a convivial nature and involved a number of persons in whose opinions on certain questions the pope was particularly interested. After due notice had been given, these meetings began in the pope's residence between 11:00 and 11:30 A.M. Thus they could discuss the matter among themselves in the presence of the pontiff for an hour or an hour and a half; then usually they were invited to dine, so that there was a rather extensive period of about three hours, from 11:30 A.M. until 3:00 P.M., during which they could analyze the topics and study them in depth. At the beginning, individual persons were invited to articulate their position, then there was an opportunity for discussion. The pope mostly listened or asked for explanations. He wanted to be informed so as to be able, then, to make the right decision. In short, it was an atmosphere of industrious activity and collaboration—a far cry from the notions still present in the collective imagination. Hence Ratzinger's summary judgment on his collaboration with John Paul II: "I have an important task; the Pope trusts me; we've always discussed very important doctrinal matters with

---

[17] J. Ratzinger, *Salt of the Earth*, 9.
[18] Ibid., 108.

each other and continue to do so. In that respect, I've had a say in the Pope's official teaching and contributed something. . . . But the Pope has very much his own course."[19]

Ecumenism

PROBLEMS AND HOPES

During the same days in which Ratzinger arrived in Rome, in March 1982, the Final Report of the Anglican-Roman Catholic International Commission was made public. Instituted in 1970, over the course of more than ten years, the commission had published various statements of agreement concerning Mariology, the Eucharist, and the ordained ministry. The final report, with two declarations of agreement and a clarification, addressed in particular the delicate topic of authority in the Church. The commission's next task, now, was to submit the document to the authorities of the two Churches and to await their respective decisions. It expressed, nevertheless, the confident conviction that "under the Holy Spirit, our Churches have grown closer together in faith and charity. There are high expectations that significant initiatives will be boldly undertaken to deepen our reconciliation and lead us forward in the quest for . . . full communion."[20] In Rome, the document was first of all submitted to the authority of the pope, who forwarded it to the Congregation for the Doctrine of the Faith.

The first major topic that the new prefect found that he had to face, therefore, was ecumenism, as evidenced by the documents and the positions on the matter contained in his anthology *Church, Ecumenism, and Politics*.[21] In it, Ratzinger not only collected his es-

---

[19] Ibid., 106.

[20] Anglican-Roman Catholic International Commission (ARCIC), *The Final Report* (Windsor, 1981). The full text is printed at the website of the Anglican Communion: http://www.anglicancommunion.org/media/105260/final_report_arcic_1.pdf. Pertinent documents can be found at the Vatican website: http://www.vatican.va/roman_curia/pontifical_councils/chrstuni/sub-index/index_anglican-comm.htm.

[21] Joseph Ratzinger, *Church, Ecumenism, and Politics*, trans. Michael J. Miller et al. (San Francisco: Ignatius Press, 2008). The volume, nevertheless, was published first in Italy, then in other languages, thanks to a special relationship of the publishing house of the Paulist Fathers with the Prefect of the Congregation for the Doctrine of the Faith, fostered by the friendship between Ratzinger and the then-director of the publishing house

says but also briefly reconstructed the history of the ecumenical movement in the Catholic world. Fostered by the renewed interest in the Church and by the return to the Church Fathers, ecumenism had finally arrived in the Catholic world, supported by individual theologians like Yves Congar or the bishop of Paderborn, Lorenz Jäger. At Vatican II, the good will with which the Decree on Ecumenism had been welcomed, highlighting the elements common to the individual confessions, made the search for unity desirable and almost obligatory. The praiseworthy initial impetus, nevertheless, quickly became, in Ratzinger's view, a search for shortcuts so as to avoid addressing the problems at the origin of the divisions in the Church.

Nevertheless, it was not possible to reach an agreement even on the subject that was supposed to lead to unity. The first solution, based on the conviction that the divisions had been caused by ministers and by theologians, called for a restoration of unity exclusively from below.[22] This analysis allowed ecumenists to skip over the established authority so as to turn directly to the laity *en masse*, who were called to bring a progressive World Church to life. This vision, nevertheless, was quickly abandoned because it was clear even to the most optimistic that an ecumenism of this sort exclusively generates small groups that divide more than unite the community.

When the attempt at unity from below failed, ecumenists then thought of proceeding in the other direction, from above, from the ecclesiastical authority, based on its ministerial mandate. This, essentially, Ratzinger said, is the thesis advanced by Heinrich Fries and Karl Rahner.[23] The thesis is forcefully rejected by the prefect of the congregation, who accuses it of being the product of a clumsy exaggeration of the sphere in which the pope and the bishops can intervene. This authority cannot deal with matters of faith freely and arbitrarily but, rather, is bound by the apostolic deposit; the bishops are at its service. One final proposal starts with the various

---

in Milan, Don Antonio Tarzia. This was also the beginning of my work as Italian curator of the cardinal's works.

[22] Ibid., 132ff. In this regard, see also Aidan Nichols, O.P., *The Thought of Pope Benedict XVI: An Introduction to the Theology of Joseph Ratzinger* (London: Burns & Oates, 2007), 192.

[23] Heinrich Fries and Karl Rahner, *Einigung der Kirchen, reale Möglichkeit* (Freiburg: Herder, 1983).

confessions that in fact exist, which are generically and indiscriminately described as "traditions" of the one Church, without referring to the presence or absence in them of a foundation in Scripture and apostolic tradition.

Given these three erroneous or incomplete forms of ecumenism, which in his opinion skirt problems without resolving them, Ratzinger proposed a form of ecumenism that includes the interaction of three elements: the faith experience of the people of God, the diligent study of theologians, the doctrinal preaching of bishops. This is a slow process that cannot easily be completed in a short time. One essential condition for attaining unity is, above all, willingness to seek God's will and to act according to his instructions.

Having said that, though, the cardinal maintained that it is possible, nevertheless, to accomplish much together: "To strengthen our common witness of charity in a world that needs it more and more. To offer the common, basic testimony of the faith, to lose nothing of it, and to try to be able to give this witness in an ever more comprehensive way . . . and thus prepare for the diverse yet one Church. . . . Perhaps we need separations in order to arrive at the complete fullness for which the Lord is waiting."[24]

THE ANGLICANS AND
THE QUESTION OF AUTHORITY

When the Final Report of the Anglican-Roman Catholic International Commission reached the Congregation for the Doctrine of the Faith, Ratzinger analyzed it carefully, then, together with his collaborators, elaborated a detailed position paper, which was sent to the episcopal conferences as a contribution to the dialogue in progress. The text was then published in the issue of *L'Osservatore Romano* dated May 6, 1982. As was his custom, Ratzinger went immediately to the heart of the question by observing that the document speaks at length about authority but overlooks one decisive point: Catholics and Anglicans have very different concepts of authority. In light of Vatican II, among Catholics authority originates from the acceptance of the mystery of the Church, which is derived from the life of communion of the One and Triune God. At the

---

[24] J. Ratzinger, *Church, Ecumenism, and Politics*, 131.

origin of the Church is the love of God, transmitted by Christ in word and in sacrament. "The Church is not to be deduced from her organization; the organization is to be understood from the Church."[25] From this comes the nature of the service proper to Saint Peter and his successors, hence the responsibility of the bishops for their own local Church but, then, in the apostolic succession, also for the universal Church.

Anglicanism, in contrast, while preserving the episcopal structure, operates according to a principle of dispersed authority,[26] whereby no institution or person can speak for Anglicans in general. Authority arises from a system of balances between Scripture, traditions, creeds, the ministry of the word and of the sacrament, the testimony of the saints, and the consent of the faithful. Many elements, therefore, combine with each other and keep one another in check. Nevertheless, one problem remains: the final decision in a matter of faith, and so there is a permanent danger that Anglicanism ultimately is "a national religion, dominated by and structured on the principles of liberal tolerance, in which the authority of revelation is subordinate to democracy and private opinion."[27] Ratzinger did not adopt the judgment of William Ledwich; nevertheless, he recalled that the danger was first seen by John Henry Newman, who for precisely this reason decided to convert to Catholicism.

Ratzinger's conclusive judgment on the Final Report of the Anglican-Roman Catholic International Commission was therefore that the document was lacking because it did not clarify the concept of authority, which had always been the invalidating factor in relations between the two Christian confessions. The position taken by the congregation displeased many who had worked on the commission; some of them described it as "chilling".[28] A pause followed for reflection before a new commission could return to the matter. After five years of work, in 1988, it produced a document, *The Gift of Authority*, which confronted precisely the themes suggested by

---

[25] Joseph Ratzinger, *Introduction to Christianity*, trans. J.R. Foster, 2nd ed. (San Francisco: Ignatius Press, 2004), 346.

[26] See Nichols, *Thought of Pope Benedict XVI*, 193.

[27] William Ledwich, "With Authority, Not as the Scribes", *Insight* 1/4 (December 1983): 14–23 at 16; cited by Ratzinger in *Church, Ecumenism, and Politics*, 92.

[28] See Andrea Tornielli, *Benedetto XVI: Il custode della fede* (Casale Monferrato: Piemme, 2005), 99.

Ratzinger: the gift of authority to the Church by God, the role of the bishops, the particular role of the bishop of Rome.

Concerning this new document, the Capuchin William Henn, a professor at the Gregorian University in Rome, declared in an authoritative comment:

> If this text were to have no other fruit than simply to associate, time and again, in the minds of its readers and of those who happen to glance at its title, that the notions of "authority" and "gift" go together, [then] it would already provide a valuable service for Christian unity. There can never be reconciliation between divided Christian communities about the topic of authority unless these communities see authority as something positive.[29]

He continued with an even more laudatory appreciation: in it are present "some of the most remarkable paragraphs to appear in ecumenical dialogue to date". The frank appeal by Ratzinger had contributed to this result.

UNITY THROUGH DIVERSITY.
THE CATHOLIC–LUTHERAN DIALOGUE

The fifth centenary of the birth of Luther occurred in 1983. In Germany, preparations were underway to celebrate the event. The pope wrote a letter to Cardinal Willebrands exhorting him to proceed in the dialogue with the Lutheran-Evangelical Church, and in the Catholic world, great expectations were connected with this event; some thought that there would be a new interpretation of the father of the Reformation, and Catholic exegetes often adopted the principle of *sola Scriptura*. For his part, the cardinal was an "outstanding expert on Lutheran theology",[30] and, according to Schütte, "the efforts of the Lutheran and Catholic theologians to reach a com-

---

[29] William Henn, "A Commentary on *The Gift of Authority* of the Anglican-Roman Catholic International Commission", in the Pontifical Council for Promoting Christian Unity, *Information Service*, 1999/1: 30–42 at 30.

[30] The judgment by Eduard Lohse, a Reformed theologian and bishop, is recorded by Heinz Schütte, "Promotor unitatis christianae: Il cardinal Ratzinger e l'ecumenismo", in Josef Clemens and Antonio Tarzia, *Alla scuola della verità: I settant'anni di Joseph Ratzinger* (Cinisello Balsamo: San Paolo, 1997), 89. It should be recalled that Schütte earned a doctorate with a thesis on Protestantism with Ratzinger as his advisor and that he was later professor of ecumenism in Bonn.

mon understanding of the Augsburg Confession . . . are almost unthinkable without the impetus provided by Ratzinger."[31] Yet he was
rather reserved. His remarks on the dialogue with Lutheranism concerned the figure of Luther himself.[32]

He remarked that historical-theological research is acquainted
with various images of the Reformer. He himself, following Harnack, recognized two faces in the former Augustinian friar: there is
the Luther of the catechism, the hymns, and the liturgical reforms,
who can be accepted by Catholics, too. On the other hand, however, there is the radical, polemical Luther, whose peculiar version
of justification by faith cannot be shared by a Catholic, for whom
the act of faith occurs in communion with the whole Church.
The principle of *sola Scriptura*, too, which is so dear to Protestant
and Catholic exegetes, worried the cardinal: "What today's average
Christian deduces from this principle is that faith comes from one's
individual perception, from intellectual application along with the
contributions of experts."[33] The result is that the Catholic concept
of Church is considered outmoded, while it seems advisable to adapt
the Protestant one.

This trend is all the more surprising since the crisis in Protestantism is certainly no less serious than the one running through
the Catholic Church. The explanation for what the cardinal considered a temptation for Catholics in those years derived from the fact
that Protestantism originated at the beginning of the modern era.
"It has acquired the form it has today largely in the confrontation
with the great philosophical currents of the nineteenth century. It is
wide open to modern thought, and, as well as constituting a threat
to it, that constitutes both its opportunity and its danger."[34] On the
other hand, there is scientific research that, on the contrary, tends to
consider outmoded the concept of *sola Scriptura*. Historical-critical
exegesis has indeed demonstrated that the Gospels are a product
of the early Church, and one can say, extending this concept, that
the whole Bible took shape and was transmitted through tradition.
Therefore, one cannot start from the Bible, which is torn to pieces

---

[31] Heinz Schütte, "Promotor unitatis christianae", 94.
[32] See Nichols, *Thought of Pope Benedict XVI*, 195.
[33] See J. Ratzinger, *Ratzinger Report*, 156.
[34] Ibid.

by the disputes of the denominations and the experts; the traditions, that is, the concrete configurations of the Christian reality in which the individual confessions live, seem to be more amenable. Dialogical irenicism suggests starting with them, but of course without inquiring into their origin and their content.

The conclusion, according to Ratzinger, is that here we no longer find ourselves facing the Scripturalist principle of Luther and Calvin, or even the Catholic and Orthodox principle of tradition that is of apostolic and divine origin, inasmuch as it transmits revelation. We are facing a factual principle that does have its positive aspects: old prejudices are put into perspective; there is a new candor and freedom to see and to understand the other's ideas. Ecumenists, however, cannot go farther in that direction. Otherwise, in the cardinal's view, "they would have cut themselves completely loose from the question of truth, and theology would then be merely a form of diplomacy, of politics."[35]

The considerations of the cardinal prefect were received harshly. Several German Catholic theologians distinguished themselves as some of the cardinal's severest critics. Ratzinger responded to them with a letter addressed to Max Seckler, editor-in-chief of the *ThQ*, the prestigious theological journal published in Tübingen.[36] After briefly chronicling the course of the interfaith dialogue in the post-conciliar era, the cardinal explained that the purpose of ecumenism cannot be irenicism at all costs, "ecumenical negotiations", but rather the attainment of the unity that is present in the Trinitarian life of God, which Jesus proclaimed and gave to his disciples. Instead, he adopted Oscar Cullmann's formula of unity in diversity. The cardinal explained that in this way he did not intend at all to restrain ecumenical momentum. On the contrary, he maintained that, from his perspective, a twofold method of proceeding unfolds with regard to the ecumenical movement. The first consists in the search for models of unity in order to overcome the oppositions with a view to unity. Alongside this search, nevertheless, there is a second, perhaps even more important path to travel in prayer and repentance. Only in this way will it be possible to achieve that unity

---

[35] J. Ratzinger, *Church, Ecumenism, and Politics*, 98.

[36] The journal is the *Theologische Quartalschrift* of Tübingen. The letter is reprinted in J. Ratzinger, *Church, Ecumenism, and Politics*, 132–38.

which we do not make but rather is given by God, "where and when [he] has seen fit", according to the saying of Melanchthon.

Although he was opposed by some theologians and by the media that gave them plenty of coverage, Ratzinger was nevertheless not alone. The bilateral document of the German Bishops' Conference and the United Evangelical-Lutheran Church of Germany more or less followed the line that he pointed out.[37] The stated purpose of the document was the communion of the Churches, not their fusion or the reconversion of one Church to the other. It was exactly the path also pointed out by the prefect of the Congregation for the Doctrine of the Faith.

The unity of the Church

Already during the years of his episcopacy in Munich, Ratzinger had displayed a growing concern with several trends and attitudes found among the faithful but also among some elements of the clergy and among the bishops themselves in Germany. This was not a matter of separatist tendencies, properly speaking, but, as Father von Balthasar had written,[38] of disaffection and dull resentment toward the Roman Curia and the papacy that did not bode well at all. As Bernard Lecomte wrote, in Germany there were still lingering consequences of the movement away from Rome;[39] in France, the Gallican tradition, which similarly imagined a national Church, free from Roman interference, was smoldering beneath the ashes.

Then there was the concern about the catechisms issued by various episcopal conferences: they ran the risk of following the model of the Dutch Catechism, which had led to a serious confrontation

---

[37] Bilateral Working Group of the German Bishops' Conference and the United Evangelical-Lutheran Church of Germany, *Ecclesial Communion in Word and Sacrament* (1984). See Adriano Garuti, *Primacy of the Bishop of Rome and the Ecumenical Dialogue* (San Francisco: Ignatius Press, 2004), 112 and 126, nn. 103 and 164.

[38] I am referring to the essay by von Balthasar, "The Anti-Roman Attitude", *Communio International Theological Journal* 8/4 (Winter 1981): 307–21.

[39] The *Los-von-Rom* (rid-of-Rome) movement started in Austria during the so-called *Kulturkampf* and was later supported especially by Chancellor Bismarck. The idea was to found a pan-Germanic state independent of Rome. Von Balthasar's polemical essay, "The Anti-Roman Attitude", also referred to this complex of ideas that then had formed the basis of the Nazi hatred of Catholics.

between the Roman authorities and the Church in Holland, creating uncertainty and bewilderment among the faithful. Faced with this danger, Ratzinger gave a conference, in Lyon on April 15 and on April 16 in Paris, in which he dared to praise the example of the Council of Trent, which had developed a uniform catechism, the so-called *Roman Catechism*.

On that occasion, Archbishop Decourtray of Lyon, vice-president of the Bishops' Conference of France, had openly distanced himself from the speech by the cardinal prefect.[40] He in turn wondered: Where is the Church going with her billions of persons if each episcopal conference publishes its own catechism with a different view of sin, the angels, the last judgment, the Holy Trinity, the virginity of Mary? His speeches reflect this preoccupation.[41] Two years later he would say to Vittorio Messori:

> Some catechisms and many catechists no longer teach the Catholic faith in its harmonic wholeness—where each truth presupposes and explains the other—rather they try to make some elements of the Christian patrimony humanly "interesting" (according to the cultural orientations of the moment). . . . [F]rom the earliest times of Christianity there appears a permanent and unrelinquishable "nucleus" of catechesis, hence of formation in the faith. Luther also employed this nucleus for his catechism, in the same matter-of-fact way as did the Roman catechism that had been decided upon at the Council of Trent. All that is said about faith, after all, is organized around four fundamental elements: the *Credo*, the *Our Father*, the *Decalogue*, the *sacraments*. These embrace the foundation of Christian life, the synthesis of the teaching of the Church based on Scripture and tradition.[42]

This was already a table of contents of the four parts of the future *Catechism of the Catholic Church*, although in a different order.

THE CODE OF CANON LAW AND
THE CONDEMNATION OF FREEMASONRY

On July 25, 1983, John Paul II signed the apostolic constitution *Sacrae Disciplinae Leges* (The laws of the sacred discipline), with

---

[40] Lecomte, *Benoît XVI*, 88.
[41] Ibid.
[42] J. Ratzinger, *Ratzinger Report*, 72–73.

which he approved and promulgated the new Code of Canon Law that was to replace the one called for by Pius X and promulgated by Benedict XV in 1917. The initiative to give the Church, in the pope's words, "the indispensable instrument to ensure order both in individual and social life, and also in the Church's activity itself", was taken by John XXIII, who had made his decision known on January 15, 1959, on the same day on which he had announced his decision to convene the Roman synod and the Vatican Council. It had then been necessary to wait for the end of the conciliar proceedings in order to take in hand a work that was intended to transmit to Church law the impulses coming from the council. Hence the duration of the work, which was not only carried out in a collegial spirit but also intended to take into account the new ecclesiology that was at the origin of the Constitution on the Church.

In this sense, the pope continued, the code is the expression of papal authority, yet it respects the collegial solicitude for the whole Church that belongs to all the bishops. John Paul II then concluded: "It could indeed be said that from this there is derived that character of complementarity which the Code presents in relation to the teaching of the Second Vatican Council." This insistence by the Polish pontiff was not accidental. He wanted to anticipate the numerous criticisms of those within the Church who, in the name of the commandment of love and of the conciliar spirit, did not even want to hear talk about a new Code of Canon Law.

All explanations notwithstanding, it was not long before the criticisms appeared. With one important exception: those who sympathized with Freemasonry were pleased to note that the excommunication with which the old code sanctioned the membership of Catholics in the lodges of the Freemasons had been dropped from the decrees of the new code. Therefore, it seemed to open the way for the reconciliation of Freemasonry with the Church,[43] but on November 26, the day before the new code came into force, a Declaration from the Congregation for the Doctrine of the Faith threw cold water on that reckless optimism. The document said peremptorily: "[T]he Church's negative judgment in regard to Masonic associations remains unchanged. . . . The faithful who enroll in Masonic associations are in a state of grave sin and may not

---

[43] See Tornielli, *Benedetto XVI*, 101.

receive Holy Communion." Then, to thwart any possible attempt to circumvent the rule, the Declaration continued, stating that "It is not within the competence of local ecclesiastical authorities to give a judgment on the nature of Masonic associations which would imply a derogation from what has been decided above."[44] This was a hard blow to Catholics who sympathized with the Freemasons, among whom there were even some monsignors of the Curia and, according to rumors, even several cardinals. From the lodges, there was no official comment. According to Tornielli, nevertheless, the origins of the persistent aversion of some of the media to the prefect of the former Holy Office are to be sought in this condemnation.[45]

THE SYNOD OF BISHOPS

In 1983, the Sixth Synod of Bishops took place in Rome. The topic on which the prelates were invited to reflect was "Reconciliation and Penance", coordinated with the Extraordinary Jubilee of Redemption that brought a large number of pilgrims to Rome that year. Ratzinger's main preoccupation, however, was a concern about unity, which is reflected also in his essay in preparation for the synod of bishops.[46] In his presentation, the cardinal recalled the fact that discussion about the nature of the synod had been urged by John Paul II. His speech had a twofold purpose: to show that the synod corresponded to the desire of the bishops assembled at the council and to the documents of Vatican II and at the same time to find a form that would preserve the unity of the Church.

From a careful reading of the individual canons and of their context, Ratzinger deduced that, according to the code, the bishops chosen to participate in the synod met to promote a closer relation between the pope and the episcopal college in order to keep alive the intimate reciprocity between the pope and the episcopal college

---

[44] See Congregation for the Doctrine of the Faith, *Declaration on Masonic Associations*, November 26, 1983.

[45] Tornielli, *Benedetto XVI*, 102.

[46] The text, originally composed in Latin, was published for the first time in Jozef Tomko, ed., *Il Sinodo dei vescovi: Natura, metodo, prospettive* (Rome: Libreria Editrice Vaticana, 1985). Later it was published in a revised form with the title "Questions about the Structure and Duties of the Synod of Bishops", in J. Ratzinger, *Church, Ecumenism, and Politics*, 51–66.

and the correct relation between the unity and the catholicity of the Church. This can be deduced from the Constitution on the Church and from other Vatican II documents. The participants in the synod can therefore offer counsel and support to the pope, drawing on their direct knowledge of the local Churches, but also on the suggestions of their confreres in the episcopate who chose them to participate in the synod. What Ratzinger meant to exclude with his clarifications was an autonomous juridical basis for the synod, independent of the pope and of the college of bishops. A permanent synod residing in Rome would no longer be representative of catholicity. A synod that merely represented the local Churches would superimpose itself on the episcopal conferences and on the personal responsibility of the individual bishops in the government of their dioceses.

Then, with a view to the reform of the synod, Ratzinger suggested that one of the tasks is mutual information, which leads also to a kind of formation and then to correction. For this reason, the participants cannot be only elected representatives who defend the mandate of their electors; rather, they are above all obliged to follow their conscience. The other task, which is even more important, is that of encouraging and strengthening the positive energies present in the Church and outside of her. From this perspective, Ratzinger concluded: "Our common work on behalf of the gospel in this time demands all our strength, and the people who live in today's world look to us, not for debates about the relation between our respective rights, but rather for the contribution that we can make toward the salvation of the world."[47]

A HARSH REPORT ON THE SITUATION OF THE CHURCH

On the occasion of the election of Benedict XVI, Vittorio Messori related how, in 1984, he contacted the prefect of the Congregation for the Doctrine of the Faith, who by then had been in office for three years, asking him for permission to interview him about the state of the Church. Contrary to the expectations of sensible people who thought that the journalist's request was unrealistic, Ratzinger

---

[47] Ibid., 66.

agreed and made an appointment with Messori at the seminary in Brixen. There, for several years, the cardinal had spent the summer holidays economically, together with his sister and brother.[48] The cardinal's consent to be interviewed, which became a precedent for the consent given then by John Paul II, sensationally broke with a culture of secrecy and a praxis of silence that had lasted for centuries. All the more so because the cardinal answered the journalist's questions courteously, but also with unusual frankness, completely contradicting the image of the *Panzer-Kardinal* and revealing himself to be a gentle, cordial person.[49]

Thus was born *The Ratzinger Report*, which became a best-seller worldwide because of the boldness and novelty of the initiative, and because of the contents, which, finally setting the clerical rhetoric aside, drew up a balance sheet of the situation in the Church. The starting point of the balance sheet is Vatican II. The cardinal began: "Today no one who is and wishes to remain Catholic nourishes any doubts—nor can he nourish them—that the great documents of Vatican Council II are important, rich, opportune and indispensable."[50] Having made this basic assertion, the cardinal, on the other hand, spoke harshly about what had happened in the years following the council. "What the Popes and the Council Fathers were expecting was a new Catholic unity, and instead one has encountered a dissension which—to use the words of Paul VI—seems to have passed over from self-criticism to self-destruction. There had been the expectation of a new enthusiasm, and instead too often it has ended in boredom and discouragement."[51] Aggressive centrifugal forces had found room within the Church in the name of a facile optimism. The defense of the true tradition in the Church is equivalent to defending the true council. It is necessary to remain faithful to the today of the Church, not to the letter of the past, as the conservatives claim, nor to a flight into the future, as the progressives hope.

As for the situation in the Church, the cardinal's diagnosis was quite clear: "My diagnosis is that we are dealing with an authentic

---

[48] See J. Ratzinger, *Ratzinger Report*, 11–12; G. Ratzinger and Hesemann, *My Brother the Pope*, 222.

[49] See J. Ratzinger, *Ratzinger Report*, 14–15.

[50] Ibid., 27.

[51] Ibid., 29–30.

crisis and that it must be treated and cured. Thus, I confirm that even for this healing process, Vatican II is a reality that must be fully accepted. On condition, however, that it must not be viewed as merely a point of departure from which one gets further away by running forward, but as a base on which to build solidly."[52] Here the cardinal stood firm in opposing those who, while appealing to a conciliar spirit, distance themselves from the conciliar documents, which they now consider outmoded. On the contrary, it is particularly important to return precisely to the conciliar texts, to discover a new equilibrium, and to break the paradigm that sees Vatican II as a sort of watershed between before and after in Church history. "There is no 'pre-' or 'post-' conciliar Church: there is but one, unique Church that walks the path toward the Lord."[53]

The cardinal, nevertheless, concluded on a hopeful note that came from the ecclesial movements. They are supported by young people who enthusiastically keep the faith of the Church, even though they cause the problem of incorporating them into ordinary pastoral ministry. This no longer worried him so much. On the contrary, he declared: "I find it marvelous that the Spirit is once more stronger than our programs and brings himself into play in an altogether different way than we had imagined."[54] Being capable of looking at the crisis with lucid objectivity, Ratzinger did not lack the courage to describe it without convenient mitigations. As the sower, nevertheless, he was attentive to the seed beneath the snow, from which unexpected fruits may come.

TWENTY YEARS SINCE VATICAN II

When questioned by Messori about the causes of the crisis among Catholics, Ratzinger had no difficulty in responding that most of the errors came from the crisis in the concept of the Church: "Herein lies the cause of a good part of the misunderstandings or real errors which endanger theology and common Catholic opinion alike."[55] In the following year, 1985, he duly took the occasion of the twentieth anniversary of the conclusion of Vatican II to present what,

---

[52] Ibid., 34.
[53] Ibid., 35.
[54] Ibid., 44.
[55] Ibid., 45.

in his opinion, was the true image of the Church that had emerged from the council.[56] His point of departure was a reconstruction of the development of ecclesiology starting with the perception of a new meaning of Church that had been developing in the awareness of Catholics in the first decades of the twentieth century. "The Church is coming to life in the souls of men"[57] had been the joyful observation with which Romano Guardini reported and at the same time introduced into theological reflection a spiritual vision of the Church. The Church, consequently, was no longer viewed solely as an organization or as one society alongside others. "She is an organism of the Holy Spirit, a living thing that encompasses all of us from within."[58]

As though to underscore the relevance of this observation, Guardini returned to the subject in his last book on the Church.[59] Continuing along this line, in the prewar decades, he affirmed, along with the interior character of the Church, the communal character, which is expressed by the formula: "Mystical Body of Christ". For Ratzinger, this meant: "Christ has formed a *Body* for himself, and I must fit into it as a humble member."[60] This ruled out, therefore, the formula of which prewar liberals were fond: Christ yes, Church no, which was adopted and became fashionable in the 1970s even among Italian Catholics.

Ignazio Silone became the interpreter of this sentiment in Italy. Having assimilated the formula during the years between the two wars, he made it popular in *L'avventura di un povero cristiano* (*The Story of a Humble Christian*),[61] a historical novel dramatizing the resignation of Celestine V from the papacy because it was impossible to reform the institutional Church, which was definitely corrupt.

---

[56] This dense article, entitled "The Ecclesiology of the Second Vatican Council", was first published in the German edition of *Communio* 15 (1986): 41–52; in English it appeared in the above-cited anthology of Joseph Ratzinger's essays, *Church, Ecumenism, and Politics*, 13–35.

[57] See above, chapter 1.

[58] J. Ratzinger, *Church, Ecumenism, and Politics*, 13.

[59] Romano Guardini, *The Church of the Lord: On the Nature and Mission of the Church*, trans. Stella Lange (Chicago: H. Regnery Co., 1967).

[60] J. Ratzinger, *Church, Ecumenism, and Politics*, 15.

[61] Published in 1968 by Mondadori, the novel won the Campiello Prize that year and sold very well for a long time. It was translated by William Weaver as *The Story of a Humble Christian* (New York: Harper and Row, 1971).

In this way, however, the cardinal argued, we end up exiling Christ to the past; on the contrary, the Church is a living body that grows and develops over the centuries, guaranteeing for Christ a place in which to be present among his faithful. At the basis of this latter logical argument is the abovementioned Henri de Lubac, author of a groundbreaking ecclesiological study, *Corpus mysticum*.[62]

With great historical erudition and theological acumen, the Jesuit priest showed that in the writings of the Church Fathers and medieval authors, the expression designated above all the Eucharist. Consequently, to say that the Church is the Body of Christ is to found a Eucharistic ecclesiology, an ecclesiology of communion. This ecclesiology became the true and authentic heart of the teaching on the Church by Vatican II, a novel element that harked back, however, to early Christianity. The Church is born with the institution of the Eucharist and grows with the celebration of Mass, which makes present Christ, who has died and is risen. And so, just as Christ always gives himself whole and undivided, "this Church of Christ is truly present in all legitimate local congregations of the faithful which, united with their pastors, are themselves called churches in the New Testament."[63]

In this regard, Ratzinger emphasized that "legitimate" means according to law and in union with the pastors. This means that no one in the Church is alone, but also that no one can proclaim himself Church, either as an individual or as a group. A group of faithful cannot gather to read the word of God and claim to be Church. The constitutive characteristic of the Church is the fact that she receives, just as faith comes from hearing. This structure built upon receiving is called sacrament. For this reason, no one can be baptized by himself, no one can arrogate priestly ordination to himself, no one can absolve himself from his sins. One cannot make oneself Church but can only receive her from where she is already present, in union with the one Lord, but also in union with those who are his body and who in the celebration of the Mass should become more and more so.

---

[62] Henri de Lubac, *Corpus mysticum: Essai sur l'Eucharistie et l'Église au moyen âge* (Paris: Aubier, 1944); trans. Gemma Simmonds et al. as *Corpus Mysticum: The Eucharist and the Church in the Middle Ages: Historical Survey*, ed. Laurence Paul Hemmings and Susan Frank Parsons (Notre Dame, Ind.: University of Notre Dame Press, 2007).

[63] Vatican Council II, Dogmatic Constitution on the Church *Lumen gentium*, no. 26.

Another key point of the conciliar Eucharistic ecclesiology is the collegiality of the bishops. This, according to Ratzinger, is not a dispute between pope and bishops about the division of power; rather, its essential purpose is the true, authentic service of the Church, the divine service, that is, the Mass, which in turn is a gift to the faithful, the people of God. The priests and the bishops, consequently, are at the service of the faithful also, to whom they administer the Eucharist and the food of the word of Scripture. The first level of collegiality is that of the bishop surrounded by his priests. This rules out any sort of autonomy whatsoever of the individual communities. A man becomes a priest through the sacrament of Holy Orders, for the purpose of the Eucharistic ministry, which implies service to the faithful, a relation with the other priests of the local Church, and obedience to the bishop, which guarantees membership in the universal Church.

In turn, the bishops, who receive the fullness of the priestly ministry for the purpose of the Eucharistic celebration in their local Church, are at the service of the faithful and cannot act alone but only in communion with the other bishops. In this way, "The communities are held together by the priests in fellowship and are inserted by the bishop into the larger unity of the whole Church."[64] Vatican II then associated the sacrament of episcopal ordination with the idea of the apostolic succession. The apostles, too, in fact, formed a community, the community of the Twelve, which represented the entire Christian community, as the twelve sons of Jacob represented the whole people of Israel. Consequently, with episcopal ordination, every bishop becomes a successor of the apostles and enters into communion with those who represent the unity of the new people of God. Indeed, from the beginning, Jesus called the Twelve to be part of a group, to be the representatives of the new people of God.

On the basis of the primacy of the pope, on the other hand, there is another fundamental principle of faith: witness for which one personally takes responsibility. In the Old Testament, this is particularly clear from the theology of the name: God has a name, although it is protected by the mystery of his transcendence; corresponding to this is the name of every believer and of every person.

---

[64] J. Ratzinger, *Church, Ecumenism, and Politics*, 21.

Basically, the theology of the name is at the origin of the concept of person. The communal principle and the principle of professing and of personal responsibility are therefore designed to last and to coexist in the Church, just as they coexist in the individual Christian, in the priest, in the bishop, and in the pope. Moreover, the principle of personal witness cannot be delegated to intermediate bodies like synods of bishops, episcopal conferences, diocesan synods, or episcopal and presbyteral councils.

Returning to papal primacy, Ratzinger recalled the personal vocation of Saint Peter, the head of the apostolic college, and the personal invitation to witness contained in the conclusion of the Gospel of John: "When you are old, you will stretch out your hands, and another will fasten your belt for you and carry you where you do not wish to go. . . . Follow me."[65] This allowed Ratzinger to emphasize vigorously what we can call the personalism of all Eucharistic, ministerial responsibilities in the Church. The priest's ministry is personal; the bishop's ministry is personal; the pope's ministry is personal. The intermediate bodies—presbyteral councils, episcopal conferences, synods of bishops—have the function of coordinating this service, but they cannot replace the ministerial responsibility of the priests, the bishops, and the pope, respectively. What is at stake here is the personal responsibility of the individual minister as well as the primacy of the universal Church over the local or particular Churches.

The schism of the Lefebvrites

The undeclared but much-feared schism on the left actually arrived from the right.[66] Its promoter was a French bishop, Marcel Lefebvre (1905–1991), originally from a Catholic family from which had come during the last two centuries a cardinal and many priests,

---

[65] Jn 21:18, 22.

[66] The clearest book on the subject of the schism of the Lefebvrites seems to me to be the one by Gérard Leclerc, *Rome et les lefebvristes* (Paris: Salvator, 2009). In my opinion, the personality of the founder, Archbishop Marcel Lefebvre, is of fundamental importance for an understanding of the movement. I was inspired chiefly by this book in reconstructing the origin of a schism that Ratzinger desperately sought to avoid, nevertheless drawing down on himself criticism that was not entirely unjustified, which perhaps did not take fully into account his intention to avoid a definitive break.

brothers, and nuns. Marcel's parents were very pious, and soon he chose a priestly and missionary vocation. Five out of the eight children of the Lefebvre family became priests or nuns. For his theological formation, he was sent to Rome, to the French seminary at Santa Chiara, not far from the church of San Luigi dei Francesi. The rector was Father Henri Le Floch[67] of the Holy Ghost Fathers, who are also called "Spiritans", who left an indelible imprint on his student. He studied theology, though, at the Gregorian University, where he completely assimilated the Scholastic thought that intensely felt the effects of the battle against modernism at the beginning of the century. Leclerc wrote: "He always declared that he was Roman. . . . He never admitted that it was possible to find support in a theology different from Thomism as he had learned it."[68]

Upon returning to France, he was ordained a priest by the bishop of Lille, Achille Cardinal Liénart, and for a short time he was assistant priest in a parish of the diocese, having admirable success in his ministry. His sympathy for Father Le Floch and the desire to work in the missions drove him, nevertheless, to enter the Congregation of the Holy Ghost, which had been founded in France in the eighteenth century but had acquired a new dynamic in the following century through the influence of Venerable Francis Libermann, an ardent promoter of the mission in Africa. After his novitiate, Lefebvre departed for Africa, where he demonstrated excellent qualities as a builder and founder of new Christian communities. "Cardinal Gantin, one of the major African figures in the Church . . . never failed to sing the praises of those missionaries who perished through the battering effects of epidemics and were immediately replaced by others who were just as heroic."[69]

In 1947, he was appointed Vicar Apostolic of Dakar, in charge of a region that coincided with present-day Senegal, and was consecrated a bishop, again by Cardinal Liénart. In 1955, he became the first

---

[67] Even though Father Le Floch was sent away from Rome following the condemnation of Charles Maurras' *Action Française*, Leclerc (*Rome et les lefebvristes*, 29) insists on pointing out that his influence on Lefebvre was spiritual, not political. This circumstance seems to me important with regard to the understanding that Ratzinger showed for the French bishop, which many thought excessive.

[68] Leclerc, *Rome et les lefebvristes*, 29f.

[69] See ibid., 30f. This detail is important, inasmuch as Bernard Gantin was created cardinal together with Ratzinger, who had a deep friendship with him.

bishop of Dakar with the title of archbishop. Under his guidance, the Church of that country undoubtedly made great progress. In 1962, nevertheless, in Rome the need was felt to appoint some African bishops. Archbishop Lefebvre would willingly have remained at his post, but in a disciplined way he submitted his resignation and was appointed bishop of Tulle, a not very prestigious see. The most disappointed were the Spiritan Fathers, who thought it humiliating for their most prominent representative to be assigned to such a modest diocese. This was one of the reasons why, after only six months, he was elected superior general of the Spiritans and moved to Paris.

After several months, Archbishop Lefebvre, who had already participated in the Preparatory Commission for the imminent council, moved to Rome to participate in Vatican II as a council Father. There he not only belonged to the conservative group of council Fathers but also assumed an increasingly critical attitude toward liturgical reform, episcopal collegiality, ecumenism, and especially religious liberty. It is necessary, nevertheless, to consider that until the conclusion of the council, his dissent remained within the limits allowed, so much so that Lefebvre signed all the documents of Vatican II. When the council was over, Archbishop Lefebvre was still in charge of the Congregation of the Holy Ghost Fathers. Even in the missionary congregation, however, the atmosphere had changed, and the enthusiasm of those who had elected him superior general had diminished to a great extent.

Having resigned, then, from his position, he was certainly not a man to be content with inaction. The year was 1968. Until then, Lefebvre, although opposed to the main conciliar documents, had remained within the limits of tolerated dissent. Now, though, in view of the abuses in the liturgical field and the intentions of many theologians, who declared that they wanted to go much farther than the letter of the conciliar documents, he slipped gradually toward rebellion. In 1969, he was one of the organizers of a position paper that was very critical of the *Novus Ordo*, the new order of the Mass promulgated by Paul VI, and in that same year he opened the Pius X international boarding school in Fribourg, Switzerland, with the permission and support of the local bishop, Pierre Mamie. But that was only the beginning.

After buying a property in Ecône, Archbishop Lefebvre started a real seminary with seminarians who came for the most part from French dioceses. It is easy to imagine the bafflement and hostility of the French bishops, who, nevertheless, had to face a growing short-age of priestly vocations. Nor was the rebel bishop's activism, which had a certain following among the faithful, especially in France, lim-ited to the seminary. His dissent even created notoriety for him, increasing the number of the sympathizers for whom he founded the Society of Saint Pius X. For his part, Paul VI suffered much from the ungenerous criticism of the former missionary bishop but agreed to meet with him in 1976. The old pope, who saw himself now near the end of his life, asked him with heartfelt insistence to accept the conciliar documents and reforms.

After yet another refusal, Archbishop Lefebvre was suspended *a divinis*. This meant that he would have to stop administering the sacraments and celebrating Mass, but he disobeyed spectacularly. The election of John Paul II seems to have been welcomed by the archbishop, who liked one passage from a speech by the new pope to the cardinals when he said that "the Council must be understood in light of the whole tradition and on the basis of the constant Mag-isterium of Holy Church."[70] Only one month after his election, the Polish pope received the French bishop, who some time later wrote to him that he had no doubt about the validity of his election nor had he ever said that the postconciliar Mass was in itself invalid or heretical.[71] There seemed to be some gleams of hope for a possi-ble reconciliation, but then the day of the interreligious meeting in Assisi in 1986 brought relations to a new, abrupt halt. For Lefeb-vre and his followers, the prayer meeting personally requested by the pope was an unacceptable gesture of religious syncretism. The archbishop wrote a letter to eight cardinals in which he asserted that the scandal in the mind of Catholics was grave and that in this way the Church was shaken to her foundations.

Lefebvre, nevertheless, was aware that he could not put off for long a decision that was vitally important for his Society. In 1987, he was eighty-two years old, and it was indispensable to think about a bishop who could succeed him in governing his followers. He announced, therefore, that he intended to proceed to consecrate

---

[70] Tornielli, *Benedetto XVI*, 127.
[71] Ibid.

several bishops. The news of a division within the Church, tantamount to a ratification of schism, was received in Rome with great concern. Ratzinger was particularly struck by it, since he was well aware of the schism of the Old Catholics following Vatican I, which had been promoted by one of his countrymen, the Church historian Ignaz von Döllinger. Now he saw on the horizon a new, dangerous division in the Church and decided to do everything possible to avoid it.

In July and October 1987, he met twice with Archbishop Lefebvre. Following these meetings, Édouard Cardinal Gagnon, himself a conservative, was appointed Apostolic Visitator to the Society.[72] The French and Swiss bishops, in contrast, were opposed to these attempts, which in their view could only create further bewilderment among the faithful who accepted the council and were obedient to their pastors. For his part, Ratzinger knew that he was running a risk; nevertheless, his concern for safeguarding unity prevailed—a desire fully shared by John Paul II. In March 1988, Cardinal Gagnon submitted his report, and the following month a three-day meeting was scheduled in Rome; the participants from Rome would be the highest authorities in the Congregation for the Doctrine of the Faith: the prefect, Cardinal Ratzinger, and the secretary, Alberto Bovone.

Meanwhile, the discontent among the bishops[73] grew; the pope personally tried to stem the tide by sending to Ratzinger on April 8, the day before the meeting with the rebel bishop, a letter encouraging the prefect to continue in the initiative. First, the pope reassured the bishops and the faithful: they would not swerve from the council. "We cherish the profound conviction that the Spirit of truth . . . spoke in a particularly solemn and authoritative way through the Second Vatican Council, preparing the Church to enter the third millennium." Then, he exhorted Ratzinger to continue the attempt to reach an agreement with the Lefebvrites: "I wish to assure you, Your Eminence, of my wish that these efforts proceed", and therefore he invited the bishops throughout the world,

---

[72] In this regard, besides the above-cited book by Tornielli, see *Storia della Chiesa*, ed. A. Fliche and V. Martin, vol. 25/2, *La Chiesa del Vaticano II*, ed. Maurilio Guasco, Elio Guerriero, and Francesco Traniello (Cinisello Balsamo: San Paolo, 1994), 680f.

[73] Even the renowned bishop and canonist Eugenio Corecco, one of the founders of the journal *Communio*, commented very critically; see ibid., 681.

inasmuch as they are concerned about Church unity, to share and to make known their own this preoccupation with the unity of the Church, thus contributing to the welfare of the entire Mystical Body, which is also the body of the Church. And at first it seemed that they had in fact reached an agreement.

After the discussions in April, on May 5, Ratzinger and Lefebvre signed a protocol in which the Lefebvrites promised to be faithful to the Catholic Church and to the Roman pontiff, to accept the teachings of Vatican II, and to acknowledge the validity of the Mass and the sacraments celebrated according to the rites approved by Paul VI and John Paul II. Finally, the Lefebvrites made a commitment to respect Church discipline and laws, in particular the Code of Canon Law promulgated shortly before. Only after these promises was it agreed that the Society of Saint Pius X would remain a society of apostolic life, thus enjoying full autonomy. The excommunication of Lefebvre was lifted, while, for practical and psychological reasons, his successor would be selected from among the priests belonging to the Society.[74] During the night between May 5 and 6, however, Archbishop Lefebvre changed his mind and privately informed Ratzinger that on June 30 he would go ahead and consecrate new bishops.

The reason for this unexpected about-face has been explained in various ways. According to the judgment of a collaborator of the schismatic bishop who was interviewed by Tornielli, Lefebvre changed his mind because he feared that Ratzinger could not keep his promise with regard to the choice of a successor, because Cardinal Gagnon's judgment at the conclusion of his visit had been against it.[75] Another hypothesis, which seems more likely to me, is that the French bishop was persuaded to retract by his own followers, some of whom were more intransigent than he himself was. Ratzinger, nevertheless, insisted again, did not give in, and on May 24, in a last-ditch effort, met again with the French bishop, who did not back off from his position. On the contrary, on June 2, he wrote directly to the pope informing him of his refusal and his renewed intention to proceed to consecrate four bishops at the end of the month.

---

[74] For the reconstruction of the negotiations, see Tornielli, *Benedetto XVI*, 129ff.

[75] Ibid., 130.

On June 29, Ratzinger sent him a telegram begging him to cancel the ordinations and to come see the pope on the following day, but not even that could change his mind. The following day, instead, assisted by the Brazilian Bishop Antônio de Castro Mayer, the now schismatic bishop consecrated four priests of the Society as bishops. Episcopal consecrations performed without the pope's authorization are valid but automatically involve the excommunication of the consecrator and of those consecrated. All that remained was to communicate that fact to the interested parties. The notification was made by Cardinal Gantin, prefect of the Congregation for Bishops.

And yet, during those crucial days of the rupture caused by the episcopal consecrations, Gérard Leclerc said that he received "several impressive testimonies of respect for Archbishop Lefebvre, despite his unacceptable attacks against the pope and the Church"[76] and his stubborn unwillingness to take into account the changing times. Among them, Leclerc recalled in particular those of Jean-Marie Cardinal Lustiger, archbishop of Paris, of Hyacinthe Cardinal Thiandoum, Lefebvre's successor in Dakar, and of the Jesuit philosopher and theologian Albert Chapelle. With this observation, Leclerc intended to show that the prefect's effort to rehabilitate a bishop who undoubtedly had good qualities was not just stubbornness. On the other hand, the failure was a difficult blow for the pope and especially for Ratzinger, who had personally conducted the negotiations, which ended up making concessions that were certainly not pleasing to the majority of the bishops.[77]

---

[76] Leclerc, *Rome et les lefebvristes*, 80f.
[77] Guasco, Guerriero, and Traniello, *La Chiesa del Vaticano II*, 681f.

IX

INQUISITOR OR DEFENDER OF
SIMPLE BELIEVERS?

In late October 1985, Ratzinger, in Foggia for a conference, took the occasion to travel to the neighboring town of Troia, situated on a steep slope of the Daunia Mountains. Accompanied by a friend, the cardinal visited with great interest the magnificent Romanesque cathedral, where his attention was drawn to a rather enigmatic bas-relief on the pulpit that dated back to 1158.[1] In the lower part, there is a lamb on which a ravenous, powerful lion has pounced. It has already caught it and holds it motionless, while the wounds on the lamb's body, from which blood is streaming, show that the slaughter has already begun. Only the anguished gaze of the poor animal indicates that it is still alive, but there seems to be no way to extract it from the lion's claws. In this highly dramatic situation, a little white dog unexpectedly pounces on the lion and at least for a moment surprises it and distracts it from its desire for food and violence. The viewer cannot tell what the outcome of this unequal struggle will be, but the intervention of the little white dog brings a gleam of hope into the violent, apparently fatal situation.

From a historical perspective, the scene could describe the situation of the Church in the mid-eleventh century, at the beginning of the struggle over investitures, when it seemed that nothing could liberate the Christian community, threatened by the imperial power

---

[1] Compare the description of it made by Ratzinger at the conclusion of the article "Teologia e Chiesa" published by the Italian edition of *Communio* 66 (1982): 36–47. The English version of the article, "The Spiritual Basis and Ecclesial Identity of Theology", was published in the anthology entitled *The Nature and Mission of Theology*, trans. Adrian Walker (San Francisco: Ignatius Press, 1995), 45–72. The conclusion of the article to which I refer here is found on pp. 69–72 of that volume.

of the Swabians. More likely, though, according to the cardinal, it is better to interpret the bas-relief according to the classical language of Christian iconography. In this case, the lamb that is about to be torn to pieces represents the Church, while the lion that attacks her is heresy, which rends and devours her. We still must ask the meaning of the little white dog that, despite the mismatch, dares to attack the lion. The guidebook says that it symbolizes the fidelity of the pastor and the theologian who give their lives for their sheep.

The cardinal preferred to remain faithful to the more properly symbolic aspect, whereby the sacrificial lamb stands for the Church, while the other two beasts, the lion and the dog, depending on the circumstances, stand for the two paths on which pastoral preaching and theological reflection can set out. They can represent the despotic violence of reason, which like a greedy lion divides and devours the ignorant, defenseless community of believers, or else the fidelity of the courageous little dog that fearlessly rushes against the aggressor to save the lamb. The iconographic image, according to the cardinal, reflects the dramatic situation of theology and theologians in the second half of the 1980s. Hence, the seriousness of his appeals to his former colleagues to protect uneducated believers. While they desired to encounter God and his Church, they were exposed instead to the rapacious jaws of those who no longer handed down the deposit of faith but instilled systematic doubt about the Creed and morality.

The man whom the media and the vast majority of public opinion stubbornly depicted as the *Panzer-Kardinal*, the Grand Inquisitor, intended to be, instead, the faithful shepherd who exposed himself to the jaws of the lion so as to save Christ's flock, which was abandoned, alone, and threatened.

Liberation theology

JOHN PAUL II AND LATIN AMERICA

In early 1979, a few months after he was elected pope, John Paul II traveled to Puebla, Mexico, for the third meeting of the Latin American bishops, who hold a plenary assembly every ten years. On the continent with the largest presence of Catholics in the world, the situation was tense. The bishops were polarized, divided between conservatives and progressives. The latter, already unhappy with the prepared text of the conference, feared that the pope's intervention would consolidate the former and, above all, would end up giving the impression that the Church sided with the parties in power.[2] John Paul II did not heed the calls for prudence; instead, he exhorted the bishops to speak with the language of the council, of John XXIII and of Paul VI. Turning to the *Indios* and the peasants, he said: "It is necessary to carry out bold changes . . . [and] urgent reforms without waiting any longer."[3] The journey to Mexico was for the pope the general test of a policy that he would recommend over the years: unity and cohesion internally, closeness to the poor and detachment from politics externally.

In Puebla, the pope saw for the first time Óscar Romero, the archbishop of San Salvador, who had been accused by various colleagues of subversive sympathies. In May of that same year, 1979, the first true meeting of the Salvadoran bishop with the pope took place: "Judging from the later developments, the outcome of that meeting was not negative, as Romero tended to think, if not at that moment, then at least in the following days, perhaps because of an instinctive comparison with the more confidential meetings with Paul VI."[4] This impression, recorded by the bishop in his *Diary*,[5] was the pretext for the critiques of many admirers of the martyred bishop with regard to the pope and to Ratzinger, also, later on.

In reality, John Paul II had esteem for the Salvadoran bishop and had occasion to show it in their second and final meeting, which occurred in Rome in late January 1980. Romero reported on that occasion: "He received me very warmly and told me that he understood perfectly how difficult the political situation of my country is. . . . The pope said that he agreed with everything that I was saying and, at the end, he gave me a very fraternal embrace."[6] Only two months later, the bishop was assassinated, on March 24, 1980, while he was celebrating Mass.[7]

---

[2] Andrea Riccardi, *Giovanni Paolo II* (Cinisello Balsamo: San Paolo, 2011), 292f.

[3] George Weigel, *Witness to Hope* (New York: HarperCollins, 1999), 286.

[4] Agostino Giovagnoli, "Romero e Roma", in Roberto Morozzo della Rocca, ed., *Oscar Romero* (Cinisello Balsamo: San Paolo, 2009), 55–81.

[5] Oscar Romero, *A Shepherd's Diary*, trans. Irene B. Hodgson (Cincinnati: St. Anthony Messenger Press, 1993), 215.

[6] Ibid., 466–67.

[7] After he became pope, Ratzinger, for his part, carried forward Romero's cause of beatification in December 2012; it had been at a standstill for several years.

Three years later, in 1983, the pope was once again in Latin America. One after the other he visited: Costa Rica, Nicaragua, Panama, El Salvador, Guatemala, Honduras, Belize, Haiti. The most compelling stop of the journey was Nicaragua, where one part of the clergy and the religious sided with the Sandinistas. Two clerics, nevertheless, were ministers in the government, against the will of the Church. One of them, Ernesto Cardenal, a poet who was well known in Europe, also, the Minister of Education, knelt down in front of the pope. Without mincing words, John Paul II exhorted him to regularize his position in the Church. Then, during the Mass, the pope had to compete with Sandinista choirs, which, throughout the ceremony, sang hymns to the *power of the people*. For his part, the pontiff called for commitment on behalf of the poor but also exhorted his listeners to cultivate their spiritual life.

Upon returning to Rome, the pope met with Cardinal Ratzinger, and they both decided that the moment had arrived to intervene with a document on the Latin American situation and on liberation theology before it was too late. The pope was not convinced of the possibility either of adopting the Marxist analysis or of using a common language with the Communists. Ratzinger shared the opinion of John Paul II and was, moreover, of the opinion that liberation theology was not entirely a way of thinking that originated in the Latin American people's cries of injustice; on the contrary, he thought that it was an intellectual construct developed on the blackboard in the universities of Germany or the United States.[8]

A MUCH DISPUTED INSTRUCTION

The instruction *Libertatis Nuntius, On Certain Aspects of the "Theology of Liberation"*, is dated August 6, 1984.[9] The document was issued by the Congregation for the Doctrine of the Faith but bears the obvious imprint of Ratzinger. First of all, it establishes the principle that the aspiration of the peoples for liberation from injustices

---

[8] See Joseph Ratzinger, *Ratzinger Report: An Exclusive Interview on the State of the Church*, trans. Salvator Attanasio and Graham Harrison (San Francisco: Ignatius Press, 1985), 175.

[9] The document was published in the Italian edition of *L'Osservatore Romano*, no. 203 (September 4–5, 1984) as a special supplement. The official edition is found now in *AAS* 76 (1984): 876–909.

and oppression has its foundation and support in the doctrine of the creation of man in the image of God and in the proclamation of the love of God and neighbor found in the Gospel. Several explanations follow, which in the mind of the drafters are fundamental. The congregation reserves for itself the right to address in a second step the topic of liberty and of liberation in the Christian vision in its entirety; the instruction, moreover, does not intend to give any support to the oppressors; it is not meant as an excuse for those who avert their gaze from injustices; it is not meant as a condemnation of those who have adopted the fundamental option for the poor.

Then comes the clear, direct thrust, which does not intend to leave room for possible escape routes: "Impatience and a desire for results has led certain Christians, despairing of every other method, to turn to what they call 'Marxist analysis.' "[10] Based on this analysis, liberation theologies are drawn to accept a set of positions that are incompatible with the Christian view. Among these postulates derived from Marxist analysis, the instruction mentions: atheism and the negation of the human person, his liberty, and his rights; class struggle presented as an objective, necessary law; the necessity of participating in the class struggle; acceptance of violence as a necessity that results from adherence to class struggle. Based on these considerations, the instruction establishes: "All priests, religious, and lay people who hear this call for justice and who want to work for evangelization and the advancement of mankind, will do so in communion with their bishop and with the Church, each in accord with his or her own specific ecclesial vocation" (XI, 3); "It is only when one begins with the task of evangelization understood in its entirety that the authentic requirements of human progress and liberation are appreciated" (XI, 5); "The class struggle as a road toward a classless society is a myth which slows reform and aggravates poverty and injustice" (XI, 11). Together with the document of the congregation, Ratzinger published over his signature a letter that added new clarifications and justifications for the rather severe admonition of the official document.[11]

The cardinal thus wrote that the intention of liberation theology

---

[10] See the Congregation for the Doctrine of the Faith, Instruction *Libertatis Nuntius, On Certain Aspects of the "Theology of Liberation"*, August 6, 1984, no. 7, 1.

[11] The text was published in *Ratzinger Report*, 174–86.

is not at all to construct a new treatise of theology alongside the others that already exist. On the contrary, it explains all of Christianity as a praxis of liberation. In its vision, all reality is political, and liberation theology itself intends to be a guide to political action. It has its center of gravity in Latin America but originated under the influence of European and North American theologians and tends to spread in other areas of the Third World. The theologians who started it are Europeans, and the theologians who caused it to grow in Latin America are Europeans or were educated in European universities. From this perspective, liberation theology is once again a product exported by the opulent West.[12]

The instruction of the congregation and Ratzinger's explanatory document gave rise to endless polemics and debates. The clarity and severity of the text reminded some of the language of Pius XII.[13]

THE BOFF CASE

In the wake of the publication of the instruction on liberation theology, the incident in which Leonardo Boff figured as the protagonist was brought to a conclusion. According to the reconstruction of the sequence of events by Andrea Tornielli,[14] a few months after Ratzinger had arrived in Rome, in 1982, a letter from Boff was delivered to the congregation defending his book, *Church: Charism and Power*,[15] which had been censored by his diocese the previous year. Born in Brazil in 1938, Boff had entered the Franciscan Order in 1959 and had been ordained a priest in 1964. After earning a doctorate in Munich, Ratzinger's city, he had returned to his homeland, where he had become a professor of systematic and ecumenical theology at the Franciscan Theological Institute in Petropolis and one of the chief exponents of liberation theology. While preparing the instruction on liberation theology, Ratzinger also studied the dossier on the Franciscan friar, and, in May 1984, he sent him a letter that set forth a series of objections to the book under consideration, which contained "a radical, ruthless attack" on the insti-

---

[12] Ibid., 175.

[13] See Andrea Tornielli, *Benedetto XVI* (Casale Monferrato: Piemme, 2005), 104.

[14] Ibid., 107.

[15] The original title of the book was *Igreja: Carisma e Poder* (Petropolis: Vozes, 1981); the volume was translated into English as *Church, Charism and Power: Liberation Theology and the Institutional Church* (New York: Crossroad, 1985).

tutional model of the Catholic Church.[16] In the same missive, the cardinal offered the theologian the opportunity to clarify matters in a conversation to be held in Rome on September 7 of that year.

Boff accepted the invitation and informed the media, which depicted the event in gloomy terms. Gustavo Gutiérrez, another liberation theologian, wrote on the eve of the encounter that if Boff was condemned, "it would be the condemnation, not of a people, but of a Church, of an ecclesial movement, and of an entire believing people."[17] In early September, Boff arrived in Rome accompanied by not one but two Brazilian cardinals: Paulo Evaristo Arns of São Paolo and Aloísio Lorscheider of Fortaleza. According to the unanimous testimony of the participants, the conversation, in which Monsignor Jorge Mejía, a future cardinal, also participated, was conducted in a cordial atmosphere and lasted around three hours. The meeting with Boff was followed by a meeting with the two cardinals who had accompanied him to Rome and feared the negative effects that a condemnation might have throughout Latin America.

The congregation's reply was published by *L'Osservatore Romano* on March 21, 1985. Two series of theses supported by Boff in his works are declared unacceptable: the statements harmful to the dignity of the Catholic Church, which remains the Church of Christ notwithstanding the weaknesses of her members and the errors of the hierarchy; the statements that dogmas are valid only for a certain time and in certain circumstances. The Franciscan was then advised to observe a year of silence, to refrain from writing, and to grant no interviews to the media. At first, Boff accepted Rome's requests positively. In March 1986, the prohibition against him was lifted. In the following years, nevertheless, Boff continued to publish and uphold his theses. In 1992, therefore, he was asked to resign from his teaching post. The Franciscan then decided to leave the Order and the priesthood.

"HE IS SACRIFICING HIMSELF FOR THE CHURCH"

The meeting in Rome did not lead to an actual condemnation of Boff; nevertheless, the media broadcast anyway the image of the humble friar, follower of Saint Francis, who was being persecuted

---

[16] See Tornielli, *Benedetto XVI*, 108.
[17] Cited by Riccardi, *Giovanni Paolo II*, 305.

by an institution that relied on power and control.[18] Andrea Riccardi maintained that behind this attitude there was an initiative orchestrated by the Soviet Union. "Among the objectives of the Soviets was precisely to widen the gap between the Vatican authorities and the radical clergy in the developing nations, especially in Latin America."[19] Another not insignificant risk was of creating serious divisions within the Church herself. The cardinals who accompanied Boff to Rome openly defended him. Cardinal Arns declared: "Liberation theology is not imbued with Marxist principles; that is a biased critique of the conservative circles."[20]

In order to suggest something of the atmosphere that still persisted several months after the publication of the instruction and the conclusion of the Boff case, even among priests and faithful who were certainly not inclined to protest, I recall an incident that I witnessed. We had met with the national directors of the journal *Communio* in early December 1985 at the residence of Father von Balthasar in Basel. During a break in the work, a small group of the younger editors formed; they asked each other in dismay what was happening in Rome and in Latin America. Then Father von Balthasar called us over and, emphasizing each word, said: "You do not understand. Ratzinger is sacrificing himself for the Church." An unforgettable moment of silent reflection followed. Von Balthasar, according to an affectionate description by de Lubac, called to mind a Father of the Church among the Helvetians. So he appeared to us on that occasion, and his appeal managed to correct a judgment that was too dependent on current events and the passions of the moment.

THE INSTRUCTION *CHRISTIAN FREEDOM AND LIBERATION*

As announced in 1984 in the first severe warning addressed to liberation theology, on March 22, 1986, the Congregation for the Doctrine of the Faith returned to the subject, proposing this time, not a condemnation, but rather a Christian view of libera-

---

[18] See Silvia Scatena, *La teologia della liberazione in America Latina* (Rome: Carocci, 2008).

[19] Riccardi, *Giovanni Paolo II*, 305.

[20] See Lucia Ceci, *La teologia della liberazione in America Latina* (Milan: Franco Angeli, 1999).

tion.[21] The point of departure, consequently, was not sociological but strictly theological. The truth is what will set men free, and this truth is brought to us by Jesus, who comes from God. Among the salient points of the instruction are several themes that are particularly dear to Ratzinger: love for ecology, respect and love for nature; a forceful appeal to morality: "When man wishes to free himself from the moral law and become independent of God, far from gaining his freedom he destroys it" (no. 19).

The instruction, however, does not intend to remain in the abstract. The first chapter dwells, therefore, on the condition of freedom in the contemporary world and on the dangers that threaten it. The second chapter, in contrast, focuses on the call to liberation, which is above all a response to God's call and the renunciation of sin, which is separation from God and from man's destiny, a temptation that recurs through the centuries. The third chapter sets forth liberation from a Christian perspective, whereby the Old Testament must be read in terms of the New, and not vice versa. Whereas the Exodus from Egypt is the central experience of the entire Bible for liberation theologians, for the instruction, the Exodus is a sign that points to the grace-filled event announced by Jesus, to which he bore witness with his death and Resurrection, which is at the origin of Baptism, the Eucharist, and all the Christian sacraments.

In continuity with the Gospel proclamation, the Church has a liberating mission to proclaim and to carry out over the centuries. Hence the preferential love for the poor according to Jesus' teaching and miracles: "But Jesus not only brought the grace and peace of God; he also healed innumerable sick people; he had compassion on the crowd who had nothing to eat and he fed them; with the disciples who followed him he practised almsgiving" (no. 67). At this point, to supplement the severe document of two years before, the instruction expresses openness toward the base communities: "The new basic communities or other groups of Christians which have arisen to be witnesses to this evangelical love are a source of great hope for the Church" (no. 69).

Having set forth the doctrinal premises, the fifth chapter presents

---

[21] On this topic, Ratzinger published an explanatory article entitled "Freedom and Liberation: The Anthropological Vision of the Instruction *Libertatis conscientia*", in the German edition of *Communio* 5 (1986): 409–24; it was reprinted in *Church, Ecumenism, and Politics*, trans. Michael Miller et al. (San Francisco: Ignatius Press, 2008), 239–55.

several lines of a possible Christian praxis in the modern world, the so-called "social doctrine" of the Church. The point of departure is the commandment of love that invites us to look mercifully on participation in the suffering of the poor and to fight against injustice, although it rejects the use of violence. In this context, nevertheless, the instruction emphasizes the role and the commitment of the laity. The principle of love then requires a true cultural transformation, centered on the person, that humanizes work, promotes solidarity, and fosters development. The conclusion is an invitation to workers—priests and laymen, men and women religious— to give due consideration to popular religious devotions. If they are not misunderstood or aimed at merely human projects of liberation, they can contribute to the establishment of a genuine civilization of love (no. 99). This final observation, too, which has in mind the shrines in Altötting, Germany, or in Guadalupe in Latin America, is a constant in Ratzinger's thought that marks his Marian devotion, which he calls the spirituality of the *Magnificat*, the song of praise and thanksgiving to God sung by the Daughter of Zion, the heir of the poor of Israel, whose hope is brought to fulfillment by Jesus.

Considering the complex way in which the delicate question of liberation theology was addressed, we can make two observations. The decision to treat the whole question in two separate documents was more in keeping with a systematic logic than with pastoral care or the demands of communication. As for the second document, then, it no doubt had strong points but was too long for it to be appreciated by the media. A pastoral concern and more concise communication might have avoided the avalanche of criticism that swept down on the prefect of the congregation in 1984. Given all that, however, we cannot help but appreciate the courage of the cardinal, who dared to call by name certain truths that were unspeakable at the time, his far-sightedness in denouncing the mixture of faith with Marxist analysis, the failure of which was about to explode a few years later in Europe.

In an enlightening essay on Latin American Catholicism, Andrea Riccardi wrote: "The years of John Paul II meant a forceful downsizing of liberation theology, which in the pope's opinion had an ambiguous role in particular because of its use of Marxist ideology."[22] The Roman historian continued, maintaining that the pope's action

---

[22] Andrea Riccardi, "Il futuro del cristianesimo", in *I cattolici e le Chiese cristiane du-*

had then caused a series of bishops with a strong pastoral commitment to emerge, on whom he could seriously rely to guide the universal Church. This observation, while certainly penetrating, must be supplemented in the sense that, notwithstanding all the criticism, Ratzinger in turn made a decisive contribution to this development.

Theology and government of the Church

THE CHURCH AND SCIENTIFIC THEOLOGY

Not surprisingly, before accepting the appointment as prefect of the Congregation for the Doctrine of the Faith, Ratzinger had asked the pope to be able to continue writing and publishing. As an expert at Vatican II and archbishop of Munich, he had understood well the importance of communication that does not rely exclusively on official documents. The interview with Messori, moreover, was a model that would be repeated at almost regular intervals over the years. It was an opportunity to explain the work done, to respond to objections, and to clarify the meaning of some interventions that otherwise would be left up to arbitrary and not always well-meaning interpretations. In addition to the interviews, the cardinal also regularly wrote articles for scholarly journals and daily newspapers and gave conferences of a scientific and pastoral nature.

As already mentioned, after his appointments both as archbishop of Munich and as prefect of the Congregation for the Doctrine of the Faith, various theologians and churchmen had asked Ratzinger to clarify his twofold role of theologian and pastor who participates in the government of the Church. Before long, the cardinal addressed this delicate subject in an article entitled "The Church and Scientific Theology",[23] in which he sought to clarify the relations between the two authorities that supervise the study and the transmission of the faith. Modern science from Galileo to Küng, the cardinal began his discussion, recognizes only itself as a criterion of judgment. In particular, after the Enlightenment, intellectuals

---

rante il pontificato di Giovanni Paolo II, ed. Elio Guerriero and Marco Impagliazzo (Cinisello Balsamo: San Paolo, 2006), 30.

[23] The article "La Chiesa e la teologia scientifica" was published in the Italian edition of Communio 53 (1980): 60–71. It was reprinted in the collection La vita di Dio per gli uomini, 195–204. Cited from the more recent edition. The article was translated for the English ed. of Communio 7.4 (1980): 332–42.

arrived at a scientific self-determination without any limits whatsoever.

In more recent times, the very same attitude is taken by the theologians who, adopting as their own the claims of science, assert full
autonomy, especially in the field of exegesis, which is increasingly
being understood as a philological and historical science and, therefore, completely exempt from the guidance of the Magisterium. To
this claim, the cardinal responded with a question: Is a theology in
which the Church no longer has any say still theology? The point
of departure, therefore, must be as follows: "The faith cannot take
up a position that conflicts with reason, but neither can the faith
allow itself to be subjected to the absolute dominion of the enlightened mind and to its method."[24] In parallel, theology is a form of
rationality that is inherent in the faith and that makes explicit the
internal coherence of the faith. For this reason, it has sought and
found support in philosophy, in the *logos* more than in myth, continuing along the course followed by the prophets and the wisdom
authors in their attempts to draw the people away from fictitious
religions so as to lead them to the encounter with a person, with
the personal God.

Today, following a merely scientific method, many theologians
invite their readers to compare important passages from the Bible
and "use the scalpels of literary criticism to reveal to us the most
intimate secrets of God".[25] But we have not grasped the heart of
the act of faith if we limit ourselves to the relation between a book
and an individual. From this perspective, Christianity, according
to Ratzinger, who cited Martin Buber, is primarily a religion of
yes. It is a yes that introduces us into the fundamental structure of
knowledge. And it is a yes that introduces us into the community
of faith, into the Church that requires an act of initial obedience.
This fundamental assent is pronounced at the moment of Baptism,
a sacrament that anticipates a close connection with the proclamation and the explanation of Christian truth. This means that the
teaching of the Church goes beyond what can be verified from the
literary form, from the connection with a book.

At this point, the task of the bishops as representatives of the
Church also becomes clear. They cannot and must not dispute the

---

[24] J. Ratzinger, "La Chiesa e la teologia scientifica", 198.
[25] Ibid., 201.

role of the specialists, whose intellectual offering of knowledge is valuable, especially in light of the recent findings in the field of exegesis. They must, instead, protect the Gospel proclamation and the faith of simple believers when it is endangered by science that sets itself up as an absolute norm. Basically, Ratzinger concluded, this is a challenge to go forward with a balance of the charisms, while respecting the faith of simple believers.

BISHOPS, THEOLOGIANS, AND MORALITY

In 1984, Cardinal Ratzinger took a trip to the United States. Although in Latin America the major risk of the moment was the temptation to adopt the Marxist analysis of society and to derive from it guidelines for the social action of believers, in North America, bishops and theologians were inclined to give in to the allurement of contemporary subjectivism, with concessions to individualism especially in the ethical field. In this regard, Ratzinger had published in 1976, together with von Balthasar and the exegete Schürmann, a slim volume entitled *Principles of Christian Morality*.[26] Faced with the serious crisis of sexual morality that resulted from and at the same time influenced the general crisis of morality, the three authors sought to demonstrate, each from his own perspective, that Christian morality has specific contents that are indispensable.

Ratzinger, in particular, insisted on the reciprocal relation between the natural law and divine revelation. These two elements are the source of the Church's authority in the ethical field. The doctrinal authority of the Church in the field of morality, indeed, was anything but exhausted with the end of the apostolic age. It is an irrevocable gift from God and includes the mission of "making concrete the moral demands of grace and of working them out in detail with regard to the contemporary situation".[27] Coming then to the present day, the first danger is the prevalence of what at that time was being called "orthopraxis" over orthodoxy. In this regard, Ratzinger responded: the practice of the faith "depends on faith's

---

[26] Joseph Ratzinger, Heinz Schürmann, Hans Urs von Balthasar, *Prinzipien christlicher Moral* (Einsiedeln: Johannes Verlag, 1975). Trans. by Graham Harrison as *Principles of Christian Morality* (San Francisco: Ignatius Press, 1986).

[27] Ibid., 69–70.

truth, in which man's truth is made visible and lifted up to a new level by God's truth".[28]

The other danger follows from subjectivism, which considers the individual and his conscience as uniquely capable of making decisions in the field of ethics. For Ratzinger, this temptation is particularly present in the Anglo-Saxon world, and for this reason he particularly insisted on it during his trip to America. He said in the first of his conferences in the United States: "Conscience is understood by many as a sort of deification of subjectivity, a rock of bronze on which even the magisterium is shattered. It is said that in light of the conscience, no other cases apply. Conscience appears finally as subjectivity raised to the ultimate standard."[29] In another passage, nevertheless, Ratzinger responded that freedom is above all a condition of the human being, characterized positively by several rights. This, in turn, presupposes moral values shared in the community, both civil and religious. Morality, indeed, is not "an abstract code of norms for behavior, but presupposes a community way of life within which morality itself is clarified and is able to be observed."[30]

Within the Christian community, moreover, the philosopher and moral theologian compare the datum of the faith with the ethical questions of the day, while the bishop, witness to Christian morality, verifies the harmony or the consistency of the moral norms with the vision of creation and redemption based on revelation as a whole. The pope and the bishops, when they offer their authoritative guidance in these questions, do not intend to replace the faithful or the specialists, but rather situate the results of the latter's research in a wider context.[31] Returning to this topic in his second conference, the cardinal suggested a clarification before resolving some specific cases. He said that in the Church there can be the case of a researcher or a specialist who dissents on individual ethical or moral norms proposed by the Magisterium. The case of the professor of theology is different, he explains. The latter

---

[28] Ibid., 70.

[29] The text is reprinted by the National Catholic Bioethics Center as "Bishops, Theologians, and Morality", in Joseph Ratzinger, *On Conscience* (Philadelphia: NCBC and San Francisco: Ignatius Press, 2007), 43–75 at 51.

[30] Ibid., 53.

[31] See Aidan Nichols, O.P., *The Thought of Pope Benedict XVI: An Introduction to the Theology of Joseph Ratzinger* (London: Burns & Oates, 2007), 170.

not only teaches his own dissent but teaches it in the name of the Church.

CHARLES CURRAN AND EDWARD SCHILLEBEECKX

Ratzinger's remark about the professor of theology who teaches his own dissent was certainly not made coincidentally in the United States. Indeed, for several years the congregation had been keeping a dossier on the American moralist Charles E. Curran. Born in 1934, in 1958 he had been ordained a priest of the diocese of Rochester, New York. Later, he had earned a degree in theology at the Gregorian University in Rome and specialized in moral theology at the Accademia Alfonsiana under the direction of Father Bernhard Häring, who at the time of the council was one of the most famous Catholic moral theologians. Returning to the United States, he became a professor of moral theology at the Catholic University of America in Washington, D.C. In 1968, he publicly opposed the encyclical *Humanae vitae*, which reaffirmed the immorality of artificial contraception, and then he extended his dissent to other moral topics such as premarital sex, abortion, homosexuality, euthanasia, and in vitro fertilization.

In response to the appeals coming from Rome, the priest had always replied that, given the delicacy of the matter, dissent was somehow justified. On the other hand, he added, he was not denying any dogma or defined truth of the Catholic faith. As had already happened with Boff, on March 8, 1986, Curran was invited to Rome, where he was accompanied by a trusted theologian. He did not depart substantially from his positions, and on April 10 he confirmed by letter that he remained firm in his dissent, describing it as "responsible" because he did not deny any truth of faith. The congregation responded to him with a letter dated July 25, 1986, in which it first of all disputed his last observation. The indissolubility of marriage had been defined by the Council of Trent; Vatican II had declared abortion an abominable crime; and therefore at least these two teachings had to be considered truths of faith. Consequently, the congregation saw itself compelled to suspend him from teaching at Catholic University because "the authorities of the Church cannot allow the present situation to continue in which the inherent contradiction is prolonged that one who is to teach in the name of the Church in fact denies her teaching."

As had happened in the Boff case, there was great disappointment in America. Catholic University sought to find a compromise, but in the end it had to suspend the professor of moral theology. Supported by some of the instructors and students, Curran sued the university, challenging his dismissal. The court, nevertheless, placed the blame on him, adopting Ratzinger's argument: the professor could not appeal to freedom of research. Teaching in a religious university bound him to respect the doctrine of that religion. As in the Küng case, finally, it should be observed that Curran then continued to teach at other universities and research institutes and to publish books and is to this day a priest of the Catholic Church.

A more complex and delicate incident concerned one of the major theologians who had played a leading role at the time of the council, the Dutch Dominican Edward Schillebeeckx, who, as counselor of the bishop of Nijmegen, had collaborated also on the drafting of the conciliar constitution on revelation. Schillebeeckx had then been one of the chief collaborators on the journal *Concilium* and among the authors of the *Dutch Catechism*, which had been very popular and widely read but had caused perplexity in Rome. Paul VI, therefore, had appointed a commission of cardinals that had asked the Bishops' Conference of the Netherlands to supplement and clarify some statements that were considered dubious or at any rate incomplete. In 1979, Schillebeeckx had been invited to Rome by the then prefect, Franjo Cardinal Šeper, to dispel some doubts contained in some of his publications concerning the Resurrection of Jesus, but after the meeting no measures were taken with regard to him. In 1984, however, a new appeal had followed because in his book on ministry in the Church "he presents a concept of the priesthood that disagrees with the teaching of the Church." In this case, too, though, the congregation took no practical steps after the clarifying meeting. Finally, in 1986, one month after the conclusion of the Curran case, Schillebeeckx was summoned to Rome a third time. In his work entitled *The Church with a Human Face*, he had partially attenuated his position. He continued, nevertheless, to maintain that the ordained ministry of priests depended not so much on the sacramental ordination conferred by the bishop that guaranteed apostolic succession as on the community to which they belonged and on its need to celebrate the Eucharist. This was certainly a delicate question, which, once again, was followed by no sanction. The impression was, therefore, that the congregation did not necessarily intend to take any restrictive measures or to suspend from teaching those professors whose orientation was different from Rome's.

THE COURAGE TO BE UNPOPULAR

Toward the end of the 1980s, the question of the relation between theology and Church governance became all the more relevant. We regularly find conferences during that time in which the cardinal tried repeatedly to explain his own idea about the function of theology in the life of the Church. Here I would like to mention a speech requested of the cardinal by the Carmelite Father Antonio Sicari, at that time the director of the Italian edition of *Communio*, and by myself, as editor-in-chief. In late September 1985, we were in Rome and had the opportunity to meet Ratzinger. We then proposed that he come to Brescia, where Father Antonio resided at that time, to give a conference promoted by our journal. Despite his workload, the cardinal immediately accepted the invitation. He asked us, nevertheless, for a bit of time.

In January, confirmation arrived and the date was set. On March 22, Ratzinger was in Brescia, where, in the Vanvitelliano Hall of the Palazzo della Loggia, he gave a magnificent conference entitled "Theology and Church". The cardinal began: "It is unlikely that any sensible Christian would contest that the care for the Word of God among men has been entrusted to the church alone."[32] Then he explained that this statement was not made by a bureaucrat of the Roman Curia but, rather, by Heinrich Schlier, a theologian and exegete, who at that time was involved primarily in the Evangelical Confessing Church. Moreover, merely academic problems were not at stake here, but rather much more dramatic existential questions. The attempt by Nazism to reduce Lutheran Christianity to a State Christianity made this clarification obligatory: the freedom of theology depends on its bond with the Church, even at the cost of having to give up teaching at the university.

Today, the cardinal continued, in more peaceful external circumstances, the question arises again. In the universities, anyone who follows a criterion that is not merely scientific meets with discrim-

---

[32] The conference, given in Italian, was then published with the title "Theologie und Kirche" in the German edition of *Communio* 8 (1986): 515–33. It is cited here in English from "The Spiritual Basis and Ecclesial Identity of Theology", in *The Nature and Mission of Theology*, trans. Adrian Walker (San Francisco: Ignatius Press, 1995), 45.

ination. The authority does not decide, but only scientific arguments; otherwise you have a usurpation and arrogance on the part of the authority. For Ratzinger, this position imperiled both the Church and theology "because a church without theology impoverishes and blinds, while a churchless theology melts away into caprice."[33] Ratzinger then focused on the relation between theology and ecclesial life, starting from the conversion experience described by Saint Paul in the Letter to the Galatians as an upsetting personal experience and at the same time as an objective reality. "It is no longer I who live, but Christ who lives in me."[34]

According to the cardinal, we are witnessing here a change of subject that implies an experience that the believer did not achieve by himself but received as a gift. "It is no longer I who live" does not refer to a private, mystical experience. Instead, it is about a sacramental event through which the individual believer is introduced into the ecclesial body, the Body of Christ. The true subject of the sacramental, ecclesial action is therefore Christ. Hence the conclusion, which is simple to the point of banality: theology presupposes faith, "it draws its life from the paradoxical union of faith and science."[35] Faith, indeed, gives rise to a new kind of knowledge, an approach to the truth that concerns, not the functioning of a particular thing, but rather the knowledge of our being itself. From this we can infer that reason is part of the essence of Christianity. Theology investigates this rationality, and the Magisterium cannot refuse to recognize this task. Otherwise, it would oppose an indispensable dimension of the faith.

On the other hand, there is no theology without faith, without conversion, which is the beginning of a new way of thinking about which Paul spoke, the beginning of a race that leads to sanctity. One result of this is the connection between theology and sanctity to which history testifies:

> Athanasius is inconceivable without Anthony, the father of monasticism, and the latter's new experience of Christ; Augustine is likewise unthinkable without his passionate journey to a radical Christian life. Moreover, Bonaventure and the Franciscan theology of the thirteenth century would have been impossible without the impos-

---

[33] Ibid., 48.
[34] Gal 2:20.
[35] J. Ratzinger, "Spiritual Basis", 55–56.

ing new representation of Christ in the figure of Saint Francis of Assisi, nor could Thomas Aquinas have existed without Dominic's breakthrough to the gospel and to evangelization.[36]

After so many examples from the past, Ratzinger also proposed contemporary models of theologians whose fruitfulness derives from their conversion. After the abovementioned Schlier, he cited the figure of Romano Guardini. As opposed to the liberal model based on individual research and self-fulfillment, the young Italian-German at the beginning of his career had a conversion experience while grappling with Jesus' saying: "He who finds his life will lose it, and he who loses his life for my sake will find it."[37] The loss to which Jesus refers, Guardini argues, is not just any loss, but only a loss for the sake of God, who is manifested in him, Jesus. But where can we truly find Jesus? The images transmitted by the scholars have a fundamental defect: they strangely resemble the idealized images of the one who proposes them. The Church is the place where we can really find the Body of Christ incarnate, where in obedience we can lose our life for him and thus gain it.

Ratzinger then concluded by recalling again the experience of Schlier, who, considering some theologians who were in favor of the German Christianity of the Nazis, asked himself: Is it better for pastors to speak up and revoke the teaching authority of possible transgressors or to look on silently, like dogs that do not bark, when abuse is committed in the name of the Church? Naturally, the cardinal was not so naïve as to fail to recognize the difference in the situations, but the risk of the transgression is ever-present. The Magisterium has the task of watching over and protecting simple believers, and this requires the courage to be unpopular.

IN DEFENSE OF LIFE

Also at the request of many bishops' conferences, in 1987, the Congregation for the Doctrine of the Faith with its instruction *Donum vitae*, "The Gift of Life", intervened in the delicate and timely topic of defending human life and the dignity of procreation, the first in a

---

[36] Ibid., 57–58. This conviction would inspire the future catechesis of Benedict XVI on the saints, which was not intended as a mere biographical account or a mere history of sanctity. He wanted to show the simultaneous development of holiness and of theological thought that must then lead to a new explanation and proclamation of the Gospel.

[37] Mt 10:39.

series of documents that would end up complicating the Church's relations with science and with the contemporary mind-set. The document's point of departure is the solemn statement that human life and the transmission thereof through the generations were given to man by God as a gift. Every person, therefore, is called to respect life. The progress of the biological and medical sciences makes effective therapeutic means possible but runs the risk of going beyond the limits of a reasonable dominion over nature. The Church is not an expert in technology, although she wants to safeguard the dignity of the human person so as to promote a civilization of love and not of exploitation. God created man in his image. Science and technology are invaluable, but they are at the service of man and must not betray that trust. Respecting the dignity of man implies respect for soul and body. No biologist can decide what the origin and the destiny of a person is. From these premises, the instruction derives the following practical directives:

- A human being is to be respected from the first moment of his or her existence. One cannot attempt to experiment on the human embryo.

- From the first moment [of conception], the adventure of a new human life begins. Therefore every form of procured abortion is condemned by the Church.

- Therapeutic interventions on the embryo are certainly justified, but those that aim to promote abortion are unacceptable.

- Human procreation and marriage: truly responsible procreation occurs within marriage. The fidelity of the spouses in the union of matrimony involves the reciprocal respect for their right to become father and mother. The good of the children and of the parents contributes to the well-being of society. The vitality and equilibrium of society require that children should come into the world in the bosom of a family.

- Heterologous artificial fertilization, which involves a donor different from the spouses, is contrary to the unity of marriage.

- The civil law must safeguard the rights of every individual human being, the rights of the family, and of the institution of marriage, which are fundamental values. Therefore, the civil laws, too, must intervene to regulate recourse to technology. Delegating decisions to the conscience of the technicians and of individual citizens is not sufficient.

THE REVOLT OF THE THEOLOGIANS

Ever since the days of Vatican II, the German moral theologian Bernhard Häring had been considered one of the great masters of the Catholic moral renewal inspired by Christian personalism and based on Sacred Scripture. An expert at Vatican II, where he had collaborated in particular in the drafting of the Constitution on the Church in the Modern World, from 1949 to 1987 he had been a professor at the Accademia Alfonsiana, the pontifical university that specialized in ethical and moral disciplines. Ever since the publication of *Humanae vitae*, the encyclical by Paul VI that opposed the use of artificial contraceptives in marital relations, he had spoken out critically against Catholic sexual morality. Repeatedly summoned for his positions, he had remained firm in his teachings, and the Congregation for the Doctrine of the Faith had limited itself to verbal appeals. In late 1988, the mass media worldwide published a rather severe document that he had written about the pontificate of John Paul II, particularly in the field of sexual ethics.[38]

The elderly theologian attacked the pope for appointing Monsignor Carlo Caffarra, future bishop of Bologna, head of the Institute for Studies on Marriage and Family of the Pontifical Lateran University. He then maintained that the encyclical *Humanae vitae* was basically only a debate on the legitimacy of artificial contraceptive methods as compared with natural ones. He concluded by asserting that what really matters is not whether a couple uses one contraceptive method or the other but, rather, that the spouses reach their decision to transmit life responsibly. Häring's article seemed to be a signal for an insurrection by dissenting theologians from various countries who were making their voices heard. On January 25, 1989, 163 theologians from Central Europe—Germans, Dutchmen, Swiss, and Austrians—made public the so-called "Cologne Declaration", in which they demanded more democracy in the Church and supported Häring's critiques in the field of Catholic sexual ethics.

---

[38] In Italy, the text was published with the title "Chiedere l'opinione di vescovi e teologi", *Il Regno-Attualità* 2 (1989): 1–4.

The Vatican spokesman Joaquín Navarro-Valls sought to scale down the extent of this challenge, describing it as a local phenomenon, but it spread rapidly to neighboring countries. Indeed, the Cologne Declaration was followed by a document by French intellectuals and theologians claiming that the bishops and the Holy See were limiting freedom of research, while sixty-two Spanish theologians, besides agreeing with the abovementioned criticisms, denounced "the strengthening of the so-called new ecclesial movements, which tend to be neo-conservative, by a significant sector of the hierarchy, while the base communities that tend to be progressive are repeatedly discredited."[39] In Italy, finally, for the first time sixty-three theologians signed a *Letter to Christians*,[40] in which they denounced the unease caused by the attitudes of the central authority of the Church in the areas of instruction, discipline, and institutions. In particular, it asserted that Vatican II with its pastoral implications should be considered a radical, irreversible change. The signers then asked the pope and the Vatican authorities to take greater account of the fact that the Church is made up of a communion of churches. Finally, they disputed a document of the Congregation for the Doctrine of the Faith that demanded adherence with religious respect to the ordinary teaching of the Magisterium as well.[41]

From this diversity of situations and demands emerged an uneasiness that could not be ignored. From today's vantage point, one can see the different approaches taken by the Vatican organizations and the representatives of the local Church. Whereas the pope, Ratzinger, and the congregation were looking at the universal Church with an eye to the future, the theologians took more into consideration the present demands of the local Churches, as the Italian theologians explicitly wrote. I think that in this regard we can adopt the judgment of Walter Kasper, the theologian from Tübingen, who at that time had just been appointed bishop of Stuttgart. When interviewed by *Il Regno*, he said that several documents presented a style that was sometimes excessively uncivil and polemical, but he recognized, nevertheless, that these stances were

---

[39] *Adista* 33/33 (1989): 12.

[40] "Lettera ai cristiani: Oggi nella Chiesa", *Il Regno-Attualità* 10 (1989): 244–55.

[41] The text was published first in the Italian edition of *L'Osservatore Romano* (February 25, 1989), then, in September, in the official Acts of the Holy See.

evidence of "justified desires and open questions on which to re-flect".[42]

THE TRUTH IS A GIFT. THE CONGREGATION'S RESPONSE

Forcibly drawn into the dispute, the Congregation for the Doctrine of the Faith responded with an instruction, *Donum veritatis*, "the gift of truth"; even the title reveals the hand of Ratzinger. Indeed, as his episcopal motto he had chosen "Co-workers of the Truth", an expression from the Third Letter of Saint John, which, as interpreted by the new bishop, underscored the continuity between the ministry of the theologian and that of the bishop. The beginning of the document is an exaltation of truth, the search for which is inherent in human nature. Indeed, the truth is what sets us free, while ignorance keeps us enslaved. Jesus came to bring as a gift the truth guaranteed by the revelation of God, which obviously surpasses man's capacity to know but is not opposed to human reason. On the contrary, it lifts him up and places him on the path that fosters the encounter between God and man.

The believer's search to understand the faith, which is entrusted to theology, is therefore a service, indeed, a requirement that the Church cannot renounce. Consequently, "theology has importance for the Church in every age so that it can respond to the plan of God" (no. 1). Hence, the vocation of the theologian, who offers his contribution so that the faith might become communicable even to those who do not yet believe. For this reason, his work cannot be detached from the spirit of love that is the source of evangelization. "Since the object of theology is the Truth which is the living God and His plan for salvation revealed in Jesus Christ, the theologian is called to deepen his own life of faith and continuously unite his scientific research with prayer" (no. 8). In fact, he cannot forget that he in turn is a member of the people of God, and in his teaching he is called to show the reasonableness of the faith. Freedom of theological research is exercised within the faith of the Church and under the direction of the Magisterium. Although it may prompt the theologian's conscience to be bold, his research bears fruit and edifies only if it is accompanied by the patience of maturation, as Saint Irenaeus said already in the second century (no. 11).

---

[42] See Tornielli, *Benedetto XVI*, 142.

The Magisterium and theologians have different functions but the same goal: to preserve the people of God in the truth and thus to make them the light of the nations. Collaboration between bishops and theologians is necessary, therefore, particularly when the latter receive the *missio canonica*, the mandate to teach in the name of the Church. To the bishops, as successors of the apostles, is entrusted the task of preserving the word of God and expounding and diffusing it among men. Therefore, the function of the Magisterium is not foreign to Christian truth, and theologians are bound to obedience to their pastors. After so many polemics, the instruction was like a breath of fresh air; it struck a peaceful, conciliatory tone in the introductory part and in the one on the vocation of the theologian. Some uncertainty remained in the definition of the collaboration between bishops and theologians and also in the attempt to extend the scope for the application of the Magisterium to objectively uncertain topics that are still being clarified. Very timely, on the other hand, was the distinction between unity of truth and unity of charity. Where tensions can always arise because of the progress of technology and the changed conditions of the times, it is important to preserve the unity of charity that is given and requested by Jesus in the Eucharist.

The dialogue with theology

THE PRAYING THEOLOGY OF VON BALTHASAR

Among the tasks entrusted by Paul VI to the renewed Congregation for the Doctrine of the Faith, there was no longer exclusively a mandate to correct eventual errors that may arise within the Catholic world; rather, it was necessary to promote, through conferences and other means, the enrichment that is likewise proposed within the Church. And although in the first half of the 1980s there was a prevalence of admonitions, encouragement was not altogether lacking. In 1985, at the initiative of ISTRA, the Institute for studies on the transition affiliated with the movement Communion and Liberation and directed by Angelo Scola, later the cardinal archbishop of Milan, a conference was held in Rome on "The Ecclesial Mission of Adrienne von Speyr". Participating in the convention were, among others, Godfried Cardinal Danneels, archbishop of Malines-Brussels; André-Joseph Léonard, Danneels' future successor; the

Jesuit priest Georges Chantraine, and Hans Urs von Balthasar; the proceedings in fact introduced a new element into theological reflection.

Adrienne von Speyr (1902–1967) was a Swiss physician who converted to the Catholic faith in 1940 after becoming acquainted with the then chaplain to the Catholic university students in Basel, the Jesuit von Balthasar. According to the priest's testimony, after her conversion, she received a series of mystical graces, following which she developed her own concept of mysticism, placing the emphasis on the objective side that does not refer to the more or less extraordinary aspects of a charismatic person but is a real service for the benefit of the Church. "Mysticism is a particular mission, a particular service to the Church that can only be properly carried out in a continual and complete movement away from oneself, in self-forgetfulness (she loved the word *éffacement*) and virginal readiness for the Word of God."[43] At the same time, she insisted vehemently that preaching and any task within the Church must be backed by a way of life that affirmed the same message.

From this, von Balthasar derived what later became a much-repeated slogan: theology done "on one's knees", as opposed polemically to theology done at a desk. Precisely by placing himself at the service of Adrienne's charism, the Jesuit had then had to leave his Order, had departed from Basel, and for a long time had remained without any diocesan faculties, and finally he had not been invited to Vatican II. On the positive side, according to von Balthasar, von Speyr's objective mysticism had then been the source of a profound upheaval in his own theological vision, which now was no longer based on the ascents of the heart, on a human movement of ascent toward God, but rather started from God's descent toward man in the Incarnation of Christ and especially in his descent into hell after his death and before his Resurrection. The Son of God had thus burdened himself with the sins of all men and had redeemed them.

For his part, Ratzinger was rather reserved about von Speyr's numerous mystical phenomena but was enthusiastic about the powerful Catholic vision of his friend von Balthasar, about his ability

---

[43] See Hans Urs von Balthasar, *First Glance at Adrienne von Speyr*, trans. Antje Lawry and Sr. Sergia Englund, O.C.D. (San Francisco: Ignatius Press, 1981), 36. See also chapters 4 and 5 of my book *Hans Urs von Balthasar* (Cinisello Balsamo: Edizioni Paoline, 1991), 109–57.

to access and to render fruitful in a new way the patristic heritage, about his staunch defense of the sanctity but also of the visible aspect of the Church, of the Petrine ministry, and of the symphony of truth that is capable of grasping and holding together the many aspects of the mystery and of Christian life. At the conference on von Speyr, Ratzinger did not speak personally, but, at the conclusion of it, he organized a magnificent reception for his friend von Balthasar at Castel Sant'Angelo. During the course of the evening, a famous pianist performed pieces by Mozart, Ratzinger's favorite composer and von Balthasar's, also; the latter in his youth had been an excellent pianist and had written important essays of musical criticism about Mozart.[44] On this occasion, the eighty-year-old von Balthasar, who had suffered much in his youth precisely as a result of his friendship with Doctor von Speyr, was visibly moved and could not keep back the tears.

HEAL THE EYES OF THE HEART.
THE RETREAT OF THE FAITHFUL THEOLOGIAN

In late May 1988, von Balthasar was in Sion, the capital of the canton of Valais, the guest of his brother and sister-in-law for a brief period of rest. One Sunday evening a telephone call, probably expected, informed him that he had been appointed a cardinal. Visibly upset, the theologian withdrew to his room, where, according to the testimony of his sister-in-law, he spent a very agitated night.[45] The telephone call was probably from Ratzinger, who had played a decisive role in obtaining approval of the nomination. The cardinal had certainly had no difficulty convincing John Paul II, who himself had very high esteem for the man whom de Lubac had described as the most cultivated man of his time[46] and to whom, in 1984, the pontiff had personally awarded the Paul VI prize, which in those days was described as the "Catholic Nobel Prize". The prefect for the Doctrine of the Faith, on the other hand, had accomplished a delicate task of persuasion, which had begun precisely with the

---

[44] In this regard, see Elio Guerriero, *Hans Urs von Balthasar* (Brescia: Morcelliana: 2006), 17–27.

[45] See Guerriero, *Hans Urs von Balthasar* (1991), 5.

[46] Henri de Lubac, *The Church: Paradox and Mystery*, trans. James R. Dunne (Shannon, Ireland: Ecclesia Press, 1969), 105.

reception described in the previous paragraph, in order to convince von Balthasar to accept the honorific title.

The Swiss scholar, indeed, together with Adrienne von Speyr, had developed a theological vision whereby he belonged to the Johannine Church, the Church of love, and he wished to keep his distance from the centers of honor and power. The Church, nevertheless, particularly in German-speaking countries, needed authoritative, faithful figures in Rome who would testify by their example on behalf of catholicity—unity in plurality—as von Balthasar himself had testified in widely circulated books. Hence, the work of persuasion by Ratzinger, who for his part had gone to Rome more out of a spirit of obedience and solidarity with the pontiff. Finally, only after long hesitation,[47] the Swiss theologian gave his consent, with the pledge that nothing would change in his life, which he would continue to live in the little Community of Saint John in Basel. His consent out of obedience, nevertheless, had been accompanied by several warning signs that had prompted von Balthasar to write: "The ones up there seem to have a different plan."[48] In fact, the theologian died on June 26, 1988, two days before receiving the cardinalatial hat.

The funeral was held on July 1 in the Hofkirche in Lucerne, with a visibly emotional Cardinal Ratzinger presiding. More than a tour of von Balthasar's thought and theology, the homily was a portrait of the theologian who is in love with God and in love with the Church. The cardinal began: "What Balthasar wanted may well be encapsulated in a single phrase of St. Augustine: '. . . healing the eyes of the heart so that they may be able to see God.'"[49] This vision, the cardinal continued, starts, not with the next life, but in the present life, in the everyday choices that often lead us by roads that are not the ones we imagined or wanted. From his youth, indeed, von Balthasar had experienced not so much choice as being chosen in his call to religious life, in his meeting with Adrienne von Speyr, in his painful abandonment of religious life, in the misunderstandings and loneliness that had accompanied that choice.

---

[47] Joseph Ratzinger, "Homily at the Funeral Liturgy for Hans Urs von Balthasar", *Communio* 15.4 (Winter 1988): 512–16 at 515b.

[48] Letter to a friend, cited by Peter Henrici, "Erster Blick auf Hans Urs von Balthasar", in *Von Balthasar: Gestalt und Werk*, ed. Karl Lehmann and Walter Kasper (Cologne: Communio, 1989), 59.

[49] J. Ratzinger, "Homily at the Funeral Liturgy", 512b.

Von Balthasar, nevertheless, knew that even "in wintertime, the root lives on"[50] and had constantly cultivated a kneeling theology. His awareness of God's love, therefore, had never been dissociated from the Petrine structure, from his love for the Church, which he saw as a living person. For this reason, in a truly Ignatian spirit, he had never renounced obedience, and his death, which deprived him of the honor, was basically a confirmation of it. The pope's gesture, nevertheless, remained fully valid: "The Church itself, in its official responsibility, tells us that [Balthasar] is right in what he teaches of the faith, that he points the way to the sources of living water."[51]

Friendship with Communion and Liberation

In chapter 6 I have already recalled Ratzinger's friendship with the Integrierte Gemeinde, the community of dialogue with Judaism, which he had recognized and supported in Munich. In those same years, as he would recall in a famous conference in 1998, the cardinal had contacts with other movements: the Neocatechumenal Way, Communion and Liberation, the Focolare Movement.[52] The cardinal testified: "This was the time when Karl Rahner and others were using the expression the 'winter period' in the Church. . . . Yet suddenly here was something nobody had planned on. The Holy Spirit had, so to say, spoken up for himself again. In young people especially, the faith was surging up in its entirety, with no ifs and buts."[53]

The movement with which the cardinal struck up more intense relations was Communion and Liberation, founded by Don Luigi Giussani. As already mentioned, on the occasion of the foundation of *Communio*, in the early 1970s, there was the meeting with Angelo Scola, Eugenio Corecco, and Sante Bagnoli, close collaborators with Don Giussani. Ten years later, in 1982, two theologians

[50] Ibid., 514a. Von Balthasar cherished the sentence by Saint Augustine as much as Ratzinger did.

[51] Ibid., 515b.

[52] Published several times, the text of the conference given on May 30, 1998, on the occasion of the meeting of John Paul II with the lay movements, is found now in Joseph Ratzinger, *New Outpourings of the Spirit: Movements in the Church*, trans. Michael J. Miller and Henry Taylor (San Francisco: Ignatius Press, 2007), 19–61 at 19.

[53] Ibid., 20.

arrived in Rome: the cardinal, as prefect of the Congregation for the Doctrine of the Faith, and Angelo Scola, as professor at the Pontifical Council for the Family within the Lateran University. This was the beginning of a collaboration that culminated in Scola's nomination as consultor of the congregation in 1986.

The breakthrough in the cardinal's relationship with Communion and Liberation seems to go back to the preceding year. In early 1985, on January 28, Ratzinger granted an interview in which he declared that the movements are instruments of the universal Church that make "the pastoral ministry of the local Church fruitful and whole . . . and they reinvigorate the regional pastoral care." He went on to say that they "cannot be reduced to the episcopal principle but, rather, rely on the [petrine] primacy both at the theological and practical level".[54] A statement of this sort could not help generating enthusiasm in Don Giussani and his followers, who in many regions of Italy and abroad were regarded by the local bishops with aloofness, if not with suspicion. *Il Sabato*, a weekly publication affiliated with the movement, entitled the article that reported on Ratzinger's interview "The Holy Pluralism of the Movements".[55] The cardinal's interview, nevertheless, seemed to be part of a larger project that involved the entire Italian Church.

That year, the convention of the Italian Church entitled "Christian Reconciliation and the Human Community" was held in Loreto from April 9 to 13. The event was designed as a sequel to the 1976 convention on evangelization and human development, but John Paul II, in agreement with Ratzinger, had a different approach. Father Bartolomeo Sorge, summarizing the outcome of the first convention, said: "Thus the result was the image of an Italian Church that is searching; although she brings certainties, she nevertheless shares with the country in the provisional dynamic that is not without ambiguity, risks, and surprises, which characterizes the historical course of events in which we are immersed."[56] Speaking energetically at the Loreto convention, the pope seemed to turn that perspective completely on its head. For him, the Church's great task was evangelization in the strong, full sense, as the ability to bring

---

[54] See Alberto Savorana, *Vita di don Giussani* (Milan: Rizzoli, 2013), 665.
[55] "Quel santo pluralismo che sono i movimenti", *Il Sabato* 7 (1985): 15.
[56] Cited in Saviero Xeres and Giorgio Gampanini, *Manca il respiro* (Milan: Ancora, 2011), 48.

Christ into the center of life and culture and therefore also of the historical process.[57] The pope said in Loreto: "The faith itself is capable of producing culture, that is, a life and a history inspired and imbued with the Word who was made flesh."[58] In this new perspective, moreover, the movements have a decisive role. Marco Impagliazzo, a historian and current president of the Saint Egidio Community, writes: "John Paul II showed from the beginning of his pontificate a profound attachment to these movements."[59]

For his part, Ratzinger was altogether in favor of the approach marked out by the pope and maintained particularly close relations with CL. With Giussani, moreover, he also had cultural affinities. He wrote in the introduction to the volume of the history of CL about the impetus at the start of the movement: "The Christian faith does not originate in theoretical proofs, but in an event: the story of Jesus Christ; this event becomes encounter, and in the encounter truth is disclosed."[60] The encounter with Jesus and the reasonableness of the faith are therefore the pivotal points from which Don Giussani set out, but also the pivotal points of Ratzinger's thought. It is not surprising, therefore, that a relationship of esteem and friendship developed between the cardinal and the founder of CL.

In the summer of 1985, the two men had a particularly warm meeting at the Elephant Restaurant in Brixen (Bressanone), where the cardinal was spending his vacation with his brother, Georg. According to the chauffeur who accompanied Don Giussani and gave a detailed account of the event, during the dinner the founder of CL asked the cardinal all sorts of questions and received clear and thorough answers from him. What surprised the driver even more was precisely "the sight of a friendship and therefore of an extraordinary familiarity and cordiality. I could not imagine that Cardinal Ratzinger would be so profoundly and, I should say, affectionately acquainted with the person, the life, the story, the thought, and the

---

[57] See Camillo Ruini, "L'impatto di Giovanni Paolo II sull'Italia e la Chiesa italiana", in Marco Impagliazzo, ed., *Shock Wojtyła: L'inizio del pontificato* (Cinisello Balsamo: San Paolo, 2010), 448f.

[58] John Paul II, Speech to the Participants in Convention of the Italian Catholic Church in Loreto, April 11, 1985 [translated from Italian].

[59] Marco Impagliazzo, "Giovanni Paolo II e l'Italia", in Guerriero and Impagliazzo, *I cattolici e le Chiese cristiane*, 117.

[60] See Massimo Camisasca, *Communione e Liberazione: Le origini* (Cinisello Balsamo: San Paolo, 2001), 7.

writings of Don Giussani. At the end of the dinner, there was a warm embrace as though between two dear friends."[61]

During the summer of 1986, there was another meeting between Don Giussani and the cardinal, at which the leader of CL asked him to conduct the spiritual exercises for around four hundred priests of the movement. The cardinal accepted the invitation, and his conferences were the source of a book that is small but significant in the thought of the cardinal and future pope.

THE REASONABLENESS OF CHRISTIANITY
AND THE RENEWAL OF THE CHURCH

As he wrote in the preface of *To Look on Christ: Exercises in Faith, Hope, and Love*,[62] when he received the visit from Don Giussani, who asked him to preach a retreat for the priests of the movement, Ratzinger had on his desk a volume in which the philosopher Josef Pieper, a disciple of Guardini, combined his three treatises on love, hope, and faith, originally published in 1935, 1962, and 1971. "This inspired me to devote the retreat to consideration of the three [theological] virtues and in doing so to use Pieper's philosophical meditations as a kind of textbook."[63] This quotation by Ratzinger seems to me to be very important. It highlights the cardinal's constant effort to start from reason so as to reach the more properly theological nucleus, in the conviction that Christianity, in adhering fully to the requirements of reason, is open to everyone. In the second place, we cannot fail to mention that two of the three encyclicals of Pope Benedict XVI address the theological virtues and, in turn, start from the standpoint of reason.

Faith. The cardinal immediately began with a previous definition of the act of faith, which is essentially a response to God who invites man to love. This, incidentally, is the reason why Pieper reversed the order, placing love first in the collection of his three treatises dedicated to the theological virtues; Benedict XVI then followed this

---

[61] Savorana, *Vita di don Giussani*, 675.

[62] The English translation by Robert Nowell was published by Crossroad in 1989; the same publisher printed a second edition in 2005 entitled *The Yes of Jesus Christ: Spiritual Exercises in Faith, Hope and Love.*

[63] Joseph Ratzinger, *To Look on Christ: Exercises in Faith, Hope, and Love*, trans. Robert Nowell (New York: Crossroad, 1991), 7, emended.

order in the sequence of his encyclicals. First, there is God, who calls to love, then man, who responds to the invitation. Hence Ratzinger took up again the line of thought already traced in his first lecture in Bonn in 1959,[64] whereby an attitude of trust is indispensable even in human relationships. There are so many achievements of technology that we do not understand yet calmly make use of every day. This opens a passage to the religious way, even though the latter is qualitatively different from simple human trust. Atheism, in contrast, especially the kind that declares itself scientific, is not sustainable at all. No one can know scientifically that God does not exist. What remains is practical agnosticism, which is a hypothesis, just as religious faith can be considered a hypothesis at this point. Confronted with these two hypotheses, though, the more advantageous is certainly the wager on God about which Pascal had already spoken.

Ratzinger, nevertheless, wanted to go farther, contrasting the image of an intelligent man who makes his calculations, counting solely on a future in this world, with the image of the wise man who takes into account his soul's aspirations for supernatural life, for eternity. While the first can be contradicted at any moment in his calculations, the wise man, even when facing everyday disasters, can experience amazement at the ways of God. From this perspective, the cardinal concluded, the intelligent proud man ultimately proves to be the real fool, while the wise man attains "a humility of thought that is ready to bow before the majesty of truth, before which we are not judges but suppliants."[65]

As Saint Thomas had already written, in the end unbelief proves to be unnatural. Nothing remains but to travel the other path, that of faith. For Christians, there is, first of all, the Word, Jesus Christ, who comes from the love of God and enters into human history to reveal this love. The gesture of John, who at the Last Supper places his head on the heart of Jesus, is the true symbol of faith. The believer, nevertheless, cannot claim to travel by himself on the way that leads to the Christian God. For God is a communion of love and makes himself known in the word of the Gospel that is entrusted to the Church and is attested by the saints. In turn, this testimony becomes the vehicle of mission: the proclamation of the Gospel to those who do not yet believe.

---

[64] See above, chap. 3.

[65] J. Ratzinger, *To Look on Christ*, 22–23.

Hope. The reflection on hope begins with the critique of the false optimism of those who close their eyes to reality. There is the optimism of progress, but also the Marxist optimism, which, in order to construct a hypothetical new world, pretends not to see the poverty and suffering that it brings with it. This programmatic optimism, nevertheless, is based on possible human achievements and in reality leaves no room at all for true hope. The Christian virtue, in contrast, is founded on a promise that comes from on high, from God, and does not ignore anyone's sufferings. The witness of Christian hope is Jeremiah, who, faced with the danger presented by the Assyrian-Babylonians, exhorts the people to have confidence in God and not in the help of Egypt; and the Book of Revelation, in which the beast is the image of the proud, arrogant person, while Christ is the image of the truly wise man. Finally, the most convincing testimony about Christian hope is contained in the Sermon on the Mount with the proclamation of the Beatitudes, of which the true subject is Christ. "He it is in whom it becomes clear what it means to be 'poor in spirit': it is he who mourns, who is meek, who hungers and thirsts for righteousness, who is the merciful. He is pure in heart, he is the peacemaker, he is persecuted for righteousness' sake. All the sayings of the sermon on the mount are flesh and blood in him."[66]

If Jesus is the true subject of the Beatitudes, the Sermon on the Mount is a powerful invitation to imitate him, and it is a sure path of hope. To the extent that one imitates and belongs to Jesus, the promises contained in the second part of the individual Beatitudes are fulfilled, also. The way of imitating Christ lasts a whole lifetime and reaches fulfillment in the life to come, but the latter is already real and present even in the today of every believer. Hence the decisive assertion of Saint Paul: "In this hope we were saved",[67] which Benedict XVI would later use as the title of his second encyclical. Hope, nevertheless, requires constant commitment and demands prayer, through which one enters into God's world. The Our Father, for example, essentially asks in the first part that the conditions for paradise be fulfilled, whereas in the second part our daily anxieties and anguishes are overcome along the lines of the Beatitudes and of hope.

---

[66] Ibid., 60.
[67] Rom 8:24.

Charity. Despair and presumption are two attitudes that in our times have been taken to unprecedented extremes. They have caused what Ratzinger described as the melancholy of the world and metaphysical acedia. The root of the sadness is the abandonment of all aspirations for the infinite, for eternity. "Today there is a remarkable hatred among people for their own greatness"[68] through which the road that had started with the pride of wanting to be like God leads to the lazy inability to believe in the greatness of the human vocation. This acedia, Ratzinger concluded, can very well coexist with frantic activity and profiteering. The crucial thing is the flight from God, the flight from one's own soul.

Diametrically opposed to metaphysical laziness is love, both natural and supernatural love. The two types of love, indeed, cannot be separated, just as one cannot separate eros and religious love. From a philosophical perspective, according to Pieper, love is above all a yes said by the lover to the beloved, a declaration that affirms: "It is good that you exist." This particular affirmation then leads to an assent pronounced about being in general: the love of the individual "thou" opens the way that leads to the love of being in general. The world to which this "thou" belongs appears worthy of being loved, and all of reality appears in a different light. This relation between particular and universal is fundamental. Only through the particular does one reach the universal. On the other hand, love for the universal cannot eliminate the particular.

This first philosophical stage of love is not eliminated by Christianity but, rather, taken to unprecedented depths. According to the path pointed out by the Teacher, the Christian knows that the way of love is above all a journey toward truth in its fullness. When a teacher of the law asks him about the best way to gain eternal life, Jesus responds by exhorting him to love God and neighbor as himself.[69] Ratzinger concluded that the first thing necessary in order to gain eternal life, the fullness of life, is an intimate agreement: "For that reason it is important throughout one's life and from one's youth onwards to learn and to practice thinking with God, feeling with God, willing with God, so that love may grow from this."[70] Hence, there is love of neighbor that consists, not of

---

[68] J. Ratzinger, *To Look on Christ*, 70.

[69] See Lk 10:25–37.

[70] J. Ratzinger, *To Look on Christ*, 103.

more or less great or heroic theories, but, rather, as the parable of the Good Samaritan teaches, of care for one's neighbor, care about his concrete circumstances.

As I have already recalled, the idea for the volume *To Look on Christ* came from the work of Josef Pieper, who, in turn, was a disciple of Romano Guardini. This detail is worth pointing out because I have the impression that from then on the prefect of the former Holy Office increasingly followed in the footsteps of the Italian-German theologian, whom he had admired since the days of his youth.[71] He was inspired by him in writing his book on the liturgy,[72] one of the most talked-about books in recent years; Guardini's volume *The Lord*[73] was the inspiration for his trilogy on Jesus. Guardini's volume on the Church (see below, pp. 644f.) presented, almost as a Last Will and Testament, on the day when he took leave of the cardinals. Finally, *To Look on Christ* marks the beginning of an impressive series of publications on Jesus suggested by the pastoral concern of presenting a unified, captivating image of Jesus.

As he would later explain in the introduction to *Jesus of Nazareth*,[74] he wanted to take into account completely the extraordinary advances of exegesis from the end of the nineteenth century to our day, and at the same time he wanted to provide the faithful with a uniform image of Jesus. Just as in a mosaic the thousands of tiles help to form the one image of the majestic face of Christ, so too the countless contributions of history, philology, and archaeology should help, not to dissolve, but rather to form a richer, more captivating image of the Lord on whom the Christian faith ultimately depends.

THE SCULPTOR AND THE BELIEVER

Ratzinger's bond of friendship with Communion and Liberation continued with the cardinal's participation in 1990 in the "Meeting for Friendship among Peoples" organized in Rimini by the movement.

---

[71] See the first two chapters of this volume.

[72] See Joseph Ratzinger, *The Spirit of the Liturgy*, trans. John Saward (San Francisco: Ignatius Press, 2000).

[73] Romano Guardini, *The Lord*, trans. Elinor Castendyk Briefs (Chicago: H. Regnery, 1954).

[74] The work was published in three volumes (2007–2012), practically speaking, from the beginning almost to the end of the pontificate.

That year, the rather odd title of the late-summer meeting was "The Admirer, Einstein, Thomas Becket". An equally allusive but rather unusual topic had been proposed to the cardinal. He preferred a more explicit title: "A Pilgrim Fellowship: The Church and Her Constant Renewal".[75]

Without wasting any words, the prefect of the former Holy Office started by noting the growing discontent, even among Christians, with regard to the Church. The disappointment starts with the observation that the Church is an institution like others, continues then with a sorrowful lament over the thought that she could be an island of liberation but is not. Hence, the zeal of those dedicated to the work of the Church, clergy, and committed lay persons in starting an ever more daring program of reforms that fundamentalists and reactionaries are seeking in vain to oppose. With the naïve assumption that earlier generations had not understood the problem correctly, they intend, with their debates, agreements, and democratic decisions, to build a better Church, a fully human Church abounding in fraternity and generous creativity. Disappointment, nevertheless, is very soon followed by frustration. The Church cannot be reformed by democratic decisions made by majority rules, since whatever is established by human beings can be changed once again by them.

We return then to the question: Who can reform the Church, and how? The cardinal responded that the odd title of the meeting can be helpful here: indeed, the admirer is someone who experiences wonder at the mystery. The true reformer, therefore, is someone who does not seek to build for himself a Church in his own image and likeness but, rather, eliminates the dross so as to discover beneath it the true face, the one that Jesus intended to imprint on the community founded by him, entrusting then to the apostles and to their successors the task of making it grow but also of preserving unchanged its fundamental characteristic traits.

In support of his reasoning, Ratzinger described an image borrowed from Michelangelo. The great Renaissance artist declared that he already saw in the raw marble the governing image that stood in front of him and was only waiting to be set free by his

---

[75] The text of the conference is now published in Joseph Ratzinger, *La Chiesa: Una comunità sempre in cammino* (Cinisello Balsamo: Edizioni Paoline, 2006), 115-37.

art. Similarly, Saint Bonaventure had said earlier that the true sculptor does not do something but rather takes away what is superfluous. "His work is an *ablatio*: it consists of eliminating, in taking away what is inauthentic. In this way, through the *ablatio*, the *nobilis forma* emerges, that is, the precious figure."[76] The image, according to Ratzinger, can be a guide both for the purification of the individual Christian and also for the reform of the Church. The latter will always need human structures, which nevertheless are exposed to the wear and tear of time. Hence the conviction already among the Fathers of Christian antiquity that the Church is always in need of reform.

The first work of purification, nevertheless, is born of the confrontation with the image of the Church that gushed from the pierced side of Jesus, from which came the blood and water of the sacraments. Generated by faith, this vision, which moves from Jesus and passes on to the Church and the individual faithful, is at the origin of all true ecclesial reform. Hence Ratzinger's conclusion that, in order to bring about the true reform of the Christian community, the simultaneous purification of every believer is necessary. Like the Church, the faithful, too, need the work of ablation, which takes away the more or less dark shadows caused by time, renews the eyes of faith, and makes resplendent the face of Jesus, who, according to the definition of Saint Bonaventure, leaves behind a very noble disposition.

Although given at the meeting of Communion and Liberation, the conference had wide influence in Italy and abroad. It signaled, nevertheless, a concern of the cardinal that would increase over the years until the proclamation of the Year of Faith during the time of his pontificate. A true reform of the Church—an effective renewal of her pastoral ministry and a new evangelization—is thinkable only in terms of a profound, firm faith. Although prompted by noble intentions, the cardinal's speech was not understood: either by those who worked for the Church, most of whom were too convinced of the benefits of pastoral programs to listen to the invitation to deepen them, or by the larger public, who were attracted more by

---

[76] Ibid., 123. Also reprinted here in a footnote is the passage by Saint Bonaventure saying that *ablatio* leaves behind in the stone the beautiful, noble form, "while knowledge of divinity leaves behind in us through ablation a very noble disposition".

the polemics of the day than by the invitation to reflection. For his part, Ratzinger, at regular intervals until the proclamation of the Year of Faith, tirelessly called attention to the divine origin of true reform in the Church, requested and accompanied by the prayer of believers.

X

"A TURNING POINT FOR EUROPE?"

The Europe of the revolutions

When he was elected pope in 1978, John Paul II already had his own geopolitical vision of Europe, of its cultural heritage, its unity, which had to be achieved as soon as possible, and its mission in the world.[1] At that time, Ratzinger's vision was more limited. As a good German, he looked with interest at what was happening in East Germany, he hoped for the reunion of his own country, and as a Bavarian he dreamed about the time when Passau and Salzburg were the bases for the religious, political, economic, and cultural exchange with the peoples of the East: Poland, Bohemia, Czechoslovakia, Ukraine. For this reason, too, he was a staunch supporter of the election of the Polish pope and passionately followed the developments of the strikes in Danzig and the birth of Solidarność. The assassination attempt on May 13, 1981, behind which he, like many others, saw the hand of the KGB, confirmed him in his opposition to Marxism-Communism,[2] which he now saw as the second evil of the century after Nazism, while the brutal martial law declared in Poland by General Jaruzelski, in December of that same year, intensified his solidarity with the oppressed Poles. He wrote to the pastors of the archdiocese: "In this situation, I invite the parish communities to pray for a peace that will make it possible for all people in Europe to shape their own future in the form that they desire, in a spirit of tolerance and liberty."[3]

---

[1] See Andrea Riccardi, *Giovanni Paolo II* (Cinisello Balsamo: San Paolo, 2011), 26.

[2] Bernard Lecomte, *Benoît XVI, Le dernier pape européen* (Paris: Perrin, 2006), 95f.

[3] See Peter Pfister, ed., *Joseph Ratzinger und das Erzbistum München und Freising* (Regensburg: Schnell und Steiner, 2006), 200.

These same events prompted him to respond favorably to the renewed invitation by John Paul II to follow him to Rome. From the Italian capital where he had arrived a few months before, the cardinal then heard with interest mixed with amazement the impassioned cry uttered by the pope to Eastern Europe, from Compostela, on November 9, 1982: "I, the Bishop of Rome and the Pastor of the universal Church, from Santiago, cry out with love to you, old Europe: Find yourself again. Be yourself. Rediscover your origins. Revive your roots. Go back to living by the authentic values that made your history glorious, and cultivate your presence on the other continents. Rebuild your spiritual unity."[4] Ratzinger was struck by the speech, by its lyrical tone, especially by its sweeping passion. More sober in his analyses, for the moment the German cardinal did not think that such a geopolitical vision could have any prospect of success. European politics, moreover, was not within the competence of the prefect of the Congregation for the Doctrine of the Faith.

John Paul II, nevertheless, could draw others into his wake. In the famous meetings at table, as well as in the private Friday meetings, the pontiff did not fail to discuss with the co-worker whom he now considered a friend these topics that he took so much to heart. Many times, in public and in private, Ratzinger heard John Paul II speak about the Europe that breathes with both lungs, about its extent from the Atlantic to the Urals, about its unification, which could no longer be postponed, about its tradition based on Christianity, about its openness to other peoples. Ratzinger listened with interest and, little by little, adopted the objectives of the Polish pope. John Paul II, moreover, did not waver in his confident expectation that change was imminent. On October 11, 1988, in Strasbourg, speaking to the European Parliament, he repeated his conviction that "Europe will one day acquire the dimensions given to it by geography and, even more, by history."[5]

The following year, again in Compostela, a few months before

---

[4] See Jean-Dominique Durand, "Giovanni Paolo II e l'Europa occidentale", in *I cattolici e le Chiese cristiane durante il pontificato di Giovanni Paolo II*, ed. E. Guerriero and M. Impagliazzo (Cinisello Balsamo: San Paolo, 2006), 39ff. The French historian reprints extensive passages from the pope's speech in the conviction, which I share, that it contains in essence Pope John Paul II's geopolitical, cultural, and spiritual vision of Europe.

[5] See Lecomte, *Benoît XVI*, 96.

the fall of the Wall, he exhorted the 600,000 young people present at World Youth Day to participate in the new evangelization of Europe. "If you remain silent, the stones will cry out!" the pope said. "In Santiago the very roots of Europe are found, and from here the new evangelization must start."[6] Until this point, Ratzinger had been an affectionate witness of the pope's convictions. However, on November 9, 1989, when the Berlin Wall fell, amid general surprise, he had finally waited and seen enough; he adopted the enthusiasm of the Polish pope and decided to go into action in his own way.

He wrote in the preface to *A Turning Point for Europe*: In this situation caused by the great revolution following the fall of the Berlin Wall, "it is an absolute obligation for the theologian and for the pastor of the Church to enter the dispute about the correct understanding of the present time and about the path into the future."[7] He agreed, therefore, to hold conferences, to write articles, and to participate in debates. At the end of this intense series of interventions, he would compile three volumes dedicated to Europe. Unlike the pontiff, who did keep in view the Christian origins of Europe but had his heart set entirely on the new millennium, Ratzinger was more sober and analytical, with the argumentative tone of the former professor. His convictions, however, began to become firm like those of the Polish pope. Most of his speeches were composed of two parts. The first consisted in a diagnosis of the crisis of the West and on the causes that generated it; the second was made up of recommendations for the future by which to avoid, possibly, the errors of the past.

A LOOK AT HISTORY

Even a rapid look at history allowed Ratzinger to identify the original sins of Europe in the modern era. The first error that had had disastrous consequences again in the twentieth century was nationalism. It is an old inheritance that took on new and aggravated dimensions in the 1800s and 1900s. Initially, the awareness of a national mission and of national diversity was formed in Spain and

---

[6] Renato Boccardo, "Giovanni Paolo II e le Giornate mondiali della gioventù", in *Il grande libro dei papi*, ed. E. Guerriero (Cinisello Balsamo: San Paolo, 2012), 177.

[7] Joseph Ratzinger, *A Turning Point for Europe*, trans. Brian McNeil, C.R.V. (San Francisco: Ignatius Press, 1994), 8.

in England with the long colonial history of the two countries. In its modern form, nevertheless, nationalism sprang from the French Revolution, when the country's unity on the basis of the monarchy was replaced precisely with the unity of the nation. Over the course of the nineteenth century, Italy and Germany, too, were established as nations, while Poland rediscovered an awareness of its own identity through various rebellions, and Russia arrived at national consciousness through the Slavophile theology of a religious character. Finally, as a result of World War I, the dismantling of Austria-Hungary, the final great edifice built on a non-national principle, gave rise to the worst fruit of nationalism, the National Socialist madness.

Common to all kinds of nationalism was the mythical over-appreciation of one's own nation. With National Socialism, however, Europeans witnessed a further step with the unique alliance between nationalism and universalism: the unity of the peoples was supposed to arise under the banner of one's own national identity, to which any other had to bow, like it or not. The national element, moreover, acquired disruptive force to the point of seeming invincible, appropriating faith in progress and the myth of the infallibility of science and technology. At this point, all the elements were in place that were to lead to an unprecedented explosion. The conviction of the superiority of one's own nation and of its mission in the world was so strong that it led to the exportation of European conflicts throughout the world. Thus was born a new form of European colonialism that gave a universal dimension to the second conflict between the nations of the Old Continent.

The catastrophic fall of German National Socialism following World War II created the conditions that made possible the unnatural division physically symbolized by the Berlin Wall. While in the West there were gradual attempts to lay the foundations for a new concept of Europe, based this time on economic collaboration and on a recovery of the spiritual genealogy of the Old Continent, on the other side of the Iron Curtain, Marxism continued undaunted in its oppressive march. Internally, it imposed by force of arms the myth of its own vision of history, with the primacy of matter over spirit. Externally, also with the connivance of Western thinkers who stubbornly refused to see the oppressive face of scientific materialism and its hostility to all freedom, it continued its work of exporting European conflicts to other parts of the world.

The unexpected collapse of Marxism, manifested in the demolition of the Berlin Wall, was for Ratzinger a historical event of epochal significance. Unlike the fall of Nazism, it was nonviolent; finally, it could start a process of liberation that was more necessary than ever.

THE DEFEAT OF MARXISM

The fall of the Iron Curtain along with the phenomena that accompanied it compel us to make two observations that, according to Ratzinger, are self-evident and cannot be ignored. Marxism as a totalitarian interpretation of reality and of history was completely repudiated. It was defeated by the force of the spirit, by firm personal convictions, by sufferings, and by hopes. Along with Marxism, the idea that matter comes first and is the origin of everything else was left definitively in crisis. It is true that more recent materialists concede that ancient metaphysics have a derivative value, but if the principle is not denied, thought remains in any case a product of matter. The result is always a materialistic arrogance present in the countries that once were on the other side of the Iron Curtain, but it is widespread also in the West with its absolute predominance of the sociological sciences, which consider themselves the new metaphysics. Such a concept of man ends up eliminating individual freedom.

Another key point of Marxist ideology that, according to Ratzinger, at least needs to be called into question is its faith in progress, which considers the increase in the power of technology as human development. For a long time this was accepted as indisputable dogma, although it has no rational principle as its basis. In this regard, Ratzinger cited Guardini, who already in mid-century spoke about the "idiocy of the belief in progress", which is unstoppable either by the freedom of the individual or by ethical considerations of any kind.

THE ROLE OF EUROPE IN THE WORLD

Marxism, according to Ratzinger, took to extremes one of the extreme theses of Hegelianism: ethics has been replaced by the philosophy of history, while the good has been identified with current opinion. This, however, made room for a style of politics that does not take respect for human dignity into account at all. A correct anthropological vision requires liberty and justice, more precisely, a juridical order based on universal moral criteria, not on the arbitrariness of individuals or of groups in power. The purpose of political institutions must be the service of human beings, who are also but not primarily citizens. Hence the conclusion that the cardinal took particularly to heart: without moral consensus about the fundamental question of the human *ethos*, morality no longer has any public relevance, but in this way it becomes impossible to have any form of coexistence whatsoever among men.

On the other hand, the *ethos* needs such solid support that it cannot be provided simply by a positive law issued according to the principles of the democratic system with the alternation of majority and minority. In this case, the winners at the polls can easily take advantage of the losers. In Europe, the transcendent good that stands behind the particular goods was formulated based on a foundation given by a tradition of a religious character: the Ten Commandments through which, however, Jews and Christians are united with the most ancient and lofty traditions of the whole human race. From this original nucleus, fundamental human rights were developed in the modern era; they serve as the litmus test that distinguishes the rule of law from a totalitarian State. The latter, as it became apparent with Nazism and Communism, thinks that it is omnipotent, empowered to formulate all sorts of laws without any limits; the rule of law, in contrast, recognizes its own limits and stops when it confronts the inalienable rights connected with the person of the citizen. The theory of human rights, nevertheless, is based on the recognition of the primacy of the dignity of the human person, which, according to the philosopher Robert Spaemann, is a postulate that is obvious to every person who suffers because of his humiliation. Hence the philosopher's conclusion, which Ratzinger adopted as his own: "If Europe does not export its faith, the faith that God is truth, that the truth is divine",[8] then it is nothing but a geographical idea. Ratzinger commented: Europe cannot export only its technology and its rationality, but must communicate also its interior origin, the acknowledgment that the *Logos* is at the foun-

---

[8] Robert Spaemann, "Universalismus oder Eurozentrismus", in *Europa und die Folgen*, ed. K. Michalski (Stuttgart: Klett-Cotta, 1988), 313–22 at 321.

dation of all things. "Then Europe will bring together the great traditions of mankind in a process of giving and receiving in which everything belongs to everyone and no one is a stranger to anyone else."[9]

A NEW ROLE FOR RELIGION?

Turning now to the future, Ratzinger pointed out three elements that, in his opinion, characterize society in South-Central European countries as the end of the second millennium approaches. They are, in order: the crisis of faith in science; a new openness to the religious dimension of the world; a new, rather vague and nostalgic spirituality. While the collapse of faith in science may clear the way for relativism, the demand for a new spirituality can be the starting point for a new influence of the Christian faith through what John Paul II called the "new evangelization". The alternative facing mankind in the West, therefore, is between relativism and a new evangelization.

Relativism, Ratzinger said, is now the real temptation, a convenient path that nevertheless does not distance itself from materialistic positivism. To give in to relativism is to fall back into positivistic scientism or else into a nihilistic skepticism that ends up blocking the path to any aspirations whatsoever to intellectual and spiritual freedom. There is no alternative, then, but to set out again on the path that leads to the recognition of metaphysics, toward the journey of faith in the living God. Unlike nihilistic relativism, faith does not imply the defeat of reason, its retreat into irrationality. On the contrary, it is "courage to exist and an awakening to the greatness and breadth of what is real".[10]

For Ratzinger, this is one of the key components of Christian thought, to which he had called attention since the time of his first university lecture in Bonn. The Christian faith implies no renunciation of reason but, rather, is the acceptance of the extreme depth of divine reason. In short, to believe is to take seriously the initial statement of the Gospel of John to the effect that at the origin there is the *Logos*, the Divine Word, creative reason. The consequence is

---

[9] J. Ratzinger, *Turning Point for Europe*, 142.
[10] Ibid., 104.

that not matter but rather spirit is at the origin of all things. By acknowledging the primacy of the spirit, man is capable of perceiving and following the traces of the reasonableness of nature, which is not subject to his absolute dominion or manipulation. This, moreover, is the ultimate reason for a sound ecology, which in our days is becoming more important than ever, not as a naïve nostalgia for an original, uncontaminated state of nature and of mankind, but as the indispensable requirement in order to escape chaos and destruction.

To sum up, the "real essence of faith . . . saves reason precisely because it grasps reason in its whole breadth and depth and protects it from the restrictions of a merely experiential verification."[11] Ratzinger thus anticipated the central themes of the encyclical *Fides et ratio*, "Faith and Reason", by John Paul II; moreover, his contribution to the drafting of it was not insignificant.

CONSCIENCE AND TRUTH

In 1991, on one of his rather frequent visits to the United States, Ratzinger gave in Dallas a conference on what was at that time one of the most debated topics in the field of Catholic moral theology: the relation between conscience and truth. The conference, however, can also be considered as a contribution of the cultural heritage of Europe to modern thought. The question was very delicate, indeed, in the United States, and the cardinal got right to the point: "The question of conscience has become paramount, especially in the field of Catholic moral theology."[12] Hence, conscience has become the bulwark of freedom against the limitations imposed by authority. One can even say that there are two somewhat antithetical models: on the one hand, the morality of conscience, also called conciliar morality, and, on the other hand, the preconciliar morality of authority.

Such an antithesis, nevertheless, leads unequivocally to the conclusion that there is no objective truth and that the teachings of the Magisterium in the area of morality are only aids to the formation of subjective moral conscience, which becomes the unchal-

---

[11] Ibid., 106.
[12] Reprinted as Joseph Ratzinger, "Conscience and Truth", in *On Conscience: Two Essays by Joseph Ratzinger* (Philadelphia: National Catholic Bioethics Center; San Francisco: Ignatius Press, 2007), 11–41 at 11.

lengeable, indeed, infallible authority in the area of morality. To this Ratzinger objected: Can fanatical Nazis who never repented of their deeds then say that they acted according to their conscience? Since this theory leads to a true aberration in the strict sense, we must infer that the principle, too, is erroneous. Moreover, this is shown by the sense of guilt. Someone who has committed serious crimes but feels no sense of guilt is a monster, a living corpse. The reduction of conscience to subjective certainty means, indeed, the renunciation of truth, and this is the true original sin "which first lulls man into false security and then abandons him in the trackless waste".[13]

Newman and Socrates as models of conscience. Rather than pursue an abstract model, at this point Ratzinger introduced two witnesses to conscience: John Henry Newman and Socrates. The English, like the Americans, have great esteem for conscience. Between conscience and authority, nevertheless, Newman introduces a connecting element, which is the truth. This allows him to say that "conscience . . . is the overcoming of mere subjectivity in the encounter of the interiority of man with the truth from *God*."[14] From this follows the duty to obey truth rather than one's own taste and one's own opinions.

In this he had an exalted example in another great Englishman, Thomas More. For the Lord Chancellor of Henry VIII, the decision to follow his own conscience rather than the king's will was not an arbitrary or stubborn decision but, rather, obedience to the truth, which comes before any social authority or personal preference. Going back in history, the example of Socrates teaches that even in a non-Christian setting, the truth can be perceived along with the obligation to obey it rather than to follow criteria of convenience. This allowed Ratzinger to conclude: "The martyrs are the great witnesses of conscience, of that capability given to man to perceive the 'should' beyond the 'can' and thereby render possible real progress, real ascent."[15]

---

[13] Ibid., 22.
[14] Ibid., 25.
[15] Ibid., 30.

Conscience and grace. After this brief tour of the testimony of conscience in history, Ratzinger proposed the Christian vision that, in his opinion, allows us to hold freedom of conscience, truth, and grace together. The first concept of the truth that imposes itself on conscience is in his opinion best expressed by the Platonic idea of anamnesis, the memory of the good that is imprinted on human hearts. In the Christian tradition, this concept was introduced rather early by Saint Basil in the East and by Saint Augustine in the West.

In short, "there is an inner ontological tendency within man, who is created in the likeness of God, toward the divine. From its origin, man's being resonates with some things and clashes with others."[16] The anamnesis of the Creator, which takes concrete form in the commandments, then needs help from outside in order to become aware of itself. This external thing, nevertheless, is not contrary to the interior anamnesis, but rather is an aid and a support to Christian memory. The pope and the Magisterium impose nothing from outside but, rather, develop and defend the Christian memory.

Among Christians, finally, the anamnesis of the Creator extends outward toward the Redeemer. This concept was explained by Ratzinger with the help of the myth of Orestes. The latter kills his mother in obedience to Apollo but is then pursued by the Furies, or *Erinyes*, understood as the personification of the conscience, who remind him that his obedience was in reality guilt. The tragic character of man's situation that is symbolized in this struggle points out the nostalgia for the *Logos*, for a truth that does not judge but gives us reconciliation and forgiveness. And this is the distinctively Christian element: "When the Truth came, loved us, and consumed our guilt in the fire of his love. Only when we know and experience this from within will we be free to hear the message of conscience with joy and without fear."[17]

A catechism amid protest and plebiscite

The twentieth anniversary of the conclusion of Vatican II fell in the year 1985. In order to emphasize the importance of this anniversary and to derive from it some guidelines for the life of the Church, John

---

[16] Ibid., 32.
[17] Ibid., 41.

Paul II convened in the Vatican an Extraordinary Synod of Bishops; contrary to what happens in the Ordinary Synods, the presidents of all the episcopal conferences were invited to it. This was to emphasize that the intention was not simply to commemorate the great event of the life of the Church in the twentieth century, but, rather, "to recall the principal intention of the Council; to ask how to make this intention our own today and to render it fruitful for tomorrow."[18] Among the tools for putting into practice the great wealth of the conciliar documents drawn up by the council, some soon thought about a Vatican II catechism that would be like the *Roman Catechism* drawn up after the Council of Trent. This was certainly not a simple undertaking, since the *Roman Catechism* was "a foundational point of modern catechesis".[19]

The first attempts along these lines after Vatican II left much to be desired. The Bishops' Conference of the Netherlands was the first to spring into action; even in the 1960s, it developed a catechism that was received with considerable interest in various parts of the world. This was, nevertheless, a text that in some parts needed considerable supplementation and revisions, as a commission of six cardinals appointed in 1968 by Paul VI determined. Once again the question arose of preparing a catechism for the universal Church. It was precisely Cardinal Frings, advised by Ratzinger, who recommended waiting: "A waiting period was necessary since, in the midst of the crisis, there was no universally accepted theology."[20]

In the meantime, other catechisms were published by various episcopal conferences, although the outcomes were not very satisfactory,[21] since they themselves were preoccupied above all with

---

[18] Joseph Ratzinger, "The Catechism of the Catholic Church and the Optimism of the Redeemed", a talk given to the priests of the Archdiocese of Milan at the archdiocesan seminary in Venegono. The text was published in the English edition of *Communio* 20.3 (Fall 1993), which was dedicated entirely to the *Catechism of the Catholic Church*. It was reprinted in Joseph Cardinal Ratzinger and Christoph Schönborn, *Introduction to the Catechism of the Catholic Church* (San Francisco: Ignatius Press, 1994), 9–36 at 11.

[19] Paola Vismara, "Il Catechismo della Chiesa cattolica e la tradizione catechetica moderna", *Communio* 128 (1993): 55.

[20] Alain Besançon, "Il catechismo venuto da Roma", *Communio* 128 (1993): 71.

[21] For Italy, the Italian Episcopal Conference (CEI) developed a catechism for children, one for young people, and a third for adults. Concerning the last-mentioned, Cardinal Ruini, President of the CEI, declared in 1993: "The last-mentioned is for the Church in Italy the text designed to promote in the Christian communities a detailed

examining the anthropological and sociological perspective and the method of transmitting the faith, with the result that along the way they ended up losing the teachings that they were supposed to transmit. In short, at the 1985 Synod, the proposal of a catechism of Vatican II for the universal Church was repeated authoritatively by many bishops. The concluding document reported: "Very many [bishops] have expressed the desire that a catechism or compendium of all Catholic doctrine regarding both faith and morals be composed, that it might be, as it were, a point of reference for the catechisms or compendiums that are prepared in various regions. . . . It must be sound doctrine suited to the present life of Christians."[22]

Responding to the invitation of the bishops, John Paul II formed in 1986 a commission of twelve cardinals and bishops with Cardinal Ratzinger presiding. In turn, the commission, at its first meeting held in November 1986, decided to avail itself of the help of a working secretariat, a commission of editors, and a college of consultors.[23] The working secretariat was provided by the personnel of the Congregation for the Doctrine of the Faith, while several bishops with complementary competencies and representing various linguistic areas were called to be members of the editorial board. From Italy, there was the bishop of Como, Alessandro Maggiolini; from France —Jean Marcel Honoré, bishop of Evreux and future cardinal archbishop of Tours, and from Lebanon—Jean Corbon.[24] Christoph

---

and systematic work of education in the faith aimed precisely at families and adults, who are the primary subjects of evangelization and catechesis, so as to serve as a basis for a solid resumption of Christian life and of incisive testimony in society." The catechism for adults was supposed to achieve its purpose through a new version that was reworked in light of the *Catechism of the Catholic Church*. One gets the impression, nevertheless, that the success of the *Catechism of the Catholic Church* ended up making both the CEI catechism and its revised version superfluous.

[22] Final Report of the Extraordinary Synod, December 7, 1985, in *Enchiridion Vaticanum* 9 (Bologna: Dehoniane), 1758, no. 1797. Quoted in John Paul II, Apostolic Constitution *Fidei Depositum* On the Publication of the Catechism of the Catholic Church Prepared Following the Second Vatican Ecumenical Council, October 11, 1992; see the *Catechism of the Catholic Church*, p. 3.

[23] See Raffaello Martinelli, "Le fasi di elaborazione del catechismo", in *Il Catechismo del Vaticano II* (Cinisello Balsamo: Edizioni Paoline, 1993), 17ff.

[24] Ratzinger wrote about him movingly: "[He] wrote the beautiful concluding text on prayer while in beleaguered Beirut, frequently in the midst of dramatic situations, taking shelter in his basement in order to continue working during the bombardments." See

von Schönborn, future cardinal archbishop of Vienna, was selected as editorial secretary. With the organizational chart established, it was finally necessary to start the working phase. According to Cardinal Ratzinger, this was an arduous task because the outlines of the initiative intended by the synod Fathers appeared vague, to say the least.[25] More explicitly, Bishop Maggiolini recalled: "It was enough to make you despair, or almost. Or else to smile."[26]

THIS CATECHISM MUST NOT BE MADE

The request of the bishops and the expectations of the faithful[27] were not shared by theologians and lay Church employees. Even before the editorial board headed by Cardinal Ratzinger got to work, there was a plethora of admonitions, distinctions, and warnings. The objections concerned, in logical order: the very idea of a catechism; the idea of a catechism with contents that would end up opposing hermeneutics, the only science capable of establishing what the word of God and revelation are in our time; the concept of a catechism of the universal Church that would end up opposing inculturation. The first two objections were clearly influenced by the ideology of the times. With regard to Italy, Cardinal Ruini described the situation as follows: "An attitude that we might call eclectic and relativistic has by now permeated the very idea of religion, our way of thinking about it and living it; no doubt this attitude is directly dependent on the widespread climate of pluralism and cultural relativism and specifically on the distrust of the idea of an objective truth that is valid for everyone."[28]

Ruini's text was not far from Ratzinger's thinking on the subject. Then there was the final objection, which in fact touched on a delicate point: the relation between the universal catechism and the catechisms of the local Churches. The journal *Concilium* dedicated

---

Joseph Ratzinger, "Introduction to the Catechism of the Catholic Church", in Ratzinger and Schönborn, *Introduction to the Catechism*, 23.

[25] Ibid., 19.

[26] Sandro Maggiolini, "Criteri per la stesura", in *Il Catechismo del Vaticano II*, 35.

[27] According to Jean Guitton, cited by Ratzinger in *Introduction to the Catechism*, 12, the universal catechism came twenty-five years late.

[28] Camillo Ruini, "Il catechismo e la nuova evangelizzazione", *Communio* 128 (1993): 25.

a whole issue to this topic in 1989.[29] The two editors of the issue,
Johann Baptist Metz and Edward Schillebeeckx, made it clear immediately in the editorial that "in all the articles, considerations
critical of the project for a universal catechism clearly emerge." In
its severity, the most drastic judgment was that of the American
David Tracy, professor of theology in Chicago, who categorically
declared: "The hope for an adequate 'world catechism' seems, at
best, illusory."[30] And he continued: The very request for a universal
catechism appears to be "a form of hubris that is clearly inspired by
cultural colonialism—something in which Western scientists and
philosophers sometimes still indulge."[31] This barrage was followed
by a more sober reflection on the problems of inculturation with
articles on history and the current scene.

What emerged, therefore, was the problem of the one and the
many, the catechism and the catechisms. Particularly important was
the above-mentioned article by Metz, which recognized that the
transmission of the Gospel cannot proceed from a previous spolia-
tion of the culture in which the Gospel itself is clothed, just as one
cannot renounce memory and narrative. These are three fundamental elements that any catechism must take into account. Similarly,
the polycentric inculturation that people talked about so much at
that time could not do without the reference to unity, which was
equally necessary. For his part, the Spanish Salesian Emilio Alberich
contrasted the possibilities and the risks of inculturation. He concluded by stating: "It is not easy to decide whether the planned
universal catechism will have a positive or a negative effect on inculturation, at least until we know the actual tenor of the final version of the text."[32] While not exactly a warm welcome, this was
at least a fair consideration that one cannot pass judgment before
even examining the text.

AT THE SERVICE OF ECCLESIAL COMMUNION

Returning to the start of the work of the editorial board that met
at the Congregation for the Doctrine of the Faith: in the midst of

---

[29] "Catechismo universale o inculturazione?" *Concilium* 4 (1989).
[30] Ibid., 42.
[31] Ibid., 47.
[32] Ibid., 122.

all the uncertainty that I mentioned above, one thing was clear: the catechism at which they were aiming should not be a generic textbook of Christian doctrine but should draw on the patrimony of faith and Christian life developed at Vatican II and transmit it to the whole Church. The procedure had had a famous precedent in the 1500s when, in order to transmit the results of the Council of Trent, the council Fathers composed the famous *Roman Catechism*, which was an effective instrument for the reform and renewal of the Church in the following centuries. The authors of the catechism turned their attention first and foremost to this model. It provided the internal subdivision of the material and also the point of departure.

As I recalled in the preceding section, the first catechisms that appeared after Vatican II dwelt above all on describing the situation in our time, and then they sought to outline an anthropology and a hermeneutic of the faith. Only after that came the contents of the faith, properly speaking. The *Roman Catechism*, on the other hand, followed the reverse order. It turned the reader's attention first of all to God, toward the mysteries of the faith that is professed (Creed) and celebrated (sacraments); only in a second stage did it shift its attention to the faith that works in charity and is expressed in Christian life (Ten Commandments) and in filial prayer (the Our Father).[33] The drafters of the *Catechism of Vatican II* also decided to follow this overall scheme. Initially, it was supposed to be divided into three parts; then they decided nevertheless on a quadripartite subdivision. A second decision, which was also made upon the Tridentine model, was to work primarily on a so-called major catechism, which means a catechism primarily directed to those responsible for catechesis, to the bishops and to their co-workers, so as to become a point of reference for future national or diocesan catechisms. "In the hands of the entire episcopate, the Catechism would foster internal unity in the faith and its proclamation."[34]

Other criteria adopted by the authors included an organic exposition of the Catholic faith in light of Vatican Council II and the

---

[33] See Christoph von Schönborn, "Major Themes and Underlying Principles of the CCC", in J. Ratzinger and Schönborn, *Introduction to the Catechism*, 37–58. See in particular 37–42.

[34] J. Ratzinger and Schönborn, *Introduction to the Catechism*, 17–18.

characteristics of conciseness, integrity, and doctrinal completeness while drawing on the sources of Sacred Scripture, the Fathers of the Church, the liturgy, and the Magisterium.[35] Another preliminary choice was the decision to use French as the basic language for composing the catechism. Initially, work had begun in Latin; then it was decided to switch to a spoken language, from which the definitive edition in Latin would be prepared in a second step.[36] On the basis of these preliminary choices, the first draft of the text was developed and was submitted to the commission of cardinals, who expressed their appreciation for the work done. They suggested, nevertheless, that for the explanation of the profession of faith, the Apostles' Creed should be followed, inasmuch as it is the ancient baptismal creed, while illustrating it and integrating it with the Niceno-Constantinopolitan Creed. After the commission's suggestions were accepted and put into practice, the project was subjected to a further examination by Ratzinger, then finally, on November 1, 1989, it was sent to the bishops throughout the world with the request to examine the text and to return it accompanied by suggestions and proposed corrections or revisions.

By the autumn of 1990, sixteen Roman congregations, twenty-eight episcopal conferences, twenty-three groups representing a total of 295 bishops, and 797 individual bishops had responded. Moreover, opinions had been sent in by twelve theological institutes and sixty-two experts, from whom an opinion had also been requested. The suggestions, moreover, came from broad geographical areas. Some episcopal conferences had preferred to respond together, others had left the task to the individual bishops, while still others, among them Italy, had given collegial opinions while some bishops had also sent in their personal opinions. The consultation was quite extensive, and the respondents generally gave a very favorable opinion, encouraging the editorial board to continue the work that had been started well.

In September 1990, the editorial board started the work of examining the 24,000 comments that had arrived. For the most part, they concerned part 3, with the suggestion to develop the description of moral growth with the virtues and grace, while maintaining the framework of the Ten Commandments, presenting them neverthe-

---

[35] See Martinelli, "Le fasi di elaborazione del catechismo", 13.
[36] J. Ratzinger and Schönborn, Introduction to the Catechism, 24 ff.

less as the fulfillment of the twofold commandment of love. Having carried out this very onerous task, the board arrived at the definitive text, which was submitted for examination by the commission of cardinals on February 14, 1992, the feast of Saints Cyril and Methodius, Apostles of the Slavs and extraordinary models for catechists. The commission unanimously expressed its favorable opinion. A round of grateful applause greeted the end of the work that had begun in 1986 and had been brought to a conclusion in record time. The text was then submitted to John Paul II for him to study; he in turn suggested a few improvements before the definitive approval that took place on June 25, 1992.

In a simple ceremony, the pope approved the text and entitled it *Catechism of the Catholic Church*. Then, thanking all the persons who had worked on it, he declared that it "is well articulated, corresponds to the guidelines of the synod Fathers, faithfully respects the teaching of Vatican II, and is addressed to modern man, presenting to him the Christian message in its integrity and completeness."[37] After this first approval, John Paul II, in order to solemnize the event, waited until October 11 of the same year—the thirtieth anniversary of the inauguration of Vatican II—to approve the text solemnly with the apostolic constitution *Fidei depositum*, "The Deposit of Faith".

Two months later, finally, on December 7, 1992, the pope presented the Catechism to the faithful with words that once again referred to the beginning of the council, to the inaugural speech of John XXIII: "The Holy Church of God rejoices today because, by a singular gift of Divine Providence, it can solemnly celebrate the promulgation of the new catechism." He then expressed thanks to all who had participated in accomplishing the work, particularly to Cardinal Ratzinger for "his wise guidance".[38]

AN UNEXPECTED SUCCESS

After the presentations and the official expressions of gratitude, on November 16, 1992, the Catechism was presented for the first time to the public in Paris because, having been written in French, the

---

[37] John Paul II, "Discorso di approvazione del *Catechismo*" (June 25, 1992).

[38] John Paul II, "Un dono per tutti: Discorso di Giovanni Paolo II per la presentazione del Catechismo della Chiesa cattolica", in *Il Catechismo del Vaticano II*, 174.

edition in the language of Voltaire and Hugo was the first to be available. As had been foreseen, the critiques followed promptly. The opening salvo was from *Le Monde*, which wrote that "the Catechism involves the risk of a breakdown in communication between a vast portion of public opinion, including Catholics, and the Magisterial authority of the Church, which is notoriously attached to a medley of prohibitions."[39] Representing the Catholic world, the journal of the French Jesuits, *Études*, wrote that "although Vatican II is frequently cited, equally strong is the influence of Vatican I, with its preoccupation with the reasonableness of faith."[40] After this observation, which was bizarre to say the least, the author of the review, the Jesuit Father René Marlé, who had contributed to the composition of the catechism of the Bishops' Conference of France, continued to express what, according to Besançon, was his real worry: that the universal Catechism might sink the national catechisms.

Father Marlé's fear was well founded. Notwithstanding all the criticism, unlike the national catechisms (sales of which stopped at a few thousand copies), no sooner did the catechism from Rome arrive in the bookstores than it sold as briskly as any great bestseller. To everyone's surprise, more than 500,000 copies were sold in three weeks, and the demand was very far from being satisfied. Cardinal Lustiger commented: "It is even more surprising when you consider the obvious contradiction between the judgment passed by those who shape opinions and the opinion of the majority, which is manifested in their purchases."[41] From this consideration, the cardinal of Paris drew the conclusion: "Some have already said that this is really about a re-centering or a call to order. This act of responsibility is none other than the exercise of the apostolic ministry as expressed by Vatican II."[42]

A few weeks later, the Catechism arrived in Italian bookstores, too. As Giuliano Vigini wrote, it was immediately understood that the Italian edition, too, would have a success surpassing all expectations. For the experienced Milanese editor, the insight of the pope

---

[39] See Besançon, "Il catechismo venuto da Roma", 72.

[40] Ibid.

[41] Jean-Marie Lustiger, "Il catechismo della Chiesa cattolica e la Francia", in *Il Catechismo del Vaticano II*, 136.

[42] Ibid.

and of Ratzinger had proved to be correct: not only the Catholic world but also the secular world needed an "important reference work", an "organic, up-to-date elucidation that serves as a sure guide for the understanding of the faith and for the practice of the Christian life."[43]

The successful sales figures of the Catechism, nevertheless, were not due solely to the need for guidance on the part of the clergy, the Church employees, and the laity. In reality, the worldwide circulation of the book in several million copies rewarded a work that was well-balanced, rich, and convincing in its contents and fluent in its exposition. About his accomplishment, Ratzinger himself wrote: "It is still a sort of wonder to me that a readable, for the most part intrinsically unified and, in my opinion, beautiful book arose out of such a complex editorial process."[44] The subdivision of the material, too, was well articulated. The first two parts, on the Creed and the liturgy, take up 60 percent of the entire Catechism, and the other two parts, on morals and prayer, the remaining 40 percent. The objection of those who feared that the new book would turn into a sort of manual of morality, full of prescriptions and prohibitions, had been fairly considered and overcome in the very design of the volume.

The work, finally, appears to be guided by a pervasive theme that is as simple and essential as it is profound and convincing. The love of God that is at the origin of the gift of faith and of participation in the sacramental life is followed by the path of conversion, supported by prayer in an attitude of trust that leads to gratitude for the love of God that moves everything.

After the commercial success of the work, the critics were reduced to silence. Some lamented certain harsh passages in the moral section; others subjected to criticism the fact that, despite the change in sensibility within the Church and in society, the Catechism still foresaw the possibility of the death penalty in cases where it was not possible to do otherwise. In March 1995, however, John Paul II published the encyclical *Evangelium vitae*, in which he affirmed that nowadays the cases in which a government cannot do without the

---

[43] Giuliano Vigini, "Il nuovo catechismo come fenomeno editoriale", in *Communio* 128 (1993): 78f.

[44] J. Ratzinger and Schönborn, *Introduction to the Catechism*, 25.

death penalty are truly rare. The typical Latin edition of the Catechism, consequently, published in Rome in October 1997, included this correction, finally bringing everyone into agreement as to the usefulness of a work that in the meantime had been welcomed with unexpected unanimity by the great majority of Catholics.

In the homily of the Mass celebrated on the occasion of the International Catechetical Congress, at which the typical edition was presented, Ratzinger again declared: "The fact that in a world full of conflicts, in a Church roiled by the collision of contradictory trends, such a testimony of unity could be prepared in a relatively short time is surprising. Personally I would not have thought it possible, and I must admit this openly."[45] Gratitude for an undertaking that initially seemed desperate goes to the authors, in particular to the editorial secretary, the Dominican friar Christoph von Schönborn, for his extraordinary organizational ability, his knowledge of the Fathers of the Church, and his literary talent. Greater credit, though, should be given once again to Ratzinger. We recognize his hand in the conception of the work as well as in the choice of collaborators and in the composition of the editorial board. Even the completion of the text in such a short period of time is due to his clarity in framing the project, his ability to work, and his choice of a reduced number of working groups composed of capable, complementary, and flexible members. When we speak, therefore, about Ratzinger and the council, we need also to take into account this important contribution to the achievement of the *Catechism of the Catholic Church*, which, according to John Paul II, is the "Catechism of Vatican II".

Between private and public life

A SORROWFUL LOSS

The workload in the concluding stages of the production and publication of the Catechism prevented the cardinal from returning home for brief periods of rest but also from spending a few days

---

[45] From the homily of the Mass on the occasion of the International Catechetical Congress during which the typical edition of the Catechism was presented, in *L'Osservatore Romano* (October 18, 1997).

together with his siblings and acquaintances. One of the regularly scheduled times for the three siblings to meet was during the early days of November. The house in Pentling would be reopened, and they would spend the feast of All Saints together. The next day they used to go to visit the tomb of their parents. In 1991, in particular, their sister, Maria, left Joseph in Rome and left for Germany, where Georg was waiting for her.[46] As usual, she took up lodgings in Joseph's house, but already on the night of her arrival, on November 1, the neighbors informed Georg that Maria was ill. They promptly called a doctor, who spoke of the possibility of a heart attack; therefore, it was necessary to call an ambulance and to transport her to the hospital. On November 2, All Souls Day, her condition worsened because of an extensive cerebral hemorrhage.

Maria died that same evening. As soon as he was informed, Joseph departed immediately for Germany, where he could do no more than bless his sister's body and then, a few days later, on November 8, celebrate the funeral Mass and give the homily in her memory in the cathedral in Regensburg. She was then buried in the family plot together with her parents, in Ziegetsdorf Cemetery, again in Regensburg. The prayer card printed for her funeral best summed up her life and expressed the gratitude and affection of her younger brother: "For thirty-four years she served her brother Joseph at all the stages of his career with tireless devotion and great kindness and humility." On the many occasions when the cardinal speaks affectionately and considerately about the faith of simple people, he certainly has in mind his parents, but he is also thinking of his sister, who devoted her time and energies to him.

THE FRENCH ACADEMY

On November 6, 1992, due also to the worldwide success of the *Catechism of the Catholic Church*, Ratzinger was admitted, as a foreign associate member, to the Institut de France, Académie des Sciences morales et politiques. Among the many honors he had received, the cardinal took his nomination to the Académie especially to heart because he had always looked with great admiration at the country

---

[46] See Georg Ratzinger and Michael Hesemann, *My Brother the Pope*, trans. Michael J. Miller (San Francisco: Ignatius Press, 2011), 221f.

on the other side of the Rhine. Moreover, he succeeded Andrey
Sakharov, the Nobel Prize winner who had not only distinguished
himself in the field of science but had fought tenaciously against
the Soviet regime. In keeping with the practice of the prestigious
institution, at the time of his admission, the cardinal gave a brief
speech that began with a tribute to his predecessor. The cardinal did
not exempt himself from this unwritten law and began his address[47]
by citing a detail taken from the biography of the Russian scientist.

In 1955, Sakharov had participated in an important experiment
with thermonuclear weapons that left two dead. The evening afterward, during a banquet that had been organized anyway to celebrate the good outcome of the experiments, the scientist expressed
the hope that the Russian weapons would never be used on Soviet
territory. Thereupon the high-ranking official who directed the research expressed the conviction that the scientist's job was only to
improve the efficiency of the weapons. It was not his duty, however,
to worry about their utilization. In turn, Sakharov commented that
a man cannot exempt himself from his own responsibility. To sum
up, the high-ranking official with his statement had denied the existence of morality and had divided mankind into classes according
to competencies. The denial of the moral principle, however, and
of that organ of knowledge which we call conscience, which comes
before any specialization, implies the negation of man.

Having finished his tribute to Sakharov, Ratzinger continued his
speech in favor of moral responsibility. Even individual freedom,
for which we all aspire today, preserves its own dignity only if it
stays connected to its own foundation and to moral duty. Moreover,
Sakharov's rebellion against the apathy and amorality prevalent in
the Soviet society of his day is no less necessary in a society dominated by liberalism. According to the description of Robert Spaemann, a Catholic philosopher and friend of the cardinal, the fall of
utopia was followed by a nihilism of banality, which in everyday
life is translated into cynicism and the cult of well-being, which
have suffocated moral responsibility even more. How, then, can we
reinforce and support what is right and good in our societies? At

---

[47] The address can be read at the website *Église catholique en France*: "Allocution du
cardinal Joseph Ratzinger à l'Académie des sciences morales et politiques", (November
6, 1992).

this point, Ratzinger recalled that he had been struck particularly by an observation of the great political scientist Alexis de Tocqueville. In his work on democracy in America, the French scholar maintained that in the 1800s a fundamental moral conviction prevailed in the great country on the other side of the ocean; nourished by Protestant Christianity, it assured the foundations of democratic institutions and structures. Institutions, particularly democratic ones, are in fact fragile and need shared ethical convictions that must be respected as a common good if we want them to last over time.

Hence, Ratzinger's conclusion: the institutions that detach themselves from the major ethical and religious forces of their own culture are in practice committing suicide. In order to preserve freedom, it is necessary to conserve essential moral judgments, to cultivate them without imposing them through constraint, and to protect them through shared conviction. Ratzinger sees in this delicate, invaluable task the public role that the Christian Churches can and must play in the modern world. One of the major achievements brought about by Christianity was the separation of Church from State. It is her task, therefore, to be responsible for the common good, also. With her freedom, the Church then turns to the freedom of all men, so that the moral force of the past might remain alive and operative in the present as well and freedom might thus be preserved. Presented in a setting that was secular by definition, the address was in reality a proclamation in defense of the Christian roots of Europe, with which the cardinal would deal more extensively in the following decade.

The cross is Germany

DIVORCED AND REMARRIED PERSONS

Cardinal Ratzinger was certainly not accustomed to resting on his laurels. New emergencies, moreover, were appearing everywhere, particularly in Germany, his country of origin, which is perhaps the European nation where the estrangement from the former archbishop of Munich continued to grow rather than diminish over the years. The disputed points, in this case, directly concerned, not the dogmas of the Church, but rather morality. With the spread of the legal recognition of divorce in Europe, the question arose more and more often about admitting divorced and civilly remarried persons to the Sacraments of Penance and Holy Communion. In Germany, then, where the population was divided almost evenly between Catholics and Protestants, the issue became particularly delicate in the case of mixed marriages.

In this context, three bishops from the Upper Rhenish Ecclesiastical Province, Karl Lehmann of Mainz, Walter Kasper of Rottenburg-Stuttgart, and Oskar Saier of Freiburg, decided to promote a pastoral program designed to demonstrate the closeness of the Catholic community to the difficult situation of the divorced, many of them with children for whom they had to provide, either by raising them alone or through the payment of alimony. In consideration of this difficult situation, the three bishops wrote together a short letter to be read in the churches on September 5 and 12, 1993, in which they exhorted the faithful to welcome divorced and civilly remarried persons as part of the parish community. Then they sent to the priests and to the pastoral workers a more extensive document entitled *Fundamental Principles for the Pastoral Accompaniment of Persons Who Are in Failed Marriages, Divorced, and Divorced and Remarried*.[48] In their letter, the bishops declared that they wished to remain faithful both to the teaching of the Gospel and to the tradition of the Church. They recalled, nevertheless, that various issues regarding biblical theology, the history of theology, dogmatic theology, and canon law have changed over time.

The three prelates, however, did not speak in favor of an official admission of civilly remarried Catholics to Holy Communion. Instead, they asked priests to respect, after having verified it, the conscientious decision of the divorced and civilly remarried to approach the sacrament. From Rome's perspective, the question was certainly delicate. On the one hand, there was the doctrine, the tradition, and the centuries-old practice of the Church; on the other, there was a situation that had certainly become more delicate because of new national laws and the increased number of Catholics who, after failing a first time, attempted marriage again, while wishing nevertheless to remain in communion with the Catholic Church and to practice their faith. To many people, exclusion from the sacraments seemed to be dictated by excessive rigor. Finally, it was necessary to take

---

[48] The text of the document is found in *Il Regno-Documenti* 19 (1993): 617.

into account the personality of the three bishops. Lehmann, moreover, was president of the German Bishops' Conference and was backed by the agreement of a large part of the episcopate, the clergy, and the faithful. Lehmann and Kasper, moreover, were famous theologians, well known to Ratzinger himself if only for the fact that both had been part of the German editorial board of *Communio*.

It was not easy, therefore, for the prefect of the Congregation for the Doctrine of the Faith to make a decision. According to the model already followed in the Boff case, he invited the three bishops to Rome for a clarifying conversation. After that, in 1994, the congregation sent to the bishops throughout the world a letter in which it exhorted them to remind divorced and civilly remarried Catholics that they are forbidden to approach Holy Communion.[49] At the same time, the Vatican urged the bishops to make Christ's charity felt. They, however, had to be conscious also of the fact that authentic understanding and genuine mercy are never detached from the truth. For this reason, the text recalled that, referring to their proposals, solutions had been suggested in various regions whereby, in certain cases, divorced and civilly remarried Catholics would be able to approach Holy Communion if they felt authorized to do so by their conscience. The congregation affirmed, instead, that it is not possible to recognize as valid a new matrimonial union if the first one was valid.

Consequently, the Catholic who is cohabiting cannot go to Holy Communion, even if, subjectively, his conscience suggests the contrary to him, since, in that case, he would have the ultimate authority to decide. Marriage, indeed, as an image of the spousal union between Christ and the Church, is essentially a public reality and cannot be reduced to a merely subjective event. The one concession at which the document did hint, and which the bishops could point out to the faithful, was the possible expansion of the causes for invalidity of the first marriage. Here, one could raise questions about the absence of a sufficiently well-formed or informed conscience at the time of the first wedding. This, however, was a procedure that necessarily involved recourse to the ecclesiastical tribunals.

---

[49] Congregation for the Doctrine of the Faith, Letter to the Bishops of the Catholic Church concerning the Reception of Holy Communion by the Divorced and Remarried Members of the Faithful, September 14, 1994.

The reason for a denial was for Ratzinger fidelity to Christ's teaching and the danger of subjectivism. In any civilization, marriage has a social value; it cannot be reduced to a contract between two citizens that can be dissolved when there are more or less serious difficulties. Then there was the fear of a headlong rush. Many times, in response to remarks about the Church's slowness in making her decisions, the cardinal replied that this was also a sign of wisdom. He certainly made it clear to the three bishops that the situation in Germany might be ripe for some pastoral decisions relative to the lack of formed or informed conscience at the time of the first marriage, recognized in an extrajudicial procedure at the diocesan (and no longer the Vatican) level, but the same could not be said of other national or continental Churches. The patience urged by the congregation's letter was also meant to preserve the catholicity of the Church.

WOMEN'S ORDINATION

Another issue that was being debated especially in the United States and in some European countries, Germany among them, was the question of the priestly ordination of women. In the mid-1990s, it became a particularly burning question because of the decision by the Anglican Church in 1992 to admit women to the priesthood officially. Given the many requests that arrived in Rome also, in 1994 John Paul II intervened directly with an apostolic letter, *Ordinatio sacerdotalis*,[50] in which he declared that priestly ordination is reserved for males. This tradition is preserved faithfully in the Eastern Churches, also. The pope then cited the similar declaration by Paul VI, who recalled that Jesus had freely chosen his apostles, and they in turn had transmitted their ministry to other men.

Proof of this free choice, for the pope from Brescia, came from the Virgin Mary. She had a function even greater than that of the apostles. No one, nevertheless, thought of including her or other holy women such as Mary Magdalen in the list of the Twelve. Anyway, according to Saint Paul, the only higher charism that one should desire is charity. The greatest in the kingdom of heaven are

---

[50] John Paul II, Apostolic Letter *Ordinatio sacerdotalis* on Reserving Priestly Ordination to Men Alone, May 22, 1994.

not the ministers but the saints. The [Polish] pope then concluded that: "the Church has no authority whatsoever to confer priestly ordination on women and that this judgment is to be definitively held by all the Church's faithful." After the publication of the letter, the ensuing debate focused specifically on this last statement. Had John Paul II spoken infallibly, or was his statement an utterance of the ordinary Magisterium that can also be changed?

The Congregation for the Doctrine of the Faith answered this question on October 28, 1995. To this *dubium*, according to the very short text of the congregation, it is necessary to give an affirmative answer. "This teaching requires definitive assent, since, founded on the written Word of God, and from the beginning constantly preserved and applied in the Tradition of the Church. . . ."[51] Ratzinger then explained, responding to a question from Peter Seewald: "It is not . . . an infallible act of the Pope, but [rather] the binding authority rests upon the continuity of the tradition."[52] This, moreover, is an idea explicated by the Vatican II Constitution on the Church (LG 25). Consequently, one cannot go against such a solemn declaration of the council. On the other hand, if one consents to the ordination of women in order to preserve the dialogue with the Anglicans, one runs the risk of breaking with the much more ancient and venerable tradition of the Eastern Churches.

THE COUNSELORS: NEW CLASH WITH LEHMANN

Following the unification of the two Germanys, in 1990 it was necessary to develop in that country a uniform law regulating abortion. There were long political negotiations, in which the Constitutional Court also intervened, and finally they reached an agreement that established that abortion is illegal. Until the third month of pregnancy, nevertheless, it would not be punishable if the pregnant woman could present a certificate attesting that, before seeking abortion, she had had a consultation in a State-approved counseling center. After the consultation, however, the counseling center was obliged to issue the certificate. Among the counselors who could

---

[51] See Congregation for the Doctrine of the Faith, Responsum ad Propositum Dubium concerning the Teaching Contained in "Ordinatio Sacerdotalis", October 28, 1995.

[52] Joseph Ratzinger, *Salt of the Earth*, trans. Adrian Walker (San Francisco: Ignatius Press, 1997), 209.

hold these consultations, and who were nevertheless bound to issue the certificate, there were Catholics as well. On this point, a new cause for dissent developed between Germany and Rome, between the German Bishops' Conference, the pope, and the Congregation for the Doctrine of the Faith.

Immediately after the German Parliament passed the law, the pope, on January 11, 1998, wrote to the German bishops asking the Catholic counselors to refuse to issue the certificate that cleared the path to abortion, even at the cost of giving up State funding. The majority of the German bishops, however, under the guidance of their president, Bishop Lehmann, were of the opinion that it was appropriate to keep the system of counselors. To the position of the pope, they objected that only by participating in the prenatal consultation provided for by law could the Church still convince a certain number of pregnant women in difficult situations to desist from their plan to procure an abortion. On this point, John Paul II was immovable. In 1999, the German bishops, backed by many lay people who sided with the counselors—who, given the papal refusal, were in danger of losing a well-paid job—tried other ways of mediation.

Finally, the bishops of Cologne, Munich, and Berlin, together with President Lehmann, were summoned once again to Rome. They were received by the secretary of state, Cardinal Sodano, and the prefect of the Congregation for the Doctrine of the Faith, who communicated to them the definitive response of the pope: If the Catholic counselors grant a certificate that is formally against the abortion but nevertheless also clears the way to the voluntary interruption of pregnancy, then the accusation of those who maintain that the Catholic message is only theoretical, without any practical consequences, is correct. It is therefore unthinkable that the Church could still remain in the public system of counselors who must issue such certificates.

Answering a question from Seewald, Ratzinger saw the matter as the pope did, but sought, nevertheless, to shift the point of view: "A primary objective is to recover the original, true view that the child, the new human being, is a blessing. That by giving life we also receive it ourselves."[53] He continued: "I think that the point

---

[53] Ibid., 201.

is to clarify the awareness that a conceived child is a human being, an individual . . . a distinct person. . . . I think that if we give up the principle that every man as man is under God's protection, that as a man he is beyond the reach of our arbitrary will, we really do forsake the foundation of human rights."[54]

The question, obviously, was too important to accept a compromise. Once again, Ratzinger gave evidence of the courage that he maintains is one of the most important virtues for bishops. It must be added also that, only several years after the events recorded here, Lehmann was appointed a cardinal, as was Kasper. A difference of opinion, even in the theological field, does not necessarily lead to a rupture of communion in fraternal charity. As for the counselors, were they not part of that excess of structures that the progressives so often lamented? In this regard, Ratzinger declared: "In Germany . . . we have far more Church institutions than we can imbue with ecclesial spirit."[55] Reducing the excess of institutions that no longer give Christian witness should not be a problem for believers.

A new report on the faith

Ten years after the book-length interview with Messori that had provoked so much debate in 1985, Ratzinger once again accepted the challenge to allow himself to be interviewed by a representative of the press, to answer his more or less troublesome questions. The author of the interview, Peter Seewald, was a journalist who had worked for some of the most famous periodicals in Germany: *Der Spiegel*, *Stern*, and *Suddeutsche Zeitung*. Raised a Catholic, he had left the Church but then was on the journey back. The procedures for the interview, explained by Seewald in the preface, were similar to those already described by Messori. The first meeting occurred in Rome; then the two interlocutors moved to the vicinity of Frascati to the Villa Cavalletti, a former Jesuit college that had been acquired by the Integrierte Gemeinde, the community for dialogue with Israel and the Jewish heritage that, at the time when Ratzinger moved to Rome, followed its protector to the Italian capital. There

---

[54] Ibid., 204.
[55] Ibid., 173.

the cardinal felt at ease, and the two men could work undisturbed for a few days.

Two major themes are addressed in the book: the situation of the Church at the conclusion of the second millennium since her foundation and an attempt to make a prognosis about society in the new millennium. Deprived of common foundations, society was in danger of dissolving, and, for this reason, faith in God is necessary, if for no other reason than as an opportunity for the survival of mankind. In the meantime, many of the analyses and judgments formulated by the cardinal have proved to be quite accurate. Here, however, we are interested not so much in the second question addressed in the volume as in the first: the situation of the Church at the end of the second millennium.

LOVE FOR THE TRUTH

After he was appointed a bishop, when he had to choose his episcopal motto, Ratzinger decided on "Co-workers of the Truth", an expression taken from the Third Letter of Saint John, to signify the continuity between his theological work and his new ministry. In the interview with Seewald, the cardinal added one striking detail: the theme of truth had not been central to his thought from the beginning. With the passage of time, though, he had gradually realized the centrality of this theme, just as he had understood that renouncing the truth does not liberate but rather leads to the "tyranny of caprice".[56] Every human being has a secret core where he finds himself face to face with God, the place of true freedom.[57] Naturally, claiming the truth for oneself can lead to pride and hardness of heart; serving the truth demands, in contrast, humility and obedience and requires acting according to one's conscience.

In this regard, Ratzinger cited two extraordinary witnesses who acted according to their conscience and are ideals and models for him: Thomas More and Cardinal Newman. These two great Englishmen had set out on the road to success but did not hesitate to renounce it in order to follow what seemed to them to be the path of conscience. We are looking, therefore, at a journey that starts

---

[56] Ibid., 66–67.

[57] Vincent Twomey, "La coscienza e l'uomo", in Josef Clemens and Antonio Tarzia, eds., *Alla scuola della verità: I settant'anni di Joseph Ratzinger* (Cinisello Balsamo: San Paolo, 1997), 123.

from the perception of reality, passes through freedom, and arrives at conscience. Ratzinger's thought continuously returned to these three themes, which are closely interrelated. This, moreover, is the reason for his growing uneasiness about a world that is becoming increasingly self-referential, which enslaves man and deprives him of his dignity. Often, Ratzinger continued, in the Church as in society, people disregard the truth, preferring consensus or a courteous atmosphere of getting along. "There is a willingness to purchase well-being, success, public regard, and approval from the reigning opinion by dispensing with the truth. . . . The fact is that under the pretext of goodness people neglect conscience. They place acceptance, the avoidance of problems, the comfortable pursuit of their existence . . . above truth in the scale of values."[58]

Von Balthasar had already denounced the career ambitions and conformism of Christians, in particular of the clergy, which with the passage of time become one of the cardinal's recurring anxieties.

THE CRISIS IN THE CHURCH

In the cardinal's opinion, an initial symptom of the crisis in the Church is attachment to institutions. Old institutions that are now devoid of any faith content are defended by the Church with a suspicious tenacity. In this regard, Ratzinger did not hide his views. This phenomenon is particularly present precisely in Germany. "It's precisely the fact that the Church clings to the institutional structure when nothing really stands behind it any longer that brings the Church into disrepute."[59] Then there are other problems that by now are deep-seated, that people continue to discuss without ever going to the heart of the question: women priests, contraceptive methods, priestly celibacy, remarriage for the divorced. Certainly these are serious questions, but the future of Christianity cannot depend on them. Just look at one example: the Lutheran Church long since gave an answer to these problems that is different from the Catholic one. It is quite obvious, though, that, like the Catholic Church, the Protestant churches have not resolved at all the problem of how to be Christian in today's world.

What is missing, instead, at least in Western Christendom, is the

---

[58] J. Ratzinger, *Salt of the Earth*, 68.
[59] Ibid., 173.

motivating force, the joy of the Christian proclamation. It is not enough to feel that one is a "good Christian"; "faith is in reality a gift to be passed on, which you don't even really have if you want to keep it for yourself."[60] This, now, is one of the fundamental convictions to which the cardinal would return insistently during the years of his pontificate. The reform of ecclesiastical organizations is a question that, in reality, hides the true crisis of faith. Faith is lacking particularly in Europe, in the countries with an ancient Christian tradition. Here, the liberalism so much feared by Newman is by now taken for granted: the separation of Church and State is no longer questioned by anyone; similarly, the conviction that the faith is a merely subjective matter is widespread even among Christians.

According to the cardinal, we are facing a historical nemesis. Christianity, indeed, is at the origin of the separation of Church and State. When it appeared in the world at the time of the Roman Empire, the State possessed a sacral character and was well disposed toward the religions present in its territory. Christianity, too, could have taken advantage of this general benevolence, provided that it recognized the cult of the State as being superior to private religions. Christians, however, were unwilling to align themselves with the other religions, thus definitively causing a crisis for the union between State and religion, except that it proposed it again once the empire became Christian. In principle, nevertheless, it had been established that the State no longer holds a sacral power; its authority is based on an order that finds its limits in a God who judges it.

At the beginning of the modern era, this achievement led to the birth of the Enlightenment and to the separation of Church and State. The process led in Western countries to the phenomenon known in Italy as "free Church in a free State". It is not a merely negative phenomenon. "Here are opportunities for a more vital [faith], because [it is] more deeply and more freely grounded."[61] At the same time, however, after Kant and Hegel, religion has been reduced to the merely private sphere and comes to lack an autonomous authority capable of proclaiming truths that are binding even for

---

[60] Ibid., 180.
[61] Ibid., 240.

the State and for the powerful in this world. Hence, the absolutism of the State and the succession of totalitarian regimes that indelibly marked the face of Europe during the twentieth century.

A PROGRAM FOR THE CHURCH OF THE THIRD MILLENNIUM

As the year 2000 approached and the jubilee events and celebrations multiplied, the elements of crisis that were amassing all over the world did not escape Ratzinger or John Paul II himself. The cardinal in particular spoke about them in a conference in which he reflected on the task of Christians and, more generally, of the Church on the eve of the third millennium.[62] The undisputed predominance of technology and the prevailing relativism brought with them the abandonment of the search for truth. For Ratzinger, here we are not facing one of the many and multifarious difficulties that man must confront in life; rather, what is at stake is the indispensable question that runs through all of human history. Without the aspiration to the truth, the search for the rationality of the world diminishes, and the memory of the Creator—the conviction that there is fundamental rationality and harmony at the origin—falls into oblivion.

Theology, too, emerges impoverished by this detachment. Deprived of its foundation in rationality, faith in God becomes a possible option without rational foundation and, hence, without any true binding force for mankind. According to Ratzinger, technology's claim to answer all questions exhaustively has led to this. In this regard, the cardinal recalled an episode that occurred at the presentation of the book by Jacques Monod, *Chance and Necessity*.[63]

---

[62] The conference, held in 1998, was included by Stephan Horn and Vinzenz Pfnür in the anthology of the cardinal's writings, *Weggemeinschaft des Glaubens* (Augsburg: Sankt Ulrich, 2002), which they edited to commemorate the seventy-fifth birthday of their former professor. In English, the anthology was published by Ignatius Press as *Pilgrim Fellowship of Faith* (2005). The conference "The Church on the Threshold of the Third Millennium" is found on pp. 284–98.

[63] Jacques Monod, *Le hasard et la nécessité: Essai sur la philosophie naturelle de la biologie moderne* (Paris: Seuil, 1970); trans. Austryn Wainhouse as *Chance and Necessity: An Essay on the Natural Philosophy of Modern Biology* (Harmondsworth: Penguin, 1997). Ratzinger had already debated with Monod in Joseph Ratzinger, *In the Beginning . . . : A Catholic Understanding of the Story of Creation and the Fall*, trans. Boniface Ramsey, O.P. (Huntington, Ind.: Our Sunday Visitor, 1990; 2nd, enlarged ed., Grand Rapids, Mich.: Eerdmans,

The French biologist maintained that, with the help of the proper hypotheses, he had made the creator spirit superfluous. Also present at the presentation of the volume was the Catholic writer François Mauriac, who made a remark that Ratzinger adopted as his own: "What this professor says is much more incredible than what we poor Christians believe."[64]

In the meantime, though, the predominance of technology has had dramatic consequences. This is demonstrated paradoxically, according to Ratzinger, by those who declare themselves agnostic about the question of God because it is not possible to prove either the existence of a Creator God or his nonexistence. On the other hand, they have no difficulty at all believing in hell because it is enough to take a look at the many forms of violence reported every day by television news programs to have certain proof of it.[65]

Faced with the dominant ideology of banality, the Church can assume the role of a prophetic opposition. This will involve the abandonment of convenient situations, just as she will have to give up structuring herself as a State or a social agency. She is a spiritual force that is unable and unwilling to give orders to the world but, in the general disorientation, can place the wisdom of her experience at the disposal of mankind. Salt of the earth, she has a function for society as a whole; she must guide the world toward God and out of itself. She, moreover, exists "so that God, the living God, may be made known—so that man may learn to live with God, live in his sight and in fellowship with him."[66] And again: "The Church is there, not for her own sake, but for mankind. She is there so that the world may become a sphere for God's presence, the sphere of the covenant between God and men."[67] In short, in Ratzinger's thought, the occasion of the millennium was supposed to be a return of the Church to herself, a reminder of her service to God and to mankind, to the whole world. Compared with this, all the possible changes, the adaptations to the world, the requests from the clergy and from the faithful themselves were secondary.

1995). He mentions it briefly in his conference on the Church on the eve of the third millennium. See *Pilgrim Fellowship of Faith*, 291.

[64] J. Ratzinger, *Pilgrim Fellowship of Faith*, 290.

[65] Ibid., 284.

[66] Ibid., 286.

[67] Ibid., 287.

The cardinal knew that this task was not simple, just as he knew that the Church was destined to become a minority in the new millennium. Nevertheless, there was no need to fear. The most beautiful presentation of the believer's journey in the world is narrated by Saint Luke in his Gospel. In what is called the episode of the two disciples on the road to Emmaus, a stranger, apparently ignorant of what has happened in the days of the death and Resurrection of Jesus, joins the two disciples and explains to them the meaning of the Scriptures. The stranger is Jesus, whom the disciples recognize in the breaking of the bread. Consequently, the Church, just like individual Christians, is never alone. With them is Jesus, who precedes them and supports them on the journey. Referring back to the preceding mention of the world, which mankind is in danger of reducing to a hell on earth, the cardinal concluded with a reference to Canto XII of Dante's *Purgatorio*.

> The pilgrim fellowship of faith, which we call the Church, should be a fellowship in climbing, a fellowship in which those processes of cleansing are effected in us that render us capable of the true heights of human existence, of fellowship with God. In the same measure as we are cleansed, the climbing, which is at first so difficult, rapidly becomes a joy. This joy must more and more shine forth from the Church into the world."[68]

With this program, the Church, even if she becomes a minority, will not be irrelevant in the new millennium—a program that can be seen as a key to interpreting his future pontificate.

Relations between Jews and Christians

In chapter 6, we have already encountered Ludwig Weimer and the Integrated Community, which would contribute to the dialogue between Jews and Christians by their testimony and call Ratzinger's attention to it. In 1994, Rabbi David Rosen, one of the eminent figures in Jewish thought and religion at the global level, organized in Jerusalem a meeting on how to provide religious guidance in a secularized world. At the suggestion of the Integrated Community, Ratzinger was invited as a representative of the Catholic Church,

---

[68] Ibid., 298.

and he gave a conference on "Israel, the Church and the World"[69] based on the *Catechism of the Catholic Church*.

As is his custom, the cardinal got right to the point by posing the question: How is it possible that the history of relations between Israel and Christianity has been characterized by tears and blood, by a hostility that is inexplicable given the affinity and closeness between the two religions? Based on the observation that, after Auschwitz, the duty of reconciliation is primarily up to the Christians, some exegetes have advanced the conjecture that they renounce those articles of the Christian faith which, in their opinion, are at the origin of such serious hostility. They mean in particular the faith in Jesus of Nazareth as Son of the living God and faith in the Cross as the redemption of mankind. This would automatically eliminate the accusation of deicide made against the Jews over the centuries, and there would no longer be any reason for contention.

Obviously, Ratzinger was not of this opinion, nor is the *Catechism of the Catholic Church*, which starts its argument based on the episode of the visit of the magi. "Their coming [to Jerusalem] means that pagans can discover Jesus and worship him as Son of God and Savior of the world only by turning toward the Jews and receiving from them the messianic promise."[70] On their journey, the Magi are guided by the star, which the cardinal regards as symbolic of the role of the world religions. They have the task of guiding men to Jerusalem, where, however, their light is extinguished because there the word of Israel's Sacred Scripture shines. "The Word of God preserved herein shows itself to be the true star without which or bypassing which the goal cannot be found."[71]

This statement is clarified and at the same time summarized by the Gospel of Saint John, which concisely states that salvation is from the Jews. This assumption, Ratzinger continued, which is fully valid

---

[69] The text of the conference was published for the first time in issue no. 1 of *Heute —pro ecclesia viva*, the journal of the Integrierte Gemeinde, which bore the significant title *Vom wider-Einwurzeln im jüdischen als einer Bedingung für das Einholen des Katholischen* (On becoming rooted again in Judaism as a condition for recovering what is Catholic) (1994): 152–69. Later, the text, again at the initiative of the Integrierte Gemeinde, was published in the volume entitled *Die Vielfalt der Religionen und der eine Bund* (Bad Tölz: Urfeld, 1998); trans. Graham Harrison as *Many Religions, One Covenant: Israel, the Church and the World* (San Francisco: Ignatius Press, 1999).

[70] *Catechism of the Catholic Church*, no. 528.

[71] J. Ratzinger, *Many Religions: One Covenant*, 26.

even today, can be explained as follows: there is no entrance into the Christian people unless one accepts the revelation of God that is present in the Scriptures that Christians call the Old Testament. Consequently, Jesus and the Sacred Scripture of Israel are inseparable. Not only that, but Jesus' mission is fulfilled through his fidelity to the law of Israel, to the point where his death on the Cross is to be considered in solidarity with the law and with Israel. Therefore, far from being the cause of the curse of Israel, of its condemnation as the people responsible for deicide, "Christ's death itself [is] the great event of atonement, . . . the perfect realization of what the signs of the Day of Atonement signify."[72] Jesus, therefore, did not abolish the law of Israel; he fulfilled it, and in the Sermon on the Mount he revealed its hidden potentialities.

A RABBI TALKS WITH JESUS

Following the *Catechism of the Catholic Church*, Ratzinger based his argument on the Gospel of Matthew. A great Hebrew scholar, Rabbi Jacob Neusner, did the same during those years. Prompted by his interest in and respect for the Christian religion, he imagined living at the time of Jesus and joining a group of his listeners. In particular, on the day of the Sermon on the Mount, Neusner wrote: "I stand there, hear words that move me, listen confidently. For Jesus' first words win my confidence. Jesus opens his preaching of the gospel of the kingdom with a message with which no disciple of Moses' Torah would take exception."[73] Then, however, gradually, as Jesus speaks, the rabbi became disturbed. What upset him was not so much the message, about which he could make objections that on the whole are not that significant, but rather the form of the teaching. According to Neusner, Matthew himself ought to have been struck by the form of Jesus' teaching, since he states: "He taught them as one who had authority, and not as their scribes."[74] To which Neusner objected: "Moses alone had authority. The scribes teach the message and meaning of what Moses had set down as the Torah on the authority of God. So we find ourselves right where we started: with the difficulty of making sense, within the framework

---

[72] Ibid., 32.

[73] Jacob Neusner, *A Rabbi Talks with Jesus* (New York: Image Books/Doubleday, 1994), 37.

[74] Mt 7:29.

of the Torah, of a teacher who stands apart from, perhaps above, the Torah."[75]

Now we understand, from the many particulars of Matthew's detailed account of Jesus' teachings, that in the end "at issue is the figure of Jesus, not the teachings at all."[76] On this point, Neusner and Ratzinger were in complete agreement. The rabbi, nevertheless, drew from it the conclusion that, given this premise, he could not accept the invitation of the Teacher from Nazareth to follow him, because he would distance himself from the law addressed to the eternal Israel. "No, if I were there that day, I would not have joined those disciples and followed the master on his way."[77]

Ratzinger considered Neusner's interpretation of the Sermon on the Mount correct, even though he did not share his conclusion. He finished, therefore, by observing: "More than other interpretations [of the Sermon on the Mount] known to me, this respectful and frank dispute between a believing Jew and Jesus, the son of Abraham, has opened my eyes to the greatness of Jesus' words and to the choice that the Gospel places before us."[78] The rabbi's point of departure was that Jews and Christians basically follow two different religions. Nevertheless, he did not wish to engage in polemics with Christians; if anything, he wanted to help them to understand in greater depth the reasons for their faith. Similarly, Ratzinger affirmed that awareness of the historical crimes of Christians committed against Jews must not lead us to take shortcuts or to renounce essential parts of the faith, such as the Incarnation and the Resurrection of Jesus, for the alleged purpose of promoting dialogue. "If the light of Christ goes out, God's light is also extinguished; for it is in the face of Christ that we have seen the light of God, the light of the one God in whom we believe, together with 'Abraham and his seed'."[79]

This is not the place to pass judgment on this form of dialogue. It is merely appropriate to recall that the relationship between Neusner and Ratzinger has been characterized by rare depth and has been continued over the years with mutual esteem.

---

[75] Neusner, *A Rabbi Talks with Jesus*, 47.

[76] Ibid.

[77] Ibid., 52.

[78] Joseph Ratzinger, *Jesus of Nazareth*, vol. 1, trans. Adrian J. Walker (New York: Doubleday, 2007), 69.

[79] J. Ratzinger, *Many Religions: One Covenant*, 13.

XI

ANNO DOMINI 2000

The cardinal's seventieth birthday

In April 1997, Ratzinger turned seventy years old. On that occasion, Father Antonio Tarzia, the general director of the San Paolo publishing house, which for several years had been his principal publisher in Italy, realized that biographical information about the cardinal was scarce and fragmentary. He asked him then for a biographical manuscript that would simultaneously give an account of his life and of his writings. Although unwilling at first, the cardinal then complied with the editor's request and drew from his memories an autobiographical sketch that manifests a rare spiritual intensity, touching kindness, and a love for thought and art.[1] In that same year, San Paolo published *Alla scuola della verità*,[2] an anthology of writings that displays the extent of the cardinal's friendships and interests and the fruitfulness of his thought, which from Rome radiates to Europe, America, and Asia. Here, obviously, we cannot review the twenty-four essays, but it may be significant to report a rather unexpected judgment.

Cardinal Martini, archbishop of Milan, said that he had known

---

[1] I refer to the book cited many times already, *Milestones: Memoirs 1927–1977*, trans. Erasmo Leiva-Merikakis (San Francisco: Ignatius Press, 1998). The original title of the German manuscript was *Aus meinem Leben: Erinnerungen 1927–1977*. Even though the subtitle speaks of memories from 1927 to 1977, the cardinal's memoir goes as far as 1982, the year of his arrival in Rome. Several times I sought to convince the cardinal to resume the narrative, which gave him the opportunity to establish a sort of red thread running through his life. He, however, no longer had time to devote to it.

[2] Josef Clemens and Antonio Tarzia, eds., *Alla scuola della verità: I settant'anni di Joseph Ratzinger* (Cinisello Balsamo: San Paolo, 1997).

Ratzinger since the sixties, from the days of the *Introduction to Christianity*. Then he expressed admiration for his confrere in the episcopate, who "since he started working at the congregation has performed an arduous and difficult task, to which the only possible response is reflection, prayer, patience, and listening. . . . It seems to me that the position taken by Joseph Cardinal Ratzinger with regard to the problem of our epoch-making turning point depends first of all on his faith and on his integrity."[3] The priest Heinz Schütte, a former student of Ratzinger, at that time was professor of ecumenical theology at the University of Bonn. Notwithstanding the criticism by many Catholics, he described Ratzinger as "a promoter of Christian unity, a theological precursor of ecumenism who looks to the future".[4] As an expert on the Bible and the Church Fathers, in particular on Saint Augustine, about whom he, like Luther, can say "Augustinus totus meus" (Augustine is totally mine), he was "very well situated to be open to some established Reformed authorities and to give witness, in keeping with the Gospel, to the faith of the one, holy, catholic, and apostolic Church."[5]

The Orthodox cleric Damaskinos Papandreou, a former student of Ratzinger from his years in Bonn, was at that time Metropolitan of Switzerland and Exarch of Europe. As such, he awarded Joseph Cardinal Ratzinger, a benefactor of the Orthodox Center, the Golden Order of Saint Demetrius the Martyr for supporting, in words and works, the construction of the Orthodox Center of the Ecumenical Patriarchate in Chambésy. At the same time, Metropolitan Damaskinos made it clear that the pope's primacy of jurisdiction remains for the Orthodox an obstacle on the way to union. His gratitude would not prevent the Metropolitan, a few years later, from engaging in lively polemics with Ratzinger.

We have already met Rabbi Jacob Neusner, at that time professor of religious studies at the University of Southern Florida in the United States. He was connected with the cardinal not only by ties of friendship but also by their common opposition to the hegemony of historicism in Judaism as well as in Christianity. Naturally, he shared with Ratzinger and with the great majority of Jewish and

---

[3] Ibid., 186f.
[4] Ibid., 89.
[5] Ibid., 89f.

Catholic scholars the conviction that ancient Israel expounded its own theology by means of thought and historical narrative. At the same time, however, together with Ratzinger, he distanced himself from historicism, which is rigidly fixed on the past. "Rabbinical Judaism, like early Christianity, found also an entirely new way of thinking about past times and of keeping all times, past, present, and future, in one and the same picture."[6] We will see that Ratzinger in turn would recognize that it was precisely Neusner who was of great help to him in understanding Jesus' Sermon on the Mount.[7]

The Bavarian Prime Minister Edmund Stoiber said that he was happy that Bavaria, which was so dear to Ratzinger, had been able to resist the constitutional ruling about removing the crucifix from public places and the decriminalization of abortion. At the same time, he verified that Ratzinger had been true to his promise that "Even in Rome, I will always be a Bavarian", and he said that he was sure that he would continue to be one in the future, also. The then president of the Austrian Parliament, Herbert Schambeck, recalled the intense ties, both familial and personal, that the cardinal had with his country. To those from his youth that have already been noted, he added the frequent vacations of the three siblings in the Austrian Republic. At Schambeck's own invitation, Maria, Georg, and Joseph spent their last vacation together in Baden, near Vienna, in 1991. There they paid a visit to the house in which Beethoven composed his Ninth Symphony, and the two brothers celebrated Mass in the parish church of the city in which Mozart composed and performed the *Ave Verum* for the first time in public. Among the essays, moreover, there is also an excerpt from a musical work that Wolfgang Sawallisch, a great composer and orchestra director of Bavarian extraction, had decided to dedicate to his cardinal friend, with whom he shared a love for music.

The only female testimony is one by the Korean Jung-Hi Victoria Kim, an instructor at Chonnam National University in Gwangju City in South Korea. A student of Ratzinger at the University of Regensburg, she acknowledged that she had succeeded in obtaining a doctorate thanks to the constant help of the professor and of the

---

[6] Ibid., 292.

[7] Joseph Ratzinger, *Jesus of Nazareth: From the Baptism in the Jordan to the Transfiguration*, trans. Adrian J. Walker (New York, et al.: Doubleday, 2007), 103.

whole group of his students. When she had returned to her country, the Marian book by Ratzinger, *Daughter Zion*, "gave me the first incentive to contribute, on the basis of Mary, to the education of women in Korea. Over the years, it became increasingly important for me to foster dialogue between the image of women in the Confucian tradition and that of the Christian perspective."[8]

Remaining for a moment in the field of publishing, I feel obliged to report a detail mentioned to me by Father Antonio Tarzia. *The Ratzinger Report* and *Milestones*, both published in Italian by San Paolo, were best sellers internationally. The cardinal, nevertheless, gave up almost completely the royalties that belonged to him. He gave the publisher addresses, especially of communities of cloistered nuns in Germany, Austria, and Italy, to which the publisher was to send the requisite sums. Moreover, Don Tarzia confirms, the cardinal led a life that was truly Franciscan in style. More than once his editor friend had to intervene to buy him a new beret, liturgical vestments, or a stole to replace a wardrobe that was more reminiscent of a rural parish priest than of a veteran prince of the Church.

The life of the Gospel in the world: The movements

Organized by the Pontifical Council for the Laity, in May 1998, a World Congress of ecclesial movements was held in Rome. The meeting, desired by John Paul II, corresponded to a concern of Wojtyła, but also of Ratzinger, to mobilize a Catholic response to the advance of the Protestant sects[9] in Latin America and the United States. Before the meeting of all the participants with the pope on Saint Peter's Square, there were study days, opening with a conference by Ratzinger that was received enthusiastically by the representatives of the movements but with some reserve as well by the bishops who were present. The title, "Ecclesial Movements and Their Place in Theology",[10] gave little sign of the innovative role described in the cardinal's speech.

---

[8] Clemens and Tarzia, *Alla scuola della verità*, 338.

[9] See Andrea Riccardi, *Giovanni Paolo II* (Cinisello Balsamo: San Paolo, 2011), 310ff.

[10] The text is found in the volume *Movements in the Church*, edited by the Pontifical Council for the Laity (Vatican City: Libreria Editrice Vaticana, 1999), 23–51, and in Joseph Ratzinger, *New Outpourings of the Spirit*, trans. Michael J. Miller and Henry Taylor (San Francisco: Ignatius Press, 2007), 17–61.

He opened his speech by recalling his joyful surprise at his first encounter with the lay ecclesial movements in Germany. "Here was something nobody had planned on. The Holy Spirit had, so to say, spoken up for himself again."[11] Some young people belonging to the Neocatechumenal Way, Communion and Liberation, the Charismatic Renewal, and Focolare were seeking to live the Gospel in its entirety with enthusiasm and dedication. Certainly, the cardinal recalled, there was one-sidedness and immoderation, which are typical of any human situation. But it was impossible to overlook the action of the Spirit, and therefore it was necessary to ask how to welcome the movements and to integrate them within the life of the Church. The Sacrament of Holy Orders is the permanent, binding structure that gives the Church her institutional order. It is just as true, however, that the sacrament can be received and lived out only by virtue of the newness of each vocation, which does not depend on the Church but comes directly from God.

For her part, the Church, too, cannot be understood solely as an institution, an exclusively human arrangement. Certainly within her there are merely human institutions relating to administration, the organization of events, and the like. Precisely because they are not essential, these organizations must be reduced to a minimum and, above all, must not extinguish listening to the Spirit, attention to his outpourings that bring renewal. This was the great newness, which for many bishops, especially those from countries with an ancient Christian tradition, seemed almost a provocation. It was not primarily up to the movements to fit themselves into the organizational structures of the dioceses and of the associations. The bishops, on the contrary, were called to reduce their organizational structures drastically and to welcome the new phenomena mandated by the Spirit. Indeed, not only are the movements not contrary to the Church; instead, they are included in what theologians call "apostolic succession".

Ratzinger arrived at this second sensational assertion on the basis of another key point in his view of the Church: the conviction that both conceptually and chronologically, the one universal Church exists first and then a local Church. Indeed, Jesus entrusted to the twelve apostles the task of bringing his message to the ends of the

---

[11] J. Ratzinger, *New Outpourings*, 20.

earth. From the apostles' missionary activity, the local Churches were born in a second phase, and they needed leaders, bishops who were to guarantee the unity of the faith and at the same time keep their community open in a twofold manner: to internal communion and to spreading outwardly. In a word, the Church could not be a federation of local Churches, just as the bishops, the successors of the apostles, could not consider their task to consist of no more than the administration of a firmly systematized Church. They also had to feel concern for spreading the Gospel, to sharpen their vision and hearing for the new outpourings of the Spirit. God, indeed, does not fail to send signs, to call persons to spread the Gospel.

While taking a look at the history of the Church, Ratzinger identified some ecclesial institutions that, in his opinion, could be considered precursors of the movements. These are monasticism, the evangelical movement initiated by Saint Francis, the missionary effort that the Church owed to Saint Ignatius of Loyola, and the social initiatives of the nineteenth century, which many times were promoted by women. At this point, we begin to see also the connection between the papacy and the apostolic movements. The successors of Saint Peter did not create the movements, but as the ones responsible for the apostolic succession and for the universal spread of the Gospel, they are their anchor, their ecclesial support.[12] Ratzinger arrived at this conclusion, however, both through a theological consideration and through historical reflection: Saint Benedict, Saint Francis, and Saint Ignatius sought and had the support of the pope, the one primarily responsible for the apostolic succession.

The anthology published by San Paolo [and, in English, by Ignatius Press] from which I cited an excerpt from Ratzinger's conference also reprints the transcript of a meeting that took place in 1999 between Ratzinger and a group of bishops. Having arrived in Rome at the invitation of the Pontifical Council for the Laity, the bishops, many of them cardinals as well, had an opportunity to express directly to the prefect of the Congregation for the Doctrine of the Faith the questions, concerns, and also reservations prompted by his conference the preceding year. Would this not burden with excessive troubles the parish communities and the priests, who receive so many requests that are often difficult to reconcile with each other? Once again the strong points of the prefect's speech emerge

---

[12] Ibid., 43.

in his reply: the bishop is not only the custodian of the institution, he also has the task of discerning and, when useful, of helping the movements to purify themselves. In the future, the bishop will be "less of a monarch, more of a brother in a school in which there is only one Master and one Father."[13] For the Church, the movements are gifts that become fruitful when the suffering that they involve is accepted. In exchange, they offer a joyous experience and the spirit of familiarity that is indispensable in today's mass society. They contribute to the revitalization of Christian culture and help to avoid the excesses of certain communities that assimilate themselves too much to the contemporary world.

The Church, finally, cannot cling exclusively to her own plans, just as she cannot devote all her efforts to social service. She is at the service of faith in God, just as she is called to defend the human being as a creature of God. Today, as in the past, Christians may even give the impression of having little influence on the events that determine the course of world history, but nevertheless their contribution will be invaluable if they continue to be "a leaven of evangelical life in the world".[14]

The liturgy

In the mid-1990s, around thirty years after the approval of the Constitution on the Liturgy and the conclusion of Vatican II, debates about the reform of the liturgy were anything but calmed. Suddenly Ratzinger had spoken up, warning against the changes, which in his opinion were excessive and too abrupt to the point of becoming arbitrary, in the search for a form that was better suited and more accessible to contemporary Catholics. With the passage of time, furthermore, the situation had become even more critical, in his view. The initial conviction that the search for a new liturgical form was only a question of praxis had soon proved to be illusory. "The liturgy involves our understanding of God and the world and our relationship to Christ, the Church, and ourselves. How we attend to liturgy determines the fate of the faith and the Church."[15]

---

[13] Ibid., 108.

[14] Ibid., 117.

[15] Joseph Ratzinger, *A New Song for the Lord*, trans. Martha M. Matesich (New York: Crossroad, 1996), ix.

And then the cardinal stopped hesitating and intervened in the problems related to the importance of Sunday for prayer and Christian life, to the construction of church buildings, and to sacred music.

These are the themes of *The Feast of Faith*,[16] which are taken up again in *A New Song for the Lord*, a volume prefaced by several essays on Christology aimed at exploring in greater depth the connection between the salvific action performed by Christ in his life, which is made contemporaneous with the believer by the liturgical celebration, which also becomes a promise of eternal life. The more complete volume on this topic arrived several years later, in 1999. The title of the book, *The Spirit of the Liturgy*, already referred to the famous work with which Romano Guardini had introduced the liturgical movement [in Germany] in 1918; Ratzinger's intention was "to encourage, in a new way, something like a 'liturgical movement', a movement toward the liturgy and toward the right way of celebrating the liturgy, inwardly and outwardly."[17] Once again, though, the publication of the book was accompanied by a chorus of protests on the part of those who had prejudged Ratzinger and labeled him strongly nostalgic, a supporter of Latin and of outmoded forms of celebrating Mass.

The cardinal, however, sought to situate the liturgy and its forms in a broad theological context of worship and common prayer to God that is both cosmic and historical. The reference to Guardini was already a signpost of this choice, even though, as the cardinal immediately noted in the preface, due consideration must be given to the changed historical context. And he accounted for this difference in the very first chapter, correcting not so much Guardini's theory of the liturgy as play as the trivializing applications of it by some contemporary liturgists who saw in that definition the source of a freedom that breaks all constraints and allows the light of heaven to shine down on earth.

Guardini, on the contrary, in mentioning play, intended to exempt the liturgy from secondary purposes. "It has no educational

---

[16] Joseph Ratzinger, *The Feast of Faith: Approaches to a Theology of the Liturgy*, trans. Graham Harrison (San Francisco: Ignatius Press, 1980).

[17] Joseph Ratzinger, *The Spirit of the Liturgy*, trans. John Saward (San Francisco: Ignatius Press, 2000), 8–9.

or deliberately artistic tasks; its deeper meaning is simply contemplation—to be precise, the contemplation of God's glory."[18] With this intention, Ratzinger provides further clarifications on the basis of an account of the events that preceded the Exodus of Israel from Egypt.

THE COSMIC AND HISTORICAL CHARACTER OF THE LITURGY

Appearing before the Pharaoh, Moses asks the sovereign of Egypt to let his people go, specifically for a cultic reason. Israel does not leave in order to be one people among others, but in order to serve God. On this basis, God manifests himself and makes with his people the covenant that involves a juridical system and a rule of life. The central point, nevertheless, consists of the manifestation of God. If God does not manifest himself, man cannot celebrate the true liturgy, which requires that God be present and respond to the one praying. This does not mean, however, that Ratzinger did not recognize the liturgies of other religions. On the contrary, whereas some biblical scholars insist on the predominantly historical character of Judaeo-Christian revelation, Ratzinger recalled that "faith in redemption cannot be separated from faith in the Creator."[19] This is the place where he recognized other religions that, although they do not have a precise revelation, nevertheless proceed from the intuition of God that is inscribed on the human heart. Just as it is crucial not to lose the connection between faith and reason, so it is necessary to keep faith in creation (its cosmic character) united with faith in the covenant (its historical character).

In 2002, when the Italian edition of the book was presented at the diocesan museum in Milan, Ratzinger was quite insistent on this point. If creation can be interpreted as the place of the *exitus*, the going-forth from God, which became tragic through sin, the *reditus*, the return to God, comes about by redemption, through the Cross of Christ, who becomes the true "Pascha", the Passover from death to life, from the human to the divine. Hence Ratzinger's conclusion: "The historical liturgy of Christendom is and always

---

[18] Hanna-Barbara Gerl, *Romano Guardini: La vita e l'opera* (Brescia: Morcelliana, 1988), 137.

[19] J. Ratzinger, *Spirit of the Liturgy*, 24.

will be cosmic, without separation and without confusion, and only as such does it stand erect in its full grandeur."[20]

JESUS, THE LAMB PROVIDED BY GOD

Another element of the Jewish liturgy that is repeated and brought to fulfillment by the Christian liturgy is that of vicarious representation. God's request to Abraham to sacrifice his own son, his only-begotten and firstborn, has vicarious significance. Isaac is sacrificed and saved on behalf of all Abraham's descendants. Similarly, in the institution of the Jewish Passover, the firstborn sons who are claimed by God and therefore to be sacrificed are saved, vicariously representing the whole people. Hence, in the New Testament, the insistence on Jesus as the firstborn Son. He is the true Lamb, provided by God, and this time truly sacrificed, for mankind and for creation.

Continuing his comparison of Jewish worship and Christian liturgy, Ratzinger pointed out a growing dissatisfaction with the Temple sacrifice, particularly in the prophets. Saint Stephen refers to this dissatisfaction when, in his speech before the Sanhedrin, he affirms that Jesus is the true sanctuary. With his Resurrection, he inaugurates the new Temple, the place of true adoration, which has a universal character. "[The] outstretched arms [of Jesus] on the Cross span the world, in order to draw all men into the embrace of eternal love."[21]

CHRISTIANS NEED CHURCHES

From the theological premises outlined briefly here, Ratzinger derived his responses for today. To those who maintain that the true Christian liturgy is carried out in everyday life lived in love, he responded that the "today" brought by Jesus embraces the entire time of the Church. In this day is found the dawn of the one-time sacrifice of Jesus and of the foundation of the Church and the "always" of the intermediate time of awaiting Christ's return. For this reason, we still need the sacred space of church buildings, liturgical seasons, and mediating symbols.

---

[20] Ibid., 34.
[21] Ibid., 48.

THE FAITHFUL FACING THE PRIEST?

One of the main novelties introduced in the Christian liturgy after Vatican II was the different position of the altar and the orientation of the priest. In order to promote the active participation of the faithful at Mass, the altar was shifted toward the center of the apse, while the priest, in reciting the prayer of consecration, no longer turns his back on those present but is facing toward them. Only this form, supposedly, corresponded to the meaning of the Christian liturgy, to the invitation addressed to the faithful to participate actively in the celebration. In Ratzinger's view, nevertheless, the innovation results from a misunderstanding. The priest who celebrated facing the altar was not turning his back on the faithful but, rather, was praying together with them facing the east, toward Jesus, who is the true Sun that comes from the east. In this way, lay people and priests have the same orient-ation. "They did not close themselves into a circle; they did not gaze at one another; but as the pilgrim People of God they set off for the *Oriens*, for the Christ who comes to meet us."[22]

Among other things, according to Ratzinger, the new orientation of the priest has fostered a clericalization such as has never been seen before. On this point, nevertheless, he was in agreement with Father von Balthasar, too, who used to speak about clericalism in a twofold sense: [a] the clericalism of clerics understood as being attached to their works, of liturgists who maintain that they always and everywhere have the last word; [b] the clericalism of priests who never stop talking and thus give the impression that they trust much more in their own word than in the word of God and even claim to suggest to the people the words in which they should turn to God. Having said that, Ratzinger did not consider himself nostalgic for the past. Some changes brought about by Vatican II were indispensable: it was right to bring the people closer to the altar, which was often too far away from the people; it was also important to distinguish the place of the liturgy of the Word from the specifically Eucharistic place.

Nevertheless, we cannot do without the orientation toward Christ. "Looking at the priest has no importance. What matters is looking

---

[22] Ibid., 80.

together at . . . the One who is to come."[23] What is to be done, then? Go back to the old way, as the Lefebvrites claim to do? This is not the cardinal's solution, because there is nothing more harmful in the liturgy than continual changes. The way out, in his opinion, is through the centrality given, not to the figure of the priest, but rather to the Crucified. Very soon in Christian tradition the east was correlated with the sign of the cross. Placed at the center of the altar, the crucifix can become the interior east of faith, the true center to which both priests and faithful look.

ART AND LITURGY

As is well known, Judaism and Islam allow no room at all for images in their worship. On the contrary, Ratzinger said, iconoclasm, the total absence of images, is not part of Christianity, which is centered on the Incarnation of Jesus, the Son of God. "Images of beauty, in which the mystery of the invisible God becomes visible, are an essential part of Christian worship."[24] It is not surprising, therefore, that Christian images should develop around the figure of Jesus, in particular around his Resurrection, rereading the biblical events that refer to him and interpreting them in a Christian sense. None of the images handed down, nevertheless, was a portrait of Jesus; rather, they were inspired by his death and Resurrection in order to guide the faithful along the path of life. This is the foundation of the icon, which, according to Orthodox theologians, is an art not created by human hands but given by God.

From these premises, Ratzinger derived his principles for liturgical art. Art finds its contents in the images of salvation history, starting from creation down to the Resurrection and the return of Jesus. Through the sacraments, in particular Baptism and the Eucharist, Christian art becomes sacred. It is centered on the Paschal Mystery of Jesus, by which Christ is depicted as crucified, as risen, as the One who comes again. Nevertheless, it also has to do with the life of Christians. Consequently, Christ and the images of the saints lead beyond what is merely visible and introduce the viewer to the mystery. Therefore, the image has a function in the liturgy and

---

[23] Ibid., 81.
[24] Ibid., 131.

must be in communion with the faith of the Church. This means that Christian art, while certainly free, cannot be merely subjective, cannot simply be produced, but must be generated by a vision of faith.

MUSIC AND LITURGY

Ratzinger started from an observation: When God comes into contact with man, mere words are not enough. Points of human existence are touched that immediately give rise to song. So it happens in the liberation of Israel from Egypt, in the Resurrection of Christ, who had crossed over the abyss that separates death from life, and so it happens in Baptism, when Christians are born to new life. This is the fundamental reason for the praise of God, which is the very essence of the liturgy. And this is the reason why the Psalter became the prayer book of the pilgrim Church. By singing the psalms, Christians express situations of need and of joy and, above all, give expression to the story of God's love for mankind, which is manifested in creation and redemption.

As praise of love, Christian music is a gift of the Spirit, an inebriation that nevertheless cannot become frantic, forgetful of reason. Indeed, the Spirit who comes from God leads to the *Logos*, leads to a kind of music characterized by the lifting up of the heart, by a kind of worship that is in keeping with reason. The meaning conveyed by the *Logos*, nevertheless, does not concern the individual alone. It takes us out of isolation and brings us into the wide, eternal spaces of the communion of saints. But it is necessary to take yet another step. The liturgy, and with it the song and music of the Church, have a cosmic dimension. "All our singing is a singing and praying with the great liturgy that spans the whole of creation."[25] Hence pure subjectivism is overcome in art. Subjective creativity cannot separate itself from the message of beauty that comes from the cosmos, at the summons of the love that is at the origin of man and of the cosmos itself. For this reason, even in a crisis, we cannot doubt the artistic inspiration that comes from the liturgy and from sacred music.

---

[25] Ibid., 152.

ACTIVE PARTICIPATION AND LATIN

One of the leading ideas of the liturgical reform of Vatican II was that of active participation. For Ratzinger, certainly, this was a good principle; he immediately specified, though, that the word "participation" refers to an action in which the principal actor is not man. In the case of the liturgy, the action we are talking about is the Canon of the Mass, the great prayer that constitutes the nucleus of the Eucharistic celebration. This prayer, however, is not so much a discourse as a divine action that is accomplished through a human discourse pronounced by the priest who acts in the person of Christ. The true liturgical action in which all the faithful are invited to participate is, therefore, the action of God himself. But how can man take part in this action? Through acceptance of the sacrifice of the Son, with the prayer that man might be transformed into the *Logos* and become, in turn, a rational sacrifice, the true Body of Christ. In this, priests and faithful are united, even if only the priest, by the Sacrament of Holy Orders, can recite the prayer of the Canon. Active participation, therefore, cannot mean a tendency to operate continually on the liturgy. On the contrary, Ratzinger maintained, we must overcome the temptation to act arbitrarily, to manipulate the liturgy, and to think of it as the object of our own invention and creativity. As for the actions such as the readings, the songs, the presentation of the gifts, it is necessary to assign them in a sensible way.

One of the most expected and characteristic innovations of Vatican II was the introduction of vernacular languages into the liturgy, which gradually were substituted for the Latin until they replaced it entirely. This development, according to Ratzinger, was desirable, and there is certainly no need to turn back. Nevertheless, he exhorted liturgists and the faithful to be more open toward Latin, more tolerant of the liturgical form that was in effect until the end of the 1960s. A break like the one that occurred in those years had never happened in the history of the Church. There was, as he put it, an exaggerated mania for change on the part of the liturgists. The danger is that the Church's whole past may be indicted in this way. On the contrary, the beginnings of the liturgical movement had been elevating: "When I think about the time of the Liturgical Movement, in which I indeed shared, it was simply marvelous . . . to understand the structure of Lent, the whole structure of the missal, and so much more. It was just a matter of finding one's way into this treasury of things that had developed and grown, and thereby into the glory that is offered to us there from God."[26] By regaining this spirit, in Ratzinger's view, it will be possible to overcome the aftermath of a hasty and sometimes disrespectful liturgical reform.

The Jubilee Year 2000

Ratzinger prepared for the Jubilee Year 2000 with interior participation and with some anxiety. In May 1998, when he saw the list of 240 celebrations planned for the Holy Year, he did not hide his bewilderment.[27] Not only was there a danger that the organizational machinery would break down with such a plethora of events, meetings, and rallies; there was also the problem of preserving the spirit of an event that seemed to be suffering from a worsening case of elephantiasis. When Seewald asked him the significance of the year 2000, he explained that the celebration of the Jubilee does not coincide at all with any great cosmic, doctrinal, or religious event. Stated positively, the jubilee recalls the birth of Jesus Christ and invites all the faithful to a renewed encounter with him and to put into practice his proclamation of love and peace. By analogy with the biblical jubilee, it is also a challenge for all mankind to free itself from old debts and to attempt a new beginning.

For this purpose, the cardinal concluded, "we really ought to make an effort to get out of this over-furnished, crammed world into an inner freedom and vigilance. It means, too, that we need penance, without which there can be no new beginning."[28]

REQUESTS FOR FORGIVENESS

Meanwhile, though, one of the key points on which the pope meant to base the celebration of the Great Jubilee, the request for forgive-

---

[26] Joseph Ratzinger, *God and the World*, trans. Henry Taylor (San Francisco: Ignatius Press, 2002), 417.

[27] Andrea Tornielli, *Benedetto XVI: Il custode della fede* (Casale Monferrato: Piemme, 2005), 222.

[28] Joseph Ratzinger, *Salt of the Earth*, trans. Adrian Walker (San Francisco: Ignatius Press, 1997), 281.

ness, was stirring up a dust storm because the pope's generous intention was at risk of being compromised, within the Church as well as outside her, by the usual progressives who tried to turn all of Christian history into nothing but a parade of corruption and degradation. Ratzinger understood that the problem was complex and assigned the International Theological Commission, of which he was president, to examine the matter in depth. A commission was also formed to which the Italian Bruno Forte was appointed president, which drew up a document, *Memory and Reconciliation*, which was presented to the press a few days before the pope's great request for forgiveness, scheduled for March 12, 2000. The ones presenting the document were Ratzinger and the theologian of the papal household, Father Georges Cottier.

The cardinal did not conceal his initial perplexity: Church history tells us about manifold sins, but to whom should they be attributed? Can the Church be responsible for them? What sort of confession, repentance, and forgiveness is possible here? The first consideration is that I do not confess the sins of others but, rather, my own; as a second point, it should be added that the confession takes place in communion with others and in the presence of God. This common confession is the premise for future reconciliation. Something of this sort occurred in the Old Testament, too, when, in the penitential psalms, Israel confessed the rebellion of its fathers against God's covenant. Israel did not pray in this way "in order to condemn those others, their fathers, but so as to recognize in the story of this sinning its own situation and so as to prepare itself for repentance and forgiveness."[29]

That being said, Ratzinger added, the pope's gesture would not be surprising at all nor should it cause a sensation. The uproar was caused by the past reaction of the Catholic Church, which had been put on the defensive by the Reformation and the Enlightenment. Having been described as the enemy of humanity, the "infamous thing" to be crushed pitilessly and relentlessly, the Church was led to develop an apologetic attitude that relegated the request for forgiveness and the purification of memory to a secondary level. Hence

---

[29] The document "The Church's Guilt", which is a revised text of the presentation of *Memory and Reconciliation*, is contained in Joseph Ratzinger, *Pilgrim Fellowship of Faith*, trans. Henry Taylor (San Francisco: Ignatius Press, 2005), 274–83 at 278.

the necessity for some criteria for a correct interpretation of this attitude of purification. The present-day Church cannot turn herself into a sort of tribunal of history; to confess means, according to Saint Augustine, to acknowledge the truth and at the same time to give praise. "In any honest examination of conscience we can see that for our part in every generation we have done much that is evil. Yet we can also see that, in spite of our sins, God has always purified and renewed the Church and has always entrusted great things to fragile vessels."[30] Notwithstanding the initial perplexity, Ratzinger had thus provided the fundamental theological support for one of the most magnificently human and religious gestures of the pontificate of John Paul II.

THE SECRET OF FATIMA

On May 13, 1981, John Paul II was seriously wounded during a general Wednesday audience on Saint Peter's Square. The attacker was not an isolated madman but, rather, an international terrorist, behind whom dark conspiracies could be glimpsed.[31] After his arrest, the terrorist marveled at the fact that two such sure shots had not killed the pope. The latter attributed his survival to Our Lady of Fatima, whose feast fell on that day. The hand of the Virgin Mary had deflected the bullet, preventing its fatal outcome. As a result of this conviction, the pope decided, in keeping with the request contained in the first two secrets of Fatima, which had already been revealed, to consecrate the world to the Immaculate Heart of Mary. For this purpose, he himself composed a prayer.

The pope, who was still recuperating, could not be present personally at the first of these consecrations, which took place on June 7, 1981, the Solemnity of Pentecost, in the Basilica of Santa Maria Maggiore in Rome. In the following years, he repeated the consecration on March 13, 1982, in Fatima, and on March 25, 1984, in Saint Peter's in Rome. Meanwhile, after the assassination attempt and such a solemn manifestation by John Paul II of his conviction that he owed his life to Our Lady of Fatima, there was a growing impatience to know the text of the third secret, written by the

---

[30] Ibid., 282.
[31] See Riccardi, *Giovanni Paolo II*, chap. 6: "L'attentato e il martirio", 190ff.

only visionary still alive, Sister Lúcia dos Santos, and delivered to the pope by the bishop of Leiria. It was known, however, that the original of the manuscript was preserved at the Congregation for the Doctrine of the Faith. Consequently, many journalists asked Ratzinger the reason for not divulging the secret. Patiently, the cardinal would repeat that the Church wanted to avoid sensationalism, but with the passage of years this did not rule out the possibility that sooner or later the document might in fact be published.

On May 13, 2000, John Paul II made a new journey to Fatima to beatify the two shepherd children, Francesco and Jacinta Marto, who had died not long after the apparitions of the Virgin in 1917. At the conclusion of the ceremony, in the presence of John Paul II and of Sister Lúcia, Angelo Cardinal Sodano finally revealed to the approximately 600,000 people present the contents of the now-famous secret that had been put into writing by Sister Lúcia at the command of the bishop of Leiria on January 3, 1944. In short, the text contained an urgent call to repentance. It spoke, then, about a bishop clothed in white, who, after traveling through a great city in ruins, was killed by a group of soldiers, shot by various firearms and arrows. After him, other bishops, priests, religious, and lay faithful died.

According to Cardinal Sodano, the text was a prophetic vision of the assassination attempt on Saint Peter's Square in 1981. For a more thorough understanding, he referred to a forthcoming publication in which the text of the secret would be accompanied by a theological interpretation written by Cardinal Ratzinger. Published on June 26 of that same year, Ratzinger's commentary[32] situated the Fatima apparitions within the context of the private apparitions that punctuate the history of the Church and of mankind. In the biblical revelation that concluded with the Incarnation of his Son, God in reality has said everything; private apparitions are to help the faithful to enter into the fray of human events and to interpret them in the light of Christ. Accurately, the visionary of Fatima said that she had seen as though in a mirror, thus acknowledging the inherent limits of the vision.

---

[32] Congregation for the Doctrine of the Faith, *The Message of Fatima: Theological Commentary by Joseph Cardinal Ratzinger* (Vatican City: Libreria Editrice Vaticana, 2000). This little volume contains a brief history of the text written by Sister Lúcia, the statement by Cardinal Sodano, and the theological commentary by Ratzinger.

According to Ratzinger, the general meaning of the vision is an urgent call to repentance, which is the right response to any historical moment characterized by great dangers. The language, in contrast, is symbolic, recalling some images from the Apocalypse. The angel with the fiery sword to the left of our Lady represents the Last Judgment, while the splendor of the Mother of God and her invitation to repentance underscore the importance of man's freedom, which can turn history in a positive direction. The meaning of the vision is not that it sets a scene in a film; on the contrary, it is "a consoling vision, which seeks to open a history of blood and tears to the healing power of God."[33] Moreover, the blood of the martyrs flows together with the blood of Christ that runs down from the Cross.

The vision, which is initially so frightful, concludes, therefore, with an image of hope. The Church of the martyrs becomes a sign of hope for mankind. The cardinal's interpretation also clarified the meaning of the consecration of the world to the Heart of Mary and of the statement "My Immaculate Heart will triumph." The pierced Heart of God is stronger than rifles and weapons of any sort. Mary's Yes changed history because she enabled God to enter the world and to direct history toward himself.

One final, important clarification concerned the type of vision that the shepherd children of Fatima had. In his typology of visions, the cardinal distinguished: a physical vision, an interior perception through images, and a mystical perception. In this case, it is obviously a vision of the second type, in which the perception of the images comes through the modality allowed by the concepts and knowledge of the children. It must be kept in mind, furthermore, that although Sister Lúcia spoke on behalf of the three, she wrote at a distance of more than twenty years from the event, when the images perceived in her childhood had grown with her. These considerations, nevertheless, from the cardinal's perspective, should not lead us to disdain but rather to value fully the faith of simple believers. This was a profound conviction of the cardinal, who always took very seriously Jesus' so-called cry of jubilation that is recorded by the Gospel of Saint Matthew: "I thank you, Father, Lord of heaven

---

[33] The text of Ratzinger's commentary can be consulted at the Vatican website: Congregation for the Doctrine of the Faith, Documents regarding "The Message of Fatima", June 26, 2000.

and earth, that you have hidden these things from the wise and understanding and revealed them to infants."[34]

AGAINST RELATIVISM

Several months had passed since the conclusion of the incident connected with the revelation of the third secret of Fatima when the publication of the Declaration *Dominus Iesus*[35] by the congregation headed by Ratzinger started a new controversy at the beginning of the celebrations for the year 2000. The genesis of the document is explained by the cardinal himself in his presentation of the text to the press. At the beginning of the third Christian millennium, the prevailing cultural orientation in the West is relativism, which in the field of religion translates into the conviction that all religions are equally valid ways to salvation. For Christianity, this way of thinking essentially involves a rejection of the identification of the historical figure of Jesus of Nazareth with the very reality of God, with the living God. Moreover, by this reasoning, the Church, dogma, and the sacraments do not have an absolute character.

In such a context, missionary work and the invitation to convert are replaced by dialogue, which places one's own faith on the same level as the religions and opinions of others. Ratzinger responds that it is understandable that in a world that is growing increasingly interrelated, religions and cultures should encounter one another, too, fostering mutual enrichment. The idea that religions are all on the same level and differ only by their respective origins and historical contexts is, nevertheless, unacceptable for John Paul II and Ratzinger. If that premise were granted, faith in Jesus Christ as Redeemer would have to fail and the foundation of the mission, the Christian proclamation to the nations, collapse.

UNICITY OF JESUS AND OF THE CHURCH

The intention of those who drafted the declaration that was made public on August 6, 2000, was to propose again the core of Christian doctrine. Hence its principal statements: Jesus is not just one his-

---

[34] Mt 11:25.
[35] The text of the declaration can be found in *AAS* 92 (2000): 742–65, and in *Enchiridion Vaticanum* 19 (Bologna: Dehoniane), 654–709, and, in English translation, on the Vatican website.

torical figure among others. The Son of Mary is the Word who was with the Father from eternity. He came into the world and dwelt among men and made himself known. "It must therefore be *firmly believed* as a truth of Catholic faith that the universal salvific will of the One and Triune God is offered and accomplished once for all in the mystery of the incarnation, death, and resurrection of the Son of God" (no. 14). Just as there is only one Christ, so, too, only one body of his exists, his one spouse, the Catholic Church. The faithful, consequently, are bound to profess that there is a continuity, based on the apostolic succession, between the Church founded by Christ and the Catholic Church.

The text then continued by affirming that the Church is the universal sacrament of salvation. Certainly, the various religious traditions contain and offer religious elements that proceed from God and are part of what the Spirit brings about in human hearts and in the history of peoples, in cultures and religions. The Church founded by Jesus Christ, however, is the instrument for the salvation of all humanity (nos. 21–22). In the future too, moreover, the revelation of Christ will continue to be the true guiding star in history. As already mentioned, the declaration caused an uproar. Against the relativism that threatened several key points of the Catholic Creed, the congregation had decided to propose again forcefully the fullness of the faith. To many observers, nevertheless, this claim appeared to be a repetition of the old axiom, "Outside the Church there is no salvation." In this regard, Tornielli speaks about an avalanche of criticism by representatives of the world religions, of the Christian denominations, and also of prelates of the Catholic Church.[36]

Particularly severe were the observations of Edward Cardinal Cassidy, president of the Pontifical Council for Promoting Christian Unity and of the commission for relations with Jews. The different sensibilities of Ratzinger and Cassidy seemed to replicate, forty years later, the different evaluations of interfaith dialogue by Cardinals Ottaviani and Bea at the time of Vatican II. The understanding between Ratzinger and the Polish pope was, nevertheless, complete, and the response of John Paul II, which Cassidy had called into question, attributing to him greater ecumenical sensitivity than that of the prefect of the Congregation for the Doctrine of the Faith, came

---

[36] Tornielli, *Benedetto XVI*, 198f.

promptly. He had commissioned and closely followed the Declaration *Dominus Iesus* as a christological synthesis of the Jubilee Year. It was a call to Christians "to renew their faith in Christ in the joy of faith".[37]

The critiques coming from Germany, too, were particularly severe. To these Ratzinger responded personally in an interview granted to the *Frankfurter Allgemeine Zeitung*, the largest daily newspaper in the country.[38] In it the cardinal said that he was displeased by the fact that the critics had focused their attention on points that, all told, are secondary. The title itself of the declaration was a profession of faith. It was "a great and solemn recognition of Jesus Christ as Lord at the height of the Holy Year, thus bringing what is essential firmly to the center of this occasion, which is always prone to externalism."[39] The most insidious reactions, finally, were those of friends who turned to the cardinal directly asking for explanations. Among these one long letter stood out, written by the Greek Orthodox Metropolitan Damaskinos,[40] who, as we have seen, had been a student of Ratzinger and had with him a bond of sincere friendship.

The Metropolitan pointed out, first of all, a discontinuity between the teaching of the professor and the document of the congregation. He then concentrated his critique on the expression "a single Catholic and apostolic Church . . . [which] subsists in the Catholic Church, governed by the successor of Peter."[41] This statement seemed to reiterate the old formulas that exclude other Churches, which are invited not so much to collaborate as to return to the Church of Rome, which maintains that she is the one, catholic, and apostolic Church. At that time, Damaskinos was, among other things, seriously ill; the cardinal responded with a very affectionate letter, reassuring him not only of his friendship but also of the continuity of his theological career. On the other hand, he specified

---

[37] Ibid., 200.

[38] The text of the interview was then published in Italian in *L'Osservatore Romano*, October 8, 2000, and in the English edition in three parts: November 22, 2000 (p. 10), November 29, 2000 (p. 6), and December 6, 2000, (p. 8).

[39] Ibid., English ed., November 22, 2000, (p. 10).

[40] The letter from Metropolitan Damaskinos is recorded by Ratzinger himself in the volume *Pilgrim Fellowship of Faith*, 217–28.

[41] Ibid., 223–24.

that between the Catholic Church and the Orthodox, the wounds result not so much from doctrine as from the lacerations of history. Therefore, these elements of a historical nature are what many times intervene as obstacles to communion, which, however, cannot be achieved by an injunction by the pope or by the patriarch but can only be granted by the Spirit of Jesus. And he concluded: "To us it is not given to resolve the paradox of the faithfulness of God and the faithlessness of men. . . . I understand *Dominus Iesus* as intended to transform the indifference with which all churches are regarded as different but equally valid, so that the validity of faith itself disappears in scepticism, once more into a lively suffering and thus to kindle anew the true fervor of ecumenism."[42]

Even more convincing, finally, was the formulation recorded in the new book-length interview, *God and the World*.[43] When the journalist asked him about the importance of prayer for the unity of Christians, the cardinal answered:

> It's not a matter of our wanting to achieve certain processes of integration, but we hope that the Lord will awaken people's faith everywhere in such a way that it overflows from one to the other, and the one Church is there. As Catholics, we are persuaded that the basic shape of this one Church is given us in the Catholic Church, but that she is moving toward the future and will allow herself to be educated and led by the Lord.[44]

Christianity and the world religions

The voices protesting the publication of the Declaration *Dominus Iesus* in the Catholic and Christian camp were joined, according to Ratzinger himself, by the cry of outrage from the major non-Christian religions, particularly of the Indian religions.[45] The wave of protest, however, did not come from India but, rather, from those in Europe who were intrigued by those noble religions without reflecting on the intellectual implications resulting from them.

---

[42] Ibid., 240–41.

[43] Joseph Ratzinger, *God and the World*, trans. Henry Taylor (San Francisco: Ignatius Press, 2002).

[44] Ibid., 452.

[45] Joseph Ratzinger, *Truth and Tolerance: Christian Belief and World Religions*, trans. Henry Taylor (San Francisco: Ignatius Press, 2004), 9.

To these protesting voices, Ratzinger responded with the volume *Truth and Tolerance*, which, from the beginning, gave evidence of the underlying concern of the declaration on the unicity of Jesus. The religion that contemporary man is disposed to accept is the one of Oriental origin that is based on mystical experience: an indefinite religion of the spirit that finally leaves behind the articles and formulas of the historical religions, especially their demands in the areas of cognition and morality.

Hence the question that Ratzinger asked himself almost obsessively in that period: "Can truth be recognized? Or, is the question about truth simply inappropriate in the realm of religion and belief?"[46] For the cardinal, there is no way out of this dilemma unless reason and religion turn to dialogue, without one being absorbed into the other. In play here are not the interests of one religion or another, but rather the interests of mankind, of man, who is in danger of being definitively defeated by a vision of religion that is confined solely to the dimension of feeling, without any influence on the lives of individuals or peoples.

This is the starting point from which Ratzinger can propose again his vision of Christianity as the religion of rationality. This journey begins already in the Old Covenant, when the God of the patriarchs appears as a personal God, the defender of human dignity, while the rationality of the world finds its foundation in the founding wisdom of God. In the great wealth brought by the Old Covenant, one not insignificant limit persisted, according to Ratzinger: that of blood. The Greeks who admired the law and the religion of Moses could only become proselytes, since full membership in the religion of Israel was bound up with descent from Abraham. Christianity broke down the wall of blood and, as the religion of the *Logos*, of the incarnate Word, presented itself immediately as a way that unites Athens and Jerusalem, "rational thought and revelation, [and] exactly answer[s] the requirements of reason and of the deeper religious longings."[47]

Finally, there is a further element that, according to the cardinal, contributed in antiquity to the victory of Christianity over the pagan religions: the moral seriousness of Christianity. The most beautiful

---

[46] Ibid., 10.
[47] Ibid., 153.

and concise expression of this Christian synthesis is found, according to Ratzinger, in the First Letter of Saint John (4:16): "We know and believe the love God has for us." He comments: "Christ had become for these people the discovery of creative love; the rational principle of the universe had revealed itself as love—as that greater reason which accepts into itself even darkness and irrationality and heals them."[48] In conclusion, the synthesis between reason, faith, and life was what enabled Christianity to establish itself as a world religion and to advance the claim of being the true religion.

The initial covenant with reason brought about in Christianity a first phase of demythologization, through which the idols of the gods were overthrown; then, however, the recognition of the religious longing present in the pagan religions inaugurated a second phase that honored the divine element present in the pagan religions. A name like Santa Maria sopra Minerva [a Basilica in Rome] makes the two phases of the transition clear: first, the truth took away from the gods the halo of divinity; at the same time, however, their truth came to light also. "They were a reflection of divinity, a presentiment of figures in which their hidden significance was purified and fulfilled."[49]

From this perspective, according to Ratzinger, another question arises concerning freedom of choice with regard to religion. He observed that today freedom is rightly considered one of the fundamental values, while the concept of truth is regarded with suspicion. Moreover, there is the skepticism, nourished by the natural sciences, that tends to consider subjective whatever cannot be explained and documented exactly. Both the intellectual and the political history of the past century showed that freedom without truth leads to destruction and slaughter. For this reason, freedom is neither a merely abstract nor a merely individual concept. Hence the necessity of a law that regulates common life, that is not simply at the mercy of majority rule but is aimed at the common good.

Ratzinger's conclusion for a West that is bewildered and in crisis is therefore as follows: "Reason needs to listen to the great religious traditions. . . . There is no great philosophy that does not draw its life from listening to and accepting religious tradition. . . .

---

[48] Ibid., 155–56.
[49] Ibid., 230.

It is precisely in connection with . . . the question of freedom's being rooted in the truth of what is good, in the truth of man and of the world, that the need for listening is most clearly seen."[50]

THE DUPUIS CASE

In his book on faith, truth, and tolerance, Ratzinger made clear once again the connection between faith and reason that, in his view, is a distinctive feature of Christianity. Only this indispensable relation allows the Christian to attain the truth and therefore to claim for it a significant place in public life. The religions that come from India, like New Age religion, are regarded with suspicion. The former, in the cardinal's view, know of no binding doctrine of faith, while they present a system of practices, a code of rituals that guarantees salvation. In this sense, they provide a system of thought resembling ancient gnosis. The divine in itself can never enter the world of appearances in which we live. It remains beyond words and thought.

In reality, the cardinal's polemic does not argue against the Indian religions but, rather, against the consequences that result from them in Europe and America. "The way that European and American thinking has turned back to India's philosophical and theological vision has the effect of further strengthening [the] relativizing of all religious figures."[51] Ratzinger said that one particularly negative example of this orientation in the West is the New Age movement, an altogether anti-rationalistic model of religion, a modern mysticism that tends to absorb the individual subject into the All. For New Age proponents, redemption consists of immersion in the fullness of life, of returning to the fatherland within the All. A preoccupation with this orientation, which at that time threatened to create a massive breach among Catholics, was probably at the origin of a new and painful theological case that played out precisely in the principal Pontifical University, the Gregorian in Rome.

Since 1984, Jacques Dupuis, an older Belgian Jesuit who had behind him a long stay in India, had taught theology of religions and Christology at the Jesuits' university.[52] An admirer of *ressourcement*

---

[50] Ibid., 252.

[51] Ibid., 122.

[52] For information about Dupuis and his thought, see the introductory essay by W. R. Burrows, editor of the posthumous volume by the Belgian Jesuit, *Perché non sono eretico: Teologia del pluralismo religioso* (Bologna: EMI, 2014).

(return to the sources), and supported by de Lubac and his confreres in Fourvière, Dupuis was the promoter of an open Christology that relied on the contributions of other religions. In Dupuis' interpretation, Jesus Christ, the Word of God, who is the ultimate criterion of value and truth in all creation, is thought of as being present in other religious traditions, also. The unsurpassable expression of this *Logos* is the sacrificial love of God revealed in the life, teaching, death, and Resurrection of Jesus. He added, nevertheless: "The Word of God, eternally present in the divine life, is also universally present in human history from the moment of creation."[53] He explained that there is an action of the *Logos* even before the Incarnation that plays the role of preparing for the Gospel, and there is a lasting, salvific action of the Spirit that is performed essentially in relation to the Christ event.[54]

For Dupuis, this was the way to give full value to religious experiences different from Christianity, particularly to those present in the Indian religions. He had expressed these convictions of his in two volumes[55] that drew the attention of the Congregation for the Doctrine of the Faith. In 1998, the congregation delivered to him a first notification. The measure, which involved prohibiting an instructor, who at the time was seventy-four years old and on the verge of retirement, from teaching seemed ungenerous. Summoned to a meeting with Cardinal Ratzinger, the professor had the impression that the cardinal was not well informed about the content of his works and about the accusations themselves that had been leveled against him. He refused, therefore, to sign the document that urged him to acknowledge the errors attributed to him by the notification.

Some other passages from *Dominus Iesus* were also interpreted as an attack on Dupuis and on his theology of religious pluralism. In fact, on February 26, 2001, the Jesuit received another notification, milder in its accusations, which he signed at the advice of his superiors, who feared more severe measures if he were to refuse. The Dupuis case had thus come to its conclusion. The elderly Jesuit, nevertheless, suffered because of the accusations, which he considered unjustified, even though William Burrows, editor of the

---

[53] Ibid., 86.

[54] Ibid., 90.

[55] Jacques Dupuis, *Toward a Christian Theology of Religious Pluralism* (Ossining, N.Y.: Orbis Books, 1997), and idem, *Christianity and the Religions: From Confrontation to Dialogue* (Ossining, N.Y.: Orbis Books, 2002).

posthumous volume *Perché non sono eretico* (Why I am not a heretic) must admit "that his ecclesiology is not high enough for his critics, and this is the main problem that the Congregation for the Doctrine of the Faith raised in reference to the work of the Belgian theologian."[56]

---

[56] Dupuis, *Perché non sono eretico*, 55.

XII

THIS LIFE IS VERY HARD

The Christian roots of Europe

The fundamental change for Europe that Ratzinger hoped for in the aftermath of the fall of the Berlin Wall in 1989[1] had not happened. Both materialism and relativism, which the cardinal feared so much, had continued their unstoppable advance. The repeated invitations of John Paul II to rediscover the unity of the continent on the basis of its common Christian tradition so as to make it the strong point in a new peacemaking and evangelizing mission at the global level had reaped the applause of young people but had gone no farther; they had almost no influence on the decision-making centers.

There was corroboration of this, during the Jubilee Year itself. While the Church was celebrating with great solemnity the anniversary of two thousand years of Christianity, on September 14, 2000, the elderly German President Roman Herzog made public the plan for a Charter of Fundamental Rights of the European Union, developed in view of enlarging the community from fifteen to twenty-seven member States. In the introduction, the document referred to the "humanistic and religious cultural heritage" of the Old Continent. France, nevertheless, which presided over the European Community that year, vigorously opposed that formula in the name of republican *laïcité* (secularity).[2] The Charter of Rights approved by the European Parliament and adopted by the Summit in Nice the following December contained only one reference to the "spiritual and moral patrimony" of Europe. John Paul II and, with him,

---

[1] See the preceding chapter.
[2] See Bernard Lecomte, *Benoît XVI* (Paris: Perrin, 2006), 98.

Ratzinger were deeply disappointed by this and did not delay in setting forth the reasons for their disagreement.

EUROPE, ITS ORIGINS, ITS VALUES

On November 28, 2000, Ratzinger was in Berlin, where he gave a short but effective conference on the present and future spiritual foundations of Europe.[3] The premise of the cardinal's reasoning was that "Europe is not a continent that can be comprehended neatly in geographical terms; rather, it is a cultural and historical concept."[4] At the origin of the two fundamental nuclei that make up Europe today was the Roman Empire that had become Christian. In the West, after the conquest of the southern shore of the Mediterranean by the Arabs, the Holy Roman Empire was formed, inaugurated by Charlemagne on Christmas Eve in the year 800. Besides the regions on the northern shore of the Mediterranean, which now make up the *limes*, or southern boundary, of the new formation, it embraces the regions of ancient Gaul, Germany, and Britain. In the East, where the Roman Empire with its capital, Byzantium, resisted the advance of Islam longer, there was also a shift toward the north, toward the Slavic countries.

These two territorial spheres, associated with the Latin and Greek languages, now constitute the European continent. They have in common the Bible, the thought of the Church Fathers, and monasticism. Nevertheless, they also have an element of differentiation that was decisive for the later development of Europe. In the East, Church and empire seemed to be almost identified, and the fates of the empire and of the Orthodox Church were closely joined. In the West, on the contrary, where Constantine had abandoned the ancient capital so as to transfer the court to Byzantium, two powers were formed: emperor and pope had different and distinct authorities. Not only did they often find themselves taking different positions, but as early as the fourth century, the idea of the two powers developed, formulated in a particularly effective way by Pope

---

[3] The conference "Europe: Its Spiritual Foundations Today and Tomorrow" lends its title to Ratzinger's second anthology of various texts concerning the Old Continent. See Joseph Ratzinger, *Europe Today and Tomorrow*, trans. Michael J. Miller (San Francisco: Ignatius Press, 2004). The text of this first conference is found on pp. 11–34.

[4] Ibid., 11.

Gelasius I in the late fifth century: "For matters concerning eternal life the Christian emperors needed the priests (*pontifices*), and the latter, in turn, abided by the imperial ordinances in the course of temporal affairs."[5]

Initially the principle of separation between the two powers was the cause of countless conflicts and disputes because of the tendency of both powers to impose on the other. In 1453, moreover, with the fall of Byzantium, the picture described thus far underwent further shifts and corrections. On the one hand, there was the dissolution of ancient Byzantium; on the other, this second Europe, until then characterized by Greek language and thought, gained a new center in Moscow, which expanded its boundaries toward the East. At the height of the Renaissance, the Greek language and culture enriched Western thought, whereas in the East the Slavic language and culture became predominant. A century later, the Latin half of the West, too, underwent a profound transformation. First, at the time of the Protestant Reformation, a large part of the Germanic world separated itself from Rome. Then, after the discovery of America, the subdivision of Europe into a Latin Catholic half and a Protestant German half was transferred to the New Continent as well, with far-reaching repercussions.

A further fundamental change occurred at the turn of the nineteenth century with the French Revolution, which rejected the sacral foundation of history, which now was supposed to depend on reason and the will of the citizens. Religion and faith in God were declared to belong to the sphere of sentiments, and so they no longer had general relevance. Consequently, they were declared a private affair that must not interfere with public life. This gave birth, for the first time, to the purely secular State, in which the citizens were divided between lay persons and Catholics, between agnostics and believers. This, in Ratzinger's view, was a schism, a separation within the Old Continent and the States that were part of it, the seriousness of which we are beginning to realize only today.

The final stage of Europe's journey seems to be that of technological and commercial culture at the global level. With these characteristics, it has extended its model not only to the New Continent, America, but has also penetrated into Africa and Asia. Here,

---

[5] Ibid., 16.

however, Ratzinger sees a paradoxical and tragic historical coincidence. At the moment when its model of living has been universalized, Europe seems to be paralyzed within; this has affected its circulatory system to the point where it constantly needs religious and cultural injections coming from other continents. These repeated transplants, nevertheless, are causing the rapid and progressive loss of its identity. Hence the need to return to the origins, to acknowledge rights that are not created by legislators and cannot be conferred by popular vote but, rather, belong to everyone and are the origin of human dignity and freedom.

Now, Ratzinger concludes, no one can deny that human dignity and the fundamental rights that are derived from it must precede any political deliberation whatsoever. The memory of the Nazi horror is, in this regard, an inescapable warning. In more recent times, genetic manipulation, abortion, trafficking in human organs, and other kinds of attacks on human life from its first moments urge us also to recognize moral values connected with the dignity of man and exempt from political control. Hence the need to recover the bond between reason and religion, to overcome laicism for the sake of harmonious collaboration between secularists and believers.

WHY DOES THE WEST HATE ITSELF?

The final question addressed by Ratzinger in his conference in Berlin concerned respect for Christian religion in Western society. He started with an observation: In our countries, if someone offends the God of the Jews, he is rightly fined. The same thing happens with the God of the Muslims and the Qur'an. On the other hand, when it comes to Christians and what is dear to them, now freedom of speech suddenly appears to be the supreme good, and therefore any request for limits seems inadmissible, harmful to tolerance and freedom. Then the cardinal continued with an observation that recurred often in this period: "Here we notice a self-hatred in the Western world that is strange and that can be considered pathological."[6]

Of all people, the proponents of multiculturalism, the very ones who prove to have so much understanding for the values of other

---

[6] Ibid., 33.

continents, see in our own history only what is objectionable and destructive. Multiculturalism is then transformed into the abandonment of and contempt for even what is great and pure about us, what is sacred. Lack of respect for the Christian God brings with it also a contempt for what is sacred for others. It is no accident that the absolute laicism that is present in Europe is unknown to other cultures, which are convinced that a world without God has no future. The Charter of Fundamental Rights could therefore be a sign that Europe is still seeking its soul, the values of the spirit. From this perspective, Christians could be a creative minority and make their own contribution so that Europe might rediscover the best of its heritage and be able to offer an invaluable service for all mankind.

THE PREPOLITICAL MORAL FOUNDATIONS OF THE STATE

Several months after the signing of the Treaty of Nice, which introduced flexibility and reforms with a view to enlarging the European Union, there was an attack on the Twin Towers in New York. It was the first and most sensational signal that made evident the weakness of the West and of Europe against international terrorism. Europeans then noticed the urgent need to arrive at a European constitution that would serve as a foundation for the modifications that were deemed necessary both within the Union and outside of it, by implementing a common foreign policy. Therefore, a commission was formed, with French ex-President Valéry Giscard d'Estaing presiding, for the purpose of composing a draft constitution to be finalized by October 2004 for the fiftieth anniversary of the signing of the first Treaty of Rome in 1954.

As a contribution to the discussion and the preparation of the European constitutional charter, the Catholic Academy of Bavaria, with headquarters in Munich, organized a debate between Jürgen Habermas, a German philosopher and sociologist of the Frankfurt School, and a well-known exponent of the laicist view of the State, and Cardinal Ratzinger. The two speakers were to present in a brief talk their respective points of view, then the invited guests —philosophers, political scientists, theologians—could ask questions. This was for Ratzinger a new opportunity to expound his theory of the prepolitical moral foundations that alone can safeguard man and his dignity with regard to the State. In the State, the rule "might makes right" must not prevail but, rather, the force of law that is opposed to the violence of the powerful. Besides, Ratzinger also argued, guaranteeing the participation of all citizens in the formation of law is the only convincing argument in favor of democracy. Even majorities, however, can be blind and approve laws that oppress racial or religious minorities. Hence, once again the conclusion: "There are then, let us say, self-subsistent values that flow from the essence of what it is to be a man, and are therefore inviolable; no other man can infringe them."[7]

Then, in order to justify the urgency of setting in motion ethical forces capable of opposing the new forms of violence, the cardinal provided a quick panorama of developments in recent decades. In the years following World War II, fear of the atomic bomb had served as a deterrent, impressing upon the two blocs the limits of their respective powers. Now, though, after September 11, 2001, new forms of terror had demonstrated that it did not take major conflicts to make the world unlivable. This new sickness of mankind originated in two particularly dangerous hotbeds: religious fanaticism and the reduction of man to a product of technology. The activity of terrorists is often justified as a defense of religious tradition against the godlessness of Western society. This in fact is undeniable. Ratzinger wonders, nevertheless, whether the observation that the religious factor may possibly deviate in the direction of intolerance and error necessarily has to lead to the elimination of religion, as though overcoming it were a prerequisite for the progress of mankind?

The cardinal's question is reinforced by another anxious observation. Not only religion is threatened. Reason, too, is at risk. The development of technology is such that now it is capable of making human beings, of producing them in test tubes. This leads to the temptation to achieve the perfect human being, to perform experiments on him, to get rid of him when he does not meet the producer's standards. And all this in the name of reason and science. Moreover, the atomic bomb, too, is a product of reason, and, for this reason, questions about its reliability can legitimately be raised. Hence the cardinal's conclusion that religion and reason have both

---

[7] Ibid., 71.

fallen under suspicion. Can we renounce both, or rather should they collaborate, "remind[ing] each other where their limits are, thereby encouraging a positive path?"[8]

REASON AND FAITH: A POLYPHONIC COLLABORATION

In antiquity, the collaboration between reason and faith took concrete form in their common recognition of so-called "natural law". In brief, faith acknowledged that reason has the ability to construct a natural law independently of religion. Natural law then allowed Christians to acknowledge secular society and other religious communities. The theory of evolution, however, radically caused a crisis in the concept of nature created by God according to rational criteria. If nature is not rational, it is useless and impossible to find criteria of rationality in it. The final element of natural law that is still partially recognized consists, according to Ratzinger, of human rights. They are, nevertheless, difficult to understand and acknowledge without the presupposition that the subject of these rights, man, is the bearer of values that are not to be invented each time but, rather, belong to the species "man". Perhaps, Ratzinger concludes, it would be necessary today to add to the doctrine of human rights a doctrine about human obligations and the limits of man.

Such a set of problems would have to be posed and confronted at an intercultural level starting both from secular culture and from religious culture. The alleged prevalence of secularist culture in the West, indeed, cannot turn itself into a global claim, at the expense of other cultures. Even in the West, therefore, both the secular culture and Christian culture are called to confront the other religious cultures so as to avoid radical tensions. And even if the secular culture considers itself predominant, the Christian understanding of reality also maintains its weight, just as the other imported cultures like Islam or Buddhism acquire it. What are the consequences of all this? The pathologies of religion have reason as an instrument of control and correction. Similarly, in order to avoid its own pathologies, which are no less serious than the religious ones, reason must demonstrate that it is willing to listen to the major religious traditions of mankind. Therefore, once again, there is a necessary

---

[8] Ibid., 74.

correlation "between reason and faith and between reason and religion, which are called to purify and help one another."[9]

This, in Ratzinger's view, is also the originality of the encyclical
of John Paul II *Fides et ratio*, "Faith and Reason", in the composition
of which the prefect of the Congregation for the Doctrine of the
Faith certainly had a hand. As he emphasized while presenting to
the press this solemn papal document, its real strong point was the
recognition of the dignity of human reason. Capable of knowing
God, it is also able to grapple with the fundamental truths of existence: the spirituality and immortality of the soul, the ability to do
good and to follow the natural moral law, the possibility of formu-
lating true judgments, the affirmation of man's freedom.[10] In short,
John Paul II together with Ratzinger postulate an open anthropology that rises up on two wings, faith and reason, toward the spirit.
This involves, on the one hand, the exclusion of reductive attitudes
such as positivism, materialism, relativism and, on the other hand,
the recognition of a great freedom for philosophical research.

NO PEACE IN THE WORLD WITHOUT
PEACE BETWEEN REASON AND FAITH

Both in 2000, with respect to the Treaty of Lisbon, and in 2004,
with respect to the fiftieth anniversary of the signing of the Treaty
of Rome, which was supposed to lead to the signing of a new European constitution, Ratzinger's appeals to Europe remained un-
heeded. The rejection of any mention of God or of the Christian
roots of Europe in the preamble of the constitution was not a matter of convenience so as to avoid offending the adherents of other
faiths present in Europe. In the cardinal's view, such an argument
is superficial and specious. Why should the Jews, the Muslims, the
Buddhists, and others feel offended? Who would ever think of denying the Jewish roots of Israel or the Islamic roots of Saudi Arabia
or of the countries of the Arabian Gulf? On the contrary, Jews
and Muslims are surprised by the lack of any reference to God in
the European charter. The real reasons for the rejection presuppose

---

[9] Ibid., 81.

[10] Joseph Ratzinger, "Fides et ratio", in *La vita di Dio per gli uomini*, nos. 208–10 of
Communio (Milan: Jaca Book, 2007), 254.

that only the radical Enlightenment culture can be constitutive of European identity. In its apparent tolerance toward all religions, the radical Enlightenment culture follows the logic of supremacy and imposition: "Alongside this culture, various religious cultures with their respective rights can coexist, on the condition (and to the degree) that they respect the criteria of the Enlightenment culture and subordinate themselves to it."[11]

This is the origin of the conflicts, all the more so because the Enlightenment culture aspires to impose its own concept of liberty, which claims the right to desacralize the symbols and values of religions, just as it aspires to impose as fundamental values some achievements of the West that are far from being shared in other historical contexts: democracy based on parties, the complete religious neutrality of States, gender equality. The cardinal then concluded with an assertion that, read years later, seems to anticipate successive developments: "If we come to experience a clash of cultures, this will not be due to a conflict between the great religions . . . , [it] will be between this radical emancipation of man and the great historical cultures."[12]

Again in 2004, in June, Ratzinger was in France on the occasion of the sixtieth anniversary of the landing of the Allies in Normandy. Recalling the event, the cardinal returned to the topic of peace, which is now threatened in Europe, particularly by the clash between Islam and the allegedly enlightened reason of the West. In his opinion, the famous phrase of Hans Küng, "There will be no peace in the world without peace among religions", should be modified as follows: Without peace between reason and faith, there can be no peace in the world because the sources of morality and law dry up.[13] Here Christians especially can make a significant contribution, since they affirm that God himself is *Logos*, the rational principle at the origin of the world's rationality.

An extraordinary synthesis of this rationality is the Decalogue, which is not only the common property of Jews and Christians: "It is an exalted expression of moral reasoning that, as such, is largely

---

[11] Joseph Ratzinger, *Christianity and the Crisis of Cultures*, trans. Brian McNeil (San Francisco: Ignatius Press, 2006), 34.

[12] Ibid., 44.

[13] Joseph Ratzinger, "In Search of Peace", in *Europe Today and Tomorrow*, 85–100 at 93.

in agreement with the wisdom of the other major cultures."[14] A return to the Ten Commandments could offer a concrete model for the rehabilitation of reason. Christians, finally, affirm that God, the eternal Reason, is also Love. He is not closed in on himself but, being the Creator, is also relation and love. This implies that the core of being itself, the first principle of morality, is love. This affirmation is the most decisive rejection of any ideology of violence and is the true apologia for God and man. This is the most convincing testimony, the most valuable service that Christians can offer in this historical moment. For this reason, Ratzinger concludes, turning to Christians, it is important that they live out their heritage in a way that is strong and sincere. "If we do not recall the God of the Bible, the God who has come close to us in Jesus Christ, we will not find the path of peace."[15]

On the way to Jesus Christ

In the first years of the third millennium, in the midst of many and various commitments, Ratzinger found the time to research and write about Jesus, a task that he considered increasingly urgent. In his opinion, indeed, the approach of biblical scholars, which was predominantly historical and exegetical, runs the risk of relegating to the past the figure of the founder of Christianity whom the faithful believe is alive and present with God but also in the liturgy, in their lives, and in world history. In this regard, he had taken up a position as early as 1996 in the first chapters of the predominantly liturgical volume, *A New Song for the Lord*. The cardinal began: "Christ is risen and therefore is not locked into the past: we do encounter him today. Even the nonbeliever cannot deny that Christ appears today and that one would not ask about his past if it were not for this present."[16]

He then continued by clearing away the reductive images introduced by early twentieth-century liberalism and by some contem-

---

[14] Joseph Ratzinger, "Political Visions and the Praxis of Politics", in *Europe Today and Tomorrow*, 47–66 at 65–66.

[15] J. Ratzinger, "In Search of Peace", 100.

[16] Joseph Ratzinger, *A New Song for the Lord*, trans. Martha M. Matesich (New York: Crossroad Publishing Company, 1997), 3.

porary theological currents: Jesus the liberator, the leader of the new exodus, the poor man among the poor. Beneath their captivating appearance, these titles err by enclosing Jesus in his own time, reducing him to a minor preacher that one could encounter in Palestine during the reign of Tiberius and Pontius Pilate. The expectations of the faith summarily expressed by the Letter to the Hebrews are quite different: "Jesus Christ is the same yesterday and today and for ever." [17] How, then, are we to overcome the distance so that Jesus might become a traveling companion for today and so that the Christian can follow him and thus enter into communion with God the Father, whom he says he has come to bring?

In *God Is Near Us*, [18] the cardinal recalls once again the three specifications of the time of Jesus to which the Letter to the Hebrews bears witness: the past, the present, and eternity. The greatest distance that we need to cross in order to become contemporaries of Jesus is certainly the one that separates the eternal God from man immersed in time. Here Ratzinger, paraphrasing Saint Augustine, observes that the believer, through this decisive union, does not have to make a long journey. The *Logos*, the Eternal Son of the Father, has covered that great distance for him by becoming incarnate, as the Creed says, through the work of the Holy Spirit in the womb of the Virgin Mary. The Son, nevertheless, is not alone in making this journey from eternity to time. At the origin, there is the Father of mercies who "so loved the world that he gave his only-begotten Son." [19] Collaborating with him is the Spirit of love, whose task, in eternity as in history, is to unite. He makes sure that, even in his distance from the Father, the Son is united with him. He guarantees that the Jesus who comes in history is the *Logos*, the Word, generated by the Father from all eternity. He is, finally, the sure guarantee that Jesus, who lived two thousand years ago, enters into communion with the faithful of today and of every era and receives their requests and their sufferings. There is, then, another person to whom the above-cited article of the Creed refers: she is the Virgin Mary. The greeting with which the angel addresses

---

[17] Heb 13:8.

[18] Joseph Ratzinger, *God Is Near Us: The Eucharist, the Heart of Life*, trans. Henry Taylor (San Francisco: Ignatius Press, 2003).

[19] Jn 3:16.

Mary, "Hail, full of grace, the Lord is with thee", refers, according
to the exegetes, to a promise of the prophet Zephaniah.[20] With this
greeting, the angel defines Mary as the daughter of Zion in person,
the dwelling place, the holy tent over which stands the cloud of the
presence of God. Thus communion with eternity is guaranteed.

Ratzinger then goes on to discuss communion with the past. In
this regard, he resorts to another pericope of the Old Testament:
the sacrifice of Isaac, preceded by the slow pilgrimage of Abraham
and his son toward Mount Moriah. This journey that seems never-
ending prefigures an era in salvation history, the time of man's awaiting but, above all, the time of God's long-suffering expectation. He
awaits man's thanksgiving but receives only outrage and violence,
as Jesus explains in the parable of the treacherous vine-dressers. At
last God himself will be the one to offer his Son as the sacrificial
victim. The ram caught in the thicket that Abraham offers instead
of Isaac is a prefiguration of Jesus Christ, who wears the crown of
thorns of mankind's guilt. As they climbed the mountain, Abraham
said to Isaac: "God will provide."

In Jesus Christ, the promise of Abraham is fulfilled to the letter. In the Son, God gives a Lamb who takes away the sin of the
world. Jesus, therefore, unites the past with the present. He brings
to fulfillment and completion the Old Covenant and unites the two
Testaments in concord. Nevertheless, it is not insignificant that beneath the Cross stood Mary and John. They witnessed the thrust
of the lance that opened Jesus' side, from which blood and water
flowed, the Eucharist and Baptism, the sacraments through which
the Church is formed; in turn the Church, with her sacramental
structure, has the task of keeping alive the communion with the
Lord after the Resurrection. Ratzinger continues: in the Roman
Canon, after the Consecration, a series of names are commemo-
rated. They are apostles, disciples, bishops, and martyrs who have
the task of transmitting the testimony of what they have seen and
touched.

The volume *On the Way to Jesus Christ* presents a hint of aesthetics with reference to Jesus Christ. The point of departure is Jesus'
reply to some Greeks who wanted to see the face of the Father,

---

[20] Zeph 3:14.

the face of God: "He who has seen me has seen the Father."[21] The desire to see God, which is present in the Old Testament and in religions in general, is satisfied in the coming of Jesus, in his Passion. The Greeks, nevertheless, like all peoples, will see Jesus, not in the flesh, but rather through his Passion. In this regard, the cardinal can cite another verse from the Gospel of John that is so dear to him: "They shall look on him whom they have pierced."[22] To the believer, therefore, Jesus crucified appears as the most beautiful of men. Nevertheless, it is not external beauty that strikes the believer and attracts him but, rather, the beauty of him whose face was disfigured by suffering. Precisely this disfigured face of Christ allows beauty to shine through, the beauty of someone who was able to love until the end. This vision, nevertheless, is allowed for those who believe, who set out to follow Jesus and understand that his death is the place of glory, of the utmost revelation of God.[23]

At the conclusion of this discourse that explains the communion and contemporaneousness between the Passion of Christ and the today of the faithful, the cardinal exhorts the readers to turn their attention anew to eternity, to complete the course that leads to full communion with the Father and Jesus in the Spirit of eternal love. In this regard, he again quotes Saint Augustine: "Eat the bread of the strong, and yet you will not change me into yourself; rather, I will transform you into me."[24] The believer is not the one who eats God and assimilates him to himself, but, rather, Jesus is the one who enters into the believer and elevates him to the world of God. Eucharistic communion, however, when it is authentic, also opens the way to solidarity and expands one's own boundaries infinitely. In Christ, every border is abolished and communion is established with the brethren of every place and of every time. The Church gathered around the Eucharist is the place of fraternity, the new people of God that performs a prophetic and vicarious function

---

[21] Jn 14:9, in Joseph Ratzinger, *On the Way to Jesus Christ*, trans. Michael J. Miller (San Francisco: Ignatius Press, 2005), 13–14.

[22] Jn 19:37.

[23] The cardinal obviously was aware of the work of his friend von Balthasar, who, starting from aesthetics, had developed his monumental trilogy, *The Glory of the Lord, Theo-Drama*, and *Theo-Logic*.

[24] J. Ratzinger, *On the Way to Jesus Christ*, 116.

toward the universal community of people with its mission, its charity, and its suffering.

The title of the last volume by the cardinal that we have examined, *On the Way to Jesus Christ*, can be read in two ways. It alludes to the journey of the faithful to encounter their Lord, but at the same time it can be interpreted as Ratzinger's journey to arrive at his major work on Jesus.

Approach to monasticism

In the first years of the new millennium, Ratzinger gradually drew closer to monasticism, as evidenced by his ever more frequent presence in monasteries. His visits, however, surprisingly coincided with the choices set before the States of the European Union and, most recently, with meetings that were decisive for his life. The cardinal was at Montecassino in 2000, when he chose the monastery as a place of refuge in which to grant to Seewald the interview that became the book *God and the World*.[25] He returned there in 2004 to preside over a meeting of the Pontifical Academy of Sciences.

Finally, he was in Subiaco on April 1, 2005, on the eve of his election as pope, to receive the Saint Benedict Prize for the promotion of human life and the family in Europe. This was the occasion for the cardinal to return one last time to the refusal to cite the continent's Christian roots in the draft of the European constitution, with a conference entitled "Reflection on Cultures that are Opposed Today".[26] In short, the cardinal repeated the historical excursus outlined above, then argued: Here we are not fighting a rear-guard battle but, rather, are advancing a discourse of responsibility for the whole world.

There are four reasons that prompted the cardinal to draw close to Benedictine monasticism: the harmonious celebration of the liturgy in the life of the monks and of the Christian, the dignity of man

---

[25] See the account of it given by Seewald in Joseph Ratzinger, *God and the World: Believing and Living in Our Time*, trans. Henry Taylor (San Francisco: Ignatius Press, 2002), 13–14.

[26] The conference "Riflessione su culture che oggi si contrappongono" is reprinted in Joseph Ratzinger, *L'Europa di Benedetto nella crisi delle culture* (Siena: Cantagalli, 2005), 29–65.

developed in the shadow of the monasteries, monastic democracy, and the centrality of Christ in the *Rule of Saint Benedict*.

LITURGY AND HARMONY IN THE LIFE OF MONKS AND CHRISTIANS

The Rule of Saint Benedict is summarized by the specialists with the expression: "Let nothing be preferred to the celebration of the liturgy."[27] The liturgy is therefore the center of monastic life, around which the day is organized and shaped. As a very down-to-earth person, Ratzinger certainly does not think that the life of the faithful can follow the rhythm of monastic life. In his youth, however, he experienced the growth of the liturgical movement and experienced the harmonious equilibrium that a correct participation in the liturgy can lend to Christian life. Liturgical prayer, indeed, can leave room both for the desire of the individual heart and for ecclesial-dogmatic truth. After a phase when a certain inebriation with innovation was prevalent, following Vatican II, the time had come for the cardinal to return to this equilibrium. Hence the need to follow a shared liturgical order. Spontaneity can predominate in individual or devotional life, not in the liturgy.

In monasticism, finally, love for conversation with God in the prayer of the heart opens the way to Gregorian chant. For Ratzinger, liturgical chant was not only an ornament or a concession to a decadent aesthetic but, rather, the attempt to conform one's own life to the order of the cosmos and to the celestial harmony. All this is at the origin of Ratzinger's growing interest in monastic life, his desire to propose it again as the source of harmony and serenity for the life of the Christian and of the entire Church.

MONASTIC HUMANISM

As is well known, Benedictine life is commonly described with the maxim "Pray and work." The hendiadys is not contained in the *Rule*, yet it effectively describes monastic life. After giving suitable prescriptions for prayer, Saint Benedict counters idleness by ordering the working life of the monastery just as carefully. Work is therefore encouraged by the *Rule*; indeed, manual work promoted the

---

[27] Rule of Saint Benedict, chap. 43.

encounter among the peoples in the West (Latins, Goths, Franks, Longobards) that, according to the cardinal, started the very concept of Europe. The Old Continent is defined not so much by geography as by a shared, beloved culture. It is formed by the foundries, oil mills, glass works, breweries, and tanneries and by the related administration developed at the monasteries, and it extends to the work of copyists, miniaturists, and archivists.

These are the premises for the development of monastic humanism, which, in turn, prepared the way for the *universitas studiorum*, to centers of research and deeper study that contributed so decisively to the physiognomy of Europe. And Ratzinger, as we know, always considered himself a professor who was attentive both to rapport with his students and to the study and research that was at the origin of his thought and his books.

MONASTIC DEMOCRACY

Saint Benedict with his *Rule* is considered also the father of Western democracy. The monk, according to the co-patron of Europe, is certainly obliged to obedience, but at the same time his life is led under the Rule, which is to say, in a regimen of law. Moreover, he is invited to participate in the most important decisions regarding the life of the monastery, just as he is called to elect the abbot. According to the historian Léo Moulin,[28] the term and the concept of parliament, a key element of European democracy, are derived from *parliamentum*, which in the twelfth century designated the council of monks that helped the abbot general of the Cistercians, an offshoot of the Benedictines, in governing the Order.

Therefore, it is not out of place to maintain that the monks were at the origin of democracy. A democracy, however, in which majority rule is not exclusively in force but in which the opinion of the minority must also receive due consideration. Otherwise, democracy runs the risk of degenerating into arrogance, and many times in his writings Ratzinger brought this point to the attention of those who are called to vote: in the most humble elections up to the election

---

[28] L. Moulin, "La vie bénédictine quotidienne hier et aujourd'hui", in *Saint Benoît père de l'Occident* (Anvers: Fonds Mercator, 1980), 412. The volume was published on the occasion of the fifteenth centenary of the birth of Saint Benedict.

of bishops and of the pope himself. The most important point for the cardinal, nevertheless, is that the life of the monks, like their legislation, unfolded, so to speak, while looking to God. This system had been preserved in Europe until the French Revolution. In times of crisis, moreover, the recognition of the inviolability of human dignity, guaranteed by God, had allowed Europeans to overcome immense difficulties. Then all this had been forgotten.

The cardinal therefore asked himself whether, at the beginning of the third millennium, with the development of forms of terrorism that explicitly declare that they aim to destroy Europe and its democracy, it is not appropriate to return to this thought. And he concluded: "What we most need at this moment of history are men who make God visible in this world through their enlightened and lived faith. . . . We need men who have their eyes fixed straight on God, and who learn from him what true humanity is. . . . God returns among men only through men who are touched by God."[29]

URGENCY OF PUTTING CHRIST BACK AT THE CENTER OF CHRISTIAN LIFE

Among the final recommendations of the *Rule of Saint Benedict* there is a warning that underscores the centrality of Christ in Benedictine spirituality: "Let [the monks] prefer nothing whatever to Christ."[30] Ratzinger not only agrees with this urgent recommendation of the Father of Monasticism, but also maintains that the most pressing task for the Church after the year 2000 is precisely that of putting Christ back at the center of Church life and Christian life. This was confirmed for me by a conversation that I had with the cardinal in early 2005. At that time, the health problems of John Paul II were well known. I asked him, therefore, about his future duties and exhorted him to finish his autobiography, both because of the beauty of the text in itself and also because it could provide a convincing reply to the many prejudices about him that were circulating.

The cardinal, who usually welcomed the editor's proposals good-naturedly, this time was firmer than ever in his response: "I cannot;

---

[29] Joseph Ratzinger, "Europe in the Crisis of Cultures", *Communio* 32/2 (Summer 2005): 345–56 at 355.

[30] Rule of Saint Benedict, chap. 72.

I must work on my *Jesus*." This was the book to which he intended
to dedicate his efforts as a scholar and a man of the Church. In drawing near to monasticism, the cardinal was certainly thinking about
the contribution that this venerable institution could still make to
the harmony of Christian life and of the existence of every human
being. At the same time, he considered conforming his life as a
retiree to the monastic model. He certainly did not imagine that it
would offer him guidelines for his pontificate, too.

Pedophile priests

The beginning of the new millennium did not bring the springtime
of peace and renewal that John Paul II had so much hoped for. On
the contrary, after the attack on the Twin Towers on September
11, 2001, the winds of war had begun to blow again. The Polish
pope did not want to resign himself to this trend. He made diplomatic efforts, invited Catholics to a day of fasting, and announced
a new day of prayer for peace that would take place in Assisi on
January 24, 2002. Ratzinger had not spoken at the first prayer meeting in Assisi, since he had reservations about an event that, from
his perspective, was not very clear theologically. This time, however, the pope wanted him at his side, and the cardinal accompanied
the elderly pontiff, whose efforts for peace moved the world. Then
Ratzinger explained that at Assisi there had been no interreligious
prayer but, rather, multireligious prayer. "They have in common an
acute concern for the needs of the world and its lack of peace . . .
and justice. . . . Hence their intention to give a public sign of this
longing, which might stir up all men and strengthen the goodwill
that is a condition of peace."[31]

Another particularly painful incident, which since the beginning
of the new millennium has been becoming increasingly embarrassing for the Catholic Church, was the revelation of cases of abuse of
minors by clergymen. Confronted with the phenomenon, which
was more extensive than anyone could have imagined, the authorities of the Church seemed to be inert and scared. Finally, on April
30, 2001, the pope decided to entrust also to the Congregation
for the Doctrine of the Faith the most serious crimes committed

---

[31] J. Ratzinger, *Truth and Tolerance*, 106.

against morality and in the celebration of the sacraments. Several days later, the congregation sent to the bishops a letter in which it informed them that the most serious crimes against morality are those committed by clerics with someone younger than eighteen years of age. And it added that every time a bishop or a superior general of a religious order receives a credible report of the abuse of a minor, he is obliged to conduct a preliminary investigation and to inform the congregation itself. The letter either will take the judgment upon itself or else will give to the competent bishop or superior instructions about how to proceed.

The rules were then further tightened in two ways: the one who has suffered the abuse and also anyone who comes to know about it, whether cleric or layman, is obliged to report it; the statute of limitations for the crime is extended to ten years from the eighteenth birthday of the minor victim of the abuse. In the first year alone, there were three thousand cases to examine, and these concerned America in particular. Here, as in other countries of the world, "after Vatican II the priests came down off the pedestal on which they had been placed by reverential fear."[32] Moreover, there had been a change of attitude, so that the victims of abuse, who once had preferred to remain silent, decided to turn to doctors, lawyers, public prosecutors, and journalists. Initially, dioceses chose to settle out of court so as to avoid further embarrassment, but soon the cases became so numerous and the financial demands so enormous that it was necessary to appear in court and to undergo judgment. This involved, besides the priests who had abused minors, also the bishops who not only had been insufficiently vigilant but often, once a scandal had exploded, had merely transferred the priest-molester to another parish or had assigned him to other duties. In this way, the discredit fell both on the priests and on the bishops. The most sensational case was that of the priest John J. Geoghan, from the Archdiocese of Boston, a city in which the Catholic Church had always enjoyed great prestige. Ordained in 1965, the priest was responsible for numerous acts of abuse before being reduced to the lay state. Hauled into court following a famous investigation by

---

[32] Cf. Chester Gillis, "Cultura americana e cultura cattolica", in *I cattolici e le Chiese cristiane durante il pontificato di Giovanni Paolo II*, ed. E. Guerriero and M. Impagliazzo (Cinisello Balsamo: San Paolo, 2006), 191.

The Boston Globe, the ex-priest was sentenced for indecency and the abuse of minors less than fourteen years old. *The Globe*, which won the 2003 Pulitzer Prize for this investigation, lifted the veil from a situation, the extent and consequences of which had long been kept hidden or had at least been underestimated.

After the trial, which made it clear that the archbishop, Bernard Law, had not taken adequate measures against the pedophile priests, the cardinal resigned and was later transferred to Rome, where he was appointed archpriest of the Basilica of Santa Maria Maggiore. It must also be said that most cases of abuse that were reported had been committed in the decades preceding the arrival in the dioceses of the bishops currently in charge, and for this reason it was not always easy to determine who was responsible. What emerged, nevertheless, was an image of a Church that was more interested in protecting herself than in her mission of proclaiming the Gospel and protecting the little ones, which is part of the Gospel message itself. Other sensational cases surfaced in Chicago, Milwaukee, New York, and Los Angeles.[33]

Serious harm was done from the financial perspective, but even more to the Church's image. Ratzinger later said to Seewald: "All this shocked us and very deeply upsets me now as before."[34] And without mincing words he acknowledged: "The greatest persecution of the Church comes not from her enemies without, but arises from sin within the Church."[35]

Dean of the Sacred College

On September 19, 2001, Ratzinger was in Cernobbio for the Ambrosetti Seminar. In the preceding days, the papers had reported the news that Cardinal Martini was getting ready to step down as head of the Archdiocese of Milan and to move to Jerusalem, where he intended to complete several specialized research projects that were dear to him. When asked to comment, Ratzinger answered: "This life is very hard. I impatiently await the moment when I will be able

---

[33] Cf. Vania Lucia Gaito, *Viaggio nel silenzio* (Milan: Chairelettere, 2008).

[34] Joseph Ratzinger, *Light of the World: The Pope, the Church, and the Signs of the Times*, trans. Michael J. Miller and Adrian J. Walker (San Francisco: Ignatius Press, 2010), 25.

[35] Interview of the Holy Father Benedict XVI with the Journalists during the Flight to Portugal, May 11, 2010.

to go back to writing some books. I understand Cardinal Martini's desire; we are both professors, we are very much dedicated to meditation, and returning to the meditative state is something normal."[36] Later in 2001, in December, to be exact, a new appointment arrived. Having reached the age of eighty, Cardinal Gantin from Benin decided to resign as dean of the Sacred College. The position is reserved to cardinals who have the title of bishop. At that time, there were about a dozen of them. Unanimously they chose Ratzinger, whose nomination was promptly approved by John Paul II.

In the system of the College of Cardinals, the title of dean is usually given to the cardinal with the most seniority. It is therefore, practically speaking, an honorary title, particularly when the dean is more than eighty years old and does not take part in the election of a new pope. In Ratzinger's case, though, he had been created cardinal by Paul VI at a relatively young age, and this appointment had decisive importance for his election as pope.[37] In 2002, Ratzinger completed his seventy-fifth year. He was approaching, therefore, the age in which bishops must present their resignation from their position. John Paul II, however, did not even want to hear about resignation from the man who increasingly appeared to be his closest collaborator.[38] As Ratzinger recalls the incident, the pope told him: "You do not have to write the letter at all, for I want to have you to the end."[39]

During the planning period of the *Catechism of the Catholic Church*, Ratzinger had realized that the Council of Trent had made available to the faithful a major and a minor catechism.[40] Similarly, around ten years after the publication of the *Catechism of the Catholic Church*, as the fortieth anniversary of the conclusion of Vatican II approached, in Rome a compendium, that is, a more summary version of the

---

[36] Cf. Andrea Tornielli, *Benedetto XVI: Il custode della fede* (Casale Monferrato: Piemme, 2005), 220f.

[37] Cf. John L. Allen, *The Rise of Benedict XVI* (New York: Doubleday, 2005), 75f. Allen goes so far as to state that Gantin's resignation should be considered a remote cause for Ratzinger's election as pope.

[38] In the *Corriere della Sera* of October 23, 2003, Luigi Accattoli describes Ratzinger as "the primary crutch of the sick pope".

[39] J. Ratzinger, *Light of the World*, 4.

[40] Joseph Ratzinger, "The Catechism of the Catholic Church and the Optimism of the Redeemed", *Communio* 20.3 (Fall 1993): 469–84 at 473.

major catechism, was planned. Consequently, in 2003, John Paul II formed a commission, obviously with Ratzinger presiding, with the task of writing the compendium. After working on it for two years, the commission had completed the draft version, which was sent to the cardinals and to the presidents of the episcopal conferences with the request for corrections and possible proposed improvements. After the proposals were received, there was a revision phase. In early 2005, forty years after the conclusion of Vatican II, the compendium was ready for publication. According to Ratzinger, the new catechetical tool being made available to the universal Church had three characteristics: its direct dependence on the major catechism; its adoption of the dialogical genre (the question-and-answer format after the model of the Catechism of Pius X), and its reliance on several recurring images throughout the catechism.

As I had the opportunity to note in the meetings in preparation for the publication and distribution of the work, the cardinal was very committed to this additional catechetical aid, which was produced to satisfy the thirst for truth of many believers and of many people of goodwill. The presentation of the work is dated March 20, 2005. One month later, Ratzinger was elected pope.

United by geography, love of Christ, and friendship: Karol Wojtyła and Joseph Ratzinger

Although different in their temperaments and personal histories, Karol Wojtyła and Joseph Ratzinger were united by their common Central European origin, by the tragedy of the Second World War, by their shared passion for Christ, and by their sincere love for the Church. With the passage of years, their collaboration had given rise to a genuine, loyal friendship that could calmly get beyond differences of opinion on individual points of doctrine and pastoral activity. As mentioned in the previous chapter, after 2000 their collaboration became even closer. The elderly pontiff, after having led the Church with a charismatic government, had seriously thought about resigning. He had then reached the conclusion that he had a "serious obligation in conscience to continue to perform the task to which Christ himself called me".[41] The sick pontiff, moreover, although forced to give up some functions that he had previously

---

[41] Andrea Riccardi, *Giovanni Paolo II* (Cinisello Balsamo: San Paolo, 2011), 527.

performed, was giving an invaluable witness to the Christian meaning of life and of suffering. He understood, nevertheless, that he needed more than ever his most trusted collaborator and entrusted increasingly serious responsibilities to him.

Together with the tasks, the cardinal-friend also received signs of gratitude. A particularly eloquent gesture of thanks was the request to write the presentation of the *Roman Triptych*, a series of poetic meditations on the origin and end of history that are intertwined with the human story of Karol Wojtyła. Since it was the pope's personal writing, there was no consideration of a theological nature that would make it inadvisable for a collaborator to present a work by the pope. The fact remains, though, that previously a gesture of that sort seemed virtually unthinkable. For his part, Ratzinger had long since proved to be, not just a faithful collaborator, but also a perspicacious and authentic interpreter of the pope's thought.

Two texts in particular deserve to be mentioned in this context: "The Unity of Mission and Person in the Figure of John Paul II" and "Faith, the Refuge of Humanity: The 14 Encyclicals of John Paul II".[42] To underscore the continuity between mission and person in the Polish pope, Ratzinger recalled the amusing remark by the Renaissance Pope Pius II, Enea Silvio Piccolomini. When reminded of the discontinuity between some of his writings as a humanist and those of the pontiff, the pope responded with a phrase that has become proverbial: "Reject Enea and accept Pius." Wojtyła, according to Ratzinger, did not need that distinction. In his career, both as a scholar and as bishop and pope, there is a continuity that is due precisely to the depth of his human journey that almost naturally gives rise to his supernatural vision: "The metaphysical, the mystical, the phenomenological, and the aesthetic—the interplay of all these aspects opened his eyes to the many levels of reality and finally became a single comprehensive perception that confronts everything that appears and manages to understand it."[43] Hence the calm assurance that John Paul II manages to convey with his teaching and with his presence to the faithful and to all

---

[42] In this regard, I take the liberty of referring to the small anthology of texts by Ratzinger about John Paul II that I edited: Joseph Ratzinger, *Giovanni Paolo II* (Cinisello Balsamo: San Paolo, 2007). The first of the two essays appeared in English in Joseph Ratzinger, *The Legacy of John Paul II: Images and Memories* (San Francisco: Ignatius Press, 2005), 7–33.

[43] J. Ratzinger, *Legacy of John Paul II*, 16.

mankind. Moreover, his is the path of man, who in order to arrive at the fullness of himself is called to be open to Christ, to his mystery of love that comes from the Father.

Again in his article on the encyclicals[44] of John Paul II, Ratzinger accentuates the basic anthropological vision that he fully shares: only if there is a truth, an absolute good for which it is worth dying, is man confirmed in his dignity: "Precisely because in man there is more than mere *bios* (living matter), biological life too becomes infinitely precious. It is not possible to dispose of man because he is endowed with the dignity of God."[45] Hence the continuity between faith and reason present in the Polish pope's encyclical by the same name. Faith, John Paul II says, does not want to silence reason. On the contrary, it exhorts it to dare; it invites it to free itself from the cataracts that have formed over the essential questions. Together, faith and reason can answer these questions and thus open man's horizon toward his supernatural vocation.

For Wojtyła and Ratzinger, finally, the decisive common element is Jesus Christ. God and man, he is the wisdom in which the world was created, the folly through which the mercy of God on Golgotha cancelled the sins of mankind, the Risen Lord who now sits at the right hand of the Father and prepares a dwelling place for those who wish to enter into God's world. This shared reason and faith soon became a communion of intentions and action, and upon it had grown a very firm understanding that was translated into a continual collaboration, in a never-interrupted nearness. Monsignor Stanisław Dziwisz, the secretary of the Polish pope, confided to me: "No important decision was made in the pontificate without first consulting Ratzinger."[46]

Nostalgia for Germany

In the first years of the new millennium, Ratzinger, busier than ever as the very close collaborator of John Paul II, was also planning his future. Already in 2003, he changed his secretary, so as to assure

---

[44] They are, in chronological order: *Veritatis splendor, Evangelium vitae, Fides et ratio.*

[45] J. Ratzinger, *Giovanni Paolo II*, 46.

[46] Statement made to the author about a month after the death of John Paul II and before the election of Dziwisz as archbishop of Kraków.

Monsignor Josef Clemens, who had been at his side for nineteen years, a future in the Roman Curia. He himself, in early 2004, was the one to ordain as a bishop his former secretary, who, after a series of intermediate positions, became the undersecretary of the Pontifical Council for the Laity. In Ratzinger's view, this was a position with great responsibility, and he assigned to it a man whom he could trust. At his side now was Monsignor Georg Gänswein, who for several years had been employed by the Congregation for the Doctrine of the Faith and as a professor of canon law at the University of the Holy Cross (Santa Croce). He proved to be a faithful collaborator not only in the few years during which Ratzinger would remain at the congregation, but also in the years of his pontificate and in those of his retirement in the monastery Mater Ecclesiae.

Important events in 2004 included in January the previously mentioned debate with Habermas about the importance of values in maintaining democracy,[47] and in June the cardinal was in France, where he gave four talks on the responsibility for peace on the occasion of the sixtieth anniversary of the Allied landing in Normandy (D-Day). On that occasion, the cardinal also connected the Christian roots of Europe with the experience of rebuilding and peace after the Second World War. "The graves of the Second World War commend to us the task of strengthening the forces of good: it is an invitation to work, to live, and to suffer for the propagation and reinforcement of those values and truths that build a united world with God as its fulcrum."[48]

And in his final speech, which was entitled "The Grace of Reconciliation", the cardinal concluded: "The memory of the sorrow and of the evils of the Second World War, together with the memory of the great work of reconciliation that, thank God, has been accomplished in Europe, shows us where to find those forces that can heal Europe and the world."[49] Above all, during the summer vacation in 2004, he took in hand what he considered his final important theological work, the book on Jesus in which once again he cites the heritage of Guardini in order to present a believable picture of the founder of the Christian religion. In the volume entitled simply

---

[47] See the preceding chapter.
[48] J. Ratzinger, *Europe Today and Tomorrow*, 113.
[49] Ibid., 117.

The Lord, the Italian-German theologian had conveyed a captivating picture of Jesus, while at the same time making it clear that, without faith in the Resurrection, there is no possible approach to a figure who is not only historical but also intends to be relevant for the today of believers. Ratzinger meant to write a similar work, while nevertheless taking into account the advances in exegesis and the new cultural context.

At the end of the year, besides his work at the congregation, he was busy completing the *Compendium*, the small catechism in question-and-answer format, which was not meant for the bishops and their collaborators but, rather, directly for the faithful. The smaller-scale edition of the Catechism by the cardinal was no less important than the larger edition. Although it was finally completed while Ratzinger was still at the congregation, the *Compendium* was published after his election as pope. Overwhelmed by the success of the large catechism, the small catechism did not have the success that the cardinal expected.

Meanwhile, he often thought about his house in Pentling, of which he was very fond, even though he had now abandoned the idea of returning to Germany definitively. His brother testified: "He wanted to keep living in Rome but also to come more often to Germany and for a longer time, so that we could be together more. Moreover, he intended to write a few more books and to finish other works he had not yet completed."[50]

THE DEATH OF JOHN PAUL II

In early 2005, Ratzinger, like many Catholics in Rome and throughout the world, was following with trepidation the pope's repeated stays in Gemelli Hospital. At the beginning of February, the pope was admitted for the first time following a respiratory crisis, and the prefect of the Congregation for the Doctrine of the Faith went to visit him in the hospital. He needed several signatures and of course wanted to visit the sick pope. About this visit he later said: "The pope was suffering visibly, but was still fully lucid and very alert. . . . He communicated his decisions to me in a few words; he

---

[50] Georg Ratzinger and Michael Hesemann, *My Brother the Pope*, trans. Michael J. Miller (San Francisco: Ignatius Press, 2012), 224.

gave me his blessing and said goodbye in German, granting me all his trust and his friendship."[51] At the end of the month, the pope was admitted again for another respiratory crisis that required a surgical tracheotomy and the insertion of a breathing tube. The stay in this case was obviously longer because of the necessary speech therapy. Ratzinger had another meeting with the pontiff on March 1. In this case, too, he reported to the journalists that the pope had had a brief conversation with him both in Italian and in German.[52] Moreover, it was the first indication that allowed him to infer that the pope was recovering and was regaining his ability to speak.

On March 13, Wojtyła, shortly before returning to the Vatican, was capable of reading a brief message to the group of faithful that had gathered at the Polyclinic to greet him. It was the last time that his voice was heard in public. He was probably discharged early because Easter that year fell in March and the pope wanted to spend at least Holy Week at home. The pope's condition, nevertheless, continued to be very serious, to the point where it was necessary to organize in the papal apartment a complete medical unit to monitor the health of the illustrious patient.[53] On Sunday, March 20, and Wednesday March 23, John Paul II made a fleeting appearance at the window of his study, limiting himself to a hand gesture to give his blessing.

Good Friday, March 25, was, in contrast, Ratzinger's day. In the traditional Way of the Cross at the Colosseum, broadcast worldwide and conducted by Cardinal Ruini, the prayers composed by the cardinal dean were read. Particularly impressive was the prayer at the ninth station, which recalls the third fall of Jesus beneath the Cross. After inviting the faithful to reflect that Jesus is often forced to suffer for the sins of his own Church, the cardinal exclaimed: "How often is the holy sacrament of his Presence abused, how often must he enter empty and evil hearts!" Then he again got down to the particulars, squarely addressing the clergy, bishops, and priests: "How often do we celebrate only ourselves, without even realizing

---

[51] Testimony taken from an interview granted by Benedict XVI to a Polish television network on October 17, 2005. The text is reprinted in Italian by Professor Renato Buzzonetti in Stanisław Dziwisz et al., *Lasciatemi andare* (Cinisello Balsamo: San Paolo, 2006), 76.

[52] Cf. Allen, *Rise of Benedict XVI*, 31.

[53] Professor Buzzonetti himself reports this in Dziwisz, *Lasciatemi andare*, 77.

that he is there! How often is his Word twisted and misused! . . .
How much filth there is in the Church, and even among those who,
in the priesthood, ought to belong entirely to him! How much pride,
how much self-complacency!"[54]

The cardinal, who during the Jubilee Year had had some doubts
about the requests for forgiveness for the Church's past, was now
inviting the faithful, in particular the clergy, to ask forgiveness for
their sins, which were no less serious, no less scandalous than those
of the past. Meanwhile, the pope's physical condition continued
to deteriorate. On Good Friday, he watched the Way of the Cross
from his private study, spiritually and physically nailed to the Cross;
on Easter Sunday, he appeared for a few minutes on the balcony
of his apartment, tried to say a few words but had to give up; he
limited himself to making a sign of the cross over the faithful in
attendance on Saint Peter's Square. The situation became desperate
on Friday, April 1, while Ratzinger was in Subiaco to receive the
Saint Benedict award for promoting life and the family in Europe.
On April 2, the cardinal came twice to the papal apartment: in the
morning, alerted by Monsignor Dziwisz, for a last goodbye to his
dying friend. Upon leaving, the usually very reserved Bavarian could
not manage to conceal his emotion and said: "He knows that he is
about to die, and he gave me a final farewell."[55] That evening, after
nine o'clock, he was in the pope's apartment again, together with
the secretary of state, Cardinal Sodano, and a few other prelates, to
verify the death of John Paul II.

A very efficient dean

According to tradition, after the announcement of the pope's death,
the cardinals and officials of the Roman Curia are obliged to submit
their resignations from their respective positions. The only ones
who remain in office are the *camerlengo*, who is responsible for dis-
patching routine business, and the dean of the Sacred College, in
this case, Ratzinger. The first task of the latter was to call all the
cardinals to Rome immediately—a job that was certainly not bur-

---

[54] Joseph Ratzinger, *Way of the Cross at the Colosseum: Meditations and Prayers by Cardinal Ratzinger*, Ninth Station (Vatican City: Libreria Editrice Vaticana, 2005).

[55] Cf. Lecomte, *Benoît XVI*, 106.

densome, given modern communications. Many cardinals, besides, were already in Rome. Others, having heard the news, were already on a plane or a train bound for the Italian capital. For all of them, it was important to arrive in time to participate in the general congregations, which have the task of organizing the funeral ceremonies and preparing the conclave.

All the cardinals can participate in these meetings, both the electors who have not yet turned eighty years old and also the octogenarians, who are excluded from the conclave. As all the cardinals now know, these meetings help to establish the general lines to be followed in the election and to identify the candidates who can best respond to the needs of the Church and the expectations of the electors. The meetings were conducted from 10:00 A.M. on in the Synod Hall, which is located right behind the Palace of the Holy Office, with Cardinal Ratzinger presiding. According to the testimony of many participants, the dean performed his duty as arbitrator and moderator very competently. In the interval of time between the day of the death of John Paul II and April 18, the date of the opening of the conclave, thirteen general congregations were held. Ratzinger presided at all of them.

Ultimately, he left a great, favorable impression on everyone. The beginning, however, was wearisome. They started by reading line by line the text of the apostolic constitution *Universi dominici gregis* promulgated by John Paul II on February 22, 1996, for the purpose of giving a new, organic system of rules for the vacancy of the Apostolic See and the election of the Roman pontiff. Since the document was widely known and every cardinal had had the opportunity to consult it, both at home and upon arriving in Rome, some of the electors considered such a minute reading superfluous. Ratzinger, however, stood by his decision, so that everyone could have the opportunity to ask questions. Consequently, they all clearly understood the manner of proceeding, and decisions would be made in a truly collegial way. Moreover, John L. Allen remarks, referring to the judgment of some cardinals, "Ratzinger seemed to be making a genuine effort to listen, and to ensure that everyone's voice was heard."[56]

---

[56] Allen, *Rise of Benedict*, 94.

To me this observation seems important because it confirms something that Ratzinger confided to me several times: that he spent much of his time at the Congregation for the Doctrine of the Faith listening to bishops during their traditional *ad limina* visits. Whereas other heads of Roman dicasteries reserved a very limited amount of time for these meetings, Ratzinger considered it precisely his duty to assure that each one had the necessary time. He inquired about their dioceses, paid attention to their difficulties, to their loneliness, and encouraged them. In short, he gave them a cordial welcome, which was, therefore, a remote cause and at the same time a proximate reason why Ratzinger's candidacy ended up winning rapidly without encountering major objections.

THE FUNERAL OF JOHN PAUL II

One of the first decisions that the cardinals who had just arrived in Rome were expected to make was to determine the date for the funeral of John Paul II. With one accord, they decided that the Requiem Mass should take place on Friday, April 8, 2005. While the first meetings were taking place in the Synod Hall, the cardinals heard the uninterrupted commotion of the crowd coming from Saint Peter's Square. They hoped for a large influx of people, but the number that actually arrived surpassed all expectations. Even on the evening of his death, the crowd was overflowing. Then, when the pope's body was transferred to the Basilica, the entire city of Rome seemed to be under attack. Coming from everywhere in the world, the faithful and the admirers of the deceased pontiff were invading the via della Conciliazione and all the streets that surround the Vatican. It was a major trial for the Italian authorities in charge of keeping public order, for the Swiss Guards, and for the cardinals themselves. The trial was even more demanding on April 8. Around two million pilgrims arrived in Rome, four kings, five queens, seven heads of State and government leaders, 2,500 religious and civil leaders who had been invited, and 3,500 journalists who had been accredited. About thirty giant screens had been positioned throughout the capital to allow those who did not manage to enter Saint Peter's Square, the via della Conciliazione, and the adjoining areas to follow the broadcast of the funeral.

Then there were the television links from all over the world except China. According to Lecomte,[57] more than a billion persons worldwide followed the ceremony live. Allen goes so far as to speak of two billion and does not hesitate to describe the funeral of John Paul II as the most-watched event in all the history of television.[58] The Mass was concelebrated by 165 cardinals, with their dean, Joseph Ratzinger, presiding. In the midst of an event of such importance, he appeared to be moved, certainly, but also in charge of the situation. The precise and substantial homily started with the invitation made by the risen Jesus to Saint Peter and to each of his successors: "Follow me."[59] A positive response to this invitation, in Ratzinger's view, marked the phases of the life of John Paul II as a priest, bishop, and pope.

It is worth mentioning Wojtyła's transition from professor to bishop, as Ratzinger interpreted it: "Leaving the academic world, leaving this challenging engagement with young people, leaving the great intellectual endeavor of striving to understand and interpret the mystery of that creature which is man and of communicating to today's world the Christian interpretation of our being."[60] To many, it seemed that Ratzinger was making an autobiographical life review, since he had been so fond of academic teaching. And then the conclusion, which was lyrical and at the same time devout, with regard to the deceased pontiff: "We can be sure that our beloved Pope is standing today at the window of the Father's house, that he sees us and blesses us."[61]

After the burial of John Paul II, the cardinals could return to their general congregations with greater serenity and concentrate on the election of a successor. First of all, there were those in favor of continuity with the pontificate that had just concluded, which had reaped so much applause throughout the world. For them, the most suitable candidate was almost naturally Ratzinger, who had a staunch supporter in Christoph Cardinal von Schönborn. The archbishop

---

[57] Lecomte, *Benoît XVI*, 107.

[58] Allen, *Rise of Benedict*, 59.

[59] Jn 21:22.

[60] The text can be found at the Vatican website: Funeral Mass of the Roman Pontiff John Paul II, Homily of His Eminence Card. Joseph Ratzinger, April 8, 2005.

[61] Ibid.

of Vienna assured the college of Ratzinger's affable character, his openness toward his fellow bishops, and his leadership ability, as the cardinals had just had the opportunity to observe. Among the opponents, in contrast, were those who wanted a more collegial government, greater attention to the Third World, and a more open dialogue with Islam.

Based on these criteria, the name that recurred most often was that of the formal cardinal of Milan, Carlo Maria Martini; nevertheless, he had Parkinson's disease and did not seem to offer a credible alternative. Some cardinals from Latin America promoted the candidacy of the Argentine Jorge Mario Bergoglio, archbishop of Buenos Aires. A Jesuit, like his confrere from Milan, he had the reputation of being a very humble and profoundly spiritual man. To some of his confreres in Latin America, however, the future Pope Francis seemed to be rather conservative in doctrine.[62] In short, Ratzinger's was the only strong candidacy, but the saying "He who enters the conclave as pope leaves it as cardinal" recommended caution.

---

[62] Allen, *Rise of Benedict*, 104.

XIII

SAINT CORBINIAN'S BEAR
STAYS IN ROME

The conclave

On Sunday, April 17, 2005, the 115 cardinals called to elect the successor of John Paul II met in the afternoon in the spacious entrance hall of the Casa Santa Marta. The residence, a sort of inn for churchmen right behind Paul VI auditorium, was already prepared for the conclave: televisions and telephones had been taken away, and the windows had been blocked so as to promote a more recollected atmosphere suited to the gravity of the moment. Given the duration of the previous pontificate, only two cardinals, Ratzinger and the American William Baum, who also had spent a long time in the Curia, had any previous conclave experience. All of them, nevertheless, were convinced of the gravity of the moment and of the necessity of finding a successor worthy of the pontificate that had just ended. On Monday morning, the 115 cardinals met in Saint Peter's Basilica for the celebration of the Solemn Mass *pro eligendo pontifice* (for the election of the pope). As provided by the rules, Ratzinger once again presided.

In his homily, the cardinal recalled that Christ's mercy, which had been central in the readings of the day, is not a cheap grace and does not presuppose the trivialization of evil. We cannot remain children in the faith and allow ourselves to be tossed about by any wind of doctrine whatsoever! Then the cardinal continued in a heartfelt tone: How many winds of doctrine in recent years! Christians themselves have let themselves be carried from one trend to another, from Marxism to liberalism, from collectivism to radical individualism, from atheism to a vague mysticism. If someone has a clear faith he is called a fundamentalist, while relativism, in contrast, appears to be the only attitude that has kept up with the times. The Gospel, however, speaks to us about friendship with Jesus, which leads to a holy anxiety to proclaim the Gospel. In view of the election, it was therefore necessary to pray for a pastor like John Paul II, who might guide people to the knowledge of Christ, to his love, to his true joy.

The homily caused a sensation. According to Lecomte, many cardinals shared the opinion of an American religious who, when interviewed by the news agency France Presse, had exclaimed: "I would not like Ratzinger as pope, but he did give a great homily."[1] For his part, John Allen says that this was strong medicine, and certainly not a political speech with an eye to the election.[2] Some drew from this the conclusion that Ratzinger was not in the running for the election. More probably, without too many electoral preoccupations, the cardinal had mentioned in his homily the themes that he had taken to heart in those years: the battle against relativism and the trivialization of the faith, the need to hold fast to Jesus in faith, hope, and above all with love. Far from intimidating the electors, therefore, the homily, pronounced in vibrant, impassioned tones, ended up making several cardinals, who were still uncertain, favorably disposed toward Ratzinger.[3]

At 4:30 P.M. that same day, the cardinals made their entrance into the Sistine Chapel. On Saint Peter's Square, there was already a small crowd of journalists and the curious, but they knew that an election on the first ballot is practically impossible. The first vote is almost an opinion poll, which serves to orient and to group the electors. In any case, the cardinal dean guided the pre-conclave phase, too, with a sure hand; when it was finished, the last outsiders present left the Sistine Chapel, and it was possible to start the election proper.

As already mentioned, almost all the cardinals were participating in the rite for the first time. Emotions ran high, especially when

---

[1] Bernard Lecomte, *Benoît XVI* (Paris: Perrin, 2006), 111f.

[2] John L. Allen, *The Rise of Benedict XVI* (New York: Doubleday, 2005), 91.

[3] Pope Francis himself, upon returning from his journey to Africa and commenting on the so-called "second Vatileaks", declared: "Thirteen days before the death of Saint John Paul II, during the Way of the Cross, then-Cardinal Ratzinger spoke about the filth in the Church. He was the first to denounce it. In the Mass for the election of the pope, he spoke about the same thing, and we elected him pope because of this freedom to say things [as they are]." Reported by Gian Guido Vecchi in *Corriere della Sera*, December 1, 2015.

every single elector approached the altar located beneath the *Last Judgment* by Michelangelo and, before dropping his ballot into the urn, recited the formula: "I declare, with Christ the Lord who will judge me as my witness, that my vote is given to the one who, for godly reasons, I think should be elected." At this point, according to one cardinal elector, "every partisan interest is forgotten; one is alone before God and one thinks only about the good of the Church."[4]

According to Lucio Brunelli,[5] on the first ballot Ratzinger won forty-seven votes, followed by the Argentine cardinal, Jorge Mario Bergoglio, the future Pope Francis, with ten votes, and by the former cardinal of Milan, Carlo Maria Martini, with nine. In the votes on the following day, support for Ratzinger continued to increase, as it did for Cardinal Bergoglio. In late morning on Tuesday, April 19, again according to Brunelli, Ratzinger had won seventy-two votes, Bergoglio—forty. The situation was still uncertain. Ratzinger needed only five votes to reach the two-thirds majority; Bergoglio, nevertheless, had reached the threshold of votes that, if he kept it, would in any case prevent Ratzinger from gaining the required majority. The election, therefore, was decided during the break for lunch on Tuesday. This is the opinion of Alberto Melloni[6] in particular, who attributes a significant role to Cardinal Martini, who, in order to avoid the election of a low-profile curial cardinal, allegedly asked some of his supporters to vote for Ratzinger, who that afternoon reached eighty-four votes and thus became the 265th Pope, the 264th successor to Saint Peter.

I PRAYED INTENSELY THAT I MIGHT BE SPARED THIS TRIAL

Judging by the numbers reported by Brunelli, this was not a landslide election. In this regard, Roberto Regoli reports the opinion that Brunelli's source could have been a cardinal hostile to Ratzinger. By making the vote count public, he wanted to prove that the German

---

[4] From a conversation of the author with Angelo Cardinal Scola several months after the conclusion of the conclave.

[5] Since the well-known Vaticanist had had access to the diary of one cardinal elector in which the votes won by Ratzinger and the other main candidates in the various ballots were recorded precisely, he published them with a commentary of his own in *Limes* 4 (2005): 291–300.

[6] Alberto Melloni, "Benedetto XVI", in idem, *Il conclave di papa Francesco* (Rome: Istituto dell'Enciclopedia Italiana, 2013), 23–61 at 38.

pope had been elected by a slim majority. The historian from the Gregorian University then points out that there are other sources with numbers much more consistently in favor of Ratzinger, and he suggests keeping in mind the rapidity of the election, the sign of a consensus that quickly consolidated in his favor.[7] Ratzinger's immediate predecessors had certainly had a larger majority. It was, though, an election that took place on the fourth ballot, therefore a very rapid one that ranks right after the record election in 1939 that elevated Pius XII to the Chair of Peter. The reasons that induced the prelates to elect the German cardinal are easily identified. Contributing factors were the indisputable intellectual and moral authority of the person, continuity with the pontificate of John Paul II, the assurance, considering his age, of a shorter pontificate than the previous one, and the convincing manner with which the dean of the Sacred College had conducted the predecessor's funeral, the general congregations, and finally the preparations for the conclave.

It seems to me more interesting, though, thinking also about his final resignation, to inquire about the reasons why Ratzinger did nothing to avoid an election that seemed in the air and that he did not desire. One possible explanation is contained in the legend about Saint Corbinian, the founder of the Diocese of Freising, and his bear, which Ratzinger recounts at the conclusion of his memoirs.

His older brother Georg, too, who had asked himself the same question, gave an answer along the lines of the explanation just recorded: "He told me [his election] had struck him like a bolt of lightning. It was so unforeseeable, it came so suddenly in the voting, that the working of the Holy Spirit was obvious. He then surrendered quickly to him, because he, too, recognized God's will in it."[8] Finally, a few days later, while receiving some German pilgrims, the new pope gave an even more detailed and dramatic explanation. When he had understood that the blade was coming close to his head, he had felt a sort of giddiness. "I was convinced that

---

[7] Roberto Regoli, *Oltre la crisi della Chiesa: Il pontificato di Benedetto XVI* (Turin: Lindau, 2016), 40–45.

[8] Georg Ratzinger and Michael Hesemann, *My Brother the Pope*, trans. Michael J. Miller (San Francisco: Ignatius Press, 2011), 232.

I had already carried out my life's work and could look forward to ending my days peacefully." Then he had prayed intensely that he would be spared that trial.

Then, however, he had received a short letter from one of his electors. "He reminded me that on the occasion of the Mass for John Paul II, . . . I spoke of how again and again, Karol Wojtyła received this call ['Follow me'] from the Lord, and how each time he had to renounce much and to simply say: Yes, I will follow you, even if you lead me where I never wanted to go." Then the letter continued: "Were the Lord to say to you now, 'Follow me', then remember what you preached. Do not refuse! Be obedient in the same way that you described the great Pope." The pope commented: "This deeply moved me. The ways of the Lord are not easy, but we were not created for an easy life, but for great things, for goodness."[9]

Ratzinger's explanation seems to me convincing inasmuch as it is consistent with the choices of his life. By nature mild, gentle, and friendly, he was called to a responsibility that he did not want and that was also very serious, but he never retreated. Besides, he was well aware of the difficulties that awaited him. In the same speech, turning in particular to the Bavarian pilgrims, he asked pardon in advance if, in conscience, in the future he would have to make unpleasant admonitions.

My program is to do God's will

ELECTORAL PROMISES?

On the evening of April 19, the cardinal protodeacon, the Chilean Jorge Medina, announced to the faithful on Saint Peter's Square and to the television viewers throughout the world that a new pope had been chosen, the German Joseph Ratzinger, who chose the name of Benedict XVI. Immediately afterward, the newly elected pope appeared on the balcony of his new apartment smiling and blessing the crowd. After the astonishing services that he had rendered in the preceding days, he now seemed tired, with bags under his eyes, as though subdued by the enormity of the weight that had been

---

[9] Benedict XVI, Address to German Pilgrims, Monday, April, 25, 2005.

placed on his shoulders. His words, too, were in keeping with his bearing: after the great pontiff John Paul II, the cardinals had elected a "simple, humble worker in the Lord's vineyard". The description hit the mark and won for the new pontiff the sympathy of those present and of the television viewers.

The following day, the pope and the cardinal electors had an appointment in the Sistine Chapel to celebrate together a Mass of thanksgiving. At the end of the celebration, Benedict XVI spoke to address his first message above all to those present who had voted for him but then also to the faithful and to those who were interested in dialogue with the Catholic Church.[10] The pontiff began his speech by recalling the two states of mind that had predominated in him during those hours. On the one hand, the sense of human inadequacy; on the other hand, gratitude and abandonment into the hands of God, who does not leave his flock alone. The new pope was preparing for the Petrine ministry by humbly entrusting himself into the hands of Providence. He truly wanted to be the servant of the servants of God. Then he continued: Peter and the apostles constituted one college. Similarly, the successor of Peter, the pope, and the successors of the apostles, the bishops, must be very closely united with one another, as the Vatican II Constitution on the Church says.[11]

Faithful to this purpose, the new pope would strive to put into practice the teachings of the council and to collaborate with the bishops. Moreover, he was beginning his ministry in the year dedicated to the Eucharist. Nourished and sustained by the Eucharistic food, Catholics cannot help being stimulated to tend toward the full unity for which Christ prayed in the Cenacle. With profound awareness, therefore, the current successor of Peter assumes the task of working unsparingly to restore the complete and visible unity of all the followers of Christ and is ready to do everything in his power to promote the fundamental cause of ecumenism. This mention of episcopal collegiality, Vatican II, and ecumenism was due, according to some commentators,[12] to a sort of elec-

---

[10] Benedict XVI, Message *Missa Pro Ecclesia*, April 20, 2005.

[11] Benedict XVI recalls in particular chapter 22 of the conciliar document *Lumen gentium*.

[12] Cf. Aldo Maria Valli, *Benedetto XVI: Il pontificato interrotto* (Milan: Mondadori, 2013), 30. Pope Benedict, nevertheless, always denied the hypothesis of the electoral agreement.

toral agreement, so as to comply with the requests of some cardinal electors.

In fact, although episcopal collegiality, ecumenism, and fidelity to Vatican II are obviously recurring themes in Ratzinger's writings, here the emphasis suggested a less cautious, more active commitment.

THE PURIFICATION OF PAPAL LANGUAGE

More in line with Ratzinger's thought, however, it seems to me, is the new terminology that he introduced into papal language. A sort of purification aimed at eliminating the claims to temporal power had already been started since the time of Paul VI. Now, though, Ratzinger replaced it with an obvious reference to the concept of service and martyrdom, of witness that in some way aligns itself with the situation of the Catholic Church in the world. Just as Catholics in many parts of the world suffer discrimination and persecution, so too the pope is called to a service, to a witness that, imitating Jesus and the apostle Peter, goes by way of deprivation and the cross.[13] Several years later, answering the question of Peter Seewald, Benedict confirmed this concept:

> Yes, I consider that correct even today. The primacy developed from the very beginning as a primacy of martyrdom. During the first three centuries Rome was the headquarters and capital of the Christian persecutions. Withstanding these persecutions and giving witness to Christ was the special task of the Roman episcopal see. . . . The fact that all the early Popes were martyrs is significant. Standing there as a glorious ruler is not part of being Pope, but rather giving witness to the One who was crucified and to the fact that he himself is ready also to exercise his office in this way, in union with him.[14]

Continuing in the work of purifying papal language, the first Mass of the new pope is no longer called "Mass of Enthronement" or

---

[13] In this regard, Ratzinger had already written an essay, in a way a forewarning, entitled "The Primacy of the Pope and the Unity of the People of God", reprinted in his anthology *Church, Ecumenism, and Politics*, trans. Michael J. Miller et al. (San Francisco: Ignatius Press, 2008), 36–50, in which he wrote, among other things: "The strength in which the Vicar of Christ must come to resemble his Lord is the strength of love that is ready for martyrdom" (47).

[14] Benedict XVI, *Light of the World*, trans. Michael J. Miller and Adrian J. Walker (San Francisco: Ignatius Press, 2010), 9–10.

more simply "of the beginning of the pontificate", but rather "Mass for the beginning of the Petrine ministry", of the service connected with succession to the first of the apostles, Saint Peter.

Present at that Mass, which was scheduled for Sunday, April 24, were a large number of civil and religious authorities and, above all, an impressive number of the faithful. To them, in his homily, Ratzinger presented himself with a new face, smiling and confident. Certainly, he noticed the weight of his new responsibility, but he did not feel alone. He explained that someone who believes is never alone; he is helped and guided by God; he is in the company of God's friends, the great saints of the past, but also of today's saints, the Christians who accompany the new pope and pray for him so that the Church might be a living reality.

GOD'S WILL AS THE PROGRAM OF THE PONTIFICATE

Benedict XVI was so convinced of being guided by God's will[15] that he did not feel any need to spell out a program for his pontificate. More concretely, the will of God was manifest in his growing Christocentrism, which was expressed not only in his writings, but also in his life. From this perspective, Benedict explained the two signs of the Petrine ministry that he put on for the first time on the inaugural day of his pontificate: the pallium and the fisherman's ring.

The pallium is a symbol of the yoke of Christ, the yoke of God, his will, which, nevertheless, is not oppressive but frees and purifies. Sometimes painfully, but it brings us back to ourselves, to our own destiny. The pallium is made of lamb's wool. This detail calls to mind the parable of the lost sheep, which the Fathers of the Church saw as an allegory of the mystery of Christ and the Church. All mankind is the lost sheep. Jesus, the good shepherd, will not and cannot lose that sheep. Therefore, he lifts it upon his shoulders and carries it back to God's house. In imitation of him, the pope, too, and the bishops are called to set out to lead mankind back to life. Here Benedict introduces one of the characteristic expressions of his thought and sensibility at the beginning of his mandate. Shep-

---

[15] Naturally there are many passages in the Gospel that speak about God's will. The one closest to Ratzinger's sensibility seems to me, nevertheless, to be the verse from the Gospel of John that says: "My food is to do the will of him who sent me, and to accomplish his work" (Jn 4:34).

herds must be moved by the holy concern of Jesus, by the desire to bring mankind back to life, to the encounter with God.

The other sign is the fisherman's ring, which Benedict explains by referring to the passage from the Gospel of John that speaks about a miraculous catch after the Resurrection of Jesus. Trusting in the Lord, the apostles cast their nets and draw out of the water an enormous number of fish. The pope comments that the net of the Gospel takes us out of the water of death and brings us into the sea of life in God. The Gospel account continues, then, with the threefold invitation to love addressed to Peter by Jesus. The fisherman's ring is a sign of this love that guides Peter on the way of the cross. Death, nevertheless, for a Christian, is not the final word. The joy of Easter follows, with the joy of the pastor who opens the door of God's friendship with man.

THE NAME BENEDICT CONFIRMS THIS PROGRAM

The choice of his name surprised many cardinals, who were ready to bet on John Paul III so as to testify to Ratzinger's continuity with his predecessor. The new pope, instead, answered the ritual question decisively: "Benedetto." Then, in order to underscore the importance of this choice, he himself explained its meaning on April 27 on the occasion of his first audience on Saint Peter's Square. The name Benedict showed his affinity for Benedict XV, who was pope during the turbulent period of the First World War, but above all it was due to his devotion to the extraordinary figure of Saint Benedict of Nursia, the co-patron of Europe.[16]

The choice of name contained two additional significant messages. First of all, with the reference to Benedict XV, Ratzinger wanted to make clear that his pontificate would be of short duration. Just as Pope Giacomo Della Chiesa lived in a tormented period because of the war and gave proof of his courage, similarly Benedict XVI knew that he was headed for a turbulent period. Courageous interventions were needed, both in the measures to be taken within the Church and also in the appeals addressed to the world. Fraught with even more significance is the reference to Saint Benedict of Nursia, who

---

[16] Benedict XVI, General Audience, April 27, 2005.

reminded Pope Ratzinger above all of the *dominici schola servitii*,[17] the school for learning to serve the Lord. This is the lifelong program of the monk, but also of every Christian.

Ratzinger was so convinced of this that he imposed on his life as pope an almost monastic routine. Differentiating himself in this from Pope John Paul II, he usually dined and prayed with the pontifical family, made up of four consecrated women belonging to Communion and Liberation and of his secretary, Monsignor Georg Gänswein. In response to Seewald, Benedict XVI himself described as follows his daily life on feast days:

> [With the papal family] . . . we celebrate Christmas together, listen to the holiday music, and exchange gifts. The feast days of our patron saints are celebrated, and occasionally we also sing Evening Prayer together. So we celebrate feasts together. And then, besides our common meals, there is above all Holy Mass in common in the morning. That is an especially important moment in which we are all with each other in a particularly intense way in the light of the Lord.[18]

This combination of reserve, study, hard work, and prayer left little room for meetings outside of official business. Hence the displeasure of those in the Curia who were accustomed to frequenting the papal apartment for reasons connected with their work, but also for advancement in their careers.

This approach to the Benedictine heritage, however, did not concern the life of the Church alone. In the view of the new pope, with his balance between reason and faith, between law and charity, Benedictine monasticism not only had given firm roots to Europe but had proposed a model that gave rise to humanism, democracy, the harmony of art and music.

Pope Benedict was not a naïve devotee of the past and certainly not an unrealistic dreamer who imagined that he could restore the conditions that had led to that movement of the spirit. With his life, therefore, he intended to propose again that balance between reason and faith that was at the origin of the particular attributes

---

[17] Rule of Saint Benedict, prologue. According to Basilius Steidle, a famous commentator on the Benedictine Rule, the expression *dominici schola servitii* summarizes Saint Benedict's whole program of life.

[18] Benedict XVI, *Light of the World*, 14.

that had made European culture and thought unique. The twentieth century had already amply demonstrated that, in abandoning that path, Europe had lost its strength to influence the world. There was no reason not to look at one's own history, one's own Christian roots with love and respect, not for the purposes of expansion, but in order to recover that ancient equilibrium that was at the origin of knowledge and wisdom of life.

The beginnings starting from Europe

CONTRASTING REACTIONS

When the election of the new pope was announced, the crowd present on Saint Peter's Square reacted with contrasting sentiments: some were exultant, others let loose an exclamation of disappointment.[19] The sentiments of Catholics worldwide were no different. Moreover, several times, Ratzinger, as prefect of the Congregation for the Doctrine of the Faith, had called bishops and theologians to adhere with conviction to the faith received from tradition and to the transmission thereof in fidelity to the Church and to the teaching of the pope and of the bishops. Only in that way could they be certain of staying in the communion of the universal Church and, above all, in the communion of the mystery of grace granted by God for the salvation of mankind.

For their part, the majority of the bishops were happy about the election of Ratzinger. The African and Asian prelates felt reassured, seeing on the Chair of Peter a man who was highly experienced and doctrinally sound, who promised to continue along the lines of his predecessor without creating further traumas in the Church. Among the Americans, in contrast, there was no lack of bishops who harbored more or less explicit reservations. The ones from South America did not forget his severity toward liberation theology; some North Americans would have liked a pontiff who was more open on moral issues and in general toward the modern world. Strangely, the ones most displeased were the European bishops[20] and, specifically,

---

[19] Cf. Valli, *Benedetto XVI*, 28.

[20] Bernard Lecomte cites the example of the Belgian Cardinal Danneels, in *Benoît XVI*, 120.

the bishops of Western Europe and the Germans.[21] Indeed, it must not be forgotten that Cardinal Lehmann, president of the German Bishops' Conference, had often come into conflict with the prefect of the Congregation for the Doctrine of the Faith, while Cardinal Kasper, president of the Pontifical Council for Promoting Christian Unity and for dialogue with the Jews, had spoken up several times in the days before the conclave in favor of a candidate with conspicuous pastoral sensitivity, thus giving the clear impression that his preference was for someone other than Ratzinger.[22]

For the sake of accuracy, it is necessary to recall that on the same day as the election, Lehmann held a press conference in which he stressed that "in today's situation of pluralism in opinions, not everyone has been able or willing to follow him, even in the Church."[23] He then added that, even in conflict, Ratzinger had won recognition for himself by his nonconformity and courage in addressing contemporary trends. Similarly, even Kasper proved to be a loyal collaborator of Benedict XVI in the following years. Nevertheless, the impression remains that the German Church in general and the Church in Western Europe were not particularly close to the German pontiff in the most delicate moments of his pontificate.

IN THE WAKE OF HIS PREDECESSOR

It certainly was not the first time in Church history that a deceased pontiff was succeeded by his closest collaborator. In the modern era, the best-known example is that of the former secretary of state of Pius XI, Pius XII, who succeeded his predecessor in record time. We should also add that in the most delicate moments, the cardinals almost naturally turn to the collaborators of the deceased pontiff. The new feature in Ratzinger's succession was, instead, the friendship and the profound understanding between John Paul II and his successor. This communion sprang, according to Pope Benedict, from a circumstance that he did not hesitate to describe as providential. Both Wojtyła and Ratzinger in their early youth had been involved in the Second World War, albeit on opposite fronts. Their

---

[21] Allen, *Rise of Benedict XVI*, 180f.

[22] Ibid., 101f.

[23] Cf. "Grusswort des Vorsitzenden der Deutschen Bischofskonferenz", text of the press conference held by Cardinal Lehmann in Campo Santo on April 19, 2005.

election, therefore, willed by Providence, was a sort of rainbow set over the nations to signify victory over the barbarity and violence that had spread from Central Europe over the whole world.

The work that Benedict set out to bring to completion was the work of increasing peace in the world, starting precisely from Europe and from its culture. Hence, once again, his insistent appeal to Saint Benedict, to the Christian origin and cultural mission of Europe in the world. As for his first appointments, according to a practice that is now customary, Pope Benedict confirmed all who held positions of authority in the Roman Curia. For the moment, he limited himself to electing or confirming his own successors: the American William Levada, whom he had known during the time when he was working on the *Catechism of the Catholic Church*, became his successor as prefect of the Congregation for the Doctrine of the Faith, while Cardinal Sodano took his position as dean of the College of Cardinals.

ATTENTION TO ITALY

Pope Benedict's first journey took him to the province of Puglia, to Bari, on May 29, 2005, for the conclusion of the Fourteenth National Eucharistic Congress of the Italian Church entitled "Without Sunday We Cannot Live." The Congress was part of the Year of the Eucharist announced by John Paul II to recall the centrality of this sacrament in the life of Christians. Only a few days had passed since the election, and the new pope might have been excused from participating in the event, but Benedict wanted to demonstrate immediately his closeness to the Italian Church. The title of the congress, taken from the statement by the Christians of Abitene, a tiny village in modern-day Tunisia, who died as martyrs in A.D. 304, provided an opportunity to stress the necessity and the value of celebrating the Eucharist on Sunday. Above all, the pope once again assured the Italian bishops about the promise he had made the day after his election to promote ecumenism. This was all the more believable since Bari, the city that preserves the relics of Saint Nicholas, originally from Myra in Asia Minor, is the meeting place between the Churches of the East and the West.

The following day, the pope and many of the bishops present in Bari met in Rome for the General Assembly of the Italian Bishops, which had been headed for almost fifteen years by Camillo Cardinal Ruini. The first thing on the agenda of the assembly was the upcoming referendum, promoted by radicals and left-wing parties, to make the laws on assisted procreation less restrictive. Guided by Cardinal Ruini, the Italian bishops had decided to fight, inviting the faithful to abstain from voting. Indeed, if more than half of the Italian citizens who had the right to vote abstained, it would nullify the referendum itself and therefore thwart the attempt to introduce a law that was more favorable toward assisted procreation, which the bishops saw as an attack against the traditional family.

The pope fully approved of the position of the Italian episcopate, which was committed, as he said, to "enlightening and motivating" the choices of Catholics and of all the citizens with regard to the referendum. He insisted precisely on this second point: "Here we are not working for Catholic interests, but always for man as God's creature."[24] Thus was announced one of the key themes of the future teaching of Benedict XVI. The Church does not want to impose Catholic morality but, rather, proposes to men and women an ethic based on a rationality that is profoundly human, not designed to achieve partisan goals but, rather, resulting from the dignity of man created by God. This dignity is at the foundation of the values that the pope describes as "nonnegotiable". Catholics must defend them in public life, even at the risk of being exposed to the hostility of their opponents. In the pope's opinion, nevertheless, the defense of these values does not involve an incorrect intrusion into the life of the State but, rather, is a sign of active participation in social life.

Benedict XVI supported this thesis also in the presence of the then president of the Italian Republic, Carlo Azeglio Ciampi. Returning the visit that the head of state had paid him on May 5, 2005, on June 24 of that same year, the pope went to the Quirinal Palace. There, the new pontiff distinguished between laicism, or dogmatic secularism, which is to be rejected, and a healthy laicity of the State, which is good for the Church as well. Healthy laicity is the sort that does not confine religion to a merely private space but, rather, makes room for it in public debate and recognizes its cultural importance. Then the pope listed his chief concerns with respect to Italy: safeguarding the family founded on marriage, the

---

[24] Valli, *Benedetto XVI*, 34.

defense of human life from conception until its natural end, and, finally, education in the schools.

Benedict XVI knew that on topics concerning human life the distance between the prevailing culture and the Christian vision was widening in Italy, too; nevertheless, he thought that the Church cannot stop offering her contribution, which is both Christian and human, to contemporary society. It is important, finally, to emphasize one fact that was paradoxical only at first glance: the election of a non-Italian pope for the second consecutive time had diminished neither the attention paid to Italy by the successor of Peter nor the deferential attitude of the head of the Italian State for the pontiffs. For the Vatican's part, the new spokesman of Benedict XVI, Jesuit Father Federico Lombardi, commented: "It has become even more obvious that the pope helps Italy to look farther into the world and into today's history."[25] For Italy's part, we may perhaps add that the fact of a foreign pope helped to reduce the interference of the Vatican hierarchy in Italian politics.

VACATION IN THE VALLE D'AOSTA

Benedict XVI also chose the destination of his first summer vacation as pope in continuity with John Paul II. Very practical reasons were probably behind the choice, given the short time that had passed since the election. In any case, on July 11, the Feast of Saint Benedict and, therefore, the day of his new *onomastico* (patron saint's feast), he traveled to Les Combes d'Introd in the Valle d'Aosta, one of the favorite vacation spots of his predecessor. There, a chalet owned by the Salesian Fathers assured a period of fairly good rest, made up of reading and not very demanding walks. It was also the opportunity for the new pontiff to meet the priests of the valley, to whom he opened his own heart in honest, sincere conversation. As he had said in Bari, Pope Benedict had confidence in Italy, where, in his opinion, the parishes still are a significant presence in the region, while the dialogue with the new charismatic groups and the movements enlivens and gives fresh sap to the trunk, which in other places runs the risk of atrophy. Moreover, given the loneliness of priests,

---

[25] Federico Lombardi, *In cammino con Benedetto XVI* (Rome: Apostolata della Preghiera, 2011), 26.

which reflects the loneliness of Western societies, the pope invited them to construct "methods of socializing the faith, so that the faith might form communities and offer living spaces".[26] Devotion or mysticism is not enough, therefore; it is necessary to communicate intelligently the beauty and the organic structure of the faith.

Benedict XVI was not a visionary, nor did he have institutions of the past in mind. He saw the disintegration of contemporary society, which was also reproduced in the Church. He was aware, too, of the phenomenon of the Catholic communities of Central Europe, in particular the German-speaking ones, which, structurally, were drawing ever closer to the Protestant communities, and he wanted to suggest a remedy. He saw the solution in collaboration between the clergy and the new ecclesial institutions, between the priests and the spirituality of the new movements. He had declared several years before to Seewald: "Catholicism in fact can never be merely institutionally and academically planned and managed, but appears ever again as a gift, as a spiritual vitality. And it in the process also has the gift of diversity. There is no uniformity among Catholics. There can be 'Focolare' or Catechumenate piety, Schönstatt, Cursillo, and [Communion and Liberation] spirituality, and so on."[27]

Then-Cardinal Ratzinger was already pointing out the response usually given in progressive circles to these arguments: whatever does not submit to academic plans or to the deliberations of committees and synods is viewed with suspicion and labeled reactionary. Therefore, he exhorted everyone to tolerance and collaboration: "I believe that a great deal of tolerance is required within the Church, that the diversity of paths is something in accordance with the breadth of Catholicity."[28] As pope, therefore, Benedict returned to these arguments and again proposed to the Italian clergy his invitation to dialogue, convinced that the Italian situation could also be a model for the countries of Central Europe, in particular in German-speaking areas.

---

[26] See Valli, *Benedetto XVI*, 36.

[27] Joseph Ratzinger, *God and the World: Believing and Living in Our Time*, trans. Henry Taylor (San Francisco: Ignatius Press, 2002), 455.

[28] Ibid., 456.

World Youth Day in Cologne

The Vaticanist Bernard Lecomte was right when he said that it was not the fault of Benedict XVI that the first World Youth Day of his pontificate was to be held in Cologne, in his native country, in the center of Europe.[29] The place, date, and theme of the meeting had already been decided by John Paul II the previous year, as is clear from the message dated August 6, 2004, that was sent by the Polish pontiff to young people.[30] The occasion, nevertheless, propitiously allowed the new pope to appear before his fellow countrymen so as to offset their rather tepid reception and to transmit to them, starting with the young people, the enthusiasm for the Christian faith that urged the Anglo-Saxon Winfrid, who became Boniface, to evangelize the eastern part of the land of the Franks, which then became the seat of the Holy Roman Empire. Benedict XVI was well aware of the opportunity that had been offered to him, and over the summer he had already prepared carefully for the event.

He disembarked at the airport in Cologne-Bonn on the morning of August 18, 2005, and was welcomed by the president of the Federal Republic of Germany, Horst Köhler, by Chancellor Gerhard Schröder, by the cardinal of Cologne, Joachim Meisner, and by the president of the German Bishops' Conference, Cardinal Lehmann. The greeting by the pontiff upon his arrival was certainly a formality, but we can believe him when he says that he considers it

a loving gesture of reconciliation, since, quite unintentionally, my first Visit outside of Italy should be to my Homeland: Here in Cologne, at a moment, in a place and on an occasion when the young people of all the world are meeting, from all the continents, in which the frontiers between the continents, cultures, races, nations disappear, in order that we may all be one thanks to the star that has shone for us: the star of faith in Jesus Christ.[31]

When Benedict speaks about reconciliation, he has in mind primarily the dark period of the Third Reich and of the Second World

---

[29] Lecomte, *Benoît XVI*, 130.

[30] Message of John Paul II to Youth, August 6, 2004, reprinted in Benedict XVI, *God's Revolution: World Youth Day and Other Cologne Talks* (San Francisco: Ignatius Press, 2006), 21–26.

[31] Benedict XVI, Address, World Youth Day, August 18, 2005, in ibid., 27–31 at 27.

War, which wounded the millennial history of his country and of
its Christian heritage, but he also has in mind what von Balthasar
called the "anti-Roman affect", the attitude of self-sufficiency and of
disdain toward what comes from the Vatican, and he has at heart the
separation of civil society from the values of the Christian tradition,
which had had exceptional witnesses. In antiquity, Saint Boniface
and Saint Albert the Great; in recent times, Saint Benedicta of the
Cross and Blessed Adolph Kolping. The presence of so many young
people can be the occasion to overcome hatreds and misunderstandings, but also to recover the desire for knowledge that urged the
Magi to undertake the journey that led them to know Jesus and,
after their death, led the Christians of Cologne to welcome their
relics on the banks of the Rhine.

LET JESUS SURPRISE YOU

On the afternoon of that same day, Benedict XVI traveled about six
miles upstream on the Rhine in a small boat toward Cologne. On
both banks, groups of young people watched as the pope embarked,
while emotions and memories crowded in on the mind and heart
of the pontiff, who had spent there some of the finest years of his
teaching career.[32] When he arrived at his destination, the pope was
almost overwhelmed by the enthusiasm of the young people. Only
with difficulty did he succeed in obtaining silence, and he extended
his greeting to those who came from near or far, particularly from
the East, from which the Magi had come also. To all of them he
cried insistently: "Open wide your hearts to God! Let yourselves be
surprised by Christ! Let him have 'the right of free speech' during
these days! Open the doors of your freedom to his merciful love!"[33]
The city of Cologne is connected with the relics of the Magi, which
are venerated there in the great Gothic late-medieval cathedral. The
pope was therefore inviting the young people to make their own

---

[32] He wrote in 1997, as he concluded his seventieth year: "At night I could hear the
whistles on the Rhine, which flows by the Albertinum. The great river with its international shipping traffic gave me the feeling of openness and breadth, of the meeting of
cultures and nations that for centuries had occurred here and made one another fruitful" (in Joseph Ratzinger, *Milestones: Memoirs 1927–1977*, trans. Erasmo Leiva-Merikakis
[San Francisco: Ignatius Press, 1998], 115–16).

[33] Benedict XVI, *God's Revolution*, 36.

the wonder of the Magi before the helpless infant who bridged the gulf between eternity and time, between the finite and the infinite, between God and man. Then he concluded: "Christ takes from you nothing that is beautiful and great, but brings everything to perfection for the glory of God, the happiness of men and women, and the salvation of the world."[34]

THE REVOLUTION OF GOD AND THE SAINTS

The pope's most original speech was held on Marienfeld, "Mary's field", an enormous esplanade about twenty miles from Cologne where around a million young people had an appointment to meet the pontiff and to spend the night in prayer, singing, and meetings in friendship and faith. The Magi were once again the leitmotif of the pope's speech. They had come to find the new king and had found themselves, instead, before a baby. They had in mind a powerful man, ready to change the world with his army, but in front of them was a frail infant who needed everything. Therefore, they had to change their ideas about power, about God, and about man, and, in doing so, they were changed as well. The Magi, who had come from the East, are, moreover, only the first in a long series of men and women who, at the sight of the star sent by God, set out and undertook a journey in search of Jesus.

In every age, the saints have turned a page of the Gospel and revealed it to their contemporaries. From Saint Benedict and Saint Francis down to Mother Teresa and Padre Pio, they are like the uninterrupted track of a comet, at the origin of which is the glowing light brought by Jesus. The real wise men, according to Pope Benedict, are those who, in the light of the Gospel, transform the reality of this world. With reference to the history of the twentieth century, they are, indeed, the true revolutionaries who carried out the revolution that comes from God, the revolution of love, which is opposed to the revolution of hatred and violence. The pontiff concluded: "In Jesus Christ . . . the true face of God is seen. We will follow him together with the great multitude of those who went before us."[35]

---

[34] Ibid., 39.

[35] Ibid., 54.

This is an image of the Church of which Pope Benedict is very fond. She is the great procession that, following God's star, travels through history and constitutes a space of unity and communion through the centuries and across the continents. For this reason, it is important to have continuity with the past and with the future, avoiding ruptures and rifts that could interrupt the procession that comes from the first Epiphany, from the manifestation of God in history.

ECUMENICAL AND INTERRELIGIOUS DIALOGUE

As he had promised the cardinals on the day after his election, Benedict XVI intended to continue on the path of ecumenical dialogue, taking as his guide the Declaration *Nostra aetate* of Vatican II; the fortieth anniversary of its promulgation occurred that year. The World Youth Day in Cologne was therefore the occasion for three high-profile meetings with leaders of the Lutheran Church, with the Jewish community in Cologne, the most ancient in Germany, and with representatives of the Muslim community in Germany.

ECUMENISM OF THE SPIRIT

Ratzinger's meeting with the representatives of other Churches and ecclesial communities present in Germany did not prove easy. Only a few years earlier, on the occasion of the publication of the Declaration *Dominus Iesus*, the then prefect of the Congregation for the Doctrine of the Faith had been severely criticized in his country by many experts, both Lutherans and Catholics, for the points concerning Jesus Christ and the Church, which were thought to impede the ecumenical dialogue that was under way. Benedict, nevertheless, went right to the point. Germany, he said, is the country where the rupture in the unity of the faith in the Western Church had its beginning. It is also the country, he continued, in which ecumenical dialogue began in the last century and where important goals have been achieved. Among these, he recalled the 1999 "Joint Declaration on the Doctrine of Justification", which, according to a generally shared opinion, is an important point of agreement.

On the other hand, the pontiff did not agree about how to continue the dialogue concerning the question of ministry and ecclesiology. What mattered to him, before entering into relatively technical inter-ecclesial aspects, was the common testimony to be given to the world and the concept of ecumenism itself, which cannot mean a denial of the history of the two ecclesial institutions, Catholic and Lutheran. We cannot and must not aim at an absolute uniformity in faith and spirituality but, rather, at unity in multiplicity and multiplicity in unity, which is above all a gift of the Spirit. "Consequently spiritual ecumenism—prayer, conversion and the sanctification of life—constitutes the heart of the ecumenical encounter and movement."[36] To confirm this statement, the pope recalled the example of Roger Schutz, the founder of the Taizé community, who had died tragically three days earlier, on August 16, 2005.[37] A precursor of ecumenism, he was at the same time a witness who had given his life for the attainment of unity. As when he was a cardinal, so too as Benedict XVI, Ratzinger did not intend to stop at compliments. He went right to the essential questions and, instead of placing his faith in the work of specialists, he relied on what he called "ecumenism of the Spirit", which is made up of prayer, conversion, and sanctity.

THE MEETING WITH THE JEWS

The intensely busy days in Cologne also included a scheduled meeting with the Jewish community of the city. Speaking in the synagogue, Benedict insisted on a concept that was certainly dear to the Jews present. The Jewish community is at home in Cologne because its presence in the city on the Rhine goes back to the time when it was a Roman colony. Over the centuries, the relations between the two communities, Jewish and Christian, had swung back and forth between periods of peace and intervals of expulsions and persecutions. Then, in the twentieth century, the insane Nazi ideology subjected the Jews to a persecution that had previously not even been imaginable.

Vatican II, fortunately, started a new phase in the relations between the two communities, based on friendship and collaboration. The Jewish community, therefore, can once again feel truly at home in Cologne, while Jews and Christians are called to grow in

---

[36] Ibid., 86.

[37] On August 17, at the Angelus, the pope had recalled the tragic death of Brother Roger, who had been assassinated by an insane woman. On that same occasion, he recalled having received from Brother Roger a letter in which he wrote: "We are in communion with you and with those who are gathered in Cologne." See *Enchiridion Vaticanum* 23 (Bologna: Dehoniane), 592.

their knowledge about each other. They have in common the Ten Commandments, which can be for the future the basis on which to build a more just and cohesive society, not only for their respective communities, but for the whole country, while Jews and Christians can and must learn to esteem and respect each other even in their differences.

MEETING WITH REPRESENTATIVES OF SOME MUSLIM COMMUNITIES

Respect and honesty were the guiding principles of the speech given by Benedict XVI during his meeting with the representatives of some Islamic communities in Germany. The point of departure was a reference to the spreading phenomenon of terrorism. The pope knew that many of those present had publicly condemned attempts to link the Islamic faith with terrorism, but he was also aware that terroristic activities were multiplying in the world, causing carnage and suffering. The task of religions, he declared, in particular of Muslims and Christians, is to resist every form of violence and to oppose all manifestations of it, based on their common conviction that human life is sacred.

The pope knew that in the past Christians and Muslims had often engaged in armed conflict in the name of God. Once again, however, Vatican II started a new phase, inviting them to forget the past and to forge relations of mutual understanding, together promoting social justice, moral values, peace, and freedom. More clearly, he continued: "We must seek paths of reconciliation and learn to live with respect for each other's identity. The defense of religious freedom, in this sense, is a permanent imperative, and respect for minorities is a clear sign of true civilization."[38] In conclusion, the pontiff recalled that he was a native of Germany and that for a long time he had been a professor. Hence, his invitation to responsibility and dedication in the formation of young people in order to respond to the challenges of the day. On this basis, Christians and Muslims can collaborate with a view to a better future.

Contrary to what many commentators and pundits in the West had expected, the World Youth Day in Cologne concluded with a true success for Benedict XVI. The new pope had not sought to

---

[38] Benedict XVI, *God's Revolution*, 76.

imitate the charisma of John Paul II but had been himself. He had won over the young people with the clarity and precision of his speeches, with his ability to argue starting from reason that then opens the way to faith. "This authenticity", Lecomte concludes, "is what enabled him to win the bet and to conquer all those young people who knew nothing about him. It was in Cologne, on Sunday, August 21, 2005, that Benedict XVI really succeeded John Paul II."[39]

A promising start

Pope Benedict returned to Rome encouraged from the meeting with the young people in Cologne. The protests in his native land feared by some had not materialized; the young people had shown him affection and enthusiasm. The pope drew from this the conclusion that the Church was alive, and this gave him peace of mind and a new awareness of his mission.

FIRST MEETING WITH THE LEFEBVRITES

After the ecumenical meetings in Cologne, in late August, the leader of the Lefebvrites, Bernard Fellay, arrived in Castel Gandolfo. The General Superior of the Society of Saint Pius X appreciated the severe admonitions of Pope Benedict in the liturgical field and expressed the desire to meet the pope, who promptly agreed to the request. In the Church and in the Curia itself, many were perplexed, but the pope did not want to abandon the attempt to put an end to the rift with the Society of Saint Pius X. They asked for the lifting of the excommunication of the four bishops who had been consecrated without authorization by the founder, Archbishop Lefebvre, and for the possibility of using the Latin Missal of Saint Pius V. The pope was willing to grant these requests, and in exchange he asked for full acceptance of Vatican II. One possible solution would be that of a personal prelature, on the model of Opus Dei. The Society of Saint Pius X could become in practice a nonterritorial diocese with its own ordinary and centers of formation and spirituality.

---

[39] Lecomte, Benoît XVI, 136.

One of the four Lefebvrite bishops, the extremist Richard Williamson, abruptly put an end to the discussions. He leaked the news about Fellay's meeting with Benedict XVI, which was supposed to remain confidential, and provoked the extremist Lefebvrites against their superior general, whom they considered too accommodating with regard to Rome. The talks were therefore suspended for the moment, but Benedict did not lose hope. Above all, he did not want to close the door on those who intended to return to Catholic communion.

Meanwhile, the pope continued his activity confidently. In September, in the first television interview of a pontiff, he confirmed once again to the Polish network his devotion to John Paul II and his friendship toward Poland, which he would visit in May of the following year. Then, over the next few days, a meeting took place that in many aspects was paradigmatic: the pope received in audience for a good four hours Hans Küng, his former colleague in Tübingen, from whom John Paul II had withdrawn the *missio canonica* in 1979, the authorization to teach theology in the German universities.[40] For Küng's part, there was a sort of openness with regard to the theologian-pope; for Benedict XVI, it was an opportunity to give some attention to erudite theologians, many of whom still had misgivings about their former colleague who had become, first, keeper of the faith and, then, universal pastor.

In mid-October, a Ratzinger whom no one would have expected from his publications stood on Saint Peter's Square, answering questions from children who had received their First Holy Communion that year. Even though they had been prepared with priests and catechists, children's questions always have something spontaneous and essential. The pope, who did not forget that he had once taught catechism and who had lavished so much effort on the preparation of the *Catechism of the Catholic Church* and of the more recent *Compendium*, answered them all in language that was simple but not trivial. The most moving answer was the one in which he recalled the day of his First Communion: "But at the heart of my joyful and beautiful memories is this one. . . . I understood that Jesus had entered my heart, he had actually visited me. And with Jesus, God himself was with me. . . . I promised the Lord as best I could: 'I

---

[40] For the previous relations between Ratzinger and Küng, see above, chaps. 6 and 7.

always want to stay with you', and I prayed to him, 'but above all, stay with me.'"[41]

The theologian who was considered cold proved to be a man with authentic spirituality, someone who loved his origins and the Church's liturgy, the sacraments, nature, and music, which are not heterogeneous realities. On the contrary, they form a harmonic whole in which one can live in the serenity that appeared to be the distinctive feature of Benedict XVI as his pontificate began.

THE SYNOD ON THE EUCHARIST

After Cologne, the most important event of the first year of his pontificate was the celebration in Rome of the Eleventh Ordinary General Assembly of the Synod of Bishops, from October 2 to 23, on the theme "The Eucharist, Source and Summit of the Life and Mission of the Church". Two hundred fifty-six bishops from five continents participated in the meeting, which took place at the conclusion of the Year of the Eucharist and forty years after the conclusion of Vatican II. Practically speaking, the bishops, who had the opportunity to meet with one another in Rome, breathed the atmosphere of Vatican II for three weeks and took the occasion to become acquainted and to discuss the problems of their Churches. Characteristically, the pope invited them to do so by adding to the program already set for those days an hour, from 6:00 to 7:00 P.M., for free exchanges among the participants. Some of the Fathers complained, considering this break a waste of time. But the pope knew very well what he was doing, and, in order to convince the more reluctant, he himself never failed to attend these sessions. He had his heart set on dialogue and listening and intended to promote it.

The rest of this first synod held during the pontificate of Pope Benedict lends itself to various considerations. First, we cannot help noting the usefulness of periodical meetings of bishops from different continents and countries. The welcoming, cordial atmosphere that they had the opportunity to experience in Rome enabled them to feel strengthened in a ministry that had been made increasingly difficult by the clergy shortage, the decrease in religious practice, and the crisis in transmitting the faith. A second consideration

---

[41] Benedict XVI, Catechetical Meeting with Children, October 15, 2005.

concerned the experience of catholicity, which invited the participants to overcome a sometimes biased viewpoint. While the European bishops lamented the lack of priests, their colleagues from Africa pointed out that their problem was to establish criteria for accepting seminarians, given the excessive number of applications. And while a bishop from Papua New Guinea asked to be allowed to ordain some older men of proven reliability for dispersed, remote islands, the Eastern Rite patriarchs, whose priests are often married with children, warned against this practice. They agreed that it is not a question of dogma, yet married priests are not considered by the faithful to be sufficiently accessible, while their bishops encounter many difficulties when it comes to replacing or reassigning them.[42]

The final point discussed was the one that had been considered many times already: divorced and civilly remarried persons and whether to admit them to the sacraments, particularly to the Eucharist. On this point, too, the bishops took different positions, and ultimately the synod was unable to make any real decisions. At the conclusion of the proceedings, nevertheless, a list of fifty propositions was prepared, which the bishops presented to the pope, who decided to make it public. Paradoxically, this liberalizing decision of the pope discredited the synod somewhat, upstaging the first two considerations. The lack of real, true solutions gave the impression that the synod was now a tired ceremony, incapable of making decisions for the life of the Church.

FORTY YEARS SINCE THE CONCLUSION OF VATICAN II

December 8, 2005, was the fortieth anniversary of the conclusion of Vatican II. On that date, the pope spoke about the Marian setting of the council, which also indicated a style, the Blessed Virgin's way of actively listening to the word of God. Much more demanding was the speech that he addressed to the Roman Curia on December 22, 2005. According to tradition, in his end-of-the-year speech, the pope gives a status report on the Church. In this specific case, Benedict XVI reflected on the first year of his pontificate, recalling the path of suffering that had led to the death of John Paul II and the intense, joyous days of Cologne. Then he recalled once again

---

[42] See Lecomte, *Benoît XVI*, 130.

the fortieth anniversary of the conclusion of Vatican II, taking the occasion to proceed to a detailed clarification of the correct way of interpreting and implementing the council itself.

Already during the council proceedings, according to Pope Benedict, there was a conflict between two ways of interpreting what was happening in the life of the Church: on the one hand, there was a hermeneutic of discontinuity or rupture, which saw a clear-cut separation between the life of the Church preceding the council and afterward. According to this interpretation, the documents themselves drawn up in Rome were the product of compromise and did not yet contain the true conciliar spirit. Only by going courageously beyond the documents of Vatican II would the Church make room for the true intention of the council Fathers. At this point, however, the pope says, the real problem with this hermeneutic arises: On the basis of what criteria can we go farther to seek the authentic spirit of the council? Is this not a path to arbitrary innovations that completely lose sight of the Lord's invitation to be wise, faithful stewards? Consequently, the hermeneutic of discontinuity, which indeed was supported by broad sectors of the press and modern theology, should be rejected.

Contrasting with the hermeneutic of rupture is the hermeneutic of reform that was proposed by John XXIII and Paul VI. It did not intend to break with Church tradition but, rather, to respond to three questions that had been raised in the modern era: the relation between faith and modern science, including historical science; the relation between Church and the modern State; and the relation between the Christian faith and world religions. With Vatican II, the Church "has reviewed or even corrected certain historical decisions, but in this apparent discontinuity it has actually preserved and deepened her inmost nature and true identity. The Church, both before and after the Council, was and is the same Church, one, holy, catholic and apostolic, journeying on through time."[43]

For her part, the Church wishes to enter into dialogue both with the State and also with the modern world and with the other religions on the basis of reason, which is the common patrimony of human beings. However, she cannot abandon the discernment of

---

[43] *Enchiridion Vaticanum* 23:1008. Benedict XVI, Address to the Roman Curia, Thursday, December 22, 2005.

the spirit, her testimony to the truth that Christians, like believers of other religions and nonbelievers of goodwill, expect from her more than ever. Anyone who had imagined that the tensions between the Church and the contemporary world would be totally gone after Vatican II obviously was wrong. In our time, too, the Church remains a sign of contradiction, and she will be so the more faithful she is to the Gospel.

JOURNEY TO POLAND

In May 2006, Benedict XVI made a pilgrimage to Poland. The visit was of course a tribute to the memory of John Paul II; at the same time, it was also a warning to the new secularized Poland and a renewed invitation to reconciliation in a country still torn by the not yet entirely healed wounds of the Holocaust and of the Communist dictatorship. Upon his arrival in Warsaw on May 25, the pope's thoughts naturally turned to John Paul II, who had traveled to the capital twenty-seven years before. He exclaimed: "How can we not thank God for what was accomplished in your country and in the world during the pontificate of John Paul II?"[44]

Although the thought of the great change brought about thanks to Pope Wojtyła was present every day during the trip to Poland, Pope Benedict also knew that Poland must now confront new challenges. One of these concerned the Catholic Church, also, in particular the clergy: it was the painful question about priests who, according to the archives recently opened to the public, had collaborated with the secret police. The pope asked the priests who were in fact responsible to find the courage to ask forgiveness, and he asked the faithful and all citizens to have the fortitude to forgive, because, although it is true that the Church is holy, it is just as true that there are sinners within the Church. This was the first of many *mea culpa*'s that the pontiff would be forced to utter during his pontificate.

On the last day of his visit to Poland, Benedict XVI traveled to Auschwitz. The German pope was courageous, knowing that the eyes of the world were on him, and he was also aware of the inadequacy of speeches. "In a place like this, words fail; in the end,

---

[44] See Valli, *Benedetto XVI*, 64.

there can only be a dread silence."[45] Then he continued: "I could not fail to come here. . . . It is a duty . . . for me to come here as [pope] and as a son of the German people . . . to implore the grace of reconciliation—first of all from God, . . . from the men and women who suffered here, and finally . . . for all those who, at this hour of our history, are suffering in new ways from the power of hatred and the violence which hatred spawns."[46] Another *mea culpa*, this time in the name of his fellow countrymen. Although he was visibly moved, the German pope was rather sparing with his words.

In reality, Benedict did not want to get into historical analyses, nor did he intend to set himself up as a judge of the German people, much less of God. "We cannot peer into God's mysterious plan— we see only piecemeal, and we would be wrong to set ourselves up as judges of God and history."[47] Furthermore, if we blame God, we are wrong and, thus depriving man of his strongest defense, we plunge further into his destruction. Nothing remains but the invocation of the psalm: "Rouse yourself! Why do you sleep, O Lord? . . . Why do you hide your face?"[48] and the invitation to the purification of memory, to reconciliation. Furthermore, the count- less inscriptions [at the memorial in Auschwitz] are not intended to provoke the visitors to hatred but, rather, to arouse the sentiments that Sophocles placed on the lips of Antigone: "My nature is not to join in hate but to join in love."[49]

JOURNEY TO SPAIN

A few weeks after the journey to Poland, in early July, Benedict XVI traveled to Spain, to Valencia, where the Fifth World Meeting of Families was being held. Less than half a century after the end of the Franco regime, Catholic predominance in the life of the coun- try was a distant memory. Among the authorities, the head of the

---

[45] *Enchiridion Vaticanum* 23:1343. Benedict XVI, Address, Pastoral Visit to the Ausch- witz Camp, May 28, 2006.

[46] Ibid., 1345.

[47] Ibid.

[48] Ps 44:23–24.

[49] *Enchiridion Vaticanum* 23:1348. Benedict XVI, Address, Pastoral Visit to the Ausch- witz Camp, May 28, 2006.

government, José Luis Zapatero, was conspicuously absent, while in the city, gay demonstrations were organized to coincide with the pope's presence. The pope, nevertheless, did not lose his serenity, and, at the concluding vigil, in front of more than a million people, he repeated one of the convictions that he had taken most to heart: "The family is the privileged setting where every person learns to give and receive love."[50] Although the institution of family is precious for the Church as an aid in transmitting the faith and love of the Lord, it is likewise indispensable for society inasmuch as it forms free, responsible persons.[51] Then came the concluding invitation, addressed to government leaders and legislators, to reflect on the obvious good secured for mankind by families, which are "a school of humanity".

After the encouraging outcome of the journey to Poland, Benedict XVI also returned from his trip to Spain with the sense of having done a good deed. His speeches had given confidence to the bishops and priests, and above all the faithful had welcomed with manifest conviction his testimony on behalf of the family and human life. The favorable overall assessment of the two journeys could, moreover, extend to the whole first year of the pontificate, during which Pope Benedict had steered the bark of Peter with growing confidence and serenity.

---

[50] *Enchiridion Vaticanum* 23:1400. Benedict XVI, Address at Prayer Vigil, Fifth World Meeting of Families, July 8, 2006.

[51] Ibid., 1405.

XIV

THE DIFFICULTIES OF GOVERNING

The decline in the approval ratings of the papacy that many had predicted when Benedict XVI was elected did not appear in Cologne, nor did it occur in the following months. On the contrary, according to Seewald, during the first year of Pope Benedict's pontificate, there was a steady increase of pilgrims to Rome, a sign of evident satisfaction with the new pontiff.[1] Benedict XVI himself noted this fact, which he attributed to "the inner continuity with the previous pontificate and . . . the abiding vitality of the Church".[2] His address to the Roman Curia at the end of 2005, however, was a signal of a difficulty that should not be underestimated. In short, the pope renewed the promise that he had made on the day after his election to remain faithful to the decisions made by Vatican Council II. However, he gave his own interpretation of the conciliar event and asked the staff of the Curia to adhere to it.

Over the years, this way of proceeding would prove to be the particular feature of Pope Benedict's governing style destined to characterize the years of his pontificate. Rather than taking concrete measures, he preferred admonitions, leaving to those concerned the freedom to adapt to the required behavior. As for the effectiveness of this way of proceeding, we can think of the parable of the sower throwing seeds on various types of soil. Some were wasted, others got trampled, while others brought forth abundant fruits. What is certain, nevertheless, is that the new pope's method of governing

---

[1] Benedict XVI, *Light of the World: A Conversation with Peter Seewald*, trans. Michael J. Miller and Adrian J. Walker (San Francisco: Ignatius Press, 2010), 18.

[2] Ibid., 19.

aimed not so much at immediate effectiveness as at conviction and bearing witness. Only time would tell if this new style would bring the desired changes.

The Secretariat of State

At the death of John Paul II, opinion about the government of the Church was sharply divided if not conflicting. In contrast to the utmost consideration for the witness and teaching of the great pontiff, there was the harsh judgment that Ratzinger himself had passed on Good Friday on Vatican leaders and more generally on the Catholic clergy. Moreover, the fear that the future pope had experienced so dramatically as he approached the election speaks volumes about the situation in the Roman Curia and, more generally, about the governance of the universal Church at the moment when Benedict XVI was elected.

The major consensus that John Paul II had earned both among Catholics and in the rest of the world had covered up the deficiencies or even the simple laziness of some curial appointees, who were much more attentive to their careers than to "the good of the Church"—an expression that they themselves abused. After all, the reform of the Curia that Paul VI had undertaken decisively and effectively in 1967 showed some sign of wear and was in need of renewal. In the opinion of Antonio Acerbi, the strengths introduced by the constitution *Regimini ecclesiae universae* on "The Government of the Universal Church" were the temporary nature of assignments, the forfeiture of office at the death of the pope, and the suppression of the right to a career. These were undoubtedly positive elements.

Paul VI, however, had also assigned to the Secretariat of State a task of coordination that had slowly turned into supervision. "With this, the Secretariat of State had become the keystone of the whole edifice: the congregations were not called to cooperate directly with the pope, but only through the mediation of the Secretariat of State."[3] This evolution was confirmed by John Paul II in the constitution *Pastor aeternus* (1988). On the basis of the new law, the Secretariat

---

[3] Antonio Acerbi, "Il pontificato di Paolo VI", in *Storia della Chiesa*, ed. A. Fliche and V. Martin, vol. 25/1, *La Chiesa del Vaticano II*, ed. M. Guasco, E. Guerriero, and F. Traniello (Cinisello Balsamo: San Paolo, 1994), 68.

of State became, according to Gian Piero Milano, "the pope's auxiliary center in the exercise of his supreme office, of his pastoral
care for the good and the service of the universal Church and of
the particular Churches".[4]

There were two areas of interest for the Secretariat of State: the
inner life of the Church, belonging to the first section, which was
also called the section for extraordinary ecclesiastical affairs, headed
by the Substitute, one of the closest collaborators of the secretary of
state and of the pope himself; then relations with the States and the
local Churches, the business of the second section, led by a secretary
also known as the Vatican Foreign Minister. Compared to the traditional duties, this second section had seen its tasks diminished as far
as relations with States were concerned, while its liaison function
with the local Churches had increased over time. Another element
that over the years ended up acquiring a prominent function within
the Curia was the figure of the pontiff's personal secretary. A leak
to the media can be more eloquent than long speeches. During the
last years of John Paul II, his personal secretary, Archbishop Stanisław Dziwisz, was nicknamed in the Curia "the little pope" with
reference to his height but also to his power. For this reason, too,
immediately after the Polish pope's death, he was named archbishop
of Kraków, to thank him for his collaboration at the side of John
Paul II, but also to remove him from Rome.

In short, any development to meet the need for a more effective
and functional government needed some preliminary groundwork
in order to restore the balance among the various governing bodies
and to respond to the grievances of the leaders of other congregations who felt excluded or even in subjection to the secretary of
state. Precisely on this point, Cardinal Ratzinger had repeatedly expressed uncertainty, both theological and practical. In order to talk
to the pontiff, even cardinals who held very important positions had
to go through a secretariat that was naturally inclined to favor its
own concerns over those of other curial dicasteries. The nuncios responsible for relations with the States, but also for keeping in touch
with the local Churches, in particular for the appointment of new

---

[4] The description by Gian Piero Milano is recorded by R. Astorri, "La segreteria di
Stato nelle riforme di Paolo VI e Giovanni Paolo II", in *Mélanges de l'école française de
Rome—Italie et Méditerranée* 110 (1998): 513.

bishops, were churchmen whose initial education was theological, but then they specialized in the study of languages and took courses on the history of Vatican diplomacy, writing diplomatic reports, and international law.

According to tradition, moreover, the secretary of state was chosen by the pope from among the nuncios who had proven their abilities in their work. There was good reason to wonder, though, whether this old practice could still stand up to the changing times. Before his election to the papal throne, Ratzinger and Cardinal Sodano, secretary of state of John Paul II from 1990 to the death of the Polish pope, had reached a sort of gentlemen's agreement. Each one had done his job without interfering in the work of the other. After the election, however, Sodano not only knew that his time was now over, but he was also aware of the theologian pope's perplexities not only about the function, but also about the formation and choice of diplomats.

Hence, the defensive attitude of the former secretary, shared by his main collaborators, who saw their own careers and acquired positions at risk. For his part, Pope Benedict decided to act prudently and to allow some time to pass before proceeding to replace the secretary of state. In any case, the turning point came with the above-mentioned address to the Roman Curia in December 2005.

Actually, the change was announced on June 22, 2006, and it was to go into effect in September of the same year. It was, in any case, a sensational replacement. Cardinal Sodano was succeeded, not by a diplomat, as was the long-standing tradition for the Secretariat of State, but, rather, by Tarcisio Cardinal Bertone, a Salesian religious, who had been bishop of Vercelli and Genoa and, above all, for a few years, secretary of the Congregation for the Doctrine of Faith when Ratzinger was the prefect. A former professor of canon law, he had collaborated with the prefect on the publication of the third secret of Fatima and the drafting of the declaration *Dominus Iesus*.

A trusted advisor of the pope, the new secretary of state was called to transmit to his collaborators what George Weigel called "God's choice"[5] of Pope Benedict. Nevertheless, there was no lack of discontent and misunderstandings, which at times led to clumsy

---

[5] Cf. George Weigel, *God's Choice: Pope Benedict XVI and the Future of the Catholic Church* (New York: HarperCollins Publishers, 2005).

errors that were aggravated by inadequate communication on the part of the Church and by erroneous and sometimes tendentious reporting on the part of the international media.

The Regensburg speech

In early September 2006, Benedict XVI returned to Germany, or rather to Bavaria, his beloved homeland, to the places where he had grown up, had been a professor of dogmatic theology and finally archbishop of Munich. In short, the trip certainly had a pastoral dimension, but at the same time it was also a homecoming, a rendezvous with the old and recent affections of life. The first destination was Munich, where on September 10, during the Mass celebrated in the presence of a vast congregation, the pope returned to the theme of a Europe that must rediscover God because it is reasonable to believe. Then, referring to the blasphemous jokes about Muhammad published the year before by a Danish newspaper, he launched into a warning to the secularist culture, which he invited to get rid of the cynicism that supposes that freedom includes the right to mock what is sacred, to be open, instead, to tolerance and to respect for religions.

After Munich, the pope spent a more spiritual day going on pilgrimage to the Marian Shrine of Altötting and meeting the religious and seminarians of Bavaria.[6] That evening, he traveled to Regensburg, where he had completed his university career, had ordered the house built where he had thought that he would spend his last years, and where his brother, Georg, lived. The city gave him an "overwhelming" welcome.[7] The following day, the most important appointment was scheduled for the afternoon, when the pope was supposed to give a lecture in the Aula Magna (great auditorium) of the university of which he had been a professor and vice-rector. As he began to speak, Ratzinger was deeply moved and openly acknowledged it. Then, he let himself go back to the memories of the beginnings of his university teaching, when the connection

---

[6] See the detailed reconstruction of those days in Georg Ratzinger and Michael Hesemann, *My Brother the Pope*, trans. Michael J. Miller (San Francisco: Ignatius Press, 2012), 236–40.

[7] Ibid., 238.

between reason and religion carried out by theology was universally accepted within the university, even by those who had no faith.

The pope had reflected again recently on this topic, he continued, reading the dialogue between the learned Byzantine Emperor Manuel II Palaiologos and an educated Persian of Muslim faith about Christianity and Islam and on the truths of both.[8] So, the emperor said to his interlocutor: "Show me just what Mohammed brought that was new, and there you will find things only evil and inhuman, such as his command to spread by the sword the faith he preached. . . . God . . . is not pleased by blood—and not acting reasonably is contrary to God's nature."[9] The pope went on to explain that: "The decisive statement in this argument against violent conversion is this: not to act in accordance with reason is contrary to God's nature." And he asks himself: "Is the conviction that acting unreasonably contradicts God's nature merely a Greek idea, or is it always and intrinsically true?"[10]

Obviously, Benedict deduced from this that the reasonableness of faith concerns everybody, Muslims and Christians, and he honestly added that in the late Middle Ages, as in the sixteenth and seventeenth centuries and even in modern times, there had also been in Christianity currents of thought that accentuated the difference between God and the creature in such an exaggerated way that: "our reason, our sense of the true and good, are no longer an authentic mirror of God."[11] The quotation from the fictitious dialogue between the emperor and the Persian wise man was an aside.

The pope then continued in his reasoning that when religion renounces the use of reason or society is no longer interested in religion, the inevitable consequence is an outbreak of violence and terrorism. In short, the speech was an exaltation of reason: "It is to this great *logos*, to this breadth of reason, that we invite our partners

---

[8] The pope cites Manuel II Paléologue, *Entretiens avec un musulman, 7ᵉ controverse. Introduction*, Texte critique, translation and notes by Théodore Khoury, in *Sources chrétiennes* 115 (Paris: Cerf, 1966). Of the twenty-six controversies, Khoury published only the seventh with notes and an extensive introduction on the origin of the text, the manuscript tradition, the structure of the dialogue, together with brief summaries of the controversies that were not translated. The volume presented the original Greek edition with the French text on the facing page.

[9] Benedict XVI, lecture, University of Regensburg, September 12, 2006: "Faith, Reason and the University Memories and Reflections".

[10] Ibid.

[11] Ibid.

in the dialogue of cultures. To rediscover it constantly is the great task of the university." [12]

A MISSTEP OR A COURAGEOUS INSIGHT?

The Regensburg lecture was meant to be a kind of meeting of old colleagues in their own *alma mater*. Suddenly, though, it became a fuse that for several weeks had incendiary effects in the world. Indeed, the media focused their attention right away almost exclusively on the quotation of Emperor Manuel II's harsh statement, completely ignoring the context and meaning of the pope's speech. *The New York Times* led the interpretation that was then adopted by the secular Western press. The front-page headline of the newspaper was at least ambiguous: "Pope Accuses West on Faith and Islam on Violence." In the article, then, Ian Fisher explained that the pope had used language that Muslims would find inflammatory. [13] In Italy, according to Marco Politi, writing in the *Repubblica*, Benedict XVI with his speech had dragged the Holy See into a true Waterloo, putting an end to peaceful relations between Christians and Muslims.

As though rallied for the occasion, the reaction of the Muslims was swift. The following day, newspapers and televisions reported the quotation from the Byzantine emperor, attributing it without further explanation to the pope. Imams and many leaders of Islamic countries raced to denounce the pope's hostility against Islam and promised retaliations. Then, in many Islamic cities, heated protests against the pope were organized, which often ended with attacks on Christian buildings and churches. For their part, Western newspapers gave broad coverage to the demonstrations against Christians taking place in the squares of the Islamic cities, not so much to denounce their violence as to highlight the alleged error of the pope's assessment. Begun in serenity and joy, the pope's journey to Bavaria thus ended beneath an avalanche of criticism that came especially from the radical Islamic media and was repeated almost complacently by the Western press.

Even some Catholic publications insisted on the pope's lack of

---

[12] Ibid.

[13] See in this regard Vincent Aucante, *Benoît XVI et l'Islam* (Paris: Parole et Silence, 2008), 37f.

attention to the consequences of his speech, his tendency to play the professor and not the pope. The journal of the French Jesuits, *Études*, once edited by Father Henri de Lubac, wrote: "The pope forgot that he is no longer just a professor in front of his students, but the head of a globalized Church, the slightest hint from whom can be exploited, even with intentions that are not at all benign. Unpleasant forgetfulness on his part, and tragic use of it by those who want to clash with the West, America, Christians and all that they represent."[14]

Paolo Rodari and Andrea Tornielli, in a particularly detailed account, tend to explain what happened in terms of the change that had occurred in those days in the Secretariat of State and in the leadership of the Vatican press office.[15] This explanation, however, cannot rule out the intention of Benedict XVI to extend the religious dialogue with Islam, initiated by John Paul II, to the cultural clash as well. From this perspective, the invitation to follow always the dictates of reason even in the religious field was an argument that deserved more attention from the Western media. It is no accident that Oriana Fallaci, anguished by the thought that Europe could turn into Eurabia, had wanted to meet Benedict XVI as a sign of gratitude for his intelligence and courage. An attack like that of September 11 in New York or other later ones on the subways of London and Madrid did not originate from a hypothetical conflict between religions, but required reflection on the need to assert reason in both the religious and the civil realm.

EXPLANATIONS AND CONSEQUENCES

Given the chorus of protests, at the behest of the Secretariat of State, the head of the Vatican press office, Father Lombardi, provided an initial explanation: "Concerning the reactions from Muslim representatives . . . what matters to the Holy Father is a clear and radical rejection of the religious motivation of violence. . . . Therefore, it is clear that the Holy Father wishes to cultivate an attitude of respect and dialogue toward other religions and cultures, obviously toward Islam also."[16]

---

[14] Pierre de Charentenay, *Études* (November 2006): 437.

[15] Paolo Rodari and Andrea Tornielli, *Attacco a Ratzinger* (Milan: Piemme, 2010), 22–26.

[16] Ibid., 20.

The clarification, nevertheless, was considered inadequate, and two days later the new secretary of state, Cardinal Bertone, had to intervene. Then, on September 17 and even more on the 20th, the pope himself returned to the incident: "This quote (from Manuel II Palaiologos) could be misunderstood. For the attentive reader of my text, it is clear that I did not want in any way to adopt as my own the negative words pronounced by the medieval emperor. . . . I trust, then, that, after the initial reactions, my words at the University of Regensburg may be a stimulus and an encouragement to a positive dialogue."[17]

Meanwhile, diplomacy was at work, and, on September 25, Pope Benedict received in Castel Gandolfo several representatives of the Muslim communities in Italy, together with ambassadors of the countries having a Muslim majority with which the Vatican maintains diplomatic relations. Benedict XVI once again explained: "Since the beginning of my pontificate, I have hoped to continue to consolidate bridges of friendship with the faithful of all religions, with a particular appreciation for the increase of dialogue between Muslims and Christians."[18]

THE JOURNEY TO TURKEY

Between the end of November and the beginning of December 2006, the pope went to visit Turkey, a country in which the history of relations between Christians and Muslims was particularly troubled.[19] At the origin of the visit was the invitation from the Orthodox patriarch of Constantinople, Bartholomew I, who wanted to strengthen his position as ecumenical patriarch in the Orthodox world and, at the same time, receive support in the face of the increasingly aggressive attitude of Turkey's religious and governmental authorities.

Then, too, the pope had the objective, which had become even more important after the Regensburg lecture, to mend relations with Turkey and the Islamic world and to obtain from the Turkish authorities greater tolerance for the Christian minority, which was

---

[17] Ibid., 29.
[18] Ibid., 30.
[19] Aucante, *Benoît XVI et l'Islam*, 62.

constantly exposed to attacks by Muslim activists[20]—objectives that are difficult to attain in a country where Orthodox and Catholics are subject to restrictions that end up contradicting the declared equality of rights with regard to the State. John Paul II considered Turkey a laboratory in which an original experiment was being conducted that had importance for all of Europe; Benedict XVI, in contrast, as a cardinal, had expressed his opposition to the entrance of Turkey into the European Union.[21] For his part, though, he maintained that Turkey's secularism was an interesting experimental model,[22] even though he called on the Turkish authorities to be consistent with the secularism established in their constitution.

During a meeting with the Ministry of Religious Affairs, the *Diyanet*, the pope declared his intention to "carry forward our dialogue as a sincere exchange between friends". "We are called to work together, so as to help society to open itself to the transcendent, giving Almighty God his rightful place. The best way forward is via authentic dialogue between Christians and Muslims, based on truth and inspired by a sincere wish to know one another better."[23]

This was a frank way of speaking that seemed to hit the mark, so much so that during his visit to the famous Blue Mosque, on the last day of his visit to Turkey, the atmosphere seemed much more relaxed. Accompanied by the Grand Mufti of Constantinople, the pope made the tour of the mosque; he did not fail to stop for a moment of recollection. This gesture, broadcast live throughout the world, won sympathy for him among Muslims.

The meeting with Patriarch Bartholomew had a favorable outcome, too. In their joint declaration, pope and patriarch confirmed their sentiments of communion, which had already been initiated extensively by their predecessors, invoked the Holy Spirit to help them prepare for the great day when full unity would be reestablished, then declared that they had positively evaluated the path to-

---

[20] In early 2006, in Trabzon, Turkey, Father Andrea Santoro was murdered only a few days after having sent a letter to Pope Benedict. The pope received it after the murder of the priest. This circumstance was a severe blow to the pontiff.

[21] Interview with *Le Figaro Magazine* (August 13, 2004); address to the pastoral workers of the Diocese of Velletri reprinted by *Il giornale del Popolo* (Lugano, September 20, 2004).

[22] Aucante, *Benoît XVI et l'Islam*, 61.

[23] Benedict XVI, Address, Ankara, Turkey, November 28, 2006.

ward the formation of the European Union. Nevertheless, they did not fail to point out: "In Europe, while remaining open to other religions and to their cultural contributions, we must unite our efforts to preserve Christian roots, traditions and values."[24]

Upon returning to the Vatican, the pope was able to draw up a favorable balance sheet of his visit to Turkey. Speaking on December 6 at the Wednesday General Audience, he commented: a journey that promised to be difficult was concluded in a positive way, in regard to both the meeting with the Orthodox and the dialogue with the Muslims. Then he thanked the Turkish authorities, hoping once again that Turkey could become a bridge of friendship and fraternal collaboration between East and West.[25]

LET US NOT MAKE OUR DIFFERENCES A REASON FOR HATE

After the furious attacks during the days immediately after the Regensburg lecture, some tentative efforts began, even on the Muslim side, to read the pope's text in its entirety and to understand its meaning. Besides the responses of individual thinkers and intellectuals, particularly important was a letter in Arabic published on October 15, 2006, by the London daily newspaper *Asharq Al-Awsat*, which bore the signatures of thirty-eight Muslim dignitaries. The same letter was then published in English by the American periodical *Islamica Magazine*. This time, though, there were a hundred signatories, a sign that people were having second thoughts. The signers belonged to different nationalities and spiritual traditions. It was the first time that such a large number of dignitaries from the Islamic world contacted the highest authority of Christianity to respond to the pope's questions.

The letter, which was obviously the result of a compromise, "shows some internal tension between the rejection of any violence and the possibility of justification of certain forms of violent reactions or war".[26] In any case, the document acknowledged the efforts made by the pope to clarify his remarks and concluded: "We

---

[24] Common Declaration of Pope Benedict XVI and the Ecumenical Patriarch Bartholomew I (from the Phanar, November 30, 2006).

[25] Aucante, *Benoît XVI et l'Islam*, 139.

[26] Ibid., 46. Besides providing an examination of the text, Aucante publishes in its entirety the letter of the *ulema* (body of Muslim scholars) on pp. 120–28 of his book.

hope to do all we can to avoid the mistakes of the past and live together in the future in peace, mutual acceptance, and respect."[27] A promising start that had a sequel the following year in a second letter undersigned by an even greater number of signatories (138). Reaffirming their willingness to enter into dialogue, the signers emphasized that Christians and Muslims have in common a faith in the uniqueness of God, in the love of God, and in the love of neighbor. They concluded: "Let us not make our differences a reason for hatred and quarreling between us. Let us compete with each other in piety and in good deeds."[28]

The Regensburg lecture was therefore not a misstep or a banal mistake, as some secular, Islamic, and even Catholic intellectuals had hastened to declare. Courageously and loyally, the pope was suggesting a path for dialogue, and although the dialogue that followed has not been very fruitful so far, it must also be said that the secular world, in particular, has done nothing to support the initiative of the German pope. Making the all-too-easy excuse that this was merely a religious dispute, cultural leaders and heads of State have done little to encourage the path of peace and understanding among people and religions.

Appointments of bishops

As is well known, Vatican Council II was convened to deal, among other things, with bishops, after Vatican Council I had addressed almost exclusively the matter of papal infallibility. The council Fathers, therefore, the great majority of them bishops, treated the episcopate in the Constitution on the Church and in the Decree on the Pastoral Office of Bishops. The first document dealt with the theology of the episcopate, in particular its sacramental nature, apostolic succession, membership in the episcopal college, the office of teaching, sanctifying, and governing. The decree, in contrast, defined more precisely the duties of the bishop, his relation to the pope, to the priests of his own diocese, and to the faithful.

One new institution that originated with the council and then gradually asserted itself in the life of Catholics was the episcopal

---

[27] Ibid., 128.
[28] Ibid., 164.

conference, an assembly of bishops designed to gather the pastors of dioceses that shared a common language or nationality, so as to facilitate the coordination of pastoral activity. This brief historical note explains the growing importance of the bishops in the life of the Church in the second half of the twentieth century, so much so that we can say, as Weigel wrote: "The Catholic Church is an episcopally ordered Church."[29]

This evolution led, in the best cases, to the development of a diocesan spirituality based on the discovery of its own origins, on a sense of belonging, and on some special devotions. More often it favored a concentration of authority whereby the above-mentioned episcopal offices of teaching, sanctifying, and governing were gradually reduced to a managerial vision that was concerned more than anything about managing consensus so as to avoid scandals and the accompanying risk of having to give up possible career advancements. This, however, put a damper on the diocesan government that the bishops had vindicated during Vatican II.

As a theologian and as a bishop, Ratzinger had intervened many times concerning the vision of the episcopate that had emerged at Vatican II. Repeatedly, the prefect for the Doctrine of the Faith had asked the episcopal conferences to avoid excessive bureaucracy; more explicitly, he had urged them to not create new curias alongside the Vatican one. He had likewise called the bishops to be bold and not to tolerate abuses by priests, religious, and diocesan employees merely to keep the peace. Now, however, he in turn was called on to act, to intervene in some difficult situations that had been left unresolved by his predecessor.

THE FAILURE TO APPOINT WIELGUS TO WARSAW

Besides the Secretariat of State, one of the most important bodies for the government of the Church is the Congregation for Bishops, which is responsible for the appointment of new leaders of dioceses. Since the year 2000, the prefect of this congregation had been Giovanni Battista Cardinal Re, from Brescia, who had behind him a career spent at the Secretariat of State, of which he had also been Substitute for General Affairs. As in other cases, the German

---

[29] Weigel, *God's Choice*, 247.

pope decided to make use of his collaboration once again, and he confirmed him in his office. In late 2006, it was necessary to appoint the successor to Józef Cardinal Glemp, archbishop of Warsaw and primate of Poland. After the usual process that starts with the nominations of the nuncio and leads to the formation of a *terna* of names, from which the prefect of the congregation, together with the pope, elects the new bishop, the appointment of Stanisław Wielgus, already bishop of Płock, was announced on December 6, 2006. The appointee was an old acquaintance of Ratzinger's, who had met him in Munich at the time when he was bishop of that city, when the young Polish priest was there completing his studies.

A few days after the announcement, however, the weekly magazine *Gazeta Polska* reported sensational news: the newly elected archbishop had long collaborated with the Communist political police, as was evident from the list of 240,000 names published and posted online two years earlier by National Memory Institute. After the initial embarrassment and the reassurance given by the person concerned, the appointment was confirmed. However, a few days after his official installation in the diocese, a daily newspaper provided accurate evidence of Wielgus' collaboration, which had started just before his departure for Munich, where the young priest had met the future pope. At that point Wielgus himself was forced to admit: "Guided by the desire to complete important studies for my academic specialization, I became involved with those contacts without the necessary prudence."[30] The bishop, nevertheless, still thought that he could keep his office; the pope, however, informed him through Cardinal Re that he had to resign.

The Wielgus case raised the veil from the weaknesses of the Polish Church, which, nonetheless, had shown great firmness and solidarity during the period of the Communist rule. Above all, the case had shown the fragility of the system for appointing Catholic bishops, in which neither the prior research by the nuncio responsible for proposing the triad of names to the Congregation for Bishops, nor the Vatican dicastery itself, nor, finally, even the Secretariat of State that was responsible for the final oversight had been able to prevent an altogether avoidable scandal. The omissions that had led

---

[30] Reported by Rodari and Tornielli, *Attacco a Ratzinger*, 43.

to misinforming the pope were so great as to lead some commentators to wonder about a true and actual attempt at sabotage.[31]

REBELLION OF THE CLERGY IN LINZ

Two years after the failed appointment of the archbishop of Warsaw, a case similar in some respects occurred in Austria, in the Diocese of Linz. On January 31, 2009, a press release by the Holy See announced the appointment of the priest Gerhard Wagner as auxiliary bishop of Linz. Usually the appointment of an auxiliary bishop passes more or less unnoticed. Basically, auxiliaries are called to collaborate with the local bishop in a geographically extensive diocese, where there are particularly large numbers of Catholics. For this reason, too, the *terna* of candidates to be presented to Rome is most often made up of names selected by the ordinary. The Vatican authorities are called to evaluate and choose from among the proposed candidates. The public's attention was focused on Linz, however, because it was generally known that the clergy of the diocese were critical of Rome, especially with regard to sexual morality.

In the summer of 2008, the bishop of the diocese with the largest number of Catholics in Austria, Ludwig Schwarz, in the right manner submitted a request for an auxiliary bishop. The request was granted, and then came the nomination of Wagner. However, in the diocese, the nomination was greeted with a veritable barrage of artillery fire. Newspapers devoted a lot of space to some incautious statements made by the future bishop, a large group of priests declared that Wagner was not accepted by the faithful, and, consequently, they themselves were not in favor of his consecration. Bishop Schwarz and Cardinal Schönborn initially sided with and defended the bishop designated by the pope. However, since the uproar surrounding the nomination was not abating, a group of Austrian bishops, headed by Schönborn, traveled to Rome, where the new auxiliary bishop was advised to lower his tone of voice and to try to win the respect of the faithful.

Meanwhile, in Austria, an assembly of the Austrian bishops was announced to deal with the situation once again. On the eve of the meeting, however, Father Wagner announced that he had asked

---

[31] Ibid., 46f.

the pope, because of the severe criticism, to accept his resignation. The following day, the assembly of Austrian bishops, for its part, criticized the process by which the nomination of Wagner had been reached and hoped that in the future the pope would be provided with better information, so that the universal service of the pontiff would not be darkened by shadows. Less relevant to the disputed position, the Austrian incident had even more disturbing implications. The accusations brought against Father Wagner were relatively trifling, while the protests by the faithful proved to be more decisive, especially those by a group of priests, some of whom made no secret of the fact that they did not observe celibacy and did not agree with Rome's decisions in the field of morality.

Bishop Schwarz, too, had taken a stance that was not very responsible. He had fundamentally delegated to Cardinal Schönborn and the pope the solution of a problem that chiefly concerned his diocese. After its conclusion with the resignation of the bishop-designate, the Wagner affair had one final development in June 2009, when the pope and his closest collaborators met with the leaders of the Austrian Church in Rome. The situation in the Diocese of Linz and the state of the entire Austrian Church were reexamined once again. At the end, the pope invited the Austrian bishops to live out more intensely their communion with Rome and to inculcate in their priests respect for canonical celibacy.

Once again the strategy of exhortation. The pope invited bishops and collaborators to remain faithful to their duties, not to give up their respective roles or the government entrusted to them. He reserved to himself the task of directing and monitoring that Jesus had entrusted to Peter and his successors. Was this sound prudence so as to avoid further splits, or was it excessive caution? There was a risk of not obtaining immediate results and of disappointing those who expected changes that they considered necessary without delay.

Marcial Maciel and the Legionaries of Christ

Marcial Maciel Degollado was born in Mexico in 1920. As a young seminarian, with the support of powerful Mexican families, he founded a religious congregation to which he later gave the name of Legionaries of Christ. This institute of pontifical right was situated within the broader context of an apostolic movement that proposed to establish in society the kingdom of Christ in accordance with the requirements of justice and charity. Conservative in its leanings, the congregation grew over the years, remaining immune to the vocations crisis in the Church in the second half of the twentieth century. Praised by John Paul II as an instrument for the new evangelization, especially in Latin America, the congregation was able to build in Rome a university, which was inaugurated in 2005 with great solemnity and in the presence of many civil and religious authorities.

During the same months, however, there was a confrontation in the Vatican of which the founder of the Legionaries was at the center. Although accused several times of abusing minors, Maciel over the years had always managed to escape what he described as infamous accusations, thanks to the support of his collaborators and his many supporters in the world and in the Vatican itself. However, in 1997, an American newspaper reported the accusations of several of his former seminarians, who declared that they had repeatedly sent to the Holy See a detailed denunciation of the abuses that they had suffered, without ever receiving any response. Again in 2004, Maciel was able to celebrate with great solemnity, with the pope in attendance, the sixtieth anniversary of his priesthood. Not until May 2006, after the change of pontificate, was an initial statement issued by the Congregation for the Doctrine of the Faith, which admitted that it had been receiving allegations of abuse against the founder of the Legionaries since 1998.

Given the priest's advanced age, however, he was ordered to renounce every office in the congregation and to devote himself to a life of prayer and penance. After resigning as Superior of the religious congregation, Maciel died in the United States in 2008, still venerated by the Legionaries. The admonition from the congregation seemed, therefore, not to have affected his reputation. However, his death caused even more disconcerting aspects of his life to emerge. Not only had he abused several of his seminarians, but he had wives and children in Spain and Mexico. A formal apostolic visitation to the congregation was initiated, and five bishops from Europe, the United States, and Latin America were put in charge of it.

At the end of their work, the five prelates gathered in Rome on April 30 and May 1, 2010, in the presence of Cardinal Bertone, and they were received by Pope Benedict. Then a statement was released by the Vatican press office. During the apostolic visitation, more than one thousand Legionaries were interviewed along with some members of the Regnum Christi movement. Although they acted autonomously, the bishops had arrived at converging conclusions. They had been received with deference and had been able to observe a genuine search for God, especially in many young men. However, that being said, they stated that they had collected incontrovertible testimonies regarding "the very grave and objectively immoral actions of Father Maciel, [which] in some cases constitute real crimes and manifest a life devoid of scruples and authentic religious meaning".[32]

The founder's life, therefore, caused serious consequences in the life and structure of his congregation, to the point where it became urgently necessary to redefine the very charism of the foundation and to review the exercise of authority in order to safeguard the young men's enthusiasm for the faith with an adequate formation. The press release ended with the announcement of the future appointment of a papal delegate, who, as it was revealed the following month, would be the Italian Archbishop Velasio De Paolis.[33] He, as specified by a decree of the secretary of state dated July 9, would have to prepare the convocation of a general chapter for the revision of the constitutions that govern the life of the Legionaries and "will have authority over all superiors, . . . communities, and the individual religious".[34] In short, a real compulsory administration, which nevertheless arrived late and contained only one reference to the system of relations built up by Father Maciel, which had allowed him to remain in charge so long, despite his crimes.

This system extended as far as the Vatican, too, where the founder of the Legionaries had had protectors among the closest collaborators of John Paul II. In particular, the magazine of the Jesuits in the United States, *America*, named names: the prefect of the Congregation for Religious, Eduardo Martínez Somalo, the secretary of state, Angelo Cardinal Sodano, and the pope's private secretary,

---

[32] Holy See, Communiqué regarding the Apostolic Visitation of the Congregation of the Legionaries of Christ, May 1, 2010.

[33] *Enchiridion Vaticanum* 26 (Bologna: Dehoniane, 2011), 1354.

[34] Ibid., 1356. Cf. "Vatican Decree Details Powers of Pope's Legion Delegate", EWTN News/CNA, July 23, 2010. http://www.ewtnnews.com/catholic-news/Vatican.php?id=1242.

Stanisław Dziwisz, did not inform Wojtyła of the complaints about the Mexican priest that had been received.[35] Although the Congregation for the Doctrine of the Faith, headed by Ratzinger, had initiated proceedings as early as 1998, it had been able to move freely and expeditiously only after the change of pontificate.

Not only the system for appointing bishops, but also the government of religious life had sprung worrisome leaks that needed to be remedied decisively and rigorously. The measure initiated by Benedict XVI finally set out on a path that was not limited to mere condemnation, often posthumous, but demanded the pursuit of the causes. It also paved the way for the possibility of "setting up study committees both with staff from within the Congregation of the Legionaries and with competent outside persons". An initial concession to the transparency called for both inside and outside the Church.

Pedophile priests again

This time Pope Benedict was not caught completely by surprise.[36] As we saw in chapter 12, as a cardinal he had already had to deal with the first wave of allegations concerning pedophile priests that came from the United States. Now, however, the big cloud of filth was coming closer, and it involved one country in particular, Ireland, which for centuries had prided itself on its membership in the Catholic Church and on its priests. In 2006, the full scandal had not yet broken. The pope, nevertheless, decided to face the issue, and on October 28, 2006, he spoke about it to the Irish bishops who had come to Rome for their *ad limina* visit. "In the exercise of your pastoral ministry, you have had to respond in recent years to many heart-rending cases of sexual abuse of minors. These are all the more tragic when the abuser is a cleric."[37] Precise orders followed: Keep addressing this problem effectively. Establish the truth about what happened; take all reasonable measures to prevent it from happening in the future; make sure that the principles of justice are respected, above all take measures to heal the victims and all those affected by those heinous crimes.

---

[35] Rodari and Tornielli, *Attacco a Ratzinger*, 230.

[36] Benedict XVI, *Light of the World*, 24.

[37] Benedict XVI, Address to the Bishops of Ireland on Their Ad Limina Visit (October 28, 2006).

The pope had not yet read the Ryan report, which later would reveal the abnormal scope of the problem of sexual abuse in Ireland; he was already convinced, though, of the need for an indispensable purification of the whole Irish Church, if she wanted to regain credibility in what once had been described as the "Island of Saints".

The movements

As I have recalled in the previous chapters, even as a bishop and a cardinal, Ratzinger had watched the ecclesial movements with interest. He saw in them the possibility of new blood flowing into the somewhat sclerotic arteries of the old ecclesiastical institutions. He had looked at them with joy and hope during the toughest moments of the student protests, when it seemed that the young people were going to abandon the Church en masse. As pope, Benedict had even more confidence in the movements, protected them, and often relied on their support, in particular for the new evangelization in Europe. At the head of the Pontifical Council for the Laity, which mainly dealt with the movements, there was still a man close to John Paul II, Polish Stanisław Ryłko, but recently his former secretary, Joseph Clemens, had landed there as well. On May 31, 2006, delegates from more than a hundred movements gathered in Rocca di Papa for the second World Congress. Prayer meetings, testimonies, and reflections were planned. In view of the meeting, on May 22 the pope had sent them a text that would serve as a guide for reflection.

The theme itself of the meeting, "The beauty of being Christian and the joy of sharing it", was taken from a sentence spoken by Benedict in the inaugural homily of his pontificate, on April 24, 2005. The expression, the pope explained, described in the most appropriate way the heart of the Christian event, the encounter with Jesus Christ, "who in flesh and blood visibly and historically brought to earth the splendor of God's glory. The words of Psalm 45[44]:2 apply to him: 'You are the fairest of the sons of men.' "[38] And again: "Christ, who is 'the beauty of every beauty', as Saint Bonaventure used to say (*Sermones Dominicales*, 1:7), is made present

---

[38] Benedict XVI, Message to the Participants of the Second World Congress on Ecclesial Movements and New Communities, May 22, 2006.

in the hearts of men and women and attracts them to their vocation which is love."[39] After the meeting of the delegates, on Saturday, June 3, the Eve of Pentecost, the pope met with the 350,000 members of the movements and ecclesial communities gathered on Saint Peter's Square for a prayer vigil.

Benedict's speech, obviously centered on Pentecost, offered him the opportunity to continue his reflection on the beauty of the figure and message of Jesus. With his advent, he made known the intimate life of God, his Triune nature, but also what man desires most, life and freedom. He is the good shepherd who gives his life for his sheep; he is the prodigal son who, in his separation from the Father, learns freedom but also responsibility. Hence, the mandate for those who belong to the movements. They are called to live life as a gift and not as a possession; they must witness to the freedom that includes responsibility for creation and for our brethren. The Holy Spirit desires the multiplicity of the Church just as he desires her unity. Hence, the invitation to preserve communion with the bishops, the priests, and the other brethren.

In the theological report to the first Congress of Movements, Ratzinger had situated them within the apostolic succession. Now, he called them together to convey to them his enthusiasm for Jesus, so that they might be collaborators in the pope's universal apostolic ministry, to help him in the reform of the Church. Obviously, Benedict did not intend to turn the movements into *missi dominici*, his envoys to eliminate abuses and scandals, inertia and resignation. He urged them, nevertheless, to be schools of communion, traveling companions, places where charity could be manifested as a passion for the life and destiny of others. And he concluded: "This is the Church's best service for men and women and especially for the poor."[40]

The Mass in Latin

On July 7, 2007, an apostolic letter urging the bishops to accommodate the faithful who wished to attend Mass celebrated in Latin,

---

[39] Ibid.
[40] Benedict XVI, Homily, Pentecost Meeting with the Ecclesial Movements and New Communities: June 3, 2006.

according to the old missal of Saint Pius V, in the revised edition authorized by John XXIII in 1962, was published *motu proprio*,[41] which
literally means "by the pope's initiative". Benedict XVI pointed out
that this missal had been the one used to celebrate Mass during Vatican II and that it had never been abrogated. He added that the
ordinary form of saying Mass remained that of the missal published
by Paul VI in 1970. However, he urged the bishops to grant to the
faithful who requested it the opportunity to attend Mass "in the
extraordinary form" according to the old missal, which "is to be
. . . duly honored for its venerable and ancient usage".

After the ban introduced by the promulgation of the missal of
Paul VI and the general introduction of the vernacular languages in
the liturgy, a first step in the recovery of the old liturgy in Latin had
already been taken by Pope John Paul II in 1988. The Polish pope,
however, had not given detailed instructions, but had exhorted the
bishops to grant to the faithful who requested it the opportunity
to participate in a Mass celebrated according to the old form. Now,
however, Benedict XVI took a further step by defining the missals
of Paul VI and Pius V as two forms, one ordinary, the other extraordinary, of the one Rite of the [Western] Catholic Church. As
a result, it was no longer the bishops' competence to authorize the
celebration of the Mass in Latin; on the contrary, they were asked
to study the best way in which the request of those who loved Latin
could be granted in harmony with the ordinary liturgical life of the
parishes and dioceses.

HARD OPPOSITION

The first rumors to the effect that the pope was thinking about the
possibility of liberalizing the use of the missal of Pius V spread in
Rome in mid-2006. Then came the many reactions, most of them
against it. Some lamented the fact that too much room was thus
allowed for the traditionalists of the Society of Saint Pius X, the
Lefebvrites; others accused the pope of calling Vatican II into question.[42] Benedict acknowledged this in the letter that accompanied

---

[41] *Enchiridion Vaticanum* 24:752–63. Benedict XVI, Apostolic Letter, Given Motu Proprio, *Summorum Pontificum* on the Use of the Roman Liturgy Prior to the Reform of 1970,
July 7, 2007.

[42] Rodari and Tornielli, *Attacco a Ratzinger*, 56–84. The two Vaticanists give ample
space to the criticisms from the Roman Curia, the local bishops, and the liturgists.

the *motu proprio* the following year: "News reports and judgments made without sufficient information have created no little confusion" and stoked "harsh opposition".[43] It was the first time in the modern era that a pope spoke so explicitly about strong opposition within the Church. Criticism came from liturgy experts and numerous bishops. Above all, many episcopal conferences unleashed a veritable firestorm against the proposal.

The most hostile were the French bishops, who said that they feared not only for the liturgical reform promoted by Vatican II, but also for the very unity of the Church. In October 2006, the archbishop emeritus of Paris, Cardinal Lustiger, accompanied by Archbishop Pierre Ricard of Bordeaux, president of the Bishops' Conference of France, traveled to Rome. Neither the prestige of the former prelate, a personal friend of the pope, nor the insistence of the president of the conference, however, managed to persuade Benedict to desist from his purpose. It seemed like a repetition of the wave of criticism that had accompanied the preparation of the *Catechism of the Catholic Church*. This time, however, the opposition did not stop even after the publication of the document. The president of the German Bishops' Conference, Karl Lehmann, interviewed by the *Frankfurter Allgemeine Zeitung*, acknowledged that the pope's intention was to "make a contribution toward a reconciliation in the Church". He concluded, nevertheless, that nothing in the life of the German Church would change.[44]

Many bishops of the Italian Church, too, who are usually obsequious toward the pope, manifested their dissent this time. This was the case with Felice di Molfetta, bishop of Cerignola and president of the liturgy committee of the Italian Episcopal Conference (CEI), and with Luca Brandolini, who was also a member of the liturgical committee of the CEI. The liturgists, therefore, were the ones who criticized the *motu proprio* openly, but the dissent was broader. It did not calm down even after several months, and it even crossed the boundaries of the Catholic world. In particular, Jews recalled that the Holy Friday liturgy in the old missal contained a prayer that spoke of the perfidiousness of the Jews and invited the

---

[43] *Enchiridion Vaticanum* 24:752–64. Benedict XVI, Letter to the Bishops on the Occasion of the Publication of the Apostolic Letter "Motu Proprio Data" *Summorum Pontificum* on the Use of the Roman Liturgy Prior to the Reform of 1970, July 7, 2007.

[44] Rodari and Tornielli, *Attacco a Ratzinger*, 70.

congregation to pray for their conversion. It was true that John XXIII had abolished the term "perfidy", but it was equally true that there were still references to blindness and conversion. That was exactly what many rabbis objected to.[45]

Nevertheless, the pope was sensitive to the dialogue with the Jews and intervened personally to modify the old prayer profoundly.[46] Then, a note in *La Civiltà Cattolica* explained that, with this change, the pope intended to avoid "any expression that could have even the slightest appearance of an offense or in any way displease the Jews".[47]

AT THE ORIGIN OF THE DECREE

In a letter to the bishops that accompanied the publication of the decree, Benedict XVI explained the reasons why he had considered it indispensable to allow the extraordinary use of the ancient form of the Roman Rite. The immediate reason was certainly to comply with the request of the followers of Bishop Lefebvre, some of whom "clearly accepted the binding character of the Second Vatican Council, and were faithful to the Pope and Bishops[;] nonetheless [they] also desired to recover the form of the sacred liturgy that was dear to them."[48] In addition to the hope, which ultimately proved to be vain, of putting an end to a schism in which the pope saw persons of goodwill involved, too, his intervention was intended to defend one of his dearest theological principles.

He referred to it at the end of the letter, when he wrote: "In the history of the liturgy there is growth and progress, but no rupture. What earlier generations held as sacred, remains sacred and great for us too, and it cannot be all of a sudden entirely forbidden or even considered harmful."[49] In other words, Benedict once again proposed the hermeneutic of continuity that he had firmly supported in 2005, in his year-end address to the Roman Curia. On the other hand, this was one of Ratzinger's deeply rooted convictions. He

---

[45] Ibid., 78f.

[46] The new text was made public by *L'Osservatore Romano* (Italian ed., February 6, 2008), accompanied by a note from the Secretariat of State.

[47] Cited in Rodari and Tornielli, *Attacco a Ratzinger*, 79.

[48] Benedict XVI, Letter to the Bishops of the World on the Occasion of the Publication of the Apostolic Letter "Motu Proprio Data" *Summorum Pontificum*.

[49] Ibid.

wrote in one of the final pages of his memoirs, in 1997: "I was dismayed by the prohibition of the old missal, since nothing of the sort had ever happened in the entire history of the liturgy."[50]

Actually, Ratzinger argued, the very expression "missal of Pius V" is improper. After the Council of Trent, Pope Ghislieri commissioned a revision of the Roman missal then in use, as did several pontiffs who came after him as well. At the time of Paul VI, in contrast, something more happened, according to Ratzinger: the old house was torn apart, and a new one was built, albeit using the old material. This certainly resulted in some improvements and a real enrichment. However, the fact that the new missal was contrasted to what had taken shape over centuries had deleterious consequences. Now the missal was no longer the fruit of a vital process, but a product of specialized erudition and legal expertise. To tell the truth, this historical reconstruction had seemed to me from the beginning a little superficial and also a bit offensive with regard to Paul VI. I expressed my misgivings to Benedict, already emeritus, and he replied:

> There is no doubt that I felt a close affinity with Paul VI, who had to put into practice the new ideas of the council in a difficult situation and at the same time defend the stable continuity of the faith. As for the liturgical question, I can understand Pope Montini's decisions very well. It seems to me, nevertheless, that greater patience in implementing the reform would have promoted peace in the Church. . . . The sudden break with the old missal caused resistance that perhaps could have been avoided. In any case, it would have been good to make clearer the continuity between the two missals. But to do that, the liturgists, too, had to help, and instead they proved to be unavailable. The real problem resulted, not from the pope's decision, but from the intransigence of the liturgists.[51]

Once again, Ratzinger's confrontation with theologians reappeared. Where specialists are prone to emphasize the novelty of their research and the goodness of their insights, the pastor focused his attention on the faithful and the effects that too sudden a change can have on them. From this perspective, the concern of contemporary bishops who feared that the restoration of the old missal in

---

[50] Joseph Ratzinger, *Milestones: Memoirs 1927–1977*, trans. Erasmo Leiva-Merikakis (San Francisco: Ignatius Press, 1998), 146.

[51] The author has the original of the letter.

Latin could lead to confusion and generate new protests was also justified. Of course, a lot depended on the attitude of the bishops and priests themselves, the majority of whom did not show enthusiasm for Pope Benedict's decision.

Everyone felt, therefore, the lack of a figure who could carry out the task that had been Ratzinger's with John Paul II. These were the first signs of that solitude which was to characterize the final years of Pope Benedict's pontificate. It was an isolation that was sought in part because of his natural reserve, through choice of a life of study and prayer, despite the duties of the Petrine office. However, it was imposed also in part by those in the hierarchy who were not capable of taking unpopular measures, of following him on the path of reform, and who preferred to leave to the pontiff alone the task of purifying and reforming the Church.

XV

THE LAST VATICAN II POPE

According to a common belief that dies hard, Ratzinger had changed his position after the Second Vatican Council, moving from progressive to conservative and doing everything possible to oppose the reforms intended by the council. One of the authors who has insisted most on this claim is the American ex-Dominican Matthew Fox, author of a work that is a concentration of gratuitous and improbable statements.[1] He dedicates an entire chapter to the coming to power of the man who had been a young and brilliant theologian, basing it, not on history, but on an analysis of the unconscious fears that in 1968 supposedly led Ratzinger to close himself off and turn in on himself rather than assent to the new ideas.[2]

In reality, as a *peritus* at the council, unanimously considered one of the most perspicacious and diligent theologians of the conciliar assembly,[3] Ratzinger never had the intention of distancing himself from this event that had marked his life as a theologian and bishop. Very soon, however, like other bishops and experts,[4] he thought that he should insist on a necessary clarification: the spirit

---

[1] Matthew Fox, *The Pope's War: Why Ratzinger's Secret Crusade Has Imperiled the Church and How It Can Be Saved*, 2nd ed. (New York: Sterling Ethos, 2012).

[2] The chapter is titled "Ratzinger's Conversion" and is found on pp. 13–32 of the work cited.

[3] Henri de Lubac in his *Vatican Council Notebooks*, vol. 2, trans. Anne Englund Nash (San Francisco: Ignatius Press, 2016), 387, describes him as "a theologian who is as peaceful and kind as he is competent".

[4] Again, de Lubac, before leaving Rome at the end of the council, wrote to his confrere Jacques Guillet: "This program is an attempt to divert the conciliar work. . . . In the coming months or years, it will be necessary for the whole of the conciliar work to be studied seriously", in ibid., 425.

of the council was not to be sought at conferences of theologians and experts, much less invented, but was present in the conciliar documents, particularly in the dogmatic constitutions: one on the Church and the other on Divine Revelation. He held to this maxim during the long years in which he was at the side of John Paul II, and he drew inspiration from this approach during the years of his own pontificate. He solemnly declared on October 11, 2012, the fiftieth anniversary of the start of the Second Vatican Council and the first day of the Year of Faith, "This is why I have often insisted on the need to return, as it were, to the 'letter' of the Council— that is to its texts—also to draw from them its authentic spirit, and why I have repeated that the true legacy of Vatican II is to be found in them. Reference to the documents saves us from extremes of anachronistic nostalgia and running too far ahead."[5]

In fact, many of his magisterial initiatives in both preaching and writing can be interpreted as attempts to overcome the controversies of interpretation surrounding Vatican II and to transmit to the faithful the fundamental intentions of the council Fathers that had found expression in the documents approved and made public by Paul VI.

The first encyclical on love

THE MEANING OF AN INVERSION

Pope Benedict's first encyclical, entitled *God Is Love*, was presented in Rome on December 25, 2005. The most original feature is the decision about where to begin. Once again confirming his disposition as a systematic theologian, from the start of his pontificate Pope Benedict had thought of dedicating his encyclicals to what theologians call the "theological virtues", the fundamental attitudes of a believer. According to tradition, these virtues are, in order, faith, hope, and love. The German pope, however, in order to underscore the primacy of divine love at the origin of revelation, the pillar on

---

[5] Benedict XVI, Homily at Holy Mass for the Opening of the Year of Faith, October 11, 2012. The homily opens with the words "with great joy", calling to mind the famous address given by John XXIII at the opening of the Second Vatican Council. With this homily, Benedict XVI proclaimed a Year of Faith in harmony, as he stated, with the authentic framework given to the Second Vatican Council by John XXIII.

which the conciliar constitution *Dei Verbum* is built,[6] inverts the order.[7] First come love and hope, given by God, then man's adherence to faith, which is likewise a divine gift.

The pope himself was the one to explain the inversion at an event promoted by the Pontifical Council Cor Unum for Human and Christian Development. Invoking the concluding tercet of Dante's *Divine Comedy*, which by now had become familiar to him,[8] Benedict XVI said: "The cosmic excursion in which Dante, in his *Divine Comedy*, wishes to involve the reader ends in front of the perennial Light that is God himself, before that Light which is at the same time 'the love that moves the sun and the other stars' (*Paradiso* XXXIII, v. 145)."[9] Then he explained that light and love are one and the same; they are the primordial creative powers that move the world. The poet's reliance on Aristotle and on Greek thought is seen in this first conviction. Dante, however, the pope continues, also sees in the light and in the originating *eros* the Trinitarian circle in which the second circle—that of the Son—has the human form depicted within it in the same color as the circle itself. With this allusion, the Christian Dante was making reference to the dogmas of the Trinity and the Incarnation. Let us return for a moment, however, to the concluding verse of the *Comedy*: "the love that moves the

---

[6] In the book interview *Entretien autour de Vatican II* (Paris: Cerf, 1985), 28, de Lubac declares to Angelo Scola: "*Dei Verbum* gave ample room to Sacred Scripture and was, in general, well accepted by exegetes", but it is not a document on the Bible, and the first chapter, "Revelation Itself", talks about Christ, "who is both the mediator and the fullness of all revelation". The personalization of revelation brought by Christ, according to the French theologian, is precisely what made it possible to resolve the separation of reason from faith that afflicted modern Catholicism.

[7] In the spiritual exercises for the Communion and Liberation movement, he himself had followed the traditional order. See above, chap. 11. In the meantime, Paul Josef Cardinal Cordes recalled that the Pontifical Council Cor Unum had already presented a draft outline of a document on charity for John Paul II, of which Cardinal Ratzinger had also been made aware. This does not detract in any way from the novelty of Pope Benedict's approach, "which so decisively places God at the beginning of the ecclesial service of charity." Paul J. Cordes, *Tre papi: La mia vita* (Cinisello Balsamo: San Paolo, 2015), 258.

[8] He had already cited it in his best-seller, *Introduction to Christianity* (see above, chap. 5), and then when speaking to the young people of the Communion and Liberation Movement (see above, chap. 11).

[9] Benedict XVI, Address to Participants at the Meeting Promoted by the Pontifical Council on Cor Unum, January 23, 2006.

sun and the other stars". This love is *eros*, yes, but it is also light, the principle of knowledge and *logos*, the ability to reflect and think. Driven to knowledge by love, man can intuit the meaning of the whole as it will later be fully revealed by the Incarnation of the Son, by the coming of Christ.[10]

This leads to the pope's conclusion: Dante's vision shows the validity of human searching and of religions as well as the originality of Christian revelation. He therefore decided to follow the poet's way insofar as knowledge through love "confirms itself". In other words, it becomes an impulse that moves man to advance in knowledge and at the same time transforms him internally so that *eros* is no longer merely a primordial force but, through the way of purification, leads to *agape*, self-giving love. In summary, in order to enter into a reflection on the theological virtues, Ratzinger followed in the footsteps of the Greeks, privileging the way of love, the way indicated by Saint John, whose Gospel the pope considers the most mature reflection on Christian originality.

THE LOVE THAT COMES FROM GOD

Looking more directly at the encyclical, it is divided into two parts. The first, which is more original, discusses the unity of love present in creation and in salvation history; the second, in contrast, is devoted to the exercise of love by the Church, which is to say, to what the experts call the "social doctrine" of the Church.

The first part, in which the pope's approach is more directly felt, starts immediately with a challenge. Love in our time has such a multiplicity of meanings and is such an abused subject that anyone who speaks about it runs the risk of being misunderstood. Despite this danger, the pope added, the effort must be made to connect the meaning of the word love in the various cultures and in contemporary language before discussing the specific meaning the term has in Scripture and in the Christian tradition. Otherwise, one runs the risk of isolation, of a mode of reasoning that does not speak to a large part of mankind. Among the many meanings of the word "love", the one that looms over the others is certainly the man-woman relationship, to which the ancient Greeks gave the name *eros*.

---

[10] Ibid.

The first consideration starts from philology. Whereas the term *eros* occurs frequently and even excessively in Greek literature, it occurs only twice in the Old Testament and is utterly unknown in the New Testament, which of all the Greek words used to designate love prefers the term *agape*. In modern times, this choice was behind the criticism claiming that Christianity is hostile to *eros* and makes the most beautiful part of life bitter. The pope responded to this criticism, which is based on the thinking of another German, Friedrich Nietzsche,[11] by pointing out that the concept of *eros* among the Greeks entailed the cult of fertility, sacred prostitution, and the thrill of power that often led to violence.

At the same time, however, the link between *eros* and the divine also becomes apparent. Love promises infinity and eternity that *eros* by itself cannot ultimately provide. "True, *eros* tends to rise 'in ecstasy' towards the Divine, to lead us beyond ourselves; yet for this very reason it calls for a path of ascent, renunciation, purification and healing."[12] Jesus indicates the manner of this purification when he says, "Whoever seeks to gain his life will lose it, but whoever loses his life will preserve it."[13] This then outlines two forms of love: the yearning for possession and the desire for self-giving. The two forms, however, are not mutually exclusive but share a common foundation, so that one who desires to possess must also be willing to give, and vice versa.

It can also be added that wherever the two dimensions do exclude each other, this gives rise to opposing yet equally dangerous pathologies. The desire for possession turns into oppression and violence, while the desire for self-giving turns into spiritualism that does not properly take into account man's bodily dimension. The pope arrived at this conclusion through the image of God and the image of man conveyed by the Bible. There is not an anonymous cosmic power at the origin of *eros* in the Bible but, rather, a personal God who loves his creation, especially man, created in his image and likeness. *Eros* is therefore preserved in creation in all its goodness, while the work of redemption is gradually revealed as a

---

[11] Friedrich Nietzsche, *Beyond Good and Evil*, chap. 4, apothegm 168.

[12] Benedict XVI, Encyclical Letter *Deus caritas est* on Christian Love, December 25, 2005, no. 5.

[13] Lk 17:33.

work of giving and purifying. It concludes dramatically with the Incarnation and death of the Son of God, whose pierced side is the most convincing evidence of the initial premise of the pope's encyclical letter: God is love. The revelation of love, however, is not merely a historical event that happened about two thousand years ago. The Sacrament of the Eucharist is for believers the guarantee that the love of God revealed by the Son's death involves the faithful in their daily life. At the same time, participation in the sacrament has an inescapable social dimension because love of God and love of neighbor are now truly united.

THE CHURCH'S CHARITY

As pointed out by several commentators,[14] the second part of the encyclical closely follows the line of Catholic social doctrine, stressing that charity is the task of all the faithful and of the entire Church. This statement finds confirmation within the early Church, whose most evident characteristic, according to the Acts of the Apostles, was precisely charity. In imitation, then, of God's love, which knows no bounds and is directed toward all people, the charity of the Church also has an internal dimension, a love directed primarily toward brothers and sisters in the faith, but also a universal dimension directed toward all people in accordance with the model described by the parable of the Good Samaritan.

One critique of the Church in modern times claims that charity has many times been an obstacle to social justice. Benedict conceded that the Church was late in realizing the need to give a new structure to the exercise of charity. On the other hand, particularly in this field, the distinction between State and Church is valid: there is a need to respect the autonomy of the State system, which is the task of politics. Charity, nonetheless, can never be excessive because, according to the words of Jesus, the poor will always accompany the journey of Christians and of all people.

Charity, furthermore, also surpasses national boundaries, so that in our time numerous forms of charity have emerged that are directed to the poor and needy of the entire world. In these interna-

---

[14] See in particular Alberto Melloni, *Benedetto XVI*, in http://www.treccani.it/enciclo pedia/benedetto-xvi_(Enciclopedia-dei-Papi)/.

tional organizations, Catholic and secular volunteers work together generously. Two points in the encyclical deserve particular attention. Christian charity must not lose its specific identity as a work of faith made manifest in love. At the same time, charity is freely given, so that the Christian faith cannot be imposed as a condition for access to the charitable action of the Church.

The pope addressed a final word to Christian volunteers, urging them not to lose heart in the face of a task that can seem vast and immeasurable. Resuming for a moment his initial reflection, the pope wrote: "It is God who governs the world, not we."[15] This observation was not meant to be an alibi for ignoring the world's needs but, rather, an invitation to humility and prayer.

In conclusion, the pope urged looking to the example of the saints. From the beginning of Christian history, from Saint Martin of Tours to Saint Mother Teresa of Calcutta, Christian history has been studded with saints who brought light to their time by their example and their love. The greatest light is that of the Virgin Mary, the result of the purity of heart that seeks not itself but simply puts itself at the service of the divine will, announced by her Son, Jesus Christ. This lyrical, poetic tone concludes the first encyclical by Pope Benedict, made public on December 25, 2005.

The uniqueness of the choice to begin the treatment of the theological virtues starting with God's love for creation and for man is confirmed in the centrality that the Eucharist takes on in the encyclical. As was the ancient conviction of Christians, and as Pope Benedict recalled with repeated insistence during the years of his pontificate, it is not only the remembrance of the Passion but is also, according to the concept of Saint Bonaventure, an ever-new event that guarantees at every moment the encounter of Jesus with his disciples and with the people of every time and on every continent. From this comes the impulse of love that is the ever-new wellspring of life, generosity, and free self-giving. This is confirmed by the lives of the saints, who in every age live out, make current, and witness to the Gospel of charity.

Pope Benedict's first encyclical was generally well received. Even the media distant from the Church recognized the originality of Ratzinger's thinking and his forceful presentation that touched the

---

[15] Benedict XVI, *Deus caritas est*, no. 35.

heartstrings with hints of lyrical inspiration. *Die Zeit* pointed out that "Joseph Ratzinger is a conservative, but not at all a preachy moralist: he is interested in the Grandeur and the Whole of the essential core of Christianity."[16] For its part, the *Frankfurter Allgemeine Zeitung* focused on the second part, which is of a predominantly anthropological character: "Never before has a pope written about human love, about 'sinking in the intoxication of happiness', in such a participatory and poetic way and, at the same time, with such theological breadth and culture as Benedict XVI."[17]

The call to holiness

At the Second Vatican Council, great importance was assigned to chapter 5 of the Dogmatic Constitution on the Church, which bears the title "The Universal Call to Holiness in the Church". The emphasis is placed on the fact that holiness is a divine attribute, transmitted to the Church by the Son of God. He loved the Church as his body and confronted death for her. For this reason, all the members of the Church are called saints—not for their works, but rather for the Baptism that they have received in Christ. At the same time, however, they are called to preserve the sanctity that they have received as a gift. Holiness, therefore, is also a calling, a pressing invitation to follow Jesus robed with "compassion, kindness, lowliness, meekness, and patience".[18]

In their pastoral letters, talking about the new teachings brought by the council, various bishops placed the emphasis precisely on holiness. Bishop Luigi Morstabilini of Brescia wrote: "It is the first time that the Church has acted with such a solemn document in order to speak explicitly to the calling of all people to holiness."[19] And the bishop of Vittorio Veneto, Albino Luciani, the future Pope John Paul I, in his pastoral letter in 1966, spoke about a Christianity that is one in the same way that holiness is one. The heart of this holiness is charity, the same charity to which those who choose the

---

[16] *Die Zeit*, January 16, 2006.

[17] *Frankfurter Allgemeine Zeitung*, January 20, 2006.

[18] Col 3:12.

[19] Luigi Morstabilini, "Vocazione dei laici alla santità", February 15, 1966, in *Lettere pastorali [LP] 1966–1967* (Verona: Edizioni Magistero Episcopale), cols. 271–82.

consecrated life are called.[20] Several years after the conclusion of the council, nonetheless, "Chapter 5 of the constitution on the Church vanished from the agenda of the Italian bishops"[21] and, according to Luigi Sartori,[22] from the agenda of theologians as well.

Pope Benedict, on the other hand, had not forgotten. During his pontificate, there was constant attention to the saints, "whose lives and example are in every age the most convincing explanation of the Gospel".[23] Echoing Benedict's affirmation, Angelo Cardinal Amato declared that in Ratzinger's intention the saints are the true workers of enculturation of the Gospel in the lives of the peoples. They do not announce the Gospel with "elaborate theories developed in the abstract, but live and manifest the *sequela Christi* in their own culture".[24]

Diocesan beatifications

Since apostolic times, some Christians who distinguished themselves by their fidelity to Christ have been venerated as saints. The first to be honored with devotion were the martyrs, who had testified to their fidelity to Christ to the point of shedding their blood. Their passion—the account of their death sentence and execution—would be written down, and their place of burial would become a destination for pilgrimages. Over the centuries, such veneration was extended to other forms of Christian life: bishops who distinguished themselves by their evangelization and preaching, monks, virgins, and others. In order to avoid abuses, several times over the course of the centuries, the Church intervened to discipline the recognition and veneration of the saints. These were the origins of the canonical practice of canonization, which essentially prescribes a two-step process leading to the Church's recognition of the

---

[20] Albino Luciani, "Lettera ai sacerdoti: I laici alla luce del concilio", in John Paul I, *Opera omnia*, vol. 3 (Padua: Messaggero, 1988), 443–79. The passage paraphrased here is found on 457.

[21] See the important article by Aldino Cazzago, "L'universale vocazione alla santità", *Il Concilio Vatican II in Italia cinquant'anni dopo*, ed. A. Cazzago (Rome: Edizioni OCD, 2015), 42.

[22] Luigi Sartori, "Il tema della santità nella *Lumen Gentium*", *Credere Oggi* 47 (1988): 57.

[23] Benedict XVI, from a conversation with the author.

[24] Angelo Amato, *I santi nella Chiesa* (Vatican City: Libreria Editrice Vaticana, 2010), 37.

sainthood of a Christian: beatification and solemn proclamation of sainthood.

According to tradition, both of these steps have been celebrated in Rome since medieval times. A few months after his election, on September 29, 2005, Pope Benedict approved two significant changes with the document *New Procedures in the Rite of Beatification* by the Congregation for the Causes of Saints. The rite of beatification, which had always been done in the presence of the pope, from now on would be presided over by a papal representative; more significantly, it would not be carried out in Rome but in the diocese of the new Blessed. The provisions took into account in a certain way the large number of saints proposed for veneration by the faithful. During the pontificate of John Paul II, the multiplication of canonizations had at times caused difficulties both in preparing the causes of the saints and in conducting the rites. For Pope Benedict, however, the new procedures were above all an urgent invitation to the faithful of the particular diocese to follow the new Blessed's path to holiness, to be inspired by his example and by his unique way of drawing closer to Christ, and to follow his advice.[25]

Holiness, in fact, never has a merely individual dimension but takes form and substance precisely within the fabric of the community to which the person belongs. Preceded by serious preparation, centered on knowledge of the new candidate's life, beatification should become for the faithful an invitation to rediscover the joy of belonging to their own community, of feeling that they are in the company of the saints. In at least some cases, the desired aim was achieved. Angelo Cardinal Amato, prefect of the Congregation for the Causes of Saints, declared at a conference held in Rome in 2009: "Beatifications celebrated *in loco* (locally) are particularly effective. They elicit enormous interest among the faithful, who are prepared by knowledge of the holy life of the beatified, with participation in prayer vigils, and a huge presence at the rite of beatification."[26]

Then, in providing examples, the cardinal declared that he had been struck by the beatification of Father Carlo Gnocchi in Milan:

---

[25] Congregation for the Causes of Saints, Instruction *Sanctorum Mater* for Conducting Diocesan or Eparchial Inquiries in the Causes of Saints, May 17, 2007.

[26] The conference "La qualità teologica della santità" (The theological quality of holiness) is found in Amato, *I santi nella Chiesa*, 27–40 at 27.

"Particularly impressive was the celebration in Milan, in the Piazza del Duomo, which was enchantingly transformed into an immense cathedral that witnessed the participation of more than fifty thousand faithful and a television link with Saint Peter's Square, for greetings from the Holy Father Pope Benedict XVI."[27]

We can also trace back to Pope Benedict's attention to holiness in the Church the Instruction of the Congregation for the Causes of Saints, *Sanctorum Mater*, published on May 17, 2007.[28] The extensive document "intends to clarify the dispositions of currently existing laws in the causes of Saints, to facilitate their application and indicate the ways of executing them both in recent and in ancient causes."[29] There are three points on which the document primarily focuses: diligent preparation of the cause by the diocese of origin, procedural accuracy throughout the various phases, and the final responsibility of the Magisterium. Greater accuracy in the preparation and procedure of the cause should not, however, give the impression that the recognition of sainthood ultimately depends on the rigor of the historical investigation. In fact, both the ascertainment of a clear reputation of sanctity and the ultimate decision regarding sainthood rest with the Magisterium. Only in this way can there be certitude that the canonization process, which starts with evidence of veneration by the faithful and is rooted in the very holiness of Christ and of the Church, Mother of Saints, concerns and definitely engages the universal Church.

Devotion to the Blessed Virgin and the saints

Benedict XVI has a great devotion to the Virgin Mary. His veneration of the Mother of God, nevertheless, has at its origin a biblical and theological vision as presented in his major Mariological writings, *Daughter Zion*[30] and *Mary: The Church at the Source*.[31] In the

---

[27] Ibid., 28.

[28] Congregation for the Causes of Saints, *Sanctorum Mater*, May 17, 2007.

[29] Ibid. On the topic, see also Angelo Amato, "*Sanctorum Mater, Instructio* della Congregazione delle Cause dei Santi circa lo svolgimento delle inchieste diocesane o eparchiali", in Amato, *I santi nella Chiesa*, 80–97.

[30] Joseph Ratzinger, *Daughter Zion*, trans. John M. McDermott, S.J. (San Francisco: Ignatius Press, 1983).

[31] Joseph Ratzinger, *Mary: The Church at the Source*, trans. Adrian Walker (San Francisco: Ignatius Press, 2005).

volume *Daughter Zion*, having observed the discredit into which devotion to the Virgin had fallen in the decade from the 1960s to the 1970s, the theologian recalled the reasons that not only justify but demand the centrality of devotion to the Virgin in the Catholic vision. Ratzinger wrote: "The image of Mary in the New Testament is woven entirely of Old Testament threads."[32] She is the woman and mother toward whom all the great women of Israel point. Eve, Sarah, Rachel, Anna, but also Ruth, Esther, and Judith are women through whom God's grace and revelation pass before definitively reaching Mary. This is why the Virgin can intone the *Magnificat* and affirm, without fear of rebuttal: "he who is mighty has done great things for me" and "henceforth all generations will call me blessed."[33]

At the same time, Mary is also the Church at the source, the Mother of Jesus, and the Mother of believers. In her life, she enacts in the best way possible the four most important seasons of the liturgical year and Christian life. She awaits the birth of Jesus and awaits the birth of the Church; she is at the center of the Incarnation, just as she is close to the Cross. Finally, as the Woman assumed into heaven, she precedes the faithful in participating in the final events of death and resurrection. Like the person of Jesus, the person of Mary witnesses to the uniqueness of the covenant established by God in the Old Testament and brought to fulfillment in the New. The covenant between God and Israel, in fact, was never revoked; rather, it was brought to fulfillment by Jesus on Golgotha, where, at the foot of the Cross, Mary, the Church at the source, was also present.

A PILGRIM TO MARIAN SHRINES

In his memoirs, Ratzinger recalled how as a child he used to go on pilgrimage with his mother and siblings to the Marian shrine at Altötting. In the years that followed, he remained faithful to this practice, and as pope he visited many Marian shrines in Italy and throughout the world. Starting with Italy, he followed the tradition of going every year on December 8 to Piazza di Spagna in Rome to venerate the statue of our Lady. The first year, December 8, 2005,

---

[32] J. Ratzinger, *Daughter Zion*, 12.
[33] Lk 1:48–49.

was the fortieth anniversary of the conclusion of the Second Vatican Council. After noting the occasion, the pope added: "For this reason, serving as spokesperson for the entire Ecclesial Community, I wish to thank the Most Holy Virgin and I turn to her with the same sentiments that animated the Council Fathers, who dedicated to Mary the last chapter of the dogmatic constitution *Lumen Gentium*, underlining the inseparable relationship that unites the Virgin to the Church."[34]

In 2006, during his visit to Bavaria, he once again returned to the shrine of Our Lady of Altötting in the company of his brother.[35] During the homily at the Mass, the pope repeated one of the pivotal elements of his Marian devotion: "Mary leads the nascent Church in prayer; she is, as it were in person, the Church at prayer."[36] Then, commenting on the Gospel of the wedding feast at Cana, he added that our Lady brings the need of the spouses before Jesus, leaving to him the decision about how to help them. On the other hand, from the Cross, Jesus entrusts to his Mother, of all people, the beloved disciple and, with him, the entire Church. It is therefore right that the faithful should turn confidently to the Mother of God. In her company, they can maintain the peaceful certainty of being in communion with the Lord.

At the beginning of 2008, Benedict XVI went to Leuca in Puglia, Italy. The name of the shrine on the easternmost edge of Italy and Europe, Saint Mary *de finibus terrae* (from the ends of the earth), seemed very lovely and impressive to the German pope, recalling the universal mission of the Church. "The Church was born at Pentecost, she was born universal and her vocation is to speak all the world's languages."[37] He then recalled that the Marian piety present in Salento had developed under the influence of the Eastern devotion to the *Theotokos* and serves as a bridge for dialogue with the East. Also in 2008, on September 15, the pope was in Lourdes. During the Mass for the sick, he invited those suffering to have unwavering confidence in the Virgin: "Mary loves each of

---

[34] Benedict XVI, Homage to the Immaculate in Piazza di Spagna, December 8, 2005.

[35] See Georg Ratzinger and Michael Hesemann, *My Brother the Pope*, trans. Michael J. Miller (San Francisco: Ignatius Press, 2011), 236ff.

[36] Benedict XVI, Homily at the Eucharistic Celebration at the Shrine of Our Lady of Altötting, September 11, 2006.

[37] Benedict XVI, Homily at the Eucharistic Celebration at the Shrine of St. Mary *de finibus terrae*, June 14, 2008.

her children, giving particular attention to those who, like her Son at the hour of his Passion, are prey to suffering; she loves them quite simply because they are her children."[38] Then he continued: "I would like to say, humbly, to those who suffer and to those who struggle and are tempted to turn their backs on life: turn towards Mary! Within the smile of the Virgin lies mysteriously hidden the strength to fight against sickness and for life."[39]

While traveling in Brazil as well, the pope did not neglect to make a pilgrimage to the Basilica of the National Shrine of Our Lady of Aparecida. In this great shrine, which is a reference point for Latin America, the pope was confident and inspired: "How beautiful it is to be gathered here in the name of Christ, in faith, in fraternity, in joy, in peace and in prayer, together with 'Mary, the mother of Jesus' (Acts 1:14). . . . I am glad to be here with you, in your midst!"[40] In short, it can be said that the pope went as a pilgrim to the Marian shrines of the world, witnessing everywhere to the confidence and hope that come from Mary and her Son, Jesus.

A PILGRIM TO THE TOMBS OF THE SAINTS

In his memoirs as in his other writings, Pope Benedict has not hesitated to reveal his particular devotion to certain saints. Among these are: Saint Corbinian, founder of the Diocese of Freising, who arrived in Rome accompanied by a bear; Brother Conrad of Parzham, a Franciscan friar canonized in the early years of his papacy; Saint Augustine, the holy African Doctor of the Church on whom his doctoral dissertation was based; Saint Benedict, the father of Western monasticism whom he chose as the patron of his papacy; and Saint Bonaventure, whose work on the creation of the world inspired his second doctoral dissertation.

On April 22, 2007, Benedict XVI went on a pilgrimage to Pavia to express, in the basilica of San Pietro in Ciel d'Oro, the homage of the entire Catholic Church to one of her most ingenious chil-

---

[38] Benedict XVI, Homily at the Eucharistic Celebration for the Sick, Lourdes, September 15, 2008.

[39] Ibid.

[40] Benedict XVI, Address at the Basilica of the Shrine of Aparecida for the Recitation of the Holy Rosary and Meeting with Priests, Men Religious, Women Religious, Seminarians and Deacons, May 12, 2007.

dren as well as his personal devotion and gratitude to the one who had played a significant role in his life as a theologian and pastor.[41] Before the tomb of Saint Augustine, the pope symbolically delivered to the world again his encyclical on love, which, especially in the first part, was largely indebted to the thinking of this African Father of the Church. All mankind, the pope went on, needs love, and Christ is love in truth. Christians should therefore have the courage to proclaim him with candor. This is the high standard of the Christian life; this is the example that Saint Augustine left for Christians of all times.

After the pilgrimage to the tomb of Saint Augustine, no one was surprised by the subsequent visit to Bagnoregio, the city of Saint Bonaventure, which took place two years later, on September 6, 2009. In his brief address to the people of the city, Pope Benedict recalled his personal connection with the saint, whose work on creation was not only the starting point for his laborious second dissertation to qualify for university teaching but was also invaluable later on, enabling him to offer an original contribution to the deeper study of the concept of revelation at the Second Vatican Council.[42] From the time of his studies in Paris, the pope began, Bonaventure was an indefatigable seeker of God, considered as the highest good to aim for with one's intellect and will. His life was therefore an uninterrupted itinerary of purification, a constant journey toward the perfection of his capacity for knowledge, toward holiness.

A disciple of Saint Francis, Saint Bonaventure, too, sang the glories of creation, considering the world a gift of love from God to man. Finally, he was a messenger of hope, as attested by the beautiful image by which "he compares the movement of hope with the flight of a bird that spreads its wings to their maximum capacity and draws on all its strength to flap them."[43] The pope's visit to Bagnoregio occurred during the year that Benedict had declared the Year of the Priest. He did not neglect, therefore, to point to the holy Franciscan teacher as a model for priests, inviting them to become, like him, tireless seekers of God.

---

[41] Benedict XVI, Homily at the Celebration of Vespers at the Basilica of St. Pietro in Ciel d'Oro in Pavia, April 22, 2007.

[42] See above, chap. 3.

[43] Benedict XVI, Address at the Meeting with the Local People of Viterbo and Bagnoregio, September 6, 2009.

Pope and theologian of holiness

An elect systematic theologian and now the reigning pontiff, Benedict, at the beginning of 2006, decided to dedicate the Wednesday
audiences for the faithful to a survey of the lives of the saints. In
his view, reflection on the saints does not result exclusively from
devotion but includes a vision of the Church, which is the house
of holiness, the place in which the presence of God generates saints
who are his witnesses in the world and in time. The link between
the Church and holiness is examined in particular by the pope in
the first[44] of the series of volumes of his collected Wednesday catecheses dedicated to the saints.

CATECHETICAL AUDIENCES ON THE SAINTS

Starting with the General Audience of March 15, 2006, his catecheses on the saints extended for a period of over five years until
July 2010. Initially, the pope did not have a well-defined plan. The
success defined by the reception of the faithful, who came in ever increasing numbers to the Paul VI Audience Hall, led him to prolong
the series for a good part of his pontificate. The series of volumes,[45]
nonetheless, shows the depth of his approach to the various saints
and the meticulous thoughtfulness with which the pope prepared
his texts. United by their following and imitation of Christ, the
saints nevertheless have their distinctive personalities, spiritual sensibilities, and charisms. Hence the usefulness of revisiting the life
of each. Here, of course, I will limit myself to mentioning briefly
the character traits that Ratzinger highlighted in some of the saints
dearest to him.

THE APOSTLES

Saint Peter. The apostle of impulsive generosity is also a fragile man.
The brazen man who had promised absolute fidelity knows the bit-

---

[44] Benedict XVI, *Jesus, the Apostles, and the Early Church* (San Francisco: Ignatius Press, 2007).

[45] The catechetical audiences were published in Italian by Libreria Editrice Vaticana in six small volumes that have been reprinted multiple times [and in English by Ignatius Press, San Francisco]. I am nonetheless convinced that they have not received the attention and dissemination that they deserve.

terness of betrayal and must learn that he is weak and in need of forgiveness. In a word, he has to experience his own fragility in order to carry out his mission. Pope Benedict greatly emphasized this character trait of the first pope. The man who defined himself as "a simple and humble laborer in the vineyard of the Lord"[46] upon his first appearance as pope found a surprising human and spiritual affinity here, far removed from the old discussions of the power and authority of the Successor of Peter in both the spiritual and political spheres.

Already the name change from Simon to Peter, the Rock, signifies the calling to a unique mission that becomes clearer, on the one hand, with the apostle's repeated professions of faith and, on the other hand, with what Benedict called the "contextualization of the Primacy of Peter at the Last Supper".[47] Peter's task is to safeguard the communion of Christ, to ensure that the net does not tear and that, thus, the universal communion can continue to last. Benedict was talking about Saint Peter but also about his understanding of the Petrine ministry, about the way in which he understood the papacy.

Saint John the Evangelist. He is the theologian apostle to whom Benedict is particularly attached. He is the beloved disciple who places his head on the Master's chest at the Last Supper but also the model of the disciple who lives out friendship with Jesus. "To achieve this, it is not enough to follow him and to listen to him outwardly: it is also necessary to live with him and like him. This is only possible in the context of a relationship of deep familiarity."[48] John, furthermore, is also the evangelist and theologian of love. Benedict himself recalled having taken the title of his first encyclical from a phrase in the First Letter of Saint John.[49] John is not a theoretician or a philosopher of love but, rather, a witness. God, in fact, is by his very nature love and has demonstrated his love concretely by entering into human history. Moreover, "having loved his own who were in the world, he loved them to the end."[50]

---

[46] Benedict XVI, First Greeting of His Holiness, April 19, 2005.
[47] Benedict XVI, *Jesus, the Apostles*, 53.
[48] Ibid., 69.
[49] 1 Jn 4:16.
[50] Jn 13:1.

Here, the pope commented, we move well beyond the ancient precept that exhorted us to love others as ourselves. The standard is now greatly extended: it is the very love of Christ, who loved his own to the point of giving his own life for them.

THE CHURCH FATHERS

The series of catechetical audiences that began with the apostles and the first disciples of Jesus was continued by Pope Benedict with a gallery of twenty-six figures who lived from the second century to the beginning of the fifth. This was the age of the great Church Fathers, writers and churchmen who distinguished themselves by their sanctity of life, excellence of doctrine, and the ability to make clear and attractive the teachings of Jesus transmitted by the Church. They wrote in Greek, Latin, and Syriac. For the most part, the pope devoted an audience to each of them, discussing first their life and then their doctrine, but in one particular case—that of his beloved Saint Augustine—he devoted five full audiences to this figure, without a doubt one of the most significant and captivating of the early centuries of Christianity.

A distinguishing feature is the pope's ability to highlight the contemporary relevance of the contribution made by each writer. In this way, Benedict was able to show the richness of thought that he obviously considered relevant and still capable of promoting communion among contemporary Christians and of proclaiming the Gospel to all who are searching. In this case, too, I will briefly mention some of the particularly important figures.

Saint Justin Martyr. This pagan philosopher who spent his life in search of the truth and then found it in Christianity is particularly dear to Pope Benedict, who credits him with having elaborated the first attempt to harmonize faith and reason. For Justin, born in Palestine around the year 100, Jesus is the *Logos*, the eternal reason. With his coming, he revealed God's eternal plan enacted with creation and redemption. All men, moreover, have within them a seed of reason, which is why both the Jews, through the words of the prophets, and the Greeks, through the words of the philosophers, have within them a ray of truth and can understand and adhere to Christian doctrine. The pope concluded: "In a time like ours, marked by relativism in the discussion on values and on religion . . . , this is a lesson that should not be forgotten."[51]

Origen. A native of Alexandria in Egypt, Origen is for Pope Benedict one of the pivotal personalities in the development of Christian thought. A passionate reader of the Bible, he is considered the first biblical scholar. His research, however, was not limited to the literal text, but he sought to draw from Scripture a moral meaning, a teaching for his own life, and ultimately a spiritual meaning, which is to say, the unity of Scripture that speaks of Christ throughout its development. Furthermore, Origen is for Ratzinger a man of study motivated by love and prayer. "Notwithstanding all the theological richness of his thought, his is never a purely academic approach; it is always founded on the experience of prayer, of contact with God. . . . Knowledge of the Scriptures requires prayer and intimacy with Christ even more than study."[52] Finally, the pope recalled incidentally that in his book on Jesus of Nazareth he sought to apply to today's situation the method already prescribed and followed by Origen.[53]

FATHERS AND WRITERS OF THE
FIRST MILLENNIUM AND MIDDLE AGES

Pope Benedict's journey through the history of holiness continued with a series of portraits devoted to the saints[54] who lived in the delicate period during which the Byzantine Empire, increasingly occupied in the East, was bounded in the West by the Holy Roman Empire established by Charlemagne. The absence of Saint Benedict is surprising, but the pope had already given the Father of Monasticism extensive homage with the choice and explanation of his name as pontiff. The selection of the saints in the second part of this volume is also marked for the most part by the monastic and imperial trend.[55]

---

[51] Benedict XVI, *Church Fathers: From Clement of Rome to Augustine* (San Francisco: Ignatius Press, 2008), 20.

[52] Ibid., 38.

[53] Ibid., 36.

[54] Benedict XVI, *Church Fathers and Teachers: From Saint Leo the Great to Peter Lombard* (San Francisco: Ignatius Press, 2010).

[55] Ibid., 163–215

Since the separation between the Churches of Greek Rite and
Latin Rite had already occurred, the protagonists of this section
all come from the West. They are the saints of the great Benedictine and Cistercian monastic tradition: Anselm, Bernard, Hugo,
and Richard of Saint Victor, down to Rupert of Deutz and Peter
Lombard. Benedict has a marked sympathy for these men of the
mind, great scholars and great contemplatives in love with Jesus.
He said, for example, of Rupert of Deutz: "Like all the representatives of monastic theology, he was able to combine rational study
of the mysteries of faith with prayer and contemplation, which he
considered the summit of all knowledge of God."[56] Once again an
autobiographical trait can be gathered here of the pastor who at the
same time yearns for the contemplation and love of God.

THE FRANCISCAN AND DOMINICAN TEACHERS

The last volume in the series of saints discussed by Pope Benedict
is dedicated to the mendicant saints, the saints from the first century of the Franciscan and Dominican Orders, from Saint Francis
and Saint Dominic to Saint Bonaventure and Saint Thomas. The
guiding principle of this series is found in the famous phrase of
Bonaventure: "Christ's works do not go backward, they do not
fail but progress."[57] For Benedict, these words imply two general
considerations: Christ is no longer the end of history, as he was for
the Church Fathers, but rather its center. The power of the figure
of Francis allows him to draw the conclusion that Christian history
is not merely a history of uninterrupted decline from its origins.
"The riches of Christ's word are inexhaustible and . . . new light
could also appear to the new generations. The oneness of Christ
also guarantees newness and renewal in all the periods of history."[58]

Proposing anew the figure of Saint Bonaventure, therefore, offered
Benedict the opportunity to read contemporary history through the
lessons of this great teacher. Even today, he said, there are those who
consider the history of the Church an unstoppable decline, just as
after the Second Vatican Council there were those who claimed

---

[56] Ibid., 203.

[57] Benedict XVI, *Holy Men and Women of the Middle Ages and Beyond* (San Francisco:
Ignatius Press, 2012), 45.

[58] Ibid., 46

that the preconciliar Church had ended and an entirely new one was about to begin. It was a spiritualistic and anarchic utopianism. Instead, there is a need to maintain the sober realism of Bonaventure and to be open to new charisms and ecclesial realities.

APPLICATIONS TO THE BIOGRAPHY OF POPE BENEDICT

As already mentioned, for Pope Benedict, the saints are not people of the past. In his vision of faith, their lives explain and transmit the Gospel of Jesus even from centuries away. With regard to his personal biography, it is helpful to take another look at the figures of the two saints who were for him examples as spiritual teachers and models of life: Saint Augustine and Saint Bonaventure. The decision of the African Father, after his conversion, to live with a group of friends while devoting himself to study and prayer was imitated by Ratzinger with his group of students, the *Schülerkreis*, to whom he tried to remain faithful even from Rome as prefect of the Congregation for the Doctrine of the Faith and as pope. Ultimately, the type of life chosen by Pope Benedict after resigning from the pontificate seems modeled upon Augustine's choice to devote the last years of his life to the study of Sacred Scripture and to prayer.[59]

From the portrait of Saint Bonaventure, on the other hand, it is worth pointing out an emphasis that almost seems to be an interpretive key for the pontificate of Pope Benedict. The German pope thus wrote:

> Thus we see that for Saint Bonaventure governing was not merely action but, above all, was thinking and praying. At the root of his government we always find prayer and thought; all his decisions are the result of reflection, of thought illumined by prayer. His intimate contact with Christ always accompanied his work as Minister General, and therefore he composed a series of theological and mystical writings that express the soul of his government.[60]

It almost seems a response to the many who during his pontificate scolded him for neglecting to govern the Church in order to devote himself to his books.

---

[59] This pairing was suggested to me by Pope Benedict himself during a meeting on September 14, 2015.

[60] Benedict XVI, *Holy Men and Women*, 47.

The Year of Saint Paul

The series of catecheses on the saints was interrupted from 2008 to 2009 by an exceptional event: the celebration of the Year of Saint Paul on the occasion of the two thousandth anniversary of the apostle's birth, determined according to an approximate calculation.[61] Announced during Evening Prayer I on June 28, 2008, in the Basilica of Saint Paul Outside the Walls, the celebration was inaugurated a year later by the pope with great solemnity in the presence of Ecumenical Patriarch Bartholomew I. The purpose of the jubilee celebration was not to be, however, simply a historical recollection: "Paul wants to speak to us—today."[62]

The apostle's message, according to the pope, comes from three experiences he had at the moment of his conversion:

- the certainty of being loved by Christ in an entirely personal way;
- the identification of Christ with the Church, which is not an association to promote particular interests: "In her it is a matter of the person of Jesus Christ";[63]
- the call to evangelization, which at the same time is a call to suffering.

Therefore, it is made clear right from the start of the Year of Saint Paul that the celebration to which Benedict was inviting the faithful, particularly the clergy, was an invitation to a change of life: "This is the goal of the Pauline Year: to learn from Saint Paul, to learn faith, to learn Christ and, finally, to learn the way of upright living."[64] In order to promote this journey, the pope personally committed himself to a series of twenty catecheses devoted to the apostle that form a little guide for understanding Saint Paul. At the same time, they are a reminder of several fundamental principles of the Christian faith: the importance of a personal relationship with Jesus, firm adherence to the Church, and the importance of Chris-

---

[61] There are no certain records about the date of birth of Saint Paul. The most reliable scholars maintain that he was born between A.D. 5 and 10. The date of the celebration mentioned by the pope was therefore established based on a calculation of probabilities.

[62] Benedict XVI, Homily at the Celebration of First Vespers for the Opening of the Pauline Year, June 28, 2008.

[63] Ibid.

[64] Benedict XVI, *Saint Paul* (San Francisco: Ignatius Press, 2009), 12.

tian preaching that essentially consists in the proclamation of Christ crucified and risen.

The pope concluded: Saint Paul was completely enthralled and fascinated by the mystery of the Son of God dying upon the Cross, to the point of renouncing his own life and devoting himself entirely to the ministry of reconciling God and man.[65] This is what is still required today of every Christian, particularly of priests and bishops. With regard to these latter, in commenting on the Letter to Timothy, Benedict recalled three traits that should distinguish a leader of the Christian community: it is necessary for him to have a good reputation among those outside the community, to be able to teach, and to have a paternal sense. It is above all this last virtue of a bishop that is particularly dear to the pope, who concluded his penultimate catechesis on Saint Paul with a prayer "that the Pastors of the Church may increasingly acquire paternal sentiments tender and at the same time strong in the formation of the House of God, of the community, and of the Church."[66]

As experts of Church history know, insistently praying for a virtue corresponds to the recognition of its absence. In the pope's intentions, the celebration of the Year of Saint Paul was certainly directed to all the faithful. It is equally true, however, that the recollection of the apostle was intended above all as a call for priests and bishops. Then again, the spiritual renewal and missionary impulse hoped for by the German pontiff could only begin with those responsible for catechesis and preaching.

This is one of the points that are both central and yet painful about Ratzinger's pontificate. Then again, the issue had already been raised for some time by more astute observers. At the beginning of Benedict XVI's pontificate, George Weigel wrote: "The suggestion here is not for an episcopal night of the long knives, in which Pope Benedict and the Congregation for Bishops depose bishops by the dozen. But when a bishop has manifestly lost the capacity to govern, or when a bishop is taking public positions contrary to Catholic teaching . . . , then something must be done."[67]

The pope's somber return to these problems concerning the clergy

---

[65] Ibid., 65.

[66] Benedict XVI, General Audience, January 28, 2009.

[67] See George Weigel, *God's Choice: Benedict XVI and the Future of the Catholic Church* (New York: HarperCollins, 2005), 252.

suggests that the response to the call of the Year of Saint Paul was inadequate.

Christian hope

Pope Benedict's second encyclical was published at the end of November 2007, and its theme was hope. At the time of the Second Vatican Council, there was intense discussion about hope. Ratzinger himself had as colleagues at the University of Tübingen both the Marxist philosopher Ernst Bloch, author of *The Principle of Hope*,[68] and Jürgen Moltmann, author of a *Theology of Hope*,[69] which became a best seller in the Catholic world. But the pope's document certainly does not have its origins in Bloch's utopian hope or in Moltmann's anthropological optimism. Forty years later, in fact, the cultural trend had profoundly changed. The optimism of the past had given way to a somber realism, the expectations of liberation had been decisively swept away by the globalization of violence.

Keeping his distance from these two opposing cultural trends, Benedict XVI began his encyclical with a citation from Saint Paul's Letter to the Romans that is at the same time an act of faith: "For in this hope we were saved" (Rom 8:24). The pope then clarified the meaning of this profession of faith with an example drawn from the life of Saint Josephine Bakhita. This humble African saint of the last century, having learned that God loved her, had gained the certainty that her life was good. "Through the knowledge of this hope she was 'redeemed', no longer a slave, but a free child of God."[70] In fact, Christian hope is not limited to this world and its time but aims at eternal life.

The pope nevertheless pointed out that a linguistic problem of significant import immediately arises. "Eternal life" cannot mean an interminable life that ends up becoming intolerable. "Eternal" is to be understood, rather, in the sense of blessed, full, free from

---

[68] The three-volume work was published over the period from 1953 to 1959.

[69] The work was published in Italy by the Queriniana publishing house in Brescia in 1970 as part of the same series in which an Italian edition of Ratzinger's *Introduction to Christianity* had been published two years earlier. English edition: Jürgen Moltmann, *Theology of Hope: On the Ground and the Implications of a Christian Eschatology*, trans. James W. Leitch (Minneapolis: Fortress Press, 1993).

[70] Benedict XVI, Encyclical Letter *Spe salvi* on Christian Hope, November 30, 2007, no. 3.

succession and the constraint of time. For now, accustomed as we are to the temporal dimension, we can only imagine such a life as a "plunging into the ocean of infinite love, a moment in which time—the before and after—no longer exists."[71] The temptation of a hope understood in this way could be that of individualism, as for those who aim solely at their own salvation without concern for their neighbors. The sacramental structure of Christianity says at the same time that Christian hope is communal and communional, concerning our neighbors in this life and as well as the deceased. At the same time, running counter to the expectations of the modern age put forward in particular by Marxism, which places its trust exclusively in science and in man's capacity for progress, the pope pointed out that hope placed solely in technical and scientific progress is what brought about the advancement from slings to nuclear bombs. Only the God who is love can be at the foundation of an authentic hope that pertains to the conditions of life in this world yet also dares to look at suffering and life after death.

In this regard, the pope presented as a model the Western monasticism started by Saint Benedict and the Cistercian reform promoted chiefly by Saint Bernard. Both monastic movements were able to recognize the dignity of work, developed a method and conditions of life, and were together based on prayer as a means of acquiring hope and awaiting its fulfillment. Hope, therefore, is linked to prayer just as it is related to suffering.

On this matter, the pope related a saying of Saint Bernard that is close to his heart: "God cannot suffer, but he can *suffer with*."[72] "God now reveals his true face in the figure of the sufferer who shares man's God-forsaken condition by taking it upon himself."[73] With his Resurrection, "this innocent sufferer has attained the certitude of hope"[74] that the sorrowful will be consoled. By this compassion, a person is able "to suffer with the other and for others; to suffer for the sake of truth and justice; to suffer out of love and in order to become a person who truly loves."[75] On the other hand, suffering can at least be mitigated by the consolation of suffering

---

[71] Ibid., no. 12.

[72] Saint Bernard, *Sermones in Cantica*, XXVI, 5, in *Patrologia Latina*, 183, 906, cited in Benedict XVI, *Spe salvi*, no. 39.

[73] Benedict XVI, *Spe salvi*, no. 43.

[74] Ibid.

[75] Ibid., no. 39.

together with God, together with our brothers and sisters and others. Prayer, furthermore, assures communion with the dead.

Pope Benedict was firm in proposing again those elements of the Christian faith that have almost entirely disappeared from preaching today and that, in contrast, in his vision are the true object of hope: death, judgment, heaven, and hell. Death and judgment are approached by Christians, not with fear and terror, but rather as moments of learning and practicing hope based on the revelation of God's mercy. Heaven and hell are likewise approached with the hope of having been preceded on this path by the Sufferer who is risen and now sits at the right hand of the Father.

Pope Benedict was well acquainted in this regard with the position of a friend and theologian like von Balthasar, who dared to speak of an empty hell. On this point, however, he was more cautious: "There can be people who have totally destroyed their desire for truth and readiness to love . . . people who have lived for hatred and have suppressed all love within themselves."[76] This state is a consequence of man's freedom, and there is nothing left to save here. This state is hell. For many, however, who have left some space for love within themselves, God is at the same time justice and grace. Even judgment, therefore, is a place and occasion for learning and exercising hope.

The pope, moreover, seemed to adopt as his own the view of several recent theologians who say that the purifying fire of purgatory is the very love of Jesus. "The encounter with him is the decisive act of judgement. Before his gaze every falsehood melts away." It is a matter, therefore, of a passage as if through fire that is painful and beautifying at the same time. "But it is a blessed pain, in which the holy power of his love sears through us like a flame, enabling us to become totally ourselves and thus totally of God."[77]

Perhaps because it was published at a time in which the reasons for looking to the future with hope seemed to be fading, Pope Benedict's encyclical on hope did not receive the reception that it deserved.[78] Even today, however, it has the merit of firmly proposing again the doctrine on life after death already expounded in the Cate-

---

[76] Ibid., no. 45.

[77] Ibid., no. 47.

[78] Interesting points from the encyclical were nonetheless taken up again by the journal *Communio* in the issue dedicated to the topic *Il ritorno di Cristo* [The return of Christ], 231 (January-February 2012).

chism of the Catholic Church. In a meeting with the Roman clergy, in response to a question from a priest, the pope highlighted the importance of the part of the encyclical that deals with the last things: "Purgatory and heaven cannot be taken away. Purgatory is a place of purification, hell is the category of those who no longer have within themselves 'a minimal capacity for loving'. Heaven is complete and definitive justice, 'brought about at last'. And where people follow the criteria given by God, a bit of heaven appears in the world."[79]

In a broader context, the encyclical is a voice above the crowd, a reminder of the dignity of human nature, an authoritative invitation to the "pursuit of virtue and of knowledge"[80] and to look beyond the boundaries of earthly life.

---

[79] Aldo Maria Valli, *Benedetto XVI: Il pontificato interrotto* (Milan: Mondadori, 2013), 148, referencing Benedict XVI, Address to Parish Priests and Clergy of the Diocese of Rome, February 7, 2008.

[80] Dante Alighieri, *Divine Comedy: Inferno*, XXVI, 120.

XVI

A NEW HUMANISM FOR
THE TWENTY-FIRST CENTURY

Commenting on the election of Benedict XVI, evangelical pastor Timothy George made a prediction about the pontificate of the new pope that proved very much on target. In his estimation, the very choice of the name Benedict showed his intention to insist, as his predecessor did, on evangelization.[1] This would bring about the birth of a new humanism, based, not on sociological analyses or philosophical reflections, but on one of the most famous maxims from the rule of Saint Benedict: "Prefer nothing to the love of Christ."[2] It was in fact the primacy of Christ above all other things that had enabled the Benedictines to create monastic humanism, based on the other famous motto, *ora et labora*: pray and work. By combining these, the monks had built a civilization that lasted centuries, traces of which remain in contemporary thought and in art.

With the motto of "a new humanism for the twenty-first century" based on Christ, Pope Benedict turned first to bishops, priests, and the faithful, then to civil leaders, cultural and academic figures, and the representatives of various religions. With regard to civil leaders, another issue arose that the pope repeatedly addressed in his travels and speeches: the issue of a secularism that he described as positive, built on mutual respect and support rather than on hostility or ostracism, as opposed to a radical or intransigent secularism that ignores or even opposes the values of the Christian tradition. For

---

[1] See George Weigel, *God's Choice: Benedict XVI and the Future of the Catholic Church* (New York: HarperCollins, 2005), 154.
[2] Rule of Saint Benedict, chap. 4:21.

the pope, Italy was in fact a model of where positive secularism produced good results.

He wrote the following on the occasion of the 150th anniversary of the unification of Italy: "The Italian State and its juridical order highlighted the two overriding principles that must govern relations between the Church and the political community: the separation of contexts and cooperation."[3] The separation served as a shelter against disputes and confusion, while cooperation could avoid reducing reality to material goods alone, preserving cultural and spiritual values.

Europe

A pope who for a long time had collaborated with John Paul II to overcome the conflict that had torn apart the Old Continent in the first half of the preceding century, who had written two books about Europe,[4] and who, according to Bernard Lecomte,[5] might well be the last European pope for a long time could not help but place the Old Continent at the center of his Petrine ministry. Truth be told, the refusal to remember the Christian roots of Europe in the European constitution had caused the cardinal great disappointment, which would be difficult to forget in such a short time. Nevertheless, as Andrea Riccardi observed, "the Catholic Church, despite the fact that many of her faithful are in the Southern Hemisphere, still considers Europe of strategic importance for upholding the vitality of universal Catholicism."[6]

Once elected to the chair of Saint Peter, Pope Benedict focused his pastoral concern on the European nations, hoping that they might have a new humanism based on the harmony of reason and faith. More concretely, according to the pope, what is needed in the new millennium is an ethical foundation, and this is where the Christian tradition can offer a decisive contribution, not by providing

---

[3] Benedict XVI, Message to H. E. Mr. Giorgio Napolitano, President of the Italian Republic on the 150th Anniversary of the Unification of Italy, March 17, 2011.

[4] See above, chaps. 10 and 12.

[5] Bernard Lecomte, *Benoît XVI: Le dernier pape européen* (Paris: Perrin, 2006).

[6] Andrea Riccardi, "Il futuro del cristianesimo", in *Storia della Chiesa*, ed. A. Fliche and V. Martin, vol. 1.26, *I cattolici e le Chiese cristiane durante il pontificato di Giovanni Paolo II*, ed. E. Guerriero and M. Impagliazzo (Cinisello Balsamo: San Paolo, 2006), 20.

technical responses and concrete political solutions, but by offering objective moral principles identified by reason with the support of faith. For this reason, too, he appointed to the Secretariat of State Tarcisio Cardinal Bertone, archbishop of Genoa, with whom he had worked at the Congregation for the Doctrine of the Faith. The nomination caused disappointment at the Secretariat of State, where the post had been for some time reserved for an ecclesiastical official with diplomatic expertise.

ITALY

The pope, who cited Dante's *Divine Comedy* in his first encyclical, was profoundly enamored with Italy. The high places of the country's spirit—Pavia, Bagnoregio, Assisi, Montecassino, Serra San Bruno—likewise became destinations along his truly unique pilgrimage to the wellsprings of Christian piety and culture. In his vision, they can again become influential cultural and spiritual centers for Italy. On June 17, 2007, the eight hundredth anniversary of the conversion of Saint Francis, he spoke as follows to the young people gathered in Assisi: "It is time that you, young people, like Francis, take seriously and know how to enter into a personal relationship with Jesus. It is time to look at the history of this third millennium just begun as a history that needs the Gospel leaven ever more."[7]

The constant recollection of the past is not, for the German pope, a historian's habit but rather a spiritual place from which to draw the strength to renew the present of the Church and of society. At the time of his election, Italy was led by a center-right government, headed by Silvio Berlusconi, that also included several Catholic representatives; more significantly, the government was supported by the Communion and Liberation movement, which for some time had enjoyed the favor of the pontiff. The country was nonetheless shaken by social turmoil that quickly led to the fall of Berlusconi and the return to power of Romano Prodi, a Catholic who nevertheless appeared more detached from the Vatican line.

---

[7] Benedict XVI, Address to Youth Gathered in the Square in Front of the Basilica of Saint Mary of the Angels on the Eighth Centenary of the Conversion of Saint Francis, June 17, 2007.

Indeed, during Prodi's administration, a regrettable incident occurred. The rector of La Sapienza University in Rome invited Pope Benedict to give a *lectio magistralis* on January 17, 2008, to inaugurate the academic year. Bitter and baseless controversies erupted, which prompted the pope to decline the invitation. Later, the newspaper *L'Osservatore Romano* published the text of the lecture that the veteran professor had prepared, which further highlighted the ideological prejudice underlying the polemics that had accompanied the invitation.

The presentation began with appreciative remarks about Roman universities: "It is in their freedom from political and ecclesiastical authorities that the particular function of universities lies."[8] Then the pope explained that he was speaking to the university as the bishop of Rome, responsible for all Catholics present at La Sapienza, and as a representative of the papacy, which has become "a voice for the ethical reasoning of humanity"[9] and seeks to preserve "sensibility to the truth".[10] In the modern university, the pope continued, the multiplication of knowledge and of scientific disciplines runs the risk of marginalizing both philosophy and theology. That way, however, the pressure of interests and the attraction of utility prevail. Consequently, not only philosophy and theology, but also reason itself becomes marginalized, and the search for truth is renounced altogether. The pope concluded by recalling once again that the purpose of his presence at the university was "to invite reason to set out ever anew in search of what is true and good, in search of God."[11]

This incident, which had no further consequences, nonetheless gave rise to an increasing coldness of Catholics toward the coalition led by Prodi. The subsequent return of Berlusconi to the government was accompanied by the economic crisis and the ongoing pursuit of embarrassing investigations into the private life of the prime minister. The Holy See, which was initially favorable toward the center-right government, adopted a more indifferent attitude. The pope found more common ground with Giorgio Napolitano, the

---

[8] Benedict XVI, Lecture at the University of Rome "La Sapienza", January 17, 2008.
[9] Ibid.
[10] Ibid.
[11] Ibid.

Italian president who remained in office from 2006 to 2015. The pope developed a cordial relationship with this veteran politician, who had risen from within the ranks of the Communist Party, and over time they became friendly. Difficult times followed for the country and for the Church. On more than one occasion, the two veteran leaders found support in each other.

Indeed, in a message to the president of the Republic of Italy on the occasion of the 150th anniversary of the unification of Italy, Pope Benedict made plain the reasons for his affection and appreciation for the country.[12] Against the backdrop of belonging together to the Catholic faith, a community was formed on the peninsula during the Middle Ages that was united by language and culture, although it was divided into a plurality of political institutions. Furthermore, the Church was able to establish educational and charitable institutions that in turn promoted the development of the arts, which were practiced by masters such as Dante, Giotto, Petrarch, Michelangelo, Raphael, Pierluigi da Palestrina, Caravaggio, Scarlatti, Bernini, and Borromini. These artists left an entirely unique imprint on the identity of the nation, as did two great saints: Saint Francis and Saint Catherine, the patrons of Italy.

The pope concluded his argument as follows: given these precedents, the unification of the country in the middle of the nineteenth century was able to occur, not as an artificial construct, but as a "natural political outlet for the development of a national identity that began much earlier".[13] The process of unification, called the Risorgimento, was initially considered a movement against the Church for reasons of historical circumstance. However, there can be no denying the contributions to thought and action that were provided by Catholics in both the nineteenth and twentieth centuries. In particular, Pope Benedict recalled the contributions to the drafting of the constitution and the signing of the new concordat in 1984, which promoted a renewal in the relationship between Church and State in Italy. This step helped establish a healthy secularism based on the separation of tasks and cooperation. Finally, the pope recognized that the State and the Italian people have

---

[12] Benedict XVI, Message to the President of the Italian Republic on the 150th Anniversary of the Unification of Italy, March 17, 2011.
[13] Ibid.

always been able to appreciate the privilege—but also the duty—of the unique situation of Rome as the See of the Successor of Peter and the global center of Catholicism. On behalf of all Catholics, he expressed his gratitude to the president and to the entire nation for this.

With regard to the Church in Italy, on the other hand, at his first meeting with the bishops on May 30, 2005, the pope asked that they "strengthen the communion between the parish structures and the various 'charismatic' groups that have sprung up in recent decades and are widespread in Italy".[14] In short, the pope was urging a Church that was alive but breathing with only one lung—the clerical one[15]—to open herself up to cooperation with movements and other lay associations, of which there was no shortage in Italy.

Benedict went to Verona on October 19, 2006, where bishops, priests, and laypeople from all the regions of Italy were gathered for the Fourth National Ecclesial Convention of the Italian Church. The meeting, which had been mired in confusion up to that point,[16] finally got under way with the pope's address. Italy, part of the secularized West that tries to exclude God from culture and public life, seemed to Benedict like a land in need. At the same time it was "a very favorable place for such a witness" because "the Church is a lively reality" and "Christian traditions often continue to be rooted."[17] It was therefore necessary to start with the love of God revealed in Christ, while at the same time keeping open the areas of rational argument so as to extend reasonableness to the authentic values of the culture of our time and to reopen rational discourse itself to the great questions of truth and goodness. On these conditions, Italian Catholics could play an important role not only in Italy but also in Europe and in the rest of the world.

The first concrete issue Benedict had to confront in Italy was the choice of a successor to lead the episcopal conference. In his many

---

[14] Benedict XVI, Address to the Italian Bishops Taking Part in the 54th Assembly of the Italian Bishops' Conference, May 30, 2005.

[15] This expression is from Saviero Xeres and Giorgio Campanini, *Manca il respiro* (Milan: Àncora, 2011), 7.

[16] See Aldo Maria Valli, *Benedetto XVI: Il pontificato interrotto* (Milan: Mondadori, 2013), 80.

[17] See Benedict XVI, Address to Participants in the Fourth National Ecclesial Convention, October 19, 2006.

years as its president, Camillo Cardinal Ruini had left a strong personal and political mark on the office. Accepting the resignation of the Emilian cardinal in early March 2007 because he had reached the age limit, the pope, at the suggestion of Secretary of State Bertone, had thought of nominating as his successor the bishop of Taranto, Benigno Papa. An Italian southerner, he had held the office of vice president for Southern Italy since 2002. As such, he could be a welcome nomination for Catholics in the South. Moreover, he was a Franciscan, a lover of the poor and simple life desired by the founder of his Order, and a Bible scholar. He could therefore represent the change much hoped for by Benedict and many Italian bishops. Learning of Benedict's intention, however, Cardinal Ruini requested an audience and noted that, according to tradition, the presidents of the Italian Episcopal Conference had to be cardinals. The numerous cardinals present among the bishops residing in the country would not have appreciated having a mere bishop as their leader.[18] Ruini's objection was certainly not unreasonable, but there was nevertheless the impression that the cardinal was trying to defend the direction he had taken during the years of his presidency.

Taking up Ruini's objection, after the meeting Benedict named Angelo Bagnasco, archbishop of Genoa, as president of the CEI (*Conferenza Episcopale Italiana*). Several months later, it was announced that he would be created a cardinal. The pope probably thought that his choice would bring peace between the two camps in the Italian Church, but the decision actually provoked a long battle. Already on March 25, the official start of his mandate, the new president Bagnasco received a letter from the secretary of state asking him to take the CEI in a new direction, prioritizing the pastoral efforts of the bishops, while leaving to the Secretariat of State the task of "promoting relations between States and tending to affairs that, always for pastoral aims, must be addressed by civil governments".[19] We cannot rule out the possibility that Cardinal Bertone meant to interpret in this way the above-mentioned

---

[18] I am indebted to Luigi Accattoli for the details on the failure to nominate Monsignor Benigno Papa as president of the Italian Episcopal Conference (CEI). The Vatican historian of the national newspaper *Corriere della Sera* further explained that Monsignor Papa had already been informed of the nomination and that the pope called him personally to apologize for making a different decision.

[19] The letter is found in *Enchiridion Vaticanum* 24 (2007), 322–25.

intention of the pope. Nonetheless, it gave the impression of trying to establish a sort of externally imposed administration that was clumsily communicated on the same day the mandate began.

An unusual coldness followed between the Holy See and the CEI, leading to several regrettable episodes that the national press covered extensively. The most sensational one was the publication of a fake document that led to the resignation of the journalist Dino Boffo, editor of the daily newspaper *Avvenire*, who had been named to that position by Ruini. After some time, however, it was proved not only that the document was fake, but that it had been fed to the newspapers from within the Vatican.[20] Boffo was later hired as the director of Sat 2000, the Italian bishops' television station. It could therefore be considered a dispute with no winners or losers, but the episode had other consequences[21] and created the impression of an absentee pope and an out-of-control Curia.

On this and other occasions, Benedict's apparently disinterested attitude can be explained by his concern with not becoming "utterly absorbed in activism" but, rather, with maintaining an "inner view of the whole, . . . interior recollection, from which the view of what is essential can proceed."[22] Another intervention—this time directly by the pope—that caused unease among the bishops and more generally among the Italian clergy was the publication of the *motu proprio*[23] that authorized the use of the preconciliar Roman Missal and Roman liturgy in general, without the need to request a dispensation from the local bishops as provided for by a previous regulation by John Paul II.

Relations between Pope Benedict and the movements were more cordial. Chiara Lubich, foundress of the Focolare Movement, died on March 18, 2008. In his message of condolence, the pope said that he was spiritually present at the ceremony and gave thanks to

---

[20] The event is reconstructed in detail in the book by G. Nuzzi, *Sua Santità* (Milan: Chiarelettere, 2012), pp. 27–52. The tone of the book is clearly sensationalist; nonetheless, the text is corroborated with firsthand documents that raised other questions upon publication.

[21] See below, chapter 17.

[22] Joseph Ratzinger, *Light of the World: The Pope, the Church, and the Signs of the Times: A Conversation with Peter Seewald*, trans. Michael J. Miller and Adrian J. Walker (San Francisco: Ignatius Press, 2010), 71, 72.

[23] See above, chap. 14.

the Lord "for the gift made to the Church by this woman of intrepid faith, a gentle messenger of hope and of peace."[24] She had carried out a silent, compelling service, always in harmony with the teachings of the Church.

For their part, Italian Catholics quickly learned to appreciate the simple, authentic piety of the theologian pope who enthusiastically traveled to Marian shrines and his catecheses on the saints who brought the Gospel to life. It was partly because of this that the feared reduction in the number of pilgrims attending the Wednesday audiences never came to pass and, on the contrary, that the number consistently grew over time. Then there was the attraction of the intellectual who, even on the Chair of Peter, was able to engage in dialogue with the prevailing currents in contemporary culture by highlighting its strong points and yet raising his voice against the dictatorship of relativism.

FRANCE

Whereas the protests against the pope at La Sapienza in Rome had come from students who identified in a general way with the left, the excessively passionate devotees of State secularism were the ones who started controversies that were as boisterous as they were baseless when Benedict XVI visited France in September 2008. In fact, the pope did not even wait to arrive on French soil before affirming that secularism is not in contradiction with faith. The protests then took aim at what was considered the excessive enthusiasm of President Nicolas Sarkozy in welcoming the pontiff first at Orly Airport and then at the Élysée Palace. A public poll by the daily newspaper *Le Parisien*, nonetheless, revealed that over 50 percent of French people respected the German pope, while the number rose to 65 percent among Catholics, more than half of whom considered him "a charismatic figure".[25]

The French Church had for some time been going through a crisis situation from which she seemed unable to escape. Churches were increasingly empty, and seminary admissions dropped to a low point. In 2009, the Catholic encyclopedia *Le nouveau Théo* published

---

[24] Benedict XVI, Letter for the Funeral of Chiara Lubich, March 18, 2008.
[25] Cf. Valli, *Benedetto XVI*, 172.

troubling statistics on the reduction in the number of baptisms and on attendance at Sunday Mass.[26] By comparison, traditionalist communities seemed more dynamic. For this reason, fearing that the pope's *motu proprio* authorizing the Latin Mass would give new confidence to the Lefebvrians, the French bishops put up greater resistance to it. In his address to the bishops during his 2008 visit, he once again called on them to promote reconciliation and unity in the Church whereby "every person, without exception, should be able to feel at home, and never rejected."[27]

The climax of Benedict XVI's visit to France was the meeting with representatives of the world of culture at the Collège des Bernardins in the Latin Quarter of Paris. The college was an old monastery of the Cistercians, called "Bernardines" in France because of Saint Bernard: not the founder, but certainly the most famous monk of the Order. It served as a house of studies for the monks until 1790, when it was confiscated by the insurgents of the French Revolution. It was acquired in 2001 by the Diocese of Paris, which renovated it so as to use it as a place for cultural encounters and education. The pope felt at home in the ancient monastery, and here he gave one of the most celebrated talks of his pontificate: a manifesto of the humanism that he sought for the twenty-first century.

This place, the pope began, was an important school of culture for centuries. Truth be told, the monks who created it were not initially aiming at culture but, rather, were seeking God. In their search, however, they made a surprising discovery. The God they desired to encounter had already turned to them with his word. Moreover, he had also given mankind the words with which to address him, especially in the psalms. For this reason, the monks surrounded the word of God with their love, which they then extended to literature, to the words of men as well. "The longing for God, the *désir de Dieu*, includes *amour des lettres*, love of the word, exploration of all its dimensions."[28] Moreover, when the word of God is directed to an individual and pierces his heart, it immediately takes on a communitarian dimension and leads to sharing and

---

[26] *Le nouveau Théo* (Paris: Mame, 2009), 1205ff.

[27] Benedict XVI, Address to the French Episcopal Conference, September 14, 2008.

[28] Benedict XVI, Address to Representatives from the World of Culture, September 12, 2008.

communion. This is why the monks must reflect on the word and learn to read it accurately, so that everyone can listen to it.

Finally, the word given by God invites us to praise, which is expressed most fully through chanting the psalms, which occurs in the presence of the angels. It is therefore necessary for chant to be cultivated well and to produce harmony. Otherwise it moves into the "zone of dissimilarity", or remoteness from God. With their prayer and chant, the monks must correspond to the grandeur of the word entrusted to them. This is handed down in the sacred books and must be interpreted correctly. Hence the need for study in order to achieve a proper hermeneutic. Moreover, the Bible cannot be studied once and for all; rather, it remains a challenging task for every generation.

After speaking about prayer and study, the pope turned his attention to work, which is the other principal activity of monks according to the Rule of Saint Benedict. It is well known that in classical antiquity, physical labor was the task of slaves. The tradition was different for the rabbis, who, in addition to their cultivation of the word, devoted themselves to manual labor. Saint Paul, too, followed this model, working as a tentmaker in order to earn a living. In this way, he influenced the monastic tradition, which coupled prayer and study with manual labor.

Returning for a moment to the word, this becomes a path for the monk who seeks. Yet it likewise drives him toward the Christian message, urging him toward knowledge. The *logos* is also at the root of modern science. Of course, the contemporary situation is certainly different from that of the past, but, the pope added, it is also similar in other ways: "the present absence of God is silently besieged by the question concerning him."[29] A merely positivistic culture would amount to a capitulation of reason, a collapse of humanism. Even today, the search for God remains the foundation of every true culture.

There was a large crowd of people at the Mass in Notre-Dame Cathedral, also. Many young people were present, and once again the secularists were surprised by the attractiveness of the Christian message, which to them seemed old-fashioned or obsolete. In the end, the great majority of French people were won over by

---

[29] Ibid.

Ratzinger, a discreet gentleman who nevertheless still dared to speak words that in contemporary society are a courageous challenge.

After his magisterial Regensburg lecture and the one in Rome that was canceled, his lecture at the Collège des Bernardins was the former professor's third academic inaugural lecture as pope. In the first, he had addressed the topic of violence and interreligious dialogue; in the second, he had dealt with freedom in universities and the search for truth. The third had encouraged the search for a new humanism for the second millennium inspired by the old monastic humanism, of which Paris and France had been an exceptionally fruitful center. The first two lectures were accompanied by controversies that misinterpreted the pope's thoughts, while the third met with general approval. Benedict, nonetheless, knew that he was planting seeds that were destined to decay in the soil before bearing fruit.

THE CZECH REPUBLIC

One year later, in 2009, Benedict XVI again took up some of the themes he had developed in Paris in another cultural capital of Europe: Prague, the city of the "Velvet Revolution" that had raised such great hopes in 1989, the year of the turning point in Europe. John Paul II had traveled here three times, and for him the Czech Republic was the heart of that second lung with which the Old Continent would breathe when it was finally united and at peace in the name of its Christian heritage. For the Bavarian pontiff, it was the door through which Germany looked to the East, a place of dialogue and exchange bringing mutual enrichment, as Cyril and Methodius, the two brothers from Byzantium, had understood very well.

Twenty years after the first trip by John Paul II in 1990, the situation in the country and the entire surrounding area had changed significantly. The great hope had been replaced by a growing disenchantment, and the land that for centuries had been a meeting place for peoples and cultural traditions was in danger of falling apart when faced with the challenges of globalization. Speaking to the president of the republic and political leaders on September 26, 2009, Benedict XVI invited the country and the entire surrounding area to reconciliation and forgiveness, putting aside the rancor caused by wars and persecutions. "Jointly we must engage in the struggle for freedom and the search for truth."[30] Then he exclaimed: "Europe is more than a continent. It is a home! And freedom finds its deepest meaning in a spiritual homeland."[31] The pope went on to say that every generation must make its own response to the search for truth. It is no coincidence, however, that Prague was called the heart of Europe. "The arresting beauty of its churches, castle, squares and bridges cannot but draw our minds to God."[32]

Benedict then argued in defense of the Christian roots of the Czech nation and of Europe, while inviting his listeners to look beyond the limits of matter toward the transcendence that is at the origin of philosophical reflection that is open to the supernatural. This is the way to avoid nihilism and relativism, to escape from the cynicism of those who care only about material well-being and from the egotism of those who seek only their self-interest. "Instead, we must reappropriate a confidence in the nobility and breadth of the human spirit in its capacity to grasp the truth, and let that confidence guide us in the patient work of politics and diplomacy."[33]

Another concern of the pope during his journey to the Czech Republic was the strong presence of widespread agnosticism in the country. Nonetheless, Benedict did not give in to polemics or discouragement. On the contrary, he invited agnostics and believers to engage in dialogue, with the conviction that even those who do not adhere to any faith understand sadness and dissatisfaction and, perhaps without knowing it, are searching for God. In short, Benedict was already thinking of the dialogue between believers and nonbelievers about which he would talk at greater length several months later in his end-of-the-year address to the Roman Curia. It was the observation that would then lead to the birth of the Courtyard of the Gentiles[34] at the Pontifical Council for Culture, creating opportunities for encounter and understanding between those who declare themselves believers and those who are seeking a fullness of meaning in their lives.

---

[30] Benedict XVI, Address to Political and Civil Authorities and Members of the Diplomatic Corps, September 26, 2009.

[31] Ibid.

[32] Ibid.

[33] Ibid.

[34] See above, in this chapter.

SPAIN

A longstanding Catholic country that in past centuries gave the Church great saints and powerful spiritual and cultural initiatives, Spain was going through a time of intense conflicts during the pontificate of Benedict XVI. The pope traveled there several times, almost as if trying to help Spanish Catholics in the delicate phase of "the present dramatic struggle between radical secularity and resolute faith".[35] His first trip to Spain was on July 8 and 9, 2006, on the occasion of the fifth World Meeting of Families, which was held that year in Valencia. The tension experienced in the country was evident even to the dispassionate observer. Right where the lines of Catholics were welcoming the pope, radical protestors were declaring that they did not want the pope's visit. Various pro-gay demonstrations were held in the Andalusian city while the pope was present.

In order to emphasize the vigor of Spanish Catholicism, the bishops of the country had invited the faithful to come in large numbers to Valencia. Together with other Catholics from all over the world, they made a truly impressive crowd.[36] The prime minister, José Luis Zapatero, however, drew attention to himself by his absence and a dismissive statement: "The Mass is nothing of my concern",[37] but that did not bother the gathering of families. While meeting with the bishops, the pope thanked them for their efforts and urged them to keep alive and vigorous the spirit that had accompanied Spaniards throughout the centuries.[38]

At the prayer vigil attended by one and a half million faithful, the pope defined the family as "the privileged setting where every person learns to give and receive love".[39] This is why the Church has always shown solicitude for the family, which is a necessary good for all people and an indispensable foundation for society. It needs the Church's support in order to be able to transmit the faith and the love of Christ to children, but it also needs the support of

---

[35] J. Ratzinger, *Light of the World*, 115.

[36] See Valli, *Benedetto XVI*, 65.

[37] Ibid., 66.

[38] Benedict XVI, Letter to the Spanish Bishops on the Occasion of the Fifth World Meeting of Families, July 8, 2006.

[39] Benedict XVI, Address to the Fifth World Meeting of Families, July 8, 2006.

leaders and lawmakers. Clearly the pope was alluding here to the troubled situation in Spain in those years. Benedict concluded by describing himself as the world's grandfather, called as all grandparents are called to be "the guarantors of the affection and tenderness which every human being needs to give and receive".[40]

Three years later, in 2010, when Benedict traveled again to Spain, the political and cultural situation had changed. While the crisis was not yet overcome, the Church nonetheless felt stronger. On this trip, moreover, the pope was operating on more favorable terrain. He went to Santiago de Compostela to make the pilgrimage to the tomb of the apostle James, then to Barcelona on the "way of beauty" for the dedication of *La Sagrada Família*, Holy Family Basilica. These destinations are obviously different, yet they are connected by two important manifestations of faith. In Santiago, the pope recalled that pilgrimage means going out of oneself in order to meet God in the place where he has revealed himself. It leads to a heartfelt defense of God and the invitation to open oneself to him: the Europe of science and technology must respect Christian truth, which in turn respects man's freedom and never harms it.

In Barcelona, the pope consecrated the Basilica of *La Sagrada Família* and acknowledged the *via pulchritudinis*, the way to God through beauty. On this occasion, the pope said: "Gaudí desired to unify that inspiration which came to him from the three books . . . : the book of nature, the book of sacred Scripture and the book of the liturgy."[41] These words were dear to Ratzinger because he saw his theology and Christocentric spirituality summarized in them. He went on to say in Barcelona that "the Lord Jesus is the stone which supports the weight of the world, which maintains the cohesion of the Church and brings together in ultimate unity all the achievements of mankind."[42] In short, his two days in Spain were an oasis of tranquility and joy in a year troubled with scandals.

A year later, Benedict XVI returned to Spain again, this time for World Youth Day, which was celebrated in Madrid. During the vigil on August 20, 2011, a windy rainstorm hit the Spanish capital,

---

[40] Ibid.

[41] Benedict XVI, Homily at the Dedication of the Church of the Sagrada Família and of the Altar, November 7, 2010.

[42] Ibid.

threatening to cancel the event. The pope remained at his post, almost amused, while the young people, drenched with water, sang choruses to support each other and to encourage the pope. The adverse weather conditions, nevertheless, did not stop the enthusiasm of the participants. The next day, about two million young people were present for the meeting with the pope. Benedict was glad. He had the image of the vigil in his heart, when tens of thousands of young people had approached the Sacrament of Reconciliation. He wished to participate personally in the celebration, hearing the confessions of four randomly chosen young people. The theme of the meeting was "Rooted and Built Up in Christ". The pope took the opportunity to invite people to become members of the Church and to urge the young people to witness even in settings where there is rejection or indifference. The atmosphere was much different from his first visit to the Iberian Peninsula, and in his parting farewell to the king, the pope pointed this out in a remark that was more than simply ceremonious: "Your Majesty, the pope felt at home in Spain!"[43]

Latin America

Ratzinger has a vivid sense of the catholicity of the Church. His concern as universal pastor therefore extended to all the continents, where, moreover, he experienced surges of enthusiasm that consoled him for the tepidity in Europe. His first trip outside of Europe in May 2007 took him to Latin America, and more specifically to Brazil. The trip was particularly delicate for the pope, who, as prefect of the Congregation for the Doctrine of the Faith, had intervened decisively to correct the trends in liberation theology that involved theology and the Church excessively in the social and political redemption of the people. At the time, these positions had elicited in that country a wave of emotional opposition to the cardinal, and many still harbored a grudge.

When questioned by a journalist on the flight to Brazil, the pope did not hesitate to state his point of view clearly. The change in the political situation confirmed that the congregation's position had

---

[43] Benedict XVI, Address at the Departure Ceremony for the 26th World Youth Day, August 21, 2011.

been right. The revolutions that had occurred in the country in the meantime had shown that it was crucial to make a distinction between politics and the Church's mission. "The purpose of the intervention of the Magisterium was not to stop the effort for justice, but to guide it along the right paths . . . respecting the proper difference between political responsibility and ecclesial responsibility."[44]

The pope arrived in the country on May 9 and met with the bishops on the 11th in the cathedral in São Paulo. One of the main problems facing the country was the issue of many Catholics abandoning the practice of the faith. Without giving in to the many complaints, the pope urged the bishops and the entire Church to embrace the duty of evangelization, starting, not from an ethical decision, but from an encounter with a person. In short, there was a need for "starting afresh from Christ in every area of missionary activity; rediscovering in Jesus the love and salvation given to us by the Father through the Holy Spirit."[45] The pope wanted to give the bishops an infusion of courage, calling them back to the duty of proclamation and witness, grounded in the centrality of Christ and of the sacraments of the Church.

FIFTH CONFERENCE OF BISHOPS OF LATIN AMERICA

Two days later, on May 13, 2007, the pope was in Aparecida in the state of São Paulo, where there is a shrine of Our Lady of Aparecida, patroness of Brazil, and where the Fifth General Conference of the Bishops of Latin America and the Caribbean was held. As with the previous conferences in Medellín, Puebla, and Santo Domingo, the purpose of the meeting was to reenergize Catholicism in Latin America and to give a specific character to evangelization on the American subcontinent. The theme chosen for the conference, however, "Disciples and Missionaries of Jesus Christ, So That Our Peoples May Have Life in Him", clearly bears the hallmark of Pope Benedict.

The pope began his address by defending the earlier history of evangelization against the facile critiques that reduce the history of the presence of Christianity in Latin America to mere exploitation

---

[44] Valli, *Benedetto XVI*, 104.
[45] Benedict XVI, Address to the Bishops of Brazil, May 11, 2007, no. 4.

and oppression. Despite her many imperfections, the Latin American Church has been able to convey the love of Christ and to preserve the unique character of the indigenous peoples through love for Christ suffering, for Christ in the Eucharist, and for the God who is close to the poor, and also through devotion to the Blessed Virgin, to which the shrines in Aparecida in Brazil and Guadalupe in Mexico bear witness. He then affirmed continuity with the preceding conferences and cautioned against those who try to start from more "concrete" factors—from "reality".

The pope asked, "What is this 'reality'? What is real?" Are material goods and social, economic, and political problems the only "reality"? This would cut off reality from its foundation, which is God, leading to the erroneous conclusions of the Marxist and capitalist movements. The first fundamental affirmation, therefore, is that "only those who recognize God know reality and are able to respond to it adequately and in a truly human manner."[46] Then the pope explained: We are not talking about a theoretical, abstract God, but about the God who revealed himself in his Son, Jesus Christ. It is therefore necessary to start with catechesis in order to learn his message and to make it the guide for one's own life and the life of the faithful. Then evangelization will promote human development and authentic liberation.

In short, the pope's proposal for Latin America was once again evangelization based on the person and message of Christ. It is up to the bishops, priests, and catechists to enact this proposal with South American creativity.

Catholics in China

The Communists took power in China around the mid-twentieth century, expelled the Western missionaries, and persecuted the Chinese Catholics. As for the hierarchy, many bishops who remained faithful to Rome had to live clandestinely, while the government established a national Church, the "Chinese Catholic Patriotic Association", and reserved the right to appoint its bishops. A situation of schism and division was thereby created between Catholics who were faithful to Rome and Catholics who, while maintaining the

---

[46] Benedict XVI, Address at the Inaugural Session of the Fifth General Conference of Bishops of South America and the Caribbean, May 13, 2007.

fullness of the Creed, agreed to join the patriotic Church. From then on, nearly all the popes, starting with John XXIII, tried to reopen dialogue with the Chinese authorities. John Paul II proved particularly active from the first years after his election.[47] In 1980, when the new leader Deng Xiaoping took power, it was confirmed that a positive development was effectively underway. Bishop Dominic Tang Yee-Ming was appointed to lead the Diocese of Canton despite never having belonged to the patriotic Church. It appeared to be the beginning of a new phase in relations between the Vatican and the People's Republic of China.

This development came to a sudden stop, however, in 1986. The Congregation for the Evangelization of Peoples led by Jozef Cardinal Tomko issued an eight-point document for the recognition of Patriotic Association Catholics that displeased both the Catholics themselves and the Chinese authorities. The response of the two offices for religious affairs in China set nonnegotiable conditions for the continuation of dialogue with the Vatican: cessation of diplomatic relations with Taiwan and noninterference with internal Chinese affairs.[48] In 2000, there were two significant events for relations between the Church and the People's Republic of China: first, the proclamation of 120 Chinese martyrs by John Paul II was interpreted in China as a provocation; then, on the other hand, the pope's broad request for forgiveness in March of that year—which encouraged a more explicit acknowledgment of Catholic mistakes during the colonial period in China—met with favorable reactions. It seemed to clear a path for a papal visit to Beijing, but a very large number of people were involved in that decision, while the pope's health was deteriorating.

The lines of communication nonetheless remained open even after the death of the Polish pope, and his successor was able to resume the dialogue. An ad hoc commission studied the unresolved tangles in relations between China and the Vatican, between Chinese Catholics and the Holy See. In January 2007, Pope Benedict convened a large meeting in Rome in which Chinese Church officials could also participate. Thanks to this preparatory effort, the pope was able to avoid the errors of the past and to prepare a long letter that was to

---

[47] See the important essay by Agostino Giovagnoli, "Giovanni Paolo II e la Chiesa in Asia", in Guerriero and Impagliazzo, *I cattolici e le Chiese cristiane*, 263–300.

[48] Ibid., 280.

open a new phase in the effort to reestablish unity among Catholics in China and in the relationship between the Asian nation and the Holy See. The letter, dated May 27, 2007, the Solemnity of Pentecost, was made public on June 30 of the same year. The explanatory note that accompanied the document and was also translated into Chinese pointed out that "Pope Benedict XVI wishes to express his love for and his closeness to the Catholics who live in China."[49]

The rich and articulate document was divided into two parts: the first started with a description of the situation of Catholics in the country and sought to interpret and remedy it in the light of the understanding of the Church that emerged from Vatican II. The issues to be addressed had no easy solutions. Above all else, it was necessary to overcome the division between Catholics who had chosen to go underground in order to remain faithful to Rome and Patriotic Association Catholics, who had chosen collaboration with the government but now wished to return to communion with the universal Church. It was therefore a question of rediscovering internal unity and overcoming tensions and divisions through mutual forgiveness and reconciliation.

The pope knew that it would be necessary to travel a long, complicated path, but "the history of the Church teaches us, then, that authentic communion is not expressed without arduous efforts at reconciliation. . . . These are urgent steps that must be taken if the bonds of communion between the faithful and the Pastors of the Church in China are to grow and be made visible."[50] The bishops in particular had had to face harsh trials in the past, but now it was a matter of looking to the future with renewed confidence. The pope could not yet recognize the Chinese Catholic Bishops' Conference because the underground bishops who were not yet recognized by the government were not members, while some bishops who had not yet regularized their relationship with the Apostolic See were members.

Another major problem was the relationship with the government. In this regard, the pope urged those bishops who had good relationships with the civil structures to come to an agreement to

---

[49] Benedict XVI, Explanatory Note regarding the Letter to Bishops, Priests, Consecrated Persons and Lay Faithful of the Catholic Church in the People's Republic of China, May 27, 2007.

[50] Benedict XVI, Letter to the Bishops, Priests, Consecrated Persons and Lay Faithful of the Catholic Church in the People's Republic of China, May 27, 2007.

resolve the questions about the selection of candidates for the episcopate, the publication of nominations, and recognition by the government authorities. The second part of the letter acknowledged the
great generosity of the hierarchy and the Chinese faithful and, at
the same time, provided guidelines for the proper celebration of
the sacraments and for the governance of dioceses and parishes. In
conclusion, the pope revoked prior faculties and pastoral directives
and declared a day of prayer for the Church in China.

The accompanying explanatory note offered two helpful clarifications that testified to the spirit in which the letter was composed.
The first, regarding the Christian community, clarified that it was
not the pope's intention to offend anyone, although he urged all
Chinese Catholics to become evangelizers in the context of their
country. Then, with regard to the Chinese people as a whole, Benedict XVI declared that he viewed "with respect and deep sympathy the ancient and recent history of the great Chinese people"
and reiterated that he was "ready to engage in dialogue with the
Chinese authorities in the awareness that normalization of the life
of the Church in China presupposes frank, open and constructive
dialogue with these authorities".[51] In short, it was a wide-ranging
document that, despite reservations toward the Chinese Patriotic
Church, helped to foster the life of communion among the Catholics in the country. Nonetheless, the invitation directed to Chinese
authorities to reopen dialogue in order to overcome division between Catholics friendly to the government and Catholics faithful
to Rome and to secure freedom for the faithful in the large Asian
country in exchange for loyal cooperation went unanswered.

In 2010, representatives of the Catholics friendly to the government held a meeting and took a very harsh tone toward Rome.
Subsequently, there were several ordinations of bishops and priests
that were illegitimate in the eyes of the Vatican as well as painful
episodes like the ban placed on Bishop Ma Daqin of Shanghai, prohibiting the exercise of his episcopal ministry.[52]

---

[51] Benedict XVI, Explanatory Note regarding the Letter to Bishops, Priests, Consecrated Persons and Lay Faithful of the Catholic Church in the People's Republic of
China, May 27, 2007.

[52] See Agostino Giovagnoli, "Cortina di Bambù meno fitta", Avvenire (October 18,
2015): 3.

The United States of America

Benedict XVI visited the United States from April 15 to 21, 2008. The Catholic Church in this country, as I recalled in chapter 12, had experienced enormous damage to her image because of the sexual abuse scandal, and the repercussions were felt in every state and almost every diocese. In most cases, the acts had occurred in the 1970s and 1980s, but they continued to come to light during the Year of the Priest that Benedict XVI had proclaimed, as if foreshadowing the need for penance and purification among the members of the clergy. In the meantime, the American bishops finally realized the gravity of the problem. They asked forgiveness and committed to taking serious measures to prevent such cases from occurring again.

In a document titled *Charter for the Protection of Children and Young People*, the United States Conference of Catholic Bishops recognized that "the Church in the United States has experienced a crisis without precedent in our times. . . . As bishops, we have acknowledged our mistakes and our roles in that suffering."[53] Above all, under the pressure of public opinion, they voted for a policy of "one strike and you're out", ensuring that anyone who abuses a child will be immediately removed from priestly ministry. The long-lasting wave of the scandal, however, seems not to have reached its conclusion yet. The pope knew that the faithful and public opinion expected authoritative and clarifying words on this matter, and on the plane during the flight he had already promised that there would be no more pedophile priests, that he was deeply ashamed, and that everything possible would be done to ensure that this would never happen again. Pedophiles would be absolutely excluded from the priesthood.[54]

The reason for Pope Benedict's journey to the United States was the bicentennial of the erection of several of the earliest dioceses of this great country: Boston, New York, Philadelphia, and Louisville were declared dioceses in 1808, and, a year later, the Diocese of Baltimore became the first archdiocese.[55] On the day after his ar-

---

[53] See Chester Gillis, "Cultura americana e cultura cattolica", in Guerriero and Impagliazzo, *I cattolici e le Chiese cristiane*, 195.

[54] Benedict XVI, Interview during the Flight to the United States of America, April 15, 2008.

[55] James J. Hennesey, *American Catholics: A History of the Roman Catholic Community in the United States* (New York: Oxford University Press, 1983), 110ff.

rival, April 16, Benedict XVI met in the city of Baltimore with the American bishops. In welcoming the pope, the president of the United States Conference of Catholic Bishops again recalled the abuse scandal and admitted that the bishops had often dealt with the problem very badly.

In his response, the pope said he was in full agreement with the condemnation of the abuses and the zero-tolerance policy that had been adopted. Moreover, he invited them to be close to the victims and to broaden the discussion. "Children deserve to grow up with a healthy understanding of sexuality. . . . They have a right to be educated in authentic moral values rooted in the dignity of the human person."[56] The bishops must pay particular attention to them, just as they are called to continue the discussion with priests. Some of them have made grave mistakes. Most of them, however, feel the weight of solitude and suspicion. "Not a few are experiencing a closeness to Christ in his Passion. . . . The Bishop, as father, brother and friend of his priests, can help them to draw spiritual fruit from this union with Christ."[57]

Indeed, as the pope saw it, the American Church presents the dark shadow of pedophilia but also many lights. The traditional generosity of American Catholics, manifested through Caritas [Catholic Relief Services] and other forms of charitable aid, has not waned. Likewise, America is a land of great faith, where the Catholic laity provide an important service, not just to the Church, but to society in general. In short, the pope expressed his gratitude to American Catholics and said that he was in awe of the nation to which so many rushed in order to breathe freedom. Nonetheless, Benedict could not avoid noting that Catholics who are loyal to the Democratic Party tend to lose touch with Catholic ethics, while supporters of the Republican Party are tempted by the subtle influence of materialism, which leads to individualistic selfishness. Hence his request that the bishops repeat the Gospel of life and recall that "we were created as social beings who find fulfillment only in love—for God and for our neighbor."[58]

The meeting with the bishops was probably the most anticipated

---

[56] Benedict XVI, Address during the Celebration of Vespers and Meeting with the Bishops of the United States of America, April 16, 2008.

[57] Ibid.

[58] Ibid.

and delicate moment of the pope's visit to the United States. The trip, however, had significant political implications as well. On April 16, his eighty-first birthday, he went to the White House, where President George W. Bush—who said he was grateful for the pope's battle in defense of liberty—offered him a warm welcome. Differences in their views remained, nonetheless. The president assured the pope of his support in the fight against abortion, embryonic stem cell research, and same-sex marriage; at the same time, Benedict XVI asked the president and the American administration not to close the country off through isolationism and to work to promote peace in the world.

During his travels in America, Ratzinger also went to the United Nations on April 18. After Paul VI and John Paul II, he was the third pope to visit the U.N. In fact, Benedict started off his address with a quotation from his predecessor recalling that "the United Nations embodies the aspiration for a 'greater degree of international ordering' . . . capable of harmonizing the day-to-day unfolding of the lives of peoples."[59] Only in this way can the U.N. remain faithful to its founding principles of the desire for peace, the quest for justice, respect for the dignity of the person, and international cooperation.

At this point, however, the pope introduced a new element in Vatican foreign policy. Ratzinger said, "Recognition of the unity of the human family, and attention to the innate dignity of every man and woman, today find renewed emphasis in the principle of the responsibility to protect."[60] The pope was thinking in particular about the situation in some African countries, but also about protecting the environment, natural resources, and the climate. If the individual nations are unable to safeguard the rights of their own citizens, the international community cannot stand by and watch. The ancient *ius gentium*, or law of nations, already evoked the principle of the responsibility to protect based on the dignity of the person. Of course, the pope did not intend to foment new conflicts but, rather, to call for "a deeper search for ways of pre-empting and managing conflicts by exploring every possible diplomatic avenue,

---

[59] Benedict XVI, Address to the Members of the General Assembly of the United Nations Organization, April 18, 2008.

[60] Ibid.

and giving attention and encouragement to even the faintest sign of dialogue or desire for reconciliation".[61]

The year 2008 was the sixtieth anniversary of the Universal Declaration of Human Rights. The pope recalled this circumstance to emphasize that the rights in question are based on the natural law written on the human heart and present in the various cultures and civilizations. If one abstracts from this framework, one gives in to a relativistic view in which rights are not founded on the universal dignity of the human person but might vary according to the social or political context.

Another of the pope's concerns is connected with the predominance of the laws of individual nations or of international bodies over justice. When natural rights are presented merely as legislative measures taken by nations, they run the risk of becoming proposals detached from ethics and reason. "Human rights, then, must be respected as an expression of justice, and not merely because they are enforceable through the will of the legislators."[62]

Finally, the pope invited the United Nations to promote the religious dimension of man and interreligious dialogue. Religious liberty falls within the fundamental rights of the person, while interreligious dialogue aims to propose a vision of faith, not in terms of intolerance and discrimination, but rather in terms of a shared contribution toward respect for truth and the harmonious coexistence of peoples. It was a wide-ranging address that was intended as a sign of esteem for the United Nations, which at the time was being called into question by the American administration, but also as a powerful reminder of those human rights recognized by the Universal Declaration in 1948 that, in the pope's judgment, were in danger of being neglected or even violated by subsequent legislative decrees of the U.N. itself.

Before leaving the country, the pope visited Ground Zero, the abyss created on September 11, 2001, by an explosion of hatred even more than by the impact of the two airplanes into the Twin Towers of New York. The pope stood, moved and silent, at this place that has become a monument to the innocent victims. Through his prayer and helpless presence, he sought to pay homage to the

---

[61] Ibid.
[62] Ibid.

sorrow of the relatives of the victims, to show solidarity with the entire nation, and to send a message of peace to the whole world.

World Youth Day in Sydney

Three months after his trip to the United States, Benedict XVI again climbed aboard an airplane for the longest trip of his pontificate, in terms of both distance and duration. The 23rd World Youth Day was held on another English-speaking continent: Australia, a distant country where Catholics number about six million out of nearly twenty-one million inhabitants. It is a young country that, nevertheless, is experiencing social problems like those in the United States and the West in general. Thus, aboard the plane taking him to his destination, one journalist's question referred to the crisis of religion in the country. The pope replied that religion and Christianity are in crisis in the West because people think that they do not need God. "Religion is always present in the world and will always be present because God is present in the heart of the human being and can never disappear."[63] Another question dealt with the issue of sexual abuse by priests. The pope did not hesitate in his response: "It must be clear, it was always clear from the first centuries that priesthood, to be a priest, is incompatible with this behavior . . . and we will do all possible to heal and to reconcile the victims."[64]

After the World Youth Day in Cologne, which still had John Paul II's imprint, this was the first time the theme was set by Pope Benedict: "You shall receive power when the Holy Spirit has come upon you; and you shall be my witnesses" (Acts 1:8). The pope spent several days resting in Australia and appeared cheerful and calm. He repeatedly talked about the beauty of nature, protecting the environment, and ecology, topics that are particularly close to his heart. The meeting with the young people began on July 17, when Benedict arrived in Sydney on a ferryboat, welcomed by a large crowd of mostly young people celebrating. As in Cologne, he came by way of water, and the scene had a moving Gospel flavor.

---

[63] Benedict XVI, Interview during the Flight to Australia, July 12, 2008.
[64] Ibid.

The pope shared the enthusiasm of the youth and seemed to put aside for a time his scholarly reserve.

The vigil at the Randwick Racecourse on July 19 had two highlights: the testimonies of representatives from each of the different continents and Eucharistic adoration. The message that the pope sought to communicate was that prayer and a personal encounter with Christ are important for the Christian life. The next day, Sunday, again at the racecourse, where many young people had spent the night in sleeping bags, the pope gave a homily during Mass that took up the principal themes of his pontificate: the proclamation of the Gospel, the strength for which is given by the Holy Spirit, whom Jesus sends and who introduces us to life, love, and Jesus himself; and Christian humanism, the guarantor of the dignity of every person. In the heart of his homily, Benedict exclaimed that "a new generation of Christians is being called to help build a world in which God's gift of life is welcomed. . . . A new age in which love is not greedy or self-seeking. . . . A new age in which hope liberates us from the shallowness, apathy and self-absorption which deaden our souls and poison our relationships."[65] The world needs this renewal; the Church needs it as well; and it requires the faith, idealism, and generosity of young people.

Humanism for the third millennium

In his first encyclical on love, Pope Benedict had proposed one of the key themes of his theology: the unity of God's love at the heart of creation and of salvation history. For Ratzinger the theologian, this observation was quite present and active both in the patristic age and in the Middle Ages. This was the foundation on which both monastic humanism and the Franciscan ecological vision of love for creation were built, the latter finding expression in Saint Francis' "Canticle of Creation".

In the modern, contemporary era, the balance painstakingly achieved over the centuries collapsed. In recent years, the biblical movement —though valuable—had unilaterally emphasized God's revelation in the redemption, to the point of obscuring acknowledgment of

---

[65] Benedict XVI, Homily at the Eucharistic Celebration of the 23rd World Youth Day, July 20, 2008.

God the Creator. Hence there is a need to highlight once again faith in God the Creator and to insist on the relation of interdependence between creation and covenant: "Creation looks toward the covenant, but the covenant completes creation and does not simply exist along with it."[66] This fundamental consideration enables the pope to develop some guidelines, following the example of monastic humanism, that can help to establish a humanism for the new millennium as well.

ECOLOGY

Pope Benedict was not the first pope to be concerned about ecology. Paul VI and later John Paul II had spoken about it, with different emphases. Nevertheless, Benedict XVI in particular was the one who authoritatively debunked the old claim that Christianity, through a mistaken understanding of the words of Genesis regarding man's position in creation,[67] gave a green light to the unbridled exploitation of nature and justified, or at least did not adequately condemn, forms of degradation and devastation of the earth's natural resources.

In fact, Pope Benedict consistently spoke in favor of a sustainable ecology, a benevolent approach to the earth, which is not merely an arena for exploitation or sport, but the place where man is born, his home. Although he wrote many different works dealing with ecology,[68] it is possible to identify a guiding thread that winds its way through three particularly important texts.

The Creator Spirit. The first text dates back to 2006. It was a homily delivered by the pope on June 3, 2006, on the Vigil of the Solemnity of Pentecost, on the occasion of a meeting with ecclesial movements and new communities. According to the pope, the hymn "Come, Creator Spirit" recited on the Vigil of Pentecost recalls the context of Genesis, which is precisely what critics claim is at the root

---

[66] Joseph Ratzinger, *The Spirit of the Liturgy*, trans. John Saward (San Francisco: Ignatius Press, 2000), 27.

[67] Gen 1:28ff. On this topic, see Patrice de Plunkett, *L'écologie de la Bible à nos jours* (Paris: Oeuvre, 2008).

[68] On this topic, see the well-done anthology by Maria Milvia Morciano, ed., *Per una ecologia dell'uomo: Joseph Ratzinger* (Vatican City: Libreria Editrice Vaticana, 2012).

of unbridled Christian exploitation. Benedict, however, notes that here it says above all that "the Spirit of God was moving over the chaos, over the waters of the abyss. The world in which we live is the work of the Creator Spirit. . . . Pentecost is also a feast of creation."[69] Hence the call for Christians to have a reverential awe and fear of nature, to cultivate it as God's garden, and to turn it into a garden for mankind as well.

Then the pope recalled another famous passage, this time from Saint Paul, which talks about creation groaning and eagerly awaiting the revelation of the children of God.[70] In Christian times, the pope said, love for nature was manifested during two particularly positive times: in the age of the monasteries, during which agriculture was developed respectfully and proficiently in the shadow of the bell towers; and in the age of Saint Francis, who had an almost mystical rapport with the earth, water, sun, and animals. In the modern era, however, a thick layer of arrogance and dirt has built up on the earth, making it difficult to see the beauty generated by the Creator Spirit.

The Trinitarian reflection, however, which developed particularly in the contemporary period, shows that in God an "I" and a "You" exist, held together by the Spirit of Love.[71] This love, which lies beneath creation and the beauty of the world, should lead Christians—following the teaching of Vatican II—to work for the protection of the environment and an appreciation of the natural resources that are part of the patrimony of mankind. In 2006, from July 13 to 20, the Sixth Symposium of the Religion, Science, and the Environment project sponsored by the Orthodox Church was held in Brazil with the title "The Rio of the Amazons, Source of Life". Since he was unable to attend, Benedict sent Roger Cardinal Etchegaray to represent him and entrusted to him a message for Patriarch Bartholomew I.

In the short text, the pope affirmed: "This immense region, where

---

[69] Benedict XVI, Homily at the Prayer Vigil and Meeting with Ecclesial Movements and New Communities, June 3, 2006.

[70] See Rom 8:19–22.

[71] I am referring here in particular to the theological aesthetics of von Balthasar, of whom Pope Benedict was a friend and admirer. While he did not agree with all of the positions of the theologian from Basel, Pope Benedict valued his theological fruitfulness and fidelity to the Church.

the waters are an unequaled source of harmony and abundance, appears like an open book whose pages reveal the mystery of life."[72] From this premise, the pope drew the conclusion that, both as individuals and as communities, national leaders are called to a dutiful awareness that must translate into consistent decisions for the protection of the environment.

Covenant between man and the environment. The second major point of Pope Benedict's teachings on the environment was developed in his encyclical *Caritas in veritate*, or "Charity in Truth", a social encyclical written at the time of the outbreak of the global crisis. The second chapter of the papal document is devoted to the development of peoples specifically on the basis of a proper attitude toward nature: it cannot be exploited savagely, just as it cannot be made more important than the human person. This is why at least some resources that are necessary for life, such as food and water, should be guaranteed for all people. The pope, therefore, called for solidarity between developing nations and highly industrialized nations, and he hoped for renewed solidarity with younger generations as well. "We must recognize our grave duty to hand the earth on to future generations in such a condition that they too can worthily inhabit it and continue to cultivate it."[73]

There is, therefore, first of all a human ecology, from which environmental ecology also benefits. "The book of nature is one and indivisible. . . . Our duties towards the environment are linked to our duties towards the human person."[74] Hence the covenant with the environment, which is welded together with the covenant with God. The truth and love that nature discloses to us are founded, not in mankind, but in God. Technology, developed through human ability, "must serve to reinforce the covenant between human beings and the environment, a covenant that should mirror God's creative love."[75]

If you want to promote peace, protect creation. The third document on ecology by Pope Benedict was written on the occasion of the World

---

[72] The full text of the message is found in Morciano, *Per una ecologia dell'uomo*, 18–20 at 19.

[73] Benedict XVI, Encyclical *Caritas in veritate* on Integral Human Development in Charity and Truth, June 29, 2009, no. 50.

[74] Ibid., no. 51.

[75] Ibid., no. 69.

Day of Peace in 2010.[76] The pope began his message, which was addressed not only to the faithful but also to all nations and to people of goodwill, with an empirical observation. Just as there are conflicts that arise from the violation of human rights, so, too, there are serious threats that are started by abuses of the environment. In order to avoid the disastrous consequences that can result from an environmental crisis, however, a profound and far-sighted review of the concept of development is necessary, based on the observation that at the origin of nature there is a God-given plan of love and truth.[77] It is therefore necessary to protect the environment with the same love, aiming for a distribution that does not exclude anyone in the world and also shows concern for future generations. For this reason, societies with advanced technology should not take advantage of the power that comes from it, but should promote life-styles characterized by moderation, so that the poorest nations can also have access to natural resources.

At the same time, the pope, far from opposing research and progress, encouraged moving forward in this direction and listed the scientific opportunities and potentially innovative paths by which it will be possible to achieve satisfying and harmonious solutions in the relationship between man and his environment. These include taking advantage of solar energy; the now-worldwide water problem, which could find solutions in the global water cycle system; appropriate, family-centered strategies for rural development; suitable policies for forest management and waste disposal; countering climate change; and fighting poverty.[78] It is obvious, according to the pope, that much is at stake and that we cannot be indifferent to what is happening around us.

For her part, the Church is fully aware of this responsibility and wishes to help safeguard the human patrimony of society. Within nature, in fact, there is a " 'grammar' which the Creator has inscribed in his handiwork by giving man the role of a steward and administrator with responsibility over creation".[79] Man cannot abuse this task, but neither can he refuse it. Hence the call for believers and for all people of goodwill to commit to a common cause, the

---

[76] Benedict XVI, Message for World Day of Peace, January 1, 2010.
[77] Ibid., nos. 5–6.
[78] Ibid., no. 10.
[79] Ibid., no. 13.

resolution of which will certainly be facilitated by acknowledging the inseparable relationship between God, man, and all of creation.

Some observers have called Pope Benedict "the green pope".[80] This designation, while certainly accurate if it refers to the German pope's constant attention to ecological themes, should nonetheless be clarified. The ecology of which Benedict speaks arises from faith in creation and from the recognition of the dignity of man, develops as a covenant between mankind and the environment, and leads to solidarity and peace among people, which proceed from the protection of creation.

ART

A lover of music and art, Ratzinger the theologian developed his aesthetic vision particularly in relation to the liturgy. During the years of his pontificate, however, a deeper exploration of the themes relating to the person and message of Jesus prompted him to reflect on the beauty that comes from God. In his works as pope, therefore, he took the beauty of Christ as a starting point for a broader vision of Christian aesthetics. The most solemn pronouncement in this regard is found in his Apostolic Exhortation *Sacramentum caritatis*, the document that harmoniously summarized and presented the suggestions that resulted from the celebration of the Synod on the Eucharist in autumn 2006.

The beauty that comes from God. Pope Benedict had no qualms about applying the words of Psalm 45 to Jesus Christ: he is "the fairest of the sons of men".[81] Whereas his friend von Balthasar focused in particular on the unpretentious beauty of Christ on the Cross, he insisted on Christ whose image—as the Eastern icons teach—always has a reference to the Triune God and the glory of the resurrection. This is the reason for another affirmation with patristic echoes that also flowed into the Constitution on Divine Revelation of Vatican II: all of Christian revelation has an intrinsic connection to beauty.[82]

---

[80] See Jean-Louis Bruguès, preface to Morciano, *Per una ecologia dell'uomo*, iv.

[81] Ps 45:2.

[82] John Paul II and Benedict XVI, *La nobile riforma: Chiesa e artisti sulla via della bellezza* (Cinisello Balsamo: San Paolo, 2009), 188.

In creation, God's beauty can be glimpsed in the harmony of the cosmos. In salvation history, the mystery of Christ's death on the Cross and Resurrection shows how God's love can transform even death into the light of resurrection. Ratzinger concluded: "True beauty is the love of God that was definitively revealed to us in the Paschal Mystery."[83] The liturgy is part of this mystery, hence its beauty, which is not an additional element but rather is constitutive to its celebration. This consideration leads also to the care with which the Church has always sought to situate the celebration of the liturgy in the most fitting framework possible.[84]

Reason and art. As I have many times had reason to emphasize, Ratzinger is one of the theologians who has raised his voice most in defense of reason. At the same time, he sees a relation between reason and art; indeed, he considers the latter a culmination of reason. Responding to a priest from Brixen (Bressanone), he said "heart and reason encounter one another, beauty and truth converge."[85] There is therefore a rationality of faith, but there is also an aesthetic that naturally does not oppose the *logos*, or reason, but opens the door to hope and becomes in a way evidence of faith. According to the pope, this is the case with the great cathedrals.

Still speaking to the priests of Brixen, he affirmed: "If I look at this beautiful cathedral—it is a living proclamation! It speaks to us itself, and on the basis of the cathedral's beauty, we succeed in visibly proclaiming God."[86] The pope made the same observation also in regard to music, from Gregorian chant to masters like Palestrina, Bach, and Mozart. "In listening to all these works . . . we suddenly understand: it is true! Wherever such things are born, the Truth is there. Without an intuition that discovers the true creative center of the world such beauty cannot be born."[87]

The pope delved deeper into this concept in the previously mentioned address at the Collège des Bernardins in Paris, taking the Rule of Saint Benedict as a starting point. In order to pray on the

---

[83] Ibid., 189.

[84] Ibid.

[85] Benedict XVI, Meeting with the Clergy of the Diocese of Bolzano-Bressanone, August 6, 2008.

[86] Ibid.

[87] Ibid.

basis of the Word of God, it is not enough to pronounce words; music is needed. Two chants of the Christian liturgy are derived from biblical texts that put them on the lips of angels: the *Gloria*, which is sung by the angels at the birth of Jesus, and the *Sanctus*, which, according to Isaiah (6:1–6), is the acclamation of the seraphim, who are in the immediate vicinity of God. Moreover, according to Saint Benedict, the entire liturgy is carried out in the presence of the angels. According to Saint Bernard's interpretation, this means "the culture of singing is also the culture of being, and that the monks have to pray and sing in a manner commensurate with the grandeur of the word handed down to them, with its claim on true beauty."[88] Great Western music arose from this inherent need to speak with God and to sing it with the words given by God himself.

The way of beauty. In the autumn of 2008, at the approach of the tenth anniversary of the 1999 letter to artists by John Paul II, on the eve of the anniversary, Pope Benedict exhorted the Pontifical Council for Culture to undertake "a renewed reflection on art, on the creativity of artists and on the fruitful yet challenging dialogue between the latter and the Christian faith." This led to the idea for a new meeting with artists, which took place on November 21, 2009, in the Sistine Chapel. On that occasion, the pope gave an address that brought to completion his reflection on beauty and art by proposing the *via pulchritudinis*, a way of beauty that is at the same time an artistic and aesthetic path and also a journey of faith.

At this point, he interpolated a citation from his friend von Balthasar,[89] according to whom the way of beauty leads us to grasp the Whole in the fragment, the Infinite in the finite, and God in the history of mankind.[90] In the context of the crisis through which the world was going in those years, the pope saw the search for true beauty as a healthy jolt that brings man out of himself, snatches him away from resignation and acquiescence to routine, and in this way reawakens him to hope and to the values of what is absolute. Hence his invitation to artists to work with the Church in reawakening

---

[88] Benedict XVI, Address to Representatives from the World of Culture, September 12, 2008.

[89] Benedict XVI, Address at the Meeting with Artists, November 21, 2009.

[90] See Elio Guerriero, *Hans Urs von Balthasar* (Brescia: Morcelliana, 2006), especially the chapter devoted to the Balthasarian aesthetic, 169–78.

men and women to the values of what is infinite. Beauty is striking, but this is precisely how it calls man back to his ultimate destiny, sets him in motion again, and fills him with new hope.

Pope Benedict's love for art, music, and concerts, which drew various criticisms from his own Curia, was not a bourgeois vice; rather, it pointed to a way—the way of beauty—which is similar to Jacob's ladder, descending from the presence of God and leading back to it.

The Courtyard of the Gentiles

Another one of Pope Benedict's initiatives in promoting a new humanism is the so-called Courtyard of the Gentiles, the founding of which was encouraged in an address by the German pontiff to the Roman Curia in late 2009. After an overall assessment of a year that was largely satisfactory, the pope also shared with his collaborators his pastoral concern for those people who consider themselves atheists and agnostics. They may still be far from a desire for true evangelization, strictly speaking, but the question of God is still open even for them. In short, the pope was thinking about a sort of courtyard of the Gentiles, which was the place in the Temple of Jerusalem where even pagans could enter and pose questions about God to the rabbis or other teachers who were present. This is precisely the area from which Jesus had driven out the merchants so as to give the Gentiles the opportunity to pray or reflect.

After the pope's address, the Pontifical Council for Culture took charge of promoting this initiative. It organized the first meeting of the Courtyard of the Gentiles in Paris on March 24 and 25, 2011, with meetings at the UNESCO Headquarters, the Sorbonne, and the Institut de France. The reasons for the decision to start in the French capital were, first, because Paris presents itself as the capital City of Light, heir of the prestigious medieval university, and because the founding address by Pope Benedict harked back to his famous speech at the Collège des Bernardins.

For his part, the pontiff closely followed the initiative and sent a warm message for the first event. "At the heart of the 'City of Light', . . . a great court has been created in order to give fresh impetus to respectful and friendly encounter between people of differing convictions."[91] The former prefect of the Congregation for the Doctrine of the Faith invited young people in particular, believers and nonbelievers, to a preliminary, fruitful dialogue aimed at building bridges between them. He did not refrain, however, from exhorting them to search for truth, which alone can make people free: "One of the reasons for this Court of the Gentiles is to encourage such feelings of fraternity, over and above our individual convictions yet not denying our differences. And on an even deeper level, to recognize that God alone, in Christ, grants us inner freedom and the possibility of truly encountering one another as brothers and sisters."[92]

The pope would return to the encounter with nonbelievers the following year, on the occasion of the twenty-fifth anniversary of the historic meeting of religious leaders in Assisi in 1986, an initiative of John Paul II. To commemorate the event, which was a monumental turning point, Benedict XVI in turn called for a world day of reflection, dialogue, and prayer for peace and justice in the world, which took place in the Umbrian capital on October 27, 2011. Religious leaders were invited to the event to reflect on the new emergence of violence linked to religion.

Benedict, nevertheless, extended the invitation also to the representatives of those whom he defined as "pilgrims of truth, pilgrims of peace". They are men and women who do not believe in God but are seeking him sincerely. They themselves, moreover, can observe that the absence of God corresponds to the decline of mankind and of humanism. It is therefore "a case of being together on a journey towards truth, a case of taking a decisive stand for human dignity and a case of common engagement for peace".[93] These are the conditions for the humanism of the new millennium.

---

[91] Benedict XVI, Video Message to the "Courts of the Gentiles" on the Final Evening of the Event, March 25, 2011.

[92] Ibid.

[93] Benedict XVI, Address at the Meeting for Peace in Assisi, October 27, 2011.

XVII

THE CHURCH IN THE TEMPEST

When asked about the character of his brother, Monsignor Georg Ratzinger gave a response that can be a good key for understanding the state of mind with which Pope Benedict faced the last, difficult years of his pontificate. The former director of the Regensburg cathedral choir said: "He is not aggressive at all, but when it's necessary to fight, he does his part, as a matter of conscience."[1]

After a few years in which Benedict was able to work with relative calm, the crisis began with the revocation of the excommunication of the four Lefebvrist bishops. Unfortunately, the initiative, which the pope intended to be a gesture of reconciliation and mercy, happened to coincide with the crazy statement by Bishop Richard Williamson denying the existence of gas chambers in the Nazi death camps. A difficult period followed with a series of scandals ranging from the administration to the governance of the Church. It reached its height with the definitive revelation of the enormity of the phenomenon of the sexual abuse of minors by priests and of the lack of vigilance by bishops.

At this point, following the example of Thomas More and John Henry Newman,[2] the pope set out on the way of truth, which turned into a long *Via Crucis* whose sorrowful stations were marked each time by an encounter with the victims, a request for pardon, severe measures taken against the transgressors, and the invitation to the entire Church to do penance and to engage in a process of purification. Nevertheless, his hope and certainty of overcoming the crisis

---

[1] Quoted by the interviewer in Joseph Ratzinger, *Salt of the Earth: An Interview with Peter Seewald*, trans. Adrian Walker (San Francisco: Ignatius Press, 1997), 67.

[2] Ibid., 68.

never failed. This confidence, however, did not come from trust in his own ability to govern but from the awareness that ultimately the Church is not upheld by men but rather is accompanied by the constant presence and support of Jesus Christ.

Once again the Lefebvrites

In the first years of the pontificate of Pope Benedict, there had already been contacts with the followers of the Society of Saint Pius X, founded by Archbishop Marcel Lefebvre, in an attempt to overcome a schism that the pope hoped could perhaps be eliminated or at least reduced in size by a greater degree of tolerance on the part of the Church, in particular on the part of bishops. Those first contacts, against which the French bishops proved to be particularly hostile,[3] were followed in later years by dialogues with the head of the Society of Saint Pius X, Bernard Fellay, and a pontifical commission presided over by Darío Cardinal Castrillón Hoyos. According to the reports of the Colombian cardinal, the four bishops illicitly ordained by Archbishop Lefebvre in 1988 had asked to return to the Catholic Church, acknowledging that they had been consecrated without the papal mandate and declaring themselves willing to pledge obedience to the reigning pontiff.

On the basis of these premises, on January 21, 2009, the Congregation for Bishops, with its prefect, Giovanni Battista Cardinal Re, made public the decree with which the excommunication of the four bishops was lifted. Almost at the same time as the publication of the decree, however, a Swedish television station aired an interview with Bishop Williamson (one of the four bishops from whom the excommunication was lifted), in which the Lefebvrist prelate flatly denied the Holocaust and the existence of the gas chambers. The simultaneous occurrence of the lifting of the excommunication and the broadcast by the Swedish television station was certainly intentional, since the interview had been recorded almost two months before.

What was surprising, however, was the fact that no one in the Roman Curia, from the Secretariat of State to the Congregation for Bishops and the Vatican Press Office, had taken seriously the previ-

---

[3] See above, chap. 13.

ous rash assertions of the Lefebvrist bishop. Even after the interview was aired, the response of the Roman agencies was very slow. Since the pope's private secretary was sick in those days,[4] no one took the initiative to inform the pope. In the meantime, in the media, in particular on the social networks, the controversy spread, and the interventions by Jewish authorities asking for explanations multiplied. Rabbi David Rosen, president of the Jewish Committee for relations with Christians, declared: "By welcoming an open holocaust denier into the Catholic Church without any recantation on his part, the Vatican has made a mockery of John Paul II's moving and impressive repudiation and condemnation of anti-Semitism."

The Chief Rabbi of Rome, Riccardo Di Segni, added: "Threatening clouds seem to be gathering over the Jewish-Christian dialogue."[5] Faced with the intense criticisms both inside and outside the Church, Pope Benedict gave an initial explanation at his General Audience on January 28: "I fulfilled this act of paternal compassion because these Bishops repeatedly manifested their active suffering for the situation in which they had found themselves." Then, referring to the criticisms resulting from the denials of Bishop Williamson, he continued: "As I affectionately renew the expression of my full and unquestionable solidarity with our fellow receivers of the First Covenant, I hope that the memory of the Shoah will lead humanity to reflect upon the unfathomable power of evil when it conquers the heart of man."[6]

Meanwhile, within the Catholic Church, requests for clarifications and distinctions were also multiplying. Finally, on February 4, 2009, the Secretariat of State, the major figure missing in the whole affair, published a note in which it attempted to respond to the objections, whether from within the Church or outside the Church. The note therefore affirmed:

A full recognition of the Second Vatican Council and the Magisterium of Popes John XXIII, Paul VI, John Paul I, John Paul II and

---

[4] This fact is reported in Paolo Rodari and Andrea Tornielli, *Attacco a Ratzinger* (Milan: Piemme, 2010), 93, and was confirmed to me personally by Archbishop Gänswein, who, having come down with a particularly severe case of the flu, did not want to go near the pontiff so as not to give it to him.

[5] Both citations are reported in ibid., 92.

[6] Benedict XVI, General Audience of January 28, 2009.

Benedict XVI himself is an indispensable condition for any future recognition of the Society of Saint Pius X. . . . The positions of Bishop Williamson with regard to the *Shoah* are absolutely unacceptable. . . . In order to be admitted to function as a Bishop within the Church, Bishop Williamson must also distance himself in an absolutely unequivocal and public way from his positions regarding the *Shoah*, which were unknown to the Holy Father at the time of the remission of the excommunication.[7]

The last statement is surprising. It is precisely the Secretariat of State, in fact, that should have been vigilant and informed the pontiff and also the two cardinals Giovanni Battista Re and Darío Castrillón Hoyos. Meanwhile, the controversy showed no sign of calming down. A request for clarifications came from Angela Merkel, the German Chancellor since 2005, while Cardinal Lehmann, the president of the German Bishops' Conference, called for the resignation of Cardinal Castrillón.

Finally, on March 10, the pope decided to intervene personally by sending, in a very unusual fashion, a personal letter to the bishops of the whole world. Returning in a sad and personal tone to the matter of the lifting of the excommunications that had caused "a discussion more heated than any we have seen for a long time",[8] the pope tried to offer a word of clarification and thus to contribute to peace in the Church. Benedict expressed regret for the fact that "even Catholics who, after all, might have had a better knowledge of the situation, thought they had to attack me with open hostility."[9] He declared yet again that he had not been aware of the denialist theses of Williamson and said that he was unhappy that a gesture of mercy toward the four bishops affected by disciplinary sanction could have been misunderstood as a repudiation of the good relations between Jews and Christians.

The pope later recalled that excommunication is a personal sanction that does not concern in any way the Society of Saint Pius X as a whole. Afterward, he added that it was clear that the Lefebvrists

---

[7] The note from the Secretariat of State is reprinted in *Enchiridion Vaticanum* 26 (2009–2010), 99f., and, in English translation, on the Vatican website.

[8] Benedict XVI, Letter to the Bishops of the Catholic Church concerning the Remission of the Excommunication of the Four Bishops Consecrated by Archbishop Lefebvre, March 10, 2009.

[9] Ibid.

must recognize Vatican II, but it was likewise necessary that those who are overly zealous defenders of the council should recognize also the possibility for mercy and reconciliation. Finally, the letter invited the bishops to go beyond the complaints and dissent that had been erroneously mistaken for freedom of expression. Written with great pathos and motivated by concern for the unity of the Church, the missive elicited many expressions of sympathy for the pontiff. It revealed, however, the growing isolation of Benedict, who had not only been let down in Rome but had also been subjected to criticisms by large groups of national episcopates. The pope experienced particular sorrow over the criticisms of the German episcopate concerning dialogue with the Jews.[10] The bishops of his country, in fact, must have known very well about the pope's attention and sensitivity to dialogue with the brethren of the First Covenant. An error of communication could not call into question a lifelong commitment.

Where is the secretary of state?

The Williamson case was the classic straw that breaks the camel's back. In the Curia, in fact, discontent was widespread because of the numerous omissions and even egregious errors that ended up casting discredit on the work of so many dedicated workers, from the most humble to the archbishops and cardinals. At first generic, the complaints focused more and more on the principal collaborator of the pope, the secretary of state, Tarcisio Cardinal Bertone. Called to be a collaborator of Cardinal Ratzinger in the Congregation for the Doctrine of the Faith, he had become accustomed to substituting for the pope, especially on journeys that fatigued Ratzinger, who was already overburdened with work.[11] Bertone probably thought that he had to carry out the same task even as secretary of state and, particularly in the first years of his mandate, took numerous trips abroad on his own initiative. His absences, however, left a dangerous void in Rome that deprived those in charge of different offices of the necessary direction.

---

[10] This was confirmed in a conversation of the author with Archbishop Gänswein, personal secretary of Benedict XVI.

[11] See above, chap. 11.

Moreover, even when he was in the Vatican, Bertone always seemed pressed for time, which easily gave his interlocutors the impression of being in a rush and authoritarian. Hence, Monsignor Georg Gänswein took on an increasingly important role; it was not by chance that Dino Boffo turned to him in order to have the news of his unjust termination as editor-in-chief of *Avvenire* reach the pope.[12] As we have seen in the Williamson case, however, Monsignor Gänswein could not be everywhere. Paolo Cardinal Sardi decided, then, to send a letter[13] directly to the pope, in which he informed him about the uneasiness in the various offices. The former "*Sostituto*" in the Secretariat of State still had strong ties to the central dicastery of the Church and, for this reason, was well aware of the widespread malaise.

And so, in April 2009, he wrote to the pope that the frequent trips of the secretary of state, who was often absent from Rome and did not dedicate the time necessary to coordinate the work of the various offices, generated confusion and mistrust among the personnel. This is what had happened in the Williamson case, and this was what was happening in the preparation of the encyclical *Caritas in Veritate*. The pope read the cardinal's missive but took no action. The malaise, however, also spread among the resident bishops and even to some cardinals who were close to Benedict, like Angelo Scola (patriarch of Venice), Christoph Schönborn (archbishop of Vienna), and Joachim Meisner (archbishop of Cologne), who intervened, asking the pope to replace his secretary of state.

At the end of the year, Cardinal Bertone turned seventy-five, the age at which bishops and curial officials must present their letters of resignation. This would have been a good occasion for making a not-too-traumatic change. On this point, however, the pope was implacable. He knew about the discontent concerning the micromanagement and often disruptive administration of his secretary of state, but he believed that these were to be attributed to personality flaws and not to a thirst for power, as his detractors maintained. As far as the rest was concerned, the pontiff also knew that the replacement of the secretary of state only three years after his appointment

---

[12] See Gianluigi Nuzzi, *Sua Santità* (Milan: Chiarelettere, 2012), 27–52.

[13] Like Boffo's letters, the one from Cardinal Sardi, too, was handed over to the journalist Nuzzi. It is reprinted on pp. 162f. of the above-cited book.

would be tantamount to an admission of his own grave error in the choice and would end up leaving him even more alone. Therefore, he decided to ask Bertone to be more present in the Curia but to continue with him, even at the expense of displeasing those who had counseled a different solution.

Furthermore, as had happened in the Williamson case, the pope did not hesitate to take upon himself the mistakes made by others. It was a gesture that revealed the generosity of Benedict and his willingness to assume responsibilities that were not really his. And this would be very clear in the matter of the pedophile priests.

Africa: The "obscured" journey

On March 17, 2009, Benedict XVI boarded a direct flight for Africa. It was the first time that he was visiting the Dark Continent as pope, and he was delighted to do so. He traveled to Cameroon and Angola, two countries of West Africa, in order to hand over to the African bishops meeting in Yaoundé the *Instrumentum laboris*, which was the basic text that would later be discussed at the Second Synod of African Bishops, to be held in the Vatican in the fall. The trip to Africa, the land of hope, as he described it, seemed to buoy him with a sense of enthusiasm and youthfulness. During the flight, according to the established custom since the days of John Paul II, he met with journalists, who one after another asked him questions. One, in particular, concerned the use of condoms to avoid the spread of AIDS, a point about which the Catholic Church seemed to hold an unrealistic and ineffective position.

Benedict was particularly sensitive to these issues and did not hesitate to say what he thought: "I would say the opposite. I think that the most efficient, most truly present player in the fight against AIDS is the Catholic Church herself." The pope recalled all the ecclesial agencies engaged in the care of people affected by AIDS and then continued: ". . . the problem [of AIDS] cannot be overcome by the distribution of prophylactics: on the contrary, they increase it."[14]

---

[14] See Aldo Maria Valli, *Benedetto XVI: Il pontificato interrotto* (Milan: Mondadori, 2013), 197f.

From the context, it is clear that he intended to speak of the interpersonal relationship that must precede every act of love, but, removed from its proper context, the news was explosive and was soon heard around the world, reported widely by Italian journalists and even more so by European and American journalists. The clarifications of the Vatican spokesman, Father Federico Lombardi, and of media outlets close to the Church and the Vatican were useless. Whereas the pope intended to situate sexuality in a broader context of an interpersonal relationship, the only message being passed along was: The pope is against condoms, therefore, he endangers the health of Africans and public health policies. The health ministers of France and Germany said this, while the Spanish Prime Minister Zapatero distinguished himself, in response to the pope's words by deciding to send a million condoms to Africa to combat the spread of AIDS.

Even more incredible was the attitude of Belgium, whose Parliament voted on a motion to condemn the unacceptable stance of the pope and asked the government to present a formal protest to the Holy See. Meanwhile, the pope arrived in Cameroon, a nation in which there is a formidable presence of Catholics. The next day, March 18, the pope met the bishops of the country, whom he encouraged to continue the work of evangelization for which they were responsible. Also necessary were a profound communion among the pastors and a loyal collaboration among the dioceses. Unlike Europe, Cameroon does not lack priestly vocations. However, the pope recommended that the bishops closely supervise the training of the young men and appoint wise, experienced collaborators to aid in their formation.

On March 19, the feast of Saint Joseph, the pope celebrated a Mass in honor of his holy patron in the Yaoundé Stadium and was transported by the joyous atmosphere of the celebration. For logistical reasons, the concluding assembly of the Second African Synod would take place in Rome, but it had already begun in the heart of the African continent. At the conclusion of the liturgical celebration, the pope went to the Nunciature where he met with the bishops who made up the Special Council for the African Synod. The pope entrusted to them the text on which they would have to reflect before arriving in Rome in the fall.

Benedict then had words of sincere praise for the dynamism of the Church in Africa, which of course also had to confront great challenges but did so with the same great self-sacrifice, the same apostolic courage and faith of the missionaries and pastors who had preceded them. Among these, the pope recalled his old friend Bernardin Cardinal Gantin, who when faced with tribal conflicts, fratricidal hatred, and violence, proposed the development of a theology of fraternity. The pope adopted this proposal, which, besides, had a firm foundation in the Word of God and in the celebration of the Eucharist.

The second stage of the African trip was Angola, where the pope arrived on March 20. The great country, having only recently emerged from a long tribal conflict, at the time seemed destined for rapid development. Speaking to young people, the pontiff joined in their contagious enthusiasm and exclaimed: Dear young friends, you hold within yourselves the dynamism of a future that needs God's support. On the other hand, turning to the politicians, Benedict warned against soulless economic development, behind which it was not difficult to perceive the great multinational oil companies. This type of development enriches only a small oligarchy of privileged individuals, excluding most of the population. As a result, the pope spoke about new forms of predatory colonialism that generate further frustrations and other forms of rancor. Material well-being is not enough to redeem a nation; great moral energies are also needed.

Benedict thus referred to the discussion that he had started with the journalists on the plane. The mechanical distribution of money or condoms is not conducive to development; rather, it causes imbalance and gives rise to injustices. Only patient educational work, for which Africans must be not only passive subjects but also conscientious and responsible promoters, can foster reconciliation among the various tribes and ethnic groups and the development of the country.

When the sensation of the first days had passed, the controversy began to wane and the originality of the message that the pope brought to Africa started to emerge. Some African episcopates, above all, took up and explained this message, and their loyal stance was comforting for Benedict. The bishops of the regional Episcopal Conference of West Africa expressed gratitude and closeness to the pope and, echoing his words, they said: "AIDS will not be overcome by putting aside the spiritual and moral resources of men. . . . From the bottom of our hearts we African bishops thank the Holy Father who is so close to us. . . . He encourages all of us to live and promote the humanization of sexuality."[15] The Congolese bishops also signed a similar declaration.[16]

For his part, Benedict, in the traditional address to the Curia, gave a very positive account of his African trip. He declared: "It was moving for me to experience the great cordiality with which the Successor of Peter, the *Vicarius Christi*, was welcomed. The festive joy and warm affection I met with along all the roads was not directed to a mere chance guest."[17]

The Year for Priests

On March 16, 2009, when the Pauline Year had not yet ended, Benedict XVI announced his decision to inaugurate a special Year for Priests. As the pope had intended, the Pauline Year, dedicated to meditation on and study of the writings of the apostle, had been at the same time a year dedicated to bishops, who are called to share the missionary zeal of the Apostle of the Gentiles. The Year for Priests, on the other hand, was to have as its theme "Fidelity to Christ, the Fidelity of the Priest", and the model that the pope offered to priests was Saint John Vianney, the Curé of Ars, whose 150th anniversary of death occurred that year. This model was in some ways a surprising one for the pope-theologian to choose— a priest who had encountered serious difficulty in studying Latin and theology—and to propose as an example for the priests of the third Christian millennium.

Over and above the simplicity of the Curé of Ars, what stood out, in fact, were his fidelity to the ministry, his dedication to the Sacrament of Penance, and his personal asceticism. Meanwhile, on March 19, the Congregation for the Clergy sent a letter to priests the better to clarify the purpose of the year that had been set aside

---

[15] The Declaration of the Regional Episcopal Conference of West Africa was published in Italian by *L'Osservatore romano* (April 18, 2009).

[16] The Declaration by the Bishops of the Congo was published also by *L'Osservatore romano* (May 1, 2009).

[17] Benedict XVI, Address to the Members of the Roman Curia for the Traditional Exchange of Christmas Greetings, December 21, 2009.

for them. The celebration, of course, concerned priests but was also meant to involve the entire Christian community: dioceses, parishes, the Catholic communities of the whole world. For their part, priests were being invited to participate in seminars, days of reflection, and retreats. Lastly, it was meant to be a year of prayer of priests, with priests, and for priests.[18]

Clearly, the pope realized that there was a problem, apparent in a lessening of spiritual fervor, which made it necessary for him to intervene. As far as the rest is concerned, the letter of the congregation speaks explicitly of priests involved in grave problems and in criminal situations, requiring investigation, judgment, and appropriate punishment.[19] The way chosen by Benedict to overcome the crisis was above all to recall the dignity, the beauty, the strength of love that are the foundation of the priestly vocation.

Three months later, on June 16, the pope sent an official Letter Proclaiming a Year for Priests,[20] dwelling on the virtues of the Curé of Ars, patron of the world's parish priests, whose moving biography is sketched in the document. The pope recalled especially an expression dear to Saint John Vianney: "The priesthood is the love of the heart of Jesus." He continued: "This touching expression makes us reflect, first of all, with heartfelt gratitude on the immense gift which priests represent, not only for the Church, but also for humanity itself."[21] The pope's thoughts then turned to so many priests who carry out their ministry with generosity and tenderness, recalling his first pastor, Max Blumschein, whose zeal had been an example and inspiration for his own pastoral work.[22] And he added a second quotation by the Curé of Ars: "Lord, grant me the conversion of my parish; I am willing to suffer whatever you wish, for my entire life!"[23]

According to the pope, this results in the identification between the person and the ministry both in the celebration of the sacraments

---

[18] See Congregation for the Clergy, *To Priests for the Year for Priests*, in *Enchiridion Vaticanum* 26 (2009–2010), pp. 373f.

[19] Ibid.

[20] Benedict XVI, Letter Proclaiming a Year for Priests on the 150th Anniversary of the "Dies Natalis" of the Curé of Ars, June 16, 2009.

[21] Ibid.

[22] See above, chap. 2.

[23] Benedict XVI, Letter Proclaiming a Year for Priests.

and in the care of souls. The Curé of Ars, in fact, was not only a man of prayer, but a priest zealous in administering the sacraments. He visited sick people and families, organized popular missions and feasts, beautified his church, called the laity to collaborate with him —a distinguishing characteristic on which the pope particularly insisted, since it was recommended also by Vatican II.

On June 19, the Solemnity of the Sacred Heart, the pope officially inaugurated the celebration of the Year for Priests. In his homily, preached on the occasion of Evening Prayer II of the feast, the pope recalled that in celebrating this festivity "the Church presents us this mystery for our contemplation: the mystery of the heart of a God who feels compassion and who bestows all his love upon humanity."[24] Thus he began to delineate the papal program for this special year. Priests were invited to regain an awareness of their dignity. At the same time, priests had to undergo purification and penance, they needed to rediscover the joy of their ministry. On the other hand, bishops were called to be vigilant, while Catholic communities and parishes were asked to draw near to their priests; to recognize their human limitations; to show them affection and, thus, to avoid exposing them to loneliness and evil temptations.

The series of celebrations in which the pope participated during the Year for Priests and at which he spoke of the priest's mission indicates the importance he attributed to the priesthood, but also the urgency of a change that was more necessary than ever. After the solemn opening of the year, the pope returned to the topic in several General Audiences; in messages sent to the European Convention on pastoral work for vocations; in an international priests' retreat held at Ars; and in a meeting with the pastors of the Diocese of Rome in February of 2010. With the conclusion of the Year for Priests in view, the pope participated in numerous solemn celebrations. On June 5, 2010, in Nicosia, while visiting Cyprus, he participated in a Mass with priests and religious men and women and spoke of the bond between the priest and the cross. On June 10, in Rome, the pope took part in a vigil with priests in Saint Peter's Square and responded to their questions. In response to a Czech priest, the pope affirmed that priestly celibacy does not mean not being married. Rather, "It is to let oneself be taken in the hand of

---

[24] See Benedict XVI, Homily for the Opening of the Year for Priests, June 19, 2009.

God, to give oneself into the hands of the Lord, into his 'I'. And therefore, it is an act of loyalty and trust."[25]

On Friday, June 11, the pope presided at a solemn celebration to conclude the Year for Priests. The pope said: "We wanted to reawaken our joy at how close God is to us, and our gratitude for the fact that he entrusts himself to our infirmities. . . . It was to be expected that this new radiance of the priesthood would not be pleasing to the 'enemy'. . . . And so it happened that, in this very year of joy for the sacrament of the priesthood, the sins of priests came to light—particularly the abuse of the little ones."[26]

In the years that the pope had spent at the Congregation for the Doctrine of the Faith, he had already had to deal with numerous cases of abandonment of the ministry and the first cases of the abuse of minors. However, he was still not quite aware of the vastness of the phenomenon, the scope of which would become clear a few months later. For this reason, later on, reflecting with Peter Seewald on the decision to have the Year for Priests, the pope defined it as providential because "the negative things do exist; that is a fact. . . . It is imperative now really to start over in the spirit of penance—and at the same time not to lose our joy in the priesthood but to recover it again."[27]

The scandal of the pedophile priests

The scandal of the pedophile priests was a cross that Benedict XVI had to bear throughout his pontificate. As has already been re-called,[28] the responsibility to examine and, as needed, to punish pedophile priests had been given him in the last years of the pon-tificate of John Paul II. According to all the evidence,[29] he acted with energy and rigor; paradoxically, though, the more he showed himself to be desirous of rooting out this scandal from the life of the Church, the more the reports arriving from many parts of the

---

[25] Benedict XVI, Dialogue with Priests, June 10, 2010.

[26] Benedict XVI, Homily, Solemnity of the Sacred Heart of Jesus, June 11, 2010.

[27] Benedict XVI, *Light of the World*, trans. Michael J. Miller and Adrian J. Walker (San Francisco: Ignatius Press, 2010), 35.

[28] See chap. 14.

[29] See: Rodari and Tornielli, *Attacco a Ratzinger,* in particular chap. 7, and Massimo Introvigne, *Preti pedofili* (Cinisello Balsamo: San Paolo, 2010).

world seemed to bring back along his path these horrendous crimes and in some way to lay the blame on him. In many cases, the abuses had been committed from the 1960s to the 1980s, but the victims of these outrages, then minors, found the courage to raise their voices and ask for justice only after 2000. Inevitably, therefore, the burden fell onto the entire Church, which, at the time, had not intervened to punish the responsible parties adequately.

In this context, the pope, as he would often declare, found that he needed to be rigorous with the guilty but also to defend the work of many generous priests who were unjustly considered responsible for crimes committed by their brothers. In short, it was a true Way of the Cross, which in some way had already been anticipated in the prayers for Good Friday composed by Cardinal Ratzinger a few days before his election.

DIMENSIONS AND CAUSES OF THE PHENOMENON

From the sociological perspective, it is necessary to make clear that the question of abuse concerned not only priests; rather, in society there are other groups of persons among whom pedophilia is much more widespread. Moreover, to provide a more exact picture with a sort of mental chart, the chronology of events goes like this: from the 1950s until the mid-1960s, the number of cases is constant, with a low median. In the mid-1960s, the line on the chart begins to rise and then reaches an apex in the 1970s and 1980s. Subsequently, it decreased until it fell below the 1950s levels.[30]

Now turning his attention to the causes, the pope himself had recourse to sociology, speaking of the rapid transformation and secularization of society.[31] This phenomenon provoked a rapid estrangement from Christian teachings and, within the Church herself, led even priests and religious to adopt models of thought and judgment of secular realities without reference to the Gospel. Thus, from the mid-1960s on, canon law simply was no longer applied, in the con-

---

[30] For this data, see the book cited above by Massimo Introvigne. The author, a sociologist and president of the Center for the Study of New Religions, cites 2004 research from the United States National Review Board for the Protection of Children and Young People.

[31] Benedict XVI, Pastoral Letter to the Catholics of Ireland, March 19, 2010.

viction that in the Church only the law of love was supposed to rule and not canon law.

As the pope saw it, this general relaxation caused a change in conscience; "this also narrowed the concept of love, which in fact is not just being nice or courteous, but is found in the truth. And another component of truth is that I must punish the one who has sinned against real love."[32]

THE CASE OF IRELAND

Almost contemporaneous with the announcement of the Year for Priests, in May 2009, the "Ryan Report" was published in Ireland, named for Judge Sean Ryan. The magistrate had coordinated an open investigation after the publication of two documents forwarded in 1998; they demonstrated the abuse and violence experienced by children in two Catholic schools. The impact was enormous, and the authorities established a government commission to investigate the industrial schools, which had been founded to care for orphans, abandoned children, or juveniles guilty of misdemeanors. The result of the nine-year-long investigation was summarized in the Ryan Report, which indicated that over the preceding fifty years around 2500 children had suffered violence and abuse by priests [and others working for the Church].

Benedict XVI, who as early as 2006 had reprimanded the Irish bishops and, through them, the priests, was surprised and saddened by the new developments. But the measure of the abuse was not yet fully appreciated. In the second half of 2009, a second document, the "Murphy Report", was published, named for the judge who had coordinated that project. This time the investigation concerned the Archdiocese of Dublin and referred to forty-six pedophile priests who had been protected or at least not punished by their bishops. Beyond the responsibility of the pedophile priests, therefore, there also emerged the grave failures of the bishops, some of whom, to avoid scandals, merely moved a priest from one parish to another.

Inability to govern, little or insufficient attention for the victims: these were not insignificant accusations against those pastors who were called to protect the littlest ones entrusted to them, not to

---

[32] Benedict XVI, *Light of the World*, 26.

expose them to the abuse of their shameless collaborators. In mid-February, the pope summoned the twenty-four Irish bishops to Rome. Together with some members of the Curia, he listened to them both as individuals and as a group; he wanted to be informed about the root causes of such odious crimes. He then proposed to the bishops the points of a letter he intended to send to the faithful of Ireland. In short, the pope showed his willingness to take control of the situation, to intervene decisively so as to put an end to the inertia of the Irish ecclesiastical authorities that had made possible "a grave sin that offends God and wounds the dignity of the human person".[33]

The *Letter to the Catholics of Ireland*, announced to the bishops and then actually sent about a month later on March 19, 2010, is the most detailed and thorough document against the pedophilia perpetrated by Catholic priests and the lack of vigilance on the part of the bishops. The pope declared immediately that, like the Irish faithful themselves, he was disturbed by the news regarding the abuse of children and young people by priests and religious. Hence the pope's decision to write personally a pastoral letter to express his closeness to them and at the same time to propose a path for "healing, renewal and reparation".[34] Then the pope made reference to the glorious history of Ireland and listed the causes that had made the crisis possible. Among these, the pope noted: the insufficient human, moral, intellectual, and spiritual formation in seminaries and novitiates; the tendency to favor the clergy, a misplaced preoccupation with the good name of the Church and with avoiding scandals. Then, the pope invited all to act with urgency to confront these factors "which have had such tragic consequences in the lives of victims and their families."[35]

The letter then became more heartfelt, addressing the different groups of affected persons. The first were the victims of abuse themselves and their families. The pope told them: "You have suffered grievously and I am truly sorry. I know that nothing can undo the wrong you have endured. Your trust has been betrayed and your dignity has been violated."[36] Then the pope recognized that it is

---

[33] See Rodari and Tornielli, *Attacco a Ratzinger,* 170–87.
[34] Benedict XVI, Letter to the Catholics of Ireland, March 19, 2010.
[35] Ibid.
[36] Ibid.

difficult for the victims of such a crime to forgive and draw near to the Church again. However, he asked them at least to regain their trust in Christ. Then, addressing the priests responsible for the abuse, the pope was authoritative: "You betrayed the trust that was placed in you by innocent young people and their parents, and you must answer for it before Almighty God and before properly constituted tribunals."[37]

The pope continued by addressing the parents of the abused children; the children and young people of Ireland; the priests and religious exposed to insults on account of the outrageous behavior perpetrated by their confreres. The heartfelt and paternal tone toward those groups again became severe when the pope addressed the bishops: "Some of you and your predecessors failed, at times grievously. . . . It must be admitted that grave errors of judgement were made and failures of leadership occurred."[38] Lastly, the pope addressed all the faithful of Ireland. He spoke of the measures needed to be taken in regard to every crime but warned that this was not enough. What was needed was a common effort to walk along the way indicated by the Gospel, to draw near to Christ, to experience a profound renewal, and thus to gain new credibility.

For his part, the pope invited the faithful to rediscover the practices of piety, Bible reading, works of mercy, and above all Eucharistic adoration. He then announced canonical visitations for the several dioceses, seminaries, and religious congregations, and a national mission for the bishops, priests, and religious. The pope enclosed with this letter a prayer for the Church in Ireland, to be recited by all the faithful, so as to invoke the grace of healing and renewal. Addressed to all the faithful of Ireland, the letter demonstrated the posture the pope intended to assume not only in dealing with the Church in Ireland but in all the countries in which the sexual abuse of minors by priests came to light.

THE SCANDALS IN GERMANY

Almost contemporaneously with the wave of scandals that came from Ireland, a new front was opening in Germany. In reality, here the credible cases of violence were much fewer; the situation,

---

[37] Ibid.
[38] Ibid.

however, was problematic for the pope because some newspapers were constantly seeking to involve Benedict's brother, Monsignor Georg Ratzinger, who from 1964 to 1994 had been the director of a famous boys' choir, the so-called "Sparrows" of the Cathedral of Regensburg (*Domspatzen*). The series of revelations of abuses committed by priests began this time with the work of a Jesuit, Father Klaus Mertes, the president of the famous College of Saint Peter Canisius in Berlin. To avoid accusations coming from the outside, the president started a transparent operation. He wrote that, as far as he knew, about thirty cases of abuse had occurred, and he invited those affected to declare that fact.

And thus, other accusations surfaced, so that the overall number of incidents of abuse from the 1970s and 1980s added up to about a hundred. A little later, the weekly magazine *Der Spiegel* began an investigation involving almost all the German dioceses. According to the magazine's data, ninety-four priests were involved in acts of pedophilia from 1994 to 2010, thirty of whom had already been convicted, while ten were currently on trial. However, as already noted, the danger came from the Diocese of Regensburg. In the first days of March 2010, the bishop of the city on the Danube had asked forgiveness of the victims and their families for the incidents that had taken place in the 1970s. Some newspapers, however, had started to mention the name of Georg Ratzinger. Dates and circumstances did not gibe, but the clarifications did not seem to put an end to the reports that were drawing dangerously close to the very person of the pope.

From Regensburg, the threat moved to Munich, where it resulted in the case of a priest accused of abuse that had been committed during the years when the pope was bishop of the Bavarian capital. Nevertheless, based on the documentation in the archives, the diocese could reconstruct the situation in detail, so that Benedict was completely vindicated, since, at the time when the priest had been accused of sexual molestations, Archbishop Joseph Ratzinger had already been in Rome for some time. Therefore, it was a clear attempt to drag the pope himself into a painful affair, while confusion among the faithful grew.

THE NEW YORK TIMES AGAINST THE POPE

Once started in Europe, the attempt to involve the pope in the sex abuse crisis continued in America with greater intensity. The first case was brought to the fore by *The New York Times*; it concerned a priest by the name of Lawrence Murphy, who from 1950 to 1974 had worked in a school for deaf and mute children in the Archdiocese of Milwaukee, Wisconsin. In the beginning of May 1974, a former student of the school accused Father Murphy of having sexually abused him and other boys. After an inquiry, the judge dismissed the case. Nevertheless, Archbishop William Cousins removed Murphy, who went to live with his mother but continued his pastoral ministry by helping the local pastor. In the meanwhile, the accusations multiplied, and the priest was interrogated by various archdiocesan officials assisted by psychologists.

In the end, it was determined that Father Murphy was a typical pedophile, and the officials in the Archdiocese of Milwaukee, where the crimes had been committed, and the officials of the Diocese of Superior, where Father Murphy was living, agreed to suspend him and to reduce him to the lay state. The priest, however, took recourse to the Congregation for the Doctrine of the Faith, which was headed by Ratzinger, pointing out that, besides having repented, he was seriously sick. Therefore, in the name of the congregation, Archbishop Bertone wrote to the two bishops of Superior and Milwaukee reminding them that reduction to the lay state must be undertaken only if it was not possible to obtain repair of the scandal, restoration of justice, and correction of the crime by other means.

Bishop Fliss, entering the case as Ordinary of the Diocese of Superior where Murphy was residing, responded by saying that the laicization process was necessary due to the gravity of the scandal. Finally, on May 30, a meeting took place in the Vatican in which Archbishop Weakland participated, along with his auxiliary Bishop Skiba, Bishop Fliss, and Archbishop Bertone. They summarized the guidelines to be followed: physical restriction of priestly ministry for Murphy; a decisive action to obtain the repentance of the priest; otherwise, the need to make provisions for his reduction to the lay state. On August 19, Bishop Fliss wrote to Bertone to bring him up to date about the measures taken and to inform him that his diocese would continue to be responsible for the cost of the therapy that the victims of sexual abuse required. Two days later, Father Murphy died, and his case was dismissed.

As a footnote to this story, which caused such a stir at the time, two observations should be made.[39] The documents published by *The New York Times* had been given to the newspaper by the lawyers for the prosecution, who were clearly interested in involving in the case not only the Congregation for the Doctrine of the Faith but also Cardinal Ratzinger, who meanwhile had become the pope. The document on which the accusatory newspaper article was based was a rough, computer-made English translation of the Italian original, which in several places ended up saying the exact opposite of the original document. Was this an oversight or a decision of the newspaper to publish a version that seemed to show that the congregation wanted to avoid a trial for Murphy? Even without wishing to question the good faith of the New York newspaper, this remains an open question.

THE LEGIONARIES OF CHRIST

In March 2009, after the death of the founder in 2008, as new grave revelations about the dissolute life of Marcial Maciel Degollado emerged,[40] Benedict XVI made plans for an apostolic visitation of the Legionaries of Christ. Five bishops were put in charge: the Mexican Ricardo Watty Urquidi; the American Charles J. Chaput; the Chilean Ricardo Ezzati Andrello; the Italian Giuseppe Versaldi; the Spaniard Ricardo Blázquez Pérez. During their visitation, the bishops were able to meet nearly all the members of the congregation. Later, they had meetings in Rome in which some members of the Secretariat of State and other representatives of the Curia participated. Benedict XVI participated in one of these meetings. Finally, the five bishops composed a document that they submitted to the Roman authorities.

In their report, they affirmed, above all, that in the Congrega-

---

[39] See the detailed reconstruction in Rodari and Tornielli, *Attacco a Ratzinger*, 170–87.

[40] See chap. 14 above.

tion of the Legionaries there were many religious who sought with authentic zeal to follow Christ and who offered their entire lives for the spread of the kingdom of God. At the same time, the bishops stated that they had verified "the very grave and objectively immoral actions of Father Maciel, confirmed by incontrovertible testimonies."[41] The founder very astutely had created alibis and gained for himself the trust, confidence, and silence of those who surrounded him. In short, he had led "a life devoid of scruples and authentic religious meaning."[42] Hence it would be necessary to redefine the charism of the Legionaries, to review their exercise of authority, in practice to replace the superiors in charge, and, lastly, to revise the formation of young people.[43] And so, a far-reaching about-face and restructuring of the entire Congregation of the Legionaries was imposed. Following this report, on June 16, 2010, the pope named Archbishop Velasio De Paolis, apostolic delegate for the visitation of the Congregation of the Legionaries of Christ. He was to govern the congregation in the pope's name, to assist the process of renewal, and to guide it toward the celebration of an Extraordinary General Chapter that would approve new statutes. The pope's letter of July 19 was accompanied by a decree of the Secretariat of State that further specified the tasks of the delegate and, above all, insisted that all the branches of the congregation and of the Regnum Christi movement had to cooperate fully with Archbishop De Paolis. The decisive intervention of Pope Benedict bore fruit with the convocation of the Extraordinary General Chapter of the Congregation of the Legionaries that took place at the beginning of 2014.

On February 6, the Chapter released a message in which it declared: "We have asked forgiveness from God and from those who have suffered because of these incidents, and we renew our commitment to make sure that they are not repeated in the future."[44] The conclusion of the Chapter also brought to an end the papal mandate

---

[41] Communiqué of the Holy See regarding the Apostolic Visitation of the Congregation of the Legionaries of Christ, May 1, 2010. English translation from the Vatican website.

[42] Ibid.

[43] Ibid.

[44] http://www.lastampa.it/2014/02/25/vaticaninsider/ita/vaticano/legionari-il-cardinale-de-paolis-comincia-una-nuova-era-713SjzBLAgljFozpb4SAPJ/pagina.html.

of now-Cardinal De Paolis, who could thus speak of a new era that was dawning for the Legionaries.

THE POPE MEETS THE VICTIMS OF ABUSE

The crisis caused by the succession of news stories about new cases of clerical sex abuse in Australia, Canada, Germany, Great Britain, Malta, Austria, and Italy[45] reached an apex during Lent of 2010. The tension was further aggravated by some inappropriate statements by representatives of the Roman Curia. Intending to defend Benedict from personal accusations being made against him especially by German-speaking countries, on April 2, 2010, Good Friday, the preacher of the papal household, Father Raniero Cantalamessa, compared the suffering of the Church and of the pope due to the accusations brought about by sexual abuse to the most shameful aspects of anti-Semitism. What followed was the indignation of the Jewish world and, of course, of the abuse victims and their relatives.

Two days later, on Easter, Cardinal Sodano, in his capacity as dean of the College of Cardinals, addressed greetings to the pope. Expressing his solidarity with the pontiff, the former secretary of state described as mere "gossip" the accusations arising from the pedophilia scandals. It was an unfortunate expression, rousing the ire even of the cardinal of Vienna, Archbishop Schönborn.[46] For his part, Pope Benedict, rather than respond to the polemics started by the new revelations, for a few years had already chosen the path of drawing nearer to the victims. Whereas often the authorities of the Church had sought to cover up or to ignore the phenomenon, the pope had decided to meet with abuse victims to ask for their

---

[45] Probably the most sensational case was that of Monsignor Lelio Cantini, a priest from Florence who was accused of numerous acts of sexual abuse over a period of twenty years and reduced to the lay state in 2008. Another case that caused an uproar was that of a priest from Lodi, Father Domenico Pezzini, professor of English literature at the University of Verona, who was sentenced to ten years in prison for abuse of minors. Another case that was the talk of Italy was that of the Irish bishop John Magee, former secretary of Paul VI, John Paul I, and John Paul II. He resigned from his post, but in reality it was a forced resignation.

[46] Rodari and Tornielli, *Attacco a Ratzinger*, 202. Cardinal Schönborn was particularly sensitive on the issue since his predecessor in Vienna, Cardinal Hermann Groër, had been ensnared in a history of abuse, leaving in the diocese a trail of controversies, for which he had to provide solutions. For more on this, see 235–44.

forgiveness; to express the closeness of the Church to their suffer-ings; to promise justice and solidarity. Almost as if to compensate for the lack of courage on the part of bishops and others in eccle-siastical authority, the pope put himself on the front line, listening to victims, weeping with them.

The first encounter came about during his visit to the United States on April 17, 2008, in the nunciature in Washington. Other encounters followed in Australia, Canada, Malta, as well as in Erfurt, Germany, and in London. The best documented of these encoun-ters took place in Malta, where one of the victims, Joseph Magro, told journalists: "The Pope wept along with me, although he is in no way guilty for what happened to me."[47] The pope, interviewed by Seewald, commented: "Actually I could not say anything special at all to them. I was able to tell them that it affects me very deeply. That I suffer with them. And that was not just an expression, but it really touches my heart. And I was able to tell them that the Church will do everything possible so that this does not happen again, and that we intend to help them as well as we can."[48]

In short, the pope reversed an established practice. While usually the intermediary authorities took the blame for possible omissions of their superiors, here the exact opposite took place. The pope, as a humble servant in the vineyard of the Lord, took upon himself the faults of priests and even the failures of bishops.

THE ROAD IS LONG

To sum up, the more severe measures imposed by Benedict XVI for sex abuse crimes committed by priests were: an apostolic visi-tation, equivalent to a sort of external administration, which took place in American seminaries; an apostolic visitation that took place in practically all the dioceses of Ireland; an apostolic visitation and pontifical delegate consisting of Velasio Cardinal De Paolis for the case of Maciel Degollado and the Congregation of the Legionaries of Christ. Pope Benedict, nevertheless, was careful to state clearly that the way of purification would be long and painful. In his let-ter to the Catholics of Ireland, he wrote: "No one imagines that this

---

[47] Benedict XVI, *Light of the World*, 33.
[48] Ibid.

painful situation will be resolved swiftly. Real progress has been made, yet much more remains to be done."[49]

In his customary address at the end of the year to the Roman Curia, the pope recalled a vision of Saint Hildegard of Bingen, who compared the Church to a woman whose countenance had a sublime splendor but was covered with dust and whose dress was torn on account of the sins of priests. "The way she saw and expressed it is the way we have experienced it this year."[50] Of course, the pope knew that pedophilia does not concern Catholic priests alone; that certain media were biased; that documents had often been provided to newspapers by the lawyers for the prosecution, who had a personal interest in making known the arguments of their clients, ignoring the possible fine points of the defense; and that the pedophiles themselves were led to highlight the faults of their superiors, so as thus to diminish their own responsibility.[51]

Nevertheless, Benedict did not allow himself to be consoled by these considerations. While traveling on an airplane to Lisbon, he told journalists: "The greatest persecution of the Church comes not from her enemies without, but arises from sin within the Church, and . . . the Church thus has a deep need to relearn penance, to accept purification, to learn forgiveness on the one hand, but also the need for justice."[52]

Finally, when asked about the media by Seewald, the pope concluded: "Insofar as it is the truth, we must be grateful for every disclosure. The truth, combined with love rightly understood, is the number-one value. And finally, the media could not have reported in this way had there not been evil in the Church herself."[53]

Anglican converts to Catholicism and the pope's trip to England

That branch of the Anglican Communion in England, in America, and in Australia, which did not share the more liberal open-mindedness of the official Anglican Communion, was called "TAC",

---

[49] Benedict XVI, Letter to the Catholics of Ireland, no. 2.

[50] Benedict XVI, Address on the Occasion of Christmas Greetings to the Roman Curia, December 20, 2010.

[51] See Introvigne, I preti pedofili, 35–41.

[52] Benedict XVI, Interview with the Journalists during the Flight to Portugal, May 11, 2010.

[53] Benedict XVI, Light of the World, 27.

meaning "Traditional Anglican Communion". In particular, TAC, which in 2009 had almost 400,000 members, refused to allow women and active homosexual persons admission to priestly and episcopal ordination. In an interview with the Australian newspaper *The Record*, Bishop John Hepworth of Adelaide (as of 2007 the former head of these Anglicans) indicated that he had already contacted the Congregation for the Doctrine of the Faith to seek admittance to the Catholic Church.[54]

After two years of frequent conversations, on October 20, 2009, in Rome and in London, two simultaneous press conferences were held. Present in the Vatican press office were the prefect of the Congregation for the Doctrine of the Faith, William Cardinal Levada, and his under-secretary, Augustine Di Noia. In London, on the other hand, Vincent Nichols, primate of the Catholic Church in England, and Rowan Williams, primate of the Anglican Communion. Together, the four prelates announced the promulgation of an apostolic constitution that Benedict XVI had prepared to welcome Anglican traditionalists into the Catholic Church. The unusual format of the dual press conference served, on the one hand, to avoid possible leaks of the news and, on the other hand, to calm Anglican and Catholic public opinion.

The welcoming of a group of Anglicans into the Catholic Church came about without breaking off the ecumenical dialogue between the two Christian confessions, as the presence of the Anglican primate at the press conference testified, along with his letter announcing the event to the Anglican bishops. After lamenting the tardiness with which he had been informed, the primate writes: "In the light of recent discussions with senior officials in the Vatican, I can say that this new possibility is in no sense at all intended to undermine existing relations between our two communions or to be an act of proselytism or aggression."[55]

Announced on October 20, the apostolic constitution was made public on November 4, 2009. It speaks above all about the insistent requests that came from groups of Anglicans who were asking to enter into full communion with the Catholic Church. The pope, therefore, decided to act upon these requests and to promote a

---

[54] Cited by Rodari and Tornielli, *Attacco a Ratzinger*, 245.

[55] http://www.catholicnewsagency.com/news/anglican_and_catholic_archbishops_say _declaration_wont_change_dialogue/.

fraternal welcome: he intended to institute personal ordinariates for the faithful who desire to enter corporately, that is, as a group, into communion with the Catholic Church. These personal ordinariates, dependent on the Congregation for the Doctrine of the Faith, are juridically set up like a diocese with lay faithful, clergy, and religious. The normative profession of faith for these faithful, who now become fully Catholic, is found in the *Catechism of the Catholic Church*, while the Code of Canon Law and the norms contained in the apostolic constitution govern their ecclesial structure.

Since the Catholic Church does not recognize the Anglican hierarchy, the ministers—bishops, priests, and deacons—can be welcomed into the Catholic hierarchy as candidates for Holy Orders; they must still, therefore, be ordained. Bishops and priests who are married can be ordained priests, and a married bishop can be appointed an ordinary but cannot be consecrated a bishop. Moreover, even in the future, the ordinary can ask, on a case-by-case basis, to confer priestly ordination on married men—an innovation of no small significance. From now on, in fact, in the Catholic Church there will be married priests in the Eastern Byzantine Catholic Churches and in the personal ordinariates coming from the Anglican Communion. Furthermore, this could be the way by which, where needed, even in the universal Catholic Church, one day there could be the ordination of married Catholic men who prove themselves worthy of sure trust (*viri probati*).[56] The provision of Pope Benedict roused not a few critics among both Anglicans and Catholics. Among the latter, once again Hans Küng weighed in with an article entitled, "The Pope Who Fishes in Waters on the Right", published in *La Repubblica*; he spoke of "a tragedy: after Pope Benedict XVI has offended the Jews and Muslims, the Protestants and reform-minded Catholics, it is now the turn of the Anglicans."[57]

More understandably, the October 21 issue of the London *Times*, too, immediately after the announcement of the upcoming publication of the apostolic constitution, expressed perplexity espe-

---

[56] This was, however, the path indicated by Ratzinger both in a series of radio talks from 1969–1970, *Faith and the Future* (Chicago: Franciscan Herald Press, 1971; repr., San Francisco: Ignatius Press, 2009), and in his book-length interview, *Salt of the Earth*, 199–200.

[57] Hans Küng, "That Pope Who Fishes in Waters on the Right Side", *La Repubblica*, 28/10 (2009).

cially about the secrecy with which the negotiations had been conducted.[58] It should also be noted that the English newspaper did not know that the silence had been explicitly and insistently asked for by those Anglicans who had desired to move over to Rome. The climate in England was not very serene when, in September 2010, having accepted the invitation of the English government, Benedict XVI prepared to visit Great Britain. However, as had already happened in the past, by his attitude and words, the pope succeeded in scattering many of the clouds that had gathered during the past year.

In keeping with the program, the pope arrived in Great Britain on September 16 and was welcomed in the royal residence of Holyroodhouse by Queen Elizabeth II. There the pontiff introduced in some fashion the theme that would be played out during his English sojourn: the risks to which society is exposed when religious faith is excluded from the public debate. And so, the German pope paid homage to the strenuous resistance put up by England to the Nazi aggression during the Second World War. It was almost a *captatio benevolentiae*, which effectively won interest and affection for Pope Benedict.

More compelling was the next day's address in Westminster Hall, where the pope was welcomed by the Speakers of the House of Lords and the House of Commons. After the customary expressions of thanks, the pope recalled the figure of Saint Thomas More, venerated by Catholics and Anglicans alike, who had been put to death "for the integrity with which he followed his conscience".[59] He is the example of a politician who knew how to keep the proper balance between the demands of the State and fidelity to one's own conscience. Moreover, the story of Saint Thomas More has continual relevance. In fact, according to the constant conviction of Benedict, the State cannot base itself exclusively on social consensus but also needs an ethical foundation.

This is precisely the point on which the Catholic Church can offer the State her own contribution, not so much by means of technical responses and concrete political solutions, but by helping to identify objective moral principles grounded in reason. And here

---

[58] See Rodari and Tornielli, *Attacco a Ratzinger*, 256.
[59] Benedict XVI, Address to the Political and Civil Authorities, Westminster, England, September 17, 2010.

the pope repeated another principle that is dear to him: "This is why I would suggest that the world of reason and the world of faith—the world of secular rationality and the world of religious belief—need one another and should not be afraid to enter into a profound and ongoing dialogue, for the good of our civilization."[60] In fact, without religion, the State can easily fall into ideology, as in the time of Saint Thomas More; without reason, religion can fall into sectarianism and fundamentalism.

The high point of the pope's visit to Great Britain arrived on September 19 with the beatification of John Henry Cardinal Newman. The very decision of the pope to participate in the celebration signaled the importance that he attributed to the event. The great man of the Church and of English culture had been a model for the German theologian from his youth. Their biographies, as well as their convictions in the political and cultural arena, had several points in common. Thus, in his homily of beatification in Cofton Park in Birmingham, the pope said:

> His insights into the relationship between faith and reason, into the vital place of revealed religion in civilized society, and into the need for a broadly-based and wide-ranging approach to education were not only of profound importance for Victorian England, but continue today to inspire and enlighten many all over the world. I would like to pay particular tribute to his vision for education, which has done so much to shape the ethos that is the driving force behind Catholic schools and colleges today.[61]

Another passage of the beatification address highlighted another feature dear to both Newman and Ratzinger: that of a Catholic laity that is well prepared, well balanced, ready to offer an apologetic for the reasonableness of their faith. Using Newman's own words, the pope said: "I want a laity, not arrogant, not rash in speech, not disputatious, but men who know their religion, who enter into it, who know just where they stand, who know what they hold and what they do not, who know their creed so well that they can give an account of it, who know so much of history that they can defend it (*The Present Position of Catholics in England*, ix, 390)."

---

[60] Ibid.

[61] Benedict XVI, Homily at Mass with the Beatification of Venerable Cardinal John Henry Newman, Birmingham, England, September 19, 2010.

As in France in previous years, by the end of the visit, the pope had conquered England, too. His invitation to welcome religion in order to escape a dictatorship of relativism had found a not-so-superficial hearing; his appeal to respect the conscience and dignity of man did not seem to fall on deaf ears.

The Pontifical Council for the New Evangelization

The most difficult year of Benedict's pontificate concluded with the establishment of the Pontifical Council for Promoting the New Evangelization. The pope announced it in his homily on the Vigil of Saints Peter and Paul, June 28, 2010.[62] Underlying the pope's decision was another insight harking back to Vatican II. Several times, in the Pastoral Constitution on the Church in the Modern World, the council Fathers had sought to redefine the meaning of the Church's presence in the world and her way of relating to the rest of mankind. Consequently, the Decree on the Missionary Activity of the Church presented concrete proposals for the task of the Christian proclamation to men—or evangelization—to take the form of witness, dialogue, presence in charity.[63]

For his part, Paul VI, who was elected during the Second Vatican Council, chose as his name that of the Apostle of the Gentiles, and in 1974, pursuing his program of conciliar implementation, he convoked a synod on the theme of evangelization in the modern world. Therefore, in the Apostolic Exhortation *Evangelii nuntiandi*, he recalled that "the effort to proclaim the Gospel to the people of today . . . is a service rendered to the Christian community and also to the whole of humanity."[64] And John Paul II, already during his first visit to Poland, used the expression "New Evangelization" whereby, according to Benedict, the adjective refers not to the contents but rather to the search for "ways that correspond with the power of the Holy Spirit and which are suited to the times and situations".[65] The newness, as the pope went on to explain, refers also

---

[62] Benedict XVI, Homily at First Vespers of the Solemnity of Sts. Peter and Paul, June 28, 2010.

[63] See Vatican Council II, *Ad gentes*, in particular chap. 2, no. 11.

[64] See Paul VI, Apostolic Exhortation *Evangelii nuntiandi*, December 8, 1975.

[65] Benedict XVI, Homily for First Vespers for the Solemnity of Sts. Peter and Paul, June 28, 2010.

to the fact that the countries that had already received the proclamation of the Gospel in past centuries needed new evangelization.

The announcement of the new dicastery, on June 28, 2010, was
confirmed on September 21 of the same year with a *motu proprio*
that then further specified the tasks of the new Pontifical Council,
whose president would be Bishop Rino Fisichella, then an auxiliary
bishop of Rome and rector of the Lateran University. Furthermore,
in the September 21 decree, the pope insisted more forcefully on
the need to promote the new evangelization in countries with an
ancient Christian tradition where, due to the ever more widespread
abandonment of Christian practice and tradition, there is need for
"a renewed missionary impulse, an expression of a new, generous
openness to the gift of grace".[66]

As Bishop Fisichella observed at the presentation of the document, this is a great challenge, starting from a realistic assessment
of the present situation in the Church. Benedict, therefore, was not
resigned to the decline of Christianity in Europe but, rather, looked
courageously at the reality and sought concrete ways to turn around
a trend that by then had lasted several decades.

---

[66] Benedict XVI, Apostolic Letter in the Form of Motu Proprio *Ubicumque et semper*
Establishing the Pontifical Council for Promoting the New Evangelization, September
21, 2010.

XVIII

I MUST RESIGN

The photographer of the BBC who took the photo that showed the dome of Saint Peter's struck by a bolt of lightning on the day of Pope Benedict's resignation admitted that he had spent three-quarters of an hour in the deluge waiting for that electrical discharge. He wanted to suggest the idea of decadence, of the end of the world, or at least of an epochal turning point.[1] The photo was a success; it soon made its way around the world and was considered by many the symbolic image of what had taken place. In reality, the photo is totally extraneous to the theological vision of Pope Benedict and to the spirit that led him to resign from the Petrine ministry. Similarly, the Italian journalist Antonio Socci wrote a book entitled *Non è Francesco*,[2] suggesting that Benedict XVI's role as pope was not over and that Pope Francis was a usurper. Here, too, nothing could be farther from the thought and the sentiment of the pope emeritus.

In his life, as in his vision of Christianity, he was always a supporter of reform in continuity, while it should never be forgotten that many years before in Tubingen he had signed a petition calling for term limits for bishops.[3] More precisely, the term called for was a period of eight years, which, as it happens, coincides exactly with the eight years of his pontificate. This does not mean that Ratzinger shared the ecclesiological view on which that petition was based or

---

[1] Joseph M. Kraus, *Il perché di una scelta: Le parole di Benedetto XVI* (Rome: Moralia, 2013), 7.

[2] Antonio Socci, *Non è Francesco* (Milan: Mondadori, 2014).

[3] See above, chap. 5 and, more extensively, Gianni Valente, *Ratzinger professore* (Cinisello Balsamo: San Paolo, 2008), 145–47.

that he considered it valid for the papacy, also. It is certain, however, that the thought of resignation had been with him both during his years as a professor and in his last years with the Congregation for the Doctrine of the Faith. And, as pontiff, while visiting Aquila, the city hit by a terrible earthquake in 2009, Benedict insisted on going into the Basilica of Collemaggio, where he left the pallium he had received on the inaugural day of his pontificate on top of the urn of Pope Celestine, the pope who, according to Dante, made the grand refusal.

Blessed John Paul II

In June 2005, making an exception to the norm that requires a waiting period of at least five years after the death of a Servant of God before initiating a cause of beatification, Benedict XVI authorized the beginning of the diocesan investigation into the life, virtues, and reputation for holiness and miracles of the Servant of God John Paul II. This very rapid start had been requested by the faithful the very day of the funeral rites for the Polish pope and in some way confirmed by the dean of the College of Cardinals, Ratzinger, who in his homily had affirmed: "We can be sure that our beloved Pope is standing today at the window of the Father's house, that he sees us and blesses us."[4] When he became pope in turn, Benedict not only authorized the much-anticipated beginning of the cause of canonization, but seemed never to miss an opportunity to show his own esteem and affection for his beloved predecessor.[5] Nor were the words of the new pope mere conventional courtesy.

The two pontiffs, who had collaborated for more than twenty years in governing the Church, were joined by friendship, affection, and veneration: an example of communion destined to go down in history. Swiftly begun, the cause was then prepared according to the rules and reached its completion at the beginning of 2011, when the commission of cardinals recognized the validity of the proposed miracle. The only thing remaining was to establish the

---

[4] Joseph Ratzinger, Homily at the Funeral Mass for the Roman Pontiff John Paul II, April 8, 2005.

[5] Joseph Ratzinger, *Giovanni Paolo II: Il mio amato predecessore,* ed. E. Guerriero (Cinisello Balsamo: San Paolo, 2007), 67.

date of the celebration. It was set for May 1 of that same year. In his homily for the beatification, Benedict himself listed the reasons that had led him to make that decision. It was *Dominica in albis*, the First Sunday after Easter, which John Paul II had established as the feast of Divine Mercy. "In God's providence", John Paul II had died in the evening of the vigil of Divine Mercy Sunday.[6] Moreover, it was May, the month dedicated to Mary, to whom John Paul II had been particularly devoted, and it was the liturgical memorial of Saint Joseph the Worker, patron of those workers for whom Bishop Wojtyła had demonstrated particular solicitude.

Continuing the homily of beatification, Benedict set aside for once his serene and rational argument and let himself be carried away by a burst of enthusiasm. John Paul II had been one of God's giants, who had transmitted to Christians enthusiasm for the faith, the strength of witness. For long years, Benedict had been at John Paul's side and had had an opportunity to verify firsthand "his witness of faith, love and apostolic courage, accompanied by great human charisma".[7] He went on: "His example of prayer continually impressed and edified me: he remained deeply united to God even amid the many demands of his ministry."[8] In short, Pope John Paul II had been a saint who had guided the people of God in crossing the threshold of the third millennium. "His profound humility, grounded in close union with Christ, enabled him to continue to lead the Church and to give to the world a message which became all the more eloquent as his physical strength declined."[9] For Benedict, this was a day of joy and enthusiasm, like an oasis in which he finally had an opportunity to divert his gaze from the clouds that seemed to accumulate over his pontificate day by day.

One cannot renounce God: A new visit to Germany

Asked by Seewald about his apostolic journeys and more generally about the years of his pontificate, Benedict XVI gave an answer that, for the most part, was positive: "Everywhere one sensed the

---

[6] Benedict XVI, Homily for the Beatification of John Paul II, May 1, 2011.
[7] Ibid.
[8] Ibid.
[9] Ibid.

awareness that the Catholic Church is alive and full of energy."[10] However, he did not hide the fact that there had also been disappointments coming, above all, from Europe, where "secularity continues to assert its independence and to develop in forms that increasingly lead people away from the faith."[11] The greatest disappointment, however, came from Catholic Germany, where there is "a rather large group of people who, so to say, are on the lookout for an opportunity to attack the Pope."[12] However, Benedict did not lose heart, and in 2011 he accepted an invitation to make a third trip to Germany, even though since the beginning of his pontificate the situation certainly had not improved among Catholics. The pope himself would allude to this in Freiburg, in the meeting with committed Catholics, when he spoke of a Church that considers herself self-sufficient and that accommodates herself to this world.

WHERE GOD IS, THERE IS A FUTURE

The theme chosen by the pope for his visit, "Where God is, there is a future", was a challenge for Berlin, for Germany, and for Europe and, at the same time, a warning for those who think they can do without God. The pope gave his most compelling address immediately after he arrived in Berlin, on September 22, 2011, before the German Parliament. Desiring to demonstrate the necessity of the presence of God in the lives of individuals and of peoples, the pope invited his audience first and foremost to reflect on the foundations of the liberal State. More directly, for the representatives of the people the question is: If politics is the search for justice, how can one arrive at the knowledge of what is just? The question becomes particularly critical when there are differences of opinion regarding the very nature of man.

Here one cannot have recourse to the law of the majority or the law of the minority; legal positivism is not enough. It is necessary once again to make room for nature and for reason, the classic sources of law. Therefore, establishing a comparison with the ecology of the world, Benedict spoke about an ecology of man. "Man

---

[10] Benedict XVI, *Light of the World: The Pope, the Church, and the Signs of the Times,* trans. Michael J. Miller and Adrian J. Walker (San Francisco: Ignatius Press, 2010), 127.

[11] Ibid., 128.

[12] Ibid., 125.

too has a nature that he must respect and that he cannot manipulate at will. Man is not merely self-creating freedom."[13] Especially as Germans, the pope added, we ought to know the abuses to which freedom built on irrationality can lead. And, therefore, should we Europeans not look to the cultural patrimony of Europe and create new space for the idea that nature presupposes a creative Reason, a creator Spirit? The pope continued: "The culture of Europe arose from the encounter between Jerusalem, Athens and Rome—from the encounter between Israel's monotheism, the philosophical reason of the Greeks and Roman law."[14] If we renounce even one of these elements, we build an edifice resembling one of those cement-block buildings without air and greenery.

IN LUTHER'S MONASTERY

The following day, the pope traveled to Erfurt, the city of Luther, the Augustinian friar who, in the sixteenth century, began the Protestant Reformation. The theme of the meetings, ecumenism, was in some way obligatory, and the pope did not shy away from it. In the chapter hall of the former Augustinian monastery, speaking to representatives of the Lutheran Evangelical Church in Germany and to numerous other Protestant communities, the pope was visibly moved. In this monastery, he said, Luther studied theology, celebrated his first Mass, sought a response to the question that never gave him any peace: "How can I have a merciful God?" This question, the pope continued, is as relevant as ever in our day, too, when even Christians seem to take for granted a generic benevolence of God who would always be ready to forgive our shortcomings. However, are our faults always so little and so cheaply forgivable? And is this not a trivialization of the faith, against which Luther rebelled? Pope Benedict concluded: "Yet it is not by watering the faith down, but by living it today in its fullness that we achieve this. This is a key ecumenical task in which we have to help one another: developing a deeper and livelier faith."[15]

---

[13] Benedict XVI, Address at the visit to Bundestag, Germany, September 22, 2011.
[14] Ibid.
[15] Benedict XVI, Address at the Meeting with the Council of the Evangelical Church in Germany, September 23, 2011.

After the meeting in the chapter hall, an ecumenical celebration followed in the church of the former monastery of the Augustinians, during which the pope returned to the theme of our common faith in God. During the days preceding the visit, there had been some leaks to the effect that the pope would make a grand gesture, a kind of gift to give a new impulse to ecumenism. However, at the risk of disappointing expectations, Benedict made it clear that in questions of faith, compromises do not work—unity is produced by the common faith in God. This common witness of faith is the gift of God to secularized society: "A thirst for the infinite is indelibly present in human beings. Man was created to have a relationship with God; we need him."[16] The contribution that Benedict sought, both from Lutherans and from Catholics, was the common witness of faith in one's personal life and in civil life.

COURAGE AND UNITY ON THE WAY OF FAITH

The trip to Germany concluded in Freiburg with Mass celebrated on the esplanade of the city's airport. In his homily, the pope addressed Catholics directly and did not hide his concern about the state of the faith in his homeland.[17] There are theologians, warned the pope, who, when faced with the evils of the world, maintain that God cannot be omnipotent. The pope disagreed. God is omnipotent but respects our freedom and manifests his power through his forgiveness and mercy. However, in order to be touched by his mercy, it is necessary to stand up to indifference and to welcome his Word. Benedict continued in a stern tone: In the civil society of the agnostics, there are those who do not find peace because of the "God question". There are, on the other hand, "routine" Catholics who live only superficially, without their hearts being truly touched by faith. Believers, too, must open their hearts to Christ anew, to hold firm to their faith in him. As Christ was totally united to the Father and obedient to him, so too his disciples must obey God and have the same mind-set among themselves.

The farewell message of the pope to his country was a severe warning to the German Church:

---

[16] Benedict XVI, Address, Ecumenical Prayer Service, Erfurt, Germany, September 23, 2011.

[17] Benedict XVI, Homily at Mass in Freiburg im Breisgau, September 25, 2011.

The Church in Germany . . . will remain a leaven in society, if the priests, consecrated men and women, and the lay faithful, in fidelity to their respective vocations, work together in unity, if the parishes, communities, and movements support and enrich each other, if the baptized and confirmed, in union with their bishop, lift high the torch of untarnished faith and allow it to enlighten their abundant knowledge and skills. The Church in Germany will continue to be a blessing for the entire Catholic world: if she remains faithfully united with the Successors of Saint Peter and the Apostles, if she fosters cooperation in various ways with mission countries and allows herself to be "infected" by the joy that marks the faith of these young Churches.[18]

Therefore, anyone who was expecting an accommodating pope was disappointed. Benedict preferred to trust the faith of the simple and the enthusiasm of young people; he was not prepared to indulge accommodation. Returning to the subject in the customary report to the Curia, Pope Benedict extended his diagnosis to all of Europe: "The essence of the crisis of the Church in Europe is the crisis of faith. If we find no answer to this, . . . then all other reforms will remain ineffective."[19]

The Door of Faith

Less than a month after his German trip, Benedict XVI announced his intention to proclaim an extraordinary Year of Faith, to begin on October 11, 2012, the fiftieth anniversary of the beginning of the Second Vatican Council and the twentieth anniversary of the publication of the *Catechism of the Catholic Church*. As he recalled in his *motu proprio Porta fidei*, with which he announced the event, the way of faith had been his constant preoccupation since his election to the Chair of Peter. With the passing of time, however, the pope had realized that, particularly in the West, proclaiming the Gospel in such a way as to open the door to introduce someone to communion with God and entrance into the Church had become so urgent that it could no longer be put off. For this reason, together with the Year of Faith, he had decided to convoke an extraordinary synod on evangelization, to begin also on October 11.

---

[18] Ibid.

[19] Benedict XVI, Address on the Occasion of Christmas Greetings to the Roman Curia, December 22, 2011.

Likewise, in his customary address to the Roman Curia at the end of the year, Pope Benedict returned to the theme of the weariness of the faith in Europe. Speaking about his trip to Benin, the fatherland of his dear friend Bernardin Cardinal Gantin, who had died in 2008, Benedict said: "None of the faith fatigue that is so prevalent here, none of the oft-encountered sense of having had enough of Christianity was detectable there."[20] On the contrary, the joyful passion for the faith was a great encouragement, while participation in the August World Youth Day held in Madrid, "was new evangelization put into practice."[21]

THE PILGRIMAGE TO ASSISI

At the end of October 2011, Pope Benedict made a pilgrimage to Assisi where, twenty-five years earlier, John Paul II had invited representatives of the world's religions to pray for peace. As already mentioned,[22] at that time Cardinal Ratzinger did not think it appropriate to participate in an event in which some bishops and cardinals saw the danger of syncretistic confusion. Now, on the other hand, the pope himself was promoting a day of reflection, dialogue, and justice for peace, to which he invited representatives of Christian confessions and non-Christian religions. To make clear that this was a true and proper pilgrimage, the religious leaders left Rome by train. In the car with the pope were the Orthodox patriarch, Bartholomew I; the primate of the Anglicans, Rowan Williams; the Armenian primate of France, Norvan Zakarian; Rabbi David Rosen; delegates of Hinduism, Buddhism, and Islam. For the first time, a representative of nonbelievers participated—Professor Julia Kristeva, a very well-known psychologist in France who, for some years now, had been in dialogue with Jean Vanier, the founder of L'Arche.

Recalling the day of prayer desired by John Paul II twenty-five years earlier, Benedict turned his gaze toward the contemporary situation, marked not so much by the danger of global war as by widespread violence. In the pope's view, at the source of this violence were two types of motivation, on which it was appropriate to

---

[20] Ibid.
[21] Ibid.
[22] See chap. 12.

reflect, engage in dialogue, and pray so as to eliminate it. The first was of a religious nature. Already for quite some time, proponents of secular thought pointed an accusatory finger at these motivations, and it was urgent to undertake an interreligious dialogue in order to "argue realistically and credibly against religiously motivated violence".[23] For his part, the pope sorrowfully recognized that above all in the past the Christian religion had also contributed to generating forms of violence. However, these were abuses of religion; the Christian Creed is built on the Gospel message of love. He supposed that the same observation could be made about other religions. At any rate, it was the task of interreligious dialogue to reflect on the nature of religions so as to avoid even a hint of violence.

The second set of motivations for violence had their origins in the denial of God and the consequent loss of humanity. "The absence of God leads to the decline of man and of humanity."[24] Therefore, the pope said, it would be necessary that even nonbelievers ask themselves about the origin of violence. Essentially, this was the same observation that Ratzinger had made at the beginning of his book *Introduction to Christianity*: "Anyone who makes up his mind to evade the uncertainty of belief will have to experience the uncertainty of unbelief."[25] Between faith and non-faith, however, Ratzinger identified a third attitude, which was that of so many people who suffer on account of the absence of God and, seeking the true and the good, are interiorly on a journey toward him as "pilgrims of truth, pilgrims of grace".[26] He invited them to accept and to make their own the journey of religions, the journey of Christians. These latter were, in their own way, warmly invited to engage in a process of purification in order to regain communion with God and the enthusiasm of the proclamation of the Gospel.

Vatileaks

After two years tormented by the scandals of sex abuse, at the beginning of 2012, Benedict XVI probably thought of giving a

---

[23] Benedict XVI, Address at the Meeting for Peace in Assisi, October 27, 2011.

[24] Ibid.

[25] Joseph Ratzinger, *Introduction to Christianity*, trans. J. R. Foster (San Francisco: Ignatius Press, 2004), 45.

[26] Benedict XVI, Address at the Meeting for Peace in Assisi, October 27, 2011.

significant direction to his pontificate by preparing the Year of Faith, which was supposed to allow the Church to turn the page. It was no coincidence that the pope had begun to work on his third encyclical on a theological virtue, to be published at the end of the year. A new ambush, however, awaited the pontiff, which would put his physical and spiritual energies to a difficult test. During the first few months of 2012, with suspicious timing, news leaked out about private documents taken from the pope's desk and handed over to journalists for publication. As in the case of Bishop Williamson, once again the Holy See found itself defenseless before the new laws of communication. It was understood this time that it was necessary to react quickly. However, no one knew where to begin. Meanwhile, publication began of the most significant documents concerning the already-mentioned Boffo case[27] and the letter sent by Cardinal Sardi to Benedict XVI to inform him about the problems in the workings of the Curia.[28] Then, however, the news began to focus on what seemed to be the true objective: the governance of the Church and the management of the Vatican finances by the Institute of Religious Works, the so-called "Vatican Bank".

THE POPE'S DESK

Faced with the repeated news leaks, on March 31, 2012, the pope decided to intervene by establishing a commission of cardinals whose members included: the Spanish Julián Cardinal Herranz as president, the Slovak Jozef Cardinal Tomko, and the Italian Salvatore Cardinal De Giorgi. Set up on April 24, 2012, according to the announcement made by Father Lombardi, the commission found itself facing an absolutely unheard-of situation. At the beginning of the investigations, the three cardinals did not have a single clue. What was certain, however, was the place from which the documents came: the pope's desk, located in the apartment on the third floor of the Apostolic Palace. Here a few, trusted persons had access: the first secretary, the German Georg Gänswein; the second secretary, the Maltese Alfred Xuereb; and the pope's *camerlengo*, Paolo

---

[27] See above, chap. 16.
[28] See above, chap. 17.

Gabriele, a sort of butler who, at the time when he was hired, had been recommended by the aforementioned Cardinal Sardi as a trustworthy man.

Less frequently, the "Memores" of Communion and Liberation came in to do cleaning, but they did not have the means to look at documents. In those days in the papal apartment, there was an unusual tension in the air. Monsignor Gänswein, who in turn was questioned by the three cardinals and succeeded in showing that he was not involved, spoke of difficult and delicate moments.[29] Besides, Monsignor Gänswein himself was the one who solved the mystery by inserting among the papers on the pope's desk a document that he alone knew about. When this document was also leaked, it was evident that the perpetrator of the theft of the documents could only be Paolo Gabriele. He was a simple man who, on the one hand, by conviction and, on the other hand, at the instigation of people desirous of greater recognition,[30] sought by his action to rein in the excessive power held by Cardinal Bertone and Monsignor Gänswein.[31]

Probably, he had also underestimated the impact of his initiative. In any case, on May 25, Father Lombardi was able to announce that the three cardinals had gathered sufficient proof to accuse Paolo Gabriele, who, in fact, had been arrested. The trial began on September 29 and concluded, after only four hearings, on October 6 with the sentence of Paolo Gabriele to eighteen months in prison for theft. Together with him, Claudio Sciarpelletti, an information expert and a employee of the Secretariat of State, was accused of being an accomplice. However, the court cut short the trial of Sciarpelletti, whose responsibility, however, was less significant. The defense itself considered Paolo Gabriele's sentence fair; he remained in jail for only a few months, since before the end of

---

[29] This was shared with me by the present prefect of the pontifical household.

[30] Also named were Frau Ingrid Stampa, former housekeeper for Cardinal Ratzinger in his apartment at Piazza della Città Leonina, and the previous secretary in the Congregation for the Doctrine of the Faith, Josef Clemens. However, given their positions, no measures against them were deemed justifiable.

[31] As was then shown, Paolo Gabriele was the one who had photocopied the documents from the pope's desk and handed them over to the journalist Gianluigi Nuzzi, who made them public by some television broadcasts and by the publication in June 2012 of his book *Sua Santità: Le carte segrete di Benedetto XVI* (Milan: Chiarelettere, 2012).

the year he was released through a pardon granted him by Pope Benedict.

The court, finally, convinced of having sufficiently ascertained the facts, did not consider it necessary to proceed against other persons who at first had been called to testify in the case of Paolo Gabriele. Beyond the judicial process, however, the evidence showed that "basically, the journalists were not the ones discovering secret, unsettling texts, but, rather, the maneuver started from within the Apostolic Palace."[32]

IS THE TARGET ONLY CARDINAL BERTONE?

The secretary of state could not be called as a witness concerning the theft of news from the pope's desk. However, the documents that had been stolen and leaked[33] took aim above all at his machinations. The documents concerning the Boffo case and the chaos caused by the trips of the secretary of state, which were considered excessive, as mentioned in the previous chapters, were joined by others related especially to the economic management of Vatican finances. The first case concerned the governorate of the Vatican City State. Since 2009, the secretary general of the governorate had been Archbishop Carlo Maria Viganò, appointed personally by Benedict XVI and charged with the task of putting into order the finances of the governorate, which had been in difficulty for a number of years, also because of the general economic crisis. The bishop, originally from Varese, thought that he had carried out his task well since the losses of the governorate had visibly declined.

In March 2011, however, Archbishop Viganò was summoned by Cardinal Bertone, who told him that his tenure at the governorate had ended. He had been chosen as nuncio to the United States; all that he had to do now was to prepare for his departure. Caught by surprise, the archbishop, who had supposed that he would succeed his direct superior, Giovanni Cardinal Lajolo, as president of the governorate, made a case based on the positive results of his work, but Bertone was not willing to change the decision. The archbishop

---

[32] Marco Politi, "L'uragano Vatileaks", in the book *Il libro dell'anno 2012* (Rome: Treccani, 2013), 371.

[33] See the previously cited book by Gianluigi Nuzzi, *Sua Santità*.

then wrote directly to the pope, informing him of the communication of Cardinal Bertone, the good results he had achieved, the personal disgrace he would experience if, after only two years, he were dismissed from the job that had been entrusted to him by the pontiff himself. In the following months, other memos of defense were sent by Viganò, who considered himself the victim of a plot.

However, the secretary of state and the pope remained firm in their decision, and in November 2011, Archbishop Viganò had to leave for the United States.[34] At that time, the mass media ignored the idea of a plot; with the passage of time, one gets the impression that the bishop had a difficult personality, which won him little sympathy. In fact, there is nothing to warrant talk of a plot.

Another particularly complicated affair that also puts the dealings of Cardinal Bertone in a negative light concerned the management of the Toniolo Institute, founded by the Catholic University of the Sacred Heart of Milan, whose board of directors is in charge of the economic management of the university and of the Gemelli Polyclinic of Rome.[35] Since 2003, Dionigi Cardinal Tettamanzi had been president of the Institute, succeeding Senator Emilio Colombo. In 2011, the secretary of state decided to intervene in the management of the Toniolo Institute. First by phone and then by fax, he ordered Cardinal Tettamanzi, who was due to retire in a few months from his role as the cardinal archbishop of Milan for reasons of age, to hand over the presidency of the Toniolo Institute. He was succeeded by Professor Giovanni Maria Flick, who had already been informed of his appointment.

The abrupt, unconventional mode of communication offended Cardinal Tettamanzi, who saw in it an unjust intrusion into an autonomous organization of the Archdiocese of Milan. Therefore, he decided to respond to the fax of the secretary of state by writing directly to the pope, with whom he had a good rapport; in that letter, he deplored both the manner and the substance of the intervention of the secretary of state. Benedict sought counsel and then invited Cardinal Tettamanzi to Rome; the pope granted him permission to

---

[34] An entire chapter is devoted to the Viganò case in the book by Nuzzi, *Sua Santità*, 53–55. The letters cited are authentic; however, they are interpreted in a rather tendentious manner.

[35] Likewise, the exchange of letters relative to the administration of Toniolo is reprinted in Nuzzi, *Sua Santità*, 163–71.

remain in office for another year. In the meantime, Angelo Cardinal Scola arrived in Milan; he would succeed Cardinal Tettamanzi in 2012 as archbishop and also as president of the Toniolo Institute. For Cardinal Bertone, this was a defeat, like his failed attempt to save San Raffaele Hospital, founded by Father Luigi Verzé.[36]

For quite some time, the Milanese hospital had been in serious economic straits. The secretary of state then devised a plan to establish it as a Catholic medical center, thereby saving the Milanese hospital through an intervention of the Vatican Bank and a private investor, and then joining it to the Gemelli Hospital and to the Roman pediatric hospital, Bambino Gesù. Bertone's plan ran into its first crisis when the investigations of an Italian court, in July 2011, led to the suicide of Mario Cal, the right-hand man of Father Verzé in administration. Later on, Angelo Cardinal Scola, who meanwhile had succeeded Cardinal Tettamanzi, opposed the secretary of state's plan to salvage the Toniolo Institute. The reasons that led Scola to oppose Bertone's project were fear of having to assume responsibility for the debt accrued by the San Raffaele Hospital and the prospect of finding himself in a very uncomfortable position, because research contrary to Catholic ethics was being advanced in Father Verzé's hospital.[37] At this point, the game was over for Cardinal Bertone.

In January 2012, despite the pressure of the banks, which considered the Vatican a good guarantor of their credit, the Vatican Bank did not exercise the option to acquire San Raffaele Hospital, which was then sold to a private investor. The difficult year of the secretary of state concluded with the resignation of Ettore Gotti Tedeschi as president of the Vatican Bank. At the end of the long term of Angelo Caloia, in 2009, Gotti Tedeschi, who had taught strategic finance at the Catholic University of Milan, had been proposed by Bertone, himself, as a candidate for the presidency of the Vatican Bank. He had distinguished himself in terms of competence, his contribution to the restructuring the governorate, and his long-time economic collaboration with *L'Osservatore Romano* on economic topics. Bene-

---

[36] The correspondence relative to San Raffaele is also reprinted in Nuzzi, *Sua Santità*, 171–77.

[37] Likewise, the letter of Cardinal Scola to Monsignor Gänswein is reported in Nuzzi, *Sua Santità*, 173f.

dict XVI had entrusted to him the task of making the Vatican Bank a model of absolute transparency.

Following the pontiff's guidelines, Gotti Tedeschi had effectively introduced into the management of the institute a series of new rules for dealing with globalization and for responding to the requests of the European Union and the International Monetary Fund against the dangers of money-laundering. Always following the pope's instructions, he sought to guarantee the necessary reserve, but not secrecy, because, according to the pope's words, the Vatican Bank must have nothing to hide. According to the experts, the results were encouraging. However, at the beginning of 2012, a stalemate was reached in the so-called Council of Supervision, which, for all practical purposes, functioned as the board of directors of the Vatican Bank, made up of lay people. On one side, there was the president, the aforementioned Ettore Gotti Tedeschi, and, on the other side, the general director, Doctor Paolo Cipriani, who was supported by the other members of the board. In short, Gotti Tedeschi was not trusted by the entire Council of Supervision, so much so that the Cardinals' Oversight Commission had to intervene.

Having ascertained the impossibility of any mediation, the Cardinals' Commission was forced to fire Gotti Tedeschi. Cardinal Bertone was then the one who communicated the decision to the banker, as it would again be the secretary of state who communicated to him, on February 7, 2013, his rehiring, by Pope Benedict's decision.[38] The incident of the president of the Vatican Bank, however, had much in common with the Viganò case, and it had the same result: the pope reaffirmed his trust in the banker but did not consider it opportune to contradict the decision of the secretary of state.

These affairs, brought to the knowledge of the public through the so-called Vatileaks, were added to the many disappointments of that first half of 2012. At the end of May, speaking on the topic, the pope said: "The incidents of these days concerning the Curia and my co-workers have filled my heart with sorrow. . . . For this reason, I wish to renew my trust and my encouragement to my

---

[38] For the whole story leading up to the dismissal of Gotti Tedeschi, see, among others: Marco Ansaldo, "È scontro tra i cardinali sul licenziato di Gotti Tedeschi", *La Repubblica*, June 2, 2012.

closest collaborators and to all who, daily, with fidelity, with a spirit of sacrifice and in silence, help me in fulfilling my daily Ministry."[39]

The theft and publication of the documents taken from the desk of the pope provoked consternation in the Roman Curia and among the world's bishops. The goal was probably the replacement of the secretary of state. The pope, nevertheless, who had already been opposed to such a possibility,[40] believed that it was already too late to think about a change. For the moment, therefore, he decided to proceed without changing the heads of the Vatican hierarchy. The idea of resignation, however, constantly came up in his mind.

The last journeys

MEXICO AND CUBA

The difficulties of the Curia did not slow down the activity of the pope or his care for the life of the universal Church. From March 23 to 29, 2012, the pope had on his calendar a particularly important trip to Latin America, Mexico, and Cuba. For many Latin American countries, the bicentennials of their independence were being celebrated that year. The most heartfelt speech of the pope in Mexico took place in León on Sunday, March 25,[41] addressed to the bishops of the country and to the many representatives of the Caribbean episcopate gathered in the city's cathedral for the celebration of Evening Prayer.

Introducing the address, the pope recalls a circumstance that bears witness to the beauty of communion in the Church: at the synod, it had become customary that when a bishop of a city or town experiencing difficulty spoke, his brother-bishops would accompany his intervention with applause of encouragement. Now addressing the bishops of Mexico and the Caribbean, the pope declared his unity with them in a great embrace of solidarity and accompaniment. Then turning his thought to the upcoming Year of Faith, the pope said that there were two objectives for which they needed to strive: a renewed encounter with Christ, whose grace permits men

[39] Benedict XVI, General Audience, May 30, 2012.
[40] See above, chap. 17.
[41] Benedict XVI, Homily at the Celebration of Vespers with the Bishops of Mexico and Latin America, March 25, 2012.

to free themselves from the chains of sin, and closeness to seminarians, priests, and religious. Then the pope made the recommendation: "Stand beside those who are marginalized as the result of force, power or a prosperity which is blind to the poorest of the poor. The Church cannot separate the praise of God from service to others."[42]

Continuing on his journey, the pope arrived in Santiago, Cuba, on March 26. The following day, he went to the Shrine of Our Lady of Charity of Cobre. In that place, four hundred years earlier, an image of the Virgin had been discovered, to which Cubans of every generation are particularly devoted. John Paul II had not been able to go there in 1998. Benedict was moved and declared: "Let all those you meet know, whether near or far, that I have entrusted to the Mother of God the future of your country, advancing along the ways of renewal and hope, for the greater good of all Cubans. I have also prayed to the Virgin for the needs of those who suffer, of those who are deprived of freedom, those who are separated from their loved ones or who are undergoing times of difficulty."[43]

The prayer anticipated the themes that the pope later addressed in his dialogue with President Raúl Castro upon his arrival in Havana. Father Lombardi explained that in the preceding days numerous requests for humanitarian aid had been made to the pope. Accepting the request of the pope, the president freed a good 2,900 political prisoners, among whom were four Italians.[44] And so, for that reason alone, the trip was a success. The high point of the visit, however, occurred on March 28 with the celebration of Mass in the Plaza de la Revolución, in which more than 300,000 persons participated. The pope again asked for greater religious freedom, declaring that the Church intended only to proclaim Jesus' message of love, reconciliation, and peace. In the late morning, at the nunciature, there was finally the much-awaited meeting with Fidel Castro, the old leader whose health condition had forced him to live a retired, private life. The pope thanked Fidel for the warm welcome, and Fidel declared that he had followed the welcome ceremony on television.

---

[42] Ibid.

[43] Benedict XVI, Words at the Visit to the Shrine of the "Virgen de la Caridad del Cobre", March 27, 2012.

[44] See Aldo Maria Valli, *Benedetto XVI: Il pontificato interrotto* (Milan: Mondadori, 2013), 344.

That trip was particularly tiring for the pope. Upon his return to the Vatican, he felt that he had reached the end of his strength and thought about what he had said to Seewald in an interview a few years earlier: "If a pope clearly realizes that he is no longer physically, psychologically, and spiritually capable of handling the duties of his office, then he has a right and, under some circumstances, also an obligation to resign."[45]

Of particular importance in this sentence is the reference to duty, which in the life of Benedict had been an ideal he constantly pursued. The pope spoke of his health condition with his personal physician, also, the cardiologist Patrizio Polisca, who could not help confirming a state of exhaustion due to the pope's advanced age, which could hardly improve much with the passage of time. In particular, the pope was worried about the trip to the next World Youth Day, to take place in Rio de Janeiro in the summer of 2013. Following the example left by John Paul II, it was unthinkable to have an encounter with young people without the participation of the pope. However, Benedict was already convinced that he did not have sufficient strength to make such a demanding trip. In brief, the idea of retirement continued to take on a more concrete form.

THE POPE IN MILAN

After returning from his trip to Latin America, the pope seemed very tired. He himself acknowledged this somewhat when speaking to the Curia on April 16, 2012, the day of his eighty-fifth birthday: "I am now facing the last chapter of my life and I do not know what awaits me. I know, however, that the light of God exists . . . and this helps me to go forward with certainty."[46] A little more than a month later, the pope was traveling again. The destination was Milan, where the Seventh World Meeting of Families was taking place, from May 30 to June 3. At that time, the Vatileaks scandal was in full swing, which had revealed to a vast public a not insignificant tension between the Secretariat of State and the Curia of Milan. However, for the occasion, all disputes were set aside. On

---

[45] Benedict XVI, *Light of the World*, 30.
[46] Benedict XVI, Homily at the Mass on the Occasion of His Eighty-Fifth Birthday, April 16, 2012.

the contrary, it seemed that the Curia and the Ambrosian diocese (now led by Archbishop Scola, one of the cardinals closest to Pope Benedict) had made very serious efforts to ensure that the event would be a success.

The pope understood what needed to be done, visibly showed his appreciation, and was full of gratitude for the glorious past, but also for the present efforts of Milanese Catholics. In particular, Benedict recalled the fund for the benefit of the families most affected by the economic crisis. This fund had been established by the archbishop emeritus, Dionigi Tettamanzi, who was present for the event. The fund was also established to aid the people of Emilia-Romagna, which, only a short time ago, had been struck by an earthquake. In his homily for Sunday Mass on June 3, the last day of the World Meeting of Families, in the presence of more than a million people who had gathered in the North Park of Milan, Benedict proposed yet again an ideal of family life characterized by Christian humanism: "Family, work, celebration: three of God's gifts, three dimensions of our lives that must be brought into a harmonious balance. Harmonizing work schedules with family demands, professional life with fatherhood and motherhood, work with celebration, is important for building up a society with a human face."[47]

Responding then to the question about separated couples who would like to be reunited with the Church, the pope showed his understanding and closeness to the broken families: "This problem of the divorced-and-remarried is one of the greatest sufferings of the Church today. We have no simple solutions. The suffering is great, and all we can do is help the parishes, the individuals, to assist these persons."[48] These words could not be taken lightly, for they showed families a closeness that was truly heartfelt and sympathetic to their sufferings.

During a break in his visit to Milan, Benedict had the opportunity for a brief encounter with the other cardinal emeritus of the Lombardian capital, Carlo Maria Martini, then seriously ill. The two elderly churchmen, who did not always have the same views on pastoral matters or on how the Church should approach the modern

---

[47] Benedict XVI, Homily at the Mass at the Seventh World Meeting of Families, June 3, 2012.

[48] Valli, *Benedetto XVI*, 351.

world, had known and respected one another for a long time. They had a very brief encounter in which communication took place more through their knowing glances than through words.

Upon the death of the Jesuit Silvano Fausti, Martini's former confessor, Gian Guido Vecchi reported a story that the Jesuit Father had repeatedly confided to his brother Jesuits, that on the occasion of Martini's meeting with Pope Benedict, Martini had told Pope Benedict: "This is the right moment for you to resign, you can't do anything."[49] This story, however, must be taken with a grain of salt and is probably attributable more to the reform-minded enthusiasm of Father Fausti than to actual confidential communications of Cardinal Martini.[50] What does remain, however, is the recollection of the moving encounter as a witness to a communion in faith much greater than possible differences of opinions on particular pastoral topics or world views.

The book on Jesus

In July 2012, although tired and physically worn out, Benedict XVI completed his third volume dedicated to the figure and message of the founder of Christianity, entitled *The Infancy of Jesus*.[51] This is a proof of the pope's fierce determination to complete a work that would have been difficult even for a theologian with no other particular tasks. It is therefore necessary to ask where the pope found the time and energy to write three such weighty volumes. According to Monsignor Gänswein, Benedict especially dedicated Tuesdays to his work. Following the practice begun by John Paul II,[52] on Tuesdays, with some exceptions, the pope did not grant audiences. Consequently, Tuesday became the day of the *Jesus* book.[53] It was also amazing to observe how the pope took up writing again in the

---

[49] See Gian Guido Vecchi, "Quando Martini disse a Ratzinger: la curia non cambia, devi lasciare", *Corriere della Sera,* July 16, 2015, 29.

[50] According to the same source, Father Fausti reportedly also said that in the first ballots of the 2005 conclave, Martini and Ratzinger were the candidates who had garnered the most votes, somewhat more for Martini. However, the story has been denied by almost all reliable sources.

[51] Benedict XVI, *The Infancy Narratives: Jesus of Nazareth*, trans. Philip J. Whitmore (New York: Image, 2012).

[52] See Mieczysław Mokrzycki, *I martedì di Karol* (Cinisello Balsamo: San Paolo, 2009).

[53] From a conversation of the author with Monsignor Gänswein on January 27, 2009.

very place where he had left off the previous week, doing so without any hesitation or uncertainty. "He had an incredible capacity for concentration, as if at the root of all he did were the thought and image of Jesus."[54]

Lastly, Monsignor Gänswein recalls, the work on *Jesus of Nazareth* was not a heavy burden for the pope that took time away from his ministry. On the contrary, it was a pleasant intermezzo, a distraction from everyday life that gave him new energy and vigor. The following day, one would see the pope more serene, more concentrated on the tasks of his agenda and on the decisions he had to make.

The order of the volumes' publication does not mirror the chronology of the life of Jesus, which is why it is necessary to summarize the content of the books here: The first part, *From the Baptism in the Jordan to the Transfiguration*, begun in the final months before his election as pope and completed in 2006 (published in English in 2007); the second part, *From the Entrance into Jerusalem to the Resurrection*, was finished in 2010 and published in 2011; the prologue, *The Infancy Narratives*, was finished in 2012 and published in the same year.[55] It is also necessary to make clear that the pontiff, as he wrote in the preface to the first part,[56] had prepared to compose this work by making a long interior journey and after writing a series of publications,[57] the last of which, not by chance, was entitled *Unterwegs zu Jesus Christus* (*On the Way to Jesus Christ*).[58]

---

[54] Ibid.

[55] In the edition published by the Vatican Press, the three volumes are reorganized in chronological order according to the life of Jesus, and not according to their order of publication. It is also important to note that the volume in the Italian edition of the complete works has a subtitle: *The Figure and the Message*, which, according to the author himself, should better clarify his intention, not to write a biography of Jesus in the technical sense but rather, "guided by the hermeneutic of faith, but at the same time adopting a responsible attitude toward historical reason, which is a necessary component of that faith" (*Jesus of Nazareth: Holy Week*, trans. Philip J. Whitmore, [San Francisco: Ignatius Press, 2011], xvii), to offer a convincing portrait of the founder of the Christian religion.

[56] Here and in the following pages, the text by Benedict XVI is cited from the translations by Adrian J. Walker (2007) and Philip J. Whitmore (2011, 2012).

[57] These writings were published in volume 6/2 of the *Opera omnia* in Italian entitled *Gesù di Nazaret: Scritti di cristologia* (Vatican City: LEV, 2015). In the preface to the entire volume, the editor-in-chief of the *Collected Works*, Gerhard Cardinal Müller, then prefect of the Congregation for the Doctrine of the Faith, speaks about "six decades of intense, in-depth spiritual and scientific study of the thematic areas of Christology" (6/1:6).

[58] In Germany, this work was published in 2004, the same year in which Cardinal Ratzinger began the first part of *Jesus of Nazareth*. The American edition appeared in 2005.

THE INFANCY OF JESUS

The question with which the pope begins his prologue, in which he discusses the infancy of Jesus, is the question about the origins of the baby announced by the Archangel Gabriel and visited by the Magi from the East. The evangelists Matthew and Luke respond to this question with the genealogies that preface those respective Gospels. The genealogy of Matthew links Jesus to David, to the people of Israel, and to Abraham, to whom God promised descendants as numerous "as the stars of heaven and as the sand which is on the seashore" (Gen 22:17). The promise made by God to Abraham goes beyond the Chosen People: therefore, starting with the genealogy, the focus is already turned toward the peoples of the earth about whom Matthew speaks at the conclusion of his Gospel, when the Risen Lord commands his disciples to make disciples of all peoples.

The genealogy of Luke proceeds along the same lines, yet it appears different from that of the first evangelist. Starting with Jesus, Luke goes all the way back to the very root, to God who is the Father of Adam, of every man, and of Jesus. The type of God's fatherhood and of Jesus' sonship, however, is different from human fatherhood, as is particularly evident in the chapter on the Annunciation and birth of Jesus. Jesus is the Son of Mary, who welcomes him with the devotion of the poor ones of Israel, and also the Son of the promise, the Son of God, who in him enters directly into contact with matter and, moreover, establishes in it his dwelling place, thus inaugurating the new humanity, the new creation. With the flight into Egypt, "Jesus, the true Son, himself went into 'exile' in a very deep sense, in order to lead all of us home from exile."[59]

Another element of great historical and religious importance, evident in this part of the work, is the development of a statement that had gradually become increasingly important for Pope Benedict: the continuity between the Old and New Testaments, which the pontiff had already highlighted in an earlier little volume in which he wrote: "According to Christian faith, on the Cross Jesus opens up and fulfills the wholeness of the Law and gives it thus to the

---

[59] Benedict XVI, *Jesus of Nazareth: The Infancy Narratives*, 112.

pagans, who can now accept it as their own in this its wholeness, thereby becoming children of Abraham."[60]

THE UNITY OF FIGURE AND MESSAGE

The first, and probably the most significant, part of Pope Benedict's *Jesus of Nazareth*, entitled, *From the Baptism in the Jordan to the Transfiguration*, proposes a methodological premise in which the pontiff explains the reason why he took time away from his serious pastoral tasks in order to propose to the faithful a unified approach to the figure and message of Jesus. He sets in motion the discourse by affirming that, in his time, in the 1930s and 1940s, there were numerous works, among them *The Lord* by Romano Guardini, that proposed a fascinating image of Jesus. From that time forward, historical-critical research offered great enrichment on individual points but, at the same time, broke up the bigger picture by severing the Jesus of history from the Christ of faith, something that is increasingly taken for granted.

If, the pope asks, Scripture transmits to us only the witness of the Christ of faith, what certitude can the faithful have of drawing close to Jesus? Does the believer still have something to do with a historical figure who lived almost two thousand years ago in Palestine, a man who at the same time claimed to be the Son of God and is accepted as such in faith? Or must he deal only with layers of tradition that transmit to him bits and pieces of witness that cannot be reduced to unity? The challenge of the pope emeritus is, then, that of reconstructing the figure and message of Jesus, not to set himself in opposition to the historical-critical method, which he also appreciates and knows, but, as Maurizio Gronchi writes, to create a dialogue between exegesis and theology, which was already called for by the Second Vatican Council in its Dogmatic Constitution on Divine Revelation.[61]

In the preface to the second part of his work, the pope writes: "If scholarly exegesis is not to exhaust itself in constantly new

---

[60] Joseph Ratzinger, *Many Religions, One Covenant*, trans. Graham Harrison (San Francisco: Ignatius Press, 1999), 41.

[61] Maurizio Gronchi, "La figura e il messaggio di Gesù di Nazaret", in *Il Gesù di Nazaret di Joseph Ratzinger* (Cittadella, Assisi: M. Tagliaferri, 2011), 61–114. The passage being discussed here is on p. 63.

hypotheses, becoming theologically irrelevant, it must take a methodological step forward and see itself once again as a theological discipline, without abandoning its historical character."[62] This will allow him to break the exclusive bond with the past, whose context he seeks to recreate conscientiously, and to turn his attention also to the present, to the praying community of the disciples of Jesus Christ. In fact, religion, Christianity in particular, looks also to the present and to the future.

From here another observation of Pope Benedict emerges that can be traced back to the Constitution on Divine Revelation of the Second Vatican Council, in particular chapter 6: "The Scripture emerged from the heart of a living subject—the pilgrim People of God—and lives within this same subject."[63] Therefore, it must be read in union with the people of God who have not ceased and never will cease their journey in history until the return of the Lord. Until that time, the people of God will have to continue to confront and deepen their knowledge of Scripture in which their Lord has spoken substantially and in which he continues to speak. For this reason, Scripture, like the Eucharist, is the place where the faithful of every time can encounter Jesus, whose figure and message, in this way, do not belong to the past, but are also contemporaneous for all the faithful in every time and place. For this reason, yesterday as today, it is important to reconstruct as one entity the figure and message of Jesus, so as to be able to proclaim him so that the faithful can draw close to him in meditation, prayer, and sacrament.

FROM THE BAPTISM IN THE JORDAN TO THE TRANSFIGURATION

In the first part of the work on Jesus, the thesis of the one covenant is proposed with the parallel between Moses and Jesus, the new and definitive prophet, who from the Mount of the Beatitudes, the new

---

[62] Benedict XVI, *Jesus of Nazareth: Holy Week*, xiv. In the same volume published by Tagliaferri, Piero Stefani, in his article "Gesù, il dono di Abramo e l'elezione di Israele", denies this point, maintaining the necessity of a rigorous historical reconstruction of the figure of Jesus, going behind the Gospels. Only by starting from a Jesus who is rigorously historical and inserted into the Jewish context is a Jewish-Christian dialogue possible. However, the question remains: What can guarantee such a reconstruction, prescinding from the Gospels?

[63] Benedict XVI, *Jesus of Nazareth: From the Baptism in the Jordan to the Transfiguration*, trans. Adrian J. Walker (New York, et al.: Doubleday, 2007, xx).

Sinai, proclaims the New Covenant. However, this New Covenant is not in contrast with the first covenant but, rather, fulfills it and brings it to completion, thus fulfilling the promise made by God to Abraham. Ratzinger's bet is that "the commands of Jesus" are not different from the teachings of the Scriptures in both the Old and New Testaments.

The previously mentioned dialogue of the pontiff with the ortho-dox Jewish rabbi Jacob Neusner is also along these lines. In a book that the pope judged quite favorably,[64] Neusner imagines being a contemporary of Jesus, being struck by the fame of the rabbi of Nazareth, and respectfully taking his place for some time among his listeners in order to come into contact with his message. At the end of the day on which he listened in particular to the episode of the young man whom Jesus invited to sell all his riches in order to be his disciple (Mt 19:16–22), Neusner goes to the synagogue in the evening to pray but also to converse with the rabbi about the teachings of the rabbi of Nazareth. The latter asks him if Rabbi Jesus omitted anything of the teaching of the Torah. Neusner re-sponds in the negative. The rabbi adds: " 'Then what did he add?' I: 'Himself.' "[65] Benedict XVI says that he agrees profoundly with this answer.[66]

On the other hand, Pope Benedict had already given a similar answer. The pope therefore, asked: "What did Jesus actually bring, if not world peace, universal prosperity, and a better world?" And he answered: "He has brought God . . . the God who revealed his face only in Israel. . . . It is this God, the God of Abraham, Isaac, and Jacob, the true God, whom he has brought to the nations of the earth."[67] The pope thought that it was possible to make progress in the dialogue between Jews and Christians on this point. The uni-versality of salvation already present in the Bible, particularly in the writings of the Prophets, is brought to fulfillment by Jesus, who does not abolish the Old Covenant, since God never revoked the covenant with his people, but, beyond every expectation, brought it to completion and fulfillment.

---

[64] Jacob Neusner, *A Rabbi Talks with Jesus* (New York: Doubleday, 1993).

[65] Ibid., 107–8, quoted in Benedict XVI, *Jesus of Nazareth: From the Baptism*, 104–5.

[66] Benedict XVI, *Jesus of Nazareth: From the Baptism*, 111.

[67] Ibid. 44.

Of course, there remains between Jews and Christians the claim of Jesus' divinity, his putting himself on the level of God the Father. This is the nucleus of the revelation brought by Jesus; for this testimony he was put to death. The Jews, however, do not need to renounce their fidelity to the covenant; nor do Christians have to renounce it. The fidelity of both can be situated in that harmony of Testaments of which the Fathers of the Church speak.

FROM THE ENTRANCE INTO JERUSALEM TO THE RESURRECTION

As underscored in the preface of the second part of the work, Pope Benedict XVI intended to write neither a Christology, that is, a theological treatise starting with the figure of Jesus, nor a true and proper biography.[68] On the contrary, the pope intended to draw near to the figure and message of Jesus, insisting on what he calls the "real Jesus". The pope wrote: "Exaggerating a little, one could say that I set out to discover the real Jesus, on the basis of whom something like a 'Christology from below' would then become possible."[69] Now, how does one discover the real Jesus? Ratzinger answered by citing no. 12 of the Vatican II Constitution on Divine Revelation —focusing on the unity and content of the whole of Scripture. This does not mean denying the historical-critical method but, rather, developing it in an organic fashion, making it become true and proper theology.

Another characteristic element of the second part of Ratzinger's work on Jesus is the accent placed on the Trinitarian life—on the relationship between Jesus and the Father in the Spirit of love. An anticipation of this theme is already present in the first encyclical of his pontificate, in the passage where the pope wrote: "*We have come to believe in God's love*: in these words the Christian can express the fundamental decision of his life. Being Christian is not the result of an ethical choice or a lofty idea, but the encounter with an event,

---

[68] Important works exist both in the area of Christological studies and in the area of biography in the strict sense. The pope himself cites some of them in German. What interested him, obviously, was to reconstruct a credible bond between history and exegesis, just as he had always fought in a wider field to keep alive the bond between faith and reason.

[69] Benedict XVI, *Jesus of Nazareth: Holy Week*, xvi.

a person."[70] Moreover, this person, Jesus, comes from God his Father and places man in communion with God the Father. This is the incandescent nucleus of Christianity. The Christian, Ratzinger continued, does not believe in a multiplicity of truths. "Ultimately he believes, quite simply, in God: he believes that there is only one true God. This God becomes accessible to us through the one he sent, Jesus Christ: it is in the encounter with him that we experience the recognition of God that leads to communion and thus to 'life'."[71] This begins with the Resurrection of Jesus, who is now the Living One and brings to life all who enter into communion with him through the Sacraments of Baptism and the Eucharist.

For this reason, Ratzinger passionately defended the classic themes connected with the event of the third day: the empty tomb, apparitions, testimonies, the uniqueness of the event with respect to other forms of apparitions in and outside the Gospels, the Ascension. Just as vigorously, he also defended matters related to Jesus' return. With the passage of time, instead of the imminent return of Jesus, a return related to Jesus' presence at the right hand of the Father has taken its place. Jesus says in the Gospel of John: "I go away, and I will come to you" (Jn 14:28). Ratzinger commented: "These words sum up beautifully what is so special about Jesus' 'going away', which is also his 'coming', and at the same time they explain the mystery of the Cross, the Resurrection, and the Ascension."[72]

This first return of Jesus is completed, according to tradition, by the final return of Christ in glory, when "he delivers the kingdom to God the Father after destroying every rule and every authority and power" (1 Cor 15:24). The themes connected to the Resurrection of Jesus have become unusual even in Christian thought and preaching. In this regard, however, Ratzinger insisted on the beauty of Christian hope in eternal life, on what tradition calls "paradise". Furthermore, he could boast of the support of the great French historian Jean Delumeau,[73] who, after extensive research on the history

---

[70] Benedict XVI, Encyclical Letter *Deus Caritas Est* on Christian Love, December 25, 2005.

[71] Benedict XVI, *Jesus of Nazareth: Holy Week*, 84.

[72] Ibid., 283.

[73] Jean Delumeau, *History of Paradise*, trans. Matthew O'Connell (New York: Continuum, 1995).

of the idea of paradise, leaves aside for a brief moment the mantle of a rigorous scholar to assume the mantle of a thinker who writes: "Paradise is a serious question: it deserves more than a reflection on the image, more than a useless nostalgia. To know better the past of paradise means also to learn a lot about ourselves and, at the same time, to shed light on our future."[74]

So it is for Pope Benedict, too. Hence, his insistence on the Resurrection, on the encounter with Jesus immediately after death, on the eschatology of the present, and on the final eschatology. Jesus, therefore, comes from God, from the past; he encounters us in the communion of the Church based on the witness of the apostles and apostolic succession. He reaches us in the present by means of his Word and the Eucharist, but he also pushes us forward toward the future, beyond ourselves, toward the definitive reality of revelation and of the encounter with God. Pope Benedict concluded: "The Lord is there, and he comes at the right moment. 'I go away, and I will come to you'—that is the essence of Christian trust, the reason for our joy."[75]

In conclusion, it is appropriate to recall once again how Pope Benedict drew our attention to Romano Guardini's *The Lord*. As has already been noted, the Italian-German theologian in his youth frequented the monastic circles where the liturgical movement began. Pope Benedict in his mature years also became increasingly close to the monastic-liturgical world. Nevertheless, although the pope shared Guardini's fundamental intention of presenting Jesus in terms of a knowledge of the faith and the context of liturgical prayer, he was also aware of the changed historical-cultural picture. Hence the need to combine the hermeneutic of faith with the historical hermeneutic. According to the pope, this was the criterion pointed out to theologians by the Vatican II constitution *Dei Verbum*.[76] Once again, the pope asserted his fidelity to the council. His last great work, *Jesus of Nazareth*, "the grace of the pontificate",[77] sprang from a desire to second the wish expressed by the council

---

[74] Ibid., introduction (translated from Italian).
[75] Benedict XVI, *Jesus of Nazareth: Holy Week*, 285.
[76] Ibid., xv.
[77] From a conversation of the author with the pope emeritus.

Fathers to make Jesus better known as the Eternal Word who enlightens all men.[78]

I must resign

THE TRIP TO LEBANON

Upon finishing the book on Jesus, Benedict XVI breathed a sigh of relief. He had completed a text that was dear to his heart, a task that was meant to help give a direction to his pontificate. The summer vacation at Castel Gandolfo, however, did not bring him, as in previous years, the recuperation of physical strength that was more necessary than ever to overcome the state of extreme exhaustion into which he had fallen after his trip to Mexico and Cuba. At the beginning of September 2012, the news of Cardinal Martini's death particularly struck Pope Benedict, especially due to the recollection of their encounter a few months earlier in Milan. In the meantime, the date of the pope's already scheduled trip to Lebanon approached; the purpose of the trip was to deliver to the local bishops the apostolic exhortation summarizing the conclusions of the Special Assembly for the Middle East that had taken place from October 10–24, 2010.

Until the last minute, the trip was uncertain due to fallout from the war in Syria, which also had repercussions on the neighboring country. However, the pope was determined to keep to the task that had been undertaken, and, as scheduled, he departed for Lebanon on October 14. The first important encounter took place in the Greek-Melkite Cathedral of Saint Paul, in Harissa, with patriarchs and Middle Eastern bishops present as well as Orthodox and Muslim delegations and representatives of the world of culture and of civil society. Before solemnly signing the apostolic exhortation, the pope observed that the date of the delivery of the document coincided with the Feast of the Exaltation of the Cross, the celebration of which goes back to 335, the day after the dedication of the Basilica of the Resurrection built on Golgotha, the site of Jesus' tomb.

---

[78] See *Dei Verbum*, no. 4.

He then continued: the exaltation of the Cross is an act of faith, of love, and of hope.

Moreover, the document that the pope had come to deliver is intended as an outline for rediscovering what is essential: the following of Christ in a difficult and sorrowful context that at times could almost suggest abandoning such a necessary path. The pope, however, continued: "In the light of today's Feast, and in view of a fruitful application of the Exhortation, I urge all of you to fear not, to stand firm in truth and in purity of faith."[79] Then, visibly moved, he concluded:

> "Fear not, little flock" (Lk 12:32) and remember the promise made to Constantine: "In this sign you will conquer!" Churches of the Middle East, fear not, for the Lord is truly with you, to the close of the age! Fear not, because the universal Church walks at your side and is humanly and spiritually close to you! . . . God grant that all the peoples of the Middle East may live in peace, fraternity and religious freedom![80]

The following day, the pope met the young people of Lebanon and the Middle East at the Maronite Patriarchate of Bkerké. There was also a delegation of young Muslims with them. The pope thanked them for their presence, "which is so important. Together with the young Christians, you are the future of this fine country and of the Middle East in general. Seek to build it up together! And when you are older, continue to live in unity and harmony with Christians. For the beauty of Lebanon is found in this fine symbiosis."[81]

And he continued: "I understand, too, that present among us there are some young people from Syria. I want to say how much I admire your courage. Tell your families and friends back home that the Pope has not forgotten you. Tell those around you that the Pope is saddened by your sufferings and your griefs."[82]

The trip continued then with the delivery of the apostolic exhortation for the Middle East to the patriarchs and bishops of the

[79] Benedict XVI, Address at the Basilica of Saint Paul, Harissa, Lebanon, September 14, 2012.
[80] Ibid.
[81] Benedict XVI, Address at the Meeting with Young People, September 15, 2012.
[82] Ibid.

Middle East in the City Center Waterfront of Beirut and the ecumenical meeting in the Hall of Honor in the Syro-Catholic Patriarchate of Charfet. In brief, this trip can be considered a success even though the conditions in which it took place were tragic because of the Syrian conflict, which was becoming more terrible with each passing day.

FIFTY YEARS SINCE VATICAN II

The month of October 2012 was rich with memories and celebrations. On October 4, the Feast of Saint Francis, Pope Benedict decided to follow the example of John XXIII, who, in 1962, in view of the beginning of Vatican II, traveled by train on a pilgrimage to Assisi and Loreto to seek the protection of the Virgin for the upcoming council. Half a century later, Benedict XVI traveled in his turn by helicopter to Loreto to seek the blessing of the Virgin on the Synod for the New Evangelization and the Year of Faith. On Sunday, October 7, the Synod for the New Evangelization solemnly opened, and the pope explained: "The Synodal Assembly which opens today is dedicated to this new evangelization, to help these people encounter the Lord, who alone fills our existence with deep meaning and peace; and to favor the rediscovery of the faith, that source of grace which brings joy and hope to personal, family and social life."[83]

On October 11, the fiftieth anniversary of the Second Vatican Council, the pope celebrated Mass with bishops who half a century earlier had been present at the council and with those present in Rome for the synod. The patriarch of Constantinople, Bartholomew I, and Rowan Williams, the primate of the Anglican Communion, also participated in the ceremony. In the homily, the pope invited all to enter more deeply into the spiritual movement that had characterized Vatican II so as to enliven the whole Church and to proclaim Christ to contemporary man: "But, so that this interior thrust towards the new evangelization [not] remain just an idea, . . . it needs

---

[83] Benedict XVI, Homily at the Holy Mass for the Opening of the Synod of Bishops, October 7, 2012.

to be built on a concrete and precise basis, and this basis is the documents of the Second Vatican Council."[84]

Then, in the evening, the young people of Catholic Action organized a candlelight gathering under the pope's window to recall the candlelight gathering that had taken place fifty years earlier before the opening of Vatican II. The pope appeared at the window and recalled that among the young people who were confidently looking up at the window of "the Good Pope" a half century ago, he, then a young theologian, had also been present, having been invited to be a *peritus* at Vatican II. Then he continued: "We are also happy today, we hold joy in our hearts, but I would say it is perhaps a more measured joy, a humble joy", which the experience of sin has caused. He meant to say that joy comes entirely from faith, while weakness has taken hold of the Church, and at times we get the impression that "the Lord is asleep and has forgotten us."[85] Having begun with a personal recollection and Pope John's famous address to the moon with his thought of bringing the embrace of the pope to the children at home, the address of Pope Benedict slid progressively toward the suffering of those days.

I HAVE REFLECTED, I HAVE PRAYED, I MUST RESIGN

In the midst of these tasks that took place between late September and early October 2012, the pope told his secretary: "I have reflected, I have prayed, I must resign from the papacy for the love of Jesus, for the love of the Church. Today it is possible to prolong physical life with pills. . . . But that is no good. Next year is World Youth Day in Rio de Janeiro, and I no longer have the physical strength to make such a long trip."[86] Then the secretary of the pope emeritus continues: "The statement was made matter-of-factly. All we could do was to listen, obey, and join with him in prayer."

---

[84] Benedict XVI, Homily at the Holy Mass for the Opening of the Year of Faith, October 11, 2012.

[85] Benedict XVI, Benediction Bestowed upon Participants in the Candlelight Procession Organized by the Italian Catholic Action, October 11, 2012.

[86] From a conversation of the author with Archbishop Gänswein on January 27, 2016.

In the meantime, there were many practical questions to be answered. At first, Pope Benedict thought about announcing his resignation in the address to the Roman Curia at the end of the year. However, a reasonable objection was raised in this regard: such an extraordinary announcement only a few days before Christmas would have overshadowed the whole meaning of the feast day and would have left the faithful even more confused. After suitable reflection, the date of February 11 was chosen, midway between Christmas and Easter, so as to give the cardinals the chance to choose a successor by the Feast of the Resurrection.

Another key decision concerned those participants in the next conclave. At the beginning of 2012, Benedict had appointed twenty-two new cardinals, ten of whom were members of the Curia and seven Italians. The number of curial cardinals could be raised to twelve, if one took into account that two others were professors with different titles working in the Roman congregations. Only ten were diocesan bishops, and only four were from outside Europe. At that time, the choice, probably made under the influence of the various Roman congregations, had aroused no small amount of criticism. In view of the conclave, the pope decided to balance things, and on October 24, he announced the convocation of a new consistory to appoint six new cardinals. This time, all were non-Europeans, and, with the exception of the American Archbishop James Harvey, who was named Archpriest of the Papal Basilica of Saint Paul outside the Walls, all belonged to sees outside Europe. In short, a course correction in view of the conclave.

The transfer of Archbishop Harvey from the Pontifical Household to the Basilica of Saint Paul outside the Walls had another purpose also: it freed up a place that the pope wanted to set aside for his trustworthy personal secretary, Monsignor Gänswein, who in those months had been the closest to the pope. Furthermore, the pope wanted to consecrate him a bishop personally on January 6, 2013, in Saint Peter's.

The other practical question to tackle was the encyclical on faith, which was almost ready. There would also be time to complete and to publish a document that was very dear to Benedict. However, there was a question of institutional etiquette, to which the pope was very committed. It makes no sense to have the new pope find on his desk an encyclical written by his predecessor. Therefore, he decided to forego its publication and to hand over the material to his successor.[87]

THE ANNOUNCEMENT

As planned, Pope Benedict announced his resignation on February 11, 2013. The words with which the pope announced his intention were very precise from a canonical perspective, so as to leave no room for potential disputes, but at the same time they reflected his state of mind. The text of the statement, which was read in Latin, is well known: "Dear Brothers, I have convoked you to this Consistory, not only for the three canonizations, but also to communicate to you a decision of great importance for the life of the Church. After having repeatedly examined my conscience before God, I have come to the certainty that my strengths, due to an advanced age, are no longer suited to an adequate exercise of the Petrine ministry."[88] Then the pope continued by recalling that in recent months his physical strength had diminished so much that he had arrived at the decision that he had to resign from the office to which the cardinals had called him in 2005.

The news quickly spread around the world, causing astonishment and consternation among the faithful and observers.[89] The sensational headlines in the newspapers were divided between highlighting the fragility and exhaustion of the pope and emphasizing the resistance he had encountered in carrying out his job.[90] The men of the Church, cardinals and bishops, for their part caught by surprise, stressed, on the one hand, the courage of Pope Benedict, while others maintained that the pope should have remained in his post even in the midst of the tempest.[91] In reality, many had in mind the decision of John Paul II, who, although challenged physically more

---

[87] Benedict, in time, would express his thanks for the "precious work" and its publication, with the supplemental material of Pope Francis. See *Lumen fidei*, no. 7.

[88] Benedict XVI, Declaration, February 10, 2013.

[89] See Roberto Rusconi, *Il gran rifiuto* (Brescia: Morcelliana, 2013), 8ff.

[90] Roberto Rusconi provides a good overview of articles from the leading newspapers of the world on the day after the resignation, ibid., 10–11.

[91] Preeminent among the critics of the pope's decision was the cardinal of Kraków, Stanisław Dziwisz, the former secretary of John Paul II, who remarked spontaneously that "one does not come down off the cross." See Rusconi, *Il gran rifiuto*, 10.

than ever, had remained in his post until the very end. Besides, Benedict XVI himself had emphasized the great witness given by his predecessor in old age.[92]

This very circumstance, however, necessarily called for greater caution: Benedict had been a witness both to the heroic decision of his predecessor and to the difficulties encountered in the governance of the Church during his sickness. Given the dysfunctionality that had already been observed over the course of 2012, the pope did not want the situation to degenerate further at the conclusion of his pontificate. Hence, once again, the pope's emphasis on the personal duty of conscience, to prove that his action was not intended to be either a critique of the different decision of his predecessor or any sort of obligation laid on his successor. Subsequently, in explaining his action, two days after the official announcement of his decision to the cardinals, Benedict hastened to offer a rationale for his choice when addressing the faithful during a General Audience in the Paul VI Audience Hall: "Dear brothers and sisters, As you know, I have decided—thank you for your kindness—to renounce the ministry which the Lord entrusted to me on 19 April 2005. I have done this in full freedom for the good of the Church. . . . I am strengthened and reassured by the certainty that the Church is Christ's, who will never leave her without his guidance and care."[93]

The faithful, who welcomed the pope's words with thunderous applause, demonstrated maturity and a capacity for understanding. The expressions of sympathy continued in the following days, helping to diminish the sadness of the time of departure. Responding to the objections that had been raised more or less quietly, the pope said in his last General Audience, on the next-to-last day of his pontificate: "I am not abandoning the cross, but remaining in a new way at the side of the crucified Lord. I no longer bear the power of office for the governance of the Church, but in the service of prayer I remain, so to speak, in the enclosure of Saint Peter."[94]

---

[92] In the homily for the beatification of his predecessor, he said: "Then too, there was his witness in suffering: the Lord gradually stripped him of everything, yet he remained ever a 'rock', as Christ desired." Benedict XVI, Homily at the Mass on the Occasion of the Beatification of John Paul II, May 1, 2011.

[93] Benedict XVI, General Audience, February 13, 2013.

[94] Benedict XVI, General Audience, February 27, 2013.

THE COUNCIL, THE CHURCH, AND JESUS CHRIST

On February 28, 2013, the last day of his pontificate, Benedict XVI met the cardinals present in Rome for a final greeting at the end of his mandate. Ever generous, the pope thanked them for their collaboration. He then left them with a thought connected with the most beautiful experiences of his life: the council, the Church, Jesus Christ. In those final months, both before and after the fiftieth anniversary of the opening of the Second Vatican Council, the pope had often thought about the days of October 1962. He had also taken in hand a book by a great friend, a teacher from the days of his youth, Romano Guardini. In the early 1920s, the Italian-German theologian made an exclamation that has continued to inspire Catholics, among whom was also the young Joseph Ratzinger: "A religious process of incalculable importance has begun: the Church is coming to life in the souls of men."[95]

Guardini himself, invited to the council as an expert like Ratzinger, had declined the invitation on account of his age and the malady from which he was suffering in those years. Nonetheless, he did not fail to follow the council's works; after the promulgation of the Constitution on the Church in late 1964, he had set to work on the project of completing his 1922 work, already announced in 1933 in the preface of its third edition.[96]

Therefore, taking into consideration the reflections of the council, in 1965 he published another volume, *The Church of the Lord*, in which the essence and mandate of the Church "are justified solely in their reference to Jesus Christ".[97] Upon the publication of this

---

[95] Romano Guardini, *Vom Sinn der Kirche* (Mainz: Grünewald, 1922). The short work, a compilation of five conferences, has been published and reworked many times. The third edition was revised by Guardini himself in 1933. In 1955, there was a new edition prepared by Johannes Spörl, who wrote in the preface: "it was then a major achievement, a breath of original, Pentecostal Christianity, when the young priest, who was still almost unknown, put his finger on the problem of the Church with such freedom and doctrinal power." It was also republished many times in Italy by Morcelliana of Brescia under the title *Il senso della Chiesa*. The 1960 edition, reprinted in 2007, carried Spörl's introduction, a short passage of which I have cited (p. 6). The initial affirmation of Guardini on the reawakening of the Church in souls is found on p. 11 of *The Church and the Catholic* and *The Spirit of the Liturgy* (New York: Sheed & Ward, 1940).

[96] Romano Guardini, *Il senso della Chiesa* (Brescia: Morcelliana, 2007), 13.

[97] Hanna-Barbara Gerl-Falkovitz, *Romano Guardini: La vita e l'opera* (Brescia: Morcelliana, 1988), 407.

volume, Guardini, even before the end of the council, sent an autographed copy of it to the young theologian Ratzinger, who, in the meantime, had become his friend. The pope now showed this copy to the cardinals, reading it as though it were a testament: the Church "is not an institution conceived and built in theory . . . but a living reality. . . . She lives through the course of time, in becoming, like every living being, in undergoing change. . . . And yet in her nature she remains ever the same, and her heart is Christ."[98] Then the pope continued: "Let us stay united, dear Brothers, in this Mystery: in prayer, especially in the daily Eucharist, and in this way we shall serve the Church and the whole of humanity."[99]

That afternoon the pope left for Castel Gandolfo, where, according to an expression that had become dear to him, the last stretch of his pilgrimage had begun. From that moment, the papal see was vacant, and preparations for the election of his successor could begin.

---

[98] Romano Guardini, *Die Kirche des Herrn* (Würzburg: Werkbund, 1965). The publishing house Morcelliana considered it wise to publish the two volumes together, giving them a single title, *La realtà della Chiesa* (Brescia, 1973). The citation is on p. 160 of the Italian edition.

[99] Benedict XVI, Farewell Address to the Eminent Cardinals Present in Rome, February 28, 2013.

XIX

MATER ECCLESIAE

For the first time in the modern era, a reigning pope resigned from the exercise of the authority connected with the mandate of the Successor of Peter. This raised the problem as to the place and way in which Benedict XVI was going to spend the rest of his life. Here again, Ratzinger proved his courage and evangelical wisdom. He could have gone away and shut himself away in silence and resentment over the unfortunate travails of his pontificate. On the contrary, he decided to stay, as he loves to say, in Peter's enclosure, and this decision immediately attested to the fact that he had not retired to private life, was not fleeing from his successor, from communion with the universal Church. To be sure, he gave up the exercise of authority but not the threefold invitation of the Lord to love him, to hold out his hands so that another can dress him and carry him where he did not want to go.[1] Hence, the decision to keep his papal name and to wear the white cassock, with no insignia of authority, however.

In Peter's enclosure

Among the many decisions connected with his renunciation of the Petrine ministry, Pope Benedict also had to choose a residence where he would spend the last years of his life. As his brother had stated,[2] as early as 2002 the then cardinal had abandoned the idea

---

[1] See Jn 21:15–19.

[2] Georg Ratzinger and Michael Hesemann, *My Brother the Pope*, trans. Michael J. Miller (San Francisco: Ignatius Press, 2012), 224.

of returning to Germany. The house in Pentling near Regensburg was now too small to accommodate all the books he had accumulated over the years; furthermore, by now he felt at home in Rome. The cardinals who had served long years in the Roman congregations customarily took up residence there, and the former prefect of the Holy Office thought of settling down there. The decision, which had been advisable in 2002, became almost obligatory in 2012, when Ratzinger was not only the pontiff who had resigned but also the bishop emeritus of the Italian capital, the city that had been entrusted to his pastoral care for almost eight years.

Moreover, he was the Successor of Peter, a status that he was neither willing nor able to renounce. It was necessary, however, to look around to find a place within the Vatican, so as to suggest closeness to his successor. At this point, the choice was limited but not particularly difficult. On the Vatican Hill, inside the Leonine walls, there was a building constructed by Pius XI to house the director of Vatican Radio, a Jesuit, who resided there with a small community of his confreres. The last director who had stayed there was Father Roberto Tucci, later created a cardinal. In 1992, John Paul II had renovated the building, transforming it into a monastery for contemplative nuns, to which he had given the name "Mater Ecclesiae". With their prayers, these nuns were to help the pope in his ministry. Initially, the nuns were to reside in the Vatican for a period of five years. After this interval, they returned to their religious houses and were replaced by religious women from another order or congregation. Experience had then suggested reducing their stay to three years.

First, the Poor Clares had taken up residence, then the Carmelites, followed by the Benedictines. Currently, the Visitandines, the Sisters of the Order founded at the beginning of the seventeenth century by Saint Francis de Sales and Saint Jane Frances de Chantal, served there. From the outset, Pope Benedict had followed life at the monastery very attentively.[3] He knew, therefore, that the Visitandines had to leave the monastery more or less at the time of his retirement. The coincidence turned out to be providential; all the more so because the monastery needed to be refurbished anyway. Therefore, based on these considerations, the decision to live in the

---

[3] See below, the interview with the pope emeritus.

monastery was almost made by itself. Moreover, for the type of life that he intended to lead, Benedict was sure to remain profoundly faithful to the purpose for which John Paul II had converted the building into a monastery. The residents were changing, but the purpose remained exactly the same: "To serve with all my heart the holy Church of God by a life dedicated to prayer".[4]

IN COMMUNION WITH THE CHURCH

The decision of the Successor of Peter, a necessarily personal one like the acceptance of the election that had taken place a little less than eight years before, had, however, an ecclesial dimension about which the pope spoke frequently in his speeches given from the time of the sensational announcement of his resignation until the day of his departure. On February 14, three days after the first announcement, the pope met with the Roman clergy. On that occasion, Benedict told the bishops and priests of his diocese: "And although I am about to withdraw, I remain close to all of you in prayer, and I am sure that you too will be close to me."[5] During the week of February 17–23, as was his custom, the pope took part in the spiritual exercises of the Curia being preached that year by Gianfranco Cardinal Ravasi. At the end of the retreat, the pope returned again to the theme of communion: "This gratitude will remain in me and even though now our 'external' and 'visible' communion is ending . . . our spiritual closeness lives on, a profound communion in prayer endures."[6]

The most beautiful and extensive statement of those days was perhaps contained in the greeting addressed by the pontiff (more sorely tried than ever) to the faithful at Castel Gandolfo. It was only a little more than an hour before 8:00 in the evening, when the See of Peter would be declared vacant, but Pope Benedict somehow pressed on, addressing the faithful as they showed him affection and recognition: "I am no longer the Supreme Pontiff of the

---

[4] See Benedict XVI, *Nulla anteporre a Cristo,* an anthology of monastic reflections by Pope Benedict, published by the Benedictine monks of Praglia (Padua, 2014), 6.

[5] Benedict XVI, Address at the Meeting with the Parish Priests and the Clergy in Rome, February 14, 2013.

[6] Benedict XVI, Address at the Conclusion of the Week of Spiritual Exercises for the Roman Curia, February 23, 2013.

Catholic Church. . . . I am simply a pilgrim beginning the last leg of his pilgrimage on this earth. But I would still with my heart, with my love, with my prayers, with my reflection, and with all my inner strength, like to work for the common good and the good of the Church and humanity."[7]

In the name of Saint Benedict, Saint Augustine, and Saint Bernard

Immediately after his election, explaining why he had chosen the name of the father of Western monasticism, the new pope had recalled the definition of a monk's life given by Saint Benedict in the prologue of his Rule: "the school of the service of God", an expression that characterizes well the monastic way of life, but also the way of life of every Christian.[8] If, however, this mention of the monastic vocation at the beginning of the pontificate could only indicate his heart's desire, now, with his retirement from the exercise of the Petrine ministry, that reference became a more concrete prospect. Several times during his pontificate, he had praised the monks' ascent of the mountain, capable of generating beauty and dignity through prayer and study. And so it is not surprising that, while reflecting on the last stage of his earthly pilgrimage, the pope's thought would turn once again to monastic asceticism, to climbing the mountain of God.

The most significant statement made by him in the period between the announcement and his departure was the one he made on Sunday, February 24, 2013. That was the Second Sunday of Lent, and the liturgy presented to the faithful for their meditation the Gospel of the Transfiguration. After briefly explaining the content of that Gospel passage, the pope applied it to the type of life that he would embrace within a few days. Benedict said: "I hear this word of God as addressed to me in particular at this moment of my life. Thank you! The Lord is calling me 'to scale the mountain', to devote myself even more to prayer and meditation."[9]

---

[7] Benedict XVI, last speech as pope, http://fjp2.com/us/news/vatican/19712-benedict-xvis-last-speech-as-pope.

[8] See chap. 13.

[9] Benedict XVI, Angelus, February 24, 2013.

Furthermore, the Benedictine way had been embedded in the mind and heart of the pope emeritus by his longtime love for Saint Augustine, who, already in the days following his conversion, had begun with some friends and disciples a way of life not very different from the life of monks, to which Augustine remained faithful even throughout his many years as a bishop. Augustine, in turn, wrote a Rule for clerics who love the common life. Lastly, after naming his own successor in 426, he lived for four years in a sort of house-monastery, where he completed important works and composed new ones. At the conclusion of his portrait of Saint Augustine in a series on the saints, Pope Benedict wrote: "The worse his illness became, the more the dying Bishop felt the need for solitude and prayer."[10]

There was, finally, in the mind of the pope-theologian the way of life of the Cistercians according to the characteristic mark given them by Saint Bernard, about whom Pope Benedict had spoken at the Collège des Bernardins in Paris. This way of life combines science and the desire for God, theology and spirituality lived out. "God is never simply the 'object' of theology; he is always its living 'subject' as well. Christian theology, for that matter, is never a purely human discourse about God, but always, and inseparably, the *logos* and 'logic' of God's self-revelation. For this reason scientific rationality and lived devotion are two necessarily complementary and interdependent aspects of study."[11]

His choice of life thus also became a model for elderly bishops and priests, for theologians, his former colleagues, to whom he addressed one last, silent warning.

AT CASTEL GANDOLFO

The pope himself had reminded the faithful immediately upon his arrival at Castel Gandolfo on February 28 that he was no longer the reigning pontiff, as people once used to say. He was, instead, a pilgrim who had reached the last stage of his journey, very tired, moreover, due to the length of the journey and the burden he had

---

[10] Benedict XVI, *Church Fathers from Clement of Rome to Augustine* (San Francisco: Ignatius Press, 2008), 177.

[11] Benedict XVI, Address during his visit to Heiligenkreuz Abbey, September 9, 2007.

had to bear. In brief, he returned to the comparison with the bear of Saint Corbinian and to the interpretation that Saint Augustine gave to Psalm 72:23 (Vulgate), "I am become as a beast [of burden] before Thee; and I am always with Thee."[12]

Closeness to the Lord, however, could not eliminate the tensions, fatigue, and emotions of the final months. In his first days at Castel Gandolfo, the pope emeritus appeared extremely tired. According to the testimony of his secretary, he spoke little, walked little, and ate little.[13] At this point, the closeness of what the pope now called "his family" proved to be decisive: the four *Memores* of Communion and Liberation who followed him and took care of him like guardian angels, as Pope Benedict loved to say, and Archbishop Gänswein, who was by now a trusted advisor, one who protected the pope from intrusions that were not always benevolent.

Then many testimonies of solidarity and affection arrived from simple people and powerful men, from believers and unbelievers, from priests and bishops, from religious men and women. These were perhaps belated gestures of gratitude that nonetheless helped to rout the feeling of solitude and abandonment, demonstrating not only ecclesial communion in the faith, but also the joy of belonging to the Church. In any case, after two months of living at Castel Gandolfo, Benedict was able to return to Rome and start the life of prayer and study of which he had spoken in the days preceding his departure.

LIFE AT MATER ECCLESIAE

On May 3, 2013, according to plan, Benedict XVI returned to the Vatican to start a sort of monastic existence that had both Benedictine and Augustinian characteristics. The rhythm of life in the new system was not very different from what he used to lead in the papal apartment on feast days, as Benedict himself recounted to Seewald in 2010.[14] For his part, Archbishop Gänswein summarized

---

[12] See Joseph Ratzinger, *Milestones: Memoirs 1927–1977*, trans. Erasmo Leiva-Merikakis (San Francisco: Ignatius Press, 1998), 155–56.

[13] From a conversation with Monsignor Gänswein.

[14] Joseph Ratzinger, *Light of the World: The Pope, the Church, and the Signs of the Times*, trans. Michael J. Miller and Adrian J. Walker (San Francisco: Ignatius Press, 2010), 14.

the new horarium of the pope emeritus in an interview with Paolo Rodari.[15]

At 7:45 A.M., concelebrated Mass with his secretary, which the Memores attend. Next the recitation of the Breviary and breakfast. Most of the morning is then dedicated to reading and correspondence, which is always abundant. In performing this task, he still has the help of his old secretary, Sister Birgit Wansing, who better than anyone else manages to read his small handwriting. Lunch is served at 1:30 P.M., according to the Roman custom, certainly not the German one. Another Roman custom is the afternoon siesta. Around 4 P.M., the pope recites the rosary and takes a walk that has become shorter and shorter due to his difficulty in getting around. Afterward, he reads and studies until dinner, which is served at 7:30 P.M. The pope then watches the news on television, followed by another visit to the chapel for the recitation of the prayer to conclude the day.

Benedict and Francis

On February 28, 2013, the last day of his pontificate, Benedict addressed a final greeting to the many cardinals present in Rome. He concluded: "And among you, in the College of Cardinals, there is also the future pope to whom today I promise my unconditional reverence and obedience." As for the phrase "obedience to the future pontiff" used by Pope Benedict, we should add the following statement of Archbishop Gänswein: "The phrase did not appear in the written text. It was spoken impromptu by the resigning pontiff, from the depths of his faith and devotion."[16]

On March 13, 2013, the Argentine Jorge Mario Cardinal Bergoglio was elected pope. Immediately after the announcement, even before appearing on the balcony of Saint Peter's, he asked Gänswein if he could place a call to Pope Benedict. The call was made, but no one answered: everyone was in the television room waiting to see the new pope appear at the window overlooking Saint Peter's

---

[15] Paolo Rodari, "Monsignor Gänswein: il mio Ratzinger segreto", *La Repubblica*, April 16, 2015.

[16] From a conversation with Monsignor Gänswein.

Square.[17] The episode, narrated by Paolo Rodari, confirms that the relationship between the two pontiffs was immediately character-ized by courtesy and fraternal communion. Of course, especially at the beginning, there were several private meetings: for the hand-ing over of the papacy, for the transmission of the work done on the encyclical on faith, for some nominations. Subsequently, the meetings became more focused on the tasks facing Pope Francis. Benedict remained steadfast in his communion with and obedience to Pope Francis, as Pope Francis remained steadfast in his respect and devotion to Pope Benedict. Particularly important, it seems to me, was Benedict's participation in some events of the pontificate of his successor. In 2014 and 2015, the pope emeritus was present at the solemn Mass when new cardinals named by Francis became part of the presbyterate of the Diocese of Rome. After the reigning pope, he was the first to exchange the kiss of peace with the new members of the Church's senate.

Benedict was also present at the canonization of Saint John XXIII and Saint John Paul II, which took place in April 2014, and at the be-atification ceremony of Paul VI in October of the same year. These were opportunities to underscore once again Benedict's closeness to the three men who had made their own mark on the Second Vatican Council and had sought to put its teachings into practice. It was not his intention to contradict those still accusing him of wanting to bury the spirit of the council; rather, he saw in each of these occasions an intimate participation in an event of grace, sharing in the gratitude of the faithful to the Holy Spirit, who had inspired and guided those great pastors of the Church. And it was gratitude to those popes who, in various ways, had called him to collaborate in the council and to guide the Church in his turn in the spirit of the council.

THE YEAR OF MERCY

The last public appearance of Benedict together with Pope Fran-cis, and probably the most important one from a theological per-spective, took place on December 8, 2015, on the occasion of the

---

[17] Paolo Rodari, "Monsignor Gänswein: il mio Ratzinger segreto", *La Repubblica,* April 16, 2015.

opening of the Holy Door of Saint Peter's Basilica and the celebration of Mass for the Solemnity of the Immaculate Conception.
Even though visibly fatigued, the pope emeritus wanted to cross
the threshold of the Holy Door personally and to participate in the
Mass, while Francis, in his greeting, demonstrated his affection by
his welcome. In fact, though quite different in terms of charisma
and temperament, the two pontiffs are very close in their vision of
a God of love, of a God whose name is mercy.

This was made clear by Francis himself, who, on October 24,
2015, at the conclusion of the Synod on the Family, which had
been particularly contentious, quoted a text of his predecessor. On
the Sunday of Divine Mercy, March 30, 2008, Benedict had said:

> Indeed, mercy is the central nucleus of the Gospel message; it is the
> very name of God, the Face with which he revealed himself in the
> Old Covenant and fully in Jesus Christ, the incarnation of creative
> and redemptive Love. May this merciful love also shine on the face
> of the Church and show itself through the sacraments, in particular
> that of Reconciliation, and in works of charity, both communitarian
> and individual.[18]

For his part, Pope Benedict, speaking at a symposium studying
justification through faith, said that he was convinced that all the
questions expressed by Luther with his insistent search for justice
in God's sight had left room for the idea of the mercy of God.[19]
Then the pope emeritus quickly outlined how the idea of mercy
has become "central and dominant" today.[20] At the beginning, there
were the visions of Saint Faustina Kowalska, who lived in Poland
in the first half of the twentieth century. God asked a humble Sister
from the country that more than any other had suffered from the
atrocities of the two World Wars to proclaim the immensity of his
mercy and to institute a feast in remembrance of this truth of faith.

It seemed to be an impossible task, but a young priest by the name
of Karol Wojtyła took very seriously the proclamation of his fellow Pole, Sister Faustina, and he sought to live this reality in his life

---

[18] Benedict XVI, Regina Caeli, March 30, 2008.

[19] The conference, organized by the Jesuit Fathers at the Gesù in Rome, took place
October 8–10, 2015. The conference papers are published under the title *Per mezzo della
fede* (Cinisello Balsamo: San Paolo, 2016). Pope Benedict's text is found on pp. 125–37.

[20] Ibid., 128.

and, after becoming pope, canonized Saint Faustina and instituted the Feast of Divine Mercy. Then, the pope emeritus continued: "Pope Francis is completely in agreement with this line of thinking. His pastoral practice is expressed precisely in the fact that he speaks to us continually about the mercy of God."[21] Discreetly, in this context, Benedict did not speak of his own contribution to the study of the theology of mercy. However, a careful reading reveals that the German pope had in his own way carved out a path for progress in thought about the notion of mercy.

The point of departure is his insistence on the link between creation and redemption, between rationality and faith. This began with his first famous magisterial lecture at the University of Bonn, during his lectures to all the faculties of the University of Tubingen, which were the basis for his book *Introduction to Christianity*. And then in his contribution to the *Catechism of the Catholic Church* and in his papal Magisterium, particularly in his encyclical on love. In this regard, it is worth relating a passage taken from one of his catecheses on Saint Augustine:

> I wanted ideally to conclude my Pilgrimage to Pavia by consigning to the Church and to the world, before the tomb of this great lover of God, my first Encyclical, entitled *Deus Caritas Est*. I owe much, in fact, especially in the first part, to Augustine's thought. Even today, as in his time, mankind needs to know and above all to live this fundamental reality: God is love, and the encounter with him is the only response to the restlessness of the human heart.[22]

And it is precisely for this reason that, returning to the above-mentioned interview on salvation through faith, Benedict thinks that the view of Saint Augustine, that Christ "had" to die on the Cross to repair the enormity of man's offense against God, is now unacceptable. The contrast between the Father who insists on an absolute way on justice and the Son who obeys by accepting the cruel paternal decree recalls the Greek mythology of Saturn-Cronos, who devours his children, but it is completely erroneous from a Christian perspective. On this point, contemporary Trinitarian theology has underscored the unity in the salvific will of the Father and the Son.

The change in perception of man's position with respect to God leads also to a different view of the role of Christians in the world.

---

[21] Ibid., 129.
[22] Benedict XVI, *Church Fathers*, 232.

They are not part of a community closed in on itself but are called "to be with Christ for others. . . . What man needs in order to obtain salvation is interior openness toward God, interior anticipation and adherence to him, and this means, conversely, that we, together with the Lord whom we have encountered, walk toward others and seek to make visible the God-event in Christ."[23]

In conclusion, Benedict and Francis converge in their vision of the merciful love of God who, like the Good Samaritan, draws near to injured and suffering man and heals him in his nature, enriching him with gifts of grace.

The legacy of Pope Benedict

On December 1, 2015, Pope Francis surprisingly declared: "Thirteen days before the death of Saint John Paul II . . . in that Via Crucis, the then Cardinal Ratzinger spoke about corruption in the Church. . . . We elected him for that, his freedom in saying these things . . . in saying such things."[24] We do not know whether with this expression Pope Francis, who in the 2005 conclave was the main contender against Ratzinger, meant to say that he himself ended up voting for Benedict XVI. In any case, his statement meant that in the conclave in which Ratzinger was elected, a majority had formed that agreed in desiring the reforms enunciated by the then cardinal dean.

The reigning pope then returned to the topic on February 19, 2016, on the airplane that was taking him from Mexico back to Rome. Responding to the journalists who were questioning him about the abuses perpetrated by Marcial Maciel, the founder of the Legionaries of Christ, who was originally from Mexico, Francis said: "And here allow me to honor a man who fought even when he did not have the power to step in, yet he did: Ratzinger. Cardinal Ratzinger deserves applause. . . . He was a brave man who helped so many open the door."[25] Another moving encounter between the two pontiffs occurred on June 28, 2016, on the occasion

---

[23] *Per mezzo della fede*, 134–35.

[24] See Gian Guido Vecchi, "Continueremo a fare pulizia", *Corriere della Sera*, December 1, 2015, 18.

[25] See *Corriere della Sera*, February 19, 2016, 2. Pope Francis, In-Flight Press Conference from Mexico to Rome, February 17, 2016.

of the celebration of the sixty-fifth anniversary of Pope Benedict's priestly ordination. On that occasion, Pope Francis said: "I wish to conclude with a prayerful wish . . . that you, Your Holiness, will continue to feel the hand of our merciful God supporting you, and that you will experience and witness the love of God." To which Pope Benedict replied: "My true home is your goodness. There, I feel safe."[26] This is a good point of departure for an attempt to summarize and evaluate the pontificate of Benedict XVI.

Faithful to his convictions and the mandate he had received, he tried above all to give a spiritual orientation to the life of the Church. For this purpose, he had recourse to what initially seemed the great accomplishment of Vatican II: the universal call to holiness in the Church (chapter 5 of the constitution *Lumen gentium*). Hence Pope Benedict's insistence on the correct celebration of the liturgy, particularly of the Mass; hence his extended preaching on the saints in the Wednesday General Audiences.

He then tried to intervene more directly in critical areas where he noticed a more urgent need to correct and encourage. The form in which he chose to make this exhortation and to express, at the same time, the nearness of the Successor of Peter was the celebration of three extraordinary years. The first, the Pauline Year, inaugurated on the anniversary of the second millennium of the presumed birth of the Apostle of the Gentiles, was an urgent invitation, addressed in particular to bishops, to become aware of their own dignity, to put themselves at the service of the Christian proclamation, and to take upon themselves the burden of the responsibilities connected with membership in the Apostolic College. The Year for Priests followed, ostensibly a year of reflection and purification for priests, announced at the very time when the scandal of sexual abuse was about to emerge in all its most upsetting dimensions.

With regard more directly to the governance of the Church, here, too, Benedict was motivated by intentions to reform. However, he did not have the ability or the good fortune to find collaborators equal to the task. It can also be said that the clergy—the bishops and the priests—were the ones who did not facilitate the task of the pope who had gone out of his way for them.

---

[26] See *Avvenire,* June 29, 2016, 17. Pope Francis and Pope Emeritus Benedict XVI, Address, June 28, 2016.

The last extraordinary year was the Year of Faith, addressed to all the faithful, in particular to those of Europe, who are increasingly exposed to the risk of atheism, proposed not so much by Marxism as by a secular materialism that seems to have benefitted greatly from the defeat of Communism. As he told his countrymen in Germany, Pope Benedict was convinced that without God, there is no future; materialistic atheism, rather than causing God harm, signals the impoverishment of man.

IN CAPITE ET IN MEMBRIS

Phenomena like the Vatileaks, which had caused such a stir in public opinion, gave the impression that the Roman Curia was a center of evil-doing and corruption for whose reform the pope needed to expend more energy. Benedict, however, had in mind not only a few thousand people, among whom there were certainly some sinners and careerists. His solicitude, instead, extended to all the Churches, since he did not want to fail in his task as universal pastor. In this regard, he wrote of Saint Paul: "Some of those Churches also caused him worry and chagrin. . . . Yet, he felt bound to the Communities he founded in a way that was far from cold and bureaucratic but rather intense and passionate."[27]

This was the model that Pope Benedict had before him, this was the example that he wanted to propose *in capite et in membris*, at the top but also in the Churches, large and small, spread throughout the world. Besides, this was the effort, starting with Vatican II, that Benedict's predecessors, John XXIII, Paul VI, and John Paul II, had undertaken. Pope Benedict, too, wanted to convey a spiritual task to a Church that, especially in Europe, seemed incapable of overcoming her sluggishness, in order to generate enthusiasm for and attraction to the Gospel. What appeared truly worrisome was the growing distance between the clergy and the faithful to which there seemed to be no effective response, in spite of the helpful proposals made so often.

Continuing along these lines already begun by John Paul II, Benedict XVI time and again invited bishops and priests to meditate on

---

[27] Benedict XVI, *Jesus, the Apostles, and the Early Church* (San Francisco: Ignatius Press, 2007), 125.

the idea of service, to draw near to the little flock, trusting the movements, the lay associations, the laity, and all who run to Jesus and seem to be like sheep without a shepherd and need tenderness and comfort. However, his example was not always followed, nor could this isolated measure probably have been enough to reverse a trend that seemed to grow rather than diminish as the years passed. Certainly, the idea of service, consistently put into practice, could be a good point of departure. Perhaps canon law should also be reworked on the basis of this concept.

HEALTHY SECULARITY AND LAICITY

Another contribution offered by Pope Benedict, this time not only to the community of believers, is the distinction between what he called "healthy secularity" and "laicity". The first refers to a correct and friendly relationship between civil society, with its just autonomy and legislation, and the Christian community, which in its own way is called to be an active and responsible part of the State. Laicity, on the other hand, is derived from a historical situation in which, perhaps even due to the fault of believers, a total and at times rancorous separation between the civil and religious community occurred.

A situation of this sort is detrimental not only for Catholics but also for secularists: the former end up being considered citizens who can collaborate in the management of public life only by putting aside their proper religious convictions; the latter, deprived of the contributions of believers, end up elaborating a positivistic law without any ethical foundation, exposed at all times to the changing views of successive majorities. Against such a drift, Pope Benedict advanced the proposal of a new humanism for the third millennium. Once again, however, Europe, and particularly Germany, showed little interest.

THE LITTLE FLOCK

Already in the years of his youth, and later in his years as a bishop in Munich, Benedict XVI realized that the community of believers was destined to become a minority in Europe. His option, therefore, was along the lines of a community that was small, but united and alive. Hence, his polemic against excessive bureaucracy, particularly in the German Church. It was also the view of John Paul II, incidentally, that it is better to give up a system of Catholic agencies that is now devoid of Christian content than to continue managing institutions without any specific faith content.

Likewise, it is better to reduce to a minimum the structural part of entities like episcopal conferences. Having fought for decades to be freed from the domination of the Roman Curia, now there was the risk of establishing as many curias as there were episcopal conferences. In sum, it is better to have a community with smaller numbers but that participates in the liturgical and sacramental life and is ready to bear witness to its own faith. Only a community of this sort, which experiences the nearness and understanding of pastors, has a future ahead of it, because it draws close to Christ, the Son of God, the Good Samaritan who heals the wounds of believers and of all mankind.

For them, the pope wrote his last book, which is not a scholarly work.[28] It was born, instead, from his desire to generate a tender and passionate love for Jesus of Nazareth. This is also a grace of Benedict's pontificate, tenaciously pursued and brought to completion with the loving care of a pastor and the mature wisdom of a theologian.

---

[28] However, it must be clearly stated that few exegetes or theologians could have successfully handled such a complex matter with such mastery and skill in writing.

APPENDIX

RESIGNATION AND
RELATIONS WITH HIS SUCCESSOR

An Interview with
Pope Emeritus Benedict XVI

In Rome the sky is heavy with threatening clouds, but when I arrive at Mater Ecclesiae, the residence of the pope emeritus, an unexpected ray of sunlight accentuates beneath them the harmony of the dome of Saint Peter's and of the Vatican gardens. "My paradise", Benedict XVI had remarked during a previous visit. I am led into the room that is also his private library, and what comes to my mind spontaneously is the title of the book by Jean Leclercq, *The Love of Learning and the Desire for God*, which was cited by Benedict XVI in his famous speech at the Collège des Bernardins in Paris. The pope arrives after a few minutes, greets me with the same smile and courtesy as always, then says to me: "We are on fifteen." I do not understand, and so he repeats: "I have read fifteen chapters." Frankly, I am surprised. Several months earlier I had sent him most of the book, but I never would have expected that he would read the entire thing. I hand him the other chapters and tell him that now I have only a little left to do. He is pleased with what he has read, and so I add: "Do you mind if I ask you a few questions by way of an interview?" His answer, as always, is polite and practical: "Ask me the questions, then send me the whole thing and we will see." Obviously, I follow his instructions. After a while he writes to me consenting to have it published. I can only thank him again for his gracious confidence.

Published in the Italian edition of *L'Osservatore romano* on August 24, 2016.

Your Holiness, while visiting Germany the last time, in 2011, you said: "It is not possible to give up God." And again: "Where there is God, there is a future." Were you sorry that you had to step down during the Year of Faith?

Of course I had my heart set on finishing the Year of Faith and on writing the encyclical on faith that was to conclude the series started with *Deus caritas est*. As Dante says, "the love that moves the sun and the other stars" drives us, leads us to the presence of God, who grants us hope and a future.

In a crisis situation, the best course is to place oneself in the presence of God with the desire to rediscover the faith so as to be able to continue on one's path in life. For his part, the Lord is very happy to accept our desire, to give us the light that guides us on our pilgrimage in life. This is the experience of the saints, of Saint John of the Cross or Saint Thérèse of the Child Jesus. In 2013, nevertheless, there were many tasks that I no longer thought I could finish.

What were these tasks?

In particular, they had already set the date of the World Youth Day, which was to be held in the summer of 2013 in Rio de Janeiro, in Brazil. Now in this regard, I had two very precise convictions. After the experience of my visit in Mexico and Cuba, I no longer felt capable of making such a demanding journey. Furthermore, with the format that John Paul II had given to those events, the physical presence of the pope was indispensable. A television link or some other form of communication made possible by technology was unthinkable. This circumstance, too, was a reason why resignation was for me a duty.

Finally, I was confident and certain that, even without my presence, the Year of Faith would be completed successfully. Faith, indeed, is a grace, a generous gift of God to believers. Therefore, I had the firm conviction that my successor, as it then actually happened, would likewise bring the initiative that I had started to the happy conclusion willed by the Lord.

While visiting the basilica in Collemaggio, in Aquila, you insisted on placing your pallium on the altar of Saint Celestine V. Can you tell me when you reached your decision that you had to relinquish the exercise of the Petrine ministry for the good of the Church?

The journey to Mexico and Cuba had been beautiful and moving for me from many perspectives. In Mexico, I was struck by my encounter with the profound faith of so many young people and by my experience of their joyful enthusiasm for God. Similarly, I had been struck by the major problems of Mexican society and by the Church's obligation to find a faith-based response to the challenge of poverty and violence. On the other hand, there is no need to recall explicitly how in Cuba I was struck to see the way in which Raúl Castro is trying to lead his country on a new course without breaking the continuity with the immediate past. There, too, I was very impressed by the way in which my brothers in the episcopate are trying to find an approach in this difficult process on the basis of the faith.

During those same days, I experienced thoroughly the limits of my physical stamina. Above all, I realized that I was no longer capable in the future of coping with transoceanic flights because of the problem of jet lag. Of course, I spoke about these problems also with my physician, Doctor Patrizio Polisca. In this way, it became clear that I would no longer be able to take part in the World Youth Day in Rio de Janeiro in the summer of 2013: the problem of jet lag clearly stood in the way. From then on, I had to decide in a relatively short time on the date of my resignation.

After your resignation, many people imagined medieval scenarios with slamming doors and loud denunciations. So much so that those same commentators were surprised, almost disappointed, by your decision to remain within the enclosure of Saint Peter, to move to Mater Ecclesiae monastery. How did you reach that decision?

I had visited Mater Ecclesiae monastery many times since its beginnings. Often I had gone there to participate in Evening Prayer, to celebrate Holy Mass for all the nuns who had succeeded one another there. I had been there for the last time on the occasion of the anniversary of the foundation of the Congregation of the Sisters of the Visitation. At the appropriate time, John Paul II had decided that the house, which previously had served as the residence of the director of Vatican Radio, should become a place of contemplative prayer, like a spring of living water in the Vatican. Having learned that the three-year stay of the Visitandine nuns was ending that spring, I became aware almost naturally that this would be the place where I could retire so as to continue in my own way the service of prayer to which John Paul II had assigned this house.

I do not know whether you, too, have seen a snapshot taken by a BBC photographer that, on the day of your resignation, depicted the dome of Saint Peter's being struck by lightning. [Benedict nods as a sign that he has seen it.] For many people this image suggested the idea of decadence or even of the end of a world. Now, though, it occurs to me to say: they expected to pity a loser, someone who would go down in history as defeated, but I see here a serene, confident man.

I agree completely. I really would have had reason to worry if I had not been convinced, as I said at the beginning of my pontificate, that I am a simple, humble laborer in the Lord's vineyard. From the beginning, I was aware of my limits, and I accepted in a spirit of obedience, as I have always sought to do in my life. Then there were the more or less major difficulties of the pontificate, but there were also many graces. I realized that I could not do alone everything that I had to do, and so I was forced, as it were, to place myself in God's hands, to entrust myself to Jesus, to whom, as I gradually wrote my volume about him, I felt united by the bond of an old and ever-deeper friendship.

Then there was the Mother of God, the mother of hope, who was a sure support in difficulties, to whom I felt increasingly close in reciting the Holy Rosary and in making visits to Marian shrines. Finally, there were the saints, my lifelong traveling companions: Saint Augustine and Saint Bonaventure, my spiritual teachers, but also Saint Benedict, whose motto "Prefer nothing to Christ" became more and more familiar to me, and Saint Francis, the Little Poor Man of Assisi, the first to intuit that the world is the mirror of God's creative love, from which we come and toward which we travel.

Only spiritual consolations, then?

No. My journey was not accompanied only from above. Every day I received many letters, not only from the great ones of the earth, but also from humble, simple people who were anxious to tell me that they were close to me, that they were praying for me. Hence, even in difficult moments, my confidence and certainty that the Church is guided by the Lord and that therefore I could place back into his hands the mandate that he had entrusted to me on the day of my election. Moreover, this support continued after my resignation, too, and for this I can only be grateful to the Lord and to all those who have expressed to me and still show me their affection.

In your farewell message to the cardinals, on February 28, 2013, you promised obedience from then on to your successor. In the meantime, I have the impression that you have also pledged to be personally close and cordial to Pope Francis. What sort of rapport do you have with your successor?

There was never any question about obedience to my successor. But then there is the sense of profound communion and friendship. At the moment of his election, I experienced, like many people, a spontaneous feeling of gratitude to Divine Providence. After two pontiffs originally from Central Europe, the Lord turned his glance, so to speak, to the universal Church and invited us to a more extensive, more catholic communion.

Personally, I was deeply touched from the first moment by the extraordinary human availability of Pope Francis toward me. Immediately after his election, he sought to reach me by telephone. Since that attempt did not succeed, he called me immediately after his meeting with the universal Church from the balcony of Saint Peter's and spoke to me very cordially. Since then, he has given me the gift of a marvelously paternal-fraternal relationship.

Often little gifts arrive up here, letters that were written personally. Before setting out on long journeys, the pope never fails to pay me a visit. The human benevolence with which he treats me is for me a special grace of this final phase of my life, for which I can only be grateful. Words alone are not proof of availability to others. He puts it into practice with me. May the Lord in turn make him feel his benevolence every day. I pray to the Lord for this grace for him.

BIBLIOGRAPHY

The Collected Works of Pope Benedict

For several years a project has been underway to publish the *Gesam-melte Schriften* (*Collected Works*) of Joseph Ratzinger—Benedict XVI, with Gerhard Cardinal Müller, former prefect of the Congregation for the Doctrine of the Faith, as editor-in-chief, in collaboration with the Pope Benedict XVI Institute in Regensburg. In Italy, four of the sixteen planned volumes have been edited by Pierluca Azzaro and published by Libreria Editrice Vaticana. In English, only one volume of *Joseph Ratzinger: Collected Works* has been published in its entirety: Volume 11, entitled *Theology of the Liturgy*, edited by Michael J. Miller (San Francisco: Ignatius Press, 2014).

The works of Joseph Ratzinger

To avoid an excessively long list, we mention here only the separate publications by Joseph Ratzinger. I will not cite, though, essays for collective works, articles, or conferences. These writings, however, for the most part have been anthologized either by Ratzinger or by his students and collaborators. If the year of the original German edition is not listed, it means that the first edition was in Italian.

Nor does this list include official documents by Ratzinger as prefect of the Congregation for the Doctrine of the Faith and as pope. These contributions have certainly been important, for instance in the case of the *Catechism of the Catholic Church* and the encyclicals. They are, nevertheless, works produced by many collaborators and experts and cannot be attributed to a single author.

Volk und Haus Gottes in Augustins Lehre von der Kirche. Munich: Zink, 1954.

The Theology of History in St. Bonaventure. Translated by Zachary Hayes. 2nd ed. Chicago: Franciscan Herald Press, 1989 (German ed., 1959).

The Meaning of Christian Brotherhood. 2nd ed. San Francisco: Ignatius Press, 1993 (German ed., 1960).

The Episcopacy and the Primacy. QD 4. New York: Herder and Herder, 1962 (German ed., 1961).

Theological Highlights of Vatican II. New York and Mahwah, N.J.: Paulist Press, 1966, 2009 (German ed., 1964).

Die sakramentale Begründung christlicher Existenz. 2nd ed. Meitingen and Freising: Kyrios-Verlag, 1967.

Introduction to Christianity. Translated by J. R. Foster, revised with a new preface. San Francisco: Ignatius Press, 2004 (German ed., 1968).

Das neue Volk Gottes: Entwürfe zur Ekklesiologie. Düsseldorf: Patmos-Verlag, 1969.

Meditationen zur Karwoche. Meitingen and Freising: Kyrios-Verlag, 1969.

Faith and the Future. Chicago: Franciscan Herald Press, 1971; San Francisco: Ignatius Press, 2009 (German ed., 1970).

Die Einheit der Nationen: Eine Vision der Kirchenväter. Salzburg and Munich: Pustet, 1971.

Storia e dogma. Milan: Jaca Book, 1971.

Die Hoffnung des Senfkorns. Meitingen and Freising: Kyrios-Verlag, 1973.

Dogma and Preaching. Unabridged edition translated by Michael J. Miller and Matthew J. O'Connell. San Francisco: Ignatius Press, 2011 (German ed., 1973).

The God of Jesus Christ: Meditations on the Triune God. Translated by Brian McNeil. San Francisco: Ignatius Press, 2008 (German ed., 1976; 2006).

Eschatology: Death and Eternal Life. Translated by Michael Waldstein. Washington, D.C.: Catholic University of America Press, 1988 (German ed., 1977).

Daughter Zion: Meditations on the Church's Marian Belief. Translated by John M. McDermott, S.J. San Francisco: Ignatius Press, 1983 (German ed., 1977).

Seeking God's Face (together with *The Lesson of the Christmas Donkey*, by Pope John Paul II). Chicago: Franciscan Herald Press, 1982 (German ed., 1978).

Co-Workers of the Truth: Meditations for Every Day of the Year. Translated by Sister Mary Frances McCarthy, S.N.D., and Reverend Lothar Krauth. San Francisco: Ignatius Press, 1992 (German ed., 1979).

The Feast of Faith: Approaches to a Theology of the Liturgy. Translated by Graham Harrison. San Francisco: Ignatius Press, 1986 (German ed., 1981).

Principles of Catholic Theology: Building Stones for a Fundamental Theology. Translated by Sister Mary Frances McCarthy, S.N.D. San Francisco: Ignatius Press, 1987 (German ed., 1982).

Behold the Pierced One: An Approach to a Spiritual Christology. Translated by Graham Harrison. San Francisco: Ignatius Press, 1986 (German ed., 1984).

Seek That Which Is Above: Meditations through the Year. Translated by Graham Harrison. San Francisco: Ignatius Press, 1986 (German ed., 1985).

Il cammino pasquale: Corso di exercizi spirituali tenuti in Vaticano. Milan: Ancora, 1985.

The Ratzinger Report: An Exclusive Interview on the State of the Church. Translated by Salvator Attanasio and Graham Harrison from the original German manuscript. 2nd ed. San Francisco: Ignatius Press, 1986.

In the Beginning . . . : A Catholic Understanding of the Story of Creation and the Fall. Translated by Boniface Ramsey, O.P. Huntington,

Ind.: Our Sunday Visitor, 1990; 2nd enlarged ed., Grand Rapids, Mich.: Eerdmans, 1995 (German ed., 1986).

Church, Ecumenism, and Politics. Translated by Michael J. Miller et al. San Francisco: Ignatius Press, 2008 (German ed., 1987).

Ministers of Your Joy: Scriptural Meditations on Priestly Spirituality. Ann Arbor, Mich.: Redeemer Books, 1989 (German ed., 1988).

To Look on Christ: Exercises in Faith, Hope, and Love. Translated by Robert Nowell. New York: Crossroad, 1991 (German ed., 1989).

A Turning Point for Europe? The Church in the Modern World—Assessment and Forecast. Translated by Brian McNeil, C.R.V. San Francisco: Ignatius Press, 1994 (German ed., 1991).

Wahrheit, Werte, Macht: Prüfsteine der pluralistischen Gesellschaft. Freiburg im Breisgau: Herder, 1993.

The Nature and Mission of Theology: Essays to Orient Theology in Today's Debates. Translated by Adrian Walker. San Francisco: Ignatius Press, 1995 (German ed., 1993).

A New Song for the Lord: Faith in Christ and Liturgy Today. Translated by Martha M. Matesich. New York: Crossroad, 1997 (German ed., 1995).

Salt of the Earth: Christianity and the Catholic Church at the End of the Millennium: An Interview with Peter Seewald. Translated by Adrian Walker. San Francisco: Ignatius Press, 1997 (German ed., 1996).

Mary: The Church at the Source (with Hans Urs von Balthasar). Translated by Adrian Walker. San Francisco: Ignatius Press, 2005 (German ed., 1997).

Images of Hope: Meditations on Major Feasts. Translated by John Rock and Graham Harrison. San Francisco: Ignatius Press, 2006 (German ed., 1997).

Milestones: Memoirs (1927–1977). Translated by Erasmo Levia-Merikakis. San Francisco: Ignatius Press, 1998 (German ed., 1998).

Many Religions—One Covenant: Israel, the Church, and the World. Translated by Graham Harrison. San Francisco: Ignatius Press, 1999 (German ed., 1998).

The Spirit of the Liturgy. Translated by John Saward. San Francisco: Ignatius Press, 2000 (German ed., 2000).

God and the World: Believing and Living in Our Time: Conversations with Peter Seewald. Translated by Henry Taylor. San Francisco: Ignatius Press, 2002 (German ed., 2000).

God Is Near Us: The Eucharist, The Heart of Life. Translated by Henry Taylor. San Francisco: Ignatius Press, 2003 (German ed., 2001).

La comunione nella Chiesa. Cinisello Balsamo: San Paolo, 2004.

Pilgrim Fellowship of Faith: The Church as Communion. Translated by Henry Taylor. San Francisco: Ignatius Press, 2005 (German ed., 2002).

Truth and Tolerance: Christian Belief and World Religions. Translated by Henry Taylor. San Francisco: Ignatius Press, 2004 (German ed., 2004).

On the Way to Jesus Christ. Translated by Michael J. Miller. San Francisco: Ignatius Press, 2005 (German ed., 2004).

Europe Today and Tomorrow. Translated by Michael J. Miller. San Francisco: Ignatius Press, 2007 (Italian ed., 2004).

L'Europa di Benedetto nella crisi delle culture. Siena: Cantagalli, 2005.

Jesus of Nazareth: From the Baptism in the Jordan to the Transfiguration. Translated by Adrian J. Walker. New York: Doubleday, 2007 (German ed., 2006).

La vita di Dio per gli uomini. Anthology edited by E. Guerriero. Milan: Jaca Book, 2007. This large, 350-page volume reprints the essays and speeches by Ratzinger published by the Italian edition of the journal *Communio* from its beginning, in 1973, until his election to the pontificate in 2005.

Jesus of Nazareth: Holy Week: From the Entrance into Jerusalem to the Resurrection. Translated by Philip J. Whitmore. San Francisco: Ignatius Press, 2011 (German ed., 2010).

Light of the World: The Pope, the Church, and the Signs of the Times: A Conversation with Peter Seewald. Translated by Michael J. Miller and Adrian J. Walker. San Francisco: Ignatius Press, 2010 (German ed., 2010).

Jesus of Nazareth: The Infancy Narratives. Translated by Philip J. Whitmore. New York: Image, 2012 (German ed., 2012).

Among the works written personally by Pope Benedict, it is worth mentioning also five volumes dedicated to the saints from apostolic times until the Middle Ages, published in Vatican City by Libreria Editrice Vaticana from 2007 to 2012. The volumes originated in the catecheses of Pope Benedict at his Wednesday General Audiences. The result is a unified work, an important introduction to the history and theology of sanctity. These volumes have also been translated into English by L'Osservatore Romano and published as:

Jesus, the Apostles, and the Early Church. San Francisco: Ignatius Press, 2007.

Church Fathers from Clement of Rome to Augustine. San Francisco: Ignatius Press, 2008.

Church Fathers and Teachers from Saint Leo the Great to Peter Lombard. San Francisco: Ignatius Press, 2010.

Holiness Is Always in Season. Edited by Leonardo Sapienza. San Francisco: Ignatius Press, 2011.

Holy Men and Women of the Middle Ages and Beyond. San Francisco: Ignatius Press, 2012.

Writings about Joseph Ratzinger

CHILDHOOD, EDUCATION, TEACHING CAREER, AND BISHOP OF MUNICH

Concerning this period of his life, we must cite first of all his autobiographical work *Memoirs*, listed above, and the book by Georg Ratzinger, written together with the journalist Michael Hesemann, *My Brother the Pope*, translated by Michael J. Miller (San Francisco: Ignatius Press, 2011) (German ed., 2011).

Borghese, Alessandra. *Sulle tracce di Joseph Ratzinger.* Siena: Cantagalli, 2007.

Hamman, Jörg, and Barbara Just. *Mein Herz schlägt bayrisch*. Munich: St. Michaelsbund, 2006.

Läpple, Alfred. *Benedikt XVI und seine Wurzeln*. Augsburg: Sankt Ulrich Verlag, 2006.

Laube, Volker. *Das Erzbischöfliche Studienseminar St. Michael in Traunstein und sein Archiv*. Regensburg: Schnell & Steiner, 2006.

Valente, Gianni. *Ratzinger professore: Gli anni dello studio e dell'insegnamento nel ricordo dei colleghi e degli allievi (1946–1977)*. Cinisello Balsamo: San Paolo, 2008.

Wagner, K., and H. Ruf, eds. *Kardinal Ratzinger: Der Erzbischof von München und Freising in Wort und Bild*. Munich: J. Pfeiffer, 1977.

Zanotti, Emanuela. *Il sorriso di Benedetto: Pellegrinaggio nella terra d'infanzia di papa Benedetto XVI*. Siena: Cantagalli, 2007.

With regard to Ratzinger's four years as archbishop of Munich, a fundamental source is the book edited by Peter Pfister, *Joseph Ratzinger und das Erzbistum München und Freising: Dokumente und Bilder aus kirchlichen Archiven, Beiträge und Erinnerungen* (Regensburg: Schnell & Steiner, 2006). In addition, the wide-ranging volume reprints several important essays on the origins and the course of studies pursued by Ratzinger until his priestly ordination and his initial teaching experiences.

THEOLOGIAN AND PREFECT OF THE CONGREGATION FOR
THE DOCTRINE OF THE FAITH

Blanco, Pablo. *Joseph Ratzinger: una biografía*. Pamplona: Eunsa, 2004.

Clemens, J., and A. Tarzia, eds. *Alla scuola della verità: I settant'anni di Joseph Ratzinger*. Cinisello Balsamo: San Paolo, 1997. This book, too, presented as a tribute to the cardinal, contains important testimonies by students and friends about the theologian and then prefect of the congregation.

Fahey, Michael. "Joseph Ratzinger, ecclésiologue et pasteur". *Concilium* 161 (1981, French ed.): 129–39.

Fermet, André. "À l'école de Ratzinger". In André Fermet and René Marlé, *Théologies d'aujourd'hui*, 93–135. Paris: Le Centurion, 1973.

Kasper, Walter. "Theorie und Praxis innerhalb einer Theologia crucis: Antwort auf J. Ratzingers Glaube, Geschichte und Philosophie". *Hochland* 62 (1970): 59–152.

———. "Das Wesen des Christlichen". *Theologische Revue* 65 (1969): 182–88.

Nachtwei, Gerhard. *Dialogische Unsterblichkeit: Eine Untersuchung zu Joseph Ratzingers Eschatologie und Theologie*. Leipzig: St. Benno-Verlag, 1986.

Nichols, Aidan. *The Theology of Joseph Ratzinger: An Introductory Study*. Edinburgh: T & T Clark, 1988. In the Italian edition, edited by Jacques Servais, S.J., and published by San Paolo, there is a serious attempt to distinguish between the works of the theologian and those of the prefect of the congregation.

O'Grady, Desmond. "The Ratzinger Round". *The Month* CCXXXIV/1276 (December 1973): 409–12.

Rollet, Jacques. *Le cardinal Ratzinger et la théologie contemporaine*. Paris: Cerf, 1987.

Segundo, Juan Luis. *Teología de la liberación: Respuesta al Cardenal Ratzinger*. Madrid: Ediciones de Cristiandad, 1985.

Siebel, Wigand. *Zur Philosophie und Theologie Joseph Ratzingers*. Saarbrücken: Saka-Verlag, 2005.

Tura, Roberto. "Joseph Ratzinger". In *Lessico dei teologi del secolo XX*. Edited by P. Vanzan and H. J. Schulz, 747–49. Brescia: Queriniana, 1978.

Twomey, Vincent. *Benedict XVI: The Conscience of Our Age: A Theological Portrait*. San Francisco: Ignatius Press, 2007.

Utz, W., ed. *Glaube und demokratischer Pluralismus im wissenschaftlichen Werk von Joseph Kardinal Ratzinger*. Bonn: Scientia Humana Inst., 1989.

Verweyen, Hansjürgen. *Joseph Ratzinger-Benedikt XVI: Die Entwicklung seines Denkens.* Darmstadt: WGB, 2007.

Acts and teachings of the pontificate of Benedict XVI

One can always consult the *Acta Apostolicae Sedis* (*AAS, Acts of the Apostolic See*), which record the official texts of the activity of the reigning pontiff.

For the pontificate of Benedict XVI, furthermore, Libreria Editrice Vaticana has published a series of nine volumes entitled *Insegnamenti di Benedetto XVI*, a collection of the writings and speeches of the German pope from the beginning of his pontificate, in 2005, until the conclusion on February 28, 2013.

In turn, the publishing house Edizioni Dehoniane in Bologna published, in the series *Enchiridion Vaticanum*, seven volumes (numbers 23–29) that reprint writings and speeches by the German pope.

It is worth mentioning also several anthologies that select speeches and essays by the pontiff on particular aspects of his teaching.

Joseph Ratzinger—Benedetto XVI. *Giovanni Paolo II: Il mio amato predecessore.* Edited by E. Guerriero. Cinisello Balsamo: San Paolo, 2007. Some of the same material is published in English in: Joseph Ratzinger, *The Legacy of John Paul II: Images & Memories,* translated by Michael J. Miller and Nicoletta V. MacKenzie (San Francisco: Ignatius Press, 2005).

Giovanni Paolo II—Benedetto XVI. *La nobile forma: Chiesa e artisti sulla via della bellezza.* Edited by G. Ravasi, E. Guerriero, and P. Iacobone. Cinisello Balsamo: San Paolo, 2009.

Benedetto XVI. *Nulla anteporre a Cristo.* Edited by the Benedictine monks of Praglia. Padova: Ed. Scritti monastici Abbazia di Praglia, 2014.

Benedict XVI. *The Garden of God: Toward a Human Ecology.* Washington, D.C.: Catholic University of America Press, 2014.

Benedetto XVI. *La gioia della fede.* Edited by G. Vigini. Cinisello Balsamo: San Paolo, 2012.

Writings about Benedict XVI

Albert, Hans. *Joseph Ratzingers Rettung des Christentums*. Aschaffenburg: Alibri Verlag, 2008.

Allen, John L. *The Rise of Benedict XVI*. New York: Doubleday, 2005.

Aucante, Vincent. *Benoît XVI et l'Islam*. Paris: Parole et Silence, 2008.

Chélini, Jean. *Benoît XVI: L'héritier du Concile*. Paris: Hachette, 2005.

Kraus, Joseph M. *Benedetto XVI: Il perché di una scelta*. Rome: Moralia, 2013.

Kuhn, P., ed. *Gespräch über Jesus: Papst Benedikt XVI; Im Dialog mit Martin Hengel und Peter Stuhlmacher*. Tübingen: Mohr Siebeck, 2010.

Lecomte, Bernard. *Benoît XVI: Le dernier pape européen*. Paris: Perrin, 2006.

Melloni, Alberto. "Benedetto XVI". In *Il conclave di papa Francesco*, 23–61. Rome: Istituto della Enciclopedia Italiana, 2013.

———. *L'inizio di papa Ratzinger*. Turin: Einaudi, 2005.

Murphy, Joseph. *Christ Our Joy: The Theological Vision of Pope Benedict XVI*. San Francisco: Ignatius Press, 2008.

Pfeiffer, Achim. *Religion und Politik in den Schriften Papst Benedikt XVI*. Marburg: Tectum Verlag, 2007.

Regoli, Roberto. *Oltre la crisi della Chiesa: Il pontificato di Benedetto Xvi*. Turin: Lindau, 2016.

Rodari, Paolo, and Andrea Tornielli. *Attacco a Ratzinger*. Milan: Piemme, 2010.

Rusconi, Roberto. *Il gran rifiuto: Perché un papa si dimette*. Brescia: Morcelliana, 2013.

Seewald, Peter. *Benedict XVI: An Intimate Portrait*. Translated by Henry Taylor and Anne Englund Nash. San Francisco: Ignatius Press, 2008.

Tagliaferri, Maurizio, ed. *Il Gesù di Nazaret di Joseph Ratzinger: Un confronto* (with essays by G. Segalla et al.). Assisi: Cittadella, 2011.

Tornielli, Andrea. *Benedetto XVI: Il custode della fede*. Casale Monferrato: Piemme, 2005.

Weigel, George. *God's Choice: Pope Benedict XVI and the Future of the Catholic Church*. New York: HarperCollins, 2005.

SUBJECT INDEX

NAME INDEX